ALSO BY JOHN HEIDENRY

Theirs Was the Kingdom:
Lila and DeWitt Wallace and the Story of the Reader's Digest

WHAT WILD ECSTASY

The Rise and Fall
of the
Sexual Revolution

John Heidenry

Simon & Schuster

Simon & Schuster
Rockefeller Center
1230 Avenue of the Americas
New York, NY 10020

Designed by Sam Potts
Manufactured in the United States of America

10 9 8 7 6 5 4 3 2 1

Library of Congress
Cataloging-In-Publication Data

Heidenry, John.
What Wild Ecstasy : The Rise and Fall of the
Sexual Evolution / John Heidenry
p. cm.
Includes index.
1. Sex customs—United States.   2. Sex.
3. Sexual Ethics—United States.   4. Sexuality
in Popular Culture—United States.   I. Title.
HQ18.U5H43   1997
306.7—dc21   96-51058
CIP

ISBN 0-7432-4184-3

For information regarding the special discounts for bulk purchases, please contact Simon &
Schuster Special Sales at 1-800-456-6798 or business@simonandschuster.com

To my wife,
Pat

Forever will I love,
and you be fair

Contents

WHAT WILD ECSTASY

Preface

All sex is divided into five parts: having, regulating, striving to understand, struggling to improve, and profiting from this mysterious neurophysical activity that pervades and often rules every aspect of our domestic, professional, creative, spiritual, and social lives.

Sex is the convulsive fiat that brings us into the world, is the force that through the hormonal fuse drives our flowering, is the consolation or torment that makes our brief stay either a pleasurable foretaste of some imagined heaven or a hell on earth, is a wish or memory that expires only with death. It predetermines our destiny, molds our personality, and for the overwhelming majority of humankind offers the only hope of immortality. Through sex we both discover and transcend ourselves, bond with and cherish others in the most deeply human way possible, and perpetuate the species.

With good reason, sex has been called the poor woman's or poor man's grand opera. Thanks to an often turbulent energy field known as libido, every woman and man on earth can and frequently does experience passion not unlike that of Juliet and Romeo or, in happier circumstances, Fiordiligi and her Guglielmo.

Regrettably, too many of us take little interest in our psychosexual identity, and the nature and significance of our sexuo-erotic roles and responsibilities, naively or arrogantly assuming that we already know all that we need to get by.

Equally vital both to our self-knowledge and to an understanding of the society in which we live is at least some knowledge of the calamitous sex-driven pathologies that, it is not too much to say, lie at the evil root of urban violence, war, sociopathic behavior, poverty, racism, class hatred, religious fanaticism, loneliness, and depression.

As a result of our ignorance, apathy, and fear, sex has to a great extent become by default the intellectual, moral, and legal property of politicians, clerics, and ideologues. The comforting idea that sex is a matter between consenting adults in the privacy of their homes is both a myth, if only because in far too many homes it is no such thing, and an irresponsible attitude, because too much that concerns our individual and social welfare is at stake.

My hope with this book is to provide an entertaining, informative, and perhaps occasionally even shocking popular historical overview of all that has happened in the wide world of human sexuality in the last thirty or so years, with particular emphasis on its epicenter, the United States. Though we are all aware that something vaguely called the Sexual Revolution occurred in the not-too-distant past, many of us are unsure when exactly it took place, or what exactly happened.

If *What Wild Ecstasy* leads some readers to read more broadly and less cynically in the field of sexual literature, to see sexual issues not merely in terms of sexual politics or the inanities of pop-sex manuals, to judge sensationalist media treatment of such issues as AIDS, child pornography, and sexual abuse in a clearer light, and to regard human sexuality in all its misery and grandeur as every bit as important as foreign policy, celebrity scandals, or professional sports, it will be, by my criteria, a success.

This serial group portrait, with numerous additional "snapshots" tucked into the frame, has four major narrative strands: sex research, pornography, sexual minorities, and contemporary sexual culture as celebrated, for better or worse, by some of its most ardent enthusiasts.

The larger message of this book is that the Sexual Revolution, far from being a pop-cultural epoch bookended between the mid-sixties and the late seventies, is in fact part of a permanent continuum of revolutionary events that has scarcely begun.

It is also a call to arms against the ancien régime of an oppressive church-state morality fueled by a dishonest, even barbarous sexual tyranny that men continue to impose on women in every culture, in every generation. Something resembling peace on earth can be achieved only when all women, in every country in the world, are sexually free at last. As Wilhelm Reich rightly proclaimed in *The Mass Psychology of Fascism* in 1933: "Sexually awakened women, affirmed and recognized as such, would mean the complete collapse of the authoritarian ideology."

It was the destiny of the flawed, all-too-human heroines and heroes of this book, in combination with other powerful medical, legal, and cultural forces, to be the pioneers of that collective, all-transforming, world-redeeming erotic awakening, which is even now only in its early morning.

Sex wise and sex foolish, this, then, is the way we were from about 1965 on, when the particles of revolt and enlightenment coalesced into a sexual Big Bang. It was a time of great courage, genius, inspired wackiness, and steady vision, and also craven duplicity, fear, and fanaticism. History had never seen its like, and probably never will again.

Note

By the very nature of the subject matter, some sexually explicit passages in this book border on the pornographic. Yet my intention throughout has been not to titillate the reader, but to give her or him as accurate, detailed, and unflinching a picture of what has recently happened in the world of sexuality as possible without crossing the line into prurience, or what moral theologians once called morose delectation.

I am also mindful, as Keats remarked, that English must be "kept up," which I have endeavored to do to the best of my modest ability. But at times, terms such as "blow job," "fuck," and "cum shot" seemed more appropriate than their clumsier, if more socially acceptable, alternatives.

In some instances, I have been obliged both by the law and by common decency to respect the privacy of certain individuals who make a brief appearance in these pages. Where only a first name is used to identify a person, that name is either fictitious and all identifying characteristics have been altered, or it is a pseudonym used by that individual.

None of the dialogue reported herein has been invented but is based on oral or written testimony.

Finally, I will be happy for the regard of any reader who thinks of this book as is sometimes said of sex itself: even when it is not great, it is still pretty good.

PART ONE

DESIRE

1965 – 1971

Chapter 1

The Orgasm That Changed the World

SHE IS COMPLETELY NUDE, LYING ON HER BACK ON A NARROW HOSPITAL BED, HER legs spread wide, droplets of perspiration forming on her body as her right hand—the fingernails painted bright red—feverishly rubs her clitoris.

Peering into the dark, pink recesses of her vagina, spread open by a gynecologist's speculum, is an eight-millimeter camera ready to record what no human eye has ever seen before.

What the camera is looking for is the Holy Grail of human intimacy. For a hundred years, a handful of scientists and physicians had sought to study the sexual arousal and climax of women under clinical conditions. Most often they were motivated by a desire to help so-called frigid women to achieve orgasm.

Theories on why an estimated one-third of all women were never able to find sexual fulfillment, and another third only occasionally, ranged from the preposterous to the enlightened. But the most prevalent hypothesis was that formulated by Freud a half century earlier—that women had two kinds of orgasm, one deriving from clitoral stimulation, the other vaginal. Freud regarded the former as immature and imitative of the male orgasm, the latter as mature and superior.

As a result, knowing older women told younger girls, doctors told patients, husbands told wives: a clitoral-centered orgasm was just fine for sexual beginners. Freud and his clinical heirs maintained that it was most likely a holdover from adolescent masturbatory practices that had to be "unlearned." By implication, women who did not experience a vaginal or true orgasm during sexual intercourse were not fully women, not fulfilled in the deepest core of their sexual being.

The problem was that a very great many women were convinced their orgasmic pleasure derived from their clitoris and wondered what they were missing, and why.

What the researchers in this secret laboratory hoped to discover was a clue as to why and how some women, a minority, were capable of orgasm, and why so many others were not, and what could be done about it. It seemed like such a humble—or maybe, given the times, frivolous—goal. Yet its social, political, and everyday ramifications were incalculable.

Nameless and faceless, the woman in the film is preserved for posterity on a single videotape (a transcription from the original eight-millimeter) on a half-forgotten shelf of the Institute for Sex Research in Bloomington, Indiana. Recorded in 1958 for showing to medical students on a portable home screen, her orgasm qualifies as the original low-tech Story of O, an earnest, clumsy cross between an industrial training film and a stag movie.

The color is faded, the voice-over almost inaudible, the title pedantic: "The Female Orgasm: An Investigation of the Anatomical and Physiological Changes Associated with Artificially Induced Orgasm in the Female Subject Has Been Undertaken [sic] by the Department of Obstetrics and Gynecology of Washington University School of Medicine, St. Louis, Mo." Masturbation was still a forbidden word.

Yet the woman's moment of pure pleasure will endure for all time, long after the video itself has disintegrated or been lost altogether. What she is about to provide for the laboratory camera is historic proof that a woman's orgasm is not penis dependent, but anatomically and psychosexually self-sufficient.

The opening segment of the film documents the woman's upper-body response to erotic self-stimulation with traditional camera techniques. The woman has already entered the first phase of what later generations would come to know as the sexual response cycle—desire. With phase two—excitement—little white arrows appear on the screen to indicate the swelling areolae of her nipples, the flushed skin across her stomach.

Then comes the lower-body sequence. The woman's hand is shown rubbing her clitoris above the speculum as the narrator points out the "sweating" on the vaginal walls. An unfamiliar landscape appears—a soft, moist, pink tunnel where countless mysterious beads form and coalesce within seconds, lubricating the entire passage.

What happens next, science has never before seen. As the woman enters the third stage of response, the plateau phase, her clitoris elevates slightly and retracts, drawing away from the vaginal entrance so that any contact between her clitoris and the penis of a man—should her lover be of the opposite sex—becomes less probable, then virtually impossible.

By the time the word "orgasm" appears on the top of the screen, the woman's muscular tension is palpable. She has reached the fourth stage, and her entire orgasmic platform—the outer third of her vagina—is seized by violent, rhythmic spasms, each contraction beginning in the upper uterus, moving downward like a wave into her cervix, and lasting less than a second. Though the contractions of a woman in childbirth are more widely spaced and much more powerful, they bear a remarkable similarity to those of a woman having an orgasm. The narrator does not enumerate, but the contractions number about ten—indicating an orgasm of above average duration.

Almost as abruptly as this anonymous orgasm began, it ends. The woman's body returns to its unstimulated state. Her labia degorge, her clitoris peeks out again from its hood, her nipples soften. Nature has rendered her, and all women, capable of repeated orgasms for as long as her libido can sustain the paroxysms of lust. Today, though, she has elected to enter the fifth and final stage, resolution. For most men—whose sexual response cycle in other respects parallels that of women—this stage is not an option, but a physiological necessity.

The film has helped to prove one simple fact: Stimulation of the clitoris has caused the woman to have an orgasm that erupted within her vagina. That mysterious bulb, in male chauvinist terms the homologue of the penis, but in fact the only human organ that exists solely to bestow pleasure, is the wellspring of female orgasm. In the average woman, no amount of stimulation of the vagina or other erogenous zone will cause the same cataclysm of pleasure.

As the film sputters to an end, the imagination of the viewer takes over. Who was this woman, sharing her body on such intimate terms with science at the dawn of the Sexual Revolution? In the annals of sex research, her name will remain forever anonymous, her identity protected by the strictest laws of confidentiality.

Broadly speaking, though, she was Everywoman, whose sexuality had for centuries been slowly and painfully emerging out of bondage to the male sex and into independence. At a slightly more specific level, she was one of 382 women—including black and Mexican prostitutes as well as graduate students and nurses (she herself was white)—who took part in the most ambitious, most incongruous, and most secretive exploration into sexual physiology ever undertaken.

That it happened at all, that it happened in America's conservative heartland, and that so many women, and men, readily volunteered their services in the cause of sexual enlightenment and freedom, was nothing less than one of the great miracles of twentieth-century science.

THE LONG PROCESS leading to the scientific proof of the clitoral orgasm began on the morning of July 5, 1954, when a balding, well-tanned, thirty-six-year-old obstetrician-gynecologist named William Howell Masters approached the librarian of the medical school of Washington University in St. Louis, Missouri, one of the most respected in the nation. The moment was paradigmatic not only for the state of sex research at mid–twentieth century, but for American sexual mores and the fragile, newborn science of sexology.

Just once in the previous half century had America briefly glimpsed the sexual light, only to recoil in horror, fear, and disbelief. That glorious, though ultimately tragic, seven-year period was just ending in that same pivotal year of 1954, which marked not only the end of one major era of sex research, but the beginning of another. It, too, had begun with a visit to the library by another midwestern professor, Dr. Alfred C. Kinsey.

In 1919, after receiving his doctorate from Harvard University, Kinsey had accepted a position in the zoology department at Indiana University in arcadian Bloomington, where he set about making a name for himself in the field of taxonomy, eventually amassing a staggering five million gall wasps for classification. In 1938 the Association of Women Students petitioned the university to inaugurate a noncredit course on marriage. A straight arrow who neither smoked nor drank, Kinsey was asked to coordinate the course and to deliver lectures on the biological aspects of sex and marriage. The course became an immediate success, with enrollment quadrupling in the first two years.

To prepare for his lectures, Kinsey went to the university library to search for data. What he found on the biological aspects of marriage was either derivative or largely opinion based. Midway in his academic career, he began to channel his enormous energy into the study of human sexual behavior.

At first Kinsey relied on a questionnaire distributed to students attending his marriage class, then to other students and faculty, and later to almost anybody he could persuade to be interviewed. Eventually he developed a 350-item questionnaire that was administered in face-to-face interviews, with questions phrased nonjudgmentally and answers encoded to maintain strict confidentiality and ensure honesty. Of the eighteen thousand interviews done under his supervision between 1938 and 1956, eight thousand were conducted by Kinsey personally.

In 1940, under pressure from community leaders concerned about the nature of the sex professor's inquiries, university officials asked Kinsey to choose between his interviews and his marriage course. To everybody's surprise, Kinsey abandoned the course that made him the most popular lecturer on campus and began to devote himself full-time to the collection of sexual case histories. He quickly secured financial support for his study from the National Research Council's Committee for Research in the Problems of Sex, at that time funded by the Rockefeller Foundation. The funding enabled him to assemble a multidisciplinary research team and expand his fieldwork.

His core team consisted of Clyde E. Martin, a student assistant who became a full-time associate in 1941; Wardell B. Pomeroy, a clinical psychologist, who joined the team in 1943; and Paul H. Gebhard, an anthropologist, who was hired in 1946.

With the interviews in the thousands and climbing, in 1947 Kinsey established the Institute for Sex Research as an independent, nonprofit organization, largely to protect the confidentiality of his subjects. He also began to amass a vast library of pornographic books and films and other erotic artifacts, some dating back to the pre-Christian era.

Kinsey's first book, *Sexual Behavior in the Human Male,* the result of ten years of research, was published in 1948 by W. B. Saunders, a house specializing in medical texts. No one, least of all Kinsey, anticipated that this dry academic tome would find an audience beyond a handful of physicians and scientists. In the ensuing brouhaha, however, the book was featured in dozens of magazines and newspapers. *Newsweek* prudishly mentioned its statistics on "onanism" (masturbation) and "sexual satisfaction" (orgasm). A runaway sensation, the book sold two hundred thousand copies in two years and remained on the best-seller list for a year, yet *The New York Times* would not accept advertising for it.

Among the scandalous findings: 86 percent of white males reported having premarital sex by age thirty, 37 percent had same-gender experiences to orgasm, two-thirds reported having sex with a prostitute. An extraordinary 97 percent claimed to have had illicit sex: 50 percent had committed adultery by age forty, while 17 percent of males raised on farms had sex with animals; three out of four males ejaculated within two minutes of penetration; and so on.

Five years later, *Sexual Behavior in the Human Female,* packed with equally startling reports of female premarital sex, masturbation, sexual contacts in childhood, and orgasm rates, was published to similar success and outrage. Only now, with the sacred honor of American womanhood at stake, the furor reached the U.S. Congress. Representative Carroll Reece of Tennessee formed a committee to investigate tax-exempt foundations and their support of un-American activities. In particular, the committee targeted the Rockefeller Foundation for subsidizing Kinsey's institute. One member of Congress commented that any study of the sex behavior of Americans paved the way for a Communist takeover of the United States.

In mid-1954, around the time Dr. Masters took his own trip to the library, the besieged Rockefeller Foundation withdrew its financial support of the ISR's work and other sex-related research. At the same time, U.S. Customs officers began seizing shipments of sex materials to the institute, including items destined for its collection of erotica.

The climate for sexual research in 1954 could not have been more hostile. Though the United States was enjoying unprecedented prosperity, a soaring birth rate, and a religious revival all at once, the international threat of Communism had given rise to a feverish hunt for subversives willing to hand over America's democratic paradise to the Kremlin. The result was an extraordinary conformity in the country's cultural life, and nowhere more so than in sexual conduct. Any display of sexual individualism, much less any explicit exploration of sexual issues in either a public or professional forum, was strongly discouraged, if not prosecuted.

In his last years, Kinsey suffered from severe depression caused by the stress of coping with the press and the conservative backlash, as well as by deep divisions among his core team of researchers. Unknown to the public, the famed institute in Bloomington was in a shambles, riven by intrigue. Yet Kinsey refused to moderate his normal fourteen-hour workday and soon developed symptoms of cardiovascular disease. On August 25, 1956, at the age of sixty-two, he died of cardiac failure following an attack of pneumonia.

What alarmed the American public about Kinsey was his utter lack of regard for sexual "normalcy." Like any good zoologist, he was more concerned with describing individual and group variations in human sexual behavior from an empirical biological and taxonomic perspective. He achieved that goal by looking at the prevalence and frequency of six different outlets to orgasm: masturbation, petting, nocturnal dreams, heterosexual coitus, homosexual responses and contacts, and contacts with animals. These findings were correlated with age, educational level, marital status, occupation, decade of birth, and religion.

The three most controversial aspects of Kinsey's data concerned female sexuality, homosexuality, and masturbation. When the female volume was published, few Americans were prepared for Kinsey's finding that women were interested in sex for more than procreative purposes. Many were shocked by data suggesting that females were as capable of sexual response and orgasm as males. Half the women interviewed said they had not been virgins when they married, and one-quarter admitted to engaging in extramarital sex.

Kinsey also found that 10 percent of male respondents were predominantly homosexual for at least three years between the ages of sixteen and fifty-five, and that 4 percent of white males were exclusively homosexual. His research further challenged the traditional mutually exclusive categories of homosexual and heterosexual, which he thought did not accurately reflect the complexities of human behavior.

Also according to Kinsey, more than 90 percent of males and 62 percent of females reported having masturbated. Like his findings on female sexuality and homosexuality, this data was a direct affront to the sexual hubris, insecurities, and hypocrisy of the Great White Penis, aka the white heterosexual male power structure.

As a result of Kinsey's heroic challenge to the monolithism of American sexual culture, he was not only denied the honors, praise, and financial patronage that were his just due, but he was hounded all his professional life by J. Edgar Hoover's Federal Bureau of Investigation, possibly the only American institution more obsessed with sex than the Institute for Sex Research.

BILL MASTERS had met Kinsey briefly some years earlier at a reception, shaken his hand, and exchanged a few pleasantries. But neither giant of sex research, the one with his life's work behind him, the other still mulling what to do with his life, talked about their favorite subject.

Though neither man knew it at the time, the young gynecologist was destined to become the intellectual and clinical heir of the great Indiana sex researcher. The reason was disgracefully simple. Nobody else in the country, nobody else in the world—it is not too much to say—gave a damn enough about whether women got any satisfaction in bed to find out just exactly why not and what to do about it.

Masters did not set off on his search specifically to find out the truth about vaginal orgasm. Passionately sympathetic to the sexual problems of his patients, he wanted primarily to study orgasmic function and dysfunction in order to discover how sexual physiology might affect infertile couples and what he could do to help them.

Born in Cleveland in 1915, the son of well-to-do parents, Masters was inspired to go into medicine by his younger brother, Frank, later a plastic surgeon and professor at the University of Kansas in Kansas City. After earning a bachelor's degree in English and science from Hamilton College, he served briefly in the service before getting a medical discharge. Masters then enrolled in the University of Rochester School of Medicine and Dentistry, with the intention of specializing in biological research. At Rochester he had the good fortune to study under Dr. George Washington Corner, one of the country's foremost anatomists and the mentor of none other than Alfred C. Kinsey.

The turning point in Masters's career occurred in 1941 when he was invited to spend spring vacation at the Carnegie Institute of Embryology in Baltimore. After taking up a new position as its director, Corner had invited several major reproductive biologists in the United States to join him, including Masters. Corner later was to discover progesterone, one of the two major female sex hormones. One day, while the group of researchers was seated around a table, a man entered, badly scratched up. He had been handling a monkey in heat. Reflecting on the behavioral changes brought on by the animal's hormonal cycle, Masters asked himself: "What do we know about the human female when she is menstruating?"

Masters's first significant assignment was to compare the estrous cycle of the female rabbit with the menstrual cycle of women. He was spectacularly unsuccessful, mainly because not enough was known about the latter. At that point the young student decided to narrow his goal to sex research in order to learn more about how and why humans mated.

Kinsey himself, then all but unknown, had only recently begun his own investigations, and publication of his surveys was still many years away. Masters thus understood he was about to undertake a voyage into unknown and possibly professionally perilous waters. To protect himself, he met on several occasions with his mentor and colleagues, trying to identify the qualifications necessary for a pioneer sex researcher.

The group decided that such an individual had to be a male (overlooking the pioneering examples of Margaret Sanger, Margaret Mead, and nineteenth-century American sex researcher Clelia Mosher); be old enough to dispel the charge of prurient motives; be established in another medical field so that his scientific dedication not be questionable; and, most important, be supported by a medical school or university. Despite the sexism and naïveté in such thinking, it was fully warranted and responsible, given the times.

The very next year Masters married, and in 1943 he moved to St. Louis, where he served first as a resident, then as an instructor, at Barnes Hospital, a teaching institution affiliated with Washington University. Over the next decade he fulfilled the remainder of those four criteria, avoiding the political infighting and high profile that would have come with being associated with a major East Coast institution while earning a reputation for research into steroid replacement and the regulation of dosage for aging men and women. In 1951 he was certified by the American Board of Obstetricians and Gynecologists.

Two years later Masters approached the reigning powers at Washington University and asked permission to study human sexual behavior. By now both Kinsey books had been published. Despite the great controversy inundating the Indiana researcher and his associates, a precedent had been set. Though Washington University authorities were duly terrified, they also had little understanding of what they were getting into. They thought Masters would do more of what Kinsey was doing—surveying people. But Masters was more interested in basic physiology—which meant observing, in a laboratory setting, people actually having sex.

Finally, after more than a year of agonized waiting, he got his answer. At the end of June 1954, the board of trustees of the university granted Masters permission, "on the basis of academic freedom," to launch his clinical investigation into human sexuality.

The day after the July Fourth weekend, Masters rushed to the library to amass all the relevant materials he could put his hands on and get to work. To his amazement, he found only a single medical book on the subject—Robert Latou Dickinson's *Atlas of Human Sexual Anatomy.* When he attempted to check out the book, the librarian informed him that he was not even allowed to look at it.

Shocked, Masters demanded an explanation. The librarian pointed out that the book contained illustrations of the sexual organs, which meant only a full professor could see it. A mere assistant professor of obstetrics, Masters was out of luck.

Eventually he was able to read the book. But lack of reference materials led him to pay another visit to Ethan Shepley, the university chancellor, for permission to work with those who knew something about sex. Specifically, he wanted to study prostitutes for one year. Shepley paled. But he gave Masters permission, on condition that he work with a review board consisting of St. Louis police commissioner Sam Priest; Richard Amberg, publisher of the far-right *St. Louis Globe-Democrat;* and Joseph Cardinal Ritter, head of the Roman Catholic Archdiocese of St. Louis. Without the backing of those four staunch defenders of public morality, who routinely, in commencement addresses, editorials, and sermons, denounced the very activities the young physician was submerged in, Masters could never have assumed Kinsey's mantle.

Masters went to see Priest, a tall, lumbering, cigar-chomping man, and explained his problem. A father of two children, a churchgoing Episcopalian, and a Republican, Masters wanted Priest to put him in touch with some prostitutes so he could find out firsthand what he was unable to learn in the rarefied precincts of the city's finest medical library.

Priest obliged by arranging for Masters to stand for hours at a time in the cramped voyeur's booths at a succession of cathouses, watching as black and Mexican whores tugged their often drunken customers by their penises into a room or squeezed their penises to keep them from ejaculating until enough time and thrusting had passed for them to feel they had gotten their money's worth.

Masters spent eighteen months working with both male and female prostitutes in brothels in the Midwest, West Coast, Canada, and Mexico, studying the varieties of sexual experience, including all known variations of intercourse, oral sex, anal sex, and an assortment of fetishes. He interviewed the female prostitutes, examined their blood-engorged labia after a sex session, quizzed them on sexual technique, and asked them what they knew about such rumored phenomena as the vaginal orgasm, multiple orgasm, orgasm occurring with no genital stimulation, and female ejaculation.

After he had learned all he could in the brothels, Masters was ready for the next stage of his research. In the greatest secrecy he opened a small, three-room clinic on the upper floor of the maternity hospital associated with

Washington University, smuggling in more prostitutes and graduate student volunteers who had heard about the laboratory by word of mouth. Visitors and staff alike entered through the office, the largest of the three rooms.

In back was a small laboratory with a one-way mirror that permitted staff persons to observe from time to time. On the other side of the hallway were the steps—a vital piece of geography—and a biology laboratory. When a volunteer was due to arrive or leave, staff members patrolled the hallway to make sure no one saw her or him arriving or exiting.

Over the next decade, the "green room" in the back of Masters's tiny laboratory was the scene of more than 10,000 orgasms experienced by 382 women and 312 men—each orgasm meticulously measured, analyzed, filmed. The volunteers, selected from 1,200 applicants, were usually paid for masturbating or engaging in sexual intercourse and ranged in age from eighteen to eighty-nine. One reason why Masters preferred volunteers over prostitutes for his physiological studies was that many of the latter suffered from chronic congestion of the pelvic area caused by prolonged excitation without release. Their condition rendered them atypical and therefore unsuitable as clinical subjects. Later Masters also began to see individuals and couples afflicted with any of a variety of sexual problems—impotence, premature ejaculation, vaginal dryness. The youngest couple he ever treated was a wife of eighteen and her twenty-two-year-old husband; the oldest, a woman of eighty-four and her husband, who was ninety-one.

Masters was obsessed with secrecy, primarily to preserve the privacy of the volunteers and clients. But as word spread of the secretive goings-on at a sex laboratory trafficking in prostitutes and surrogates, snoopers became a serious problem. Once Masters caught a doctor from a neighboring suite eavesdropping with his stethoscope.

In March 1956 Bill Masters had the great fortune to meet a very attractive prostitute with a Ph.D. in sociology who sold her services to enhance her university salary. As she talked to Masters about the subjective aspects of female sexual arousal, she could see that he had no frame of reference for what she was talking about. Finally, in exasperation, she said: "You know, you're never really going to know anything about the subjective aspects of female sexual functioning, are you? What you need is an interpreter."

The more he thought about that, the more he agreed with her, and later he gave her credit for developing the concept of the dual-sex team for research and therapy. In the fall he placed a hubristic—and ungrammatical—job description at the university placement office, stating that the successful female candidate for the position had to be "(a) good with people, because I'm not; (b) have to work; (c) married and divorced, and at least one child; (d) intelligent; and (e) no post-graduate degree." Masters included this last criterion because he did not want the responsibility of having a woman risk the loss of her degree, even though he knew he himself still stood a good chance of losing his medical license. Perhaps more important, he did not want someone with graduate school theories of her own that might interfere with his.

In December 1956 he interviewed a twice divorced, middle-aged mother of two named Gini Johnson, who joined him the following January. The gynecologist was convinced that her lack of education and experience rendered her an Eliza Doolittle of sex research.

VIRGINIA ESHELMAN was born into a Springfield, Missouri, farming family in which any discussion of sexuality was rigidly forbidden. After studying music at a local college, she was briefly married to a much older lawyer who did not want children. They divorced, and Eshelman moved to St. Louis, where she took a job as a secretary while pursuing a singing career on an amateur level. In June 1950 Eshelman wed St. Louis band leader George Johnson, with whom she had two children, and performed with his ensemble at a variety of local venues. When that marriage, too, ended in divorce a few years later, she worked as a secretary at a local radio station and as a ballroom dance instructor.

By 1956, one year after Masters began his investigations, Gini Johnson was in search of work when she registered for a job in the placement bureau of Washington University. She had no degree and no experience in much of anything except singing. But Bill Masters was astute enough to realize her personable manner ideally complemented his own stern, circumspect bearing. In their immaculate white laboratory smocks they were to present a remarkable study in contrasts—he with his deep-set eyes, fixed powerful gaze, long straight nose, strong chin, and uncommunicative air; she with her auburn hair swept back from her face into a ponytail and her ready smile. Johnson joined Masters on January 2, 1957, and was put to work in the physiology laboratory. She quickly became a zealot for the cause, working literally around the clock, though promising herself that after ten years she would quit and return to her singing career.

The research that Masters and Johnson now jointly embarked on was unique in respects other than its unprecedented scale. Masters—later assisted by Johnson—also devised a variety of highly sensitive instruments to measure literally every microsecond of female and male arousal and climax. One of these was a recording drum that monitored the number and intervals of vaginal contractions; another sought to explain the mystery of vaginal lubrication and aspiration. Other props and instruments included an electrocardiograph, an electroencephalograph for measuring blood-volume change in a penis, biochemical equipment, floodlights, and color movie cameras. Most crucial of all was a nine-inch-long clear Lucite phallus with a ray of cold light emanating from its glans so that the camera lens housed inside the shaft could venture deep inside a woman's vaginal walls to discover other secrets of human sexual response.

Masters and Johnson chose to study female physiology first because they thought women would be much more difficult subjects than males. (Later they learned that males, burdened with the lion's share of sex hangups and problems, posed the greater challenge.) To assure volunteer anonymity, they also worked odd hours and a grueling seven-day week. Beginning July 1, 1954, Masters personally did not take one day off for seventeen years—not even Christmas or New Year's.

Kinsey and his associates had also studied sexual intercourse and other sexual practices in a laboratory setting. But in the wake of the storm of controversy following the publication of his works on the sexual behavior of the human male and female, those findings were never publicized.

Though Masters and Johnson's research was motivated primarily by a desire to help infertile couples conceive, the two sex researchers were determined to solve the mystery of female orgasm. Both ardent feminists, far in advance of their time, they soon surmised that the Freudian distinction between clitoral and vaginal orgasm was not only erroneous but sexist.

Kinsey had also contradicted this Freudian premise in *Sexual Behavior in the Human Female,* noting: "There are no anatomic data to indicate that such a physical transformation has ever been observed or is possible." Rather, he postulated that "the concept of a vaginal orgasm may mean, on the other hand, that the spasms that accompany or follow orgasm involved the vagina." Since the vaginal opening lay near the clitoral shaft, it seemed possible that the shaft was stimulated indirectly during intercourse.

But during arousal, as Masters and Johnson learned, the clitoris did not become erect. Rather it withdrew beneath its protective foreskin. As climax approached, its length was also reduced by at least half.

Kinsey had also argued that the main difference between male and female sexual response was psychological—that men depended more on mental stimuli than did women. The basis for that opinion was the view that the clitoris was a miniature penis, since it is an anatomical homologue of the male sex organ.

Yet Masters and Johnson demonstrated two major differences between the penis and the clitoris. The male organ ejaculated, and except in very rare cases—usually very young teenagers—was incapable of another orgasm without first undergoing a refractory period.

But in some women, if stimulation was immediately resumed after orgasm, the clitoris could repeat the pleasure cycle over and over again; it had no refractory period. Masters and Johnson recorded some women who experienced from twenty to fifty orgasms in a single session.

Also the clitoris rarely if ever made contact with the penis of the male during sexual intercourse. What stimulated the clitoris during intercourse was friction not against the penis or male pubis, but against its own hood.

Most significant, the clitoris responded to general pressure in the mons area. Though the outer third of the vaginal area was highly sensitive to sexual stimuli, Masters and Johnson concluded that it played no direct role in female orgasm.

This reinvention of the female orgasm, on an almost Copernican scale, had several major ramifications for sex therapy and sexual politics. In the first place, it established the erotic independence of women insofar as their sexual fulfillment was no longer modeled after that of the male. Moreover, women were shown to be not only independent of men, but capable of more and deeper orgasms than even the most potent of young men. Indirectly, Masters and Johnson's findings also meant that well-endowed males had no right to feel sexually superior, because penis size was irrelevant to a woman's gratification.

In addition to their physiological explorations, Masters and Johnson struggled to devise treatments for the variety of sexual difficulties afflicting both women and men.

To help treat male patients, they found it necessary to resort to the use of sexual surrogates—another radical innovation that went virtually unnoticed by civil authorities. At first, all the surrogates were prostitutes. Before long, however, Masters encountered intense opposition from members of the university administration and fellow faculty members, who regarded the use of prostitutes as not only illegal but immoral, or at the very least questionable from the point of view of medical ethics.

Masters eventually stopped using prostitutes and began advertising for volunteers from among female graduate and medical students. Out of thirty-one volunteers, thirteen women were selected, ranging in age from twenty-four to forty-three. All but two had been previously married. One was a physician interested in sexual dysfunction.

Despite later rumors to the contrary, no dysfunctional men or women were ever asked to perform in the physiological laboratory—Masters and Johnson would not have considered putting such pressure on their clients. Rather, the researchers always worked with two different populations, those they studied in the research laboratory and those seen in clinical practice.

Masters and Johnson also rarely used the one-way mirror. Clients were shown where it was and how it could be blocked from the inside if they so desired. A far more important goal was to gain the clients' trust, which Masters and Johnson often obtained by introducing a distraction factor. For example, after an initial session Masters and Johnson usually sat and worked in an adjacent room, with the door ajar, thus assuring the couple that the two researchers would neither observe them nor enter the room. In this way the couple undergoing therapy became accustomed to having other people around.

The next step was for Masters and Johnson to enter the room occasionally and tell the couple just to continue with their activity. Actual observation did not begin until patients felt comfortable with occasional entrances and exits.

Usually there were at least two observers and occasionally a physiologist or two who monitored the EKG or polygraph or ran the cameras. If they were measuring, for example, vaginal lubrication at certain intervals, the researchers did not necessarily remain in the room the entire time; on other occasions they might just sit and stare for an hour at a four-inch-square patch of skin, trying to determine significant color changes.

As word of the sexual goings-on reached beyond the precincts of the university, Masters and Johnson pleaded with the local press not to publish anything before their study was complete. Ironically, the *Globe-Democrat,* one of the most right-wing publications in the country, was not a problem since publisher Richard Amberg had been a powerful supporter of Masters's research from the very beginning. But the progressive, Pulitzer-owned *Post-Dispatch* could not entirely be trusted.

By the end of the 1950s Masters and Johnson also had to contend with sabotage that went beyond people trying to identify their volunteers. When the pair borrowed the medical school's two-channel recording equipment, parts began to disappear, making it necessary for someone to stand guard over it around the clock. Most alarming were the personal attacks against Masters's children, who were socially ostracized. Masters ultimately felt it necessary to send his daughter to a school out of town.

By 1958 Masters and Johnson had become convinced of the multidisciplinary nature of their specialty. Though neither had any training in psychotherapy beyond Masters's three-month course in psychiatric interview technique, they saw this as positive, enabling them to develop a rapid method of sex therapy, which they saw as an educational process. Eventually the three-week course of treatment was reduced to two weeks to accommodate most people's vacation schedules.

During those two-week treatments, the social isolation of the couple from the cares and distractions of their workaday life was strongly emphasized. Masters viewed sex as a natural function, and dysfunction as akin to respiratory, bowel, or bladder malfunction. In some cases the problem *was* purely mechanical—for example, ejaculatory incompetence might have a urological cause. In other cases the solution might be mechanical regardless of the origins of the problem—most famously the "squeeze technique" used by prostitutes that later became an established part of sexual therapy after Masters and Johnson discovered it was an almost surefire method to prevent a man from ejaculating prematurely.

* * *

WHILE GYNECOLOGIST BILL MASTERS labored to unlock the mysteries of sexual physiology, hoping that his findings might help infertile couples conceive, another gynecologist at Harvard was taking an entirely different tack. In his attempts to cure infertility in women, Dr. John Rock, the tall, handsome, debonair chief of gynecology and obstetrics at the Harvard Medical School, had come to believe that administering the female hormones progesterone and estrogen might stimulate conception.

In 1944 Rock was the first scientist ever to fertilize a human egg in a test tube and among the first to freeze sperm cells for a year without impairing their potency. By 1945 it was known that progesterone inhibited ovulation, but how was uncertain. In his experiments administering progesterone to "infertile" women, though, Rock noticed that a significant number of them got pregnant after the treatment stopped.

Dr. Gregory Pincus, a Harvard-educated biologist, was also carrying out extensive laboratory tests related to infertility. In 1934 Pincus had achieved in vitro fertilization of rabbit eggs and subsequently built a research center at Clark University in Worcester, Massachusetts.

In the late forties Margaret Sanger, founder of Planned Parenthood, and Katherine McCormick, a wealthy American dedicated to the birth control movement, asked Pincus if a drug were possible to stop conception. After he replied in the affirmative, Planned Parenthood provided him with the first of several grants. Applying the basic research of others, particularly Russell Marker, who had produced a chemical imitation of progesterone from the roots of the Mexican yam tree, Pincus developed a contraceptive pill combining synthetic estrogen and progesterone. He eventually enlisted the help of Rock, who in 1954 experimented on three women with a powerful new synthetic version of progesterone.

A Catholic, Rock had not set off on a quest for a birth control pill. But he was also becoming alarmed at the population explosion and had begun to fit some of his patients with diaphragms, leading several of his Catholic colleagues to attempt to have him excommunicated. A daily communicant, devoted husband, and loving father who was monogamous to the core, Rock was never to waver in his devotion to the church, but he never flagged in his crusade against church doctrine on birth control, either. Moreover, he encouraged hysterectomy candidates to have intercourse just prior to their operations—which meant, in effect, that he was arranging potential abortions to facilitate his experiments. His historic test-tube fertilization of a human egg was also, in the eyes of the church, the moral equivalent of an abortion.

In 1956 Rock skillfully conducted a series of clinical trials with his new pill on two hundred women in Puerto Rico—birth control being still illegal in Massachusetts. The following year the pill was approved by the Food and

Drug Administration (FDA) for treating women with menstrual disorders. Next came another double-blind clinical trial involving 897 more women in Puerto Rico—a method that many would consider ethically questionable today. Those trials led directly to a scant two-inch notice in *The New York Times* on May 10, 1960, that the world was about to change—the FDA had approved for public consumption a birth control pill called Enovid, produced by G. D. Searle & Co. in Chicago, and for the first time in history millions of women were potentially free from unwanted or untimely births.

By the end of 1961 more than four hundred thousand American women were taking the pill. The following year that figure had jumped to more than a million, and in 1963 it more than doubled again to three million, with coeds leading the way. By 1966 six million American women and another six million around the world were on the pill. Ambassador Clare Boothe Luce said of it: "Modern woman is at last free as a man is free, to dispose of her own body, to earn her living, to pursue the improvement of her mind, to try a successful career."

Rock had argued that the pill was a totally natural variant of the rhythm method, which the church blessed. But the church ignored him, just as it later ignored the special 1965 Vatican commission on birth control, which unanimously favored a reversal of traditional doctrine. In 1968 Pope Paul VI's encyclical *Humanae Vitae* condemned the pill and all other forms of artificial contraception.

With good reason, Margaret Sanger, who died in 1966, looked upon the Catholic Church as the most formidable of her enemies.

IN 1960 Bill Masters taught a required course for medical students on reproductive biology. In the first hour he concentrated on female infertility, which the overwhelmingly male student population took in stride. The second hour, on male infertility, raised hackles. Masters devoted the final hour to female sexual physiology, which led to pandemonium. A quarter of the students went to the dean and demanded that the lectures be discontinued. Three members of the executive faculty did likewise.

The dean, a friend of Masters's old mentor, George Washington Corner, told Masters, "Bill, they just complained, they didn't put it in writing, and down here in the small print it says I don't have to bring it up in executive faculty unless I have it in writing."

As a result, nothing ever happened.

Even so, Masters was beginning to feel confined by university politics and knew that he could broaden his sex research only if he went independent. That same year he and Johnson also submitted their first publication on sexual physiology to both *Obstetrics and Gynecology* and a psychiatric journal. The latter rejected the material outright as pornographic, while the former published their groundbreaking "The Sexual Response Cycle of the Human Female."

In 1964 Masters and Johnson decided to break from Washington University and create a public foundation for the study of sexuality, which they christened the Reproductive Biology Research Foundation.

When they began offering sex therapy in 1959, all patients were local, and all were married. Most were referred by doctors, judges in divorce cases, or the Missouri Division of Family Services, which worked with couples trying to conceive. Initially Masters and Johnson conducted five-year follow-ups of clients, but after thirteen years they concluded that more than 90 percent of sexual problems reappeared within the first two years after therapy. Follow-up was then reduced to two years. For the first five years of their program they also provided the sex therapy free of charge.

Now, out of economic necessity, they began to charge for therapy. The intensive two-week course cost $1,000, exclusive of hotel and other living expenses. Couples usually booked into a room at the nearby Chase-Park Plaza Hotel overlooking Forest Park. Though many of the patients included anorgasmic women, numerous others were couples who never even had intercourse. One couple's marriage had been unconsummated for twenty-three years.

In November 1964 the secrecy surrounding Masters and Johnson's research was destroyed irrevocably when Washington, D.C., psychoanalyst Leslie Farber attacked the still unknown researchers in *Commentary* with an article entitled "I'm Sorry, Dear." A nasty, stupid, shortsighted snicker, the article poked fun at the "moviemaking" the researchers had described in an article published in *Obstetrics and Gynecology* and at some of their findings, such as the minute changes in coloration in the vagina as a woman headed toward orgasm. Farber jokingly mused on the true degree of Masters's detachment from his work and disparaged the researchers' attempts to isolate the orgasm in the laboratory as a clinical obsession that would destroy the mystery of sex.

Fearful that their work was being reviewed even before it was published, Masters and Johnson pushed up publication of *Human Sexual Response* by a year. It reached bookstores on April 26, 1966; the first printing, despite intentionally turgid prose, sold out in one week and ultimately sold more than three hundred thousand copies. After an *AMA Journal* editorial pronounced the work worthy, requests for interviews flooded in. Overnight the pair went from being covert sex researchers to international celebrities who felt secure enough to decline offers to appear on talk shows hosted by Merv Griffin,

Dick Cavett, and David Frost. They also turned down a $100,000 offer for movie rights to their book.

But they did appear on NBC's *Today* show and gave interviews to *Time, Newsweek, Life,* the *Atlantic,* and *The New York Times,* and they accepted speaking engagements at medical conventions all over the country. Each took a third of the royalties, and they gave another third to their foundation. It was a welcome influx, since after 1962 they had been turned down for federal research funding, even for research that had major implications for birth control. (For example, their studies of female sexual response showed that in some women genital secretions destroyed sperm.)

In their public personae, Johnson came across as intelligent and sophisticated. Masters appeared grimly serious. Both looked important. She smiled quickly. He seldom if ever smiled. Mistrustful of the press, he also never forgave *Time*—later to assume the role of career-long adversary—for reporting the "fact" that Masters and Johnson had trained seven thousand sex therapists at the institute when the actual figure was thirty.

Despite the immense public welcome, however, many publications ignored the book altogether. Some critics even charged that Masters and Johnson's volunteers were unconscious exhibitionists and their reactions the product of the "artificial excitement" produced by observers and cameras. Masters countered by saying that he selected average people with average experiences. A few critics even questioned the unconscious motives of the two researchers, implying they had gone into sex research for prurient motives.

Among the first major critics of *HSR* was sexual anthropologist Margaret Mead, who claimed the study was skewed because data was from a laboratory, not real life, and involved people who were predisposed to be fitted for electrocardiograms and to be involved in studies to begin with. The study "obtained a little not very exciting data on such matters as the circulatory and respiratory effects of sex arousal and the subsidence of sex excitement," she objected, rather myopically. Mead also worried that the book would be read by the general public primarily as a form of pornographic entertainment.

Defenders countered that both in their research methods and in their results, Masters and Johnson had significantly brought about an openness of scientific discussion about human sexual behavior. By helping to remove the hypocrisy and cant surrounding sex, they were in fact helping to decrease the amount of pornography and exhibitionism in society.

Masters and Johnson had debated with themselves which book to do first. If they published the physiology book first, they feared being labeled as "mechanics." But if they wrote the sex-therapy book without being known in the field, critics might dismiss them as "kooks." The former seemed preferable, but what they had not anticipated was the deluge of hate mail that also greeted their work.

In their writings the sex researchers avoided the word "love" because it meant different things to different people, but they did constantly stress the need for caring, touching, holding.

Masters's personal sexual philosophy was that any form of sexual expression between consenting adults in private was acceptable. Most sex laws, in his opinion, were totally out-of-date. He also scorned the very notion of a frigid woman. "There is no such thing as a totally non-orgasmic woman," he insisted. "She may be non-orgasmic in her current marriage with her current mate, but this proves absolutely nothing."

At the time *HSR* was published, Johnson thought the women's movement then gaining ground was much too intense to hold any meaning for her personally. But she did complain that 95 percent of what was written about female sexuality in the past was written by men.

Later Masters and Johnson became embarrassed by the archaic language used in *HSR,* and Johnson could not bear to reread it.

AFTER KINSEY died in June 1956, his place was taken by anthropologist Paul Gebhard. Wardell Pomeroy had expected to be named Kinsey's successor after the latter died unexpectedly, but he lacked a Ph.D. Consequently, Gebhard was named, though he was not as qualified.

Under Gebhard's leadership, new sources of private and public funding were secured for the renamed Kinsey Institute in Bloomington. During the ensuing years the institute concentrated on analyzing and publishing the interview data gathered under Kinsey, as well as sponsoring new research and publishing a number of books on such diverse topics as pregnancy and abortion, homosexual preference, sex offenders, and sexual nomenclature.

In the spring of 1969 eight staff members of the Kinsey Institute, seven men and one woman, flew to St. Louis for a summit conference on the erotic science. It was the first joint meeting of the staffs of the institute and the Reproductive Biology Research Foundation headed by Masters and Johnson, who were old friends of Gebhard. For the next day and a half the two groups talked about sexual inadequacy, male and female homosexuality, sex among students, sex and the computer, and sex for the aged and infirm. All were subjects of studies under way at the only two centers in the country engaged in a continuing investigation of a broad range of human sexuality. Yet the two organizations had scarcely fifty employees between them, only a third of them professional, and each got by on paltry half-million-dollar annual budgets derived from federal and foundation grants, royalties, and lecture fees.

By now Pomeroy and Martin had left the institute. It was not generally known that Kinsey, dissatisfied in later life at dealing only with reported data, had begun a small, informal project to analyze and film mammalian and human intercourse. The study was dropped when Masters began his more detailed work. Kinsey also wanted each member of his staff to engage in sex while being photographed, an idea he arrived at after he "turned homosexual," in the opinion of Masters, who saw two of the films Kinsey had made. (Pomeroy appeared in several.) The ill feelings and animosities generated by this project contributed to the eventual breakup of Kinsey's team. (In subsequent years the Kinsey Institute denied the existence of the films, though during Gebhard's tenure copies were given to Hugh Hefner, an avid collector of sex on film, along with copies of the institute's eight thousand other sex films, in return for a grant.)

Also not too well known was that Masters and Johnson had collected data not just on conventional intercourse and masturbation, but on all varieties of heterosexual and homosexual intercourse and numerous other sex acts. (Curiously, the same-sex encounters were not recorded on film.) Yet the St. Louis researchers withheld that material from their book because they believed its inclusion would make it more difficult to gain professional and public acceptance—a most reasonable assumption—though they hoped to publish those findings eventually.

The two organizations had begun approaching sexuality from opposite points. Kinsey tabulated the stark facts of sexual experience, such as type, frequency, and age at first encounter. Masters and Johnson measured blood pressure, organic changes, and other physical symptoms. Increasingly, the two groups seemed to be working toward each other.

In contrast with the austere and humorless Kinsey, Gebhard was easygoing and anecdotal. The Colorado native had joined the institute in 1946, only a few months before receiving his doctorate from Harvard. He later estimated he had conducted 10 percent of the roughly eighteen thousand interviews in the files. A connoisseur of the sexual underworld, he was also friendly with such colorful figures as girlie photographer Irving Klaw and dominatrix Monique Van Cleef, whose recent deportation brought tears to scores of flagellants whom she had made literally her slaves.

Among the Kinsey Institute's most important current undertakings was its study of homosexuality, begun in 1966. In the first phase, four hundred white gay men were surveyed on the Near North Side of Chicago, a high-rent district equivalent to New York City's Upper East Side. The second phase, a study of eleven hundred white and black homosexuals of both sexes and five hundred nonhomosexual members of their families, was about to begin.

Preliminary assessment of the Chicago data showed that gays held some surprising views. Researchers asked whether they would take a "magic pill" that would turn them into heterosexuals. A significant majority said no. Most knew by the time they reached their early teens that they were sexually different, but for many others their homosexuality did not become apparent until much later. A majority admitted to engaging in numerous brief affairs and one-night stands, though a substantial number were also involved in long-term relationships.

The subjects of the Kinsey study were questioned for two hours each, responding to a questionnaire running to 145 pages. Many of the questions concerned occupation, social stability, love, and friendship. The survey showed that many gays led double lives, pretending they were straight to business associates and friends. Only a few affected stereotypically effeminate mannerisms.

In his study of men, Kinsey had estimated that 4 percent of males and 2 percent of females were predominantly or exclusively homosexual. Gebhard thought those figures were substantially correct, even though homosexual activism had lately made it seem there were even more. Homosexual acts between consenting adults were still forbidden by federal statute and in forty-nine states, the only exception being Illinois. Even so, Chicago police were particularly rough on gays, resorting often to such practices as entrapment and beatings.

Perhaps the most controversial statistic in Kinsey's study, however, was his claim that 37 percent of men had at least one homosexual experience. For years that number had haunted the institute. Kinsey used many prisoners for his interviews, mostly because he had access to them and thought their experiences typical of lower socioeconomic groups. But such was not the case at all, as Gebhard and his associates later realized. Also much overt homosexuality, particularly among youngsters, had a heterosexual impulse—for example, adolescent boys who masturbated with one another simply because they lacked a female partner.

Under a grant from the Russell Sage Foundation, the Kinsey Institute was also preparing to publish all eighteen thousand of its case histories, the raw material of its publication, for possible use by other researchers. As always, the anonymity of its subjects was to be preserved, including that of the hero of *Sexual Behavior in the Human Male,* a New York lawyer who reported an average of thirty orgasms a week for thirty years. Recently, Gebhard, who conducted the interview, saw him again. The lawyer reported that, despite the encroachments of age, he was still going strong.

In contrast with the shabbily academic quarters of the Kinsey Institute, those in St. Louis were dazzlingly ultramodern—a world of black leather, stainless steel, glowing walnut, muted phones, silent tape recorders, and technology to record everything visual or aural. Masters and Johnson seemed dazzling, too, in their starched white frocks and well-modulated, earnest voices.

Masters pointed out at the meeting that overwork and mental fatigue were the greatest enemies of a healthy sex life, yet admitted that he still regularly put in seven long days a week. "You know doctors," he quipped. "They never take their own advice."

Masters and Johnson also reported to their peers on the progress of their next work, to be entitled *Human Sexual Inadequacy.* Most of the 382 female and 312 male subjects were as close to "normal" as possible, the two researchers related. Psychological screening had eliminated 40 percent of the volunteers, many from Washington University.

Masters and Johnson had also found that, the authors of pornographic novels to the contrary notwithstanding, women did not ejaculate at climax. (That issue was to lie mostly dormant, however, until the G-spot controversy of the early eighties.) The trouble with pornography, Drs. Masters and Gebhard agreed, was that by providing inaccurate and exaggerated descriptions of sexual activity, it failed to perform the one service it might render: instead of enlightening the inexperienced, it filled them with unrealistic expectations. In any case, the most intense female orgasms measured were induced by masturbation.

Masters and Johnson also reported that, of four hundred couples treated over the past ten years, 80 percent showed immediate improvement, and in all but a small number of cases there had been no relapse during the five-year follow-up period. Some couples even returned with Polaroid photos of themselves to show how they were progressing. Nonorgasmic women were encouraged to familiarize themselves with their anatomy, to caress themselves, and to permit their husbands to do so. Many women were simply unaware of their clitoris's sensitivity to stimulation—a discovery that had initially shocked Masters and Johnson. Many others simply had a taboo against touching themselves.

As for men, primary impotence, in which the husband was never able to sustain an erection long enough to achieve penetration, was rare in marriage. Secondary impotence—the most common sexual difficulty among men, along with premature ejaculation—was usually caused by alcohol, fatigue, or tension, and responded readily to treatment.

The meeting ended on a note of high optimism, with the future of sex research looking brighter than ever before in history—which in fact it was. The only fly in the ointment seemed to be the matter of Johnson's education. She had been referred to in most publications, ever since the publication of *Human Sexual Response,* as a psychologist and was often introduced by Masters at professional meetings as Dr. Johnson. Johnson also used the initials D.Sc. (for doctor of science) in programs for professional conferences. She even once signed a paper with the title. But she had never earned any kind of college degree. The D.Sc. was strictly honorary, granted by the University of Louisville, best known for its basketball team.

Though Johnson was later awarded a doctorate by Washington University, many critics, including highly placed colleagues of Masters, claimed it was not legitimately earned—a relevant accusation in light of the furious controversies later to engulf the team when they published their dubious findings on homosexuality, and yet again when two prominent California sex therapists raised serious doubts about the seemingly miraculous 80 percent success rates Masters and Johnson claimed to achieve in treating various sexual dysfunctions.

Chapter 2

The Merchants of Venus

ONE DREARY, WET LONDON MORNING IN JANUARY 1965, AS MASTERS AND JOHNSON hurried *Human Sexual Response* to print, a young American expatriate named Bob Guccione looked out the window to see if the police were still there. They were. That was good—also scary.

After making a strong cup of coffee and lighting up another cigarette, Guccione went back to his cramped dining room table, strewn with galley proofs, contact sheets, piles of unanswered correspondence, layout sketches, and dozens of glossy color photographs of provocatively posed women.

Cocksure, inexperienced, possessing no more than a rudimentary knowledge of photography, Guccione was fumbling his way along through trial and error. But he knew he had one of the best ideas in British publishing history, and he was determined that *nobody* was going to stop him—not the two plainclothes detectives still parked outside his little Chelsea town house, not the MPs who rose almost daily to denounce him in the House of Commons, not the parliamentary subcommittee formed to investigate the tidal wave of pornography he threatened to unloose across one of the most sexually repressed countries in Europe; not even Bertrand Russell, the country's most prominent philosopher, who was also about to join the fray.

Little did anyone suspect that the most feared and reviled man in all of England was also, at that moment, dead broke.

At the age of thirty-four, Guccione had already run through a lifetime of careers. His second wife had recently left him, taking their four children, because she could not believe he was really going ahead with this latest crazy scheme. Every day the tabloids ran another story about the swarthy, handsome, would-be smut merchant. Almost as ominous to the British public as the American's pornographic intentions was his Sicilian heritage.

But inside the house, hope burned brightly. The day he left the seminary back in New Jersey in the summer of 1948, Bob Guccione had embarked on the voyage that would one day make him the Sultan of Soft-core and the most successful publisher of a pornographic magazine in history.

Unlike many young men who answered the call to the priesthood, Guccione was untroubled by Catholic guilt about sex or questions about his sexual identity. Unlike his future arch-rival Hugh Hefner, he did not suffer from sexual shyness and repression. He liked girls, pure and simple, like any average healthy Italian boy from New Jersey, and he was no virgin.

But he possessed a powerful idealistic streak, which briefly first expressed itself in that disastrous three-month stay in the seminary, when he thought he might devote the rest of his life to God. On second thought, he decided to devote himself to painting.

Soon after leaving the seminary, Guccione married his high school sweetheart and moved to Rome, where he set up an atelier and began painting. For three years he painted, sometimes going for two or three days at a time without sleep for the sheer love of putting paint on a canvas. He painted peasant women in a Tuscan field, still lives of apples and pears, nude female bathers.

He went to museums to study the Impressionists, Postimpressionists, and Old Masters, trying to discern the secrets of their technique. By night he hung out with other struggling artists in the cafés and dreamed of one day having his own gallery show—the supreme ambition of his life. Every day was like a fantasy come true, until the day came when his wife announced she was tired of his womanizing and intended to return to the United States, taking their infant daughter.

Having not earned a single lira from his painting, Guccione began auditioning for bit parts in movies. The motion picture industry was hot in Italy at the end of the war, turning out masterpiece after masterpiece—*Open City, Bicycle Thief, Bitter Rice.*

Fluent in Italian, Guccione soon made a reputation for himself as Roberto Sabatini, borrowing his mother's maiden name as his *nom de cinéma.* Before long he wound up starring in a film called *Il Rematore di Amalfi* (*The Oarsman of Amalfi*) opposite Nadia Gray, later to become internationally famous for her striptease during the orgy scene in Federico Fellini's *La Dolce Vita.*

Soon tiring of the film business, however, Guccione took a ship to Tangier, where he fell in with William Burroughs and his crowd of misfits and castaways. Days and evenings were spent in idle talk, interminable games of chess, passing the kif pipe, and sexual adventurism with a variety of Arab prostitutes and other women with exotic sexual proclivities, including one who forbade him to bathe for weeks at a time.

One evening in a café, Guccione struck up a conversation with an English girl named Muriel Hudson, a cabaret singer, and they became lovers. For a while Bob and Muriel lived in Spain and the south of France, doing odd jobs along the way. Back in London, he met her folks and they were married. But Guccione was homesick, they were desperately broke, and there was simply no way for an ex-painter with a little acting experience to earn a living in postwar England.

For the next four years the couple lived in a cold-water walk-up flat in New York's Greenwich Village. Guccione supported his family by working on the Van Heusen shirt account for Grey Advertising, selling cartoons to magazines, and designing Studio Cards—elongated greeting cards with a cartoon on the cover and a punch line inside. His enormous energy and entrepreneurial genius soon translated into the then astronomical income of fifteen hundred dollars a week.

But success frightened Guccione because, like his acting career, it took him away from painting. In 1957 he, Muriel, and their young son returned to Paris so that Guccione could pursue his dream of being an artist. For a while he continued to freelance for Van Heusen and Studio, and he also wrote a humor column that appeared in eighty-five college newspapers. But distance and cultural isolation soon made those arrangements impractical.

By 1959 Guccione realized that he had to get a real job. He moved to London, where he found work overseeing a string of dry cleaners, along the way introducing the first pickup and delivery service in the country. His industriousness soon earned him a promotion to managing director and a salary sufficient for him to lease a town house in an exclusive Chelsea neighborhood and buy a Cadillac convertible.

The same year Guccione went to work for the dry-cleaning chain, a weekly tabloid called the *London American* started up. Painting was incompatible with a full-time job, but cartooning—an old love—was not. Guccione submitted a cartoon for the very first issue, which was accepted, and after that the paper ran one of his cartoons every week. Later he also wrote a few humor columns like the one he had written years earlier, called "The Solemn Column." He started going to the paper on Thursdays, writing captions and helping with layouts. He also became friendly with the publisher's companion, Barbara Taylor, later best-selling romance author Barbara Taylor Bradford. At Taylor's urging, publisher Richard Boult hired Guccione as a full-time general manager. Six months later he was made managing director and editor in chief.

One of the paper's problems was that it had more English than American readers, despite a sizable American art and business colony in London. If its readers were English, the advertisers asked, why go through an American paper to reach them? That taught Guccione a very valuable lesson—no publication should ever rely on advertising, because advertisers were fickle.

In his routine spot checks of newsstands to see how the publication was faring, Guccione kept noticing the American edition of Hugh Hefner's *Playboy,* at the time one of the most celebrated magazines in the English language. It seemed to be everywhere. Guccione learned that *Playboy* sold about 110,000 copies a month in the United Kingdom, or about what the popular humor magazine *Punch* was selling. That meant *Playboy* was at the very top of the pyramid of glossy magazines in England—and there was no English equivalent. Why not adapt the formula, Guccione reasoned, to an editorial package designed to meet the interests of an English readership?

Meanwhile, the *London American* was failing for lack of advertising, and there was nothing Guccione could do to save it. As staffers dropped away or quit because they were not getting paid, he stayed on, even though he was not getting paid, either, to the absolute bitter end. He then spent the next three years trying to raise a few hundred thousand dollars to publish his British version of a *Playboy*-like magazine. (Over time he ran through something like a dozen titles. The penultimate, used just before the actual launch, was *Playgirl.*)

In his sales pitch to potential investors, Guccione argued that a magazine like *Penthouse* could sustain a high cover price, allowing it to survive on newsstand sales alone rather than relying on advertising. Had not the market already been tested by *Playboy*? He went to see investors in Germany, Scotland, Canada, and the United States. He visited investor Bernie Cornfeld in Switzerland. But everywhere he went, the response was: "Sounds great. But if it's such a good idea, why hasn't anybody else done it?"

Guccione kept saying, "It's being done *now.* I'm the guy who's doing it." But to no avail.

By now Muriel had given birth to a daughter and another son, with another baby on the way. Eventually, out of desperation, he decided *Penthouse* had to be launched on no money at all. The only way to do that was on a subscription basis.

He did have some previous mail-order experience. After leaving the *London American,* he had borrowed a few thousand dollars from his father to buy back issues of secondary American girlie magazines in bulk from wholesalers in the States, then placed small advertisements in the newspapers offering magazines like *Cavalier* and *Gent* at discount. He soon learned that the British were very vulnerable to mail order. Unlike the Americans, whose mailboxes even then were stuffed with junk mail they tossed out unopened, the British looked at anything that came to them by post.

The next step was to design a direct-mail brochure. That meant he needed photographs of nude women in order to advertise the magazine's most important product.

Around that time an American photographer friend of Guccione was in London to do a fashion assignment for *Cavalier.* He told Guccione, "If you and your wife pose for the shoot, I can save the money I'll have to pay any models."

Guccione agreed, on condition that the photographer teach him how to use a camera. Later all three went to Piccadilly Circus and Trafalgar Square, and the photographer shot Bob and Muriel sporting the latest fashions. That Saturday night the photographer visited the Guccione town house. Bob made dinner and afterward received his first lesson on how to use a Roloflex.

After the lesson was over, the photographer said, "I'll come back tomorrow night and give you your next lesson."

"That won't be necessary," Guccione replied. He had already lined up three models for the next day—one in the morning, two in the afternoon. Writers, cartoonists, artists, and models had agreed to donate their services. But no photographer would work except for money. "You can't just go take pictures like that," the photographer said. "I've been taking pictures all my life. I can tell you it takes more than an hour to learn how to take photographs."

"I'm sure you're right," Guccione answered, "but I have no choice. I have to move quickly. Besides, as a painter I understand all that other stuff about lighting and composition. And I have a flair for design. All I needed to know was the mechanical side—how to read a light meter and translate that to film."

The next day the three models showed up, and they became three of the eight discreetly draped nudes he used not only in the brochure, but in the first issue of the magazine. One of them wore boots and a sweater of Muriel's. Another looked over her shoulder at the camera in a photo that would become particularly controversial.

Muriel was not present for the shoot and, on returning home, was not amused to find that her dresser had been raided. This only added to her growing alarm that Guccione was actually serious about proceeding with this magazine idea of his. After a series of arguments, she gave him an ultimatum: "*Penthouse* or me." He bridled at the very idea of having to make a choice, and she left him, taking their four children.

Getting credit from the printer, H. L. Vickery, to produce the brochure was no problem. Impressed by the Chelsea town house and the Cadillac convertible that took up half the block in front, Vickery assumed Guccione had all kinds of money. The next step was to buy a test list of twenty-five thousand names. It included dentists, company directors, lawyers, and five thousand doctors—Guccione had once read they were very sex oriented because their profession required them to be intimate with women.

Guccione's grand scheme was to send out one million pieces of direct mail, the biggest ever undertaken in England. The plan was to do an inverted pyramid, sending the next fifty thousand on the income of the first twenty-five thousand, then the next hundred thousand on the income from the first fifty, and so on up to a million, using what was left at the end to pay for the first issue of *Penthouse* and to use the income from the sale of the first issue for the second.

He decided to launch the mail campaign on a Thursday, remembering that when he had sent out some mailers for back issues of American girlie magazines, he had received his first responses the next morning, thanks to the efficiency of the post office. That meant he would have some money on Friday, more on Saturday, and the most on Monday, the third day bringing the biggest returns.

To pay for the postage on the first twenty-five thousand brochures, Guccione had written a check without having any money in the bank. As he hoped, the first returns arrived the next day. On Monday morning he was parked outside the bank when it opened, sitting in the backseat of his Cadillac, tearing open piles of envelopes, taking out the checks and money orders and writing deposit slips. The check cleared and he never had another problem with credit.

Around four o'clock that afternoon the BBC carried a news item about a vicar in a small village who had complained that he was receiving pornography in the mail. Guccione had failed to account for the fact that the mail-order business in England was still a most unsophisticated science. An address remained on a list for year upon year, even though the name belonging to it had moved away or passed on. Inadvertently, it turned out, thousands of the brochures wound up arriving at the homes of old-age pensioners, members of Parliament, and little old ladies.

Before long, complaints were pouring in from all over the country, and Parliament quickly created a special subcommittee to investigate. It was one thing for *Playboy* to send its airbrushed magazine through the mail to subscribers. But never before had anybody sent a cold mailing featuring pictures of nude women through the royal post. The authorities could not invoke any criminal law, because the brochures were not deemed obscene under the Obscene Publications Act. But the police raked up Section 11 of the Post Office Act, which was outside the criminal code and dealt with the sending of indecent materials through Her Majesty's post. "Obscene" had a legal definition, but "indecent" was defined by whatever judge was looking at the material.

After a summons was issued, the police attempted to serve it, but Guccione refused to answer the door or leave the house. Three shifts of policemen rotated through the patrol car parked out front each day, waiting for him to appear. The siege lasted three weeks.

At nine o'clock on this wet, dreary January morning, Vickery telephoned to say that the next fifty thousand brochures were ready for mailing. Guccione told him to send out ten thousand pieces from Shepherd's Green. Then he called his lawyer, Ben Baker, asking him once again how long the siege was going to last. "Stay in until I tell you to come out," Baker told him. "Right now, if you accept the summons, they'll prosecute you in the boondocks, and they'll strip you alive, because the magistrate will be the local butcher. You want to get prosecuted in London to have any chance at all and to maximize publicity."

At ten, Joe Brooks showed up. A thin, long-haired young designer just out of art school, Brooks had answered Guccione's advertisement for an assistant art director some weeks earlier and had immediately gone to work for not much more than the promise of future rewards. But he was reliable, competent, and unfazed by the bobbies. He delivered layouts and galleys, along with gum, cigarettes, a sandwich, potato chips, and a few other supplies, then waited as Guccione handed back yesterday's corrected layouts, more galleys, and letters to be mailed.

All afternoon Guccione worked at the furious pace he had sustained for the past six months—eighteen to twenty hours a day, seven days a week—fueling himself with endless cups of coffee.

At three o'clock Vickery called again, to report that he had gone to the post office as directed, only to be accosted by a postal inspector who impounded the brochures as evidence.

"Okay, we'll use another post office," Guccione replied. "Tomorrow take five thousand brochures, only this time use the Brixton post office."

The next day Vickery went to Brixton, and again a postal inspector confiscated the mailing. This happened several more times, until finally Guccione remembered that the post office owned the telephone company. Obviously someone was listening in on his line. Immediately he called Vickery and said, "Come over for a meeting tomorrow."

That evening Guccione heard a member of the parliamentary subcommittee say on the radio that *Penthouse* would get published only over his dead body. It was the first time he ever heard his name on the radio. But hearing the attack made him only more determined.

The next day he told Vickery, "I'm sure my phone is being tapped. So we have to come up with a new tactic."

Guccione showed him seven ballpoint pens, each a different color, and a stack of different-size envelopes. "You've got a hundred different home workers who knock out labels for you all the time," he said, knowing that the firm addressed labels for other publishers as well. "Give each of them seven different-colored pens and seven different kinds of envelopes, and tell them to hand-address every single one of the lists. And I don't want them all dumped into one mailbox. Hire two trucks with two men on each, and have one go to John o' Groat's in Scotland and the other to Dover, and have one of them drive and the other jump out at every single red pillar box. I want them to drop off mail in every single village and hamlet along the way."

And that was how the mailing finally got through.

Afterward Ben Baker called and said, "Now's the time to come forward. Now if they try to arrest you, you'll be tried in London."

Guccione went to court and was fined about one hundred pounds. Afterward the man charged with prosecuting him stepped forward to apologize and shake his hand, saying he had only been doing his duty, was embarrassed by the whole affair, and thought *Penthouse* was just what the country needed. As Guccione stepped out into the sunlight, he saw a "pitch" placard at a newsstand with a bold headline written in black crayon—the kind used to announce big stories like "Germany Invades Poland." This one said: "Sex Mag Man in Court!"

Guccione printed 120,000 copies of the first issue and sold all but 1,500, instantly overtaking *Playboy* in Great Britain. The other copies were destroyed by rain. The issue sold for three shillings, or about fifty cents, and within days was selling on the after-market for five pounds—the average weekly salary for a secretary.

The MP who declared that *Penthouse* would be published only over his dead body died the next day.

GROWING UP in the tough Kinsman Road neighborhood on Cleveland's South East Side, where he was born in 1924, Reuben Sturman got his first taste of the publishing business delivering newspapers door to door on his bicycle, like thousands of other American kids. The oldest son of Jewish immigrants from Russia, he also inherited a keen business instinct from his father, Nahum, who operated a small grocery store and owned a number of apartment buildings.

In 1943 Sturman enlisted in the army, serving a three-year stint. After getting an honorable discharge, he put himself through Case Western Reserve University on the G.I. Bill in two and three-quarter years, earning a degree in business administration while he worked four days a week to support himself.

After graduation Sturman and a friend bought out a candy-and-tobacco wholesale company and went into business for themselves, distributing their line of goods to dozens, then hundreds, of mom-and-pop stores in Cleveland and the surrounding region. Sturman had a natural-born genius for wholesaling. It was his métier, his art, his calling. He also had a gift for gab, a talent for small talk with the little people of the retail world who were his customers and the cornerstone of his fledgling empire. He genuinely liked them, and they liked him, because he always looked out for their best interests as well as his own.

The late forties and early fifties, when Sturman first got into wholesaling, was also the dawn of the golden age of the comic book. In those pretelevision years, just about every kid in America eagerly awaited the next ten-cent adventure of Captain Marvel or Batman. Possessed of a near infallible instinct for mass-market trends, Sturman quickly began to specialize in this new genre and built up a substantial clientele.

Three years later, Sturman's partner got married and asked to buy him out. Although he was the idea man, Sturman sold back his half of the business and headed off for a two-week vacation in California. He stayed for a year, eventually marrying a transplanted New Yorker named Esther, whose six-year-old daughter, Peggy, he later adopted. But after a time, homesick for the Midwest and needing a familiar territory where he could reestablish his wholesale business, he persuaded Esther to move with him to Cleveland.

Back in Cleveland, Sturman, now twenty-seven, went to see his old partner and said, "Look, I need those comic books back." His friend replied, "Take them." The rest, as Sturman later liked to boast, was history.

Operating out of his garage, he began peddling new and used *Archie*s and *Superman*s from the back of an old Dodge, traveling from one mom-and-pop store to the next, at first in Cleveland and later expanding to Toledo and Youngstown, then Buffalo, then Detroit. Covers of unsold comic books were routinely torn off and returned to the publisher for credit, and eventually Sturman got the bright idea to repackage the coverless comics in cellophane bags and sell them three for a dime—an immense hit with hundreds of mom-and-pops and hundreds of thousands of kids.

But not with Dell Publishing, a major purveyor of comics, which obtained a court injunction to force Sturman to cease and desist. Ignoring the order, he continued to sell new and used comic books of every description, eventually expanding his line to include crossword, automotive, true detective, and Hollywood gossip magazines, mostly cheap pulps that the bigger distributors could not be bothered with. Esther kept the books and looked after her daughter and their two boys, David and Lee. Later she helped manage the small candy store she and Reuben opened near Cleveland's downtown. The last thing they ever thought about was going into pornography. Like everybody else in the booming fifties, they just wanted to get ahead.

Then a new product came along. Hugh Hefner's *Playboy* had made girlie magazines respectable. For years no major distributor would touch it because the magazine published pictures of nude women. So Hefner depended on small wholesalers around the country to distribute his publication. When *Playboy* finally made the big time, Hefner insisted his wholesalers get paid off. Suddenly they found themselves without a hot property to peddle, but with a great deal of money to subsidize their own publishing operations.

Sturman later claimed the birth of legitimate hard-core could be traced to that collective moment. Unable to compete with glossies like *Playboy* and its many imitators, wholesalers began cranking out grainy black-and-white pulps by the truckload. What they lacked in sophistication, they made up for in raunchiness.

Though he had never distributed *Playboy,* Sturman now found himself besieged by dozens of fellow wholesalers who wanted him to push their products. As far as he was concerned, girlie magazines were just another line to sell. The idea of competing with Hefner never occurred to him. He was a wholesaler, not a publisher.

Instead, all his enormous energy and marketing genius went into establishing more and more warehouse colonies in cities like Milwaukee, St. Louis, Chicago, and Toronto—and later London and Germany. For twenty straight years he worked indefatigably, putting in eighty-hour weeks, until he had established an unrivaled network of wholesale warehouses from coast to coast.

Each warehouse bore a regal name like Royal News or Crown News and serviced a string of a hundred or more shops—many of which Sturman owned either outright or on a fifty-fifty basis with a partner. Headquarters was the Sovereign News warehouse, a windowless, three-story red-brick fastness that was an outgrowth of Esther and Reuben's little store in what had now become the heart of Cleveland's black ghetto.

Sturman remained a devoted son and father, who moved his family to Cleveland Heights to be near his mother. He continued to go bowling with Esther on Friday evenings and to play poker with his pals on Wednesdays. But now he could afford to drive around town in a Cadillac instead of an old Dodge, to indulge his taste for expensive clothes, to treat himself to a Cuban cigar now and then. Looking in a mirror one day, he also decided it was time to get rid of his growing gut, and he started going on his lunch hour to an exercise class at the YMCA just down the street from the Sovereign warehouse. Before long, a natural leader, he was conducting the workouts.

Esther and Reuben's marriage was good, but not great. The most serious source of contention concerned Esther's wish to keep her hand in the business, managing the books. Reuben had no objection to her desire to combine a career with raising their three children. But the business was expanding so rapidly that he thought Sovereign needed a full-time professional accountant. As the marriage began to fall apart, Sturman started having affairs—some long-term and passionate—with several of the Cleveland housewives in his exercise class.

It was a good life. An average, reasonably successful guy heading into early

middle age, Reuben Sturman, the future King of Porn, asked for and expected no more.

Then the feds made their first house call and changed his little world forever.

AT THE TURN OF THE CENTURY, sexually oriented moving pictures could be
found on midways and carnivals and in nickelodeons. The films were called
peep shows because each viewing was semiprivate. An average of one hundred thousand people enjoyed such shows each year, giving Hollywood
much of the money it needed for feature films.

Although newspaper editorials attacked them as pandering to the lowest
instincts, peep shows were merely naughty, mostly showing attractive young
women bathing, disrobing for bed, and exercising. So-called stag or hard-
core films were not yet available to the public except at such places as pre-
Communist Cuba's infamous Shanghai Theater, which offered a continuous
program of sexually explicit films. Yet there was a worldwide market for stag
films even before World War I, most of them produced not in Europe but in
Latin America, primarily Buenos Aires, the Hollywood of first-generation
hard-core. Consumers were of two kinds: the wealthy who could afford the
expensive equipment necessary for private showings, and brothel owners
who exhibited blue movies as separate attractions or combined showings
with their primary service.

Very few early examples of cinematic erotica survive; production was limited, storage not scientific, and confiscation by authorities a very real threat.
Since viewers were often community pillars, most prosecution was aimed at
producers and distributors. Even so, production only increased over the
years. The earliest known stag movie was *Le Bain,* an 1896 film version of a
French postcard. By 1908 humorous one-reelers like *Making Love in a Ham-
mock* often had sex as a finale; but by 1915 the pattern of the stag film was set.
When sixteen-millimeter film equipment became available in the early twenties, the stag party, or smoker, was born. Finally, eight-millimeter technology
brought the stag film into the home market.

The story line of a typical stag film was exclusively erotic: rapid seduction
followed by assorted sexual acts, with the women as sexually avid as the men.
Heterosexual intercourse was portrayed in almost all of the films, also fellatio and cunnilingus. Lesbianism was popular, but homosexual acts between
men were infrequently shown, and violence was extremely rare.

Eventually the bare outlines of plot and character emerged, with certain
stock variations: the pompous banker, the priest, the robber. When the male
performers removed their clothes, most kept on their black socks; the ubiquitous tattoos came much later. By the late fifties and early sixties, the per-

formers were younger and far more attractive, especially the women, who were often in their late teens. But the plots remained so formulaic that stag films made in the twenties were still being distributed in the sixties. The only stag film to achieve any prominence was *Smart Alec,* made in 1951 and notable not for its cinematic creativity, but for the notoriety of its star, striptease artist Candy Barr.

Meanwhile, mainstream exploitation films emerged in the early thirties, with pre–ratings system teen pictures like *Hot Saturday.* The term "exploitation film" was not meant to be derogatory but referred to niche marketing. Some, like *Reefer Madness,* were to become camp classics. If the forties overflowed with B-movies, the fifties boomed with biker, beach, sci-fi, monster, and rock 'n' roll exploitation films.

The breakthrough year for the mainstream celluloid orgasm was 1955, when Robert Aldrich's *Kiss Me Deadly* portrayed a male actor performing a sexual act that was not only illegal in most states, but still a taboo subject even in private conversation. Based on Mickey Spillane's torrid novel, the film opened with a shot of Cloris Leachman running barefoot down a moonlit Route 66, wearing nothing under her skimpy raincoat. Flagging down a Corvette driven by detective Mike Hammer (Ralph Meeker), she asks for a lift to Los Angeles. Just then a man in polished wingtips, brandishing a monkey wrench, knocks Meeker out and forces Leachman onto a gantry. The viewer sees only her naked, fluttering legs and hears her heavy breathing escalate orgasmically. Then Mr. Wingtips strolls away, the first character in a Hollywood movie to perform cunnilingus.

Hollywood still strictly adhered to the Hollywood Morality Code, popularly known as the Hays Code after Postmaster General Will H. Hays, a list of anathemas drawn up in 1930 by the Reverend Daniel Lord, a Jesuit, and Martin Quigley, the Catholic publisher of a movie trade paper. According to the Hays Code, movies could not show two people living together who were not married, use the word "abortion," display nudity in any form, show lustful behavior, or capitalize on "impure love" as the subject for comedy or farce.

Enforcement of the code was left to an elderly, British-born widower, Geoffrey Shurlock, who took no orders from state or municipal censorship boards and kept to himself in order not to be compromised. If he did not like something in a movie, Shurlock phoned a studio head and firmly told him what to change. Plenty of violent movies received the seal, though: *Scarface, Little Caesar, Public Enemy.*

The first movie openly to defy the Hollywood Morality Code was Howard Hughes's *The Outlaw,* released in 1943. Although the film did not receive a seal of approval, Hughes got away with it. (Busby Berkeley musicals also frequently had seminude women "hidden" in the crowd scenes.) Other successful movies that lacked the seal included *The Moon Is Blue* and *The Man with the Golden Arm,* both produced by Otto Preminger. Not until 1959, though, with *The Immoral Mr. Teas* by Russ Meyer and producer David Friedman's *Adventures of Lucky Pierre,* did modern-day soft-core pornography get under way. In that year, half-clad women and simulated sex emerged from the stag film underground and became respectable. Natalie Wood and Warren Beatty next debuted the first cinematic French kiss in 1961, in *Splendor in the Grass.* That same year, Gualtiero Jacopetti's "shockumentary" *Mondo Cane,* featuring naked Trobriand islanders chasing prospective mates, brought *National Geographic*–style nudity to the big screen.

After that, barriers began to fall. In 1963 alone Friedman made *Bell, Bare and Beautiful*; *Blood Feast*; and three other soft-core films. A stocky, cigar-chomping caricature of the Hollywood producer, Friedman, who once owned a small circus, had formed his own production company to make so-called "sexploitation" films, which were just then gaining notoriety.

But the next great leap forward did not occur until 1965, when *The Pawnbroker* revealed a bare-breasted woman on the American screen for the first time. The movie was condemned by the National Legion of Decency, a widely followed Catholic movie-rating organization. That year the Hollywood Morality Code was revised. Eric Johnston, head of the Motion Picture Association of America (MPAA), led the fight, which originated over a movie version of Mozart's *Don Giovanni* titled *Don Juan.* The case began in Chicago when the distributor refused to let censors see the picture before it was shown to the public. Though the MPAA lost its case before the Supreme Court in a five-to-four vote, the battle against censorship had begun, and the movie industry was soon joined by publishing and television to form a united front. Ultimately, in 1968, the MPAA affixed its own ratings to films: G for general audience, M for mature, R for restricted—no one under sixteen without parent or guardian—and X for adults only.

Foreign-film houses, just then entering their golden age, were another important front in the battle against censorship. Around the country, two hundred art houses routinely showed films like *And God Created Woman* with Brigitte Bardot. Facing increased competition from television in the early 1960s, the local art houses also began showing daring European and Asian movies that the major chains would not touch. As the big studios continued to favor mainstream metropolitan theaters for their high-budget releases, some art houses also began to exhibit soft-core movies.

In 1966 Michelangelo Antonioni's *Blowup* became the first legitimate film to give viewers a glimpse of pubic hair. Finally, the next year, an earnest Swedish film titled *I Am Curious,* directed by Vilgot Sjöman, made the world safe for adult films. The movie came in two editions, *I Am Curious (Blue)* and *I Am Curious (Yellow).* The former, more controversial in Sweden than the yellow version, focused on political issues and attacked social democracy. The yellow version, which told the story of a young Swedish woman who tries to cling to her philosophy of nonviolence and free love until reality forces her to adopt a broader ideology, concentrated on the emergence of sexual liberation. The movie made history for the simple reason that it was the first to show full-frontal nudity of both its male and female performers. It was later declared obscene in the United States.

A number of underground films also centered on nudity. At the 1968 International Experimental Film Festival at Knokke-le-Zoute, Belgium, a full-length film titled *Number 4* by Japanese avant-garde artist Yoko Ono consisted of close-ups of the buttocks of 365 London artists and intellectuals in sequence for twenty seconds each.

That same year, the Adult Film Association of America (AFAA) was formed, with Friedman one of the founders and a membership of nearly one hundred producers, distributors, and exhibitors. Most legal problems occurred in the South, and to defend local exhibitors, the AFAA began to hire top-of-the-line First Amendment lawyers. In the late eighties and early nineties other First Amendment lawyers became the focus of federal prosecutors who suspected them of money laundering and other illegal activities on behalf of pornographers.

ONE DAY IN 1964 one of Sturman's managers told him that a man named Les Aday in Fresno, California, had developed a line of paperbacks he wanted Sovereign and its satellites to distribute. Aday was among those wholesalers who had helped distribute *Playboy* in the early days. With his payoff money he began publishing a series of detective and adventure novels, tame by today's standards but spicy enough back then to be considered daring or even dangerous.

The sample Sturman was given to inspect was called *Sex Life of a Cop*, which he thumbed through and deemed fairly innocuous. "Listen," he told his manager, "if you want to try it, go ahead."

Sovereign put the book out, an unusually large number of retailers took it, and *Sex Life of a Cop* became an instant success. Before long every publisher of smut pulp and girlie magazines in the country was knocking on Sovereign's door, eager to do business with the man who had built up such a colossal warehousing empire. As far as Sturman was concerned, it was just product. Comic books, crossword puzzles, and movie star magazines were still Sovereign's bread and butter.

Unfortunately, federal prosecutors in Grand Rapids, Michigan, did not agree with Sturman's benign assessment of *Cop* and brought charges against Aday for publishing obscene material. After he was convicted and sentenced to twenty-five years, Cleveland prosecutors decided to go after Sturman.

Sturman's lawyer, Ralph Hertz, advised his client to make a deal with the government—to abide by whatever happened in Aday's appeal.

"Are you crazy?" Sturman asked. "You want me to risk twenty-five years in jail?"

At that point he was ready to drop his sex line in an instant. But he followed Hertz's advice, only to learn that the appellate court in Grand Rapids merely cut Aday's sentence back to fifteen years. Having no other option, Sturman joined him in an appeal to the Supreme Court. He also decided to take a closer look at *Cop*. What he read was a book that he still judged harmless. He was also incensed that prosecutors were trying to tell people what to read in the privacy of their homes. Slowly the case worked its way up to the Supreme Court, which tossed it out. In a separate ruling, the judges declared that such material was protected by the First Amendment.

Earlier, in 1957, the liberal Warren Court had restricted the definition of obscenity to material judged to be "utterly without redeeming social value." That defining word—"utterly"—opened the floodgates, and thereafter no obscenity trial was complete without a clergyman, literary critic, psychologist, or First Amendment advocate spotting at least a soupçon of redeeming social value in even the most sordid examples of hard-core.

Reuben Sturman liked the taste of victory. His aggressive business style was fueled by the discovery that this product called pornography had a still largely untapped mass market. He decided to exploit it with a vengeance.

Also with a difference. Shrewdly, he saw that *Playboy* and its imitators had a stranglehold on the world of girlie magazines. But in the world of hard-core, Hugh Hefner had no counterpart. Reuben Sturman decided to be that man. Besides, who else was in a position to saturate every city and small town in the country with this new product that bore the seal of approval of the Supreme Court and that the great American public seemingly could not get enough of?

The only serious problem was supply. Having operated underground like a hunted wolf for so long, hard-core had no manufacturing base in the United States. But when Denmark decriminalized hard-core in 1969, it became the Wild West of XXX-rated porn. Sturman began flying to Amsterdam, the international crossroads of porn contraband, the way he used to drive from Cleveland to Detroit. He bought whatever he could lay his hands on—shock-porn photos of straight sex, gay sex, child porn, bestiality, bondage. As long as it was legal, he sold it. It was, after all, just product.

To attract the crowds, because advertising in the respectable media was impossible, Sturman also created the adult bookshop—garish, neon-lit sanctuaries for men with no sex outlet except looking at pictures of people having the kind of sex they were not. And if the community and police did not like it, then the community and police be damned. Fed up with ongoing federal harassment and a police raid of his Detroit warehouse, Sturman first revealed his aggressive, cocky side in public by filing suit against J. Edgar Hoover and the FBI. Not surprisingly, it was dismissed.

By now Sturman had moved out of the house, but Esther kept her hand in the business. He also brought in his kid brother, Joseph, though neither Esther nor Joseph was particularly comfortable with the content of the publications Sturman was importing. Increasingly, he was also doing his own manufacturing. Unsold magazines were simply repackaged with new covers and put back on the racks. Sooner or later, everything sold.

One morning Esther showed up for work, only to find her office occupied by a new bookkeeper. Later Sturman changed the locks, barring her altogether, and used phony papers and a forged signature to drop her name from the boards of five companies she had helped to build.

Not long after, Esther and Joseph were indicted, along with Reuben, on another obscenity charge. It was a shock for them to see their pictures in the local paper. Joseph decided to get out of the business. Reuben was just moving too fast.

By now, though, Reuben knew his way around the First Amendment the way he knew Amsterdam, and he had no trouble beating that obscenity rap, either. But Esther and Reuben's marriage was over. Her one request: not to bring the kids into the business. Reuben did not promise.

MODERN MASS-MARKET hard-core pornography (which explicitly showed vaginal, anal, or oral penetration, unlike soft-core) was introduced to the world by Scandinavian magazine publishers beginning around 1967. The catalyst was the advent of photolithographic color-printing techniques, which dramatically reduced manufacturing overhead while improving picture quality. Other factors included the liberalized sociopolitical climate engendered in the late 1960s by a series of European and American court rulings and the success of such soft-core magazines as *Playboy* and *Penthouse.* So great was the potential market in Europe that over the next two decades more than 250 billion copies of hard-core magazines were published.

In 1969 technology also fostered the loop, the grandfather of video porn— Super 8 porn films, for use on home projectors, though most customers viewed them through coin-operated peep-show booths installed in sex clubs. (These films had begun to be mass-produced in the United States for home consumption starting about 1964, though color and quality were poor. Simultaneously, from England black-and-white Carnaby Street pornography, with much better production values, was being smuggled into the United States.) Typically ten minutes long, loops were shot in color and often included sound, unlike the old black-and-white sixteen-millimeter.

As international hard-core pornography grew, about a dozen people came to control more than half of the gross revenues. Given its multicultural appeal, no one race dominated either its manufacture or distribution, though admittedly Irish hard-core was an oxymoron. In the beginning, though, before it was embraced by Americans and Europeans, Asians, Jews and gentiles, hard-core was decidedly Scandinavian. Most of the child pornography that flooded into the United States in the years before it was outlawed in 1974 also came from Sweden and Denmark.

Three early pioneers were Sweden's Berth Milton, publisher of *Private,* the world's best-selling hard-core magazine; and the Theander brothers of Denmark, who specialized in porn loops. By far the most powerful figure of all, however, was a woman—the formidable Beate Uhse, whose chain of sex shops supplied Germans with every known variety of the sex toys and gimmicks they so enjoyed.

Born during the war years, Peter and Jens Theander started out driving taxis and later pooled their savings to open a secondhand bookshop in downtown Copenhagen in 1966. To alert customers to under-the-counter material, they featured naturist and pinup magazines in the shop windows. At the time, hard-core was still illegal, but the brothers covered the genitals of models in their hard-core merchandise with tape, which satisfied the police.

As demand outstripped supply, Peter and Jens decided to become producers, capitalizing their venture by selling all of their inventory and not reordering. Before long their supplies were almost completely diminished and they were reduced to selling even the naturist wares in the window. At the same time, responding to public outcry, the police rounded up Denmark's known hard-core retailers and hauled them into court. But the raid on the Theander brothers netted nothing because their inventory had been depleted.

By a lucky stroke of fate, the Theanders were now in a position to corner the market, even though they had to proceed clandestinely. For the next two years they resorted to false identities, anonymous printers, and secret warehouses, gradually creating an underground monopoly on Danish hard-core, until 1969, when public pressure led to the reform of Danish pornography laws and the decriminalization of hard-core.

The first Theander creation, a magazine called *Color Climax,* appeared in 1968. With decriminalization, they expanded into mail order, mailing even to countries where hard-core was prohibited, in violation not of Danish but possibly of another country's law, such as Britain's. Rodox, their company, also at first cooperated with smugglers bringing in hard-core to countries like Britain; trucks carrying Danish bacon to English supermarkets served as a convenient cover, though after 1969 the Theanders decided such covert operations imperiled their now legitimate enterprise.

In 1969 the Theanders also established Candy Film in downtown Denmark, soon to become one of the world's biggest producers of Super 8 film. As their output quickly exceeded the capacity of local processing plants, the brothers bought an existing film laboratory and in 1975 joined all operations—design studio, production, warehouse, administration—in a single facility in a drab industrial park on the outskirts of Copenhagen. Over the next two decades the Theander brothers produced more than ninety million magazines, nine million Super 8's, and one million videocassettes. By far their biggest customer was Reuben Sturman.

The redoubtable Beate Uhse, on the other hand, was a twenty-five-year-old war widow who had piloted a small plane out of Berlin on the day Hitler committed suicide, landing in Flensburg near the Danish border with her two-year-old son, Klaus, by her side. Finding work in a birth control clinic, she began advising local women about a technique later known as the rhythm method. Nazi ideologues had discouraged birth control, and Uhse, recognizing a need for sex education, was soon operating a thriving cottage industry direct-mailing contraceptives, sex aids, and marriage manuals.

In 1962 Uhse opened the world's first sex shop, the Sex Institute for Marital Hygiene, in Flensburg, offering a full range of products. Before long she had opened a similar sex shop in every major German city and become a minor national celebrity.

When West Germany legalized hard-core pornography in 1975, the government stipulated that such materials could not be sold through mail order, but only in sex shops. Uhse's string of sex shops were not only the ideal venue, but they constituted a ready-made monopoly. At the same time, foreseeing a demand for XXX-rated cinema, she opened a string of "blue movie" theaters. In order to present loops that were of a better quality than those produced by the Theander brothers in Denmark, she established her own subsidiary, Beate Uhse Film Distribution, with her youngest son, Uli—the offspring of a second marriage—in charge. Reuben Sturman was both a major customer and a supplier.

Though Berth Milton was to reap nothing approaching the fortunes created by the Theander brothers and Uhse, he outdid them in one respect—by inventing the hardest hard-core in history.

In the mid-1960s, when hard-core porn was still not completely decriminalized in Sweden, young Berth decided to pursue a fantasy and open a bookshop specializing in soft-core. By 1966, deciding he could do better than what he was selling, he expanded into magazine publishing. Hard-core magazines at the time were stark, simple, and basic: thirty-six pages of black-and-white photographs, one to a page. An average edition sold about five thousand copies.

Milton elected to use color and attractive layouts and to incorporate text.

To avoid being harassed by the police, he took some sample photographs to the Ministry of Justice to determine what was legally publishable.

"You tell me," he told an official. "If I steal a bicycle, you can tell me that's against the law. Look at this picture and tell me if I can publish it."

"Oh," came the reply, "we don't know! You publish it, then we'll see what happens."

"I am asking *you*—you're the Ministry of Justice, you should be able to tell me."

Receiving no satisfactory reply, Milton felt he had no choice but to proceed with caution, publishing at first only photos of naked women.

To recoup his investment, Milton needed to sell ten thousand copies. Though *Private* was twice as expensive as any porn magazine on the market, the first issue quickly sold out, generating for the average newsstand dealer more profit than all of his other publications combined. But *Private* was still basically a girlie magazine, with none of the editorial window dressing of a *Penthouse* or *Playboy*. Milton had a different intention. He wanted his pictures not merely to be of better quality than his Danish competitors, but to depict sex acts in explicit detail.

In 1967, with the sixth or seventh issue, he began using male models as well; and though their penises were not visible, it was obvious to the viewer that the male and female models were engaged in actual intercourse. Soon afterward, hard-core was decriminalized, leading to the breakthrough issue, *Private No. 8,* whose hard-core content catapulted the magazine to a circulation of forty thousand. Most of Milton's and other manufacturers' female models for hard-core came from England, Germany, and Sweden. Few were professionals, who were in fact discouraged in order to prevent the same face and body from appearing in different magazines.

Though the reputation of the magazine soon began to spread worldwide, Milton remained so suspicious of the police, distributors, and anyone else involved in his operation that for many years he continued to stow all the cash that accrued from his mail-order business in an old suitcase under his bed. One night in the late sixties he decided to count the money and learned he was literally sleeping over a fortune that amounted to about a half million dollars.

AFTER RENOVATIONS, the four-story mansion on Chicago's North State Parkway boasted one hundred rooms. Some were used for photo shoots, others to entertain advertisers or put up visiting writers and artists. Though the magazine's offices were only a half mile away, the mansion also featured a suite of offices and a conference room. Two dozen Bunnies also called the biggest house on the prairie home.

Lord of this castle, the most decadent domicile in all America and maybe the entire world, was Hugh Hefner, already a legend in his own time, the publisher of *Playboy* magazine and the man who epitomized—at least in the pages of his own publication—male sexual prowess and sophistication.

One flight up from the gleaming white marble reception area, the visitor was greeted by a stark white door with a brass plaque warning in Latin: *Si Non Oscillas, Noli Tintinnare* ("If You Don't Swing, Don't Ring"). Paintings by Pollock, de Kooning, and Picasso seemed to be hanging everywhere. To maintain a sense of timelessness, virtually all the windows in the mansion were shaded. There were secret doors, tunnels, passageways, and entire walls that moved with the touch of a button.

Deep within the heart of the mansion, Hefner had created a mammoth, windowless apartment, totally sealed off from the rest of the house, where he retired when he wanted privacy. On a typical day he went to sleep at eight A.M. and arose at three P.M., when his workday began.

An unhealthy-looking, hollow-cheeked man whose eyes were sunk deep in their sockets, his longish brown hair tinged with gray, the fortyish Hefner nevertheless exuded energy and enthusiasm. He hated to sleep, because life was too short, and he often worked thirty-seven hours or more at a stretch. When he did sleep, the house whispered the news, and a hush fell.

The *Playboy* publisher did most of his work in his heavily mirrored bedroom, which was equipped with an Ampex videotaping console to record his lovemaking. His private collection of more than one thousand blue films was among the largest in the world, with the best of the lot reportedly starring Hefner himself.

During the course of his career, Hefner had made love to more than two thousand women and publicly admitted to having tried nearly every variety of sex, including homosexual. Every Wednesday night, the oak-paneled main drawing room was the scene of a huge Gatsbyesque party attended by virtually every celebrity in Chicago. What was not acknowledged was rumored: conga lines of nude bodies snaking from floor to floor, hookers imported by the dozen, horses and other stud animals delivered in the dark of night; SM dungeons, lesbian orgies, men sleeping with children; "a sexual phantasmagoria, a Grand Hotel of the libido," in the words of ex-*Playboy* editor Frank Brady, "that takes place every night in scores of the one hundred rooms, all of which contain hidden closed-circuit television cameras."

From early 1963 to mid-1965 Hefner, the hermit of sex, left his Chicago mansion only nine times. Beginning in 1963 he also embarked on the writing of the "Playboy Philosophy," a rambling, droning, but at times insightful twelve-part editorial ranging from the Sexual Revolution to *Playboy*'s editorial magnificence and sensibly adult approach to life, to American Puritanism, divorce, free love, and pornography.

At the conclusion of the seventh marathon installment, Hefner admitted that his magazine would probably not change much in a censorship-free society, a tenet that would play a significant role in his imminent rivalry with Guccione: ". . . an easing of the censor's tight control would only bring to wider distribution and sale a host of bolder imitators of this publication that have long been a bane to our existence and a source of not a little embarrassment."

Hefner went on to admit that *Playboy* "has never attempted to push to the outer boundaries of what was censorable or what could be considered objectionable by the more sophisticated part of our society. We have always chosen to set our own standards of taste and propriety, and to communicate with that number of other urban fellows whose view of life is similar to our own."

After concluding his lengthy diatribe on American morals, Hefner expressed the wish that his mother would simply give him the approval he sought. When she later told an interviewer, "I would have been just as happy if he'd been a missionary," he exclaimed in exasperation, "But I was, Ma!"

Hefner had begun rehearsing for *Playboy* while editing *Shaft*, the University of Illinois humor magazine, in which he instituted a feature in the center of the publication called "The Coed of the Month." When the first Kinsey report was published, he lauded it in an editorial.

After graduating from college, Hefner also tried to make his way as a cartoonist. While working in the subscription department of *Esquire*, he learned the fundamentals of direct mail and later decided to start his own magazine, originally to be called *Stag Party*. The initial investment consisted of $600 in savings and $6,000 in loans. Borrowing from "Esky," *Esquire*'s man about town, Hefner chose a bunny to symbolize the new enterprise because rabbits were the playboys of the animal world. The first issue, published in December 1953 and featuring the now legendary calendar photos of a nude Marilyn Monroe, sold an extraordinary 53,991 copies.

In 1955 the concept of the Playmate, the name given to each month's featured centerfold model, underwent a revolutionary change when subscription manager Janet Pilgrim (a statuesque 36-24-36) walked into Hefner's office and asked for an Addressograph machine. Hefner (reputedly eight inches) had been having trouble finding suitable professional models for the centerfold and half-jokingly suggested she might want to pose. No doubt influencing both his offer and her acceptance was the fact that the two were having a serious affair at the time. Pilgrim quickly became the new ideal of the fresh, wholesome girl next door—a down-to-earth fantasy who was literally in reach of every male subscriber.

Not until 1959, though, did Hugh Hefner, Methodist midwestern boy, start becoming the kind of person he wanted to be, and even then for a considerable period, during the early years of editing *Playboy*, he lived a double life. Though his marriage was faltering, he kept up the pretense of being a family man for the sake of his daughter, Christie. Only after his divorce did he begin the task of reinventing himself as Mr. Playboy, getting out from behind his desk, buying a mansion, doing a TV show called *Playboy's Penthouse,* and opening the first Playboy Club.

By 1967, two years before the American launch of *Penthouse,* Hefner had made the cover of *Time,* and the circulation of *Playboy* stood at a towering four million. Another 450,000 men were members of sixteen Playboy Clubs in the United States, London, and Jamaica, where both steaks and drinks cost $1.50. A $9 million luxury Playboy Resort was also in the works on the shores of Lake Geneva, Wisconsin.

The public view of Hefner was the hip but conservative one he projected at those Friday evening parties for the benefit of public relations. Arriving at the appointed hour with his latest girlfriend on his arm, usually a receptionist or assistant editor, Hefner and date sank into the reserved love seat while a full-size movie screen silently descended against a side wall. Instantly, the buzz of cocktail chatter and the clink of ice cubes stopped. Just before show time, a butler appeared, bearing a bowl of popcorn and bottles of Pepsi.

After the movie, usually a first-run film, a buffet supper was served in the dining room. Once Hefner left, the guests were free to amuse themselves as they wished, though the top floor—a Bunny dorm—was off-limits.

But the kidney-shaped first-floor swimming pool was much used, with bathing suits optional; for seclusion, guests swam to a hidden grotto furnished with soft cushions where background music gently played and orgies were common. The grotto was also observable through a trapdoor in the main hall above, while a downstairs bar gave patrons an underwater view of the Playmates and other guests swimming nude.

In the early sixties Hefner also signed a sixty-three-year lease on the thirty-seven-story former Palmolive Building on Chicago's Michigan Avenue. Playboy products ranged from calendars and albums to cuff links and Caribbean cruises—ninety mail-order items that brought in more than $1 million a year. One nonprofit venture, the Playboy Theater in Chicago, was a showcase for film. Failures included *Show Business Illustrated,* which after only nine issues racked up a $2 million loss. Yet the newly formed Playboy Press was thriving on annual sales of $1 million in books.

Not only was Hugh Hefner the most visible and successful sybarite in modern times, not only did *Playboy* have a virtual monopoly on sophisticated sex entertainment and advice for the male masses, but the rabbit kingdom seemed destined to endure and thrive forever in a world that was just heading into a Sexual Revolution. Symbolic of its potency was the famed Bunny Beacon atop the company headquarters, which was allegedly visible for five hundred miles in a clear night sky.

* * *

THE FIRST ISSUE of *Penthouse* contained an excerpt from a new work by Bertrand Russell that the aspiring publisher had personally negotiated with the philosopher's young American aide. A naive Guccione concluded the deal with a handshake. After the first issue of the magazine appeared, amid enormous tabloid coverage, Russell and his aide denied having made the agreement and sued Guccione in court. The young entrepreneur wound up paying Russell a substantial sum, but it taught him a valuable, if elementary, lesson: Put it in writing.

The first issue had literally been produced on Guccione's dining room table in Chelsea, but for the second issue he leased a small apartment in Chelsea Studios near Fulham. Furniture consisted of one borrowed chair and six wire milk crates stolen from neighbors. After stacking the crates, he removed the bathroom door to create a crude desk, where the next issue was created.

The staff consisted of assistant art director Joe Brooks, Guccione's sister-in-law, who worked as a secretary, and freelance editor Bill Hopkins, who had ties to England's Angry Young Men movement and was able to obtain the services of such writers as John Osborne for little or nothing.

That second issue changed Guccione's life in ways he could not have foreseen. The big movie playing in London at the time was John le Carré's *The Spy Who Came In from the Cold,* starring Richard Burton. Among the minor players was a lithe, blonde, doe-eyed dancer named Kathy Keeton, a native of South Africa and a graduate of Sadlers Wells, the dancing academy of the Royal Ballet. In its promotional handout, Paramount mentioned that Keeton, who played an exotic dancer in the film, owned a zoo in Mozambique. That struck Guccione as funny, and he made a tongue-in-cheek reference to it in the magazine's editorial section.

As soon as the magazine hit the stands, Keeton's manager called Guccione to complain. Guccione told the man not to get so exercised—he was just being satirical and had no idea who Kathy Keeton was. "Well, you ought to know her," the manager said. "Why don't you come and see one of her shows?"

Guccione agreed, and a date was set for him to see Keeton in a popular song-and-dance revue. Afterward he went backstage. Keeton's dressing room was at the end. When he entered, the first thing he noticed was that the mirror and walls were bare, unlike those of the other performers, which were cluttered with pinups, postcards, and photos. On the bare desk was a neat stack of the pink-papered *Financial Times* of London.

That night Keeton, her manager, Guccione, and his father, who was visiting, went out for dinner. Guccione was impressed not only by her dancing, but by her business acumen. Over the next few weeks they went out to lunch on several occasions, until finally he asked her to work for the magazine as an advertising representative—at the time an exclusively male occupation.

Keeton, who was bored with dancing, immediately agreed, even though the salary was only fifteen pounds a week—one-tenth of what she made dancing. Figuring he was on a roll, Guccione added, "But I have to defer five pounds a week until later."

Again Keeton agreed. She sold advertising in the morning and continued to dance, doing a show in the afternoon and another in the evening. Only after about a year did the two begin dating, and for a considerable period thereafter they continued to live on Keeton's dancing income of one hundred and fifty pounds a week.

For the first eighteen months of publication, all the income generated by *Penthouse* was hypothecated to the printer, various accumulated debt, and day-to-day expenses. At one point, Guccione's mystified banker even called to wonder how the magazine could be selling all over the country while the company had only one pound sixteen shillings and threepence in its coffers.

As the magazine grew, Guccione continued to take most of the photo sets, since few British photographers of any caliber were shooting erotica at that time. Occasionally he also visited the United States to purchase sets.

One day, after the second or third issue hit the stands, he received a letter from a man named Mr. Bumstead, who said he had a problem. On occasion his thirteen-year-old daughter became so naughty that it was necessary to administer a spanking, which Mr. Bumstead found sexually arousing. He was writing to *Penthouse,* which he took to be an authority on all things sexual, for guidance. While he thought disciplining his daughter was necessary, he felt guilty about the pleasure it gave him.

Guccione published the letter, not realizing what a storm of interest it would create. Immediately, thousands of other letters flooded into the tiny studio, some commenting on Mr. Bumstead's plight, others containing their own ardent reveries of being spanked by schoolmasters or governesses. Guccione realized he had touched a very sensitive nerve in contemporary British culture.

Seizing the opportunity, he began to orchestrate letters, editing them to be as controversial and reader involved as possible and even writing a few himself. Before long the reader-letters section, called *Forum,* proved almost as popular and controversial as the pictorials, and Guccione decided to spin off a second magazine, called *Forum,* to be sold at first by subscription only. The magazine cost virtually nothing to produce since all editorial content consisted of letters from readers discussing their sex lives. Like *Penthouse,* it was an instant success. Later Guccione hired an expatriate American TV producer, Al Freedman, as editor. Under his guidance it evolved into the first and only mass-market magazine devoted exclusively to sex information, advice, and entertainment, eventually reaching a circulation of nearly one million.

As *Penthouse* continued to grow, Guccione was frequently approached by investors or distributors who wanted to launch a U.S. edition. Though he saw that the magazine could easily reach an American circulation of about thirty thousand, thereby creating a much needed revenue flow, he held back. Increasingly, he was beginning to perceive the United States as the ultimate market, which meant the American edition would have to be launched with the same ferocity as the British edition or be lost in the welter of *Playboy* imitators. Moreover, Guccione continued to be conflicted about his art, telling himself that once the English edition was established he could turn his attention again to his painting. As a result, *Penthouse* gradually came to be sold in nearly every country in the world except the United States.

The sales figure that most fascinated Guccione, though, was that his magazine was vastly outselling *Playboy* in, of all places, Vietnam, among U.S. soldiers. That insight into the tastes of young American males finally gave him the heart and courage to bring the magazine into the United States.

For tax reasons, Guccione discovered it was impossible to use revenues derived from the English edition of *Penthouse* to launch the American edition. As a result, he once again found himself in the position of having to launch a magazine on no money.

On a visit to the United States he met with officials of Curtis Circulation, a major magazine distributor, who declined to take on the magazine. Having nowhere else to turn, he signed a contract with Cable News, which had a reputation for seizing magazines that got behind in their debt. A substantial number of magazines that Cable News distributed it also owned.

Guccione next flew to Los Angeles to meet with representatives of the *Los Angeles Times-Mirror,* whose subsidiary the New English Library was the U.K. distributor of *Penthouse.* His proposal: a loan of $100,000, with the payments to be taken out automatically each month from revenues in England. After much arduous negotiation, he got the loan.

Now realizing that his contract with Cable News put him at too much of a handicap, he returned to Curtis, where he hinted to officials that the British edition of *Penthouse* was circuitously owned by the *Los Angeles Times-Mirror,* though it did not want to advertise the fact. Impressed, Curtis signed Guccione on. He then returned to Cable News, where he paid dearly to get out of his contract—$50,000, or half of his loan.

But at least, and at last, he was ready to take on Hugh Hefner centerfold to centerfold on his home turf.

Chapter 3

The Pubic Wars

IN NOVEMBER 1966, THE FIRST TOPLESS WAITRESSES APPEARED IN NEW YORK City when two young women wearing only pasties began serving tables at nine P.M. at the Crystal Room on East Fifty-fourth Street.

Not long after, reports began to appear in the media on the new permissiveness in society. In its issue of November 13, 1967, entitled "Anything Goes: Taboos in Twilight," *Newsweek* enumerated the unsettling signs of moral upheaval: an increasing nudity and frankness in films, blunt and often obscene language on TV talk shows and in plays like Edward Albee's *Who's Afraid of Virginia Woolf?*, candid pop lyrics—particularly those of the Rolling Stones—undress in avant-garde ballet, and erotic art.

Other signs of the times included Joseph Papp's exciting new Public Theater, where teenagers in a musical called *Hair* were singing "gutter profanity with the cherubic straightforwardness of choir boys." Show World, a Times Square magnet for the raincoat crowd, featuring live performers, drew more customers and made more money than any other theater on Broadway.

Movies like *Bonnie and Clyde* and *In the Heat of the Night* showed barebreasted starlets. Books like Jacqueline Susann's *Valley of the Dolls* used language once reserved for books smuggled in from Paris. And those books, including *Story of O* and the works of Henry Miller and de Sade, brought pornography to the corner drugstore. A sultry model in a TV advertisement for shaving cream urged men, "Take it off, take it all off." The Maidenform bra campaign pioneered a new niche market—intimate apparel. British fashion designer Mary Quant claimed her daring creation, the miniskirt, was symbolic of women who wanted to be with a man in the afternoon and not wait until dark.

The hippie Haight Ashbury/East Village alternative lifestyle, which started in the early sixties, also helped integrate sex, drugs, and rock 'n' roll, and nudity was a large part of this movement toward sexual liberation. The Grateful Dead/Hog Farm collective was a traveling proselytization for this radically new way of life.

Playboy, meanwhile, was inching toward the five-million mark in circulation—second only to the *Reader's Digest,* the mother of all mass-market magazines. Sex best-sellers included *The Sensuous Woman* by the pseudonymous J, and Masters and Johnson's *Human Sexual Response.*

A thoughtful piece, the *Newsweek* story suggested that society in transition seemed to be losing its consensus on such crucial issues as premarital sex and clerical celibacy, marriage, birth control, sex education, and standards of conduct. Conservative, born-again cultural commentator Malcolm Muggeridge gave good ominous quote: "At the decline of the Roman Empire, the works of Sappho, Catullus and Ovid were celebrated. There is an analogy in that for us."

Despite the increasing popularity of the pill, however, the Sexual Revolution was still pretty much a highbrow affair. While millions read *Playboy,* few practiced the Philosophy. Pioneering sex radicals included cello player Charlotte Moorman, who performed in the nude and was once arrested in midconcert; and Julian Beck and Judith Malina, co-directors of New York's Living Theater, who in May 1968 participated in the student takeover of the Odéon, Paris's national theater. With *Paradise Now,* their experiment in guerrilla theater, Beck and Malina hoped to bring about a similar revolution in the United States—unlimited artistic freedom of expression, uncensored drama, fraternal love. Standing in the aisles every night, Beck announced, "I'm not allowed to take off my clothes," then promptly stripped to a G-string. Though some older women usually got up and left, two thousand others in the audience remained. Critic John Simon, writing in *New York* magazine, called such sexual bullying fascistic.

Guerrilla theater went public, in a manner of speaking, the following year when four hundred thousand young people descended on the small town of Bethel in upstate New York to establish the Woodstock Nation. Widely covered in the media, the open-air rock festival for the first time focused the attention of the American people on nudity, marijuana, psychedelic drugs, and open displays of sexuality in a way unparalleled in the nation's history. More than any other event, Woodstock signaled that the new generation—the first ever to be sexually liberated by the pill—was casting off the constraints of traditional morality and testing new sexual mores with revolutionary fervor.

Things heated up even more in 1969—a year like no other in the sexual history of the world, radically altering the cultural, moral, and political landscape of the United States and Western Europe forever.

In *Dionysus in 69,* Richard Schechner's Performance Group went even further than *Paradise Now* in erasing the inhibiting barrier between audience and actors. After remodeling an old warehouse in Greenwich Village, with scaffolds instead of seats and a multilevel stage, he loosely adapted Euripides' *The Bacchae,* with Pentheus standing on the side of law and order and Dionysus the champion of rebellion. In an ecstasy of revolt, audiences were invited, "Do what you will! Drink wine, make love, be free!"

Leaping from a platform into the play arena, Schechner then stripped naked, while all the other actors did likewise, circulating in the audience and leading spectators in a Bacchanalian dance. As the audience gradually left the safety of their scaffolds, jackets and shoes came off. As the music reached a feverish pitch, some stripped all the way. Occasionally a distraught actor, actress, or spectator had to be led away, weeping or hysterical. At the end, Bacchae tore Pentheus limb from limb, bathing the arena in blood, with spectators joining in. Audience participation–wise, it was a long way from *Sing Along With Mitch.*

In 1969 Philip Roth's *Portnoy's Complaint* became the first best-seller ever to explore the agony and ecstasy of male masturbation. Dr. David Reuben's *Everything You Always Wanted to Know About Sex (but Were Afraid to Ask)* told millions of readers precisely that. A Gallup poll showed that a historically high 55 percent of college females did not think premarital sex was wrong. Rock star Jim Morrison was arrested for indecent exposure at a Doors concert in Miami. John Lennon and Yoko Ono launched their Fuck for Peace Campaign, giving interviews while lying naked and entwined under the sheets in a luxurious Montreal hotel bedroom.

On June 17, Off Broadway saw the debut of *Oh! Calcutta!,* featuring satirically sybaritic full-frontal skits by Lennon, Jules Feiffer, Sam Shepard, and others. Directed by British literary critic Kenneth Tynan, the play—the first to bring erotica to the legitimate stage—derived its coy title from a play on a French phrase translated as "Oh, what a pretty cunt."

On a warm Friday evening in late June, gays harassed raiding police, for a switch, during a riot outside the Stonewall Inn, a popular New York gay bar. The protest continued over the weekend, and within a month the Gay Liberation Front appeared, advocating radical social change and adopting the tactics of the antiwar movement. Fisting, the first original sex practice in centuries, was also introduced into the world of the gay baths at around this time.

A cabaret singer named Bette Midler developed a cult of admirers for her performances at the Continental Baths, in which she did campy Mae West routines and covered hits from the thirties and forties. *The Queen,* the first documentary about the transvestite subculture, revealed that life was a drag in small and large towns all across America. Miss Harlow, a gorgeous nineteen-year-old Philadelphian, starred.

The ultimate upscale swingers' playground opened at Sandstone Ranch, fifteen acres of hothouse lust in Topanga Canyon outside Los Angeles.

Even so, as of 1969 *Playboy* and other men's magazines still airbrushed female genitals into oblivion, Hollywood still shied away from full-frontal nudity, and mass-market American hard-core had not yet been invented.

Only in the seventies did sex get really down and dirty. Only then, too, did the winds of change and the temples of tradition enter into a life-or-death struggle for supremacy. Not so coincidentally, the year 1969 also ushered in the deeply puritanical administration of Richard Milhous Nixon.

BOB MCGINLEY was an aircraft engineer working for the Bendix Corporation in Japan in the mid-sixties when he first heard about wife swapping. A bearded, muscular man heading into his thirties, he was in the mood to swap his own wife permanently, since their marriage was obviously not working. One very big problem was monogamy. McGinley was pro-marriage. He just did not understand why marriage had to be the sexual equivalent of going into solitary confinement with one woman for the rest of his life.

Wife swapping, or swinging, as some people back in the States were beginning to call it, seemed to take the hypocrisy out of conventional extramarital sex. It sounded to McGinley like the ideal tribute to the variety of sexual pleasure. Not only did it neutralize the proprietary aspect of a relationship, but it allowed all participants to benefit in an open, loving way.

After answering a personal advertisement in a swingers' publication, McGinley struck up a correspondence with a couple back in the United States. Soon he began exchanging letters exclusively with the wife, whose extremely erotic replies, all with the approval of her husband, suggested to McGinley that he had finally met up with some people who were in the vanguard of the dawning age of sexual enlightenment.

However, since McGinley was involved in the air force's top-secret SR-71 spy plane project, the post office routinely intercepted his mail. When the inspectors read his letters, they contacted his employer and said that as a result of his steamy correspondence, McGinley was vulnerable to blackmail. Bendix immediately annulled his security clearance.

After returning to California, McGinley sold real estate for two years. It was an extremely traumatic time, as he struggled to regain his security status and witnessed the final disintegration of his marriage. It was also a time of intense sexual searching for something better for an average guy like himself than Saturday night sex with the wife and a little cheating on the side.

Most swinging activity around that time took place in California and New York, although it existed in Florida, Ohio, Texas, Illinois, and, curiously enough, Indiana. In Berkeley, McGinley joined the Sexual Freedom League

(SFL). Though the SFL was the granddaddy of all swingers' organizations, with particularly large memberships in Los Angeles and San Francisco, enough smaller clubs preceded it that by 1964 William and Jerrye Breedlove had published a book about the phenomenon titled *Swap Clubs*. The SFL had its roots in the New York City League for Sexual Freedom, a mainly political organization founded in 1963 by Jeff Poland. After moving to Berkeley, Poland organized a nude "wade in" to protest laws against public nudity. When participants indicated continued interest in socializing in the buff, the SFL was born in 1967.

At an SFL party in Berkeley, McGinley met Geri, a petite, attractive woman in her early thirties with auburn hair and a lilting laugh. Like him, she was in the process of divorcing her first spouse. They got married and moved in together, along with their eight children and stepchildren, but a basic tenet of their marriage was that each was free to have sex with other people.

After winning back his security rating, McGinley went to work on the McDonnell-Douglas DC-10 project. But the turmoil in his private life had also given him an opportunity to think about making a big career change. In 1969 Bob and Geri founded Wide World of Contemporary People, destined to become the biggest, longest-lived, and best known swingers' organization in the country.

Unlike Sandstone Ranch in nearby Topanga Canyon, which attracted a mostly upscale crowd, Wide World was the swingers' equivalent of an Elks Club, appealing to blue-collar Middle Americans, dentists and other mid-level professionals, men with a flair for polyester and women with bell-bottoms, just like Bob and Geri.

At first the pair decided to keep their swinging and personal lives separate. They bought a suburban tract home to be used exclusively for their swing parties, held every Saturday night of the year. Over the next five years they purchased and sold five party houses, each slightly more luxurious than the last, until they found the perfect home in Orange County, midway between Knott's Berry Farm and Disneyland.

On Saturday mornings Bob trimmed the bushes and hosed down the patio furniture, while Geri planned her menu for the evening buffet—lasagna, salad, pies—and hurried down to the laundry room to wash load after load of sheets, clean the house, and make the beds—all sixteen of them. Meanwhile, Bob skimmed the bugs off the pool, took a break to splash around with his children, and later iced the beer and wine, cleaned the whirlpool, and got everything ready down by the firepit. The last order of business was to deliver the children to a nearby hotel, where they were looked after by a sitter.

Around seven-thirty Bob and Geri slipped into their party clothes—matching kimonos and sandals were a favorite. An hour later the first guests began to arrive. Usually about thirty couples showed up—mostly regulars, but always a few newcomers. At every party the men and women were evenly matched to make sure nobody was left out in the cold. Single males who wanted to party were put on a waiting list until a single female decided to attend. Then the two were paired. Nobody was ever allowed to attend a Club Wide World party without a date. Reservations were a must, and partygoers checked in at a front desk when they arrived.

Once the party got under way, the men exchanged their coats and jackets for towels, while the women donned negligees or teddies. Some changed outfits several times in the course of the evening.

Around nine-thirty Bob stood in front of the fireplace to introduce new members and tell a few jokes. Then it was time to get down to serious sex.

Swinging etiquette ranged from parking (never in a neighbor's driveway) to asking for sex. Polite euphemisms ("Would you like to go upstairs?") were preferred to "Do you want to fuck?"

The erotic environment was highly structured, with group, semiprivate, and private rooms; the latter were by far the most popular. The group room, consisting of two large beds surrounded by mirrors, was used for threesomes and couple-to-couple couplings. The back room contained eleven beds on carpeted platforms and lofts. In the TV room guests rested or geared up for another round by watching porn movies. At three P.M. the party officially came to an end.

Orgies were only a small part of swinging, maybe 15 percent at Wide World. In the swinger's worldview, swinging was not synonymous with promiscuity. Most swingers insisted that the social element predominated.

Later Bob and Geri also started up Lifestyles Tours and Travel, a travel agency offering cruises and vacations for swingers. Once a year they led a swing trip to Japan, to party with members of the Mickey Mouse Swing Club, their Japanese equivalent. The annual Lifestyles convention usually attracted nearly a thousand swingers from around the world.

Bob also served as president of the North American Swing Club Association (NASCA), a group of swing clubs and magazines that promoted swinging as a way of life, and over the next ten years he appeared on hundreds of TV and radio talk shows, preaching the gospel of sexual freedom within the context of mutual sharing. Later he earned a doctorate in counseling psychology, writing his dissertation on swinger marriages.

In the *NASCA Membership Handbook,* McGinley stated, "Swinging enables a couple to explore sexual and social feelings and needs together, permitting a demystification of sex which allows sex to assume a place in the relationship unhindered by the standard ties to love, duty, sex roles and morals of others."

Estimates of the number of Americans swinging in the late sixties and early seventies ranged from a low of one million to a high of twenty million. McGinley himself guessed there were between three and five million, based on the number of swing clubs throughout the country, their membership size, and the circulations of swing magazines.

Membership questionnaires revealed that 40 percent were married, with an average family income for responders of $42,500. Eighty percent were Caucasian, while 40 percent had a college degree. A third rated themselves liberal, 28 percent middle of the road, 19 percent conservative, 13 percent no political preference. In contrast with the celebratory and communal aspect of swinging on the West Coast, swinging in the Midwest and on the East Coast was still mainly confined to old-fashioned, just-between-friends wife swapping. In certain parts of the South swingers were reluctant to include black swingers in their midst, but there was no such bias in California.

Because it was a semiclosed structure, where most swingers knew one another's sex histories, sexually transmitted diseases were relatively rare in swinging circles—usually no more than one or two cases of gonorrhea a year. Anyone exposed was immediately contacted. Yet it was also a time of sexual near innocence, when consciousness about the dangers of sexually transmitted diseases (STDs) was nearly subzero. Many swingers boasted complacently that they were not merely STD free, but virtually STD immune—at a time when Eugene Schoenfeld's "Dear Dr. Hip" sex-and-drug advice column, which appeared in the *Berkeley Barb* and other underground and alternative publications from 1967 on, was documenting the seriousness of the STD epidemic at large.

A constant problem was infiltration by homosexuals, who tried to make passes at straight men. Then as now, male swingers were not comfortable being sexually affectionate with other men, in contrast with women, who were much more receptive to bisexuality. Upon being discovered, gays were usually eased out. SM was almost nonexistent in the swing culture.

About half of the single swingers who dropped out to marry a traditional partner returned to swinging in due course. The median age for men was thirty-nine, for women thirty-six. Most swingers had spent their twenties looking for a significant other and only after getting married felt a need to extend their relationship to include sex with others.

Perhaps the most sensational instance of mate swapping occurred in 1973 when Yankee pitchers Mike Kekich and Fritz Peterson announced what Susanne Kekich gigglingly called "the most unique trade in baseball history." Susanne and her two daughters had swapped places with Marilyn Peterson and her two sons. Soon afterward, however, Kekich found himself mired in midlife crisis. Marilyn, feeling guilty, moved out, taking her children. After the Yankees traded him to Cleveland, the lefthander wandered the big leagues, having lost his wife, children, home, and best friend's wife. Later he pitched in Japan and the minors before retiring. Proving that God surely does work in mysterious ways, Fritz and Mrs. Kekich moved to Chicago, where his playing days ended, he found religion, became an evangelist, and established the Baseball Chapel, a nondenominational house of worship for ball players.

ONE FATEFUL DAY in 1967 or 1968, which would later come back to haunt him, Reuben Sturman was driving through Gary, Indiana, and spotted a shop called Jack and Jill's. Hungry and looking for a place to buy a Coke and ham-and-cheese sandwich to eat on the long drive, he decided to stop in. While waiting for his sandwich, the ever-affable magazine salesman struck up a conversation.

"You must be Jill," he said. "Where's Jack?"

"Jack is in jail," Jill replied.

"In jail?" Sturman said, surprised. "Why is he in jail?"

"He's in jail because he sold a dirty magazine," Jill told him. As proof, she showed him the magazine rack, and Sturman was astonished to see some of his own titles on display.

"If I had known about this," Sturman vowed, "Jack would never have gone to jail."

Whenever any of Sturman's mom-and-pop stores got busted, he either provided them with legal help or awarded them a generous bonus for jail time. When he got back to the Sovereign News Warehouse in Cleveland, he sent Jill three hundred dollars' worth of new racks and titles. It was a gesture of friendship and solidarity, but it was also good business. Without the little people to sell his magazines, he could not be King.

The next time he stopped in at Jack and Jill's, Sturman learned that Jack was due to get out in a month. On his third visit Jack was there to shake his hand personally.

"I got to get out of this pigsty," Jack told Sturman. "I'm moving to Chicago and opening up some real stores."

"Fine, Jack," said Sturman. "Good luck." That was just how he and Esther had gotten into the business—start small, have no fear of the consequences, think big.

After Jack and Jill moved to Chicago, Reuben Sturman dropped in to have lunch with them from time to time. Jack and Jill prospered, but one day Jack said to his friend Reuben, "I know a place where we can *really* do some business. So I want to sell you my store."

"You're crazy, Jack," Sturman replied. "You're making more money now than you ever made in your life. Where are you going?"

"Las Vegas," said Jack.

"Las Vegas?" Sturman exclaimed. "What, are you crazy? That's a police state. The motorcycle cops got dark glasses and white helmets. They'll put you away forever."

"No, I'm going to Las Vegas. That's where it's at," said Jack.

Jack and Jill sold their two Chicago stores to Sturman and moved to Las Vegas, where they opened a bigger store called Talk of the Town. Jack put classified advertisements in newspapers around the world, inviting porn-starved tourists to visit. Asians in particular flocked to the place. Jack and Jill were getting very rich.

But nothing like Reuben Sturman. As the sixties came to a close, the prospects for pornography never looked rosier. Lyndon Johnson's Commission on Obscenity and Pornography had just urged an end to all bans on pornography for consenting adults. Sturman decided to up the ante with his latest brainstorm—the peep show/masturbation booth. He had gotten the idea from an old gentleman in Cleveland who owned a few tobacco shops with a couple of wind-up carnival machines in a back room into which customers put a quarter and, by working the crank, watched dirty pictures flip past. One day Sturman saw a machine in operation, thought it was a natural for his stores, and directed employees to create in the back of each one a private "cabin" containing a projector, screen, and inside lock to ensure privacy.

In 1970 he placed a call to an Italian named Alberto Ferro, a ne'er-do-well diplomat's son who had gone to Denmark to make his fortune as an entrepreneur in hard-core. Under the *nom de porn* of Lasse Braun he directed a film called *Delphi in Greece*. Sturman told Braun he was excited by his first sight of a "double penetration" (a woman having simultaneous vaginal and anal intercourse with two men) in the film and that he wanted to buy U.S. rights and convert it into Super 8 loops for his ever-expanding peep-show operations. These also included adult bookstores in which Sturman paid for the installation (between $22,000 and $60,000) and the store kept 50 percent of the gross.

Peep shows had become a coast-to-coast craze, like pinball machines in the fifties, with everyone from Wall Street pinstripers to Oregon lumbermen popping into an arcade at noon hour or after hours to drop a few quarters while they dropped their pants.

Braun was only one of Sturman's thirty or more suppliers, and he ultimately supplied Sturman not only with *Delphi* but with thirty more films, then another twenty. Over the next four years Sturman made several thousand copies of each. By now Sturman also owned three porn-loop manufacturing companies in Los Angeles. According to a local police report at the time, 580 of the city's 765 video arcade machines were likewise owned by companies controlled by Sturman.

The arrangement with Braun not only made the Italian rich, but earned him the sobriquet "the Pope of Porn." Few outside the industry, though, knew that the Pope served the King. Over the next two decades, Sturman's own grosses from porn loops alone may have exceeded a staggering $2 billion.

The man of the people was increasingly becoming one of the Beautiful People as well. Membership in American Airlines' 500,000-Mile Club attested to his international lifestyle. He also owned a credit card from the Sahara Casino in Las Vegas and was a regular at London's Victorian Sporting Club. Two passions were hand-tailored clothes and beautiful women, whom he always treated generously, usually arranging a job for them somewhere when the relationship ended.

Yet the King chose not to live in Los Angeles or Las Vegas, which he often visited for business and pleasure. He remained in Cleveland, partly to be near his aged mother, but also because he felt more comfortable with his management team there, many of whom were from his old Kinsman Road neighborhood.

Sturman's latest castle was, by Hefnerian standards, modest—a sixteen-room mansion in Shaker Heights, Cleveland's most exclusive neighborhood. Perched on a small hill overlooking a swan-filled lake, the house boasted a traditional formal dining room that sat twenty-four and walls lined with expensive art. Next door was the Shaker Heights Country Club, which Sturman was never allowed to join. By now Cleveland's leading citizens had become uncomfortably aware that a certain millionaire in their midst was bringing their hometown a dubious distinction as the world's crossroads of pornography.

Around this time, Sturman also decided to bring his eldest son, David, into the business. Walking to his grandmother's house one evening, David listened to his father enthuse about the commercial possibilities of vibrators. Many of Sturman's stores featured a small glass case containing prehistoric "marital aids," usually packed in faded, cracked cellophane and covered with a layer of dust. Such items sold in spite of themselves. To Sturman, that meant an immense market was waiting to be exploited. If David was interested, Dad was prepared to install him as head of this new division in the empire.

David enthusiastically agreed and suggested they come up with a name for the enterprise.

"Good idea," said Sturman. "But it has to sound medical and have substance to it. How about Doctor Something?"

"No, make it Doc," said David.

"Good idea. Doc what?"

Sturman also intended to market sex paraphernalia throughout his stores in Europe, and to those of Beate Uhse, so he wanted an international-sounding name. Partly in homage to the president, whose commission had koshered porn, and partly because the name was a synonym for penis in many parts of the English-speaking world, but mostly because the name had a Swedish and ergo sexy ring to it, Doc Johnson was born—an instant Goliath.

IMPROBABLY ENOUGH, the father of the modern dildo whose commercial possibilities so intrigued Reuben Sturman was a happily married, wisecracking forty-three-year-old ventriloquist named Ted Marche, who in the mid-sixties opened a small dildo factory in North Hollywood.

Before 1966 the high point of Marche's professional career was a glowing mention in Walter Winchell's gossip column touting his act at industrial shows across the country. From morning to night Marche and his hand-carved dummies helped drum up business for products ranging from auto springs to patio furniture.

One day Marche paid a visit to an old friend, John Francis, a jack-of-all-trades who was building a boat in his backyard and supporting himself by printing greeting cards and making prosthetic phalluses for the Gem Company, a surgical supply company. At that time the sex-toy market was virtually nonexistent, and many people desperate for a little sexual variety still made their own dildos, fashioning crude devices from broom handles and foam.

"You can make these, too," Francis advised Marche, showing him a very straight wooden phallus copied from an art book. "I make them for white people. You should make them for black people. A lot of people in the black community are impotent, too."

Marche carved his first dildo on the dining room table while the family was having dinner. Later he became sole supplier of the "ebony division" of the Gem Company, gradually improving his product from a straight wooden tube to a semilifelike phallus sporting fancy wrinkles and folds.

Sensing an opportunity, he also began selling phalluses both white and black through mail order, advertising in true-detective and other pulps. Mom, Dad, and teenage son, Steve, when he was not in school, slaved away in a fifteen-foot-square garage behind their modest Venice home, working around the clock to keep America supplied with dildos. As the company grew, Marche rented a small warehouse in North Hollywood. Only once did he get into trouble with the post office, after claiming that his product provided men with a "real" erection. A stickler for detail, the post office required that Marche's advertisements and brochures promote a device that only "simulated" erection.

Later Marche experimented with a plastic phallus, using aluminum molds filled with liquid plastic, which were then baked in an industrial oven for ten minutes. The result was even more lifelike, pliable, and wrinkly, and sales boomed.

Before long the Ted Marche Manufacturing Company had thirty employees and was supplying novelty store distributors from coast to coast. To avoid prosecution in those early days, however, Marche continued to market his wares as prosthetic devices, much as girlie magazines once masqueraded as uplifting reading matter for nature lovers.

All of Marche's products contained preaddressed postcards that customers could mail back with their comments. Though the original dildo measured six inches and remained the best-selling item, accounting for 55 percent of all dildo sales, Marche later acceded to customer demand by introducing five, seven-and-a-half, and nine-inch models, while also accommodating kinky customer demand for an outsized glans or a thinner stalk.

Ted Marche also invented the first primitive vibrator and the first artificial vagina. The former was "mass-produced" by son Steve, then only sixteen, and his schoolmates in the family garage. The other kids did not know what they were making, and curious neighbors were informed the boys were busy on a "science project."

Starting with a two-by-four-inch plastic box, the boys installed a snap lid on top, then soldered in a battery connection with a switch on the side. The final step was to attach a flange to accommodate a dildo. The item was a huge success, and Marche Manufacturing sold hundreds of thousands.

Marche's nonphallic vibrator consisted of a battery-powered back-scratcher, which he purchased in bulk. Strapped on top was a plastic flower held on by a rubber band, and voilà! Other Marche marvels included a curved vibrating prostate massager, Squirt Bananas, and a massage mitt covered with plastic nodules that either women or men could use to stimulate themselves. The mold for that one came from a welcome mat.

The world's first mass-produced artificial vagina came into being after plastics technology pioneered by toy manufacturers permitted them to market soft, pliable, lifelike dolls. Several of those same manufacturers soon became serious competitors on the dildo front as well.

To compete, Marche bought a defunct fishing-lure company, which used the newly created hot-melt plastic process. One of Marche's associates was Freddy the welder, who had an intimate knowledge of industrial plastics. Freddy took the lure machines apart and remade them into an apparatus that churned out penises more realistic looking than ever.

Later Freddy fashioned a vaginal mold suitable for dipping into rubber. The form was then baked, cured, provided with a sleeve insert to keep it clean for repeat usage, and equipped with a four-way heavy strap. Marche was convinced that his primary customers for this gadget consisted of women having their period and homosexuals eager to fake heterosexual intercourse.

Marche sold his dildos to wholesalers for $1.50 to $2.00 each, and they in turn sold them to retailers who charged up to $25.00. Still, Marche thought he was making good money, and his showroom now boasted hundreds of dildos, blow-up Judy dolls made in Japan, and such curious novelties as the Penis Pacifier "for women who talk too much." Yet another was a heavy thrusting dildo that ran on a back-forth, back-forth windshield-wiper motor, which proved so popular it starred in several hard-core films.

By 1976, in that golden age of sex novelties, Marche Manufacturing was turning out 350 different sexual products, though dildos remained the mainstay, with total unit sales reaching 4,975,000 and annual revenues at $250,000. Business was primarily through mail order, though sex toys were also becoming increasingly visible on retail counters across the United States—in newsstand and novelty stores, barbershops, and even a few beauty parlors. At the same time, condoms were also coming out from behind the counter. In the vibrator market, Marche found himself competing with such giants as Hitachi and General Electric.

Other popular sex toys on the market around that time included ben-wa balls (vibrating and nonvibrating), cock rings (vibrating and nonvibrating), anal reamers, and a masturbation machine called the Accu-Jac. A pump-action mechanism with assorted attachments—sleeves for men, dildos for women—it was at $200 the most expensive sex toy on the market at the time.

Marche's heyday as a sex gadgeteer came to a sudden and unfortunate end, however. Since the hot-melt process he used to make plastic phalluses was still in its infancy, Marche reinforced them with wire. One day, during a bout of exuberant lovemaking, one man thrust a Marche phallus into his lover's anus a little too energetically, and it ripped the man's colon. A jury later awarded him $14 million—forcing Marche to bail out.

In 1976 Reuben Sturman made Ted Marche an offer he could not afford to refuse. Under Sturman, with Doc Johnson's two hundred retail shops providing the retailing oomph, sales of Marche Manufacturing rose tenfold to $2.5 million annually in only two years and continued to increase an average of 28 percent annually. Ron Braverman, an old Sturman school chum, was installed as president.

Ted Marche, meanwhile, went back on the road as a ventriloquist, wowing crowds at industrial trade shows from coast to coast.

THOUGH REUBEN STURMAN, Bob Guccione, and Hugh Hefner were chiefly responsible for bringing the consolations of hard-core and soft-core to the American masses, several other individuals played significant supporting roles. Foremost among them was Ralph Ginzburg.

Two events that took place in June 1963 exemplified how the fates conspired to make one man inordinately prosperous and the other doomed to end his days in tragicomic failure. One afternoon in that month, Hugh Hefner was asleep in his mansion in Chicago when four men from the local vice squad came calling. The police were perturbed by a spread in the June *Playboy* of actress Jayne Mansfield, in bed and bubble bath, revealing everything except what a tiny G-string managed to conceal. At the time, Hefner's, magazine had reached a very respectable 1,250,000. Though that circulation was dwarfed by *Life*'s 7,000,000 and somewhat lower figures for *Look* and the *Saturday Evening Post,* those three mass-market dinosaurs were all on the verge of extinction, victims of television in the competition for a lowest-common-denominator audience and megarevenues from advertising. Excluded from that race, *Playboy* alone among American magazines, even at its tamest, broke new editorial ground with each new issue.

Hefner easily beat the charge, afterward noting that the photos were really no more revelatory than what others had shown. The only explanation, the publisher laconically observed, was that "Jayne has more than most. She makes people nervous."

That same month a loudmouthed, left-wing, Jewish intellectual from New York was found guilty on twenty-eight counts of mailing obscene matter, for which he was liable to fines up to $140,000 and 140 years in prison.

Though the charge was easily beatable, Ralph Ginzburg chose to place a higher value on truth than on his own personal fate.

The son of Lithuanian immigrants, Ginzburg was a wiry, nervous young man with a trademark mustache. Born in Brooklyn in 1931, he majored in accounting at the City College School of Business with a minor in journalism, served a two-year stint with the army, and returned to New York. Soon after joining *Look,* he was appointed promotion manager at age twenty-three, quickly mastering the economics of publishing.

In 1956 Ginzburg moved to *Esquire* as articles editor, after impressing publisher Arnold Gingrich with an article on the Library of Congress's restricted collection of erotic literature. Soon afterward he self-published a book-length expansion of his article called *An Unhurried View of Erotica,* which sold at the then unheard-of price of $4.95. To ensure that the book wore the fig leaf of socially redeeming value, Ginzburg enlisted prominent psychoanalyst Dr. Theodor Reik to write the introduction.

If Ginzburg had a genius, it was in promotion—which also turned out to be his Achilles' heel. Taking out full-page advertisements in *The New York Times,* Ginzburg touted his coyly written bibliography as if it were humankind's first prurient peep into the archives of lust. The promotional blitzkrieg, virtually unlike anything ever seen before in the staid world of book publishing, was a spectacular success. *Unhurried* sold 125,000 copies in hardcover and 275,000 in paperback, becoming in the process the first big sex best-seller in an America starved for sex information, pictures, and titillation of almost any kind. In Ginzburg pornography found its first huckster.

After Gingrich fired Ginzburg for identifying himself on talk shows as an *Esquire* editor, Ginzburg began to make preparations to publish his latest brainchild—an elegant quarterly called *Eros,* after the Greek god of love.

Ginzburg was influenced by the Supreme Court's 1957 ruling in *People* v. *Roth,* which stipulated that only hard-core pornographic literature could be banned. For the first time, the Court had formulated a three-part legal definition of the word "obscene." First, "to the average person, applying contemporary community standards, the dominant theme [of the work in question] taken as a whole [must] appeal to prurient interest." Second, it must go "substantially beyond customary limits of candor." Third, it must be "utterly without redeeming social importance."

The launch of *Eros* took four years partly because Ginzburg encountered unexpected difficulties in obtaining copies of long-suppressed masterpieces from the world's leading libraries and archives. It was just as difficult to line up artists and writers willing to wait for payment until after the first issue appeared. Living off *Unhurried* royalties and writing—improbably—for such magazines as *Reader's Digest* and *Redbook,* Ginzburg worked alone in a small office overlooking the main branch of the New York Public Library.

Finally, in September 1961, he succeeded in mailing ten thousand copies of a brochure announcing *Eros,* a lush, full-color, hardbound quarterly "devoted to the joy of love" and selling for $25 a year. Contributions from the world of great art included drawings and sketches by Rembrandt, Picasso, Dalí, and Rubens, as well as Edgar Degas's monotypes illustrating de Maupassant's *Madame Tellier's Brothel.* For text, Ginzburg excerpted from the works of Shakespeare, D. H. Lawrence, and such long-suppressed classics as Frank Harris's *My Life and Loves,* John Cleland's *Fanny Hill,* Mark Twain's *1601,* and Robert Burns's "The Merry Muses of Caledonia." Contemporary contributors included philologist Eric Partridge, science-fiction writer Ray Bradbury, and journalist Mimi Sheraton, author of "My Quest for a French Tickler in Japan," who later achieved eminent respectability as the restaurant critic of *The New York Times.*

The response to the mailing exceeded anything even Ginzburg expected. Soon he repeated with another one hundred thousand brochures, then another five hundred thousand, then millions more, adding up to nine million altogether, with revenues reaching $3 million. America was clearly ready to welcome the Greek god of love into its midst.

The first issue of *Eros* was published, in a typical Ginzburg touch, on Valentine's Day 1962, and like an ardent lover, he spared no expense in producing the most sumptuous collection of erotica ever published before or since for the general public. Printed on expensive, heavy stock between hard covers, *Eros* reeked of redeeming social value. The U.S. State Department even included representative selections of *Eros* in a portfolio of leading American graphic art to be displayed in Moscow. Publications like the *Saturday Review* hailed it, while the magazine's art director was voted Art Director of the Year by the National Society of Art Directors.

Six weeks after publication, though, U.S. Representative Kathryn Granahan, a devout Roman Catholic from Philadelphia who was chairman of the Post Office Operations Subcommittee, vilified both *Eros* and Ginzburg on the House floor. Other Catholic vigilantes rose up. At the time, the country was home to some three hundred smut-hunting organizations, led by the Legion of Decency and the National Office for Decent Literature.

Then volume two came out, featuring an excerpt from an Arizona woman's sexual autobiography called *The Housewife's Handbook on Selective Promiscuity,* which she had been selling for two years through direct mail before Ginzburg acquired the rights. Reik called it "a work of admirable moral courage," and it received similar testimonials from sexologist Albert Ellis and others. The issue sold twenty thousand copies.

By now the U.S. Post Office was receiving up to nine hundred letters of protest a day—thirty-five thousand complaints in all, the greatest in its history. Ginzburg later claimed the post office was receptive to the complaints because "virtually every top postal official since the turn of the century—including almost every postmaster-general—has been a devout Catholic."

Meanwhile, Ginzburg continued his massive mail-order assault, driving even his defenders to despair. In a move calculated to garner even more outrageous publicity, he applied for mailing permits from such Amish towns as Intercourse and Blue Ball, Pennsylvania.

On December 19, 1962, in the middle of an *Eros* Christmas party—a few bottles of Scotch, an FM radio playing classical music—two U.S. marshals served the enfant terrible of erotica with a subpoena. The Justice Department, under Robert Kennedy, planned to prosecute Ginzburg in Philadelphia on twenty-eight counts of mailing obscene matter, claiming that the contents "go beyond the customary limits that society tolerates."

Ginzburg always expected trouble to come from the post office, not the Justice Department. In all previous censorship cases, the government had brought civil charges against a publisher in an attempt to ban the book from the mails. But Kennedy had deliberately resurrected the Comstock Act, named after the most notorious smut suppressor in history, in order to bring criminal charges.

Unperturbed, Ginzburg still expected to get only a slap on the wrist, more to mollify Catholics than anything, followed by exoneration by the appeals court, plus invaluable nationwide publicity. He hired the best legal counsel money could buy, however, mindful that this was the first time in the ninety-year history of the Comstock Act that a defendant had to defend himself outside the locality where his offenses occurred. Moreover, the City of Brotherly Love not only boasted a large conservative Catholic population, but was the smut-hunting capital of the country, headed by a Catholic-sponsored vigilante group that had gotten *Tropic of Cancer* and *The Scarlet Letter* banned from local libraries. To celebrate those and other victories, the group later held a massive burning of obscene books, complete with choir, on the steps of the Catholic cathedral.

Fearful of the average Philadelphian, Ginzburg waived his right to a jury trial and put his faith in Judge Ralph C. Body, a slight, graying man of sixty-six who, though a Shriner and American Legionnaire, at least had the advantage of being a Protestant.

When the trial began the following June, Ginzburg showed up in court wearing a boater, black pin-striped blazer, and a white carnation in his lapel, prompting Judge Body to ask, "Where does he think he's going to, his wedding?"

The prosecution did not focus as expected on *Eros*, which was virtually ignored, but on the *Handbook*, saying it was both pornographic and symptomatic of Ginzburg's "intent to pander." Prosecutors also focused on an article in volume 1, number 4. Contributors to that issue included poet Allen Ginsberg, sexual gadflies Phyllis and Eberhard Kronhausen, and Aristophanes. But that issue also contained a full-color "photographic tone poem" by Ralph M. Hattersley Jr. called "Black & White in Color" which juxtaposed a nude white woman and a nude black man engaged in an assortment of tender, romantic, noncoital embraces.

Ginzburg had been intent on publishing not only America's best, but its most in-your-face specimen of erotica ever. But in those turbulent times, when America was deeply divided over civil rights, any hint of interracial sex was too far over the top. Two southern congressmen had immediately taken to the floor to denounce Ginzburg as a race-mixing pinko pornographer.

In his defense, Ginzburg had marshaled sixty-five psychologists, sexologists, and assorted literati to testify, including Lillian Serett, author under the pen name of Rey Anthony of *The Housewife's Handbook*, who told the court: "Women's role in sex is widely misunderstood. Women do have sexual rights." Essayist Dwight MacDonald, on the other hand, conceded under examination that he found *Housewife* of "no literary value."

On June 14 Judge Body announced his verdict: guilty on all counts. What especially disturbed him, the magistrate said in his opinion, was the photographic essay. While admitting he had not read all of the *Handbook*, he allowed that he also found what parts he did read "extremely boring, disgusting, and shocking."

All during the trial, the American press had remained silent. In reporting the outcome, few showed any sympathy to Ginzburg personally or seemed concerned about First Amendment issues. *Time* even playfully whooped it up over his conviction and, Ginzburg later claimed, falsified a few facts in order to get off some wisecracks at his expense—for example, that the magazine was in fact mailed from Intercourse and Blue Ball. Only *Newsweek* among the major print and TV media showed any concern, quoting Mac-Donald to the effect that Ginzburg was the victim of a "persecution."

Sentencing was on December 19. This time Ginzburg showed up in the squarest blue serge suit he could find. Unmoved by a plea for clemency from Ginzburg's lawyer, who pointed out that the publisher was the sole support of his wife, three children, his widowed mother, and his blind sister, Judge Body meted out $42,000 in fines and five years in prison.

Shortly afterward, the Philadelphia Court of Appeals affirmed Ginzburg's conviction, the three-man court's opinion rendered by Gerald McLaughlin, a seventy-two-year-old bachelor and presumed Catholic. The possibility that Ginzburg might actually be sent to prison for five years began to seem, for the first time, grimly real.

Three separate amici curiae briefs were then filed on Ginzburg's behalf— by the ACLU, by the Authors League of America, and a third by such literary notables as Kay Boyle, Harry Golden, Paul Goodman, Joseph Heller, James Jones, Christopher Isherwood, Kenneth Rexroth, Henry Miller, Arthur Miller, John Crowe Ransom, Robert Penn Warren, and William Styron, as well as assorted museum directors and members of the clergy. While appealing his sentence, Ginzburg suspended *Eros* and in 1964 launched a new, fiercely muckraking publication called *Fact* whose agenda appeared to be to savage Ginzburg's more outspoken persecutors such as Republican senator Barry Goldwater and the *Reader's Digest.*

Having purchased the mailing list of the American Psychoanalytic Association, Ginzburg sent each member a detailed questionnaire on Republican presidential candidate Goldwater's mental stability. Twenty percent of those questioned replied. Ginzburg carefully culled the responses to portray Goldwater as a manic depressive, paranoid, anally arrested homosexual with sadistic tendencies. Responses affirming Goldwater's mental health were ignored.

Furious, Goldwater sued Ginzburg and *Fact* for $200,000, ultimately winning $75,000 in punitive damages. Ginzburg's reputation was muddied just as the Supreme Court justices were pondering his fate. As journalist Robert Stein remarked at the time: "As a publisher, Ralph Ginzburg seems to have an instinct for his own jugular."

On March 21, 1966, the Court upheld Ginzburg's conviction. Three of the leading liberals, Chief Justice Earl Warren, and Justices William Brennan and Abe Fortas, ruled against him. The majority decision rested not on the contents of *Eros,* but on its promotion. By applying for mailing permits in Blue Ball and Intercourse, the Court declared, Ginzburg had demonstrated his intent to pander to prurient interests.

A stunned Ginzburg heard about the ruling over the radio while working in his office. The Court had upheld his conviction over a postmark. He was being sent to prison for a bad joke.

After the Supreme Court affirmed the obscenity conviction, declaring that a lurid promotion can make obscene a borderline work that would otherwise pass judicial muster, Sidney Zion wrote a story in *The New York Times* citing legal experts who thought another wave of censorship was now in the offing. Similarly, Russell Baker suggested in a column that the Court was confused about smut and in over its head.

In the aftermath of the ruling, smut dealers in Times Square panicked, hastily removing all titles dealing with SM, fetishism, and homosexuality. But advertisers took some comfort in the ruling. Dr. Ernest Dichter, founder of modern advertising, noted that the Court had accepted a long-standing claim of advertising people, that the image of a product produced by advertising and promotion was part of the product itself.

While his attorneys fought for a reduction in or suspension of the sentence, Ginzburg folded *Fact* and launched yet another handsome new publication in 1968—*Avant Garde.* A typical full-page advertisement showed a comely young woman in bed, her eyes closed and mouth gasping in ecstasy, over the copy line: "*Avant Garde,* an Orgasm of the Mind."

When the magazine failed to catch on, Ginzburg suspended publication in 1970, only to immediately launch *Moneysworth,* a four-page, five-dollar-a-year, biweekly consumer newsletter. Ginzburg spent hundreds of thousands of dollars promoting this latest and least of his publications with full-page advertisements in *The New York Times* and elsewhere in what was perhaps the most heavily promoted publishing venture of the decade. Filled with superficial money-saving tips and virtually no original reporting, *Moneysworth* mostly mined current book reviews to crank out tidbits such as "Dentistry and Its Victims" and "The Great American Food Hoax."

Yet the real purpose of the publication was not to make money on subscription revenues, but to sell the rapidly expanding mailing list to other publishers. Within a very short time, the *Moneysworth* list became one of the hottest on the market, with one broker calculating that it netted from $2 million to $3 million a year in rentals.

By now the country was wallowing in pornography. What began as a delaying tactic now seemed almost like a victory, and by 1971 Ginzburg had reason to hope his sentence would be suspended.

But on January 28, 1972, at a time when Reuben Sturman, Bob Guccione, and Hugh Hefner were flooding America with unprecedented amounts of hard-core and soft-core, while at the same time successfully fighting off federal and local prosecutions and expanding the legal interpretation of the First Amendment almost on a monthly basis, Ralph Ginzburg lost his last plea to vacate his conviction. On the other hand, an embarrassed appeals court did reduce his sentence from five years in prison to three.

A few weeks later, Ginzburg traveled to Lewisburg, Pennsylvania, where he turned himself over to a federal marshal. On the street outside the courthouse he waved a parchment copy of the Bill of Rights before the assembled media, then crumpled it into a ball and flung it into a litter basket. Moments later he emerged from federal district court in manacles.

Eight months later, in October 1972, the federal government released Ginzburg on parole from its prison farm camp at Allenwood. Soon after, Ginzburg disappeared into anonymity, finally winding up as a photographer for the tabloid *New York Post*.

The conviction of Ralph Ginzburg was the last hurrah of sixties-style censorship by the Great White Penis. Yet his ordeal probably had more impact on the Sexual Revolution than earlier Court rulings on such long-suppressed works as *Fanny Hill* and *Lady Chatterley's Lover,* because it later shamed the Court into broadening the constitutional freedoms they had so egregiously denied Ginzburg. The eight months he spent in jail constituted the greatest travesty of the First Amendment in this century.

As of November 3, 1968, despite the eruption of sexual freedom all across the country, explicit visual pornography was virtually nonexistent. Comedian Lenny Bruce's courageous articulation of the word "cocksucker" stood as perhaps the high point of public sexual daring.

Steadily, though, the pressure cooker was building up a head of steam. On November 4, 1968, it began to whistle—and shortly thereafter it blew its lid. On that date, Al Goldstein and his X-rated newspaper, *Screw,* stepped onto the world stage—or, as Goldstein himself later described it with characteristic hyperflair, "This jizz-frothed sexual tsunami roiled about a bit, belched, erupted, and deposited me on its crest, to ride a wild tidal wave with only a soggy tabloid surfboard called *Screw* to keep me afloat. I was a man who was in the right place at the right slime."

Screw hoped to become the *Consumer Reports* of the sexual netherworld, intent on calling a penis a cock and not a phallus or male organ, a vagina a cunt, and sexual intercourse fucking—and, moreover, depicting the same with the uncensored eye of the camera. Over the next two decades it was to publish probably more sexually explicit photographs than any other publication in history.

Screw had come about a few months earlier when a young journalist named Jim Buckley, a staffer on the alternative paper *New York Free Press,* met Al Goldstein, a bearded, overweight, thirty-three-year-old ex–cab driver, ex–insurance salesman, and erstwhile journalist. Deciding it was fruitless trying to raise people's political consciousness, they agreed to launch *Screw,* since, after all, as Goldstein was fond of saying: "A hard-on is its own redeeming value."

If Hefner merchandised himself as the dapper, self-assured playboy, Goldstein became the antihero of raw sex—fat, self-deprecating, filling his publication with stories of his sexual obsessions, failures with women, and humiliating need to buy sex from prostitutes because of his obesity. The raunchy humor, gross sex, porn movie reviews, and endless columns of advertisements for prostitutes seemed only a sideshow.

In issue number four, the Peter Meter was born to evaluate the quality of celluloid eroticism. In its eleventh issue *Screw* published an article titled "Is J. Edgar Hoover a Fag?" which reported on the censorship of a book called *The Homosexual Handbook* and the deletion of the FBI director's name as a possible homosexual. Twenty-four hours later Mrs. Goldstein, Al's mother, was subpoenaed to appear at a grand jury investigation, and Goldstein himself was arrested. After a later issue similarly made fun of New York mayor John Lindsay, Goldstein was taken in handcuffs to prison. Since Lindsay was an antipornography candidate, Goldstein did all he could to harm him by endorsing him in the pages of *Screw.*

Finally brought to trial in 1970, Goldstein and Buckley were found guilty of promulgating and distributing obscene material for sale and were fined. In all, during the first four years of publication, Buckley and Goldstein received eight convictions.

In 1970 *Screw* also got a little hard-core competition from a cheesy, documentary-style film called *Man and Wife*—me man, you woman, this sexual intercourse—that nevertheless made pornographic history as the first movie ever screened in New York to show actual sexual intercourse. An enthusiastic *Screw* gave it a 95 on the Peter Meter. Before anyone could say "cunnilingus," another landmark film, *Sexual Freedom in Denmark,* explained to the burgeoning "sex education" market the ups and downs, ins and outs, of male and female oral sex.

In the summer of 1970 *Screw* also began accepting advertisements for model and massage studios, which invited customers to bring their camera and pay $10 or $20 to take photographs of young nude women. Soon tiring of at-lens-length intimacy, patrons expressed a need for something a little more intimate, like touching, and body painting was born. The logical next step was to figure out a way for patrons to ejaculate. Soon massage studios began performing hand jobs and blow jobs.

By 1972, places like Caesar's Retreat on East Forty-sixth Street were luring

Screw readers with images of toga-clad girls who pampered men with full-body massage in a champagne bubble bath. Other advertisers, who had few other places to publicize their services, included SM studios and leather-clad dominatrices.

The government also tried to deny *Screw* second-class mailing privileges, but the case was successfully defended in federal court by the ACLU.

By 1969, the British circulation of *Penthouse* had reached 180,000 when Guccione, who considered himself the tortoise to Hefner's hare, brought his magazine over to the United States to challenge *Playboy* in earnest. Following the lesson he learned at the *London American,* Guccione concentrated on newsstand sales as opposed to direct mail and subscriptions. In only nine years *Penthouse* not only outdistanced *Playboy,* but became the third most profitable magazine in history and catapulted its sole owner into the ranks of the world's wealthiest men.

Guccione had long been an admirer of the advertising innovations of Ralph Ginzburg. In order not to be lost in the crowd of girlie magazines, Guccione knew, *Penthouse* needed to be launched with a similarly bold media campaign. Resorting to his cartoonist's skills, he created full-page newspaper advertisements depicting a hapless-looking rabbit caught between the crosshairs of a telescope. The tag line brazenly announced, "We're going rabbit hunting," with Guccione promising his potential advertisers that within only five years his magazine would catch up with, and then surpass, *Playboy.*

The media campaign, which ran in New York, Chicago, Los Angeles, and other major cities, was an instant success, guaranteeing Guccione much needed advertising revenue—though still far below that harvested each month by *Playboy*—as well as prime newsstand display.

At the time, *Playboy* was sixteen years old, with a circulation of nearly seven million—a seemingly unsurpassable lead. No other men's magazine even had a circulation above one hundred thousand—what Guccione considered an "unnatural gap" and the very inspiration for his American launch.

Guccione further intuited that *Playboy*'s strength was also its most vulnerable weakness—its centerfolds, which were still airbrushed, as were those of all other above-the-counter girlie magazines. No longer a revolutionary, Hefner now cautiously strove to be accepted as a respectable member of the publishing community. Guccione had none of Hefner's Establishment aspirations. Rather, he possessed an appetite for controversy and confrontation that *Playboy* traditionally recoiled from.

Hefner's only daring gambit, in fact, had been to print those famous photographs of Marilyn Monroe in volume 1, number 1. Somebody else had thought up the magazine's name. The individual mainly responsible for circulation growth was Vincent Tajiri, a first-generation Japanese American and former editor of *ArtPhotography,* where Hefner had once worked in sales promotion. Tajiri created *Playboy's* photo department, which revolutionized pinup photography and gave the world the "girls next door" who were little more than real-life Varga girls.

Hefner was halfway to disassociating himself from the label of pornographer altogether when Guccione, within months of arriving on America's shores, upped the stakes with the April 1970 issue of *Penthouse*—perhaps the boldest and most defining moment in soft-core—by becoming the first slick commercial magazine to show pubic hair.

Hefner was delighted when he saw the photos of Miss Holland, standing on a beach in the dim middle distance but unmistakably not airbrushed, because he suspected his upstart rival had finally made a strategic blunder and would at any moment be closed down by federal prosecutors. But nothing happened—much to Guccione's surprise as well. Over the next few months he grew still more daring, until finally *Penthouse* readers were rewarded with a close-up of a centerfold Pet in full-frontal glory.

Screw, hailing the advance, predicted the sequence of events: "First pubic hair, then cunt, and finally opening the way to spread shots in a year or so. In three years they'll be fucking across the shiny centerfold of *Penthouse!*"

In fact, that gray area between hard-core and soft-core—the teasing hint of penetration by either tongue, penis, or finger—was to remain a no-man's-land for another fifteen years. Along the way, though, until he broke that barrier as well, Guccione was to claim assorted other firsts, with—as *Time* magazine once sniffed—the air of a man who had invented penicillin: open vagina, simulated masturbation, lesbians, threesomes, full-frontal male nudity, erect penis. *Penthouse* was also the first to employ such props as whips, chains, and leather. A Guccione mantra, one that earned him hundreds of millions, was: "All men are voyeurs, and all women are exhibitionists."

In forty years, by contrast, *Playboy* was to make only one modest adjustment—throwing away its airbrush when, beginning with the December 1970 issue, a resigned Hefner finally realized he had to keep up with Guccione or go the way of the dinosaur.

The editorial contents of the two magazines were also radically different and reflected the temperaments of their publishers. Elements of the editorial in *Penthouse* were every bit as radical, explicit, and provocative as the pictorials—notably the famed "Forum" section comprising unexpurgated letters from readers writing about their fantasies and experiences, and a sex advice column by Xaviera Hollander. Though Guccione did not like the banished ex-madame from Holland, he recognized the advantages of having her brand of raunchy sensibility represented in his pages. The magazine's other editorial strength was its investigative journalism, which aggressively exposed corruption in the worlds of science, medicine, politics, and law.

Playboy editorial, by contrast, was almost prim, with nothing more risqué than the mild "Ribald Tales" and "Party Jokes." Instead of investigative journalism it concentrated on essays and commentary by the respectable likes of J. Paul Getty and John Kenneth Galbraith, thereby combining sex with upward mobility, and fiction by Vladimir Nabokov and James Baldwin. *Playboy* editorial was for the most part virtually interchangeable with that of *Esquire, Saturday Review,* and other lifestyle/literary magazines with a predominantly male readership. Socially redeeming value, in the language of the courts, *Playboy* had in excess.

Yet even the magazine's formidable editorial product was not Hefner's creation, but that of editor Auguste Comte Spectorsky. With top-flight art director and editor in place, Hefner had retreated to his mansion to play with his toys and Bunnies, emerging occasionally in his pajamas to deliver another installment of the Playboy Philosophy.

Though Guccione never took his intense rivalry with Hefner personally, the latter did, and as a result the two men were never to meet. The closest thing to an encounter between the two occurred in the winter of 1972, when the *Penthouse* publisher was a guest of American investor and art patron Bernie Cornfeld at his home in Los Angeles.

Hefner, who by now had taken up permanent residence at Playboy Mansion West in Los Angeles, was also a friend of Cornfeld. One evening the latter suggested both publishers join him for some popcorn, a movie, and perhaps a visit to a nightclub later. Guccione agreed, but Hefner refused. Accompanying Guccione were eleven Pets, along for a photo shoot, who had been looking forward to the night out. Not wanting to disappoint them, Guccione told Cornfeld to go out with Hefner and bring the Pets along, while he remained home alone.

"But give him a message for me," Guccione told Cornfeld before he departed. "I once announced I was going to catch up with *Playboy* in five years. Now I'm going to take away a year. Tell Hefner it's down to four."

Hefner's response, when Cornfeld delivered the message: "Fuck him."

Guccione nearly kept his word. By 1974, after only five years in the United States, *Penthouse* circulation had vaulted to 3.8 million a month. *Playboy* still stood at a commanding 6.4 million, down from a 1972 high of 7 million, yet the figures were deceiving. While *Penthouse* was up 22 percent, *Playboy* was in an irreversible decline, losing 400,000 readers annually. Its stock was also down from $23.50 to $4 per share after going public in 1970, and both magazines were now engaged in the publishing equivalent of a barroom brawl.

Securities and Exchange Commission documents further showed that from 1973 to 1975 net profits from *Playboy* and *Oui* declined from $24 million a year to $8 million. *Oui* was an especially costly mistake. When *Playboy* learned that Daniel Filipacchi, publisher of *Lui,* a raunchy French imitation of *Playboy,* planned to bring out an American edition, a panicky Hefner remembered how he had smirked at the idea of *Penthouse* and decided to collaborate. The result, *Oui,* lost millions more.

To no avail, some forward-looking executives at *Playboy* had advised Hefner to buy Simon & Schuster, *Rolling Stone,* and Grove Press. Instead he built the Great Gorge resort in New Jersey for $30 million; by 1976 it carried a mortgage of $14 million and was worth at best $10 million. Among Playboy Enterprises' many holdings, only a London gambling club attracting Arab bettors was a clear success. Hefner's bad black private DC-9 and other playthings were costing the company $3.5 million per year, for a total of $16 million and counting. The Playboy Clubs, except those in Miami and Boston, were another $4.5-million-a-year money drain.

Guccione also made his share of mistakes, some of them, like Hefner's, exorbitantly expensive. Casinos in London and Krk Island off Yugoslavia lost millions. *Lords,* a lavish quarterly for the British country gentleman, failed to catch on. In September 1973 Guccione launched a magazine for women titled *Viva,* featuring discreet nude male centerfolds, a year before Douglas Lambert came out with *Playgirl.* The magazine reached a circulation of seven hundred thousand but had trouble attracting advertisers. An even bigger headache were the newsstand dealers, who routinely displayed it among men's sophisticates instead of among women's magazines, where its primary audience could find it. After six years and a loss of nearly $30 million, the magazine was folded.

Chapter 4

A Love That Dared to Speak Its Name

ONE MORNING IN SEPTEMBER 1965, A WARMLY PERSONABLE, BROAD-SHOULDERED, rather tall young Indiana woman named Roberta White decided to iron her penis.

Roberta's problem was not sexual performance, but sexual identity. She had no interest in the mysteries of orgasm that Masters and Johnson were so exhaustively exploring in a laboratory just a few hundred miles away. Her consuming obsession was anatomy. Roberta felt trapped inside a male body and wanted out so badly, she had already attempted suicide three times.

Almost as burdensome a problem as her anatomy was what a very few progressive psychologists were already calling "gender role"—a term that the unsophisticated Roberta had never even heard of, but which defined the way she was supposed to act in public just because she had a penis. Because of this alien appendage, Roberta was forced by society to look, behave, and talk like a man. Because of her penis, her parents had raised her as a boy and christened her Robert Leslie White. Society and her penis had also conspired to lure her into a conventional marriage and into fathering a child.

But in her heart Roberta knew she was a woman, even if she did not have breasts or a vagina, even if she could not yet comb her hair out in long, pretty curls, even if she might be arrested if she dared to wear a dress in public.

As much as she longed to *be* a woman, Roberta craved the pleasure of acting, dressing, and talking like one in front of family and friends. This man business was all somehow a terrible mistake, she wanted to tell everybody. Yet she had to keep it a shameful, dreadful secret, even though she did not know why.

Gender was still very much a genetic and sexuo-erotic terra incognita in

1965. At the same time, the medical and psychotherapeutic communities, as well as the churches and the public, were in unanimous agreement: anatomy was destiny, and the only moral, legal, and socially acceptable sexual outlet imaginable for anatomy was heterosexual marriage. Not only was homosexuality still listed as an official mental disorder by the American Psychiatric Association, but such notions as transvestism and transsexuality, esoteric terms that drifted up from the sexual underworld or across the Atlantic from countries like Denmark, seemed the very definition of depravity or medical perversity.

But for Roberta, having to deny herself the freedom to groom and ornament her body in a ladylike way, and use the body language and vocal intonation of a woman, was unbearable. She had reached the point of suicidal despair because nobody had an answer to a question that had plagued her since puberty—not medicine, not science, not even religion, though Roberta was a devout, even prim middle-aged woman.

Her question was twofold: Why had she been cursed with a penis? How could she get rid of it? For forty-seven years she had been trapped inside her anatomically male body, like a prisoner living the worst form of solitary confinement. The ironing episode, brutally painful and miserably unsuccessful, was just one more in a series of increasingly desperate attempts at escape.

Roberta did not know it at the time, but she was one of thousands of people living in a sexual twilight zone that only a few visionary sexologists and doctors were beginning to pay attention to. Like the legions of volunteers at the Masters and Johnson clinic, she was also a sexual pioneer, fated to become a first-generation American transsexual and living lifelong proof that not only nature, but nurture, with a little help from science, was also destiny.

Roberta's parents, Roscoe and Anna Belle, had eloped when they were only seventeen because Germany had just sunk the *Lusitania* and he was about to be drafted. After he went off to war, their daughter, Roberta, was born on a sweltering August 5, 1918, with temperatures hovering at one hundred degrees. Seeing a penis bobbing from the baby's legs, the family physician proclaimed her a boy. The child was named after a farmer friend and Hollywood actor Leslie Howard. When Roscoe returned home after the war, he thought he had a baby son.

Growing up, Roberta did not like playing with boys because they were too rough. A strict disciplinarian, Roscoe sent her to a country school. The family was fundamentalist, and all forms of drinking, smoking, and card playing were strictly forbidden. Even so, Roberta could not help secretly dressing up in her mother's stockings and sister's panties.

When the Depression came along, Roscoe became a tenant farmer like his parents, and the family moved to the country. Roberta and her brother, Ben, worked as field hands at harvesttime. As the Depression deepened, the family moved into a three-room shack. During high school, Roberta wanted to study home economics but was forced to take shop and woodworking because, after all, she looked like a boy. Even so, she experienced stomach cramps once a month.

Roberta did not like sports. One day a boy who thought her swing was too girlish threw a baseball at her in disgust. The ball struck Roberta near the temple, and she lost her left eye. She became a loner. She was embarrassed whenever she had to take her clothes off in the boys' locker room at the school gym. An inner voice seemed to whisper, *You're in the wrong place.*

In high school Roberta finally determined to do some research into her problem and went to the public library. She knew there had to be an answer. But not only were there no answers, she barely knew how to formulate the questions.

In one book, though, Roberta read that a tribe in Africa made certain young men ride horses until their testicles were so damaged that their breasts enlarged. She also read about an early American male governor named Lady Cornbury who dressed as a woman. Those two options seemed to suggest there might be an answer to her torment, but how exactly she did not yet know.

Roberta's penis was much smaller than average—she usually wet herself while urinating unless she squatted—and she thought she might eliminate it step by step. One day she tried to cut off her foreskin but succeeded only in slicing off a piece of prepuce with a kitchen knife—an extremely painful episode. Later she experimented with trying to liquefy her testicles by dunking them in near boiling water.

Having not much interest in sex, she rarely masturbated and felt guilty when she did.

After graduating from school, and with the Depression still on, Roberta began having severe nightmares of herself spinning around and around in a black void. To calm her, her parents put wet cloths on her forehead even though she had no fever. She earned money doing construction work, washing dishes at a restaurant in the small town of Fiskville, and doing minor repairs and delivery for a furniture shop.

One day a preacher from a nearby church came to visit Roberta, and she began attending the local Nazarene church, studying the Bible and helping out with small chores. Later she was elected Sunday school superintendent and taught classes. During this time she also dated two girls from the neighborhood, though she felt no physical attraction for either.

When America went to war after the bombing of Pearl Harbor, Roberta found a job in a defense plant. She also attended Bible school, where she met a young girl who, after a series of dates, proposed marriage. Roberta, still a virgin at age twenty-four, accepted, mainly so as not to hurt her feelings. After their marriage, Roberta's wife conceived a child. But the childbirth was extremely difficult, and the mother lost a great deal of blood.

Roberta and a sister with whom she was especially close looked at the baby and thought it was a girl, even though she had a penis. The sister knew what Roberta had been going through. The doctors told Roberta there was not a sufficient blood supply to save both the mother and the child and asked whom to save. Roberta asked that her wife be given the blood. Privately she was racked by a fear that a gene in her body had caused her baby's problem.

After that, Roberta's marriage fell apart. Her wife realized her husband had no interest in sex and began having numerous affairs, many with Roberta's approval. After fifteen years, though, Roberta decided she did not want to be married to a woman any longer and walked out. For the first time in her life she felt hopeful and happy, even though her weight had ballooned up to 265 pounds.

By now Roberta was quite familiar with the story of George Jorgensen, an ex–U.S. soldier who in 1952 went to Denmark, underwent hormonal and surgical treatment, and returned home an international sensation as Christine. In fact, the first modern sex-change operation had occurred in Germany in 1931, and references to hermaphrodites (people with the genital characteristics of both sexes) could be found in Greek mythology, ancient Rome, and seventeenth- and eighteenth-century Europe, when several prominent hermaphrodites wrote their autobiographies.

But the Jorgensen case marked the beginning of public awareness of the fact that it was now possible for a person to make the almost unimaginable psychological and physical leap and actually change her or his sex. Inspired by Jorgensen, Roberta kept saying to herself, "If she can do it, so can I."

There was one insuperable problem, however. Transsexual surgery was not available in the United States. Roberta started saving up her money for a trip to Europe, naively assuming she could walk in off the street, somewhere in that enlightened, faraway continent, and have her penis lopped off much as she might have an abscessed tooth pulled.

Meanwhile, settling in the small Indiana town of Crawfordsville, she began to experiment with cross-dressing. In a desperate gambit to grow breasts and bring her voice to a higher pitch, she also purchased jar after jar of Rubenstein's Beauty Cream, which contained the female hormone estrogen, smearing it over her chest and throat and even ingesting it by the spoonful.

One day while Roberta was buying estrogen cream, the pharmacist said, "I don't see why you women don't ask your doctor to give you estrogen tablets so you won't have to buy this kind of beauty cream." Later Roberta traveled to nearby Bloomington to pay a visit to Dr. Alfred Kinsey, who was sympathetic and interested in her problem, but at the time could offer only moral support.

Now in her forties, Roberta supported herself as a nurse's aide and continued to be involved in her church. Yet despair crushed down on her night and day, since it seemed she was doomed to spend the rest of her life in this horrible prison that was her own body. It was during this period that she attempted to iron her penis and three times tried to commit suicide.

The lowest point in Roberta's life occurred in early 1961 when, full of hope, she finally sailed for London, with a thousand dollars hidden in her suitcase, and from there took a train to Scotland. Arriving unannounced at a clinic she had heard of that she thought might be of help, she was informed that the doctors could do nothing for her because she was an American and not eligible for treatment under the country's national health plan.

Returning home aboard the *Queen Mary*, a deeply depressed Roberta seriously contemplated throwing herself into the sea and ending her life once and for all. But somewhere in the back of her mind she remembered hearing a "rumor" that some doctors in Baltimore were also involved in helping anatomical males like herself become women.

Her lifeline was that thin thread of hope, and she decided not to jump into the water. Arriving at the Psychohormonal and Gender Identity Clinic in Baltimore, again without an appointment, Roberta succeeded in meeting Dr. John Money, who, like Kinsey, showed not only great sympathy but a keen interest in her problem. The clinic was affiliated with the Johns Hopkins School of Medicine.

Roberta said to herself, "If I could marry him, I'd be all right."

Money had Roberta admitted into the hospital's psychiatric ward, where she underwent a battery of psychological, endocrinological, and other tests. Surrounded by people who were obviously suffering from severe mental problems, Roberta told herself, "I may be poor white trash, but I'm not crazy."

After three weeks she returned home. Money promised Roberta he would be in touch.

Living in Crawfordsville had become impossible for Roberta after her three suicide attempts, so she moved to Indianapolis. Immediately she went to see a psychiatrist, who agreed to prescribe estrogen tablets, which offered some relief. For the time being, she lived as a transvestite. She also discovered, after a painful, two-mile walk in high heels, that she could not transform herself into a woman overnight.

In 1967 Money wrote to Roberta, asking her to come to Baltimore for her operation. But Roberta replied that she needed more time to raise money. Eventually a date was set for November 1968.

At the time, Roberta was working as a maid for an elderly bachelor with whom she had a flirtatious but not sexual relationship. When she informed him she was going to Baltimore for a "female operation," she was only telling the truth. He offered to pay her plane fare.

Back in Baltimore, Roberta learned that she suffered from a syndrome Money labeled "dysphoria." Her body appeared to be biologically male in all respects, yet her mind and psychology were entirely female.

After another go-round of tests, to make sure Roberta understood all the risks involved, she was asked by the head surgeon whether she wanted a vagina. Previous male-to-female transsexual operations had created a vaginal facsimile out of a section of intestine.

"Wait a minute," Roberta replied. "Why don't you make it out of the fore-skin?"

"Good idea," the surgeon replied. "That makes sense." Another advance in transsexual surgery was born.

As Roberta lay on the operating table, the surgeon asked: "Are you ready?"

Her enthusiastic reply: "Let's do it!" She felt no fear, no sense of impend-ing loss. After fifty years of misery, she was about to have her dream fulfilled.

The doctors operating on Roberta went through four steps. First they cas-trated her, removing the testicles, which were discarded. They then per-formed a penectomy, or removal of the penis, an intricate task in which the difficulty lay in preserving a functionally normal though greatly shortened urethra. Next they created female-looking external genitalia, achieved by us-ing the scrotal tissue to fashion the labia majora. The skin of the penis was used to form the labia minora–like folds. All of those tissues contained sen-sory nerve ends that could later help to convey sexual satisfaction and possi-bly even orgasm.

The most crucial part of the operation lay in the fourth stage, the creation of an artificial vagina. After a channel was fashioned, one of three materials was used for the lining of the artificial vagina: skin from the thigh, buttocks, or back; skin stripped from the amputated penis and inverted like the finger of a glove (which enabled it to bear the closest resemblance to a sex organ); or, the most complicated, using a part of the gut, a loop of ileum, which required opening the abdominal cavity.

An artificial clitoris was, at the time, not possible, but also the last thing on Roberta's mind. For the next two weeks she recuperated, and for six months thereafter she was required to wear a rubber form inside her new vaginal barrel to prevent the muscles from joining together again.

"Hallelujah!" she told the doctors and nurses who gathered around her every day. "I'm a woman now! Even if I die, I'm a woman!"

Slowly, the hormonal treatment she had been undergoing for years re-sulted in substantial hair loss throughout her body, breast development, and a higher-pitched voice. Through dieting she lost nearly a hundred pounds.

When Roberta returned to Indianapolis, she treated her aged bachelor friend as well as herself to a previously impossible entertainment—appearing before him in a see-through negligee. For the first time in her life, she was not ashamed to display her body.

Her CB moniker, as she traveled down the Indiana highways, working as a nurse's aide or going to the local Nazarene church for services, was Dysphoria. None of the truckers knew what she was talking about, and Roberta never bothered to explain.

On a September evening in 1965, around the time Masters and Johnson were concluding their marathon research into the mysteries of female orgasm, a team of surgeons and clinical psychologists was about to make a different but equally important kind of sexual history in Baltimore. This time, though, the center of attention was not a woman lying on her back, but a young white man in his early twenties lying on an operating table at Johns Hopkins Medical Center. Born a female inside a man's body, he was about to surrender his penis in order to achieve his goal of becoming an anatomical woman. The chief surgeon was Howard W. Jones, who later went on to head an in vitro fertilization clinic in Norfolk, Virginia.

A few days later a black adolescent male underwent similar surgery. Both were charter transsexuals in Johns Hopkins's program to become the first American hospital to perform sex-change surgery. By now Johns Hopkins had nearly a hundred requests for transsexual surgery on hand, about ten of them anatomical women.

Yet the most important figure in this drama was the hospital's director of psychohormonal research, Dr. John Money. A courtly, acerbic transplanted New Zealander whose wiry hair sticking out at right angles suggested to one observer that he looked as though electrified, Money nevertheless reserved for the sexual minorities and misfits of this world a profound compassion. In time, his very specialized interest and empathy would establish him among the greatest sex researchers of the century, and for that same reason also one of the least known and understood.

If the Kinsey reports had raised questions about the very concept of so-called normal sexuality, even less was known about pathological, deviant behavior, or the sex lives of women and men whose genitalia, chromosomal makeup, and psychosexual history rendered them unfit for anything like a traditional sex life. If Bill Masters had embarked on his research in order to find out why so many women did not experience orgasm, John Money had an even more basic problem to contend with—how to help society's erotic outcasts discover and come to terms with their misplaced sexual identity.

Money had made the decision to proceed with the controversial surgery both because he was interested in the welfare of transsexuals and because there seemed no better way to establish the legitimacy of sexological medicine and change the medical profession's attitude toward people with severe sexual problems. The not-so-rare children with anomalies of sex organs or endocrine systems, in Money's view, were "nature's experiments."

Born in 1921 in Morrinsville, New Zealand, Money had been delivered by midwife, a traditional custom in the northern region of the country. A by-product of that procedure was that he was not circumcised. By age five, already a keen observer of the cosmetics of sex, Money had became envious of the large, mushroom-shaped, exposed glans of his same-age circumcised playmates.

As a child Money also collected dried worm casts from his family's lawn after a rainfall and arranged them as miniature sculptures on the crossbeams of a water tank. Later that habit translated into a passion for collecting—art and artifacts, books, sculptures, painting, and, above all, research data.

A thin, delicate child, though he later became an expert camper and mountain climber, Money lost his father early on and grew up in a female household. As in many other New Zealand and Australian families, a tragic number of males had been decimated at Gallipoli in World War I. Surrounded by spinster aunts, Money suffered from the guilt of being male and was overwhelmed by the antisexualism and antimasturbation hysteria of late Victorianism.

Early on he also became aware that he was a potential sacrificial victim in a *Lord of the Flies* schoolroom atmosphere where the other children were the grandsons of either rugged British colonialists or Maori warriors. Outwitting his tormentors instilled in him, however, a tenacity and shrewdness that later became hallmarks of his research activities in psychoendocrinology, sexology, and psychopathology.

At the University of Otago, where he was appointed junior lecturer in psychology, Money first encountered the world of human sexuality when he read Havelock Ellis's *Studies in the Psychology of Sex*. Obtaining any kind of book on sex was virtually impossible because they were all locked away in the librarian's office, and even those were routinely pilfered. Later he read the works of Karen Horney, whose study of the dynamics of attraction and response in love and lovesickness, male and female, made a profound impression. (In 1979 Dorothy Tennov coined the term "limerence" to denote lovesickness.)

During this period, he also both lost his religious faith and became enamored of the cross-cultural psychology of Franz Boas, Ruth Benedict, and Margaret Mead. Feeling the need for some theoretical foundation on which to build his career, he elected to pursue his doctorate in psychology, not then offered in New Zealand, in America.

After a year in Pittsburgh at the Western State Psychiatric Institute, Money won a scholarship to the Psychological Clinic of the Harvard Gradu-

ate School and chose to write his doctoral thesis on the subject of hermaphroditism—not only because he found pathological phenomena inherently interesting, but also to discover what light it might throw on so-called normal
human sexuality.

Needing hospital case records of hermaphrodites, Money contacted Dr.
Lawson Wilkins, head of the Department of Pediatrics at the Johns Hopkins
Medical School in Baltimore, who agreed to cooperate. In 1951 Money joined
the Johns Hopkins faculty, and the following year his thesis was accepted by
Harvard. Three years later, assisted by a young woman psychiatrist named
Dr. Joan G. Hampson, Money began in earnest to study hermaphroditism
and related problems like transsexualism. After Hampson moved away and
Dr. Wilkins died, Money became head of psychohormonal research.

An intensely private bisexual, Money enjoyed several love affairs throughout this period with a number of men and women, some briefly, others over
a longer duration. One love affair in particular, with a woman brilliantly accomplished both professionally and sexually, affected him deeply. After their
traumatic breakup, he vowed to spend the rest of his life living alone, though
giving up parenthood meant a great sacrifice.

Wilkins's pediatric endocrine clinic had been devoted to the study of endocrine syndromes of childhood and adolescence, before and after hormonal
treatment and in long-term follow-up. Sex hormones had been isolated in
the 1920s, then synthesized and marketed in the thirties, but endocrinology
was still a relatively young science. Many at the time thought those somewhat
mysterious hormones might eventually be shown to determine personality.

Every Saturday Wilkins convened his outpatient follow-up clinic in a
shabby hospital annex. Attendance was compulsory and included the Hopkins pediatric endocrine staff, visiting pediatricians, and one psychologist—
John Money.

Those Saturday clinics were a gold mine of research information. Many of
the patients who attended suffered from impaired statural growth or pubertal delay or failure. At that time, the very existence of a pituitary growth hormone was still deemed questionable. The only effective hormonal treatment
of dwarf children, or those who had not advanced into puberty, was a sex
hormone, male or female, to induce secondary sexual maturity. Most hermaphrodites and preoperative transsexuals who went to Hopkins for treatment also required not only hormone therapy and surgery, but psychological
guidance and counseling.

During the 1950s, Money's findings seemed to indicate that human sexual
behavior was determined by the sex of assignment and rearing rather than by
prenatal hormonal influences—that is, nurture over nature. The two extreme positions in this debate pitted biological against cultural determinism.
The former argued that a person's identity and behavior could be explained

exclusively in terms of biological factors and genetic inheritance. Cultural determinists thought such factors as socialization and sexual scripting—the conditioning a person is subjected to by family, parents, society, religion, and peers—explained identity and behavior. Ultimately Money came to believe that nature and nurture met and reciprocally complemented one another at critical periods of development. Such critical periods, whether fetal or postnatal, were defined as moments when a person was highly receptive to a particular stimulus.

In dealing with hermaphrodites and transsexuals, though, Money thought he was confronting a radically new sexual problem: not only their copulatory roles, but also the mind-sets of people whose social or legal sex was discordant with their chromosomal, gonadal, or body status. Though society was absolute about male and female, he reasoned that nature was not.

To avoid that semantic trap he borrowed the word "gender" from philology, the study of languages, where gender signified a person's personal, social, and legal status as male or female without reference to sex organs. From that he coined the terms "gender roles" and "gender identity," both of which later became universal. As Money soon learned, most hermaphrodites and preoperative transsexuals were convinced they were either female beings trapped inside a male body or vice versa.

Basic gender identity, or a person's sense of herself or himself as a female or male, was usually completely formed within the first thirty months of life. Gender identity comprised two elements: chromosomes, hormones, and genitals that determined sex; and social roles taught from birth that determined gender. When sex and gender were in agreement, the result was a male who was masculine, or a feminine female. The problem arose, as in Roberta's case, when gender and sex disagreed.

The fetus also contained the seeds of dual sexuality. At conception the baseline of sexual tissue was feminine, meaning it would develop as a girl unless it received some male sex hormones in the womb. What determined the latter possibility was a set of double chromosomes: XX in the female (the second X necessary for the ovary to fully differentiate) and XY in the male (the Y causing the testes to differentiate).

For Money, gender identity was one's private experience of gender, while gender role meant the things a person said or did to reveal himself or herself as having the status of a boy or girl, man or woman. Yet he also soon found it necessary to combine the term into gender identity/role. Eventually his research led him to the realization that the ultimate criterion of a hermaphrodite's gender identity/role as masculine or feminine was the body sex of the partner who, whether male or female, evoked limerence and erotic attraction. Limerence superseded every other criterion of masculinity or femininity, whether chromosomal sex, gonadal sex, hormonal sex (prenatal and pubertal), genital sex (internal and external), and sex of assignment and rearing. None of those criteria accurately predicted the sex of limerence. Roberta White, in short, was psychosexually speaking a heterosexual woman because she was incapable of falling in love with another woman.

Though John Money advanced the treatment of gender-displaced persons more than any other, the father of medical treatment and intervention regarding transsexuals was Dr. Harry Benjamin, a Berlin-born, Manhattan-based physician who popularized the word "transsexual" and wrote a standard reference work on the subject, *The Transsexual Phenomenon,* published in 1966. He also served as Christine Jorgensen's physician when she returned to the United States after her pioneering operation in Denmark. The term "transsexualism" was coined by American sexologist D. O. Cauldwell.

Benjamin had seen his first transsexual patient, a referral from Kinsey, as early as 1948. He became interested in the syndrome through his study of hormones in the twenties and thirties, thought its cause was biological, and later gave the syndrome both a name and a theory.

In a survey conducted in the early seventies, Benjamin found that 40 percent of male transsexuals were found to have hypogonadism (underdeveloped gonads), while other researchers reported the presence of an unusually enlarged clitoris in many female transsexuals. But the majority of transsexuals, like Roberta White, had no easily observable somatic defect. More likely, in Roberta's case, a special sex identification gene may have become attached to the wrong chromosome during her fetal development.

Then as now, transsexuals were widely regarded as the Uncle Toms of sexuality, devoutly believing, like Roberta, in old-fashioned sexual stereotypes and taking a conservative position on nearly everything, including sexual relationships. Most were willing to sacrifice even sexual pleasure to be women, and to remain celibate forever afterward, just for the deep, gender-existential satisfaction of being able to *be* a woman. Roberta, not atypically, also harbored little sympathy for homosexuals, whom she thought could be "cured" of their problem just as she had, by taking hormones.

Another reason why few male-to-female transsexuals had little interest in sex was that a surgical vagina, though capable of sex, was often poorly constructed and easily infected. Female-to-male transsexuals had to be content with clitoral orgasms, even with a surgically constructed penis. Soon after Roberta's surgery, Christine Jorgensen was obliged to undergo additional surgery at Johns Hopkins to correct her surgically constructed sex organs. Even so, many transsexuals considered the day of their surgery their real birthday, feeling they were truly reborn on the operating table.

Soon after the two breakthrough operations in September 1965, surgeons on the Johns Hopkins staff also began to perform similar sex-change operations on women, enclosing the urethra in a pseudopenis and reducing their breasts through hormonal treatments. A sex change from female to male consisted of three steps: mastectomy, hysterectomy, and the creation of an artificial penis, which only a small percentage of patients underwent.

After a long and expensive series of plastic-surgical procedures, the final result looked convincing, and the patient was able to urinate through a tube constructed in the middle of the penis. Sometimes a plastic splint even enabled it to appear somewhat erect. Yet there was no known way for an artificial penis to change from flaccid to erect during sexual activity, nor was it sensually sensitive like a normal penis.

A third and permanent stage in the metamorphosis of a transsexual, following the preoperative phase and surgery, was lifelong maintenance. At the beginning of this stage, all legal matters were taken care of—name change, status on personal documents. The dosage of hormones was also adjusted at that time.

In 1966, the same year Masters and Johnson published their landmark work, Money was among the founding members of the first U.S. gender identity clinic specializing in sex reassignment and transsexualism. That same year he also created a research program for the psychohormonal treatment of paraphilias ("perversions") and sex offender syndromes.

Despite such pioneering efforts, the American public and the medical profession alike continued to regard such surgery as mutilative, and crossover transsexuals as deviates. Over the ensuing decades, various defenders of orthodox psychiatry were to wage an aggressive counterattack against the new frontier of forensic sexology that Dr. Money was exploring and, in fact, inventing.

IN THE SUMMER OF 1969, New York's Greenwich Village was not yet an archipelago of gay and lesbian bars and boutiques appealing to the most exotic and rarefied of sexual tastes. Mostly there were just a few known hangouts where homosexuals of every type, from college kids and leathermen to drag queens and butch lesbians, hung out together.

Among the most popular and longest lived of the city's gay hangouts was the Stonewall Inn on Sheridan Square at the intersection of Christopher Street and Seventh Avenue, the Times Square of New York's gay subculture. A no-frills establishment, the Stonewall did not even boast a bar sink. Used glasses were merely dunked into a barrel of bilge and refilled. Yet it was the closest thing in town to a gay dance hall, and on most nights the place was packed.

The police permitted the Stonewall to operate for one simple reason—it was run by the Mafia, who paid them off. To keep up appearances, the police raided the bar every so often, though usually only after forewarning the proprietors. Patrons of the Stonewall called the police Betty Badge, or sometimes Lily Law.

Early in the morning of Saturday, June 28, 1969, two patrolmen, two detectives, and two policewomen descended on the bar. As police raids went, it was a modest operation. But this time Betty Badge blundered her way into history. The day before, on Friday, June 27, Judy Garland, a patron saint of gay men everywhere, had been buried. Betty Badge was oblivious of the intense emotions generated by the singer's funeral, which had drawn thousands of gay mourners.

One o'clock on a Saturday morning was also the bar's peak hour for business, and this time the proprietors had not been told about the raid in advance. Moreover, this was the second police raid within days. A light went up on the dance floor, signaling male couples to separate while Betty Badge carried out her humiliating ID checks. As usual, only the drag queens were detained.

But as patrons were released one by one onto the street, a crowd began to gather. Initially it was a festive gathering, composed mostly of men waiting for friends still inside. A few began to strike a pose and swish by the detectives with a "Hello, there, fella." Wrists went limp, hair was primped. Quips—"I gave them the gay power bit, and they loved it, girls." "Have you seen Maxine? Where *is* my wife—I told her not to go far"—met with cheers and applause, evidence that the raid was being taken in stride.

Suddenly the paddy wagon arrived and the mood of the crowd changed. Three queens in full drag were loaded inside, along with the bartender and doorman, to a chorus of boos and catcalls. A cry went up to push the paddy wagon over, but it drove away before anything could happen. After it departed, the crowd grew momentarily silent. Then a tough-looking lesbian emerged, putting up a struggle as the police tried to force her into a police car, and she threw a punch at Betty Badge.

That riled the crowd again, only this time they began pelting the police with coins, bottles, cans, and dog feces. Retreating to the bar, the police found themselves cornered with a terrified *Village Voice* reporter. As the crowd surged through the door, someone poured lighter fluid through a broken window and ignited a blaze. Immediately the police turned on a fire hose and cleared a path to the street, though they managed to escape only when backup arrived.

By now the angry crowd had swelled to the thousands and the Tactical Patrol Force was called in. Helmeted and heavily armed, they marched up Christopher Street in wedge formation, still pelted by the retreating crowd. When they reached the Stonewall, they were met by a chorus line of queens kicking their heels into the air and singing, "We are the Stonewall girls / We wear our hair in curls / We wear no underwear / We show our pubic hair."

The protesters were brutally dispersed, but not for long. Later that day word of the raid spread rapidly throughout the Village, and a protest march—a tactic borrowed from the antiwar movement—was hastily arranged. That Saturday night thousands of gays and lesbians gathered in Sheridan Square, outside the Stonewall Inn, bearing signs that read "I'm a faggot and proud of it." "Gay Power!" "I like boys." The protesters continued to rally all day Sunday and into Monday morning, and within a month the Gay Liberation Front appeared in New York, an entirely new kind of gay organization advocating radical social change.

Yet the Stonewall riot was not just a beginning, but a culmination of nearly twenty years of intense homosexual activism. Though the gay rights movement flowered virtually simultaneously on both the East and West Coasts, its roots were indisputably Californian.

The rise of the gay rights movement in the fifties coincided with the worst political witch-hunt in modern times, led by Senator Joseph McCarthy, Republican senator from Wisconsin, who equated homosexuality with the Communist menace insofar as the founders of the gay civil rights movement were former Communists and radicals. Harry Hay, who first called for a gay movement in 1948, had been a Party member for twenty years and had also been active in labor organization and cultural affairs.

In the winter of 1950, a group of seven gay men gathered by Hay in Los Angeles founded the Mattachine Society, named after troupes of men who traveled from village to village in medieval times, taking up the cause of social justice in their ballads and dramas. Conceived as the gay counterpart to the National Association for the Advancement of Colored People and the Anti-Defamation League, the Mattachine Society, later rechristened the Mattachine Foundation, soon sprouted branches in San Francisco, New York, and Washington, D.C. In 1951 the foundation began sponsoring discussion groups and that April adopted a statement of missions and purposes: "Mattachine holds it possible and desirable that a highly ethical homosexual culture emerge, as a consequence of its work, paralleling the emerging cultures of our fellow minorities . . . the Negro, Mexican, and Jewish peoples."

The following year, after a Mattachine discussion-group meeting, activist member W. Dorr Legg formed another group, One, Inc., which on February 7, 1953, started publishing *One,* a magazine purporting to deal "primarily with homosexuality from the scientific, historical and critical point of view and to aid in the social integration and rehabilitation of the sexual variant."

Meanwhile, in September 1953 Hall Call, president of the San Francisco Mattachine Society and the man most responsible in the fifties for organizing gays, began publishing the *Mattachine Review,* a newsletter. Though the local group had only two hundred members, circulation of the *Review* soon reached twenty-five hundred. Many of the articles described the bitterness gays felt toward the straight world. Call also organized discussion groups on such topics as how to avoid being arrested or what to do if arrested, since police harassment was nearly as big a problem as social ostracism by the heterosexual community.

Adding to the frustration of many gay activists was a policy of harassment adopted by the FBI toward both the Mattachine Society and One, Inc., from their very beginnings. The FBI justified its harassment by accusing branches of both groups, particularly in Los Angeles and Washington, D.C., of being Communist fronts. The U.S. Post Office also refused to mail the October 1954 issue of *One*—a decision later upheld by the Ninth Circuit Court of Appeals.

The FBI policy of harassment stemmed from the November 1955 issue of the *Mattachine Review,* which claimed homosexuals occupied "key positions" in the agency. Both the FBI's director, J. Edgar Hoover, and his top aide, Clyde A. Tolson, were known in certain homosexual circles to be closet cases themselves. Tolson's response to the article, according to an FBI internal memo, was to tell Hoover, "I think we should take this crowd and make them 'put up or shut up.' " The director concurred.

By March 27, 1959, an FBI field report was claiming that "60% of the officers of the chapters [of One, Inc.] are known homosexuals and individuals who have allegedly participated in Communist 'front groups.' " On April 19, 1961, another FBI field report also disclosed that the Mattachine Society "appear[s] to have been infiltrated by certain Communists."

Homosexual women were also beginning to organize, though they faced a huge hurdle that gay men had no trouble with—wondering what to call themselves and where to turn in order to discover more about their sexual identity. Like Roberta White, discovering her transsexuality through trial and error, many lesbians in the fifties knew mainly what they were not—heterosexual. Yet they were unable at the time to call themselves lesbians since the word simply had no vernacular currency. No popular literature (and very little professional literature) existed that talked about women having sex with other women. Everything about their sexual yearnings seemed a mystery, often clouded over with feelings of guilt and self-doubt. Two cases in point were Phyllis Lyon and Del Martin, destined to become the founding mothers of the lesbian rights movement.

Martin had married at nineteen, soon divorced, and then settled in Seattle, where she spent the next ten years trying to determine who and what she was sexually. Though she was not attracted to any woman in particular, she knew that from puberty onward she had always been more attracted to women than men, but at the same time could never talk about it. Radclyffe Hall's *The Well of Loneliness,* one of the first modern books to deal explicitly with lesbianism, though not lesbian sex, proved a great help.

In 1950 Martin, a bookkeeper, met Phyllis Lyon, a twenty-six-year-old journalist. They became close friends, and one day over drinks at the Seattle Press Club Martin broached the subject of homosexuality. Until that point Lyon—who had never married—had virtually no awareness that there was such a thing as a female homosexual. During the course of the conversation, though, Martin finally worked up the courage to say:

"I am one."

Lyon thought it was one of the most exciting things she ever heard in her life. The rest of the conversation was a blur, but Lyon immediately realized she was one, too.

The next day Lyon phoned several of her friends to say, "Guess what! I'm a lesbian." She had not considered that such information might jeopardize either those friendships or her career, but fortunately nothing happened. Thereafter she and Del became close friends, though not lovers. Lyon was still not comfortable with the idea of homosexual sex.

In 1953 Lyon decided to move to San Francisco. In the weeks before her move, Martin finally made a pass and the two women became lovers. For a time thereafter they struggled to keep their long-distance affair alive, with Martin occasionally visiting San Francisco. Just when she was growing discouraged, Lyon wrote an impassioned letter inviting Martin to move to San Francisco and live with her. Martin took an all-night bus ride in order to get to San Francisco by Valentine's Day.

During their visits to the city's few lesbian bars, mostly on North Beach, they felt too shy to approach the other women who collected in discreet groups. So they decided to found a lesbian social club. Neither woman had ever heard of the Mattachine Society or One, Inc.

In time four couples began to meet secretly each week at one another's homes for dancing and socializing. As the group grew in size and courage, Lyon and Martin decided to go public. Several members wanted to keep the group small and secret, but Lyon, Martin, and one other couple felt it necessary to reach out to other women like themselves—particularly after meeting Hall Call of the San Francisco Mattachine Society chapter.

In October 1955 Lyon and Martin founded the first lesbian rights organization, the Daughters of Bilitis, named after Pierre Louÿs's epic poem *The Songs of Bilitis,* about a contemporary of Sappho. Like the Mattachine Society, the DOB began holding discussion groups that soon attracted not only lesbians, but transvestites and would-be transsexuals. Fear of social ostracism, loss of employment, and police raids required that the group keep as low a profile as possible, and indeed the FBI was keeping watch. A report to the head office stated that the group was Communist infiltrated.

Lesbianism was also coming out of the Hollywood closet. Back in 1936 director William Wyler had made a watered-down version of the Lillian Hellman play *The Children's Hour,* about a lesbian relationship. Unable to use such taboo terms as "homosexual" or "lesbian" or explicit imagery, Wyler called the movie *These Three.*

Not until 1966, though, was the first large-scale study of lesbianism undertaken. The main conclusion of the study, headed by Dr. Ralph E. Gunlach and Dr. Bernard F. Reles, was that the pattern of lesbian development did not seem to parallel the development of gay men, who were commonly believed to be the product of dominant mothers and withdrawn fathers.

Though the gay subculture still operated in secret in most cities, by the early sixties openly gay communities existed in New York, San Francisco, Chicago, Los Angeles, Miami, and New Orleans. Already the word "gay" was in use. San Francisco even had an SM scene in the warehouse district, replete with motorcycle and black leather motifs.

In 1961 Illinois had become the first state to revise its criminal code concerning consensual activity between adults, removing long-standing penalties for private consensual sex, fornication, adultery, and homosexual relations. As other states began to update their laws regulating adult consensual behavior, the rights of victims of spousal abuse and rape were also slowly established.

Internal debate among the various gay rights groups was also helping to clarify issues in the movement and draw a line between accommodation and activism. After One, Inc., proposed a Homosexual Bill of Rights, a bitter debate ensued, with the Mattachine Society and the DOB arguing that such a document, even for discussion purposes, took "a demanding attitude towards society." Yet the Homosexual Bill of Rights served as a virtual prototype for the gay civil rights movement of the seventies.

The first significant show of gay power occurred in 1960, during the San Francisco mayoral campaign. In a desperate move to gain support, the challenger accused the incumbent of harboring sexual deviates, specifically the Mattachine Society, whose "national headquarters" were located in the city. Though the smear tactic failed, the homophobia of both candidates alienated a sizable group of gay voters and kept at least nine thousand of them away from the polls.

In 1961 police extortion of gay bars in San Francisco erupted into a media scandal when several bars refused to pay and went to court instead. The following year, several bar owners formed the Tavern Guild, working cooperatively to fight police harassment. In 1964 several liberal ministers who were concerned with gay rights formed the Council on Religion and the Homosexual (CRH). Later that year, the CRH sponsored a New Year's ball for the gay community. Though the police showed up in force and arrested several of the ministers, the resulting outcry effectively reduced police harassment thereafter, although it remained a threat to gay communities on both coasts.

In 1963 the East Coast Homophile Organization began to push for a larger gay rights movement. In 1965 the Washington, D.C., Mattachine Society took the stand that "homosexuality is not a sickness, disturbance, or other pathology in any sense, but is merely a preference, orientation, or propensity, on a par with, but not different in kind from, heterosexuality."

That same year the new metropolitan editor of *The New York Times,* A. M. Rosenthal, was astounded to discover while house hunting that Manhattan's East Fifties was a popular cruising neighborhood for gays and assigned a reporter to do a front-page story. The reporter found that estimates of the gay population of the city ranged from one hundred thousand to six hundred thousand, that one thousand gays a year were being arrested for overt activity, and that underworld involvement in gay bars was pervasive.

Before long, activist organizations had formed in Seattle, Kansas City, Chicago, and Miami, and in New York the Student Homophile League at Columbia University became the first gay student organization. Yet as late as 1964, southern states such as North and South Carolina were still sentencing homosexuals to prison. In 1967 a police raid in Los Angeles sparked a vociferous street demonstration of several hundred gay people.

In 1968 a group of gay journalists and writers founded *The Advocate,* the first truly national gay publication; and that same year Troy Perry's Metropolitan Community Church initiated another important trend: the development of social and cultural institutions for gays and lesbians.

By 1968 radical feminism was an important force in lesbian organizations. Militant feminists staged their first bra-burning protest at a Miss America pageant, and lesbianism began to come out of the closet. A lesbian feminist was also elected president of the San Francisco DOB, sparking a debate between old and new ways of doing things. The radical feminist position held that women's liberation was the first priority for lesbians. Increasingly, lesbians were joining the feminist movement, and many feminists were coming out as lesbians.

In England a wave of sexual reform had been swelling since 1959, with the defense of literary merit being pioneered in obscenity cases. In 1967 the Sexual Offences Act—one of several pieces of permissive legislation that included the decriminalization of suicide and the easing of laws relating to abortion and divorce—partially decriminalized homosexuality, largely as a result of a 1963 Report of the Committee on Homosexual Offences and Prostitution presented to Parliament by a distinguished committee of physicians, psychologists, sociologists, lawyers, and clergymen under the chairmanship of Lord Wolfenden. The so-called Wolfenden Report declared that the issue of homosexuality—like that of prostitution—was confused by society's attempt to equate what the churches called sin with what the law punished as crime. The report found homosexuality to be neither a sin nor a crime, although it depicted homosexuals as sick people in need of treatment. Yet a report by the Committee on Public Health of the New York Academy of Medicine found that homosexuals saw themselves as leading "a desirable, noble, preferable way of life."

The bars—like the Stonewall Inn in New York and Maud's in San Francisco, a legendary lesbian hangout run by Rikki Streicher that flourished throughout the sixties, seventies, and eighties—remained the lifeblood of the gay and lesbian community. Maud's served as a virtual sorority house for a generation of lesbians, many of whom regarded the gay rights movement of the seventies as a fraternity party that excluded women and blacks.

Another place where gays congregated, usually in the greatest secrecy, was the baths. In 1960 only three existed in New York, notably the St. Mark's Baths, the "flophouse of the tubs." All three had in common an ingrained seediness that dismayed all but the hardiest. The rooms were filthy, torn sheets covered stained mattresses, the latrines were unspeakable, and the atmosphere was bleakly degenerate.

Though bathhouse conditions first began to improve on the West Coast, a Manhattan entrepreneur named Steve Ostrow, riding the wave of gay consciousness in the late sixties, made history by opening the Continental Baths in the basement of the Hotel Ansonia on New York's Upper West Side.

Ostrow introduced a number of radical improvements: a policy of absolute cleanliness, a coffee shop, young, good-looking attendants. Above all, Ostrow was intent on erasing the sense of illicitness that had haunted homosexuality's dark days. The new keynotes were cheerfulness and acceptance. Virtually overnight, gay men of all stripes flocked to his self-proclaimed mecca, and in short order the Continental added a dance floor, live entertainment on weekends, a small gymnasium, masseurs, yoga classes, beach furniture at poolside, incandescent plastic stairways, and access to a sun deck on the hotel roof.

Soon other baths around town began refurbishing and new bathhouses opened, including the Club, which before long was operating a chain in twenty cities around the country. To attract customers, the rival baths began to specialize. One targeted the college crowd, another the smart set, others the sadomasochists, while yet another was popular with middle-aged businessmen looking for a quick turn before catching the train back to the wife and kids in the suburbs. Yet at the core of all the bathhouses was an architecture designed to provide the highest probability of sexual contact possible.

With gay bars and spas leading the way, gay culture soon saw an extraordinary proliferation of gay churches, gay counseling centers, gay newspapers and magazines, gay movies and theater groups, and gay political parties. Homosexuality was becoming big business, catering to a clientele with an above average disposable income. In Florida, Southern California, and certain desert resorts, the baths evolved into motels and spas offering outdoor swimming pools, horseback riding, nature trails, beaches, and accommodations for extended stays. Los Angeles led the field with Big Sky, a million-dollar, seven-acre resort with a panoramic view of the San Fernando Valley and an architectural design right out of Cecil B. DeMille.

Yet New York's Continental Baths remained the ne plus ultra of the bath and sauna culture, where regular entertainers included Bette Midler and Cab Calloway, and the dress code mandated not black tie but narrow black towels. Open around the clock, 365 days a year, the Continental had an ambience all its own. Thick, windowless walls blocked out light and noise. Morning and night were indistinguishable, a libidinous limbo where women were not allowed. On a good night more than a thousand men crowded in.

By the late sixties a few states had repealed their sodomy laws, while many cities adopted civil rights protection for gays and lesbians. Presidential candidates had endorsed gay rights. Disco was the anthem of gay men celebrating the triumph of their struggle against self-hate and denial. Off Broadway, *The Boys in the Band* trumpeted gay sexuality in a way that *Oh! Calcutta!* did for heterosexuals. Groups such as the National Gay Task Force, founded in 1973, hired professional lobbyists to influence legislation and obtain media coverage of gays, with some success. For the first time in history, gays were openly becoming a visible—and often noisy—political and cultural force.

Finally, in 1973, the American Psychiatric Association removed homosexuality from its diagnostic manual, declaring that gays and lesbians did not suffer from a mental disorder.

Chapter 5

Intimations of Immorality

AT THE AGE OF EIGHTEEN SHE SPENT FOUR DAYS IN THE WOMEN'S HOUSE OF Detention in New York City after being arrested in a demonstration against the Vietnam War. Two doctors administered such a brutal internal examination that she hemorrhaged for fifteen days.

An alumna of rad-chic Bennington College in the mid-sixties, when the first alarums of women's liberation were being sounded, she took a cynical view of feminist consciousness-raising, dismissing Betty Friedan's *The Feminine Mystique* as a book for "housewives." She also thought of herself not as homosexual or heterosexual, but as an artist. Her favorites were the "wild men" of letters—Dostoyevsky, Whitman, Baudelaire, Rimbaud—and the lesbian Greek poet Sappho.

The daughter of first-generation Russian Jews, she had grown up in Jersey City estranged from her domineering mother. Her father, a teacher who worked nights in the post office to cover his wife's medical bills, inculcated in her a love and respect for ideas—one of them being an absolute commitment to the First Amendment. An overweight ugly duckling, with a preference for bib overalls, she refused to wear makeup or conform in any other way to society's idea of femininity. In 1969 she fell in love and married a left-wing radical like herself. At last she felt free of her mother's "ignorant demands."

Marriage, though, turned out to be a hell unlike anything she ever imagined. Her husband raped her, routinely beat her, kicked her in the stomach, punched her in the breasts and burned them with cigarettes, and mercilessly battered her about the legs with a piece of wood. Every day, every night, she cried, screamed, begged for mercy, for a little love and kindness. Her first thought, on waking up from a battering that left her unconscious, was despair that she was still alive.

At twenty-five, almost catatonic, she somehow worked up the determination to walk out. Desperately needing money, she agreed to carry a briefcase full of heroin through customs for a junkie. When the deal fell through, she financed her escape by stealing. A year later, out of nowhere, her ex-husband sprang on her again, hitting and kicking her, then disappeared again. She began to think of him as a "ghost with a fist."

Yet she also thought of herself now as "one year old, an infant born out of a corpse, still with the smell of death on her, but hating death." Hating death translated into hating men. Her name was Andrea Dworkin, and within the decade she would become the most celebrated, outrageous, and influential enemy of the male sex that America, or perhaps any country, had ever produced.

After leaving her husband, Dworkin tried to support herself as a writer, contributing to obscure magazines and beginning work on a book entitled *Woman Hating.* Well-paying assignments from the women's magazines disgusted her, and she turned them all down.

At the time, she also felt deeply masochistic—not so much in a personal sense, but as part of her lot as a woman. Yet one thing she knew—she had not inherited those masochistic feelings from her parents. Trying to determine where they did come from, she turned to a modern SM classic then enjoying early renown, *Story of O* by the pseudonymous Pauline Réage.

From that beginning Dworkin embarked on an investigation of other pornography, as well as fairy tales and such refinements of male cruelty toward women as Chinese foot binding. During this period she also came to a deep realization of herself as a woman and established a new, healthier relationship with her mother. She also read the first seminal feminist tract of the decade, Kate Millett's blockbuster *Sexual Politics,* published in the fall of 1970, which converted her fully to the feminist cause. Heavily indebted to Wilhelm Reich's 1930 classic, *The Sexual Revolution,* and Simone de Beauvoir's *The Second Sex*—though she cited the French author only twice—Millett painted a nightmare vision of endless female subordination to and suffering at the hands of men. "Sexual dominion [is] perhaps the most pervasive ideology of our culture and provides the most fundamental concept of power," Millett wrote, claiming that the status of woman was that of "chattel" perpetuated through marriage—"an exchange of the female's domestic service and (sexual) consortium in return for financial support." Millett virtually coined the term "sex object" and the idea of sexism as applied by men to women. The way men kept women subordinate, Millett argued, echoing Friedan, was by making an elaborate pretense of placing them on a pedestal.

The product of a midwestern convent education, Millett had been molested by an older man when she was thirteen. For ten years she kept her secret. Then one day she joined a group of women friends who were driving downtown, and the conversation turned to rape and exhibitionism. Every one of the eight women in the car was able to recount an experience similar to her own. She began to perceive that women were constantly the victims of male violence. Women did not attack women, men did. Violence had become sexually institutionalized in the United States. "Men equate their power with their balls," she wrote, "so when they think they're losing their power, they start screaming that they're losing their balls."

Though Millett's heaviest fire was directed against Freud, her most outlandish suggestion was to call for the abolition of the family, a social institution virtually coextensive with history. One reader who believed in that message, however, was Andrea Dworkin, whose writings and lifestyle took up where *Sexual Politics* left off.

"[Rape] remains our primary model for heterosexual relating . . . a right of marriage," Dworkin now wrote, revealing a pornographic streak of her own that was to deepen over the years. By contrast, "Being a lesbian means . . . there is an erotic passion and intimacy which comes of touch and taste, a wild, salty tenderness, a wet sweet sweat, our breasts, our mouths, our cunts, our intertangled hairs . . . a sensual passion as deep and mysterious as the sea." She found strength and inspiration not so much in lesbianism as in a radical man-hating ideology, which sought to explain why all men did what they did to all women.

Radical feminism was Dworkin's way out of madness, though not necessarily back into sanity. At the time, the movement was splintering into liberal and radical factions. The liberal wing, whether it found pornography distasteful or appealing, was above all committed to the First Amendment and leaned away from characterizing all women as victims and all men as villains. But the right wing took issue with the First Amendment's protection of pornography, leaning toward a polarized view of male and female sexuality that demonized men and idealized women and dismissing liberal feminists as co-conspirators in their own enslavement.

In April 1974 *Woman Hating* appeared. Dworkin hoped its publication would establish her as a writer of recognized talent, but she was disappointed. The following year she earned less than $2,000. *The Village Voice* refused to publish her essays and reviewed her work with seething contempt, and she was scorned by the Village's left-wing lesbian community. In succeeding years Dworkin continued to have difficulty placing her work.

The turning point, both in Dworkin's life and in the history of radical feminism, came in October 1974 when she spoke at a three-hour New York City "speakout" on sexual issues, values, and experiences sponsored by the

National Organization for Women and attended by eleven hundred women. The title of her talk was "Renouncing Sexual 'Equality,' " and afterward she received a standing ten-minute ovation. Many in the audience were crying and shaking. It was not the last time she would inspire such a reaction.

Extremely skillful in evoking pathos, Dworkin often succeeded in her talks and debates in bringing women in the audience to tears by vividly condemning the "millions and millions of pictures of real women bound, gagged, and hanging from meathooks for men's entertainment," as she later wrote and lectured. Shaming her liberal listeners, she insisted that "men do to women in pornography what men do to political prisoners in those third world countries we're all against. How many women's bodies does it take to equal one injury to one male body?"

A fundamental tenet championed by Dworkin and other radical feminists was that male sexuality depended for its pleasure on victimizing others. Dworkin had a high stake in maintaining this patronizing view of female sexuality—that women, when they were not victims of rape, were essentially whores. In her books and lectures she claimed that not marriage but sexual intercourse should be abolished because it was the cause of many if not most of women's problems.

As for men, they were, not surprisingly, mere "creeps" who wanted only to "occupy," "violate," "invade," or "colonize" women's bodies. "Physically, the woman in intercourse is a space inhabited, a literal territory occupied literally: occupied even if there has been no resistance, no force; even if the occupied person said yes please, yes hurry, yes . . ."

It seemed unlikely that Dworkin would be able to find a man with whom she could live on her terms. But then a palm reader told her she would. In 1974 Dworkin met John Stoltenberg, an openly gay magazine editor who had a master's degree in divinity from Union Theological Seminary, at a meeting of the War Resisters League. They began living together, in a brother-sister arrangement intended to demonstrate Dworkin's contention that a union between a man and woman need not be penis centered. The two also agreed that each could have sex partners outside the relationship as long as they were not brought home to the four-room co-op they jointly owned, making their sexless union an open nonmarriage—a sexual first of sorts.

Dworkin took charge of the fun aspects of their lives: picnics in Prospect Park, trips to the theater. The second most radical issue in their lives after pornography was housework. Frequently, after Stoltenberg washed a dish, Dworkin good-naturedly returned it for a more thorough cleansing. What Dworkin most feared was losing the ability to make decisions—even in such minor matters as what kind of toothpaste to buy. Stoltenberg and Dworkin solved that problem by buying two different tubes.

In 1977 Dworkin met a divorced young law professor named Catharine

MacKinnon, who shared her notion that sexual intercourse was an "aggressive intrusion" into a woman's body. Incorruptible, brimming with righteousness and limitless zeal, MacKinnon was an attractive blonde who wore tailored suits and gold jewelry, in sharp contrast with Dworkin's studied dishevelment. Endowed with ferocious legal cunning, she was to play Robespierre to Dworkin's pamphleteering, emotional Marat in the radical-feminist Reign of Terror against men that was to wash over the country in the coming decade.

A child of privilege, MacKinnon grew up in rural Minnesota, the daughter of George E. MacKinnon, a staunch Republican and a member of the U.S. Court of Appeals for the District of Columbia, who once wrote an opinion saying sexual activity in the workplace was "normal and expectable." After earning a Ph.D. in political science at Yale and graduating from Yale Law School, MacKinnon worked with the Black Panthers and opposed the Vietnam War.

Though not among the first women lawyers to become involved in the issue of sexual harassment, which first entered the cultural lexicon around 1975, she began to pioneer a novel approach toward the issue—seeing it, too, as a form of sex discrimination—soon after meeting Dworkin in the late seventies. In support of that contention, a 1976 *Redbook* survey reported that 88 percent of women responding said they had experienced overt sexual harassment and regarded it as a serious work-related problem. A later survey of more than twenty thousand federal government workers showed that 42 percent of women and 15 percent of men said they had been sexually harassed in the previous two years, with 78 percent of the harassers male. Harassment behavior ranged from suggestive conversation to touching.

Above all, Dworkin and MacKinnon agreed that pornography was at the root of all evil suffered by women. According to Dworkin, not only did sex itself have to move away from its "penis-centricity," but pornography could no longer be seen simply as the harmless objectification of women for the entertainment of men. That was because men's sexuality, meaning their very nature, was rooted in the victimization of others. Women, as a result, lived their entire lives as victims, whether they knew it or not.

MacKinnon and Dworkin began giving speeches and lobbying together for antipornography ordinances. Yet their writings continued to seem oddly pornographic in their detail. "The fuck, the fist, the street, the chains, the poverty are the hard end," MacKinnon wrote. "Hostility and contempt, or arousal of master to slave, together with awe and vulnerability, or arousal of slave to master . . ."

Alarmed by the rhetoric and activism of the radical feminists, liberal feminists belatedly organized into anticensorship groups. As American Civil Liberties Union (ACLU) president Nadine Strossen pointed out, most liberal feminists opposed censoring sexually oriented speech even when they found it offensive—recognizing that censorship would ultimately play into the agenda of male-dominated institutions intent on reversing progress in abortion rights, contraception, and other gains toward full sexual equality made by the women's movement.

Liberal feminists also disputed any empirical link between sex crimes and pornography and feared that forcing pornography underground would bring out the worst in both the manufacturers of XXX-rated materials and those intent on suppressing them—as the analogous example of Prohibition suggested.

Among the most notable feminist groups opposed to the MacKinnon-Dworkin tide were the Feminists' Anti-Censorship Taskforce, formed in 1984 by the poet Adrienne Rich, Columbia University professor Carole Vance, Betty Friedan, and others; the Feminists for Free Expression; and the National Coalition Against Censorship's Working Group on Women, Censorship, and "Pornography," the quotation marks in the latter's title underscoring the word's inherent ambiguity.

THE MOST COMPREHENSIVE EXAMINATION ever undertaken of the effects of hard-core pornography on human criminal behavior was contained in the 1970 Report of the President's Commission on Obscenity and Pornography initiated by Lyndon Johnson shortly before he left office. (Nine "technical reports" were subsequently published in 1971–1972.) Soon after Richard Nixon was inaugurated as his successor, he added another name to the panel—Charles Keating, a wealthy Catholic investor and a founder of the Cincinnati-based Citizens for Decency in Literature, the most vociferous antipornography group in the nation.

The commission spent two years researching the extent of the sexually oriented motion picture, book, and magazine industries, mail-order erotica, hard-core pornography, the relationship between the manufacture and distribution of pornography to organized crime, community exposure to erotica, and even information on patrons of adult bookstores and movies.

The report, submitted to Nixon in April 1970 in ten volumes, found no substantial basis for the belief that exposure to erotica caused sex crimes or bad moral character. Volume VII, subtitled *Erotica and Antisocial Behavior,* reported on nine studies on the relationship between explicit sexual material and criminal sexual acts. None found any reason to conclude that pornography encouraged sex crimes; in fact, the available data pointed to quite the opposite.

Dr. C. Eugene Walker of Baylor University, for example, had interviewed a sample of jailed sex offenders, along with a control sample of nonoffenders.

"In terms of their experience with pornography," he concluded, "the control groups tended to be exposed to pornography more frequently, to have been exposed at a younger age and to respond more positively to this material than the sex offenders."

But Nixon, the most bluenosed of modern presidents, was shocked by the report and immediately repudiated the $2 million, two-year study, calling its conclusions "morally bankrupt." At the same time, he ordered his Justice Department to crack down on pornography—hard. The U.S. Senate also rejected the report, by a vote of sixty to five. Critics accused the commission of being packed with liberals; feminists noted that it was dominated by men. The dissenting minority characterized its conclusions as "a Magna Carta for the pornography industry."

Yet the technical reports contained perhaps the two best defenses of pornography ever mounted. Both dealt with Danish pornography, at the time virtually the only hard-core available anywhere in the world. The "Danish experience," according to researcher Richard Ben-Veniste, was a turning point in public attitudes about the effects of explicit sexual representation. He and Berl Kutchinsky, director of the Institute of Criminal Science in Copenhagen, found that when the availability of pornography mushroomed in Denmark during the sixties, the sex-crime rate actually decreased, leading Kutchinsky to speculate about a "direct cause." In the second instance, the commission's executive director and director of research, W. Cody Wilson, concluded after a statistical analysis of sex crimes: "In sum, analyses of United States crime and illegitimacy rates do not support the thesis of causal connection between the availability of erotica and either sex crimes or illegitimacy."

The commission found that "there are two elementary, but fundamental, questions about erotic materials upon which nearly all concerns with the subject are based. First, does exposure to erotic sexual stimuli sexually excite and arouse the viewer? Second, does such exposure affect the subsequent sexual behavior of the user?"

Clinical tests proved that between 60 and 85 percent of both male and female subjects were aroused by looking at visual or printed explicit sexual material. Men more often reported arousal from visual stimulation than from reading, while women showed the opposite tendency. Females also reported more "disgust" than males. Not content to rely on indirect measures such as increased heart rate, sweating, and heavier breathing—which might, for example, indicate disgust as well as arousal—researchers used a plethysmograph (a device for measuring changes in volume) to measure the degree of men's erections after exposure to stimulus. With some difficulty, a similar technique was adapted to measure female subjects' increase in vaginal lubricity and temperature and the slight change in color as the vagina became suffused with blood during arousal. Several such clinical tests left no doubt as to the effectiveness of pornographic material.

Males were far more aroused than females by depictions of oral sex, whereas coitus produced equal degrees of arousal. Also there appeared to be a connection between the amount of pornographic material a man consumed or viewed and his general amount of sexual activity; the more sexually active he was, the more pornography he consumed.

In its report on the Danish experiment, the majority of the presidential commission recommended "that federal, state, and local legislation should not seek to interfere with the right of adults who wish to do so to read, obtain, or view explicit sexual materials."

Critics of the pornography commission charged that it overlooked several serious factors: that, first of all, one study had shown a marked relationship between exposure to pornography and moral character, and that exposure to pornography was a strong predictor of sexual deviance. Other critics contended that major consumers of pornography were often sex starved, and/or suffered from assorted sexual difficulties such as premature ejaculation, anorgasmia, and impotence, and that reading or viewing pornography only increased their sense of frustration and social isolation—a dangerous set of circumstances.'

Feminist Robin Morgan declared that the presidential commission was male biased, and that evidence contradicting its findings was suppressed. The claim of suppression of evidence had originally been made by the two conservative clergymen on the presidential panel—Jesuit priest Morton Hill and Methodist minister Winfrey C. Link. Morgan further intimated that results of the commission were slanted because of pressure from "the porn industry's political power"—an unfounded charge. It was at this point that the bizarre seed of an alliance between radical feminists and Christian fundamentalists was planted.

In June 1973 the conservative Supreme Court, reconstructed along Nixonian lines, responded to the fierce criticism of the presidential commission by fundamentalists, antipornography activists, and radical feminists. It did so by taking the nine justices altogether out of the business of reviewing allegedly objectionable work altogether.

The Burger Court now declared that local juries would have to decide what offended standards of taste, and convict if they found that a work taken as a whole seriously lacked literary, artistic, political, or scientific value. In effect, the decision allowed all fifty states to frame their own new antiobscenity laws.

Not surprisingly, the Court's ruling generated mass confusion, with defense lawyers and prosecutors agreeing on only one thing: prosecution of pornographers would increase. Some legal experts forecast a profusion of vigilante movements, while others thought the rulings would have no effect on the availability of hard-core. Meanwhile, the Association of American Publishers, representing two hundred and fifty publishers, resolved to fight the Court's obscenity decision and took the first step toward forming an alliance with librarians, booksellers, magazine publishers, and moviemakers.

For the time being, though, as events soon proved, pornographers had little to worry about. With community standards in disarray, few localities were in the mood or single-minded enough to take on the porn lords. Police and prosecutors were also reluctant to campaign against so-called victimless crimes. Even in San Francisco, a major center of pornography, prosecution of pornographers was at a virtual standstill. Boston officially approved a "combat zone" on Washington Street to contain the spread of adult material.

But it was a different story at the federal level, where the Justice Department—responding to Nixon's edict—was busy prosecuting eighty-five obscenity cases, many in the Bible Belt. Many federal prosecutors also thought organized crime dominated not only the traditional pornography industry, but massage parlors, topless bars, and strip joints.

Ironically, however, it was the 1973 Supreme Court ruling that gave the Mob its foothold in the industry. Fearful of prosecution for interstate activities, many independent producers turned the risky business of distribution over to organized crime. In turn, the Mafia began pirating prints, then going to film producers and offering to take over future distribution in exchange for calling off their piracy.

The profit potential, even in distribution, was enormous. In 1976 an eight-millimeter film cost only $1 or $2 to manufacture but retailed for $16. A peep-show machine showing a customer two minutes of pornography for 25¢ or a full twelve minutes for $1.50 grossed more than $10,000 per year. A hard-core porn movie for theatrical showing was made for between $15,000 and $50,000 and could return hundreds of thousands of dollars and in some cases millions.

BETTY FRIEDAN's impassioned 1963 best-seller, *The Feminine Mystique,* was the first to explore the inequalities prevailing in male-female relations and marriage, and more than any other single book or event helped to galvanize the incipient feminist movement and fasten public attention on women's rights.

Friedan, née Goldstein, had moved to New York's Greenwich Village after graduating from Smith College, finding work as a reporter for a labor newspaper. In 1947 she married Carl Friedan. Like many other postwar couples, they eventually moved to the suburbs, where Friedan became a full-time mother, transporting her children to school and joining the PTA.

Though motherhood was fulfilling, Friedan still felt a need to pursue a career and began writing for magazines like *Cosmopolitan,* although an article on actress Julie Harris's natural childbirth was declined because the editors deemed it too graphic and because it did not explore a woman's role vis-à-vis her husband and children.

In 1957, for her fifteenth college reunion, Friedan got an assignment from *McCall's* to write an article based on a questionnaire she planned to distribute to the class of '42. Among the questions: "What difficulties have you found in working out your role as a woman? What are the chief satisfactions and frustrations of your life today?" The answers suggested that an overwhelming number of women felt unfulfilled and isolated, envying their husbands who had other lives, friends, colleagues, and challenges away from home.

Friedan's article for *McCall's* recounted the frustration and hopelessness of the Smith alumnae, but the magazine turned it down. She then submitted it to *Ladies' Home Journal,* which accepted the piece but rewrote it to portray women as being generally happy with their lot. Angered, Friedan pulled the piece and showed it to *Redbook,* which also declined it.

At this point Friedan realized she was challenging the very raison d'être of women's magazines and was being censored. The only solution seemed to lie in a book, which she tentatively titled *The Togetherness Woman,* though along the way the title was changed to *The Feminine Mystique.* This first investigation into the unhappy, unfulfilled, needlessly male-centered lives of so many American women sold three million copies—a clear sign that sexual emancipation through the pill and changing mores was not enough. Women wanted a much more fundamental revolution than anything most men had in mind. They wanted not only the freedom to have sex with whomever and whenever they chose, without fear of pregnancy—just like men. They wanted the freedom to realize their full potential as human beings and to be themselves—as women.

In fact, the Sexual Revolution that began in the mid-sixties was primarily male-driven, even though many of its goals and achievements benefited millions of women. Alfred Kinsey, John Rock, William Masters, John Money, and many others exhibited profound compassion for the sexual and cultural predicament of women and often worked in collaboration with female colleagues. Though male protofeminists risked their careers to explore the sexual unknown, their gender was the most decisive factor in enabling them to do what they did; no woman could have done likewise for the simple reason that their gender prevented them from being in the right place at the right time. Pornographers were also, of course, primarily male, while activists for homosexual rights concentrated on their own special concerns.

The grass-roots feminist movement, on the other hand, was of necessity almost entirely composed of women, most of them anonymous and not a few heroic. Though the agendas of the Sexual Revolution and the women's movement intersected at numerous points, and were to converge most conspicuously on the narrow issue of pornography in the mid-eighties, at the onset they were distinct and separate.

Back in the early decades of the century, the first wave of feminism had narrowly concentrated on women's right to vote, a cause that attracted a mass following. After universal suffrage was achieved in 1920 with the passage of the Nineteenth Amendment to the U.S. Constitution, that wave dissipated.

The second wave that developed both in the United States and Europe in the early sixties was of an entirely different nature, fueled by the discontent many women felt that their political, legal, economic, and social status was not keeping pace with the dramatic inroads they were making in education and the workforce.

A model and forerunner of this second wave was the black civil rights movement, which had already brought national attention to bear on the immorality of discrimination and legitimized mass protest and activism. New feminist issues included legal equality, women's control over their own bodies, the elimination of discrimination based on gender, race, ethnicity, and sexual orientation; greater political power; and the abolition of institutional and social roadblocks to professional and personal achievement. By the mid-seventies feminism was a mass movement with more than half of American women supporting many of its principles and demands.

But this second wave advanced on two separate fronts that underscored different styles and values. Though both fronts consisted primarily of white, middle-class, college-educated women, what differentiated them was age—a generation gap. Younger women tended to abjure hierarchical structure and the traditional political system in favor of engaging in such activities as consciousness-raising groups, women support services (health clinics, women's bookstores, rape crisis centers, battered-women's shelters), and the organization of public awareness campaigns and marches. Younger women were also more active than their older sisters in the pro-choice, environmental, and antinuclear movements. By the early 1980s this kind of grass-roots activism had helped to establish more than three hundred women's studies programs and thirty thousand courses in colleges and universities, as well as a national professional association, the National Women's Studies Association.

The second front comprised older, more traditional women, whose organizations were replete with officers, boards of directors, and paid staffs, among them the Women's Legal Defense Fund, the Center for Women's Policy Studies, the Feminist Majority Foundation, the National Coalition Against Domestic Violence, and most notably the National Organization for Women (NOW), with Betty Friedan as founding president.

NOW became the first feminist group to develop a mass membership. At the national level its purpose was to become a powerful political voice for women's causes, and one of its first major causes was passage of the Equal Rights Amendment (ERA), guaranteeing legal equality for women. The proposed wording of the ERA read: "Equality of Rights under the Law shall not be denied or abridged by the United States or by any State on account of sex."

Previously the Supreme Court had upheld laws excluding women from jury service and had ruled that the rights of women did not merit constitutional guarantees—that to extend guarantees would be to deny the states their lawful rights to impose discriminatory and restrictive laws on women.

Though the ERA was endorsed by Congress and sent to the states for ratification in 1972, it encountered strong opposition from well-organized conservative and right-wing political and religious groups who depicted feminism as an attack on family values and the American way of life. In 1982 the Stop ERA campaign won after the amendment failed to pass within the allotted time frame by seven votes in three states. Yet feminism itself was victorious, and many states passed their own equal rights amendments and revised discriminatory state and local laws.

Meanwhile, the publication of Friedan's book and the FDA's approval of the pill had occurred within only a few years of each other and quickly reached their peaks in popularity and acceptance on college campuses, where a new generation of women was preparing to challenge traditional male prerogatives and prejudices across the board. Among the issues of surpassing concern to women, the most immediate and pressing was abortion—a medical procedure that many women felt was their fundamental right to choose and yet was denied them by a male-dominated coalition of state and church.

The move to legalize abortion was made all the more urgent by several developments in the early sixties. The first of these was the invention of the vacuum curettage method in Hungary, which made abortions medically safe. The dilemma of women carrying a severally crippled fetus was made poignantly clear with the unfolding of the thalidomide tragedy, in which a powerful sedative unexpectedly turned out to have a devastating effect on the formation of a fetus's arms and legs. Women who had used the tranquilizer, and now found themselves faced with the possibility of carrying a child who might be born without limbs, created pressure in the mass media for the reform of abortion laws. A 1964 epidemic of German measles, another threat to fetal health, caused many women to seek and obtain legal abortions. Finally, the American Law Institute took a formal position advocating the legalization of abortion, and in 1970 Alaska, Hawaii, New York, and Washington legalized abortion in the first twenty-four weeks of pregnancy.

The abortion debate finally culminated in victory on January 22, 1973, when the U.S. Supreme Court in a seven-to-two decision voted to legalize abortion, basing their position on a woman's right to privacy. The justices ruled that a woman and her physician had sole discretion on an abortion in the first trimester. In the second trimester a state could intervene only to protect the woman's health. In the third trimester the state could regulate an abortion to protect fetal life. Few feminists realized that the Playboy Foundation played a significant and perhaps decisive role in *Roe v. Wade* by funding a series of court cases that culminated in the Supreme Court's ruling.

Immediately an antiabortion backlash developed, particularly within the Roman Catholic and some fundamentalist churches. Nevertheless, by 1980 three out of every ten pregnancies in the United States ended in abortion, for a total of about 1.3 million abortions a year. Six out of ten abortions were by young women, including 26 percent by teenagers. White women accounted for 70 percent of abortions, though nonwhite abortion rates were twice that of whites. Half of all abortions were performed in the first six weeks of gestation. More than four out of ten abortions in the United States were repeat abortions. Eighteen- and nineteen-year-old women had the highest abortion rate for any age group.

Feminists also very early on took an interest in gender differences, disputing the biological bases for sex differences and arguing that changing the environment would change the animal itself. In *Sexual Politics,* for example, Kate Millett wrote: "Groups who rule by birthright are fast disappearing, yet there remains one ancient and universal scheme for the domination of one birth group by another—the scheme that prevails in the area of sex." New research, she wrote, "suggests that the possibilities of innate temperamental differences seem more remote than ever. . . . In doing so it gives fairly concrete positive evidence of the overwhelmingly *cultural* character of gender, i.e., personality structure in terms of sexual category."

Anthropologist Lionel Tiger, defending the biological view, admitted that "the most dismal difference between males and females is that men create large fighting groups." Though feminists associated that grim pattern with machismo—the need for men to assert themselves in an aggressive way, Tiger pointed out "a simple and clear biological factor the feminists overlook—the effect of sex hormones on behavior."

At adolescence, testosterone among boys increased at least tenfold, and possibly as much as thirty times; among girls the testosterone level only doubled, and from a lower base to begin with; and both those levels remained stable throughout the life cycle.

Yet sex researcher John Money pointed out that it was dangerous to draw sociological conclusions from biological data—that is, to use cultural stereotypes as a basis for defining biological men and women. In a famous study he conducted with fellow researcher Anke A. Ehrhardt, he studied twenty-five girls born with somewhat masculinized genitals caused by an excess of androgen in the womb. The two researchers found that according to cultural stereotypes of femininity, the girls were more tomboyish than a matched set of "normal" girls. Money and Ehrhardt also tested ten genetic males who were unable to respond to the male hormones in their system, much as some diabetics are unable to use the insulin produced by their bodies. Those ten males had been reared as female because they lacked external male genitals; all tested as extremely feminine; they wanted to be wives and mothers and preferred playing with dolls to other games.

Pointing to various recently disproved sexual myths—that all women suffered from penis envy, that women were limited to vaginal orgasm, that pornography led to sex crimes, that women did not respond to sexual pictures and stories—Money declared that the only unalterable biological difference between the sexes was that women menstruated, gestated, and lactated; men impregnated. Yet even those boundaries could be hedged.

By 1974 at least five hundred transsexuals had undergone sex-change surgery, many at Johns Hopkins, while hundreds more had opted to skip the preoperative counseling sessions and hormonal treatments in favor of a quick fix at transsexual mills in Mexico, Puerto Rico, Canada, and Europe. Unscrupulous doctors in Tijuana and Casablanca did land office business, surgically altering the genitals of patients who had not been properly screened. In that respect they were spiritual kin of the *hijras* of India, whose history was lost in the mists of time. Gypsy transsexuals who roamed India, begging for money and playing at weddings, the *hijras* numbered about a half million. Some were born hermaphrodites, others castrated themselves with rocks or a knife without benefit of anesthesia—a rite of passage, as all shunned surgical castration. *Hijras* routinely replenished their ranks with runaway teenagers who were disgracing their families by being too effeminate. The ultimate stage in a *hijra*'s life was to work up the courage to have her penis and testicles amputated—without benefit of anesthetic or hormone treatment. One curious characteristic of a *hijra* was that she preferred to look like a man impersonating a woman than like a woman per se.

IN ADDITION TO Kate Millett's *Sexual Politics,* other blockbusters of the late sixties and early seventies by women included Marilyn French's *The Women's Room,* Erica Jong's *Fear of Flying* (which introduced the phrase "the zipless fuck"), Alison Lurie's *The War Between the Tates,* Marge Piercy's *Small Changes,* and Alix Kates Shulman's *Memoirs of an Ex–Prom Queen.* Written in the years before legalized abortion, most included scenes of women trying to procure an abortion either for themselves or for a friend. Most also featured long digressive passages aimed at raising the feminist consciousness of women who did not read feminist literature or even know what feminism was.

Broadly speaking, the mother and father of feminist studies were French protofeminist Simone de Beauvoir and Harvard professor David Herlihy. De Beauvoir, author of *The Second Sex, The Coming of Age,* and *The Prime of Life,* much of them autobiographical, found both rebellion and fulfillment in her escape from bourgeois married life and its attendant womanly responsibilities of nesting and raising children. At the same time she existed completely under the rule of her longtime companion and mentor, Jean-Paul Sartre, a male chauvinist of the old school, who gave her lists of books to read so she could discuss them with him. In 1922 they became a couple while devising a pact in which each would be central to the other's life but have multiple lovers and make full disclosure about their affairs. When he told her he did not find her exciting in bed, she accepted his judgment without complaint.

Herlihy, one of the most eminent medievalists of his generation, and later president of the American Historical Association, was a founding member of the Women's Studies Committee at Harvard. In the early sixties he called for the establishment of women's studies in a famous lecture. He also gave powerful impetus to lesbian and gay studies when he encouraged his doctoral student John Boswell to write his massive study of homosexuality and the Christian Church. At the time, the Harvard faculty did not contain a single woman or noncloseted gay man. A devout Catholic, Herlihy (in contrast with de Beauvoir) was dedicated to home and family and radical only as a scholar.

Perhaps the most notable pioneering work in gay studies was *Greek Homosexuality* by Kenneth Dover, a leading ancient historian, though despite his eminence he had difficulty finding a major press that would publish his work. French philosopher Michel Foucault, a homosexual and devotee of SM who was later to die of AIDS, earned a considerable reputation as a sexual theorist by arguing, among other things, that such modern categories as heterosexual and homosexual had no precise equivalent in classical antiquity—a view pioneered by Kinsey to cover all sexual behavior. In the Foucault worldview, the fundamental distinction for males was between passive and active roles; for so long as one took the active role, the gender of the partner was of no great importance.

Yet the most powerful and prominent feminist of the seventies was a young journalist named Gloria Steinem. At a 1970 feminist speakout to protest a New York State abortion hearing at which fourteen men and a nun had been invited to testify, Steinem listened as an endless stream of women told of doctors demanding preabortion sex, operations without anesthetics, and other horrors. It was the first time Steinem ever heard women telling the truth about their lives in public.

Inspired, she rose to tell her own story, for she, too, had undergone an abortion soon after graduating from college and now revealed her secret. If one in three or four adult women had this experience, Steinem later asked herself, why was it illegal? Why were women's bodies in control of someone else? After reporting on the event for *New York* magazine, Steinem found that even her well-meaning colleagues treated the women's movement with condescension and alarm. Many told her not to get involved with those "crazy women."

In the months that followed, Steinem temporarily set aside her journalism career to become an organizer and speaker, crisscrossing the country to talk about how to start a nonsexist multiracial childcare center, where to find women's fiction and poetry, what to do about violence against women, how to get a father/husband/boss to change.

By 1971 Steinem and several other women writers and editors determined that a new kind of women's magazine was necessary to address these and other issues. Clay Felker, editor of *New York,* was looking for a special feature for a double issue for the year-end holiday season and suggested a trade. He would pay out-of-pocket expenses for a new monthly to be called *Ms.* if *New York* could choose a third of its articles for its own double issue. The result was an insert that contained Jane O'Reilly's "The Housewife's Moment of Truth," Judy Syfers ("I Want a Wife") on why women needed wives as much as men did, and Vivian Gornick's "Why Women Fear Success."

Steinem's opposite number, and an editor with a constituency that numbered not in the hundreds of thousands, but in the millions, was Helen Gurley Brown, editor of *Cosmopolitan* and author of *Sex and the Single Girl*—the first modern sex advice blockbuster. Brown's advice to women was not how to get married, but how to stay single with sexual style—a shocking message in 1962. Typical advice: "A man is talking to you, nothing very personal. Look into his eyes as though tomorrow's daily double were there. Never let your eyes leave his. Concentrate on his left eye . . . then the right . . . now deep into both." A few years later she published *Sex and the Office,* in which she revealed that she relied on "padded bra, capped teeth, straightened nose, Pan-Cake, false eyelashes and wig" to get ahead and meet men.

Among those who heard Brown's message was the Hearst Corporation, publishers of *Cosmopolitan,* which was then on the chopping block. Deciding on a stay of execution, company executives agreed to turn it into a magazine for single career women. Brown's husband, David, a former editor of the magazine, heard of the plan and submitted a dummy copy of *Femme,* a proposed magazine he and Helen had put together and targeted at the same audience.

Though she lacked any editing experience, Helen Gurley Brown was hired as editor. Over the next two decades, and in the fiery midst of the rise of feminism, Brown delivered her main message—how to win and hold on to a man—in a breathless, peppy, girlish style that became the magazine's trademark.

Each month *Cosmopolitan* delivered beauty and decorating tips, sex advice, admonishments to stop "being a slug" and get out and work for what a woman wanted, and other self-improvement inspiration liberally adapted from Norman Vincent Peale and the *Reader's Digest.*

The result: *Cosmopolitan* was transformed from a wallflower with a mere eight hundred thousand circulation to prom queen with a circulation of three million and a readership of eleven million. Like *Playboy's* Playmate and *Penthouse's* Pet, That Cosmo Girl on each month's cover soon became a cultural icon and not only a role model for young women, but one of the most famous sex objects in the world.

Though radical feminists continued to focus their outrage on pornographers, women like Brown were condemned in even harsher terms because they were, in Dworkin's words, "collaborators, more base in their collaboration than other collaborators have ever been: experiencing pleasure in their own inferiority; calling [sexual] intercourse freedom."

PART TWO

EXCITEMENT

1971 - 1978

Chapter 6

Virgins and Gypsies

ONE SUMMER EVENING IN 1960 AN EAGER, GRINNING NINETEEN-YEAR-OLD AIRMAN, fresh out of Yale's Institute of Far Eastern Languages where he had spent an intensive year studying Chinese, asked a San Francisco cab driver to take him to a whorehouse. Ferdinand D'Acugno was a virgin, and an overwhelming curiosity about this thing called sex had finally got the better of him.

After selecting a woman in the lounge and paying his money, D'Acugno was led up to a drab, darkened room, where he nervously undressed. Outwardly, he was just another first-time john—slight of build, with a ready, impish smile and dark Latin good looks inherited from his Italian father and Puerto Rican mother. As sexual endowments went, his was merely average—a standard scarce six inches. Only his intense, lingering stare suggested he might be a little out of the ordinary. Clumsily mounting the prostitute, he thrust once or twice when, suddenly, a delicious spasm shuddered through his body. Then it was all over.

Moments later D'Acugno found himself out in the street again, dazed and uncertain about what exactly had happened. Eventually he realized he had prematurely ejaculated almost as soon as his hair-trigger penis brushed against the prostitute's thighs.

A week later, Airman D'Acugno arrived in Japan, where prostitution was still legal. Near the air base was a polymorphous pleasure dome unlike anything back in the States—five hundred bars overflowing with bar girls and cheap whiskey.

D'Acugno had been given top-security clearance, and by day he intercepted and translated radio broadcasts from mainland China for the intelligence services. In letters home to his devout Catholic parents, he described an

129

idyllic, full life. But by degrees he was discovering within himself a secret identity that set him radically apart from other people. Like some latter-day wolfman or vampire, who underwent a bizarre and uncontrollable transformation with the rising of the moon, he had been cursed, or blessed, with a libido of monstrous proportions and a sexual imagination and spirit of erotic adventure such as befall few men or women in a generation, or maybe a century. In the whorehouses of Japan he incubated, waiting for his hour to come at last.

In the meantime, like any good ex-Catholic boy, D'Acugno also had to contend with guilt, another lifelong affliction, which surfaced in the person of a Japanese woman named Hatsue, a kindergarten teacher. Though she was tall and attractive, with a touch of Russian blood, he felt no lust for her. He was a veteran now, and their chaste necking sessions reminded him, depressingly, of his adolescence back in New York's East Harlem. Yet it troubled him that he had yet to sleep with a woman who was not a whore. His conscience told him it was time he gave up his profligate ways and got serious with an honorable woman.

He borrowed a friend's apartment, attempting to remedy his lack of desire by forcing the issue. But the apartment was in a raucous neighborhood teeming with prostitutes and screaming children, and he found himself for the first time unable to perform. The experience left him despondent for a week. The dilemma he posed to himself was: "How am I going to fuck this girl when I'm a total degenerate?"

Determined to succeed, he took Hatsue to a traditional Japanese inn with sliding doors, tatami mats, and a tranquil rock garden. But when they made love, it was under the sheets, and once again he felt no passion. The sex was so obscure that he was not even certain that he had an erection or penetrated her. In the morning, though, he discovered blood on the sheets and concluded he had broken Hatsue's maidenhead. Feeling a sense of obligation, he proposed. She accepted. Against the advice of his distraught family, the base chaplain, and various friends, he went through with the wedding, although later he suspected Hatsue had used chicken blood to trick him. He was only twenty-two. D'Acugno was stripped of his security clearance and put to work in the laundry room. He requested a discharge, returned to New York, leaving Hatsue temporarily behind, and enrolled in Brooklyn College to complete his college degree. Soon he forgot all about his wife back in the Far East. The pill, introduced onto the market only a few years earlier, was transforming the sexual mores of America's college campuses. D'Acugno found himself in coed heaven. Then one day his mother tapped him on the shoulder and said, "Oh, by the way, didn't you get married?"

"Oh, right. I got married," D'Acugno replied. With a loan from his parents, he sent for Hatsue and they moved into an apartment together. He supported them by working as a night clerk at the American Society for the Pre-vention of Cruelty to Animals (ASPCA).

One night he collapsed at the ASPCA office and a friend brought him home, where he vomited bile for twenty-four hours and tried to come to terms with his hopeless, sexless marriage to a Japanese stranger. Sensing the cause of his misery, Hatsue approached his sickbed and, for the first time, fel-lated him.

At school D'Acugno failed one course after another, except for psychology, his major and a lifelong passion. He became friends with a group of Com-munists living in a commune called the First Williamsburg Soviet on Brook-lyn's Atlantic Avenue. Fueled by a hatred of the capitalist system, the members read Marx, Engels, and Trotsky, talked of blowing up banks, played Pete Seeger records, and sang the ballads of the Spanish Fifth Brigade. Hanging out at the commune gave D'Acugno a preview of the hip-pie road show soon to barnstorm through the sixties—a Barnum & Bailey psychocircus featuring three-ring political anarchism, free love, psychedelic drugs, Eastern mysticism, strange new foods, the psychology of the human potential movement, and free-floating hostility against the established order.

D'Acugno realized he wanted to play a starring role, not sit in the audi-ence. One day he calmly fried two frankfurters, washed the pan, packed his clothes and books in a suitcase, and moved into the commune. After much indecision, Hatsue finally moved back to Japan. Years later D'Acugno's mother received a note saying she had remarried and found happiness—a goal D'Acugno would spend a lifetime futilely pursuing.

AT THE DAWN of the sixties a new word entered the American lexicon—guru. D'Acugno seemed determined to sample them all. Having already pondered deeply the works of P. D. Ouspensky and G. I. Gurdjieff, he was only just getting started with Marx when abruptly the man who recruited him into the commune was exposed as an FBI informer and tossed out. Disillusioned, D'Acugno turned to hatha yoga, studying the writings or attending the workshops of the Maharishi, Satchidananda, and the Yogananda Brothers Psychic Circus. To earn a living he wrote alternative journalism and fiction for pulp magazines like *Escapade* and *Caper.* He also experimented with LSD, Scientology, and Gestalt therapy. Nothing seemed to satisfy him—least of all his own stumbling, inept progress toward enlightenment.

Determined to reinvent himself, he changed his name to Marco Vassi—anglicizing his mother's maiden name, Vasquez, and combining it with the first name of his spiritual forebear, Marco Polo, the first Westerner to explore the Far East—and moved to the promised land, San Francisco. He settled in the Mission District, one of countless hippie migrants, and quickly became associated with the Experimental College (EC), an anarchistic offshoot of San Francisco State. More mild-mannered than its radical siblings—the Third World Liberation Front, the Black Student Union, and numerous other splinter groups—the EC hoped to revolutionize the world through astrology, dance, poetry, and assorted other nonmartial arts. Anybody could teach anything she or he wanted, and Marco decided to teach "Relaxation, Awareness, and Breathing."

Though no credits were given, more than a hundred students signed up, letting their official schoolwork drop. Marco found himself no longer a disciple but a guru. He shaved his head and went barefoot, wore a leopard-skin coat, and carried a wooden staff. Instead of talking, he played the harmonica. If he wanted to dance in the street, he danced in the street. If he wanted a particular girl, he had only to smile at her. After one class Marco watched as his beautiful, stoned students, having formed a circle to communicate with one another better, launched into a full-fledged orgy. Just before he was hauled down into the sea of flesh, he called out, "Stop!"

Later he drifted to Tucson, where he continued to play the role of hippie Zen master, conducting fantasy and relaxation classes in the open air. Peyote and other psychedelic drugs were a routine diet for him and students of his rambling Socratic colloquies. He briefly changed his name again, to Cloud, after a man asked him his name one day and, looking up, a spaced-out Marco saw a clue in the heavens.

Marco was almost permanently high throughout the sixties, a period he recorded in *The Stoned Apocalypse,* a collection of nine tales mixing sexual escapade and anarcho-Zen psychobabble.

One day, as he was walking down a Tucson street, a woman came up to him on a motorcycle. She took him home and they made love. When he came, he noticed that she turned her head to one side. It made an impression on him, but he thought no more about it and did not see her again. Eventually he returned to San Francisco.

The woman's name was Jane. In time she got in touch and informed Marco that she was pregnant and living in Los Angeles, where she was minding the dogs and house of a wealthy couple. He borrowed a car and went to see her, accompanied by three women friends. Jane told Marco she wanted the two of them to get married in order to give the child a name and a legal father. He agreed. They tripped for three or four days, then Jane introduced Marco to her mother. When he said they intended to get married, she told him that Jane was mentally unstable and had spent the last six months in an insane asylum. Stunned, he replied, "We're going to go to Nogales and we're going to get married and then I'm going to split."

Accompanied by Marco's friends, they went to Nogales, where for the second time Marco married a woman he scarcely knew and did not love. Then they all returned to Tucson for a honeymoon-night orgy. But the next morning, when Marco announced his intention to leave, Jane started to cry. Marco began to have doubts, wondering, "Maybe I really love her and it's destined by God." But he wrenched himself away and headed back to San Francisco. When Jane followed him there a month later, Marco sternly told her he did not want to be married, and she returned to Los Angeles. Later he heard through the grapevine that she had an abortion and became a junkie.

WHEN LINDA BOREMAN got pregnant, she had the child put up for adoption, then enrolled in computer school in upstate New York. Life seemed to be getting back on course when a skidding Chrysler struck her Opel Cadet, propelling her to a chaise longue outside her parents' Fort Lauderdale retirement home. Her face had smashed into the windshield, breaking her jaw, while the steering wheel snapped her ribs and lacerated her liver.

One day, while lying under the white-hot sun, she had a visitor—an old high school friend named Betsy, who had driven up from Miami with her friend Chuck Traynor, a handsome photographer with wraparound sunglasses, in his burgundy Jaguar XKE convertible. Betsy revealed that she was a barmaid in North Miami. She invited Linda to join them on the ride back, and Linda was thrilled to get away from the suffocating environment of her parents' home. As they raced south the three shared a few joints and Linda learned that Traynor had been a marine, knew how to sky-dive and skin-dive, had worked as an assistant cameraman on the TV series *Flipper,* and had once won a date with Natalie Wood after winning a marksmanship contest.

Linda reveled in the ambience of the Vegas Inn. In the strict Catholic environment of the Boreman household in Yonkers, just north of New York, Linda had been beaten frequently by her mother for minor infractions, and for a time she had wanted to be a nun. The blinking lights and Day-Glo of the inn promised freedom, especially after a friend of Traynor's named Benny asked her out on a date. They formed a foursome until Linda found out Benny was married; she broke up with him. Then Traynor, who had stopped seeing Betsy, asked Linda out. She agreed.

At first, Traynor was always the gentleman—opening car doors, lighting cigarettes, spending money freely. Never once did he come on to Linda sexually, and he always made sure she got home by the eleven o'clock curfew imposed by her anxious parents. One night, though, Traynor delivered Linda to her home fifteen minutes late. When she walked through the door, her mother greeted her with a vicious slap in the face.

The next day, Linda told Traynor what had happened. When he invited her to move in with him, she agreed, and that night they became lovers. Only later did she realize he had trouble sustaining an erection. Only much later did Linda also learn that her new boyfriend had acquired a police record for assault, had once run a prostitution business, and was facing charges of drug smuggling.

In 1970, while living in New York's East Village, Marco saw an advertisement in the *Village Voice* that read: "Wanted: Writers for adult novels." Desperate for money, as always, he dashed off a chapter and posted it. Back came the manuscript with a rejection note explaining: "It's too literary for the fuck market and it's got too much fucking in it for the literary market."

He showed the chapter to his friend, fledgling agent Richard Curtis, who said: "Finish the book and let me see what I can do with it." Marco worked furiously, entitling his novel *Mind Blower* and setting it in a futuristic sex therapy institute dedicated to fulfilling clients' wildest sex fantasies. Curtis dubbed it one of the most arousing works of erotic literature since Henry Miller. Maurice Girodias, Miller's own publisher and owner of the legendary Olympia Press, had just set up shop in New York, and the logical next step was to show him the manuscript.

Perhaps the world's most battle-scarred and illustrious veteran of the porn wars, having taken on the establishments of France, England, and the United States, the fiftyish Girodias was a charming Gallic dandy whose keen eye for women matched the sharpness of his literary genius. He had inherited a Paris publishing house called the Obelisk Press from his father in 1939, and soon after he also started publishing art books under the Éditions du Chêne imprint. During the Occupation, he took his mother's name, since it was safer to be identified with his French mother than his British/Jewish father. In 1951 Girodias lost Obelisk Press and Éditions du Chêne in bankruptcy to Hachette and two years later began Olympia Press on a shoestring, housing the operation in the rue St. Severin, a narrow thirteenth-century thoroughfare in the Latin Quarter.

By 1967 Girodias had transplanted his publishing operation from Paris to New York after losing a $1.2 million suit against the French Ministry of the Interior for denying him the right to publish books in English that were published in French. In retaliation, the puritanical Gaullist regime had ordered him not to publish works of any kind for eighty years and six months, a term later reduced to three years. Girodias himself was sentenced to six years in prison, a term subsequently reduced to three months. After a series of appeals, he spent two days in a Paris jail.

Sex fiction was the stock in trade of the Olympia Press. Other Olympia titles included J. P. Donleavy's *The Ginger Man*, Samuel Beckett's *Watt*, *The Black Book* by Lawrence Durrell, *The Naked Lunch* by William Burroughs,

Our Lady of the Flowers by Jean Genet, *Lolita* by Vladimir Nabokov, and *Candy,* the all-time best-seller, by the pseudonymous Maxwell Kenton—actually expatriate Americans Terry Southern and Mason Hoffenberg.

Most of Olympia Press's sex writers were male, but two notable exceptions were Marilyn Meeske, a graduate of a prim Boston girls' school, who wrote porn under the pen name of Henry Cranach, and Iris Owens. Probably the best works of unadulterated pornography published by Olympia were the series written by Marcus Van Heller, a pseudonym that originated with John Stevenson (who was responsible for *Roman Orgy* and eleven other titles) and was then passed on to other writers. Another outstanding work was *The Pleasure Thieves,* coauthored by Meeske and the equally pseudonymous Harriet Daimler, with an assist from author Terry Southern, who had worked on a screenplay with Meeske. Angela Pearson, another popular writer who specialized in books about governesses who administered punishment to naughty boys, was in fact an English schoolmaster who lived in Greece.

Girodias was a shrewd judge of the porn market. He liked a ratio of approximately nine dirty passages per book, scattered throughout. He knew that there was no money in necrophilia, but that whipping themes were especially popular in England, where such books were known as "flaggies." He also knew that there was a vast, untapped, mostly male audience for porn on the theme of good old-fashioned male-female sex. A fundamental publisher's rule for all porn, then as now, was that it was always healthy, never merely degenerate; that at the end of the sexual gauntlet, the players emerged as renewed and glowingly energized as any participant in a human potential workshop.

In 1968 Girodias predicted that a new, more refined form of porn fiction—more autobiographical and with greater erotic content—was about to emerge from "the dungheap of pornography." "After the sexual revolution we are in for a mystical revolution," he told one interviewer. "From the hippie-yippie business and drugs and the fusion of yoga and Zen and Oriental eroticism will come the basis of tomorrow's style and research."

Marco Vassi fit the bill with eerie exactitude, and a delighted Girodias told him, "You are the best since Henry Miller. Write us another book." Marco's second book, *The Gentle Degenerates,* was a blur of autobiography and fiction. While he was writing it, the woman he was living with grew concerned about their romance and pressed him to tell her what was going on with them. Marco replied, a little too nonchalantly, "I don't know. I haven't written the next chapter yet." She did not speak to him for six months.

Soon Marco began to develop both a reputation and a following. *Screw* asked him to be a columnist, and he also wrote erotic stories and commentary for *Gay, Penthouse,* and *Oui.* In time he was to develop into one of the most original and shocking writers of erotica since the Marquis de Sade. Girodias published two more of his erotic novels, *Contours of Darkness* and *The Saline Solution*. Altogether he wrote twelve novels, a collection of fables, numerous essays, and a 1972 autobiography, *The Stoned Apocalypse*. However, despite such fans as Norman Mailer, Kate Millett, Saul Bellow, and Gore Vidal, and translations of his novels into a half dozen languages, none of his books became best-sellers, and he continued to support himself with translations from the Chinese, reading manuscripts for publishers and agents, and writing for the sex magazines.

Meanwhile, in June 1971 Girodias's own hacks formed a group called Dirty Writers of America and picketed Olympia's offices on Park Avenue South with signs reading "Give Us Our Dirty Money" and "Pornographers' Kids Need Clothes, Too." The strikers were demanding better royalty deals in the ever-expanding smut market. Even so, the sixteen picketing men and women had kind words for Girodias. "He will take manuscripts that are too raw for other publishers," one protester told a reporter. "He has more taste." But they were also upset that not even Girodias would permit humor— *Candy* being a notable exception.

After marrying the daughter of a senior U.S. diplomat, Girodias eventually returned to Paris, French government actions against him having subsided at last.

AFTER SETTLING IN with Chuck Traynor, Linda Boreman started helping out with the management of the Vegas Inn. The daily routine was invariable: wake up, clean out the bar, drive to a fast-food restaurant for breakfast, return to the bar to check the beer supply, fill the cash register, do other errands in the afternoon, and go to a movie at night. After returning home, they dozed, woke up, closed down the bar, then went back to bed. It was a relationship of sorts.

Since the bar featured bottomless as well as topless dancers, there was a constant hassle with local law enforcement agents. The law prohibited the girls from showing their pubic hair—a restriction Traynor got around, at least for a few weeks, by having the girls shave their pubises. At Traynor's urging, Lindas also shaved off her pubic hair. But her smoking continued to bother him.

"Why don't you just quit?" he once asked her.

"I can't."

"Sure you can," he replied. "I could help you quit. I've helped dozens of people to quit smoking. By hypnotism."

Traynor hypnotized Linda, and after a half dozen sessions he ordered her to stop smoking. She complied.

He also had another request—to perform fellatio when they made love. But her Catholic upbringing got in the way, and she refused. Later he forced himself on her.

"You know why you don't like it?" he told her. "It's the gagging mechanism. Well, I can cure you of the gagging mechanism the same way I cured you of cigarette smoking. It's just a conditioned reflex, and you can control it. You can learn to relax your throat muscles completely."

When she objected to the taste of his semen, he taught her a sexual trick he had learned in Japan—how to overcome the gag reflex and take the penis past her epiglottis, so she would not taste a thing when he ejaculated.

One night, when Linda and Traynor returned to shut down the bar, they found a barmaid lying spread-eagle atop a table, taking on three male customers. Linda was stunned and sickened, and she turned to leave. But Traynor would not let her go. It never occurred to her that he had staged the display.

Later an old friend of Traynor's named Theresa came to visit and told Linda how she always looked up to Chuck as a big brother. When she was gone, Traynor mentioned that Theresa had once been a "working girl."

"A working girl?"

"A hooker," he explained. "She was one of the best prostitutes that ever worked for me."

Though startled by yet another glimpse into Traynor's murky past, Linda had more pressing things to worry about. By now she was doing the bookkeeping. The bar was doing badly, and Traynor was routinely ignoring bills. The telephone was disconnected, and even the electricity got turned off for a couple of days. More and more, Traynor began to reminisce about "the good old days" when he ran a string of prostitutes. By now he was pocketing the money directly from the register, and he sold the Jag. One day he told her: "Linda, I've got to start up the old business again and I want you to run it for me."

"Chuck, I can't," she replied. "I don't even want to talk about it anymore."

"Maybe you don't want to talk about it anymore," Traynor said, "but you're going to do it. One way or the other."

After yet another argument, Linda told Traynor she was thinking of returning to New York. She never got a chance to complete the sentence. Traynor hit her on the side of the head, and after she slumped to the floor he continued to kick her with his boots. As she continued to scream, he became fully sexually aroused with her for the first time, and the beating concluded with him raping her on the floor.

"You're not going anywhere," he told her afterward. "You're not fucking going anywhere without me."

The hurting eventually stopped, but not the fear. Long afterward she realized why he did not simply hire a hooker. Anyone with experience would have been too smart for him. But she was too gullible, too stupid, too frightened, to say no.

ONE HOT JULY AFTERNOON, Chuck said to Linda: "Let's go for a ride." By now she had learned never to disagree because then he would hit her, kick her, or menacingly toy with his .45-caliber Walther automatic pistol.

Linda assumed they were going to his dealer to pick up some pot, but instead they drove to the Holiday Inn in South Miami. Spotting an advertisement for the buffet lunch, she hoped they might eat because it was lunchtime and she was famished. Instead he told her he had to see some people on business.

Chuck led her down a corridor to the last room, knocked three times, and the door opened. Inside were five middle-aged men in suits. One greeted Traynor like an old friend. Linda learned that two were bankers, while the others ran small businesses. Excusing herself, she went to the bathroom. When she opened the door to return, Traynor was waiting in the dressing area. He said: "You know those five guys out there."

"Well—"

"You're going to fuck all five of them." To prove it, he pulled a revolver from his pants pocket.

"Don't do this, Chuck," she begged.

"Say your prayers," he replied. "Those guys out there got everything to lose and nothing to gain by saying anything. And that about sums it up for you, too. Take off your clothes or you are one fucking dead chick."

Trembling, too scared even to pray, she took off her clothes and, after composing herself, walked out naked into the room. Two of the men were already undressed.

For the next few hours the quintet played musical chairs on Linda's body, including a painful introduction to anal sex and double vaginal penetration. When all sexual possibilities and energy had been exhausted, Traynor looked down at her semen-splattered body and said, "You're a fucking mess. Go take a shower."

In the days, weeks, and months that followed, there came an unending stream of other johns, along with reinforcing threats, punches, kicks, and chokings from Traynor. As the business grew, he hired three other hookers—Moonshine, Debbie, Melody. They got any johns who were young and handsome, while Linda was always given the 350-pound mama's boys or the ones who liked to spank and whip. One wealthy customer just liked to watch her take a luxurious bubble bath.

Most of all, though, Linda's customers liked her unique knack of being able to swallow their penises without gagging. And if they were happy, Chuck was happy and did not beat her so often. Never once in all that time, though, or all the while she lived with Chuck, did she ever experience an orgasm. Deep-throating became just a way of keeping a man from putting his penis inside her and coming.

As THE SUMMER OF 1971 wore on, Traynor became increasingly obsessed with his upcoming trial on drug-smuggling charges. According to the prosecution, Traynor and two confederates had been caught carrying bales of marijuana and cocaine to their cars in a wooded area just south of Miami. The bales had been dropped from a plane. Traynor's defense was that he and his friends were forming a sky-diving club and accidentally stumbled on the bales while reconnoitering a possible landing sight.

Meanwhile, Linda Boreman had been offered $40,000 as an insurance settlement stemming from the injuries she sustained in her automobile accident. Traynor used the money to form a partnership, L. J. Enterprises, with his lawyer, who also advised Traynor that since Linda was not his wife, she could be called to testify against him. The next day, Traynor told her, "We're getting married tomorrow." When she objected, he struck her to the floor, then stomped on her.

Early the next morning, Chuck and Linda drove to the little town of Valdosta, Georgia, six hours from Miami. Along the way, he stopped at a novelty shop to buy a plastic wedding ring. After a brief ceremony performed by a justice of the peace, the newly wedded couple headed for a local diner and a banquet of cheeseburgers. That night he told her she could never charge him with a crime now, because he was her husband. Linda believed him.

At the end of the summer, Chuck and Linda headed for Aspen, Colorado, where one of his friends had opened a bar and needed a go-go dancer/after-hours hooker. Along the way, though, he informed her they were making a slight detour—to Juárez, Mexico, where he was going to enter her in a donkey-fucking contest. Linda never prayed so hard in her life: *Dear God, please don't let us get to Juárez, Mexico; please stop us from going to Juárez.*

Just outside Little Rock, Arkansas, God answered her prayer. Traynor's Volkswagen was rammed from behind by a station wagon, swerved into a ditch, and turned over. Neither was seriously hurt, but the car was totaled. With Juárez out of the picture, not to mention Aspen, Traynor decided they should bum a ride to New York.

In Jersey City, just across the Hudson River from Manhattan, Traynor found a cheap apartment for Linda and himself. With his last fifty dollars he went out and bought every sex tabloid he could find. "This is some town!" he told her while perusing the Help Wanted ads—French Instruction, English Leather Fanciers, TV Specialists. "They get away with stuff they haven't even thought of back in Miami." He was particularly attracted to the Models Wanted listings.

That first week Chuck and Linda visited a number of photographers, who referred them to sex club owners, who passed them on to madams, peep-show operators, and adult-bookstore owners. Everybody knew everybody, and by the end of the week Traynor knew them all, too. Later an eighteen-year-old hooker named Brandy, who had worked for Traynor in Miami, also arrived in Jersey City. Over the next few weeks, Brandy and Linda performed for a few Super 8 peep-show loops shot in a string of dingy studios off Times Square.

One day a director said to her, "We've been thinking of making a dog movie. Would that interest you?"

"No," she replied.

But Traynor was interested. He informed Linda and Brandy they would be starring in a dog movie the next day. When Brandy balked, Traynor threatened her for the first time. Later she drew Linda aside and told her she was leaving.

When Chuck and Linda returned later that night from a meeting with yet another director, Brandy was gone. Traynor fell into a dark rage, turning over furniture. Linda dreamed of dogs and decided even the worst beating of her life—which was surely in store for her if she refused to cooperate—was better than being raped by an animal. Not for the first time, she wondered why she did not have the courage to flee, like Brandy.

Early the next morning Traynor took her to a cluttered studio in the East Village. The director, large, greasy, black haired, at first complained that only one woman had shown up instead of the two as planned. Finally he turned to Linda and told her how much he appreciated her cooperation.

"I'm not letting any dog near me," she informed him.

The director exploded, but Traynor calmed him down. Then he ordered Linda to do the movie.

"I'd rather take the beating," she replied.

Traynor led her into the main room, where by now the director and his assistant were sitting beside a small table on which lay a revolver in plain view.

"Now are you *sure* you don't want to make the movie?" the director asked.

"You better be sure," the assistant said.

"Take off your clothes, cunt," Traynor commanded.

The odds against her—three men and a gun—seemed suddenly overwhelming. She reached up to unbutton her blouse, knowing that she was about to give up the last vestige of self-respect.

The plot was simple: a male actor fondles her enough to get her aroused, then abruptly departs on some pretext. Frustrated, she casts about, sees the dog, and has a bright idea. Traynor—the irony of his name stunned her. As directed, she got down on all fours, and a German shepherd mounted her from the rear—as it had obviously been trained to do. For more than an hour Linda, terrified of being bitten, fought off acute revulsion.

Finally the session ended.

"He could've handled two easily," the dog's owner proudly boasted.

The experience left Linda feeling totally defeated, more submissive than ever. It was the saddest, most wretched day of her life.

In 1978 a radical twenty-five-year-old Dutchman named Willem de Ridder was released from a Rhode Island jail, along with a fledgling porn star who performed under the name Annie Sprinkle, after her urological specialty. The charge: producing and modeling for, respectively, an artsy porn magazine that had just established a new benchmark in the hippie sport of *épater les bourgeois.*

A nationally known radio personality in Holland as well as a prominent figure in the anarcho-hippie Fluxus art movement, de Ridder was the European intellectual/sexual anarchist impresario par excellence. A charter member of the Organization for the Elimination of Time and Space, which refused to recognize the conventional limits set by dates, appointments, deadlines, pressures, and assorted social responsibilities, the bearded, macrobiotic Dutchman preferred instead to place a premium on the seemingly unending inspirations of the moment.

Back in the mid-sixties, after his first museum show convinced him that art was "finished," de Ridder had opened two nightclubs in Amsterdam, the Paradiso and the Fantasio, both of which immediately became extremely successful. To communicate with his customers, and to enable them to communicate with each other, he also began publishing a newspaper, *Hit Week,* whose main focus was ostensibly rock 'n' roll.

In fact, though, the lack of editorial censorship—or even of an editor— soon transformed much of the content into a freewheeling discussion of nearly every aspect of sexuality and sent the circulation skyrocketing. In true anarchist fashion de Ridder printed verbatim or uncropped whatever copy and photos his readers mailed in. In a small country, *Hit Week* was a big hit, and its cultural influence was enormous.

Meanwhile de Ridder also started up his own dance troupe, which performed in his clubs. The troupe always featured a series of unpredictable sexual images in its shows, which soon attracted the attention of various European newspapers. One of these was the *International Times* in London, edited by an American, William Levy. Two expatriate friends of Levy's from

Louisiana, James Haynes and Jack Moore, ran an arts laboratory. The three approached de Ridder, asking him to edit and lay out an international sex newspaper from Amsterdam since such an undertaking was too big a legal risk in England.

When de Ridder expressed interest, a delegation went to see him: journalist Heathcote Williams and his lover, fashion model Jean Shrimpton; Haynes; Levy; Williams; and a gangly, Australian-born sex radical, academic, part-time actress, and occasional contributor to the *London Sunday Times* on feminist issues, Germaine Greer. Greer, who had once been married to a truck driver for three weeks, had decided that marriage was debasing and espoused a group lifestyle. She was currently working on a seminal feminist tract, soon to be published as *The Female Eunuch,* that would become an international best-seller and instal. her as the Sexual Revolution's reigning intellectual.

At the meeting the group decided to call the new publication *Suck,* with Greer agreeing to serve as European editor. Its editorial philosophy was simple: sexual relationships should be open and unpossessive. Unlike *Screw,* which the group thought sadistic, treating female flesh like so much meat, *Suck*'s editorial policy was to renounce such imperialist, demeaning attitudes and, as its name implied, to orient itself around pleasure, not penises. The day after the first issue was printed, a delegation from Scotland Yard arrived. But they could not do anything. De Ridder smuggled the paper into England. Levy was thrown out of the country and started living in Amsterdam. Together the group began to prepare the second issue.

Greer was by far the most prominent and dominant voice of the publication and used it as her bully pulpit in a way that she could not when writing for the *Times.* In one issue Greer wrote: "To know cunt, it is also necessary to know how it works, and what it can do. While Masters and Johnson have done much to dispel those absurd presumptions about cunt, they could not be better than their subjects, and there is no reason why we should believe that what American middle class women taped to electrodes could do, is all that could have been done. . . ."

Responding to the frequently voiced criticism that feminists were puritanical, Greer noted that feminist puritanism was a reaction to the demands of an alternative culture that men put on women when they discovered sexual liberation. Suddenly women were expected to become sexual gymnasts and technicians.

Greer also railed against the missionary position, which placed the male in full control. Not only did it allow him to set the tempo and the degree of penetration, but the position removed the clitoris from contact except for "the shattering impact of pubic bone on pubic bone." Moreover, the missionary position required the woman, generally the lighter partner, to bear the man's weight. Far preferable, in Greer's view, was the female superior position, which left the hands of both parties free, allowed the woman to accept the penis without having to take on her partner's weight, permitted her to stroke his testicles and penis root, and even gave her the freedom to swivel or turn around.

"Any woman can be a good fuck lying on her back," Greer fumed, "but poised over her man and his rigid penis she must proceed with sensitivity and control, and with all her strength. Now she must cooperate, responding to her lover's spasms and trembling with delicate alterations in the speed and pressure of her movements. She can control the degrees of penetration, drawing herself up so that the smooth lips of her vagina nibble at the velvety head of her lover's penis, letting herself down again, slowing or swiftly, violently or softly, fluttering and squeezing him with her vaginal muscles which are now free to respond to her desires, instead of being deadened by the impact of the heavy male body. She is at last conscious of female potency, the secret power of her lovely, complex genitals."

De Ridder did not much care for Greer, who he thought used *Suck* as a mouthpiece for political statements. When a sadist wrote a piece on male domination, she vehemently protested, insisting the magazine should publish only material that was woman-positive. Such diatribes caused the anarchic, insouciant de Ridder gradually to lose interest in the publication.

Greer eventually resigned from *Suck* after receiving a letter from the editors requesting a nude picture of herself. All the editors wanted to publish nude photos of themselves, and Greer replied that she would do so when *Suck* had obtained a nude photo of Shrimpton. The editors replied that they already had a photo of Shrimpton, but it turned out to be a small photo of her montaged as Williams's erect penis. Greer herself appeared to *Suck*'s readers with both legs over her head, exposing her vagina. Later she complained that publication of the photos was a tasteless example of exhibitionism; she also criticized the degree of sadism in the publication and had been appalled that the issue was peddled at the Frankfurt Book Fair. In sum, she resigned. In sympathy, all the other editors resigned, too, while also managing to publish a full-frontal photo of Jean Shrimpton. Though unrepentantly penis oriented, Al Goldstein's *Screw* shamelessly reprinted many of Greer's articles, including one called "Do You Like Boobs a Lot?" and another in praise of masturbation, as well as the notorious nude photograph of the author.

Emboldened by *Suck*'s critical success, de Ridder and Levy decided to launch the world's first porn film festival. In late November 1970 an international collection of weirdos and sex freaks gathered in Amsterdam to observe the first international Wet Dream Festival, a de Ridder–inspired erotic free-for-all that, in fact, turned out to be a rather tedious, unerotic affair. The festival was sponsored by de Ridder's own Sexual Egalitarian & Liberation

Fraternity (SELF), which claimed 270 members and whose manifesto stated: "It is sexual frustration, sexual envy, sexual fear, which permeate all our human relationships and which pervert them. The sexually liberated, the sexually tolerant and the sexually generous individuals are open, tolerant and generous in all their activities. Therefore SELF wishes to encourage sexual freedom, sexual tolerance and sexual generosity."

The following year de Ridder got smart, scheduling the second Wet Dream Festival right after the Frankfurt Book Fair, which drew thousands of foreign visitors to Europe. The quality of the entries was notably better. Membership in SELF rose to 422.

At the film festival, held in one of de Ridder's nightclubs, the first three rows of the screening room were reserved for mutual masturbators, while elsewhere in the audience blow jobs were everywhere in evidence—all in accordance with SELF's dictum that if sexual freedom comes first, liberation follows.

Socializing took place at the Lido Club, large and homey, with an orgy room, eight-millimeter stag films, and hash cakes among the attractions. (Corpulent Al Goldstein, assuming they were simply food and being a cake freak, ate three at once.) The day before the festival ended, four hundred patrons crowded aboard a boat. As it toured the canals over the next seven hours, passengers were treated to more sex films, exotic food, and an orgy room featuring four water beds, while Dutch police remained discreetly in the background.

First prize went to *A Summer Day,* starring a farm girl and a canine. *Screw* publisher and festival judge Al Goldstein shrilly insisted that *Adultery for Fun and Profit* be declared the winner instead and wrote as much in his magazine. Greer, who was also a judge, was similarly outraged.

If anything, the atmosphere in Amsterdam was too liberated. Sales of *Suck* were plummeting in the wake of Denmark's legalization of pornography in 1969. De Ridder resolved to capitalize on the sex boom in more puritanical America by relocating to California.

In all *Suck* published only eight issues, which were distributed widely throughout Europe and America, compared to *Screw*'s weekly, advertiser-packed issues. Each issue was edited from the home of a person with a special interest in sex—the last in Stinson Beach, California, at the home of Dr. Hip (aka Eugene Schoenfeld). *Rolling Stone* staffers used to come over from San Francisco to help lay it out. Lack of nine-to-five editorial and advertising staffs contributed to *Suck*'s short life span, though the major factor was probably de Ridder's indifference to financial success.

After the magazine folded, de Ridder decided to move to Los Angeles and resume his old role of anarchic radio announcer. He also pioneered a toll-free sex line, using cassette tapes.

One day while browsing at a newsstand he discovered a magazine called

Finger, which announced that its next issue would be dedicated to the "legendary European publication *Suck.*"

"This is interesting," de Ridder said to himself, and went directly to Beverly Hills, where the *Finger* folk were flabbergasted to see the legendary editor himself in the doorway. De Ridder personally edited the next issue, changing the format from a newspaper to a magazine and introducing America in the process to the first completely reader-written sex magazine. It was a big success. Letters poured in, and each subsequent issue of the magazine sold out. Each letter was published as written, full of raw language and misspellings, with the briefest of introductions. De Ridder thought of himself as publisher of America's autobiography on the installment plan.

Unfamiliar, though, with the sensibilities of Americans, de Ridder also found himself reading letters he was not prepared for. About 80 percent were about incest, mostly from people talking about how they had great memories of sex with their parents and now did it with their own kids. There was also the letter from the college professor who collected his feces for months in a bathtub, then took a bath in it—and Polaroid shots. But perhaps the most gruesome was the letter from a surgeon who claimed he was slowly amputating parts of his wife's body—a finger here, a toe there—with the goal that she might ultimately wind up as a human suitcase. By his account, she loved it.

De Ridder surmised that his reader-writers were testing him, but he published whatever was sent in. As marketing strategy, his unblinking commitment not to censor paid off: on newsstands where it was displayed, *Finger* outsold *Playboy.*

De Ridder had rented the penthouse next to the magazine's office, but he had a lot of problems with the Los Angeles Police Department. To evade raids, every week he had someone in the office signal via telephone who was waiting for him. Ultimately the magazine relocated to a mansion that had been owned by Gary Cooper.

Like most hard-core sex magazines, *Finger* was distributed by the Mafia. That arrangement proved to be mutually beneficial until one day the high-flying Dutchman announced he was now going to publish an even more outrageous magazine called *God.* All hell broke loose. De Ridder agreed to change the name to *g,* but some agents from the FBI, alerted by all the media coverage about the impending publication of the magazine, paid a visit. Even the Manson family began to send cassettes to radio stations, saying that the makers of the magazine *g* were corrupting the morals of America and were targeted for murder.

With the Mafia, the FBI, and the Manson family threatening him in succession, de Ridder justifiably began to feel a little paranoid. He started getting calls in the middle of the night. His partner, Maxmillian "Mickey" Leblovic, a half-Italian, half-Czech pornographer who claimed royal blood and called himself a prince, was scared out of his wits and wanted to leave the country as soon as possible.

To placate him, de Ridder returned to Europe, where the two resumed publication of a magazine called *Love*, first in Holland, then in a villa in Santa Margherita Ligure, Italy. Intermittently, de Ridder continued to be involved in numerous non-sex-oriented enterprises, such as a performance-art radio program that got thirty thousand listeners simultaneously to stop their automobiles in a simulation of Orson Welles's broadcast of H. G. Wells's *The War of the Worlds*.

After a while, Leblovic and his family returned to the United States, settling near Newport, Rhode Island, where they continued to publish *Love* on their own. De Ridder chose to continue with another magazine, called *Hate*.

One day Mickey phoned de Ridder and said he had just found the most incredible porn star, Annie Sprinkle, who had performed in something like fifty porn flicks and now wanted to publish her diary. Mickey asked de Ridder if he would be willing to do the layout. When de Ridder agreed, Mickey sent him a ticket and he flew to New York.

AFTER GRADUATING from high school, Marco Vassi had briefly entered a Franciscan monastery as a novice, only to leave a few weeks later to enroll at Iona College, a Catholic institution in a suburb of New York City. College had not suited him well, either. Now that he was Marco Vassi, sex visionary, he often liked to claim he was a priest without a church, an apostle without a savior. His religion was to explore the depths of degradation, the towers of ecstasy, his roles as erotic artist—male lesbian, perfected bisexual, androgyne.

In his journalism Marco frequently inveighed against monogamy, claiming it was a form of sexual slavery imposed by church and society. (Marriage, though, was another thing. He married for a third time, to a woman named Royce, whom he had dated for only three months when he was living with another woman and she was seeing two other men.)

In an article for *Screw* in 1972 entitled "Beyond Bisexuality," Marco presented three portraits of himself: one with a long, feminine braid of hair down his back; another with half his face shaven, half sporting a beard; and a third showing him in black tights. In the accompanying text he declared that he had "fucked or been fucked by over five hundred different women, and twice that many men, in circumstances ranging from brief graspings in alleys and whorehouses to lengthy relationships. . . . At the far edge of bisexuality I realized that all that had gone before was but the task of perfecting the instrument, the mindbody that is myself." The many modes of sex—heterosexuality, homosexuality, bisexuality, abstruse psychological states and practices, yoga, the so-called perversions—"were now at my command, to be used the way a director uses a cast of characters to realize a vision."

Lacking an adequate term to describe his sexual constitution, he coined the word "metasexuality" and referred to himself as a metasexual—the only one, moreover, that he knew. Though a priest of perversion, he had no desire to proselytize or change anyone, only to describe the mysteries of lust he had seen. To go beyond bisexuality meant first of all the "healing of the male-female split within the individual." Many were called, very few chosen.

In the spring of 1975 Marco gave a series of talks on eroticism at Anthos, a human potential center in New York, telling the audience: "I have transcended bisexuality. I am capable at any time, with any person, of any kind of erotic trip whatsoever. I have mastered the eroticum. I can call forth instant passion, instant expertise, instant involvement, all of these things, like a master actor on the stage."

He considered his sexual calling a "high, pure, austere path," or sexual Zen. Metasex, Marco elaborated, meant taking a woman through a "two-hour ritual" consisting of a half hour of foreplay, "an hour of solid fucking," and another half hour devoted to "mutual appreciation." Except for the occasional orgy, when he found the stamina to endure for hours, he considered such two-hour programs the "rice and beans" of his erotic life.

When Marco turned thirty-five, he marked the occasion by getting a tattoo on the inside of his left forearm. He had spent three months composing the design—a half-inch symbol consisting of Gurdjieffian concentric circles and jagged lines that he fancied provided a key to the occult world. Later he met Spider Webb, a lanky longtime hippie who ran a tattoo parlor in Mount Vernon, just north of New York City. In 1977 tattooing was still associated with circus freaks and drunken sailors and was illegal in New York City. Webb did Marco's second tattoo, a stylized three-inch-long vagina in three colors, just below his navel.

Throughout the seventies Marco frequently had sex with strange men behind the trucks near the Hudson River in Greenwich Village while police cars prowled past, flashing searchlights into the shadows. Once, at four in the morning, he decided to make a spontaneous statement about sexual freedom by lying down in the middle of Columbus Avenue and masturbating. Fortunately, he chose a moment when no cars or pedestrians passed by.

Once a man rimming him asked Marco to defecate in his mouth. Marco was shocked to the point of being sickened. Yet later he realized that coprophiliacs, though suffering from abysmally low self-esteem, were perhaps the only people who had the courage to face the most primitive of all inhibitions: the inability to defecate in front of another. This gave him the insight that what is called perversion is the most useful map for understanding the true nature of fascism, and the most powerful key to unlocking its hold on people.

As a result of that insight, the next time he was being penetrated and felt the pain closing in on him, Marco allowed his bowels to loosen freely. "Oh, beautiful, baby," said his partner, his pelvis whipping frantically with re-newed energy. Marco simply lay there, no longer afraid of what might pour out of him, rejoicing in the man's joy. Who he was, what his name or personal history was, did not matter. He was a man, he was a human, he was a meta-sexual.

While visiting the baths, being taken from behind six or eight times in the evening by different men, Marco often felt himself become pure malleable flesh. Each time he tried to assume a different persona to suit the personality of the man doing him, while feeling cold liquid flashes up his spine as his deepest muscular tensions melted away.

After several encounters, though, came the pain, and with it a conceit of himself as the eternal victim, an erotic Christ suffering for the gratification of others, giving himself up entirely to satisfy the needs of hungry men. Enter-ing the kingdom of Genet, he now viewed himself, with characteristic self-absorbed aplomb, as the holy degenerate.

Chapter 7

The Scene

GERARD DAMIANO WAS A MARRIED MAN WITH CHILDREN WHO LIVED IN QUEENS, New York, and a successful hairdresser. But operating three salons and owning three Cadillacs was not satisfying enough. In fact, he felt miserable and unfulfilled. In 1967 he began hanging around porn sets and locations and before long had worked his way into directing films.

Damiano had seen Linda Boreman in several stag movies and eventually hired her to be in some of his own. For Linda it was a giant step up—going from a dirty loft in Times Square to a studio operated by the hard-core equivalent of Cecil B. DeMille. When *he* made films, Damiano actually used a crew.

Traynor had told Damiano about Linda's ability to swallow a penis without gagging. Damiano thought he might be on to something. One day while driving into Manhattan he had a vision—a thirty-five-millimeter film about a woman whose clitoris was in the back of her throat. Only by performing deep-throat fellatio could she ever climax. When he got to work, he excitedly told Traynor about his plan.

"Hey, that's cool," Traynor said with a shrug.

"I've even got a title," Damiano went on. "*Deep Throat*. It came to me all at once."

Damiano's partner, Lou Peraino, though, was not impressed. "No one will understand it," he told Damiano. "It's not catchy enough."

His alternative: *The Sword Swallower.*

But Damiano was resolute. "*Deep Throat* will become a household word," he replied, or so he claimed later.

As plans moved slowly forward to make the film—for a budget of $25,000, or many times that of the usual Super 8 loop—Peraino began to have other reservations. So what, he asked aloud, if Linda Boreman could do this deep-throat thing? She was too skinny and her breasts were too small to appear in a porn film, especially an expensive one.

By now Traynor was fretting. Linda had been promised $100 a day for her role in the film—for a total of $1,200. That was big money.

"We could get Lou to change his mind," he told Linda, "if you just go in there and give him a blow job."

Soon afterward Traynor met with Peraino in his office, then signaled for Linda to join them. When she was alone with Peraino, he told her to lock the door.

"C'mon," he said. "Let's get this over with."

He had already undone his zipper.

Every day afterward, the same routine was repeated. Even so, Peraino continued to complain to Damiano that his investment was going down the drain.

Deep Throat was shot in Miami. For the role, Damiano had come up with a new name for Linda—Linda Lovelace, the alliteration modeled after Brigitte Bardot and Marilyn Monroe. To Linda the new surname seemed better than Boreman or Traynor. Several members of the production crew also befriended her and offered to help if her husband ever beat her again. But he did beat her regularly, and she did not protest. By now being physically and emotionally abused had become habitual.

Linda's costar was Harry Reems, who had entered the New York theater scene in the mid-sixties as a member of the avant-garde ensemble at Cafe La Mama and the National Shakespeare Company. After meeting a husband-and-wife team who made stag movies, he performed in a Super 8 loop with actress Tina Russell and was soon working a stunning three hundred days a year.

The big scene in *Deep Throat* occurred when Reems, playing a doctor, discovers that Linda's sex-starved character has a misplaced clitoris and offers his penis as a means of relief.

After shooting, Traynor, Linda, Damiano, and the others returned to New York, where the film was to be edited. Traynor expected *Deep Throat* to be reviewed in a few underground sex newspapers, then vanish. In his view Linda was little more than a one-trick pony, and the only way to establish her as a real porn actress was to endow her with breasts.

During the six months between postproduction and premiere, Traynor forced Linda to undergo silicone injections to increase her bust size from a 34B to a 36C. Payment for the injections, performed after hours in a doctor's office, was oral sex.

In June 1972 *Deep Throat* opened at Bob Sumner's New World Theater in

Times Square. But after assorted underground New York critics gave the film rave notices, it immediately took off as both a box office hit and a media event. One of the first to call for an interview with the star was *Screw,* which had bestowed on the movie its first 100 rating on the Peter Meter.

After the interview, *Screw* publisher Al Goldstein asked Linda if she would personally deep-throat him. She agreed. He found it a very lonely experience and suspected it was the same for her. Nothing about the encounter was spontaneous; it was a mere mechanical reenactment of her cinematic prowess. As his penis disappeared into her mouth, he could not have been more miserable. But not as miserable as Lovelace herself.

In Los Angeles the film opened at the Pussycat Theater on Santa Monica Boulevard, part of the Pussycat chain co-owned by David Friedman. At first the *Los Angeles Times* refused to allow even the title of the movie in its advertising columns. The movie took in $24,000 the first week, but sales declined the second and third week. Then *Time* magazine came out with a story about the *Deep Throat* phenomenon, the *Times* reversed its advertising policy, and the weekly gross shot up to $90,000.

Within days, Traynor and Linda, who had remained in New York, began receiving invitations to parties from the rich and famous. Sammy Davis Jr. turned out to be an especially big fan of Linda Lovelace and invited her to his suite at the Waldorf-Astoria. Virtually overnight Linda Lovelace, abused wife and recalcitrant porn star, became an international celebrity.

Then *Playboy* invited the pair out to Los Angeles for an interview and a photo spread. At a party, the bedazzled Traynor and Lovelace met guests like Warren Beatty, Goldie Hawn, Elizabeth Taylor, Peter Lawford, and Clint Eastwood. Hefner told Lovelace how much he enjoyed *Deep Throat,* which he had screened several times at the mansion. Later he also complimented her on the movie she made with the dog.

As celebrities of the moment, Traynor and Lovelace quickly became members of Playboy Mansion West's inner circle, joining the other freeloaders every Wednesday—orgy night—for movies, buffet dinner, and wee-hour sex. Pinnacle Books gave the pair a $50,000 advance to write a book on deep-throat technique. Traynor used part of the money to buy himself another Jaguar, now that they were driving in the fast lane. Every week, it seemed, Linda was being whisked away for an appearance on *The Tonight Show,* a cover shoot for *Esquire,* or an interview with a newspaper.

Yet Traynor always kept his eye on the next big prize: *Deep Throat Part II.* He was also plotting how to get Linda in bed with Hugh Hefner, a man who could be of inestimable help in advancing her—that is, Traynor's—fame and fortune. There was just one slight problem. Lately Hefner seemed more interested in backgammon than sex, sometimes playing for up to twenty hours at a time.

One Wednesday orgy night, though, Hefner showed up. All the regulars sporting about the pool and grotto looked up expectantly. When Hefner stepped into the Jacuzzi, Traynor nudged Lovelace to join him. But the *Playboy* publisher made no move to seduce her.

Instead of approaching him directly, Linda and another woman began to perform cunnilingus on each other, while everybody gathered in a circle to watch. Finally an aroused Hefner approached, quickly entered Lovelace doggie style, and came. As soon as it was over, he left. Traynor, though, was very pleased.

A few nights later, Lovelace was summoned to the mansion's bathhouse. All the guests had gone home, and she noticed that security guards were posted. Inside the bathhouse she found Hefner and Traynor waiting for her. As usual, the publisher was dressed in pajamas and bathrobe, and as soon as she entered he began talking about how excited he was. Also waiting was a large dog named Rufus.

"Okay, Linda," Traynor said, "take off your clothes."

Linda stripped as told, knelt down, and waited, knowing it was useless to resist. Hefner was unaware that she was submitting to this performance against her will, though that certainly did not exonerate him from moral culpability in her degradation. Rufus mounted, then backed off. Hefner was very understanding.

"Well," he said, sighing, "these things happen."

As the whirlwind of publicity continued, Linda gradually began to have a sense of herself as her own person. On a trip to New York she also entered into an affair with Sammy Davis Jr. and became a member of his jet-set coterie as well. They even talked of marriage.

One night Davis, Linda, and Traynor were watching a porn film in the entertainer's private screening room, and Davis—high on either cocaine, amyl nitrite, or both—asked Linda for a lesson in deep-throating. At that moment, she saw how she might finally get her revenge, pathetic as it was, on her husband. Whispering to him in the darkness that he should unzip his pants, she gestured for Davis to crawl over to Traynor and fellate him. Only after a few moments did Traynor realize what was happening, and for the duration of Davis's eager performance he silently glared at his wife.

Soon afterward, having achieved a measure of financial independence, Linda finally worked up the courage to leave Traynor. For a long time after she would only appear in public disguised in wigs and sunglasses. Renouncing porn, she also tried her hand on the legitimate stage. When that flopped, she did another X-rated film. Later she wrote a tell-all autobiography, *Ordeal,* revealing many of the sordid details of her treatment at the hands of Traynor—who in turn vigorously denied using Linda in bestiality films and prostitution.

By some estimates *Deep Throat* was one of the all-time top-grossing films in moviemaking history, earning a reputed $100 million. Damiano's profit amounted to a mere $15,000. The rest went to Lou Peraino and his associates.

In 1972 Damiano made *The Devil in Miss Jones,* starring Georgina Spelvin, about a woman who commits suicide, cannot go to heaven as a result, and cannot go to hell because she has not sinned enough. Detouring to Hades, she meets Harry Reems, who agrees to boost her sin count. Though Damiano was able to command a $200,000 fee, most of that money went to defending himself against obscenity charges federal prosecutors brought against *Deep Throat* in New York, Tucson, Memphis, and elsewhere, determined that no movie like it would ever be made again.

IN THE FALL OF 1969 a pale young music teacher in the New York public school system took a sabbatical from his job to go on tour with the General Platoff Don Cossack Chorus, at the time a well-known company. In the spring he joined the chorus on another tour. Crisscrossing the country on the bus, he found himself with lots of time to think and fantasize.

All his life he had been consumed by fantasies of submissive and masochistic sex, but every time he got up enough courage to tell a girl, or later a woman, how he felt, the relationship fell apart. On the road, he resolved that when he returned to New York, he would finally do something to make his fantasies of being whipped and dominated come true.

Aware of the growing crop of underground sex publications sprouting up, he decided to run a personal advertisement seeking compatible SM partners, but with a difference. In particular, the teacher also called on other masochists like himself to band together and do something for their common interest. The publication he chose to run his advertisement in was *Screw,* which seemed the most popular and outrageous of the lot.

The advertisement ran: "Masochist? Happy? Is it curable? Does psychiatry help? Is a satisfactory life-style possible? There's women's lib, black lib, gay lib, etc. Isn't it time we put something together? Write Box . . ."

Five people answered the advertisement, and a meeting at the teacher's small apartment on the Lower East Side was set up for a Sunday afternoon in January 1971, though only two people actually showed up. One was a man named Terry Kolb; the other failed to appear at the second meeting.

Although the Stonewall riot was almost two years old, the SM subculture was still diffuse, surviving mainly as an informal sideshow in a few gay leather bars. Unknown to the teacher at the time, others were also championing virtually all aspects of consensual sex, including SM, over New York's radical radio station, WBAI. Kolb, the teacher, and another man decided to rerun the advertisement in *Screw* and also to place it in the *East Village Other* and *The Village Voice*. But the latter turned down the advertisement, explaining: "We don't run ads for masochists."

Undeterred, though not exactly swamped with replies, the three masochists agreed to call their fledgling organization the Masochist Liberation Society. Later the name was changed to the Eulenspiegel Society, after a connection made by Theodor Reik in *Masochism in Modern Man* between the psychology of masochists and the personality of the legendary German folk character Till Eulenspiegel, who preferred to climb rather than descend mountains. Kolb also picketed the *Voice* until a sympathetic columnist interviewed him. The resulting publicity brought in a substantial number of new members, and Kolb later wrote an article for the publication entitled "Masochist Lib," along with an article by P. N. Dedeux called "Sade Lib." Once those articles were safely published, the picketing of the *Voice* resumed until the advertisement was accepted.

When the first consciousness-raising sessions began, there were usually no more than a dozen people at a meeting. Almost all the participants testified that only when they heard others speak out were they finally convinced that they were not alone in their sexual proclivities.

By July 1971 the members of the Eulenspiegel Society had screwed up the courage to hold their first public meeting. Since the teacher was scheduled to work in an elementary school that fall, he resolved to use another name just in case the media showed up. The name he planned on adopting was Prometheus Bond, which he often used for writing letters to the *Voice*. Someone later called him Pat by mistake, and from that point on he became known as Pat Bond.

After a series of organizational meetings, the Eulenspiegel Society decided to broaden its focus from masochists to all orientations of SM—tops, bottoms, straights, gays, bisexuals, lesbians. At the same time it also elected chairs, none of whom ever showed up again. Obviously organization was not an SM strong point. Over the years, though, something like an informal board of directors—with names like Candy, Brother Leo, Goldie—finally took shape. Pat Bond, though, remained Eulenspiegel's driving force, lecturing and holding public seminars on SM lib. While all members agreed on the principles reflected in their creed, most were so pansexual in orientation and inventive in sexual exploration that Bond was often led to think, "I am *not* a normal pervert!"

Not surprisingly, one of the Eulenspiegel Society's charter members was Marco Vassi.

In 1974 another SM organization open to all sexual orientations, the Society of Janus, was formed in San Francisco. Samois, a strictly lesbian group, was later replaced by the Outcasts, led by Pat Califia, a well-known writer/activist in the SM community.

*   *   *

As a shy, gangly teenager, Ellen Steinberg volunteered on archaeological digs to ancient volcanoes deep in Latin America, visited Colombia and Costa Rica, went deep-sea fishing, swam in the Panama Canal, and hung out at local casinos in Panama City, where her family had moved when she turned thirteen. The oldest of four children in a Jewish Unitarian family, she had been born in Philadelphia on July 23, 1953. After eight years in Los Angeles, her father was transferred to Panama, where Ellen went to high school.

Growing up, Ellen enjoyed a loving, nurturing relationship with her progressive, middle-class parents. Yet she had a wild streak that nothing could harness. At age seventeen, after graduating from high school, she ran off with a twenty-six-year-old motorcyclist named Van whom she met at a hippie coffee shop in Panama City. Not only was she a virgin, she had never even masturbated.

But that year all orgasmic hell broke loose. Heading for Tucson, Arizona, the pair lived as hippies in an artist community in the desert for six months. During that time she had sex with fifty-two men, keeping a list of their names and writing down brief descriptions of what they did. Sex was not only fun, a creative outlet, it was also liberating. Barefoot and braless, she panhandled for cigarettes and Tampax, occasionally smuggled pot from Mexico, and lived in a house where the rent was seldom paid.

After she and Van broke up, Ellen asked a friend who claimed to be a witch to cast a spell over her. The friend obliged. A week later Ellen went to work as a masseuse. Since she was fluent in Spanish, many of her clients were Hispanic. Ellen thought of herself not as a hooker, but as a very horny, promiscuous woman. The job seemed tailor-made.

Later she took a job as cashier at a porn theater in Tucson, which was showing a movie sweeping the nation called *Deep Throat*. Unfortunately, the state of Arizona was prosecuting the producers and distributors of the film, and Ellen was subpoenaed. In the witness waiting room she met Gerard Damiano, the film's director. Awestruck, she flirted, asking if he would teach her how to deep-throat, and the two became lovers. At the time, he was forty-six and married with two children; she was eighteen. After the trial, Ellen flew back with Damiano to New York.

Through Al Goldstein, Damiano got Ellen a job at Spartacus Spa on East Fifty-third Street, a twenty-four-hour, seven-day-a-week establishment where male clients were attended by two women with a program including sauna, cream or oil rub, hot compresses and lemon facial treatment, and champagne, at a cost of $50 an hour. At Spartacus Ellen turned tricks on the side.

During the week she apprenticed filmmaking at Kirt Studios, a maker of hard-core films, though refusing owner Leonard Kirtman's offer to be in the movies herself because she still hoped one day to be a high school art teacher and thought a porn background would ruin her chances. Her scruples lasted eight months—until Kirtman persuaded his protegée to star in a crude sexvid called *Teenage Masseuse,* playing opposite Harry Reems, star of *Deep Throat.*

The persona of Annie Sprinkle was not long in emerging. Whereas Ellen was excruciatingly shy, Annie was an exhibitionist. Ellen wore orthopedic shoes and flannel nightgowns. Annie favored six-inch spiked heels and fetish lingerie. The daily rate for acting in a porn film was $150—not enough to live on since shooting seldom lasted more than two days. To earn extra money, Annie, like many porn stars, continued to work as a prostitute on the side.

In her first few films, Ellen was billed as Annie Sands. The change to Sprinkle flowed naturally from her uninhibited *joie de urolagnie* on screen. As Annie, she also adopted a stage lisp that accentuated the silly-naughty roles she usually played—a bored suburban housewife in *Seduction,* a jungle nurse in *MASH'D.* She also got into the magazine end of porn, both as model—her first centerfold was in *Cheri*—and as photojournalist, writing articles about the sex world for *High Society* and other publications.

Altogether Annie spent eight years in the massage parlors. Some clients treated her roughly, others simply left without paying. Once she heard a friend in another booth scream when a patron tried to bite off her clitoris. Annie also lived in constant fear of arrest and was forever bailing friends out of jail. For long periods she also became sexually jaded and confused, not wanting to be touched. Yet she never got arrested or contracted a venereal disease, and for the most part she found the job of prostitute satisfying—a way of helping people, like being a nurse.

In her first few years as a porn actress, Annie made fifty feature films and two dozen Super 8 loops and ultimately starred in 150 features, 20 videos, and 50 loops. In 1978 she met Mickey and Susan Leblovic, a couple with two children who lived in Rhode Island and published a cottage-industry sex magazine called *Love,* written entirely by its readers.

Raw, honest, crude, *Love* published whatever its readers sent in, not only without censorship but without editing, including outrageous sex pictures. The Leblovics invited Annie to make her own special edition of the magazine, using excerpts from her diary and photos other magazines would not touch. Best news of all was that their friend and partner, Willem de Ridder, was flying over from Holland to be the issue's art director.

ARRIVING FROM AMSTERDAM at JFK Airport, de Ridder took a commuter plane to Jamestown, Rhode Island, where Mickey Leblovic met him with a limousine. Sitting in the backseat was Annie Sprinkle, star of the show, dressed in Salvation Army castoffs. De Ridder, who had never heard of her, was less than impressed. Not only did she not look like much of a porn star, but she did not even seem particularly sexy. But he adored her high, girlish voice, which to his European ear sounded typically American.

At the rented villa, Mickey had amassed all the necessary equipment, including a secretary to perform typesetting and other chores. The special was a *Love-Hate* joint issue on Annie Sprinkle's diaries, and de Ridder was determined to make it a masterpiece.

Previously de Ridder had proposed that they invite as extras some friends with whom he had worked in Los Angeles—among them a huge "mountain girl" named Queen Andrena who appeared in dominance flicks under the name Queen Kong. Queen Andrena arrived in Jamestown with Long Jean Silver, a beautiful young amputee whose leg was so small at one end that it resembled a large penis. As a result she was a popular attraction in porn flicks and sex shows.

After the photo session, all three were sitting around the fireplace when in marched the typesetter, who turned out to be an undercover policewoman. Following behind the typesetter was a phalanx of twenty-five FBI agents, local police, and press, complete with TV cameras and lights. In the advertisement that Mickey placed in a local college paper, he had warned that the material would be sexually explicit, and a suspicious reader had alerted police. The police confiscated everything from tampons and diaries to magazine paste-up boards. Prince Mickey defiantly proclaimed, "You can confiscate all of our magazines, all of our pictures, all of our materials. But you cannot take away our minds." De Ridder, who got chained and handcuffed with Annie, suddenly felt very important.

Both the Leblovics and de Ridder were booked on charges of sodomy, violating state law on child pornography—on the unfounded assumption that the Leblovics' two children were involved—and circulating obscene adult pornography. Annie was arraigned on felony charges of sodomy, conspiracy to commit sodomy, and conspiring to circulate adult pornography. Bail was set from $1,000 to $6,000 for the various defendants, while the Leblovics' children were seized by child welfare officials.

The next day the headlines announced that members of an international porn ring with connections in Italy, Los Angeles, and Amsterdam had been arrested in a local villa.

The jail was cold, and all six were deprived of blankets and toothbrushes. Yet Susan, Jean, Queen Andrena, and Annie, who shared a cell, kept their spirits alive by singing freedom songs: "Ain't nobody gonna turn me 'round / Turn me 'round / Turn me 'round / I'm gonna keep on suckin', keep on fuckin', march into the freedom land." When they were finally taken before a judge, Annie found herself handcuffed once again to de Ridder, and at that moment they fell in love. She was twenty-four, he thirty-nine.

Released after forty-eight hours, the Leblovics, Annie, and de Ridder retired to a nearby motel to regroup and plan their next move. While they were there the motel owner appeared and said a lawyer would be arriving shortly to see them. It turned out that the *capo di tutti capi* of the regional Mafia lived in Newport, and the lawyer was his consigliere. Mickey Leblovic explained how they were going to defend themselves, and the lawyer was quite amazed. They gathered the Mafia did not look on them as competitors.

De Ridder tried to explain that they were publishing pornography because they wanted to develop sexuality. But the lawyer could not understand why anybody would publish or read such materials except to make money. He offered to help defend de Ridder and Mickey.

Mickey, though, insisted on defending himself. Eventually all charges against Annie and Willem were dropped. If they had been prosecuted, every handicapped person in Rhode Island would have been liable. But Mickey spent a year in jail and Susan several months. She was pregnant when she went in, and she went into labor while wearing handcuffs. The Leblovics' two children, meanwhile, were temporarily sent to foster homes.

After being released from jail, Willem and Annie drove back to her New York apartment and created an Annie Sprinkle *Hot Shit* magazine in three days, with friend Bobby Hanson reshooting photos of Annie and Long Jean. The issue sold out quickly. Meanwhile, de Ridder wanted to move back to his Villa Genesi in San Felice Cerceo, halfway between Naples and Rome, and asked Annie to join him. By now she was suffering from prostitution burnout, and she agreed.

For the next eighteen months they lived idyllically in de Ridder's blue-terraced, twelve-bathroom villa with its lush garden overlooking the Mediterranean that cost an astronomical $1,800 a month. He taught her cooking, macrobiotics especially. Soon she was making her own tofu, grinding her own grains, reading, and meditating. They also worked on radio plays together. Willem earned a living recording his radio show for broadcast in Holland; it was the first and last time a man supported her. Meanwhile, both also practiced the weirdest sex they had ever known—monogamy. They even flirted with the idea of getting married, and Annie was tempted to go off birth control and have a baby. Though never more than a casual drug user, she also gave up all drugs during this period.

But after a year Annie found herself growing bored and longing for the excitement and wild sex of New York. Willem, though, had seen enough of America for the time being. He returned to Holland, and they went their separate ways.

* * *

THE SCENE, as the SM world was known, was dubbed by Al Goldstein "a great greasy beast, coiling around in the bowels of the nighttime populations" of three or four cities in America—San Francisco, Los Angeles, maybe Chicago, and, of course, Scene Central, New York. Only around two o'clock in the morning, when the rest of the world was safely abed, did the beast emerge from its daytime camouflage in a handful of anonymous clubs in some deserted part of town.

One indication of the burgeoning popularity of the Scene was the experience of a San Francisco sandal maker who called himself Nick O'Demus. In 1968 Nick was quietly asked by a few customers to custom-make harnesses for some SM games they liked to play. Word got around, and he soon found himself with a new product line.

By 1976 Nick employed eighteen people at his Trading Post Enterprises, grossing $500,000 a year from the manufacture of bondage fashions, whips, chains, and other devices, mostly for the gay trade, and selling them on the premises in a cluster of boutiques. SM had become, if not big business, a significant niche market.

America got its first real peek at subterranean sex in December 1965, when a police raid on dominatrix Monique Van Cleef's Newark torture chamber was smeared across the nation's tabloids. At the same time, a superb film version of Jean Genet's *The Balcony,* set in the bordello of a dominatrix, was playing in the nation's art houses. Men who ruled society went to the brothel to act out masochistic fantasies and be humiliated by whores and others occupying the lowest rungs of the social ladder.

Apart from such tame clues, however, and despite a wave of promiscuity engulfing almost every state of the Union, the Scene remained the Sexual Revolution's dirtiest little secret, a world where conventional sexual values were not only inverted but stomped on, in the form of sadomasochism, bondage and discipline, infantilism (involving men who liked to dress up in diapers), and every variety of paraphilia.

Like tennis, SM was a game played according to very strict rules, and no responsible dominatrix (or "top") ever transgressed beyond the limits set, often moment by moment, by the humiliated or violated victim (or "bottom"), a situation that led to endless speculation over who was really in command. An intricate method of physical and psychological control, SM was not only the most physical but also the most intellectual variant of kink.

The masochist also usually possessed the "safe-word"—such as "yellow" for "caution" and "red" for "stop now." Most sadists were interested, conversely, in giving pleasure as well as receiving it. Many SM relationships were loving ones, which was in essence the difference between SM and mere acts of violence sometimes depicted in sexually explicit materials. And it was a common predilection. Even as early as the 1940s Kinsey had found that book dealers sold as much SM material as all other sex-related material combined. Most people engaged, moreover, in mild sadomasochism: bites, scratches, hickeys. In the masochistic libido, a link existed between pain and eroticism. As the masochist became sexually aroused, his—or, less often, her—pain threshold commensurately rose. He was able to tolerate pain that in other circumstances would be unendurable because the person or act inflicting or causing the pain was charged with erotic significance.

Many animal and insect species also engaged in SM-like behavior, most famously the male mink, which during copulation virtually raped the female, sinking its teeth deep into her pelt before inserting his penis. Some researchers suggested, based on that and other observations, that SM behavior might be part of a genetic inheritance.

The Scene began in the late sixties when an obscure club called the Hellfire opened in Manhattan's meat-packing district near the wharves along the Hudson River. Housed illegally in a damp, anonymous, black-on-black basement with its own water-sports room, a dark labyrinth of doorless cubicles, and an impressive array of hardware, the Hellfire reeked of stale sex and urine. A visitor's first impression was one of unremitting foulness, random globs of dripping black water, a challenge to the stomach as well as the libido.

Its name harking back to the notorious secret society founded by Sir Francis Dashwood in eighteenth-century England, the Hellfire attracted sexual adventurers of every description: straights, bisexuals, drag queens, sadists, masochists, fist fuckers, masturbators, voyeurs, and especially gay leathermen, who were then reveling in their he-man heyday.

Miniscenes within the Scene varied from night to night: a pretty, flat-chested, long-nippled blonde upended and hung by her heels, as a team of four doms—three men and a lesbian—worked her over, inserting two dildos into her anus, one after the other. In a corner an elderly gentleman with the body of a white slug, hairless and naked except for black-framed glasses, sat on a love-chair, legs propped up on struts, offering his puckered anus to the crowd. A frequent fixture in the doorless toilet was the crouching figure of the Psycho Wimp, a pale young white man whose open mouth perpetually invited use as a urinal.

In addition to alcohol and drugs like amyl nitrite or "poppers" to enhance orgasm, jars of K-Y jelly and a variety of SM gear were also on sale. In back was a maze of glory holes, body racks, and staging areas for whipping or other exhibitions. Patrons ejaculated, urinated, and defecated anywhere they wanted. Guys from New Jersey, couples from Wall Street, good old boys from Texas mingled with the regulars, disgust and excitement on their faces.

In subsequent years, as SM doms began to advertise their services in magazines, places like the Anvil and Mineshaft began to compete with the Hellfire. But for a long time it was the only and biggest game in town.

In this dank and dangerous paradise of perversion, and others like it, the seed of an apocalyptic plague was also probably first incubated and indiscriminately transmitted. At first a relatively weak virus that attacked the human immune system, it was passed from one person to another through the repeated commingling of blood or semen. Those whose immune systems had already been weakened by drug use or a previous sex-disease history were particularly vulnerable. In the Hellfire dungeon all those conditions were not merely met but exceeded in wretched excess.

Yet the AIDS epidemic still lay in the future—though not a very far-off one. In the meantime, the "great greasy beast" roamed free in at least one place on the planet, where the only thing banned was the mere thought of a sexual inhibition.

A week after Annie returned from Italy to New York, she became not only a regular at the Hellfire, but a club attraction. After eighteen months of monogamy with de Ridder, she had stored up an A-bomb's worth of libidinal energy. The Hellfire was her ground zero.

Every Friday and Saturday night Annie went to the club, outfitted in zany, outrageous costumes that she created herself, careening from one wild sexual encounter to another, doing what most women, or men, were almost incapable even of fantasizing about.

What made Annie popular was an erotic exuberance that few could match. She thought up little sex games, like a schoolmarm trying to keep her wards entertained. Once she invented something called oatmeal wrestling, then enlisted two dozen men to wash the oatmeal off her body with urine. Another time she orchestrated a circle jerk of twenty men around her. Often she was asked by gay men to be their first female lover. She had sex with a forty-two-inch-tall dwarf, a black man with a penis three times normal length, a man named Erhardt who liked to have sex in a Nazi uniform, and countless other denizens, including many who wanted to be whipped or caned on their buttocks until they bled. Samuel, a Hasidic masochist, liked to eat her Tampax. Timmy, a fire victim whose lips, fingers, eyelids, ears, and nipples had been burned off, found in Annie a tender, caring lover. She also accommodated foot-worshiping slaves, slutty transvestites, novice transsexuals, piercing scenes, a Great Dane that enjoyed fellatio, an eight-foot boa constrictor, men who liked being danced on by women in eight-inch spike heels, and Billy Kerr, who was able to take an entire rack of billiard balls up his rectum. (Annie fist-fucked him up to her elbow.)

It was performance art before the term came to be, with everybody putting on a spectacular show. Annie was the star and, in tribute, was ultimately voted Queen of the Hellfire Club.

Soon after her return to America, Annie also made the movie that established her as a porn superstar—*Deep Inside Annie Sprinkle,* which she both wrote and directed and which became the number two best-selling video of 1982 after Marilyn Chambers's *Insatiable.* After the film was removed from the market when the FBI deemed it obscene, it quickly became a collector's item.

Talking to her viewers directly, Annie revealed in her film that her real name was Ellen. She showed snapshots of her parents and herself as a young girl. Then she asked the viewer: "Would you like to see what I can do with two hunky men, right now?" Whereupon she launched into a highly idiosyncratic tour of her body and all the interesting things it could do.

In addition to posing for spread-leg shots for *Chic, Hustler, Oui, High Society,* and other mainstream erotic magazines, Annie also appeared in a variety of poses in *Foot Fetish Times, Enema News, Sluts and Slobs, Battling Babes,* and *Bazoombas.* She modeled for the high-tech masturbation machine Accu-Jac, shot a catalog of sex toys for Pleasure Chest, and joined a masturbation session for the pro-porn lesbian magazine *On Our Backs.* Sometimes she also did standard photo shoots, including one with comedian John Belushi for *National Lampoon Foto Funnies,* and posed for the artist Alice Neel.

MARCO VASSI first witnessed fist fucking one Saturday night in 1969 in the orgy room of the St. Mark's Baths. Observing a crowd gathered around a bunk bed, he edged his way to the center, joining a dozen other young men whose eyes were straining out of their sockets in total disbelief as a young blond boy lay spread-eagle on the mattress, a burly man in front of him methodically pushing his arm into the boy's entrails.

The first original sex practice in centuries, fist fucking was just then gaining notoriety. Neither ancient erotica nor the Kinsey reports mentioned it. Within a short time the practice gave birth to several works, including *The Fist Fucker's Manual.* The first published photo of heterosexual fist fucking—a man's hand and wrist inserted into a vagina—appeared in *Screw* under the headline "Fist Fucking Femme."

Before long fist fucking evolved into an onstage act in many gay bars, the gay equivalent and forerunner of Linda Lovelace's deep throat. At first it was viewed as an act of sadomasochism, the epitome of sexual degradation, submission, punishment, and pain. Later enthusiasts transformed it into the ultimate in lovemaking and trust—a supremely erotic act, tender, gentle, voluptuous, complete, and not an athletic demonstration or freak show. The person doing the fisting had to be capable of deep caring and sensitivity.

Fist-fucking orgies were also popular, with poppers passed around while everyone fisted and watched the film *2001* on a home projector, timing their final orgasm with the color sequence at the end of the film.

In 1975 this perhaps most difficult of all sexual feats was taken to its logical culmination when some three hundred men gathered for a fist-fucking convention sponsored by the Fist Fuckers of America at a resort near Ossining, New York. The two-day fete was topped with a contest won by a man who was able to take two fists simultaneously and have six orgasms by masturbating, all within one hour.

The immense pressure on the prostate gland was, of course, of tremendous help in the production of erections and the secretion of semen. Soon fist fucking appeared in gay porno films, magazines, stage shows, and slang. The use of the word "Crisco" (the gay lubricant of choice, though axle grease was also favored) also usually suggested fist fucking. The actual percentage of gays who engaged in the practice was never established but almost certainly was extremely low.

THE TERM "SADOMASOCHISM" derived from a conjunction of two aristocratic literary names: the Marquis de Sade, an eighteenth-century French noble, who had virtually no opportunity to experience the sadistic activities he wrote about; and Leopold von Sacher-Masoch, born in Austria in 1836, a century after de Sade, whose novels, tame by today's standards, suggested he was very much involved in the masochistic activities he described.

Psychiatrist Baron Richard von Krafft-Ebing was the first to recognize the typology of sadistic and masochistic sexual behavior and attached the name of those two noblemen to their respective passions. But not until 1895 did psychologist Albert von Schrenk-Notzing link sadism and masochism into algolagnia, a reference to the connection between sexual excitement and pain; and in 1938 Freud first conjoined the two terms into "sadomasochism."

In 1969 Paul Gebhard's pioneering study, "Fetishism and Sado-masochism," made an important contribution to the study of SM by laying the foundation for its examination as social behavior rather than as a manifestation of individual psychopathology. But serious scientific research into SM did not begin until the late 1970s. Perhaps the most notable was that eventually published in 1984 by Colin Williams, Martin Weinberg, and Charles Moser, who found that SM behavior usually contained five components: dominance and submission, role playing, consensuality, sexual context, and mutual definitions.

Dominance referred mainly to the appearance of rule over one partner by another and the reciprocal appearance of obedience. Role playing implied an exaggeration of expectations surrounding the interaction between dominant and submissive roles. Consensuality was defined as a voluntary agreement to enter into dominant/submissive play and to honor certain limits. Sexual context suggested that SM was primarily sexual behavior, even if it did not lead to orgasm or even an erection on the part of a male participant. Mutual definition simply meant that the partners agreed on the parameters of what they were doing.

In sum, healthy, nonpathological SM was erotic, consensual, and recreational, heavily dependent on fantasy and the illusion of control, requiring collaboration and mutual definition in order to be satisfying, and bearing no resemblance to Hollywood's Central Casting portrayals of homicidal sadists and psychotic masochists.

EARLY ONE WEEKDAY EVENING in the spring of 1975, Marco Vassi decided to pay a visit to the Continental Baths, where Metropolitan Opera star Eleanor Steber was the headlined singer.

Guests could rent either a locker or a room with a cot and a night table. Marco chose a room. He handed over his valuables for safekeeping and was admitted to the inner sanctum.

After undressing and donning his towel, he set out to explore, starting at the top floor. The layout was similar to that in many baths, with rooms lining long, wide corridors that were packed with an endless stream of men, endlessly prowling. Occasionally a pair would exchange a few words and go off together. Some of the doors were open. In one room a naked man lay facedown on the bed, his body an open invitation. In another a man sat on his mattress, his back against the wall, holding his semierect penis in one hand and staring insolently ahead, like a model in a stud magazine. Another knelt on the floor, a leather belt draped invitingly over his bare buttocks.

The second floor was much the same, except for the addition of an orgy room—a large, dorm-style open space holding about fifty cots and, against one wall, a platform covered with enough mattresses to hold twenty people. Voyeurs rested and watched while exhibitionists performed in the dim light.

On the first floor Marco encountered more restless wanderers. A deep silence pervaded the corridors, except for an occasional cry of pain or pleasure. A man of about fifty came up and put his hand on Marco's buttocks. "I have a room," he said, "and poppers." Marco shook his head and the man left. The unspoken code in the baths was that anyone could propose anything to anyone, with no offense ever given. Similarly, anyone could also refuse any invitation without risk of offense.

In the steam room Marco found couples embracing in the intense heat, sweat running down their bodies, threesomes and foursomes in the dark corners, shrouded in white mist. As always, the sheer volume of sexual activity astounded him. Lying on a plank, he let the hot, wet air relax his muscles. Soon he experienced the eerie sensation of a disembodied mouth descending between his thighs. Yet he could not get an erection, and after a few minutes the ghostly presence disappeared.

He went out and plunged into the cold pool, showered, and entered the coffee shop. Here the atmosphere was not so fiercely sexual, and it was possible to be alone with one's thoughts or to strike up a conversation. It was barbecue night, and free refreshments were being served in the lounge. Later a dance contest was scheduled, followed by a Judy Garland movie. But it was all a little too campy for Marco's tastes, and after another swim he left the building, experiencing a mild culture shock as he stepped back out onto the noisy street.

As he walked along, Marco reflected that balling with the boys was just as healthy as bowling with the boys, that the ugly male conditioning of competition and aggression tended to melt away in the baths. At the same time, he wondered if there was also a dark side to so much promiscuity, if liberty was being confused with freedom. Many of the patrons seemed like lonely souls, stifled by their jobs, unable to form lasting relationships with either men or women. The brazen sexuality they affected—though understandable after centuries of fear and persecution—often seemed to lack real passion or joy.

It seemed to Marco that the gay baths were betraying the basic concept of the gay movement. "The revolutionary idea," he noted in his journal, "was not that a man could have sex with another man, but that a man could *love* another man." He hoped for the day when gays could get past senseless promiscuity to arrive at a truly viable gay culture.

Of course Marco himself haunted the St. Mark's Baths primarily because he wanted to experience degradation and because the Felliniesque tableaux he witnessed there electrified him—one man fellating another who was being fist-fucked by a third, and so on. Oddly enough, it was there that he found love, with Bill, the sixty-five-year-old ticket taker. Bill was old and had lost his sexual enthusiasm, but he had a lecher's refined taste and in Marco saw a young, energetic, talented neophyte—an SM virgin.

Soon Marco began visiting Bill in his musty furnished room on East Sixth Street. As soon as he walked into the building, he felt a deep dirty thrill going right down to his anus. In the beginning they experimented with Bill hitting Marco with a belt or dropping burning wax on his nipples, which quickly brought him to a level of pain that seemed intolerable. But the wax always cooled immediately, and he learned to distinguish between pain—which in SM parlance never hurt anybody—and damage. Damage would have been letting Bill cut his flesh with razors, but Marco kept putting him off. "When are you going to do it?" Bill kept asking. "When are you going to stop playing around?"

Whipping sessions were the compromise. After each hard lash, Marco pulled back with a posed "Ooooohh!" And Bill would say, "When are you really going to feel the pain of the thing?" When Marco squirmed girlishly, Bill asked again in disgust, "That's all very cute, but when are you going to be the thing you want to be?"

They also did master/slave, owner/dog scenarios with leash and collar, and they played urinary games. Marco crouched in the shower and alternately pleaded, "Oh, don't pee on me," and "Yes, do." Bill replied, "Look. Do you want to drink piss or don't you? If you're a piss drinker, we'll get on with it. And if you're not, why are you doing this thing?" Marco's standard reply was: "I'm only here for the experience." After a while, though, they began to have a real, loving relationship. They told each other about their lives and loaned each other money. Bill confided his loneliness, and they talked and cried together for hours. One night Bill asked, "Do you want to do father/son?" Marco—whose actual father also happened to be named Bill—consented. While he was fellating Bill, the old man said, "That's it, son. Suck your father's cock."

After a while, they lost touch. Then one day Marco called the baths and learned that Bill had been put in Bellevue Hospital, catatonic and paranoid. At the hospital, Marco discovered that Bill had recently died. Asked if Bill had any relatives who could claim the body for burial, Marco nearly said, "Me. I'm his son." Later he consoled himself with an observation by Wilhelm Reich: "Underneath every bit of distorted, grotesque behavior, I always found a little bit of human simplicity."

Chapter 8

Sex for Advanced Students

A YEAR AFTER AMERICA'S FIRST EROTIC SUMMIT CONFERENCE ATTENDED BY THE staffs of the Kinsey Institute and the Reproductive Biology Research Foundation in St. Louis, Masters and Johnson published *Human Sexual Inadequacy,* on April 27, 1970. One awestruck observer was inspired to characterize their St. Louis clinic as the "Lourdes of America for people with sexual hangups." Publication of the book not only reaffirmed their seemingly unassailable standing in the scientific community, but launched the brand-new profession of sex therapy. By making the study of human sexuality respectable—and big business—Masters and Johnson set an inspiring example for countless others, and the decade was to witness the greatest blossoming of sexual research, experimentation, and activism in history. On the downside, countless self-styled sex experts and phony sex clinics also set up shop, hoping to parlay America's infatuation with virtually any kind of sex advice into a big paycheck.

In *HSI* the St. Louis sex researchers divided sexual dysfunctions of each sex into four main classifications: in the male, primary and secondary impotence (respectively, men who were incapable of an erection either always or under certain circumstances), premature ejaculation, and ejaculatory incompetence (inability to ejaculate into a vagina despite prolonged erection and coital thrusting); in the female, primary orgasmic dysfunction (women who had never had an orgasm) and three categories of situational orgasmic dysfunction (women who sometimes had an orgasm), whether coital, masturbatory, or random. Other innovations pioneered by Masters and Johnson included seeing only couples and pairing each with a team of two therapists; and an intensive course of treatment over a period of two weeks, with daily sessions. The two researchers sought to change bedroom behavior by assigning patients sexual homework rather than just relying on talk about sexual feelings and fantasies. Moreover, Masters and Johnson emphasized current obstacles, not unconscious conflicts or childhood events.

Not a few critics noted, however, that the two researchers devoted four-fifths of *Human Sexual Response* to the female and a corresponding amount of their subsequent *Human Sexual Inadequacy* to the male. Their prime accomplishment was to formulate sex therapy along the model of female, not male, sexuality—by helping men become the kind of sexual partner a woman needed, rather than by considering an anorgasmic woman as an inferior partner of the male.

Four months after *Human Sexual Inadequacy* was published, Masters divorced his wife and began dating his longtime collaborator. Masters was the suitor in the relationship, the lovable curmudgeon who once told a reporter from *Life:* "I'm sort of a bastard. I'm no good with people." Johnson was the warm, womanly, independent spirit who transformed him into someone reasonably human. Friends were struck by the resemblance of their relationship to the screen chemistry between Spencer Tracy and Katharine Hepburn.

Around the time of his divorce, Masters also quipped to a writer for *The Atlantic* that neither he nor Johnson planned to run off to Mexico. "But I do take it upon myself to chase as many women eighteen years and older as a slightly bald fifty-four-year-old can catch." Whether or not Masters was suffering from a midlife crisis, he did marry his collaborator and lover, Virginia Johnson, on January 7, 1971, in a secret ceremony in Fayetteville, Arkansas. The ceremony was performed in the home of Dr. LeMon Clark, a physician and Unitarian minister. Only their closest friends knew, and months passed before the official union of the first couple of sex was reported in the media.

At their suburban home, Masters and Johnson employed a white-jacketed butler to serve dinner and pour the wine. Without the burden of housework, they were able to resume their research immediately after dinner. Two Doberman pinschers, trained to attack on command, slept outside their bedroom door, a precaution necessitated by the hate mail their books had generated. "When things are going rough we don't drink, we go to bed, hold tight, and go to sleep. It's a helluva lot better than drinking," Masters told a reporter around that time.

Things got very rough in August 1970 when George E. Calvert, an Englishman living in Westfield, New Hampshire, filed suit against the researchers, claiming they had, in effect, prostituted his wife by persuading her without his knowledge to engage in sexual intercourse with two different men on successive occasions. The couple had undergone a sex-therapy session, under the direction of Masters and Johnson, for a fee of $2,000. Calvert claimed he "lost the conjugal society" of his wife and suffered "great humiliation and disgrace in his social and domestic relationships" because of his wife's involvement in the men's treatment, for which she was paid $250 on one occasion and $500 on the other. The suit further stated that Masters and Johnson had known Barbara Calvert was married and induced her to keep her activities a secret from her husband, thus breaching the doctor-patient relationship. Calvert asked for $750,000 in damages, a figure later amended to $2,500,000.

In *HSI* Masters and Johnson estimated that half of all marriages suffered from one sexual problem or another—a sexual desolation affecting thirty million couples, not counting millions more single people with sex difficulties. Masters and Johnson deemed it highly unethical for a therapist to have sex with a client, terming it a form of rape. But they had defended the controversial use of partner surrogates in sex therapy as a way of establishing a therapeutic environment. Surrogates were used only with male patients, however, because Masters and Johnson thought the practice might be counterproductive with single female patients.

By the time the lawsuit was settled out of court, in 1972, Masters and Johnson had prudently stopped using surrogates. The legal risks, on top of considerable professional disapproval, had simply proved insurmountable. The pair had also stopped observing subjects engaged in sexual activity, and most of their subsequent published work was based on their existing research.

The sex life that the world's foremost sex researchers enjoyed was still a source of fascination to the rest of the world, however, and finally journalist Gay Talese decided to investigate. At a 1973 convention of the American Society of Newspaper Editors, he stood up and asked Johnson how often she and her husband had sex.

"Who keeps score?" she gracefully replied. "I could not or would not, and he could not or would not, give you an accurate count."

Masters added, "There is no such thing as normal. How often do you breathe? As often as necessary."

The famed two-week Masters and Johnson sex-therapy course now cost $2,500 per couple, and demand was heavy. On occasion, out of economic or other considerations, they reduced the fee, but on the whole they felt that the investment provided additional motivation.

Upon receiving an application from a couple seeking therapy, Masters and Johnson first took a thorough medical and sexual history. Some applicants were disqualified as psychotic or the marriage simply deemed unsalvageable. One in five couples owed their sexual woes to a physical cause—diabetes or medicines used to treat high blood pressure—or to an emotional problem.

A maze of corridors and rooms, the offices of the Reproductive Biology

Research Foundation were austerely clinical, but each therapy room featured a different color scheme so that patients—who used whatever room was available during their two-week stay—did not get bored. A strictly clinical approach also ensured against a personal relationship with a therapist. If Masters, Johnson, or an associate discerned an emotional bond developing between patient and therapist, the latter was replaced.

On the first day of the course, the couple split up, with the man going off with a male therapist, the woman with a female therapist, to discuss their problems. The partners were instructed not to discuss with each other what they told the therapists until the third day, when a roundtable was scheduled.

On day two the couple returned for another history-taking session, only this time the male therapist sat with the woman partner, and vice versa. This crossover technique seemed to reveal truth more quickly.

At the roundtable on the third day, all four discussed the results of the history taking, with the therapists suggesting where they thought the couple was going wrong. All problems, however, were treated as joint problems, and the therapists took pains to avoid giving either the female or male patient any sense that she or he was being graded or judged. At this point, the couple was also given homework: two sessions of fondling and massage—so-called sensate focus—back at the hotel, with no demand for performance.

On the fourth day, the couple discussed their hotel experiences and were told to repeat them again. On the fifth day, Masters and Johnson selected a specific treatment designed to help the couple's problem, whether premature ejaculation, anorgasmia, impotence, or whatever.

Only one other U.S. center offered a similar two-week intensive therapy program, the Center for Marital and Sexual Studies under the direction of Drs. William Hartman and Marilyn Fithian in Long Beach, California—sometimes referred to as "the Masters and Johnson of the West Coast." But there were notable differences between the two centers. Rather than send couples to a hotel for "homework" after the history taking, Hartman and Fithian began their sensory retraining at the center's treatment room, where couples were shown videos of a woman and man successfully performing intercourse. The therapy was based not on talk, but on touch and self-awareness. Couples were encouraged to look at themselves in the mirror and accept all that they saw, to practice caressing their partner's feet and face, breasts and genitals; and then to learn better sex techniques that would eventually culminate in mutual though not necessarily simultaneous orgasm. Hartman and Fithian's treatment also included therapist involvement in stimulating sexual response, and many sex therapists regarded them as too radical.

California in the mid-seventies was, of course, the perennial boom town of other popular, often sex-related therapies, including Gestalt therapy, psychodrama, rational emotive therapy, bioenergetic therapy (an outgrowth of the work of Wilhelm Reich), transactional analysis, encounter groups, and primal therapy. A growth industry, the self-help movement also included Synanon for drug addicts, Weight Watchers, and an endless variety of "Anonymous" organizations. Eastern approaches incorporated the Taoist, Zen, and Hindu traditions, hatha yoga, tai chi, and transcendental meditation.

Even swinging tried to assume a new identity now that it was becoming marginally respectable in some major cities. It tried to ride the wave of the human potential movement roaring out of California by dressing itself up as "growth swinging" and emphasizing its conservative, marriage-based constituency. Though many of the old accoutrements remained, including buffet diners, hot tubs, and, of course, sex, now the participants emphasized that they belonged to a community, not a "swing club." Swinging, Bob McGinley now proudly proclaimed, had become part of the humanistic revolution—community oriented, nonsexist, self-aware.

As the art or science of sex therapy quickly developed, new sex problems also began to crop up. Helen Singer Kaplan, an associate professor of psychiatry specializing in sex therapy, claimed the most common sex problem was lack of desire, a problem she had not even alluded to in her own *The New Sex Therapy,* published in 1974. Nor was it mentioned in *Human Sexual Response* or *Human Sexual Inadequacy.*

According to Kaplan, she became aware of the problem only when she began to study the failures in her psychosexual therapy practice. Reviewing case records, she discovered a hidden lack of sexual desire in a large percentage of those patients she failed to help significantly. That problem, she now saw, was very distressing to many patients and often led to severe sexual anxiety that was disruptive of a relationship.

People with a low libido were allegedly also more susceptible to being emotionally injured and tended to set up more rigid psychological defenses than persons whose orgasms were perhaps impaired but at least indicative of desire.

Kaplan divided her time between private practice and a low-cost clinic at New York's prestigious Payne-Whitney Center. Unlike Masters and Johnson or Hartman and Fithian, Kaplan approached all sex problems via a treatment that was a mixture of direct sex therapy and psychotherapy, believing almost all sex problems were in the mind. Originally she had treated all sex problems with lengthy psychotherapy—looking for psychological causes like guilt, anxiety, fear of rejection, fear of failure, inability to let go—but later found that sex therapy brought faster results. Kaplan now reserved analysis only for patients whose sexual problems were compounded by obvious psychic disturbances.

Despite its popularity, sex therapy in the mid-seventies, like psychotherapy, was mostly a middle-class phenomenon. According to Masters and Johnson, only about fifty therapists in the United States were suitably qualified—even though an astounding five thousand sex-therapy clinics sprouted up in the wake of *HSI*. Moreover, many private clinics were expensive and outside the reach of the poor. A good number were attached to hospitals, and the fee did not usually include the cost of travel, hotels, and food.

Though only a few of the clinics admitted it publicly, up to 70 percent probably used surrogates. Only in California, though, were surrogates taken for granted. One prominent therapist who routinely worked with five female surrogates was psychiatrist Bernie Apfelbaum, director of the Berkeley Group for Sexual Development. Apfelbaum's clinic was unusual in that it treated men who wanted treatment, whether or not they had a partner. Some of the patients were married, others were single, all were desperate. Apfelbaum considered each surrogate a co-therapist.

The qualifications Apfelbaum looked for in a surrogate were that she be sexually well adjusted and responsive, sensitive and warm, and able to communicate easily. Among the most celebrated was Sue Green, a surrogate with schoolteacher looks, who had worked with twenty-six clients. In her view, a prostitute dealt with fantasy while she dealt with reality. Typical Apfelbaum-Green therapy called for her and the client to engage in sex, stroking, and nondemand pleasuring, interwoven with meetings attended by all three.

Not a single sex clinic in the country offered surrogate therapy for single women, for which demand was virtually nonexistent. But consciousness-raising groups often emphasized the importance of women's getting to know their own bodies, using a speculum and mirror to explore the vagina and cervix, and learning how to enjoy their genitals.

In early 1981 the American Association of Sex Educators, Counselors and Therapists (AASECT) finally established a code of ethics regulating the use of a sex surrogate. Above all, AASECT said that if a surrogate sex partner was used, the spouse of that person had to be informed. Critics of that stand included Wardell Pomeroy, who termed such a limitation "ridiculous." In Pomeroy's view, a wife who knew her husband was involved in sex therapy with a surrogate could be devastated.

Probably the most respected sexologist in the country apart from William Masters, Pomeroy once cataloged some of the new sexual myths being spawned in the seventies: that sex problems were easily cured, masturbation was more satisfying than intercourse, women's orgasms should be earthquakes, there was no significant difference between clitoral and vaginal orgasm (based on the belief that no matter where a woman's orgasm originated—clitoris, fantasy, breasts—it occurred within the structure of the vagina), or that penis size was irrelevant to sexual satisfaction (in fact, a small penis could cause less satisfaction, a large penis discomfort).

BY THE EARLY SEVENTIES, in New York, Chicago, Los Angeles, and a few other major cities, prostitutes—posing as sex therapists, masseuses, escorts, or mentors in "role-playing" games—were able to advertise their services openly in underground newspapers, complete with phone numbers. But state laws governing the oldest profession varied widely, and in most cities call girls, hookers, and bar girls operated subversively. Only Nevada lacked a statute deeming prostitution a crime, but a prostitute was forbidden to enter the state, and it was a crime to live off the earnings of a prostitute. Nevertheless, three of the state's seventeen counties had licensed brothels—though not Clark County, which encompassed Las Vegas. To get around the earnings prohibition, the brothels simply charged their permanent female residents a steep fee for room and board.

One of the most notorious Nevada brothels was the Mustang Bridge Ranch eight miles east of Reno, where manager Joe Conforte wore two diamond rings and paid the county $1,000 a month in lieu of a license. Prices for services started at $10, compared with $50 in Las Vegas. At Mustang, prostitutes averaged ten to fifteen tricks in a twelve-hour tour; some boasted "personal bests" of up to forty a day. Though the prostitutes earned less money at Mustang, they enjoyed more security, as well as a weekly medical checkup. In such illegal venues as hotel bars, prostitutes had to deal with a host of problems ranging from police bribery and customers with STDs to thieving johns and sadistic freaks.

In 1973, Atlanta prostitute Margo St. James formed a prostitutes' rights group called COYOTE (Call Off Your Old Tired Ethics) for the purpose of improving the working conditions of prostitutes and ultimately legalizing their profession. Despite considerable media attention given to the group, old tired ethicists did not budge an inch.

The most liberal part of the world for prostitution was the Orient, where it played a significant role in the economy. The number one customer: the American serviceman. The biggest red-light districts in the world were in Thailand and the Philippines, both of which attracted not only thousands of U.S. and other soldiers and sailors every year, but droves of Asian businessmen. In Hong Kong, British and American businessmen created a strong demand for high-class call girls. Pedophiles flocked to Vietna, India, where child prostitutes of either sex could be purchased for as little as a quarter. In Turkey a man could legally sell an adulterous wife into prostitution. In Israel most prostitutes were Arabs. The downside of so much unregulated commercial sex was a shameful legacy of illegitimate and traumatized children, battered women, and an epidemic of drugs, violence, and STDs.

An admirable and enlightened exception was France, where the government regulated prostitution in the interest of hygiene; every prostitute had to carry a card certifying that she had had her weekly checkup and was currently STD free.

An international sex survey of college-age and adult men and women published in the May 1969 issue of the *Journal of Marriage and the Family* found that Englishmen were the most avid patrons of prostitutes and also reported the highest involvement in whipping and spanking. A distant second in whipping were American men, with German men bringing up the rear. Norwegian men were the least likely to patronize a prostitute.

Kinsey had estimated that 65 percent of the total white male population in the United States had experience with prostitutes at some point but, for most men, only once or twice. Most who did frequent prostitutes were unmarried males: bachelors, divorcés, widowers. Kinsey did find that young bachelors were less inclined than the generation of their fathers to frequent prostitutes, though his survey techniques in that respect were flawed, and hard data was still difficult to come by.

FOR MORE THAN A CENTURY, the *Kama Sutra,* an ancient Indian love manual probably dating to the fourth century A.D., was in English or French translation the only explicit celebration of erotic techniques available to Western readers. Though not widely available, it exercised a profound influence on European and American works dealing with sexual technique when they did appear, most notably Dr. Theodoor H. Van de Velde's revolutionary and immensely popular 1926 *Ideal Marriage,* first translated from Dutch into English in 1928. Among other achievements, *Ideal Marriage* was the first Western marriage manual to pay explicit attention to foreplay, oral sex, and different coital positions.

By the late sixties, a ragtag brigade of journalists, therapists, physicians, and others were lining up to cash in on the new sexual openness with a flurry of how-to and sex advice books ranging from the earnest and thoughtful to simple trash. But not until a Cambridge-educated British classicist turned medical biologist named Alex Comfort published *The Joy of Sex* did the century produce a worthy successor to the great Hindu book of love.

Decades earlier, while lecturing at University College, London, Comfort had published an iconoclastic book of essays titled *Sexual Behaviour in Society,* which held that Christian morality was so much "temporary scaffolding" that eventually would have to be dismantled. In 1972, at the age of fifty-five,

Comfort began the dismantling of that morality with the publication of *Joy*. He was the unlikeliest of sex popularizers—a senior fellow at an exclusive ivory tower encampment, the Center for the Study of Democratic Institutions in Santa Barbara. But while reviews were generally disapproving, popular acclaim was enormous, and by 1974 this best-selling sex manual of all time had sold eight hundred thousand copies in hardcover and nearly two million in softcover.

A rival work, though it did not achieve the same stellar success, was *Open Marriage* by anthropologists Nena and George O'Neill, who claimed marriage was "an equal partnership between two friends." The O'Neills insisted that a marriage based on mutual trust and communication had to be flexible enough for each partner to grow and develop, even in unexpected directions, including sexual attraction to and relationships with other persons. By 1983 sex researchers reported that nearly 15 percent of married people claimed to have a sexually open marriage, while 30 percent of cohabiting couples identified themselves as sexually open.

Other promoters of the joys of sex took a less theoretical and more pragmatic approach, founding communes for the enlightened few rather than publishing books for the millions. Perhaps the most sincere and admirable of these erotic visionaries was a disenchanted inventor named John Williamson, who came to believe that too many social ills were caused by people who were alienated from themselves, from people they supposedly loved, and from their social environment.

With his wife, Barbara, Williamson, who had made a modest fortune in electronics, bought fifteen acres in Topanga Canyon, outside of Los Angeles, where they founded Sandstone Ranch in 1969. In a dense, closely reasoned paper entitled "Project Synergy," the bearded, boyish-looking Williamson—like his nineteenth-century forebears who had founded Oneida and other free-love settlements—outlined his vision for an erotically based utopian community.

Many of Sandstone's early members were scientists, engineers, and successful midlevel businessmen, mostly in their thirties and forties, who shared Williamson's enthusiastic belief that society was in trouble and needed sexual help. Among those who made a pilgrimage to Topanga, besides the usual Hollywood contingent of actors, directors, and producers, were Alex Comfort, journalists Gay Talese and Max Lerner, artist Betty Dodson, sex therapists William Hartman and Marilyn Fithian, singer Bobby Darin, sex pioneers Phyllis and Eberhard Kronhausen, and Daniel Ellsberg, the Defense Department staffer who later leaked word of Nixon's secret bombing of Cambodia to *The New York Times*.

At its high point, membership rolls reached 275 couples, despite a 1970 fire and a 1971 ordinance requiring the licensing of all "growth centers and nudist camps." Together with the legendary Ed Lange, who had founded Elysium, a neighboring nudist colony, Williamson challenged the ordinance on First Amendment grounds and won. But the protracted legal battle had been a financial disaster, decimating plans for growth. Morale dropped, as did attendance, and the holdouts felt as if the Sexual Revolution were passing them by, even though once, for about fifteen minutes, they had been at its epicenter.

Rancho Rajneesh, also known as Big Muddy Ranch, in rural Wasco County, Oregon, was arguably the biggest, best, and baddest sex commune of all time. It was the creation of an Indian sex swami, Bhagwan Shree Rajneesh, also known as Rajneesh Chandra Mohan—or, to his devoted disciples, God. (*Bhagwan* was one of three Sanskrit words for Almighty.)

A lithe, dark-skinned man with big almond eyes, long gray beard, gray robe, and diamond-encrusted watch, Bhagwan was born in 1931 in India, the son of a wealthy cloth merchant. From the age of sixteen to twenty-six he ran sixteen miles a day, eight in the morning and eight at night. During this period he lost all interest in sex. At the age of twenty-one, while sitting under a maulshree tree one evening, he achieved enlightenment, and he remained celibate ever afterward.

Later Bhagwan became a professor of philosophy at the University of Jabalpur, where he mastered the esoteric ideas and meditation techniques of Buddhism and Taoism and learned to repackage them for Western sensibilities. An electrifying, iconoclastic speaker, he soon attracted a following, especially among wealthy Europeans and Americans who liked the Perfect Master's freewheeling lifestyle, and founded his first major ashram in Poona. But Bhagwan also soon ran afoul of the Indian tax bureau. Beset by legal and medical problems (he had a heart condition), he jetted out of the subcontinent with ten followers.

After a first stop in New Jersey, to tend to his health, Bhagwan moved on to Oregon, where he put a $2.5 million cash down payment on a $6 million sale for 265 square miles in the heart of Marlboro country.

Located two hundred miles from the nearest major city, Portland, the community—twice the size of San Francisco—contained a shopping mall, a small university, a 145-room luxury hotel, a public transportation system, a casino, a disco, bars, and gourmet restaurants. The ranch also produced sixty different kinds of vegetables and hundreds of cattle. It even owned its own airline, Air Rajneesh. Perhaps its most famous occupants, apart from Bhagwan himself, were the hundred-plus Rolls-Royces—more per capita than any other place in the world, including Kuwait and Beverly Hills.

Above all, though, what drew people to Rancho Rajneesh was tantric sex. Common in India since at least A.D. 500, tantra cults also flourished in ancient Japan, China, and Greece. Though in some cases practiced in secret, tantra was never a religion, but a way of life. It was rediscovered in the West in the sixties, and Bhagwan was undoubtedly its most important teacher.

"Real tantra is not technique, but love," Bhagwan preached. "Is not head oriented, but a relaxation into the heart. . . . The ordinary sexual orgasm looks like madness; the tantric orgasm is a deep, relaxing meditation. Tantra is not teaching sexuality. It is simply saying that sex can be a source of bliss."

The primary difference between the sexual philosophy of the *Kama Sutra* and that of the Ayurvedic or tantric tradition in India was roughly that between a California free-love community and seventeenth-century New England Puritanism. While the one celebrated the uninhibited enjoyment of sex, the other saw it as a dissipation of energy and a distraction from the search for the cosmic self. The latter also espoused the conservation of "vital fluids," that is, semen. What most outsiders never realized, in other words, was that at the core of Bhagwan's teaching lay an ascetic message: If sexual (or any other form of) excess was necessary in order to reach inner peace and enlightenment, then be excessive until you were able to do with less. Though many Rajneeshees did indulge in group sex and other forms of unorthodox sexual behavior, in fact the goal for all was rigorous sexual discipline and—if possible—celibacy. By the same token, the parade of Rolls-Royces symbolized capitalism's garish excesses, and the faithful were encouraged to use them until they realized that all forms of luxury were a distraction to the soul.

Some 52 percent of Bhagwan's thirty-five hundred disciples were women. The average age was thirty-seven, and one in four came from outside the United States. A high percentage were Jewish. The commune was supported by an international string of nightclubs and restaurants, publishing and video arms, and a travel agency. It was also part of a worldwide chain of five hundred meditation centers that serviced 350,000 devotees, known as *sannyasins*—making it perhaps the largest sex cult in history. Bhagwan also offered room, board, and bus transportation to thousands of the homeless and derelict so they could start a new life on the commune.

Each evening, Bhagwan held meetings for favored *sannyasins.* Everyone had to shower beforehand, since he was allergic to perfumes and colognes. At those audiences, Bhagwan repeated his main message: Do what you want as long as you do not hurt anyone. Work hard, respect the rights of others, question authority, and use technology to build your utopia.

But as the commune prospered, rumors about it began to circulate among its conservative neighbors. Some thought Bhagwan was a member of the KGB. Then former Rajneeshee and born-again Christian Susan Hafouche serialized her memoirs in *Oregon* magazine, revealing that Rajneeshees at the meditation center in Los Angeles spent a lot of time "drinking, partying, remaining unemployed, changing bed partners almost nightly, and getting high." She also claimed that names of new arrivals who had been medically approved for promiscuity were posted on a bulletin board near the dining hall.

In the wake of the mass suicide/massacre of Jim Jones and his hundreds of followers at Jonestown, Guyana, groups like the Rajneeshees were having serious public relations problems. Hafouche charged that the community was a "cult" preying on emotionally vulnerable young women and men. A powerful conservation group called the 1000 Friends of Oregon began questioning Rajneeshee compliance with local land-use planning laws. The state's attorney general wondered aloud if the ranch might have to be dismantled because of laws separating church and state.

Hunters and ranchers were another problem, and Bhagwan's followers were repeatedly threatened by local biker gangs and others. When the Rajneesh Hotel in Portland was bombed, commune members began to arm themselves with Uzis and established a security force.

Then Ed Bradley did a segment on *60 Minutes* that included a portion of a tape purportedly made in Poona showing people beating each other as part of their therapy. The program also disclosed that the real power behind Bhagwan's throne was an American woman who called herself Ma Anand Sheela, president of the Academy of Rajneeshism and personal secretary and soul sister to the master.

As opposition to the commune grew, the U.S. Immigration and Naturalization Service began to investigate. In January 1982 the State Department announced that Bhagwan had either faked or seriously exaggerated his medical condition in order to transfer his ashram to the United States and escape tax difficulties in India.

In the summer of 1983 Bhagwan announced that the end of the world was coming, probably between 1984 and 1999, during which period there would be floods not known since the time of Noah, "along with earthquakes, volcanic eruptions, and everything else that is possible through nature. . . . Tokyo, New York, San Francisco, Los Angeles, Bombay, etc.—all these cities are going to disappear." But it was only Bhagwan's little world that ended when in 1987 he accused Ma Anand Sheela of trying to kill him and later held a book burning to rid his free-sex-for-all commune of her influence. By November he had been charged with violating immigration laws and fled the country. His fleet of Rolls-Royces was sold, and the commune was disbanded. By year's end, the town had readopted its former name, Antelope.

A SANDSTONE-LIKE ENCLAVE in Robert Park in a tiny Sonoma valley north of San Francisco, the More House commune was an offspring of Jeff Poland's near legendary Sexual Freedom League devoted to free love. Here, by 1975, eighty-five men, women, and children sought to live together in complete, radical sexual freedom, or anarchy. Members believed they were sexual gods, choosing fantasies that other members went out of their way to fulfill. A bulletin board featured erotic want lists. Typical: "I want: (1) A new Cadillac. (2) A blow job three times a day. (3) A night with Sally and Sue. (4) A gold-plated revolver to wear with my new cowboy suit."

Beneath the adolescent veneer, however, lurked an alluring hypothesis. The commune's origins went back to the summer of 1968, when Victor Branco, a middle-aged refrigerator salesman turned acid freak, founded an organization called the Institute of Human Abilities, housed in a formerly condemned nine-bedroom Victorian mansion in downtown Oakland. LSD had convinced Branco he was a god. Like Reich, he was also convinced that full orgasmic release was the key to happiness and financial success. He called his philosophy "more" and taught people how they, too, could become gods, enjoying all the sex they had ever wanted and earning lots of money in the process.

In the loopy, LSD-saturated fringes of the West Coast, this gospel found an instant following. Branco became immensely successful, bought a mansion in the Oakland hills and a Cadillac limousine, surrounded himself with female devotees, and by 1975 had receded like a sultan into semiretirement.

One of his disciples, though, a man named Patty Matlock, expanded Branco's philosophical concept into a way of life. In 1970 he founded More House, which in only five years became one of the most stable and financially successful sex communes in the world—and also, perhaps not so coincidentally, by far the most radical. Reality, in the More House philosophy, was merely a matter of social agreement.

The commune consisted of four main dormitories, each with its own dining room, kitchen, and house parents. It supported itself through sexuality courses that members offered to outsiders and through a salvage business tearing down old barns and reselling the wood and hardware. Most of the adults were married, as More House was not opposed to marriage—only monogamy.

An obese forty-four-year-old who bore a passing resemblance to Colonel Sanders, Matlock himself was married to a fifteen-year-old named Robin. His greatest inspiration was to study the works of Masters and Johnson and work out in practice the most efficient way for a man and woman to have the most intense possible orgasms. Armed with Masters and Johnson's discovery of the clitoral orgasm, and their finding that only the outer third of the vaginal barrel contained erotically responsive nerve endings, he declared intercourse an inefficient method of obtaining pleasure; oral sex was it. The logical More House conclusion: not *we* do, but *you* do, or *you* are done. Sucking, not fucking, was the watchword.

Matlock also took Masters and Johnson's squeeze technique for men and expanded it to a practice called stroking: an alternating sequence of light manual masturbation, licking, and squeezing to defer orgasm and build up tension, until finally climax was permitted. Masters and Johnson had found that the average male orgasm contained four to six contractions; but at More House, by squeezing, the orgasm could be continued indefinitely. One member claimed to have experienced an orgasm lasting up to twenty minutes, with up to four hundred contractions—a record the group was inordinately proud of.

For women the process leading to orgasm began with a light teasing massage of the clitoris called tumescing, followed by gentle licking, with the person performing cunnilingus elongating the orgasm by stopping and changing rhythm at peak points. Girls as young as seven were taught how to masturbate, using plaster models of vaginas to show them just where to touch.

Matlock and his followers taught these and other theories at regular weekend seminars that all members and guests were obliged to attend. Women were encouraged to be the aggressors. Members practiced an art called hexing: forcing a person to face his or her negative self-projection to the breaking point, then revealing how good they were and how worthy of praise. Sex was both bait and reward, withheld until the person being harried projected herself or himself as a god.

Later More House expanded to at least three northern California communes. Basic Sensuality was an explicit course based on Masters and Johnson's explanation of the human sexual response cycle and the personal observations and experimentation of Sue and Victor Branco. Techniques included peaking, pushouts, and pull-ups to expand and intensify orgasms. A pushout was a technique to deepen an orgasm by expanding (as opposed to contracting) pelvic muscles and directing pressure out on the genitals at the moment of orgasm to engender greater bliss. The More House alternative lifestyle experiment officially ended in the mid-seventies. In 1978 More University was founded in the town of Lafayette, California, where the teachings continue in greatly modified form.

The common denominator—and inherent error—of More House, Sandstone, and other California sex communes was their simplistic ideal that an inhibition-free sexuality was the solution to all societal and individual problems. Their doctrines urged sexual overachievement and discouraged contentment, tantalizing people with illusions of perfect orgasms and preaching the paramount importance of sex. Only a very few sexual pioneers were exploring the notion that freedom of sexual expression, while fundamental to a person's growth and identity, was ultimately a search for love.

*   *   *

IN THE LATE SEVENTIES sexology made a quantum breakthrough when John Money advanced the idea that every person had a unique mental template that orders and controls her or his sexual satisfaction. Money called that template the lovemap and described it in *Lovemaps: Clinical Concepts of Sexual/Erotic Health & Pathology, Paraphilia and Gender Transposition in Childhood, Adolescence, and Maturity.* That slender volume, virtually unknown outside the community of sex professionals, ranks among the seminal works of sexology in the second half of the twentieth century.

Money compared the infantile lovemap to a satellite map of a planet in which the details have only begun to be resolved. The topography of the lovemap evolved in the womb, where the developing brain was open to the influence of the sex hormones. Erotic play continued throughout childhood for most people, further etching the contours of the lovemap. At puberty the child matured into a healthy lover. Adults sought to match lovemaps with someone else, an idealized lover, in a pair-bonding experience.

Thwarted childhood sex play, on the other hand, often led to a "vandalized lovemap." A person with a vandalized lovemap was usually incapable of normal or pair-bonding adult sex relations and sometimes went without sex altogether. At the other extreme, some people with vandalized lovemaps engaged in sex with compulsive frequency—again, without pair-bonding. In a third scenario, the person with a vandalized lovemap found release and a solution to the problems created in childhood in a paraphilia—essentially a detour around so-called normal sexual functioning.

First used by I. F. Krauss and adopted by Wilhelm Stekel, whose pupil Benjamin Karpman introduced it to American psychiatry in 1934, the term "paraphilia" was initially used officially as a replacement for the legal term "perversion." Paraphiliacs, or "paraphiles," as Money called them, were capable of experiencing erotic excitement only when the genitals worked in the presence (in fantasy or reality) of some special substitute imagery, object, or ritual. Many paraphilias were as benign as a shoe fetish, while others were as bizarrely complex as cross-dressing or as deadly as asphyxiation, rape, or lust murder. In street language, a paraphilia (or love, *philia,* that is altered, *para*) was kinky sex; but to the law it was a perversion. A paraphilia probably developed when sexual arousal became related to a particular activity. In a classic example, a boy gets an erection upon being called down to the principal's office for punishment. The equation erection = sexual feeling = beating translated into a sadomasochist in the making. A pedophile most likely had a sexual relationship with an older person as a child; he seldom advanced sexually beyond adolescence and often even dressed and behaved like a teenager. His pedophilia was a repetition of the earlier affair. As for a rapist, Money theorized that most likely he was a victim of incest as a child. The sexual marauder or rapist, in his view, could simply not conceive that anyone would ever get involved in sex on a consenting basis. Therefore sex always had to be taken by force.

Paraphilias shared one principle: each represented a tragedy turned into a triumph. If tragedy was the defacement of an ordinary lovemap, triumph was the rescue of lust from wreckage and obliteration. A paraphiliac's lovemap gave lust (the erotic side of a relationship) a second chance, but at a price—saintly love and sinful lust were separated. When the brain acquired language, Money theorized, it developed an intense degree of plasticity, which allowed languages to be logical, coherent systems and yet be variable. That same brain was also freed up regarding sexual excitement and partnering. But why did some men need a partner to dress them in diapers, feed them a baby bottle, and smack their bottom in order to enable them to get an erection and climax? And why did there not seem to be any women who enjoyed diapering them? Extremely few women had paraphilias, probably because their psychosexual development was much less subject to distorting or traumatizing experiences at those critical periods—fetal or postnatal times when a person is highly receptive to stimulus—where nature and nurture interacted. When a lovemap formation was distorted in the early years, lust asserted itself in circuitous ways in males. But in women lust tended to turn off altogether. (The occasional exceptions were female amputees and paraphiliacs of amputation, whose lovemaps often matched.)

Did paraphiliacs have more intense sex lives? Though a paraphiliac probably experienced neurochemical changes in his brain and entered into a trancelike state to carry out his rituals, Money suspected his experience was probably not too different at heart from that of a normal person caught up in a hopeless love affair.

Though the neurochemistry of falling in love was a mystery, Money thought it made sense to think of pair-bonding as an aspect of human existence with special programming in the brain. Two other kinds of experience were analogs to falling in love: sudden, intense grief, and sudden, intense religious ecstasy. While all three could be both overwhelming and unexpected, each could also develop gradually, build to a crescendo, and fade slowly.

Money dismissed the idea that a paraphiliac acquired his paraphilia by looking at pornography. If that were so, then by extension a homosexual, for example, could "catch" heterosexuality, given all the romance in Hollywood movies. Money was uncertain, for that matter, whether homosexuals had lovemaps or vandalized lovemaps. The final criterion of homosexuality or heterosexuality was the morphological (body) sex of the partner with whom an individual was able to fall in love. Love, not sex, really determined orientation, Money thought; therefore the proper terms were not homosexuality and heterosexuality, but homophilia and heterophilia. That was because a person had no voluntary control over the sex or anything else about the object of his or her desires. In short, Money's radical idea was that love was the determining factor in sexual behavior.

It was very difficult to change a lovemap; changing meant allowing a small branch of a lovemap that had been stunted to grow. In the same way, it was often extremely difficult, for example, for a German to speak English without an accent because some things about learning became imprinted on the mind and were resistant to change. Money and two associates were also the first to attempt the pharmacological suppression of a paraphilia by administering the antiandrogenic hormone medroxyprogesterone acetate (Depo-Provera) to pedophiles, rapists, and others whose lovemaps brought them into conflict with the law. But a far more important agenda was the prevention of vandalized lovemaps in the first place.

ANOTHER MOMENTOUS EVENT in the seventies was the founding of the Institute for the Advanced Study of Human Sexuality (IASHS) in San Francisco. The IASHS was to became the first—and only—fully accredited institution in the United States to grant a doctorate in human sexuality. It was also responsible for training the first generation of professional surrogates for use in sex therapy and in time, improbably enough, came to possess the largest collection of film pornography ever assembled.

The driving force behind this singular institution, all but unknown outside the professional sex community, was a Methodist minister named Ted McIlvenna, a complex man who was half philosopher and half sex entrepreneur. Unlike many of his colleagues in the sex profession, McIlvenna regarded erotology—the study and dissemination of pornography and sex aids—as far more important in the long run than all the sex therapy in the world, for the simple reason that it showed people what sex was like, demystified it, and gave them relief. A friend of Reuben Sturman and other major pornographers, McIlvenna also considered the federal government and the Catholic Church the two worst enemies of freedom of sexual expression.

Growing up in Oregon, McIlvenna had traveled the river towns with his father, a Methodist minister who inculcated in his son a sex-positive attitude. In the McIlvenna household sexuality was seen as one among many ways to seek and find God. But while studying theology at Garrett Evangelical Theological Seminary in Evanston, Illinois, McIlvenna first encountered people who feared or hated sex. Later he traveled to Scotland to study at the University of Edinburgh and while there met his future wife, Winni, a young Danish beauty. After being ordained a minister, McIlvenna settled in Hayward, California, where he looked after his parish and established a family. It was a quiet, fulfilling pastoral life until one day in 1962 when the Methodist Church asked him to study the needs of San Francisco's young adults.

One of the first things McIlvenna discovered was that many young people, males in particular, were uncertain about their sexual identity. Looking for medical and psychological guidance, McIlvenna was appalled to find that the literature on the subject was virtually nonexistent and the so-called experts as much in the dark as everyone else. He was also shocked to discover the degree to which homosexuals were persecuted, a point brought home shockingly one evening when he saw two gay men get their genitals kicked in by the police.

Seeking out the leaders of the city's homosexual community, McIlvenna familiarized himself with gays' lifestyles, sought to understand their problems, and befriended Phyllis Lyon, Del Martin, and Hall Call, establishing with Lyon in particular a working relationship that was to endure for decades. He also asked the United Methodist Church for permission to make films that would combat the ignorance and antisexual bias he found everywhere. Nobody was attending his lectures, and he thought graphic pictures and language might help. It did.

In 1964 McIlvenna developed his first breakthrough, the Sexual Attitude Restructuring (SAR) process, as part of the Young Adult Project sponsored by the United Methodist Church and other Protestant denominations. Using films, slides, and tapes, SAR relied on techniques of desensitization and resensitization. Viewers were exposed to a barrage of sexually explicit films until they reached a point of satiation—that is, a complete demystification of sexuality. Then it was possible to begin the process of resensitization, equipping people with practical suggestions for improving their sex lives and specific information about other sexual matters. Eventually the SAR process was incorporated into the curricula of numerous medical schools.

In 1966 McIlvenna attended an international meeting in London of professionals in the sex field. The group concluded that persons in the helping professions were woefully lacking in their knowledge of human sexuality and that a center specifically designed for the training of professionals should be initiated. In the spring of 1967, after a further meeting with members of the Kinsey Institute and representatives from several church bodies, the National Institute of Mental Health, and several foundations, McIlvenna determined that the Glide Foundation in San Francisco should be the home of the proposed center. So it was that the National Sex Forum (NSF) was founded in October 1968.

The main task that McIlvenna set for the NSF was to study what helping professionals needed to know about sexuality and to develop effective educational methodologies. Assembling a team of seven women and men, including himself, McIlvenna and his group set about on a formal study of sexology, which lasted until 1974. In the process McIlvenna earned a Ph.D. in sexual research and counseling. He also began to produce explicit films that explored every aspect of human sexuality—the first so-called sex education films.

In all, over the next decade McIlvenna produced more than one hundred Sexual Pleasure Education tapes, ranging from ten minutes to an hour long. They covered every aspect of sexual behavior: heterosexual, homosexual, male and female masturbation, sex aids, abortion, general sex education, anal sex, sexual positions, sensual massage, the needs of sexually dominant females, threesomes, and two-couple exchanges. Though created primarily for doctors, therapists, and teachers, McIlvenna's series also launched the home-video sex education revolution, which by 1980 accounted for about 2 percent of the pornography market.

In 1975 sponsorship of the NSF was transferred to the nonprofit Exodus Trust, whose sole purpose was to promote sexual, mental, and physical health. The following year McIlvenna formally established the Institute for the Advanced Study of Human Sexuality in the Cathedral Hill section of San Francisco, incorporating it as a private nonsectarian graduate school and employing his six associates as the core faculty. Guest lecturers ranged from Phyllis Lyon to Al Goldstein. Wardell Pomeroy was dean. Initial financing came from a number of churches, including the Board of Christian Social Concerns of the Methodist Church, and from the Presidential Commission on Obscenity and Pornography appointed by former President Johnson.

In 1978 the state of California approved the institute for the granting of graduate degrees: master of human sexuality, doctor of arts in human sexuality, doctor of human sexuality, doctor of philosophy in human sexuality. Students were mostly midcareer professionals such as physicians, nurses, and social workers. Over the next two decades more than seventy thousand people were to attend its courses.

A MUCH MORE IMPORTANT WORK on female sexuality than Kate Millett's *Sexual Politics* or Germaine Greer's *The Female Eunuch,* and—in the post-Kinsey era—second only to Masters and Johnson's *Human Sexual Response,* was *The Hite Report,* which appeared in 1976, became an international best-seller in thirteen countries, and was banned in nine more. Author Shere Hite was the first to report that women were increasingly taking responsibility for their own sexuality. She also introduced a new verb, "to orgasm," to denote that women were no longer leaving their pleasure to luck or to a man's attitudes and needs. A vote of confidence in the penis *The Hite Report* was not.

"You have to take care of yourself and want to pleasure yourself," she wrote, addressing her female readers directly, "and you have to feel it is your *right*. You have to do it, whatever it is—or ask for it, very clearly and specifically."

Hite's most important findings were, first and foremost, that most women did not orgasm as a result of penile thrusting during vaginal penetration, and that this unrealistic expectation placed a great burden on women (not to mention men). That was not to say women did not enjoy intercourse; most did, *pace* Dworkin and other radical feminists. But more women experienced orgasm from masturbation than from intercourse and considered intercourse itself not as important as intimacy, touch, and freedom to "be." The 30 percent of Hite's respondents who did orgasm during intercourse usually resorted to body maneuvers learned over time that allowed sufficient clitoral stimulation for orgasm to occur. If there was any lingering doubt, Hite's book—the first large-scale work ever devoted specifically to female orgasm—made it abundantly clear that the only orgasm the penis accomplished was its own.

This revolutionary message made Hite a millionaire and was the culmination of a rags-to-riches journey. Born Shirley Gregory in St. Joseph, Missouri, she kept the name of her husband, whom she divorced after a brief marriage. In 1968 Hite left the University of Miami in Gainesville, Florida, with a master's degree, to pursue a doctorate in cultural history at Columbia University. But, disillusioned with her professor and Columbia's program, Hite left after two semesters to eke out a living as a model, putting her fragile, Pre-Raphaelite beauty to work posing nude for both *Playboy* and *Oui* and modeling fashion in both Paris and Milan.

Yet it was not her experience as a centerfold that set Hite on the path to feminism. Rather, it was an assignment for Olivetti, the Italian typewriter company, whose print advertisement for its sleek new product portrayed Hite as a secretary over a caption reading "The typewriter that's so smart that she doesn't have to be."

Soon after posing for the advertisement, Hite learned from a newspaper clipping that a women's group had organized to picket the company. Hite joined the picket and quickly immersed herself in the women's movement, attending seminars and discussion groups. When she learned that the medical establishment regarded a woman who could not orgasm through intercourse as having a medical problem, she decided to send out a questionnaire to determine how women really felt.

After obtaining permission from the recently formed National Organization for Women to use its letterhead, Hite began distributing the questionnaire in 1972. Lacking a foundation grant or other means of financial support for her undertaking, Hite resorted to the services of a small cooperative press

called Come! Unity Press, which was available to anyone for whatever dona-
tions she or he could afford, so long as the printed material was free to everyone. Over time Hite printed one hundred thousand questionnaires at the
press, with the help of several female volunteers, using all sorts and colors of
paper, including recycled Bingo cards. As the project grew larger, Hite decided to make the results available in book form and in 1974 published *Sexual Honesty by Women for Women* at Come! Unity Press. That paperback led
to a book contract and advance from a mainstream publisher, which with the
help of several loans from friends enabled Hite to continue sending out, col-
lating, and indexing questionnaires. Eventually seventy-five thousand questionnaires were mailed, while the remainder were distributed at feminist
conferences and other meetings attended by large numbers of women.

Over a period of five years Hite sent out four different versions of her
questionnaire, each an improvement over the previous one. The mailing
drew a relatively standard 3 percent return, though many went to abortion
rights groups and subscription lists for *The Village Voice* and *Ms.,* among
other outlets, giving her study a strong feminist bias. In all, 3,019 women
aged fourteen to seventy-eight responded anonymously to Hite's fifty-eight
very personal, and often very profound, questions. The first three, in the final
version, were

1. Do you have orgasms? If not, what do you think would contribute to your having them?
2. Is having orgasms important to you? Would you enjoy sex just as
   much without having them? Does having good sex have anything
   to do with having orgasms?
3. Do you have orgasms during the following (please indicate
   whether always, usually, sometimes, rarely, or never):
   masturbation: _____
   intercourse (vaginal penetration): _____
   manual clitoral stimulation by a partner: _____
   oral stimulation by a partner: _____
   intercourse plus manual clitoral stimulation: _____
   never have orgasms: _____

Nine-tenths of the *Report* was taken up with quotations from the respondents themselves. Though many sexologists criticized Hite for treating statistics cavalierly—much of her data was raw and unanalyzed—many of the
questions had the virtue of never having been asked of women before. As a
result, *The Hite Report,* for all its flaws, was both a milestone and an emancipation proclamation, or, in the words of psychotherapist Leah C. Schaefer,
"the first opportunity for women themselves to define their own sexuality."

Hite's second important finding concerned female masturbation. What first prompted her study was a question: Why did women orgasm relatively quickly when masturbating and yet were so slow or erratic to climax during intercourse? Hite discovered that there was a strong taboo against women touching themselves. They *waited* to be touched, waited for men to read their minds, and were often angry and frustrated when men failed to comply.

Hite further noted that no word existed to describe the clitoral stimulation of a woman by her lover. Cunnilingus implied oral stimulation. And masturbation usually meant an act done by the individual to herself, while she was alone. But manual or some other form of clitoral stimulation was subsumed under the general term "foreplay," which suggested that such touching was only a sexual preliminary to something else.

"Although sharing sex with a man can be wonderful," Hite also asked, "why does 'sharing' for a woman mean that the man must 'give' her the orgasm? Why can't a woman use her own hand to bring herself to orgasm?"

According to Hite, women were afraid to ask for more stimulation, one fear being they would no longer be supported economically by men. She further claimed that to "have an orgasm" was passive and suggested that the verb "to orgasm" implied that a woman "takes charge." She also attacked men's magazines for "incorrectly" posing models with their backs arched to simulate orgasm, whereas she thought women should bend their backs outward during orgasm.

The report's many detailed descriptions gave scientists a knowledge of what female masturbation was really like. The same was true for its many descriptions of orgasm, easily the best and most comprehensive source in a hitherto skimpy literature. Hite's respondents provided minute descriptions of many types of orgasm along the continuum, but they tended to place greater value on the process of sex than on orgasm per se.

After the success of the *Report,* Hite established the Feminist Sexuality Project, with herself as director, and immediately set about compiling a similar survey of men.

What Shere Hite did for orgasm and masturbation, journalist Nancy Friday did for female sex fantasies. The first of her best-sellers, *My Secret Garden,* published in 1973, helped change American consciousness by collecting women's fantasies at a time when most people assumed only men harbored forbidden sexual dreams. As a treasury of female lust, it proved a minor masterpiece. Friday herself offered little interpretative analysis, but she did contribute her own secret fantasy: having sex in the bleachers during a football game.

Garden was followed by *Forbidden Flowers,* a second helping of women's fantasies. After that, Nancy Friday the reporter evolved into Nancy Friday the sexual and cultural expert. In *My Mother/My Self,* she declared (with only anecdotal proof) that the primary influence in a woman's life was her mother.

It, too, had a sequel, *Men in Love,* wherein Friday insisted that all men were in a rage against their mothers. Though men did not talk about their anger, she contended, "the rage is still there. It has merely been repressed." Similarly, in *Jealousy* she stated that everyone, male or female, was consumed by this deadliest of sexual sins, and that anyone who denied it was merely in denial. Since her assumptions could be neither disproved nor believed (as David Hume remarked of the fanciful idealist philosophy of Bishop Berkeley), Friday's works were not taken seriously by the sexological community, though they continued to meet with popular success.

ONE OF THE MOST impassioned gay people in America in the seventies was a Harvard-educated former *Time* magazine editor named Boyd McDonald. In a small, cluttered room in an SRO hotel on Manhattan's Upper West Side, McDonald devoted his life to compiling a collection of volumes rivaling in importance—though certainly not in sales or publicity—*The Hite Report.*

Talkative, gaunt, and sardonic, the chain-smoking McDonald kept his personal needs to a minimum—a small cot covered with an army blanket, a tiny stove and refrigerator, a writing table. Lining the walls were overflowing bookcases and rows of shopping bags stuffed with letters from gay men around the country. McDonald's ongoing mission was to collect and publish these letters, which described the writers' sexual experiences in graphic detail, along with his often droll commentary, in a journal he titled *Straight to Hell: The New York Review of Unnatural Acts,* popularly known as *STH.* He dubbed the accounts "true case histories in the tradition of Kinsey and the great sex researchers of this country" or, less loftily, "true stories of men's groins and rear ends."

McDonald had gone into voluntary exile from respectable society. Born and raised in a small town in South Dakota, he had been drafted in 1943 and later guarded Nazi POWs at Fort Dix, New Jersey. After his discharge he enrolled in Harvard, where he immersed himself in his books but developed a serious drinking habit. Upon graduation he went to work as a staff writer for *Time,* staying five years and hating every minute. Bored and drunk most of the time, he bounced around from IBM to Merrill Lynch to the American Stock Exchange, editing in-house publications.

After twenty years of drinking, McDonald entered a detoxification program at a state hospital. On his release, he found himself jobless and broke. Determined to go into publishing for himself, he decided to publish a newsletter containing gay personal advertisements geared toward foreskin fetishists. An advertisement for the newsletter in *The Village Voice* elicited a substantial response. Best of all, though, subscribers began to send along accounts of their sexual experiences with their copy, inspiring him to create *STH.*

Before long, some of the most explicit and extensive true case histories ever written filled the journal's pages, and the personal advertisements were relegated to a department called "The Men's Room Wall." It was not long before the publication achieved legendary status among gays. Renowned gay writers like William Burroughs and Christopher Isherwood offered him praise and encouragement, and Gore Vidal called *STH* "one of the best radical papers in the country."

In the early eighties Winston Leyland of the Gay Sunshine Press and Gay Presses in San Francisco contracted with McDonald to edit anthologies of *STH* material, and by 1985 eight titles had been published, each with a brazen one-word title: *Sex, Flesh, Meat, Smut, Cum, Juice, Wads, Filth.* They outsold every other gay book on the shelves except Harvey Fierstein's *Torch Song Trilogy*—about fifty thousand copies in all.

Unlike gay video porn, which featured sexual automatons with huge penises, *STH* letters, whether garden-variety lewd or extravagantly debauched, rang true. McDonald's stringent editorial policy was that contributors had to include "just the facts, the sight, taste, touch, and smell of sex. How men look, act, dress, undress, and talk. What happened, in A-B-C, 1-2-3 order." McDonald thought sex was the one subject that did not need to be written "up." The plain truth was more interesting, more pornographic, than pornography.

STH's contributors included doctors, soldiers, lawyers, other professionals, laborers, prisoners, and an unusual number of clergy, particularly Catholic priests. All contributors were anonymous unless they requested a byline. Differences in class and education were evident in the writing, but even those with bad grammar and misspellings were often memorable reading.

If McDonald found a contribution particularly intriguing, he often asked the writer to provide more information in an "embarrassingly detailed" questionnaire for publication. Like a Kinsey researcher, he asked his subject such nosy things as "Do your jockey shorts have encrusted urine deposits? Embarrassing fecal stains? Do you ever sniff your asshole? What does it smell like?" Other questions related to penis size, frequency of orgasm, density of body hair, and the like.

At Harvard McDonald had joined the left-leaning John Reed Society, and all his life he remained a Socialist. Favorite targets of his commentaries were Ronald Reagan, Jerry Falwell, William F. Buckley ("the Liberace of literature"), neoconservative Norman Podhoretz, and Norman Mailer ("America's most obsessive exponent of joy through strength, virility through violence").

Unapologetic about his gay chauvinism, McDonald thought heterosexuality had nothing to do with sex and was more about status, respectability, and power, none of which was offered by homosexuality. "How can women go to bed with Spiro Agnew, Richard Nixon, or Ronald Reagan?" he asked. "It's because sex is one of the least things in heterosexuality. It's all money, houses, reputation, mortgages." The objects of his teasing criticism of straights were men: "Most women are decent, and we wish them power," he once editorialized in *STH*. Yet one reason for the popularity of his books was that they featured numerous accounts of ostensibly straight men (known as "trade" in gay jargon) being serviced by, or servicing, gay men.

McDonald also edited a monthly column of true-sex accounts for the *New York Native* and wrote a monthly film review for *Christopher Street,* the gay magazine of arts and letters, leading *Mother Jones* to call him "one of the nation's least appreciated and most astute film critics."

PART THREE

P L A T E A U

1975 - 1983

Chapter 9

The Sleazing of America

WHEN HE TURNED FOURTEEN, HE RAN AWAY FROM HIS APPALACHIAN HOME AND alcoholic father to join the army, lying about his age. Six months later, after failing miserably on a battery of tests, he was discharged. Moving to another state, he lied about his previous military record, enlisted in the navy, and was ultimately assigned to the USS *Enterprise,* America's first nuclear-powered aircraft carrier. At the height of the 1962 Cuban missile crisis, President Kennedy visited the ship before it departed for the Caribbean to head up the blockade. As the crew was being reviewed, he stepped forward onto the president's shoes just so he could say he was sorry.

It was probably the first and last time Larry Flynt ever apologized for anything.

Unlettered, truculent, rowdy, a wild child of the hills, Flynt learned only one thing while serving his country. Picking up a paperback copy of Harold Robbins's *The Carpetbaggers* one day, he saw revealed, as in a vision, a mesmerizing world of wealth and power. Right then and there, he decided to become a carpetbagger himself.

After getting his second service discharge, Flynt returned to western Appalachia and used his meager savings to open up a go-go bar. Inspired by Hugh Hefner's Playboy Clubs, Flynt christened it the Hustler Club, drawing his blue-collar clientele from the hill country of southern Ohio and neighboring Kentucky. Members paid a nominal fee at the door—a stratagem that allowed the club to circumvent county liquor restrictions while giving it the air of a semiprivate establishment. What the Hustler Club lacked in big-city sophistication it made up for by recruiting the sauciest dancers and serving up the raunchiest, honky-tonky-est good time around, with Larry and his brother, Jimmy, leading the way on most nights.

As the string of Hustler Clubs expanded, Flynt began publishing a newsletter to hype featured dancers and editorialize about local politics. Keeping mathematical pace with his go-going concerns, Flynt married four or five times—a number that even his several wives were unable to pin down—fathered five children, and got himself frequently arrested up and down the Ohio Valley for barroom brawling and other disturbances of the peace.

Those disturbances took an ugly turn in the early seventies, when Flynt was sitting in the back of a Cincinnati bar with a woman. Another woman approached, jealous of the attentions Flynt was showing her rival, and pulled a gun. Flynt wrestled it away, but not before several shots were fired into the ceiling, at which point the sobbing woman laid her head on his lap.

This time, though, Flynt was prosecuted for discharging a firearm in a public place and sentenced to thirty days in jail, despite supporting testimony from the woman and brother Jimmy, who was also in the bar. Flynt went to jail mainly because his go-go joints and newsletter editorials had incurred the wrath of Simon Leis, the Hamilton County prosecutor. The two men had been bitter enemies from the start.

Upon Flynt's release from jail, Leis summarily charged him with perjury. Since Flynt had been convicted, Leis told the jury, he must have been lying. Then, while the perjury rap was still pending, Leis slapped Flynt with a sodomy charge, stating that the woman with the gun had actually been performing fellatio on him. Once again Flynt was convicted, though this time the judge wisely set the verdict aside and ordered a new trial. Leis's tactic established his MO in his war with the hillbilly hell-raiser: take a misdemeanor and turn it into a felony.

In July 1974 the Hustler Clubs' two-page, two-color newsletter underwent a radical metamorphosis and emerged as *Hustler* magazine, with an initial paid circulation of 160,000. If Hefner's centerfolds presented lush visions of the girl next door, and Guccione's served up fantasies of women almost beyond any mortal man's reach, Flynt went in the opposite direction. *Hustler* models were the good-time bar girls who posed, legs splayed gynecologically wide, without benefit of postsession airbrushing, fancy props, or trendy clothes. What the truckers, factory workers, and telephone linemen saw when they picked up a copy of the magazine was exactly the kind of girl they went home with if they ever got lucky at closing time.

Equal parts *National Lampoon, Playboy, Rolling Stone,* and *Screw,* the magazine struggled through its first year, but turned the corner spectacularly with its August 1975 issue, which featured a five-page pictorial of Jackie Kennedy Onassis sunbathing nude on her Greek island, Skorpios. The pictures not only made national news, but gave *Hustler* both the circulation and the notoriety Flynt was seeking—even though the photos were not nearly as much of a coup as he later claimed. The same set had appeared a few years earlier in the Italian skin magazine *Playmen* and had been offered to both *Playboy* and *Penthouse,* which had declined to publish them out of consideration for the widow of the slain president.

The Jackie O issue enabled *Hustler* to achieve the million-copy mark, and within a few years it reached a circulation of three million while selling at the high cover price of $2.25, making it one of the most financially successful American magazines of the decade. To avoid Leis and Cincinnati's aggressive pack of vigilantes, Flynt had relocated to upstate, more liberal Columbus, where the offices of *Hustler* were housed in a grim, four-story building downtown.

In 1976 one of Flynt's former go-go girls and the July 1975 centerfold model, a twenty-four-year-old woman named Althea Leasure, took over the responsibilities as executive editor. Though inexperienced in publishing, she was endowed with a sexual imagination even more calculatedly perverse than Flynt's, and circulation under her guidance immediately shot up 375 percent. In quick succession she became associate publisher, editorial director, and Mrs. Flynt.

Though Flynt had a reputation for being promiscuous, Leasure was to remain the only woman he ever loved. Occasionally he beat her, which she once even admitted in the pages of *Hustler,* explaining to an interviewer, "I don't see anything wrong with a man striking a woman. In fact, many women are turned on by it." Occasionally Althea also joined in Larry's indiscretions, as well as carrying on several love affairs with women.

In addition to *Hustler,* Flynt also published *Chic,* designed to be competitive in the upmarket against *Penthouse* and *Playboy,* just as the latter attempted to compete in the downmarket *Hustler* realm with *Oui.* Other profit centers included Leasure Time sex accessories and a magazine distribution company. A typical occasional publication, *Hustler Rejects,* featured women who were judged not good enough to appear in the main magazine. In centerfolds they were pictured with bags over their heads.

Before long Flynt was earning $15 million annually—a redneck millionaire with an enormous pot belly in pullover sports shirt, lacquered fingernails, gold rings and bracelets, and a gold necklace supporting a pendant that read "#1" in diamonds. His red Rolls-Royce was carpeted in fur, and he flew around the country in a pink jet. Yet he continued to prefer the food he was raised on—beans over cornbread, with Skippy peanut butter and thick slices of raw onion on the side, and more cornbread dipped in molasses for dessert.

Though Flynt's Columbus mansion featured such standard luxury items as swan-shaped gold bathroom fixtures, the basement was further evidence that he was never far from his Appalachian roots. In the subterranean Kentucky Room, Flynt was able to retire into a life-size reconstruction of the cabin where he had grown up. Plastered along the entryway were straw and chicken wire, while extending from a basement wall was a replica of the porch. Elsewhere in the museumlike display was a collection of plows, shovels, washboards, jugs, and plaster chickens. But it was all a typical Larry Flynt joke: housed inside this down-home shack was something no poor Kentuckian could afford—a luxurious sauna.

As the Jackie O photos demonstrated, Flynt's bad taste knew virtually no bounds. In ensuing years the magazine regularly ran jokes and cartoons about bestiality, dismemberment, castration, Tampax, feces, even First Lady Betty Ford's mastectomy. Other subsequent Flynt firsts included a life-size nude foldout, a pubic scratch-'n'-sniff centerfold scented like lilacs, pictorials of pregnant women fondling each other, a fifty-year-old model, and a hermaphrodite who after the his/her photo finally chose to become a man.

Self-styling himself the "Eighth Wonder of the World," sometimes on the cover of his own magazine, Flynt also frequently attempted to give away a million dollars, sometimes for good causes and at other times just to get a little free publicity—as when he offered the sum to Elizabeth Taylor to pose nude in his pages.

IN THE WAKE of *Deep Throat,* a surprising number of sex-oriented films outside the pornographic genre established cult followings. Among the first, in 1973, was writer-director John Waters's *Pink Flamingos,* a campy exploration of sexual evil. Anything but erotic, the story revolves around a feud between lead character Divine, a transvestite, and a clan named the Marbles as they vie for the title of being the "filthiest people in the world." Filthy deeds included mailing human feces; kidnapping female hitchhikers, impregnating them, and selling the babies to lesbian couples; spreading saliva over an enemy's furniture; incest, castration, cannibalism, torture, rape, and murder. Perhaps not so coincidentally, Waters was an admirer and friend of his fellow Baltimorean John Money, the world's leading authority on paraphilias.

Art films also grew more explicit, notably Bernardo Bertolucci's controversial 1973 hit, *Last Tango in Paris,* with Marlon Brando and Maria Schneider. The story of a guilt-ridden lonely American in Paris, the film follows Brando's character as he looks for an apartment. He finds one, but a pretty young French girl wants it, too, so they argue, then agree to share the apartment but not their names, with the search ending in a brutal, animalistic bout of sex in which Brando forces Schneider to the floor and she submits to anal sex facilitated by a bar of butter.

Russ Meyer's soft-core *The Supervixens,* made for $213,000 in 1974, was to gross more than $20 million. By 1978 porn accounted for about 17 percent of a total of $365 million in box office receipts.

In 1981 Jim Sharman's *The Rocky Horror Picture Show* became the all-time favorite midnight-movie show, outcamping even *Pink Flamingos* and inspiring its fanatical followers to appear weekend after weekend at theaters around the country dressed in the extravagant drag of their favorite performers. A musical based on a smash hit London play, *Rocky Horror* recounted the adventures of a young middle-class couple motoring in the countryside on their wedding night. When their car breaks down in front of a mansion, they ask to use the phone and enter just as its garter-belted master, Dr. Frank N. Furter, is conducting an experiment—the unveiling of his newly made creation, Rocky. Before long the young couple, caught up in a strange household populated by lavishly eccentric guests of uncertain gender, succumb to Dr. Furter's charms.

The finest sexually explicit art film ever made, *In the Realm of the Senses,* still managed to draw gasps of astonishment as late as 1979. Directed by Nagisa Oshima, and starring Eiko Matsuda and Tatsuya Fuji, this wonderfully plotted and expertly acted erotic fantasy turned nightmare was based on the true-life 1936 Abe Sada case.

Soon after opening Doc Johnson, his sex toy and sex aid mail-order division, in the mid-seventies, Reuben Sturman visited Las Vegas and stopped in to see Jack and Jill. Much to his amazement, Jack said: "I want to sell Talk of the Town."

"Are you out of your fucking mind?" Sturman replied. "Where are you going to make more money than this?"

"I know where the promised land is," said Jack.

"Where is that?" Sturman asked.

"Los Angeles."

Sturman knew Jack was netting maybe $20,000 a month from Talk of the Town, which was a lot of money. But Jack was insistent. He wanted $75,000 for the store, plus inventory. Sturman said he would think about it. But he did not have a management team in place that he trusted.

Back in Cleveland, Sturman was playing poker one Wednesday night with his buddies when he mentioned this stupid guy who wanted to sell his Las Vegas store. The next day one of his poker pals, Ralph Levine, called and said he wanted to get out of Cleveland, move to Las Vegas, and buy the store with Reuben. That was all Sturman needed to hear. They bought the store in partnership, opened a few more, and made Talk of the Town bigger than ever.

Sturman trusted his partner and his son, David, so much that he decided to use their names to help solve a little problem—what to do with all the money he was making. Every day his warehouse office crowded up with scores of briefcases stashed with cash from his retail stores and peep shows, most of it skimmed profits. Sturman just hated the idea of paying his fair share in taxes.

In 1974 Sturman bought a Dutch passport in the name of Paul Bekker and used it to open several Swiss bank accounts. He also asked David and Ralph to sign the accounts. Both obliged, though they may not have understood what they were getting into.

What happened next was a Keystone Kops version of criminal ineptitude. Authorities in Zurich quickly caught on to the ploy and arrested Sturman, who good-naturedly blurted to the arresting officer that he was only trying to hide his money in Switzerland to avoid paying U.S. taxes. He was sentenced to a month in prison and barred from Switzerland for the next three years.

Brazen and unrepentant, Sturman sent David and a lawyer to yet another Swiss bank to close down an account. To avoid creating bank transfer records, the two men withdrew money in the form of twenty-two gold bars and $400,000 in cash. But the load was so heavy that it had to be carted out on a dolly, which was not the most inconspicuous way to move money around in the banking capital of Europe. The pair then deposited the money in a third Swiss bank.

Sturman's confession and the gold-bar escapade attracted the attention of the IRS, which logically assumed the owner of Sovereign News and a number of other corporations was not only avoiding taxes, but laundering cash. In 1975 the FBI even resorted to using a battering ram on the Sovereign Warehouse's reinforced door to serve a subpoena. Soon afterward, Richard Rosfelder, an IRS criminal investigator based in Cleveland, began looking full-time into Sturman's affairs. He tracked Sturman's paper empire from Switzerland to the Cayman Islands to Cleveland, learning far more about creative corporate financing, state-of-the-art money-laundering techniques, and the role of lawyers and money couriers than about smut. Successful prosecution, however, meant the IRS had to prove Sturman's receipts were being skimmed or kept off the books. Rosfelder also had to document cash flow through bank accounts under Sturman's control. Yet the maze devised by Sturman and his tax lawyer, Bernard Berkman, was so intricate that none of thirty bank accounts scrutinized by Rosfelder and his associate, Tom Ciehanski, could be traced directly back to the King. One problem was that names of corporate officers of Sturman enterprises were often fabricated or lifted from phone directories. To avoid signatures, rubber stamps bearing the bogus names were used on bank account signature cards and corporate tax filings.

Sturman seemed invincible. His high-priced lawyers won every obscenity prosecution brought against him. On paper he was the most law-abiding pornographer alive. And by now he was universally acknowledged as the most brilliant and ruthless player in the game, a business genius whose triple-tier manufacture-wholesale-retail operation was a textbook example of Harvard Business School vertical integration that assured him of a monopoly in one of the world's most lucrative trades.

UNTIL 1974 Bob Guccione still divided his time between his penthouse apartment in the Penthouse Club in London's Shepherd's Market and a suite at the Drake Hotel in Manhattan. In 1975 he purchased the combined town houses on Manhattan's East Side that had belonged to Jeremiah Milbank Jr., board chairman of Commercial Solvents. The price was a then record $650,000, though brokerage and other fees upped it to close to $1 million. Guccione renovated the town house to include a photography studio, swimming pool, and garden, furnished it with rare European antiques, a museum's worth of Impressionists and Old Masters, and a gilded grand piano formerly owned by Judy Garland, and moved into it with his companion, Kathy Keeton, and a kennel of purebred Rhodesian Ridgebacks.

Favoring black leather pants and a print sports shirt with a plunging neckline that revealed a half dozen gold chains, Guccione radiated sexual radicalism. Yet by every account the quiet, almost monastic precincts of the Guccione town house were never once disturbed by orgies, and drugs were banished. For that matter, nobody ever swam in the swimming pool, either. Guccione worked late into the night at the layout board on his coffee table, usually not waking until noon the following day. Taking neither breakfast nor lunch, he fueled himself on diet soda and coffee. Guccione the public radical was almost straitlaced in private life. A devoted family man, he scoffed at those who saw a parallel between his character and Hefner's, beyond the fact that each man owned a soft-core magazine and lived in a mansion. In Guccione's view, Hefner's was more like a circus tent, with the ringmaster surrounded by phonies and cronies.

Indeed, Hefner had never cast himself, or been perceived by the American public, as a sexual rebel, a threat to traditional values. Yet he managed to live out a sexual lifestyle in virtual full view of the public, although there were aspects that the public never saw: the nightly orgies with some of the most famous faces and bodies in America, his cocaine habit, his custom of filming himself while engaging in group or private sex.

As a result, Hefner was able to portray himself as a slightly wayward friend of the Establishment, the black sheep who was doing openly what all the boys in the back room privately lusted to do themselves and could do vicariously by reading his magazine. Guccione's fondness for gold chains and his Sicilian ancestry stereotyped him as the hood on the corner, waiting to seduce the girl next door on her way home, while Hefner's increasing disposition to appear in public wearing only pajamas, bathrobe, and slippers seemed merely the odd affectation of a nice young Protestant man in the prime of life with a predilection for pretty young girls. If his magazine made a cult out of publishing lush pictorials of the girl next door, Hefner was the guy next door.

In 1975, having worn down editor Spectorsky and fired art director Tajiri, Hefner hired his twenty-two-year-old daughter, Christie, as liaison to his vice presidents. Tall and slender, with the perfect teeth and light brown hair of a *Playboy* centerfold, Christie was only a few months older than the magazine. It was only a matter of time, appropriately, before a girl next door would be running the magazine; and in the long run Hefner's nepotism proved to be sound strategy. As she matured, Christie became the personification of the level-headed publishing executive during the politically fraught upheavals and turmoil of the eighties and nineties.

In addition to waging war with *Playboy,* Guccione—one of the most litigious men in America—was frequently in court as a plaintiff or defendant, often as a result of the magazine's aggressive investigative journalism. One of the most serious cases involved organized crime. In 1975 the principal officers of Rancho La Costa, a luxurious California resort, filed suit against *Penthouse* seeking $630 million in damages—one of the biggest libel suits in American legal history. Guccione and his insurance company, which later went broke, spent $20 million defending him, and the four plaintiffs paid out an equal amount.

In an article called "La Costa: Syndicate in the Sun," freelancers Lowell Bergman and Jeff Gerth claimed the 5,600-acre resort near La Jolla was a haven for members of organized crime and had been financed with a questionable $250 million loan from a Teamsters pension fund and skimmed profits from a casino.

The four plaintiffs were Moe Dalitz, a longtime racketeer and associate of the late Lucky Luciano and Bugsy Siegel; Allard Roen, who had once been convicted of stock fraud; and two real-estate developers, Merv Adelson and Irwin Molasky. Adelson and Molasky were also principal officers of Lorimar Productions of Hollywood, producers of *The Waltons,* a major TV series.

Worried that real-estate prices would be disastrously affected by the article, Dalitz and Adelson personally went to see Guccione and complained that it was full of inaccuracies. Adelson also mentioned that celebrity interviewer Barbara Walters refused to marry him until he refuted the charges. Guccione defended the article's assertions, but did offer La Costa's owners space in the magazine to refute the charges. They refused.

One evening soon afterward, Guccione was sitting alone in his fourth-floor office on New York's East Side and heard a tinkling of glass. After diving to the floor, he looked up and saw a tiny hole in the window. Crawling across the room, he discovered a bullet hole near the baseboard. Someone had obviously shot at him from a rooftop about eighty feet away. Guccione had no doubt the gunman missed intentionally and meant only to frighten him—though he had no evidence then or later as to who hired him. But he did not call the police for fear that the publicity might inspire a deranged copycat gunman. However, he did hire a bodyguard.

Prominent attorney Louis Nizer led La Costa's legal team. *Penthouse*'s chief litigator was Roy Grutman. During the trial, a male *Penthouse* lawyer and a female assistant—the daughter of a prominent businessman—went to California to gather legal documents about the resort and were secretly photographed having sex at their hotel. Later Nizer went to see Grutman and said, "Okay, the time has come to settle."

"How much are you going to give us?" Grutman asked.

Nizer replied, "We're not going to give you anything. We want money from you."

Grutman laughed and said, "I don't have any time to waste." Hoping that *Penthouse*'s legal team would want to avoid a sex scandal involving the young woman, Nizer then informed Grutman about the photographs, whereupon Grutman laconically remarked, "I just fired the bastard."

Throughout the trial, the plaintiffs packed the court with movie stars. On the day the jury was charged, they even put up a tent serving lemonade and food to onlookers. To no avail—in 1982 the jury found for *Penthouse* on every count. Later the judge overturned the jury's verdict and the suit was reinstated. After another three years, both sides realized that neither could win and that any victory would be Pyrrhic. In an out-of-court settlement, *Penthouse* declared it had never meant to suggest that Adelson and Molasky were involved in organized crime, and La Costa acknowledged the magazine's numerous journalism awards.

Despite the suit, the FBI suspected that Guccione was financed by Mob money and in the late seventies tried to entrap him as part of its Abscam operation, named after a fictitious sheik code-named Abdul. At the time, Guccione was trying to open a casino in Atlantic City, but needed to borrow massive amounts of money to realize his dream. One day he was approached by Melvin Weinberg, a con man turned FBI informant and the middleman in the sting, who told him about a Sheik Abdul who wanted to invest $150 million in the operation, but only after the casino had obtained a license. To that end, Weinberg authorized Guccione to pay up to $300,000 in bribe money to New Jersey gaming officials. Guccione's response: "Are you out of your mind?" Only in 1983, when testimony before a Senate subcommittee on organized crime became public, did he learn that he had been the target of an attempted sting. The Senate subcommittee criticized the FBI for its handling of the episode, saying it was "a chilling reminder of the risks imposed by lax procedures and inadequate supervision of an informant like Weinberg." Guccione later filed a suit against the Federal government, claiming that the sting attempt was the reason why, despite his immense personal fortune, he could obtain neither financing nor a casino license. The suit was dismissed without comment. Undeterred, he continued to spend tens of millions annually in his bid for a casino—an obsession that was ultimately to be the iron-willed Guccione's undoing.

The seventies, though, were the boom years. By 1978, nine years after it set out to dethrone *Playboy, Penthouse* finally overtook its competitor where it mattered—in high-profit newsstand sales, by a 37 percent margin. *Forbes,* in announcing the news, said *Penthouse* "may be the single most profitable magazine in publishing history, save perhaps *TV Guide* or *Reader's Digest.*" In due time *Forbes's* fun-loving publisher, Malcolm Forbes, and the workaholic Bob Guccione were to become best pals.

Penthouse now averaged 4.3 million newsstand copies per issue in the United States and Canada alone at $2 per copy; *Playboy* only 3.1 million at $1.75 per copy. That translated into monthly gross revenues of $8.6 million for *Penthouse,* $5.5 million for *Playboy.* Still stinging from the loss of *Viva,* Guccione and Keeton were preparing to launch *Omni,* a lush pop science/science-fiction magazine, which debuted in September 1978 and within a few years reached a circulation of nearly one million.

In overall circulation, including subscriptions, *Playboy* stood at 5 million, compared with *Penthouse's* 4.6 million and *Hustler's* 2 million. At the back of the pack were *Gallery* (backed by attorney F. Lee Bailey), *Genesis, Club,* and *Oui.*

By 1977 *Screw* claimed a readership of one hundred thousand, and by now federal prosecutors were resolved to bring the magazine down. Instead of prosecuting Goldstein in New York, however, the government decided not to take any chances. In the words of Harvard law professor Alan Dershowitz, "The feds took out a map of Middle America and sought out a Bible Belt jurisdiction where Goldstein was likely to be viewed as the devil incarnate and *Screw* magazine as his *Gehenna Gazette.*"

The choice fell on Wichita, Kansas, which had less than a dozen subscribers to the publication in a city of 375,000. Newsstand sales were nonexistent. No Wichitan had ever complained to the authorities, so the government created its own bogus case. During the very week of the Watergate break-in in July 1972, several postal inspectors, apparently operating on instructions from Washington, had filled out subscription applications to *Screw.* When the sealed envelopes containing the newspaper arrived in Kansas, they were placed intact in another envelope and sent on to Washington. An alleged felony had been completed; obscene material had entered the territory of Kansas.

The stage was now set for "the monkey trial of sex," as Goldstein later termed it. Grand jurors literally got down on their knees and sought guidance from God each day before hearing evidence of *Screw*'s blasphemies. Ultimately they rendered a thirteen-count indictment charging Goldstein and his partner, Jim Buckley, with the use of the mail to distribute obscene material.

Goldstein bought out Buckley, who had lost interest in the magazine and regarded the outspoken Goldstein as irresponsible, although Buckley still had to stand trial. Goldstein's lawyers, who eventually obtained a change of venue, to Kansas City, were among the best in the business of defending the First Amendment: Paul Cambria, a tough, young New Yorker, and the legendary Herald Fahringer, fiftyish, stately, self-assured, quick on the draw. The prosecution was handled by Washington lawyer Harold Damlin: young, short haired, neatly dressed. Despite the considerable publicity the trial was generating, Judge Frank Theis issued a gag order on the press. The trial began in the fall of 1976.

During testimony, New York postal inspector Raphael Lombardi confirmed that orders from Washington had initiated the series of events leading to the trial. Cambria and Fahringer argued that the mailing of phony subscriptions was entrapment, claiming that the government had even done a demographic study to determine where it was most likely to get a conviction. Among the defense experts were Brendan Gill of *The New Yorker* and Dr. W. Walter Menninger of the Menninger Foundation. The trial lasted four weeks. Before the case went to the jury, Judge Theis reduced the counts against Buckley and Goldstein from thirteen to twelve. The jurors, most of whom had not gone beyond high school, deliberated only seventeen minutes. Then they convicted the two New Yorkers on every count.

In April 1977 Larry Flynt's macho empire struck back at feminism by publishing a portfolio of seven nude photos of author Shere Hite in *Hustler,* captioned "The Hite Report Exposed." They included one shot of the most famous feminist in the world lying on a bed, her legs spread wide apart, wearing only wig, nylons, high heels, and a feathered headdress. The photographs had been taken in 1968 during Hite's modeling days in New York by Sam Menning, who specialized in selling sex photos to adult bookshops in Times Square.

Hustler also voiced a common objection among male readers of Hite's book, taking issue with her contention that it was all right for men to have sex without orgasm, and that the reason why some women did not climax during intercourse was because men controlled sex and society. That complaint was to be repeated frequently over the years by both men and women, who claimed Hite was an angry woman using her data to vent her hostility toward men. Feminists criticized her for getting rich off feminism, especially after *The Hite Report on Male Sexuality,* published five years after her first book, sold three hundred thousand copies and earned her another $1 million. Nearly a thousand pages long, the tome dealt with women's disappointments with male-female relationships and was featured in a *Time* magazine cover story titled "Back Off, Buddy."

But Flynt had other fish to fry as well. He continued his million-dollar giveaways, offering $1 million to President Jimmy Carter in 1977 to reinstitute the Commission on Obscenity and Pornography to "get the truth behind erotic materials." The offer was ignored. But just when it seemed impossible that he could ever shock anybody again with his antics, an uncharacteristically pious Larry Flynt announced that, with the help of President Carter's evangelist sister, Ruth Carter Stapleton, he had become a born-again Christian and vowed to change *Hustler.*

Ostensibly, Flynt and Stapleton got together because both were opposed to child abuse. *Hustler,* in fact, had published several extraordinary essays on the subject, including one by National Institutes of Health (NIH) administrator Dr. James W. Prescott that cost him his job. (In a misguided attempt to understand sexual perversion, Stapleton also escorted Flynt into the subterranean world of SM parlors—as observer, of course, not participant.) Flynt also donated generously to the cause and at one point offered $1 million to Congress to fund a study on child abuse. He even shared a pulpit with Stapleton at a San Antonio revivalist church, telling the congregation, "I feel I owe every mother here an apology for *Hustler"*—even though Flynt's own mother, who lived with him, had never complained.

Everybody he knew told him they were offended by his magazine, Flynt confessed, which led him to ask himself, "Are they right?" Looking through its pages, he found that indeed he was offended "by almost everything." Among the more egregious examples of bad taste was the Beaver Hunt section, where men sent in pictures of nude girlfriends, or women sent them in themselves. A cartoon showing feces offended him. Pictures of lesbians making love offended him, not that he had anything against lesbians or homosexuals. "But lesbians humiliating themselves for our readers—that offends me. And a lot of what doesn't offend me bores me. I'm bored with pornography."

Yet he kept publishing because men all over the country needed *Hustler.* Not only did they feel inferior, but they *were* inferior, Flynt told his readers. That was because women were naturally superior. "They're our only hope," he contritely admitted.

Flynt vowed to turn his magazine toward a healthier vision of sex and religion. He warned, though, that it would take months for the changes to ap-

pear, owing to the long lead time necessary in magazine publishing. He repeated his message in numerous press conferences and TV appearances.

Perhaps it was not a coincidence that in January 1977 Flynt, Althea,
brother Jimmy, and production manager Al Van Schaik had gone on trial in
Cincinnati, where the magazine was distributed and sold, on charges of obscenity and trafficking with organized crime. Not so coincidentally, Cincinnati was also the home of Charles Keating, founder and director of the
Citizens for Decency through Law. His brother, Bill, served as president of
the city's most influential paper, the *Cincinnati Enquirer,* whose editorials and
investigative stories kept up a relentless attack on pornographers.

In the January issue, *Hustler* also fired the first salvo in what promised to
be a lengthy battle fought not only in the courtroom but through the media—a horrific pictorial entitled "The Real Obscenity: War." Since few residents of Cincinnati were likely to buy that or any other issue of *Hustler,*
reprints of the photo set were sent to four hundred thousand residents of
Hamilton County. The sickening photos consisted of scenes of the Vietnam
War that no family newspaper, or even other magazines, dared to run. The
mailing cost $50,000 and soon had the city up in arms.

Defense lawyer Herald Fahringer had also defended Goldstein in Kansas
City. Prosecutor Simon Leis, like Judge William J. Morrissey, was Catholic.
(During the trial, Leis characterized fellatio as a repulsive act, leading *Hustler* in its report on the proceedings to speculate on the prosecutor's sex life
with his wife, adding that "it would seem unlikely that Leis can tell a clitoris
from a rutabaga.") The prosecution used its quota of twenty peremptory
challenges to eliminate jurors under thirty, as well as those who were obviously well educated and those who had ever read a men's magazine or seen a
porn movie or thought adults had the right to read what they wanted. In
turn, the defense removed those of clearly conservative background or with
little education. As a result, the trial was essentially a battle between the
morals of different generations.

In its defense, *Hustler* claimed that once the printed copies of the magazine
were in the hands of the distributor, the publisher no longer had control over
where the magazines were eventually sold. That was determined by the distributor, who in this case subcontracted to the J. L. Marshall News Company
for distribution in the Cincinnati area. Marshall had the option of refusing to
distribute issues it felt exceeded community standards and had done so with
other publications on more than one occasion. But Marshall had been
granted immunity in exchange for testifying on behalf of the prosecution.
And Judge Morrissey refused to admit into evidence magazines comparable
to *Hustler* that were sold in Hamilton County during the same period as the
indicted issues, ruling that the jury itself constituted a sufficient gauge of
community standards.

208 ■ WHAT WILD ECSTASY

Among those testifying for the defense was Wardell Pomeroy, who spurned the notion that the photos and text in *Hustler* would incite the average person to commit sexual acts that were degrading and shameful. In his view, the average person's response to pictures of bestiality and stories of incest would be repulsion. Those who responded pruriently were already, by definition, not average. Novelist Harold Robbins, Flynt's hero, showed up in Cincinnati. Though Robbins did not testify, he did make a statement to the press in defense of the First Amendment and mentioned that he was writing a novel entitled *Dreams Die First,* about the publisher of a successful girlie magazine.

It was all to no avail. Althea, Jimmy, and Van Schaik were acquitted, but Flynt was convicted on all counts. After he was handcuffed, he was led before the judge. A defense attorney asked for a temperate sentence. Then Flynt requested to speak in his own behalf. "You haven't made an intelligent decision during the course of the trial," he said, "and I don't expect one now."

The judge sentenced Flynt to seven to twenty-five years in prison, plus $11,000 in fines—the maximum—and further ruled that he could not be released on bond. For the next six days, until his lawyers got the remand order overturned, Flynt remained in jail. As consolation, Al Goldstein sent a deluxe package of dildos with a card reading "To Althea for those long cold nights when Larry's in jail."

Flynt's lawyers appealed. At the same time, to almost nobody's surprise (except perhaps Ruth Carter Stapleton's), his fervor for his newfound religion began to wane. In June 1978, *Hustler* published what was destined to become the most outrageous and offensive magazine cover, whether soft-core or hard-core, of all time: a photograph of a woman's long legs sticking up from a meat grinder under the caption "We will no longer hang women up like pieces of meat. —Larry Flynt." Outraged, Women Against Pornography and other antiporn organizations immediately gave the cover even greater notoriety and currency by reproducing it as a fund-raising poster—much to Flynt's delight.

"No one can tell me what I can or can't say," he remarked at the time. "I have the right to yell 'Fire' in a crowded theater if I want. Hell, I can yell 'Cunt' in a convention of feminists. It's in bad taste, and you can arrest me for disturbing the peace, but don't go violating my First Amendment rights."

In Flynt's uncompromising view, *Penthouse* and *Playboy* were "copouts," while their respective publishers, Bob Guccione and Hugh Hefner, were "artsy-fartsy types." He was momentarily seized by the idea of distributing *Mother Jones,* one of the decade's boldest left-wing publications, though he scarcely knew anything about its content. On an impulse he visited the magazine's home office and flew back with the publisher to Cincinnati to discuss distribution, which did not work out. Yet he remained convinced that *Hus-*

tler and *Mother Jones* had the same mission—to expose America. What was disgusting in his magazine only mirrored what was disgusting about the country itself.

Flynt's appeal coincided with Al Goldstein's trial in Kansas City. Flynt was certain Goldstein would be found guilty, and he had planned to fly his pink jet to Kansas City to sell *Screw* on the courthouse steps after the verdict. It was not only a gesture of solidarity, but a cunning business maneuver. Flynt had also just contracted to distribute an extra 250,000 copies of the New York newspaper.

But his distribution company would turn out to be Flynt's one serious miscalculation. Many of the less successful and raunchier men's magazines were distributed by companies under Mafia control. But Flynt thought he was invincible, a superman who could buck not only the federal government, but the underworld. And setting up his own distribution company had made good business sense, at least on paper. Though its circulation was less than that of *Penthouse* or *Playboy*—both distributed by legitimate companies—*Hustler* was equally profitable to the retailer because it had a higher cover price and fewer returns. Flynt asked himself why he should pay a percentage to the Mob. After all, he reasoned, it amounted to only a few cents a copy. They probably made so much money elsewhere, they would never miss it anyway.

But the Mob did miss that extra few cents, multiplied by several millions twelve times a year. Nor did it like an uppity hillbilly showing it no more respect than he displayed toward a centerfold with a bag over her head. Most ominously, Flynt was deeply in debt to Mob moneylenders, and was ignoring their demands for repayment.

THE CORONATION of Reuben Sturman as King of Porn took place sometime in the mid-seventies. During this period his fortune not only doubled but quadrupled, then grew tenfold. What catapulted Sturman to the throne were two great thunderbolts that made it necessary to reinvent the realm of porn all over again.

The first was *Deep Throat,* which became the *Gone With the Wind* of XXX-rated sex, the first porn flick to make a significant profit (although the year before, *Mona,* another hard-core offering, had landed on *Variety*'s list of the fifty top-grossing films of the year). The success of *Deep Throat* jump-started the mass-marketing of full-length hard-core movies, which by decade's end were being produced at the rate of at least two a week, mostly in North Hollywood, where there was a plentiful supply of part-time actresses, actors, camera and sound people, studios, and developing and editing labs.

Seizing the day, Sturman's old friend Lasse Braun quickly produced a quasi-documentary on the life of a porn filmmaker—*French Blue,* which in 1974 became the first hard-core film ever exhibited at the Cannes Film Festival. Sturman himself had always shunned films, preferring to concentrate on peep shows, which offered an uninterrupted cash flow and did not require a large investment up front. But after *Variety* praised *Blue,* his opposition softened. Braun flew to Cleveland and offered to produce a classy porn flick that would make "the whole world horny." Sturman enthusiastically agreed to provide $250,000 in backing and to distribute the film in the United States.

Shot in England, Belgium, and Holland in early 1975, *Sensations* starred Brigette Maier, a former *Penthouse* Pet, playing Margaret from Minnesota sampling such kinky—or kooky—European "sensations" as sex with a woman chained to a wheel, or with a man whose right hand was a steel hook. Once again Cannes applauded, and the film went on to gross millions—how much, exactly, not even the IRS knew for sure.

In 1974 federal prosecutors in Cleveland succeeded once again in hauling Sturman into court on obscenity charges. Like Flynt and Goldstein, he chose Herald Fahringer as his lawyer. Wardell Pomeroy again appeared as a star witness. The trial gave Sturman his first opportunity to sit down and watch the XXX-rated films with which he was inundating America. Prosecutors had chosen thirteen as being particularly offensive and disgusting, including one called *Cake Orgy,* in which three women and two men smeared cake all over themselves before, during, and after assorted sex acts.

All through the screening of *Cake Orgy,* Sturman guffawed, as the jury of six women and six men watched in stony silence. He thought the movie was genuinely hilarious. The jury, though, was ready to convict. Only one remarkably persuasive female juror held out, arguing that it was impossible for a normal person to have a morbid and degenerate interest in sex—exactly what Fahringer had hammered home in his ringing summary. That meant it was impossible for an average person to be corrupted by pornography. All the other jurors eventually came around, and once again Sturman was acquitted.

Despite an increasing number of prosecutions by local DAs, XXX-rated movies did a land-office business in the seventies. Nearly one thousand adult theaters sprouted up on America's busiest thoroughfares, many of them supplied by the King. Hard-core box office receipts now accounted for 17 percent of the motion picture industry, with gross revenues in excess of $500 million. As an industry, pornography (including soft-core) had gone from under-the-counter obscurity to a $2 billion high profile in less than ten years.

In one of a series of moralizing cover stories that *Time* issued during the Sexual Revolution, this one titled "The Porno Plague," the magazine complained that by 1976 every major American city now sported "a garish, grubby, mile-long gauntlet of sex-book stalls, theaters and 8-mm. peep shows for voyeurs, and massage parlors and sexual encounter centers for those who want direct action." Nowhere in the article was there any mention that the individual chiefly responsible for the plague was an improbable jet-setter who now divided his time almost equally between Cleveland (the warehouse), North Hollywood (film production), Amsterdam (Euro-porn), and Switzerland (secret bank accounts).

IN SEPTEMBER 1976 a sex club called Plato's Retreat opened in a New York brownstone under the proprietorship of a divorced veteran swinger and father of three named Larry Levenson. After being forced by angry landlords to move from seven other locations, the bearded, heavyset Levenson finally wound up paying a rent of $100,000 per year on twenty-four thousand square feet in the basement of a decrepit, peeling residential hotel called the Ansonia, once the epitome of belle epoque elegance and now popular with penurious musicians and opera singers on the Upper West Side. The previous tenant had been the Continental Baths.

In its new quarters, Plato's instantly became the biggest, most celebrated, and ultimately most notorious heterosexual pleasure dome in the world—though not the first. New York's original on-premises swing club was the short-lived Percival's. On an average night, more than two hundred couples flocked to Plato's basement cave to see, to conquer, to come. Most of them were straight, aged twenty to fifty, and well educated—but the only common denominator was lust, and they included both the ugly and the beautiful, and anomalies like female couples, though single men were banned. Unattached women, of course, got VIP treatment.

Only the year before, the Bronx-born, forty-one-year-old Levenson, a high school chum of Al Goldstein, had been collecting unemployment checks. A former McDonald's manager and obsessive masturbator, he had financed Plato's by borrowing $150,000. He foresaw a nightly admission of eight hundred couples and an annual net profit of $1 million. With his partner, Mike Ross, Levenson hoped eventually to open a string of franchises around the country—a McDonald's of sex—on the assumption that Plato's would be to the seventies what the Playboy Clubs had been to the fifties.

The admission price of $25 included such amenities as a swimming pool, steam room, disco, bar, restaurant, exercise room, two porn flick parlors, free liquor, a television lounge, and forty cubicles for private romance. All rest rooms were supplied with gallon-size jugs of mouthwash. But the main attraction was the mat room, a square, darkly lit, sex-smelling chamber of carnality decorated in a black-and-white leopard pattern.

Arriving late one evening at Plato's, accompanied by a young woman, Marco Vassi felt eager to recharge himself erotically, having just emerged from a month of "negativity." Already three hundred horny patrons had gathered, though everybody was still fully clothed, awaiting the witching hour in the bar area.

By one A.M. the crowd had grown to five hundred and the orgy began. By now most of the guests had shed their clothes, and group gropes were everywhere—in the pool, whirlpool, baths, or steam room. Couples and threesomes made love in the cubicles or out in the open. Women gave random blow jobs in the hallway or lay spread-eagle on a table as two or three men worked them over. As any male swinger knew, a ratio of two or more men to one woman was always better than two or more women to one man, despite Hollywood fantasy scenarios to the contrary, since many women under such circumstances became incredibly aroused.

Joining another couple, Marco and his companion headed for the mat room, where hundreds of people were having sex in every imaginable position, like the *Kama Sutra* run amok. Men masturbated into women's open mouths, a woman was urinating onto a man's tongue. Everywhere he saw cunts and cocks and asses, breasts and thighs and tongues. All that he saw proved his metasexual thesis. In such a setting it was impossible to retain any notion of one's individuality. Everywhere he looked, he saw himself. All those thrashing bodies were incontestable evidence that everybody, men and women, enjoyed sex in exactly the same way.

In the middle of his own scenario, Marco glimpsed the woman he had arrived with, lying on her back, her legs wide apart, a man thrusting into her. The expression she wore was the same as when *he* made love to her, and momentarily he was seized by a spasm of jealousy. Later he decided that that moment of jealousy was the only obscene thing he had experienced that night. Jealousy, he confided to his diary, was based on "the myth of specialness. . . . It was obvious that all of us were merely variations on a major theme. She was just another creature. We were all just creatures."

In November 1977 Plato's first competition opened: the Fifth Dimensional Jazz Club on West Fifty-fifth Street. Though it offered no pool, sauna, or whirlpool and was not too spacious, entrance was only $15 per couple. By 1978 New York boasted a dozen clubs where the floor show was a full-tilt orgy. Swing clubs had opened in nearly every state in the Union, with twenty-seven in California alone, and most of Canada.

DESPITE ITS SPECTACULAR GROWTH and *Time*'s dismay, pornography was also in serious trouble by 1976. Not only had saturation point been reached in the market, but federal and state prosecutors were getting downright vicious in their lust for obscenity convictions.

Salvation came in the form of the videocassette recorder that Sony quietly unveiled that year—the most significant event in adult-film history and, along with *Deep Throat,* the impetus for a revolution in hard-core pornography. Producers immediately began transferring their film libraries onto cassettes, which in some cases sold for as much as $300 per tape. Price wars and product glut soon brought the cost down to that of a regular film, and the spread of cable systems widened the availability of pornography even further.

A versatile technology, video was a double boon because it allowed manufacturers both to package affordable pornography for home use and to repackage existing features, or strings of three or four loops, into new films—and, ultimately, to shoot pornographic features directly onto recording tape. Video also made pornography once again available to cottage-industry entrepreneurs, giving rise to numerous amateur videos that lasted as long as the sexual encounters they recorded. Many of these were widely swapped.

Many diehards thought video was an ephemeral phenomenon. But Sturman immediately sensed its potential and was quick to order his new North Hollywood–based video company, Vidco, to begin transferring Super 8 loops to videocassettes. The distribution network centered on Sturman's General Video of America in Cleveland. Sturman also had an interest in Caballero Control Company, a producer and distributor of porn known for its line·of Swedish erotica.

By decade's end, 40 percent of all VCR owners polled would say they had bought or rented an XXX-rated cassette within the past year, and fifteen million–plus hard-core videos were being rented per week, with an annual gross of more than $1 billion. Video freed porn from its bondage to adult bookstores and the raincoat crowd, a liberation cable and satellite TV would continue. It also made community standards for obscenity—the lethal instrument prosecutors were using to convict pornographers—much harder to define. Now the community was reduced to a viewing audience of one—or, with luck, two. As a result, porn also began to get a lot kinkier. Bondage and rape fantasies, group sex, and anal intercourse became commonplace.

The video revolution also caused hundreds of porn theaters to close, and many of those that remained open functioned primarily as brothels. Production of thirty-five-millimeter films dropped to fewer than twenty a year. Meanwhile, the video version of *Deep Throat* was reputed to have sold five hundred thousand copies. Video producers like Sturman's Vidco manufactured about four hundred feature-length videos per year. Every day in California, seven days a week, at least one new porn video started production and was usually "in the can" by day's end. Produced for about $10,000 apiece, they usually earned back fifteen times that amount. Sturman also began to expand into the suburbs, building compartments behind swinging doors of America's latest franchise—video stores—for his hard-core product.

Sturman later claimed he always steered clear of child porn, bestiality, and other depictions of obviously depraved or nonconsensual sex. Whether he actually did so was virtually impossible to determine. But after Congress finally passed legislation in 1977 making child porn illegal, no major player in the game would have risked an empire for the sake of relatively few dollars. The market for such material was limited, and clear-cut federal convictions carrying very stiff penalties were easy to obtain.

Out in Las Vegas, though, Sturman's Talk of the Town partner, Ralph Levine, had fewer scruples about selling child porn and bestiality films through direct mail. Ralph was a mathematical genius, and in Las Vegas that translated into compulsive gambling. Whether Sturman was aware of Ralph's activities on the animal front and was cocky enough to think they could get away with it, or was honestly in the dark, Ralph the gambler was his weakest flank.

Sturman's son, David, meanwhile, had gotten to be a royal pain in the neck. At Doc Johnson he developed a drug problem and later married one of his father's ex-girlfriends. Sturman fired him. David drifted off to San Francisco, and for several years the two lost contact. Finally David met a woman who helped him put his life back together. They married and eventually had three children, and Sturman helped his son get a toehold in the wholesale business, starting him out where he had begun—with comic books.

WORLDWIDE, pornography was becoming a multibillion-dollar industry, though not all profits went to the manufacturers and distributors; international companies like Kodak, TDK, Canon, Panasonic, Sony, and Fuji took their share. In fact, hard-core quickly provided a model for global manufacture and distribution later emulated by multinational companies in the eighties and nineties, with the photo shoots for a hard-core magazine taken in one country, designed in another, printed in a third, and distributed in multilingual editions.

In the wake of *Deep Throat*, other XXX-rated blockbusters included the Mitchell brothers' *Behind the Green Door*, starring Ivory Soap girl Marilyn Chambers; and *The Opening of Misty Beethoven*, starring Constance Money and directed by Henry Paris (real name: Radley Metzger). Many porn connoisseurs regarded the latter, a takeoff on *My Fair Lady*, as the best hard-core film of all time. A stock feature of Hollywood porn was that most were patterned after well-known movies rather than having plots of their own.

Within the world of kink porn, SM remained by far the most popular, though still accounting for less than 10 percent of the Theander brothers' material. The biggest European market for SM was Germany, while it was least popular in Scandinavia. Animal and child sex were universally strictly forbidden.

By the mid-seventies, Berth Milton's off-size bimonthly *Private*, with an international circulation approaching two hundred thousand, had long ceased to be a one-man operation. Milton now drove a Rolls, frequently appeared in his magazine's pages surrounded by adoring naked women, and even developed a Hefnerian philosophy, writing editorials denouncing sexual violence and promoting "erotography." Al Goldstein ultimately dubbed *Private* the "best porno magazine in the world." Though an inferior, copycat version was published by the Mafia under the same name in New York, the real *Private* remained too hot to be sold on or under U.S. counters.

According to federal law, hard-core pornography retailed in America had to be manufactured in the United States. As a result, only a small amount of European mail-order pornography got through. Canada used a similar stipulation to keep out U.S. hard-core and to harass such soft-core publications as *Penthouse* and *Playboy*.

Another problem lay in the many variations in state obscenity statutes, which fragmented the hard-core market even further. Magazines like *Hustler* even appeared in a variety of editions, the softest in Bible Belt states. Even women's magazines like *Cosmopolitan* sometimes encountered community-level resistance with their explicit sexual advice. In 1972, when *Deep Throat* premiered, actor Burt Reynolds broke the male centerfold barrier by posing nude for Those Cosmo Girls.

Britain remained the last hard-core-free country in Europe. Under the Obscene Publications Act, customs officials were free to seize whatever they felt like at ports of entry. Obscenity laws were not only extremely restrictive, but enthusiastically enforced by the police and courts. As of 1984 it was still illegal in Britain to publish photographs showing erections, vaginal penetration, ejaculation, explicit cunnilingus or fellatio, or anal sex.

After West Germany decriminalized hard-core in 1975, that country quickly became the biggest porn market in Europe, five times that in Sweden. At the same time, German laws were also stricter: child sex was strictly forbidden and acts of violence frowned on, and only licensed shops were permitted to sell hard-core. Sending porn through the mails was also banned. As a result, however, German pornography was able to achieve a level of respectability that set the standard for the rest of the world. German porn headquarters were in Wiesbaden, an old spa town near Frankfurt, where Georg Schmitt and his four sons dominated the distribution of porn from three warehouses.

Though the Theanders' partnership was probably the most lucrative in the history of hard-core, it ended in 1985. A photographer, Jens wanted to expand the Candy Film studio to make hard-core features. Peter preferred to close the studio down and buy European rights to films produced by others. After Jens retired to London, Peter continued to operate Rodox single-handedly. Still the largest hard-core publishing house in Europe, it generated annual sales in the late eighties of about $15 million—sufficient to allow the reclusive Peter to indulge his grand passions—opera, modern art, and an extensive wine collection.

The second biggest porn consumer in Europe was Spain, which had not only a substantial native population of thirty-six million, but a huge tourist population, particularly English. Spain was also the gateway to the expanding South American market. Yet quality was very poor and competition intense.

Porn was also legal, or unimpeded by law, in Portugal, Greece, and Italy, which in June 1987 became the first country to elect a porn star—La Cicciolina, or Little Chubby—to office when she was elected to the National Chamber of Deputies as a member of the Radical Party. In addition to Britain, Ireland and the Soviet countries also outlawed hard-core.

By conservative estimates, more than 250 billion hard-core sex magazines were printed in Europe from the end of the 1960s through the mid-1980s. At any one time, more than one thousand hard-core porn magazines were being published, with a global inventory of perhaps fifty million copies per year and estimated annual revenues of about $400 million.

IN THE WORLD OF KINKY PORN, the entrepreneurial counterpart of Guccione, Hefner, Flynt, and Goldstein was a former Brooklynite turned Hollywood resident named Larry Rosenstein, publisher of such offbeat porn papers as the biweekly *San Francisco Ball* and the monthlies *Gaytimes, Fetish Times,* and *National Swing.*

Tall, bearded, energetic, Rosenstein got into the business when publisher Irv Munch asked him and a friend to lay out a girlie magazine. The pair pooled their resources—$200—and created *Seize,* the first "lesbian" magazine ever—though certainly not edited by lesbians for readers with lesbian sensibilities. Though tame by later standards, it caused a sensation when published in 1969. After Rosenstein and his partner sold the issue for $1,500, Munch commissioned them to do another but later pulled out. With credit from the printer the two men published the second issue and hawked it personally to stores in San Francisco, San Diego, and Los Angeles, reaping a profit of $8,000 each.

Subsequently Rosenstein purchased the *San Francisco Ball,* which was sinking fast after only twenty issues. Rosenstein turned it around by injecting adolescent fun and sick humor into its pages, which later became its trademark as a sort of milder competitor to *Screw.* A few years later, with *Ball* booming, Rosenstein began to look for a new venture. With gay liberation in full swing, he decided that a gay sex paper was the logical next addition to his Jaundice Press "family of friendly perversions." The result, *Gaytimes*—a mixture of gay sex stories, reviews of books and films, explicit photos, and articles on gay liberation—was an immediate success.

Two more papers followed, *National Swing* and *Fetish Times.* The former had been taken over from a young swinging couple who had been publishing a newsstand paper in California. When laws leveled at sidewalk sales from local vending machines were enacted, they asked Rosenstein to help them put together a national paper. Soon afterward the husband was stricken by a heart attack and retired. Rosenstein took over both editions and later sold off the local paper. Meanwhile, *Fetish Times,* the most outrageous of Rosenstein's publications, gave him a chance to complete his coverage of the sexual arena. In any given issue readers were treated to stories about bondage and enemas, spanking and humiliation, water sports and scat (the popular term for scatophilia, or coprophilia, a condition in which sexual arousal depends on the smell or taste of feces). The cover of one issue featured a bloody Kotex.

In 1979 Rosenstein acquired three more swing publications, *International Action, Friends & Lovers,* and *Loving Couples.* By that time he was also financially involved with Roxbury Press Publications, which included *Enema Hotline, Bottom Line,* and *Power Line,* publications aimed at enema, excrement, spanking, and SM aficionados. Rosenstein also packaged sex magazines for other publishers and even launched a new mail-order business under the imprint of the Permanent Press, which offered marital aids, penis enlargers, aphrodisiacs, leather and rubber goods, books, and magazines.

Unlike Guccione, Hefner, and Goldstein, Rosenstein never had a brush with the law in ten years, which he attributed not to high-priced lawyers, but to attitude. That translated into maintaining a low public profile and not attacking or confronting the Establishment.

For many years, the Eulenspiegel Society remained a voice in the wilderness of kink. Then, in the late seventies bondage chic developed. The Rolling Stones recorded "When the Whip Comes Down," trendy department stores began carrying handcuff jewelry and black-leather fashions, mainstream magazines ran covers and feature articles with SM themes, and shy SMers started to emerge from the closet.

Yet the flowering of SM never received the slightest acknowledgment in the pages of *Playboy,* whose girls next door were to remain demurely wholesome. *Penthouse,* though, early on introduced leather gear and such props as Doberman pinschers into its pictorials. Rushing over the top as usual, *Hustler* published explicit bondage scenes almost as soon as word of the SM trend reached Columbus, Ohio.

New York contained the biggest colony, featuring dozens of independent dominatrices and small SM-oriented brothels, which advertised their unique services in the sex tabloids. In the world of commercial SM, female submissives, or slaves, were a precious commodity, able to charge up to $100 an hour for their services. A dominant mistress cost $60 an hour. Enema sessions were $115 an hour.

Among the most popular clubs was the Castle, located in midtown and run by a couple prominent in the SM establishment, Jay and Diane Hartwell. In the field for thirty years, they also published the *S&M Express,* a serious tabloid for advanced practitioners.

Inside the club, rows of folding chairs faced a stage equipped with sawhorses, ratchet-run pulleys, and a whip rack. So-called session rooms were serious environments containing a functioning rack and a slanted cross, among other popular props.

Weekly performance of SM theater at the Castle drew audiences ranging in age from their mid-thirties to the golden years. Very few women or men in their twenties seemed drawn either to the lifestyle or to the spectacle, and couples were also a rarity. The most common audience members were conservative-looking, intellectual-seeming men in business suits. On a typical night they were greeted by master of ceremonies Jay Hartwell, a thin, bearded, spectral-looking man who in his articulate, witty monologue often told his audience: "We love you, even if you're straight and just here to watch the freaks play."

After the lights dimmed, a bare-breasted black woman, wearing a bandolier of nipple clamps, rode on stage mounted atop a nude male wearing a black leather face mask and a horse's tail attached to his scrotum. As she cantered him across the stage, he whinnied and she slapped his buttocks until they trotted off stage to moderate applause.

Another attraction was Carol the Slave Girl, who slipped her hands into a pair of overhanging wrist bracelets in order to be hoisted by two female attendants via a pulley mechanism until she stood on her toes. One of the women then brought out a bowl of large, industrial-duty clips, which the other attached to the Slave Girl's breasts.

As each clip was attached, Carol sighed audibly, until her breasts sprouted eight clips in all. Then a like number were affixed up and down the front of her body, with a final clip applied to her panty-covered labia. As the tension mounted, the audience shuffled nervously, then lit cigarettes in relief as the clips were ceremoniously removed, leaving welts visible from across the room. When the women left the stage, the grateful voyeurs thanked them with deafening applause.

Several more scenes followed, but the highlight of the night always came last—the audience-participation session. For many male submissives, domination was never satisfying unless their humiliation was made public. Many males in the audience repeatedly returned to attend the show for that very reason. As several mistresses assembled on stage, inviting victims to step forward, none seemed willing to break the ice until, more often than not, a man of circumspect appearance arose and announced, "I'll give it a try."

After boldly disrobing on stage, the victim was manacled and lightly paddled. Then the rush began: waves of men crowding the stage to have their buttocks swatted and physiognomies insulted. Despite the heavy punishment meted out all around, the atmosphere was almost frivolous, with MC Jay shouting, "Stand still! What, are you crazy, lady?" When the audience convulsed in laughter, he continued: "You see, you might think we're all whips, threats, and punishment, but we really have fun!"

Another sex mecca, Club O at Fantasy Manor, was a sprawling complex second only to Plato's Retreat in terms of size and facilities. Owned by two women, Judy and Lois, it specialized in swingers and SMers because many of the former often "graduated" to SM. As a result, Club O boasted an unusual mix of gay and straight clientele. Since the eternal surplus of single male submissives in the SM world resulted in a massive buyer's market, sexual nomads shuttled from club to club, looking for a mistress to call their own. Most ended up unfulfilled unless they paid a professional.

Many submissive males were proud of their capacity to endure pain. One evening at Club O, when Mistress Precious ferociously began to paddle a submissive, causing his buttocks to jump six inches off the bench with each thwack, the man retreated after the second blow. Shrugging, Mistress Precious commanded a large hulk of a man, Otto, to drop his trousers and bend over the bench. After attendants tied Otto's arms to the legs of the bench, Mistress Precious methodically paddled his buttocks with all her strength. Perhaps hardened from previous beatings, Otto's posterior merely reddened a little at first. Only after a dozen vicious swats did he permit himself an "Ouch!"

Finally the paddle broke off at the handle, eliciting polite applause from the audience of mistresses and slaves. But it was no record. On the wall of Chateau 19, another club, hung another paddle that Mistress Precious had broken on Otto's rump. This time, perhaps going for a new record, Mistress Precious continued beating Otto's buttocks with a leather strap until she got bored. Otto did not even break a sweat. Later he retired to a couch to rest, a blissful expression on his face.

In mellower San Francisco SM was becoming known as bondage and discipline, or B&D. Disdainful of the New York style, SF BDers thought the East Coast scene was too heavy and weird and wondered why so many of its clubs had to be so dark and dingy. West Coast clubs, by contrast, were airy and light, like hotel lobbies. Many SM scenes in San Francisco even took place poolside.

Chapter 10

See Dick Run

IN THE SPACE OF ONLY FIFTEEN YEARS, THE WORLD OF FEMALE SEXUALITY HAD undergone three major revolutions. The pill granted women erotic independence, recognition of the clitoral orgasm acknowledged their potential orgasmic superiority over men, and *The Hite Report* authorized them to guarantee their own pleasure by literally taking it into their own hands if necessary.

In the minds of some radical feminists, the next step was to banish the once omnipotent penis altogether. The only thing the penis seemed to be good for was procreation, and in vitro fertilization and other reproductive technologies were rapidly freeing that problem from the messy exchange of bodily fluids or the entanglements of who's-on-top politics. As a result, a small but highly articulate group of radical lesbians declared war on the penis, claiming it was not only a sexual anachronism, but the cause of most of the terrible oppression and suffering of women at the hands of men down through the centuries. They had a point.

Until 1948 the only set of genitals that tacitly enjoyed anything like social status, sexual rights, and assorted licit and illicit perks was the white heterosexual penis. Most laws governing marriage, divorce, birth control, abortion, and sexual practices were written specifically to satisfy the requirements and to accommodate the insecurities and prejudices of that overindulged organ. By contrast, the genitals of women, gays, black or ethnic males, and such invisible sexual minorities as transsexuals, hermaphrodites, or others with deformed sex organs had few rights and little medical, legal, or social recourse and were usually paid the ultimate insult of being ignored altogether. The single exception was the mythic size attributed to the black penis—not only an indication of white male sexual anxiety, but also perhaps a racist comment on the supposedly ungovernable size of black families.

As for the maze of labia, clitoris, vagina, cervix, and uterus that constituted the female sexual conundrum, many men hardly knew which was where and could not have cared less. Like the great white lion hunters of Africa, they simply marched into the bush when the desire to shoot arose, aimed, and fired. Though countless men obviously cared about the erotic rights of their partners, the written and unwritten laws of the land reflected a belief that female genitals were subject to male authority. Until Kinsey published *Sexual Behavior in the Human Male* in 1948, except for a few esoteric religious texts and ancient phallus cults, a grab bag of anthropological and medical citations, and some pornography, the penis had lacked anything resembling a literature. Kinsey was the first to peek behind the curtain, dispelling myths, assembling charts and statistics, and reducing euphemisms to dry clinical descriptions. He subjected the penis to all sorts of scientific scrutiny: how many times it was inserted into a vagina, or somewhere else, how often stroked by its owner's hand, how many times a week it provided orgasm, even its angle when erect. In so doing, he destroyed forever the mystique of the white heterosexual penis. (Though the data was not published in his *Male* volume, he even confirmed a long-standing white man's fear: at an average 6.15 inches when erect, the white penis was shorter than the average erect black penis, at 6.44.)

Many people refused to believe that so many white heterosexual males engaged in so many different sex practices, that so many of them were not in fact exclusively heterosexual, that premarital sex and adultery were commonplaces of the bedroom—in brief, that the Great White Penis was not exactly behaving itself, not abiding by the conventional morality that had been set for it. Indirectly, Kinsey was demonstrating the virtual futility of telling men, or women, what they must do with their bodies, at least when hormone levels were high.

Kinsey's work set the stage for Masters and Johnson's *Human Sexual Response,* which gave the penis its first really serious fall from grace by demonstrating that during sexual intercourse the clitoris produced an orgasm without having direct contact with the thrusting male organ. The St. Louis sex researchers added insult to injury with *Human Sexual Inadequacy,* a virtual inventory of male sex hangups that deprived women of their sexual fulfillment. One of the primary achievements of Masters and Johnson was to turn sex therapy 180 degrees around—to redirect it toward the needs of women, not men. "With orgasmic physiology established," they wrote, "the human female now has an undeniable opportunity to develop realistically her own sexual response levels."

In some quarters of the emerging world of radical feminism, that "undeniable opportunity" was interpreted to mean not merely the physiological independence of the clitoral orgasm, but the irrelevance of the penis. In a cele-brated essay entitled "The Myth of the Vaginal Orgasm," New York jour-nalist Anne Koedt wrote that "lesbian sexuality, in rubbing one's clitoris against the other, could make an excellent case, based on anatomical data, for the extinction of the male organ. . . . It forces us to discard many 'physical' ar-guments explaining why women go to bed with men. What is left, it seems to me, are psychological reasons why women select men [to] the exclusion of other women."

So the battle was joined. And almost immediately it moved to the battle-ground of pornography, where some women suspected the penis kept their sex prisoner.

Now, apart from the historic opportunity the pornography boom of the mid-sixties and early seventies gave vast numbers of men to examine in mi-nutest detail women posing naked or performing sexual acts, it also amounted to the first significant counterrevolution of the penis. Whatever other pleasures men derived from pornography, it enabled them to reach or-gasm when a sex partner was not available or when libidinal energy was low. With pornography, the penis was freed from performance anxiety, was ac-countable to no one. Pornography was almost, one might say, a Darwinian adaptation to the situation at hand. It also dispensed, at least temporarily, with the need for a real woman, just as radical feminists were proposing to dispense with men.

In 1975, in *Against Our Will*, radical feminist Susan Brownmiller argued that rape was not an isolated act by a sick or criminal individual, but the way all heterosexual men conspired to repress all women. It made no difference if some men took responsibility for their penises. All penises were, by defini-tion, evil adherents of a dark creed: that what a woman really needed, to be reminded of her place (in bed, in society), was a violent intrusion into some orifice. Many rapists did expect their victims to enjoy the act and to be grate-ful for the attention, but Brownmiller did not allow for the possibility that while such attitudes might say a great deal about the sexual repression and erotic pathos of some men, they might have very little to do with the sexual aggression of the species.

Perhaps not so coincidentally, Brownmiller was writing during the years when *Deep Throat* was at its zenith. Never before had there been such a bla-tant public display of female obeisance to the almighty penis—at a time, moreover, when many American men and women hardly knew what fella-tio was, much less how to pronounce it. The sight of Linda Lovelace swal-lowing Harry Reems's enormous penis was perhaps the single most offensive sexual act in history to one group of viewers, while to another group it was the most amazing and most enviable.

Brownmiller's book shocked the country into recognizing the true monstrousness of rape, but it also laid the groundwork for blaming an increase in sex crimes on pornography. Robin Morgan's slogan, "Pornography is the theory and rape is the practice," helped to inspire a wave of protest against not only soft-core and hard-core pornography, but also nonexplicit images of women in movies, TV, and advertisements that were considered degrading.

At the same time, a fellow traveler of the radical feminists, the onetime erotic libertarian Germaine Greer, now a frequent lecturer on American campuses, was among those urging women to assess the personal cost of sex, in light of bad pill and IUD experiences, abortions, and infections, not to mention STDs. An intermittent stream of unsettling reports had begun to unearth a variety of new health hazards—circulatory problems, pregnancy complications, liver and gallbladder disease, diabetes—associated with the pill, which ten million American women were now taking. In the early seventies a type of IUD known as the Dalkon shield resulted in numerous cases of pelvic inflammatory disease and spontaneous miscarriages. Women and their husbands or lovers were beginning to ask whether birth control was worth the risk.

Another drug, diethylstilbestrol (DES), had been given to some six million American women in the years between 1941 and 1975 to treat gestational diabetes, to prevent miscarriage, and as a postcoital contraceptive in cases of rape or incest. Now DES was discovered to increase the risk of vaginal and cervical cancer in daughters born to mothers who used DES during their pregnancies.

Greer suggested that since female orgasm did not occur in the vagina, there was no need for male ejaculation to occur there, either. She pointed to Burmese villagers, Java natives, and Xinguano Indians and suggested that the prevalence of male abstinence in those cultures could be a model for men in Western, industrialized society, whom she considered too lustful. Abstinence did not lead in those cultures to stress or unhappiness but was a normal part of life, even when it was extended up to six years after the birth of a child, as a form of birth control. Greer also pointed to a 1973 study of American prison populations, in which some prisoners were found to be "relatively unconscious of sexual tension and uninterested in sexual activity."

Greer's advocacy of group sex over marriage at the beginning of her career, and of male abstinence over intercourse a decade later, was at least consistently extreme, and as a result her work became increasingly irrelevant. But she was justified in calling attention, along with other feminists both female and male, to the risks of contraception, the unfair and often dangerous burden they put on women, and the need for men to assume a greater role in preventing pregnancy.

* * *

WHILE THE ANTIPORNOGRAPHY, antipenis, and antisex counterrevolutions continued to build momentum, one small but troublesome problem for America's publishers and writing community was what to do about so-called four-letter words, not to mention legitimate words designating intimate body parts or practices.

Book publishers and literary publications took the lead, inspired by the 1960 trial in England that found *Lady Chatterley's Lover* not obscene. In 1961, in *Herzog,* Saul Bellow used all the words. The *New York Review of Books,* which began publication in 1963, spelled out "cunt" in an early issue and before year's end had gone through virtually the entire maledicta. The *Atlantic* and *Commentary* ventured into "fucking" in 1965, *Harper's* in 1968. In 1965, though, prudish *Playboy* still quoted actor Peter O'Toole as saying, "So, I thought, well f——— it." In 1966 it published a long article by Ray Russell defending taboo words without putting a single one in cold type.

The New York Times suffered from the worst case of sexual anxiety. In 1948 it had refused to publish advertisements for Kinsey's volume on male sexuality and for Gore Vidal's novel *The City and the Pillar.* (A decade earlier, even the *Reader's Digest* was advocating divorce, contraception, and abortion reform and paved the way for public acceptance of such words as "syphilis," "orgasm," and "penis.") Not until 1976 did the *Times* work up the courage to print the word "penis," and then only under pressure from health columnist Jane Brody, who had pioneered with the word "ejaculate," and in a brave story on female orgasm upped the stakes with "penile thrusting." That particular column was so controversial within the gray-suited ranks of the *Times* that an editor brought the column home for his wife to read before deciding whether to publish. She told him it would be the most important story the *Times* would run that year. Did he not know how many divorces were caused by this problem, which men and women found so difficult to discuss?

Despite the paper's editorials lamenting the number of unwed teenage mothers, a subsequent Brody column on proper condom use upset one editor so much that he insisted Brody's future sex-related columns be screened by a special editorial panel. The *Times* also worried about how to report such matters as an offensive but widely reported joke told by Earl Butz, secretary of agriculture under Nixon, which avowed that the three things blacks most wanted in life were "loose shoes, a tight pussy, and a warm place to shit." In the end, the paper timidly substituted "good sex" for the middle *desideratum.*

WHILE SOME WOMEN were trying to kill pornography and dispense with the penis, a few well-intentioned if misguided men were trying to lay claim to an area that had been almost exclusively women's—multiple orgasm. The phenomenon of male multiple orgasm had first been investigated in depth by

Kinsey, though his findings were singularly unscientific. Half of the boys in his preadolescent sample claimed to have repeated climaxes regularly. Since young boys did not have a functioning prostate and seminal vesicles, their orgasms occurred without ejaculation. Only one in five retained that capacity by age twenty, and by age thirty-five the heroic few had dwindled to 7 percent. But since Kinsey did not distinguish between multiple orgasms on the same arousal curve and several orgasms experienced in the course of a marathon bout of sex, his statistics were virtually worthless.

Only 1 or 2 percent of adult males were multiorgasmic in the sense of being able to achieve more than one orgasm on the same arousal curve. In *Human Sexual Response,* Masters and Johnson shed little new light on the topic. "Many males below the age of thirty," they wrote, "but relatively few thereafter, have the ability to ejaculate frequently and are subject to only very short refractory periods [the hiatus necessary for the male glands to refill]. . . . One male study subject has been observed to ejaculate three times within 10 minutes from the onset of stimulate activity. The seminal fluid volume progressively was reduced in amount with each ejaculatory episode. This example, of course, marks the exception to the basic rule of severe male psychophysiologic resistance to sexual stimuli (refractory period) immediately after an ejaculatory experience."

But male multiple orgasm, or MMO, was too intriguing an issue to lie dormant for long. In 1978 Dr. Mina B. Robbins and Gordon D. Jensen, M.D., resurrected it in an article entitled "Multiple Orgasm in Males," published in the *Journal of Sex Research.* The authors departed from established male physiology, hypothesizing that "the orgasmic response and the ejaculatory response can be separate physiological reactions in a normal state." For their study, Robbins and Jensen had looked for male volunteers who believed they were multiorgasmic, eliminating those who experienced multiple ejaculations. That left a tiny sample of thirteen men, who "described their repeated orgasms as including most or all of the following aspects of orgasmic response: increased respiratory rate, increased heart rate, myotonia, hyperventilation, urethra contractions, and an altered state of consciousness, all without ejaculation. These men apparently inhibit or control ejaculation and thereby withhold it until the final orgasm of the series, which they describe subjectively as being the most intense."

But Robbins and Jensen eliminated a key criterion: release. In his study of orgasmic physiology Kinsey had noted: "The most important consequence of sexual orgasm is the abrupt release of the extreme tension which preceded the event and the rather sudden return to a normal or subnormal physiologic state after the event," notably an instantaneous drop in heart rate. Robbins and Jensen had merely discovered *karezza,* an ancient Indian technique by which a man allowed himself to approach orgasm, then let himself down, for as often as he was able, until finally he ejaculated.

But by now MMO was the Holy Grail of male sex research. William Hartman and Marilyn Fithian of the Center for Marital and Sexual Studies in
Long Beach, California, were the next to jump on the bandwagon. As if men
did not have enough performance anxiety to deal with already, Hartman and
Fithian informed them that any penis sputtering out only one orgasm at a
time was virtually shirking its duty. They claimed MMO could be experienced in one of two ways, according to a ten-year study they had conducted:
"multiple orgasm discrete," "a series of single orgasms usually five to ten
minutes apart"; and "multiple orgasm continuous," "several peaks and several orgasms in five minutes," which was their most common clinical observation. Although the relatively long refractory period in the first type
invalidated it as a true MMO, and the second was merely another definition
of *karezza,* Hartman and Fithian knew a golden opportunity when they saw
it. In their book *Any Man Can,* they outlined three easy steps to MMO: so-
called male Kegel exercises designed to strengthen the pubococcygeal muscles supporting the penis, lots of masturbation practice, and now and then a
little squeeze technique.

Dr. Alan Brauer was next in line, with the best-selling *ESO: How You and
Your Lover Can Give Each Other Hours of Extended Sexual Orgasm,* co-written
with his wife, Donna Brauer. A California psychiatrist trained in biofeedback, Brauer claimed to have invented a method of "extended sexual orgasm" that could also eliminate headaches and high blood pressure. Brauer's
definition of orgasm was loose indeed, requiring no ejaculation and only a
feeling of inevitability. "Unlike women, men have a two-stage orgasm," he
claimed. "The first is called the internal emission stage, or 'point of no return.' That's when the orgasmic reflex is triggered, and about three seconds
later it is inevitably followed, so it is thought, by ejaculation, which is the second state." His advice was for men to use biofeedback to maintain themselves
at the edge of this feeling for more than an hour, even though most sexual literature claimed that that three-second moment vanished in most men
around the age of thirty. Regardless, by dividing male orgasm into two
stages, the Brauers were, like Hartman and Fithian, merely giving *karezza* a
new name.

Yet among gay men the MMO was a well-known phenomenon. A receptive male partner in anal intercourse often experienced a series of dribbling
orgasms as his prostate was being "massaged" by his partner's thrusting penis, while subsequent penile stimulation resulted in a total, ordinary climax.
The primary difference, of course, between a straight and a gay MMO was
that the latter did not require an erection; a straight male who ejaculated
upon orgasm almost always lost not only his erection, but any hope of another orgasm until the refractory period passed.

* * *

MEANWHILE, antiporn feminists were getting some help from the feds. Desperate to cripple the porn colossus, the FBI launched its Miporn (for "Miami porn") investigation when two agents established a dummy business, Golde Coaste Specialties, Inc., in a rented Miami warehouse equipped with hidden microphones and video cameras. The operation had its origins in a 1976 investigation by the Dade County Public Safety Department, in which an Organized Crime Bureau detective, Alberto Bonnani, set up Amore Products, a fictitious company. Within months he was doing business with organized crime figures, mostly from outside Miami. In September 1977, after a nationwide web of pornography distributors was uncovered, Dade County turned its operation over to the FBI.

Agents met with major distributors and producers of pornography across the country, though never with Reuben Sturman. Two prime targets were Lou Peraino and his brother, Joseph, who were connected to the Columbo crime family and had distributed *Deep Throat*. During the same period, IRS investigator Richard Rosfelder was still trying to pick his way through a corporate maze to determine whether Sturman even did business with organized crime syndicates involved in porn (such as Star Distributors of New York, run by Robert DiBernardo), much less paid them off. Or had he created his paper labyrinth just to avoid taxes? In his memoir *The Last Mafioso*, Jimmy "the Weasel" Fratianno, a Mafia figure turned informer, claimed Sturman paid protection money to a major Mob figure after Fratianno sent thugs to intimidate him. But Sturman, who did not use a bodyguard, personally reported that attempt to the FBI, as well as several other efforts by thugs to muscle in on his territory. He even went to agency headquarters and pointed to pictures of the men who had paid him a visit. As far as anyone knew, nothing ever happened.

One snowy day in late 1978, Rosfelder and his associate Tom Ciehanski decided it was time to officially notify Sturman that he was under IRS investigation. The two men waited in their car outside the Sovereign warehouse in downtown Cleveland until at last a man emerged who looked as though he might be Sturman, though they were not sure because Sturman often used disguises when entering or exiting a courtroom. Approaching him, they politely asked if Reuben Sturman was on the premises. The man suggested they ring the buzzer. As they headed off, Sturman wiped the snow from the windshield of his Cadillac and drove off. He had won round one.

In 1980 Miporn prosecutors indicted the Perainos, DiBernardo, and more than fifty others, including Harry V. Mohney of Durland, Michigan, a major importer of European pornography and the third largest producer and distributor of pornographic movies, and Anthony Arnone, of Plantation, Florida, who once owned thirteen adult theaters in south Florida and worked with the Peraino brothers to gain distribution control of *Deep Throat*.

Sturman was arrested, too. According to Miporn investigators, the King was America's number one pornographer, controlling more than a dozen wholesale outlets and between 150 and 700 adult bookstores in the Midwest and East and servicing thousands more. Overall, adult bookstores were now a fixture in most American cities, numbering somewhere between fifteen and twenty thousand.

Prosecutors also believed Sturman's close association with DiBernardo confirmed him as a "made" member of the Mob, but they lacked proof—and also, apparently, any awareness that only Italians received this honor. FBI agents did receive information, though, suggesting Sturman paid off large sums to Cleveland organized crime syndicates, and that he probably operated with the Mob's blessing. Fratianno claimed Sturman's protection was Terry Zappi of the Gambino family.

Yet the charges against Sturman were eventually dropped for lack of evidence. At the age of fifty-six, the King had taken the feds' best punch and survived unscathed. No prosecutor had ever convicted him of obscenity. No tax collector ever hauled him to court. Best of all, he had fallen madly, wildly in love, for the first time in his life.

Little did he know that the long-persevering Rosfelder, a mere accountant, was about to ruin his life.

A HALF HOUR BEFORE NOON, on March 6, 1978, a four-door sedan that witnesses later said was either a Buick or a Pontiac turned right onto Perry Street and parked in front of an abandoned hotel in the little town of Lawrenceville, Georgia, about thirty miles northeast of Atlanta.

The front-seat passenger, a blond, mustached man wearing an expensive leather jacket, quickly exited from the car and entered the building. A passerby later testified he thought the pair might be real estate agents come to inspect the property or maybe detectives, because on second look a large pistol appeared to be bulging from the stranger's belt. Later police identified the weapon as a .44 Magnum hunting rifle.

Earlier that same morning, on the other side of town, Larry Flynt awoke in his hotel room, shaved, and put on a conservative dark suit, carefully sticking an American flag pin in his lapel. Despite his ferocious independence outside the courtroom, he knew it did no harm to look his respectable, patriotic best in front of a jury.

Flynt had no doubt he was going to win. The government's case was as phony as a porn star's orgasm, and his star witness was none other than Wardell Pomeroy, who by now not only routinely testified for the defense at high-profile pornography trials, but wrote for publications like *Hustler* as well. Nor did it hurt, here in the Bible Belt, that Flynt was a born-again

Christian, brought back to the fold by none other than evangelist Ruth Carter Stapleton. Even better, she had offered to be another witness for the defense. With God and the president's sister on his side, the jurors—five men and a woman—could not help but be impressed.

Flynt felt at home in towns like Lawrenceville. It reminded him of his hometown in Kentucky. And these were his readers, after all. *Hustler* was the soft-core porn of rednecks, truck drivers, and other blue-collar types. All in all, Flynt found the atmosphere so friendly that he decided not to bring along his bodyguard.

The bad boy of porn was on trial in Lawrenceville because Gwinnett County solicitor Gary Davis had sent an investigator to buy copies of two Flynt publications, *Hustler* and *Chic,* from Stan's Shopette in Lawrenceville, then charged Flynt with distributing obscene magazines. Like Flynt, Davis was also banking on Middle America to help him win.

In his testimony Flynt spoke calmly and with conviction, telling the jury he saw no hypocrisy between being born again and publishing pornography. "I agree that scratch 'n' sniff could be offensive to some people," he admitted in court, "but we did it strictly as a put-on. . . . *Hustler* is as much humor as sex." He even confessed that as a Christian, he was now personally offended by much of the content of *Hustler,* but he sadly explained to prosecutor Davis that "what you're seeing is the extension of the neuroses of the creators of this magazine," much as any successful TV series was an extension of "the neuroses of the creator of the show. But we're all neurotics responding to a neurotic environment."

Flynt finished his testimony just around the time the blond man in the expensive leather jacket disappeared into the abandoned hotel. The judge called a recess. As usual during the trial, Flynt and his associates walked two blocks to the V&J Cafeteria. At lunch, the overweight Flynt had limited himself to grapefruit juice. On the stroll back to the courthouse, he walked along beside Gene Reeves, Flynt's local attorney. Aide Dennis Sims hurried ahead to make travel arrangements for Flynt's two-week fasting vacation. Two journalists covering the trial, Neil Shister and *New West* magazine contributor Grover Lewis, also went ahead, talking shop. Suddenly, Reeves felt a burning sensation in his arm and stomach and realized he had been shot. The impact of the bullet did not knock him down but seemed to go right through him. But, looking over, he saw that Flynt had also been shot and knocked down.

Later, doctors theorized that a second bullet, fired from less than fifty feet away, had hit Flynt's spine, causing him to lose sensation in his legs, which instantly buckled. Reeves, who was on the curbside facing the building from which the shots were fired, had been struck first. The bullet that hit him split, hitting his pancreas and liver. Even in Korea, where he had been wounded in action, he had never felt that kind of pain.

Flynt lay on his back, clutching his stomach. "What happened?" he asked. Reeves, now on his knees, told him they had been shot and to lie still, knowing that shock was probably the biggest danger at that point. He also knew he had to get off his feet because he was pumping blood heavily. He later needed eleven pints of blood. Flynt required twenty-four.

Up ahead, Sims and Shister at first thought the shots, fired about five seconds apart, were firecrackers or a truck backfire. Turning around, though, they saw Flynt lying on the sidewalk. Sims ran back and saw what he believed was water or urine everywhere. But when Flynt rolled over, Sims saw two big holes in his stomach and ran off to call an ambulance. When he returned, Flynt cried in agony, "Help me. Oh, the pain. Get me to the hospital." Paramedics rushed to the scene and took Flynt and Reeves to Button Gwinnett Hospital a mile away, which was prepared for the emergency only because some doctors were on the premises doing elective surgery.

When they operated, doctors found that one bullet had entered the right side of Flynt's stomach and gone out the other, with a large exit wound, while a second was lodged near the spine. A doctor performed two operations within hours, removing Flynt's spleen and several feet of intestine. After three days, the publisher was moved to Emory University Hospital in Atlanta, where another doctor removed bone fragments and metal from the spinal canal. The lodged bullet had come to rest near Flynt's buttocks, damaging some nerve roots and paralyzing his legs.

For nearly a week, Flynt hovered near death as a result of internal bleeding and infection. Doctors gave him only a 50 percent chance of regaining the use of his legs. The pain, coupled with the morphine and Valium, frequently made him delirious. He gave no interviews and saw very few visitors, mainly his wife, Althea, and the room was kept under heavy security. Ruth Carter Stapleton also went to Flynt's bedside and prayed for him. "At first I thought God was unhappy with me," he told his visitors, "but I realized that was my ignorance. It was presumptuous of me not to be protected."

After it appeared he would pull through, Flynt offered a $100,000 reward for information leading to the arrest and conviction of those responsible for the attack. Possible suspects included a religious fanatic (though the shooting seemed too premeditated and well planned), an enraged relative of a *Hustler* centerfold, the Ku Klux Klan, or a competitor. Even Billy Carter, the president's brother, was a target of suspicion. A few weeks earlier Billy had said on *Donahue,* "I've got a man looking out for him [Flynt]. The first thing he's going to do is beat the hell out of him." Billy was angry because Flynt had used his mother, Lillian, as a centerfold in a spoof called "The Plains, Georgia Monster," depicting her as a Madonna with a black Jesus, surrounded by third world children. But Billy was soon eliminated as a suspect.

Government agents were also suspected. Flynt told Althea he thought the

CIA did it, just as he thought the CIA was also behind what he claimed was a poisoning attempt at a Washington, D.C., hotel three months earlier. But some inside the porn industry knew the Mob was angry that Flynt had been distributing his own magazine and decided to send him a serious message.

In the September 1978 issue of *Hustler,* Flynt published some of the most shocking photographs ever to appear in its pages—bloody close-ups of the publisher lying in his hospital bed, his face partly obscured by an oxygen mask, his bare stomach showing gaping, sutured, unbandaged wounds. The message was stark and simple: Violence, not sex, was the real obscenity.

BACK IN 1977 investigative reporter Jack Anderson and his associate Les Whitten had recounted in their syndicated column an allegation that former Atlanta mayor Andrew Young, now U.S. representative to the United Nations, was paid a sum of money by pornographer Mike Thevis to arrange for the latter's transfer from a federal prison to a prison hospital.

At the time of Thevis's transfer to the prison hospital, Young was a member of the U.S. House from Thevis's district. Young later admitted urging such a transfer, but for humanitarian reasons, and insisted he had received nothing in return. An FBI investigation later showed there had been no impropriety.

The story was a potential blockbuster because, after Reuben Sturman, Michael G. Thevis was the most important hard-core pornographer in the country—and in many respects his forerunner, much as Ralph Ginzburg was the soft-core precursor of Hugh Hefner and Bob Guccione.

Raised by his Greek immigrant grandparents, Thevis—like Sturman—had used his savings to open his own newsstand in Atlanta after graduating from high school. He quickly discovered that sex-oriented materials brought in more profit than newspapers and greeting cards. By the early sixties his wholesale and retail network, a prototype of Sturman's, extended from California to New York. His legitimate businesses included an auto dealership, a liquor store, a mail-order cheese and fruit club, luxury real estate, and the production of movies starring such nonpornographic actors as Shelley Winters and Leslie Uggams. Though Atlanta police arrested him eighty-eight times over the years, his attorneys kept him out of prison. But in 1970 the federal government targeted Thevis as America's porn enemy number one. Acting swiftly, U.S. attorneys in New Orleans indicted Thevis for shipping obscene materials across state lines and through the mails. For the first time, Thevis was convicted.

That same year, his former associate, Kenneth "Jap" Hanna, went to attend what his wife later described as an "urgent" meeting with Thevis. Hanna's gold Cadillac was later found in the airport parking lot with his body stuffed into the trunk. The murderer was never found. In September 1973, while Thevis's appeal dragged through the courts, former Thevis bodyguard James A. Mayes Jr. walked out of his peep-show shop on Atlanta's Peachtree Street and switched on the ignition of his truck. A dynamite blast blew him through the roof.

After the Supreme Court denied Thevis's appeal in July 1974, his attorneys claimed Thevis sold his porn empire for $5.7 million in 1973, though no buyers were identified. But federal authorities valued his empire at $100 million, saying it accounted for 40 percent of all U.S. pornography. In a last-ditch effort to win public support, Thevis donated his $5 million mansion to the city of Atlanta for use as a school and vowed to spend another $3.3 million restoring a historic theater for public benefit—to no avail. In December 1974 he began serving an eight-year federal prison term. The *Reader's Digest* celebrated with an article, probably written with help from the FBI, claiming the agency had finally put away the "Sultan of Smut." Unlike the reclusive Sturman, Thevis conformed to the public image of what a sleazy, Mafia-befriending, murderous pornographer ought to look and act like.

In April 1978, Thevis escaped from a jail in New Albany, Indiana, where he was being held while testifying in a civil proceeding. Federal authorities, who promptly put him on their "10 Most Wanted List," assumed he had fled the country because murder and arson indictments handed down by a federal grand jury in Atlanta were pending. The indictment also quoted the FBI as calling Thevis the King of Porn. Six months later, a key witness against Thevis, Roger Dean Underhill, died after an ambush shotgun attack in Atlanta. The testimony of Underhill, who was about to enter the witness protection program, was a vital part of the government's plan to convict Thevis in the murder of Mayes.

In November Thevis tried to cash a $31,000 check at the Connecticut Bank and Trust Company in Bloomfield, Connecticut. Officials became suspicious and called police when he asked for the large withdrawal from a checking account held under an assumed name. A female companion, Anna J. Evans, a real estate agent from Marietta, Georgia, was waiting outside in a car containing another $600,000 in cash, $1 million in diamonds, and several pistols. Police arrested the pair without a struggle.

Evans was held on $2.5 million bond on charges of harboring a criminal. Thevis, now forty-six, was wearing a toupee and had shaved the distinctive beard and mustache that he had worn as one of Atlanta's most easily recognized public figures. Using the name of Evans's brother, Thevis had been traveling the country, collecting cash in accounts from North Carolina to Connecticut.

In August 1979, Thevis again went on trial, this time on federal charges that he used murder, arson, mail fraud, and extortion to create his nationwide porn empire. Evans and her cousin Bart Hood, a former South Carolina police officer, both pleaded guilty in separate trials to helping Thevis escape from jail. On October 26, 1979, Thevis was sentenced to life in prison for conspiring to murder Underhill and received an additional twenty-year sentence on charges he used murder and arson in a pattern of racketeering. Evans and Hood were also sentenced to life on the murder conspiracy. In 1982 Thevis lost his appeal and died soon after while still in prison.

EARLY IN 1978 Marco Vassi began to keep a sex diary in order to discover, as he confided with typical Weltschmerz, whether "the esthetic pleasure I derive from my search was worth the sorrow of consciousness." At the time, he had just moved in with a professional singer who, like Marco, wanted to explore the outer limits of sexual expression.

Not long after he moved in, Judith announced that her former live-in boyfriend was coming to visit. Marco greeted the news with misgiving, dreading a stilted encounter or the "compulsory ménage." Just in time, though, he remembered his Oscar Wilde and concluded that "the only sin is mediocrity." Just before the old boyfriend was due to arrive, Marco handcuffed Judith to the bed, tying her arms over her head and positioning her feet wide apart. Then he pulled down her blouse to expose one breast, hiked up her skirt, and as a final touch blindfolded her. When Dan rang the bell, Marco greeted him with a handshake and led him into the bedroom, where the two men ravished Judith for more than an hour. Then they all sat down to lunch, which was followed by more sex, this time with Judith unbound.

Marco had begun reading tantric texts, and though he considered one teaching too extreme—that a man should never ejaculate unless a baby was wanted—he did begin experimenting with allowing himself to ejaculate only every third time. He also divided sensual experience into five kinds: (1) tantric, or sensual; (2) Reichian, or "complete vegetative release"; (3) fantasy, which included acting out, for which purpose he kept a few whips and friends on hand to join in various scenarios; (4) contextual, or "*New York Times* reality," in which a person's primary social identity always remained in view during lovemaking, no matter how intense; and (5) simple affection, "the sine qua non of true eroticism, without which the fanciest games are no more satisfying than adolescent pranks."

He still visited Catholic churches regularly, making peace with his Catholic upbringing and enjoying the flicker of candles and the smell of incense. But occasionally the "man mood" became too strong to deny and he visited the baths, to fellate other men and be the passive partner in anal intercourse. Taking inventory from time to time, Marco was astonished at the array of women, men, strangers, and friends he had made love to. Yet he also experienced long days of silence and solitude, nights devoted to contemplation and sleep, hours spent reading or walking, visiting his parents and friends, afternoons or evenings with meditation groups.

One night, a tearful Judith phoned to say, "I loved you all alone, in the deepest shelters of my heart. No one else knew what that love was, no one else believed it was real."

Moved, he replied: "I feel the loss of you in pangs of sorrow like long lonely cries piercing the endless dark of eternal night."

There was a silence on the phone. Then they laughed, pleased with the doleful sentimentalism of their words.

Marco's most frightening sexual moment occurred when he was asked by Judith and a lesbian dom to help break in a young woman who had never been tied down and worked over before. Though she was turned on by the idea, the woman always became extremely skittish when the moment arrived.

Finally, Marco and the two women, both dressed in black leather outfits, succeeded in shackling the woman spread-eagle onto a bed. The woman immediately panicked and begged to be let loose. Marco refused, but to calm her fears he set an alarm to go off in one hour, at which time he would free her if she so desired. That put the woman's mind at ease.

The two doms and Marco then proceeded to give their virgin "bottom" their full attention, licking and whipping her, applying nipple clips, penetrating her with fingers and dildos, taking turns sitting on her face—all the while keeping up a stream of insults, abuse, and threats.

Later, as the lesbian lay between the woman's legs, putting acupuncture needles through her clitoris, Judith grabbed Marco by the hair, forced his face between her thighs, and slipped a choke collar around his throat. Marco was not new to the experience, and he enjoyed the sense of oblivion it provided. But he was just beginning to swoon when he observed Judith snap a popper under her nose and lose contact with conventional reality.

In the world of SM, everyone knew someone who had an "accident" because someone else got carried away. Marco thought his own time had come. Under the influence of the drug, Judith was no longer keeping the proper tension on the choker but was literally strangling him. Even more bizarre, he did not care. He decided it was all right to die. He felt no pain but was flushed with the unique, keen erotic pleasure that comes with asphyxiation. Such a death seemed the perfect conclusion to his erotic career.

Then, as though from a great distance, he heard a buzzing sound. He thought it was the blood pouring into his ears. But it was the alarm going off. Judith jumped up. Literally, he had been saved by the bell. Later Judith admitted she had gone over the edge. But when she realized what was happening, she decided to go for it anyway. Marco had often claimed that at its greatest intensity, sex was transformed into the death experience. "After all," she later told him, "how many chances do you get to try for the big one?"

A more compliant lover during that period was Marco's inflatable doll, for which he professed real love and desire. She never protested anything he did. She just lay there and received all of him—his anger and hatred, as well as his tenderness and caring. Crying out his pain to that doll, he fancied, meant more to him than having any real woman pretend to be interested in what he had to say.

One night, though, drunk, stoned, tired of himself and of humanity, he was making love to his beloved inflatable doll when she sprang a leak in her neck. Hearing the *whoosh* of escaping air, he tried to stanch the "wound" with his finger. Then a second seam burst, at the base of her spine, then a third. As the doll deflated and collapsed, Marco found himself holding a wrinkled sheet of plastic in his arms. He cried himself to sleep.

Marco found that he was growing "a trifle impotent," an inconvenience he attributed to sexual excess, drugs, and the strenuousness of many of his encounters. Yet he also knew he was aging, and he began to refer to himself as a "metaphysical eunuch." Increasingly, too, he was plagued by anxiety attacks. Dread gnawed at his mind, and at times he felt as though he were "fifteen billion years old."

After finishing his fifteenth book, Marco visited tattoo artist Spider Webb at his New Hampshire farm. While there he confided to his diary: "My reputation is assured. And I have many friends, all over the world. I'm in the prime of life. And yet, I am not happy." Rather, he was tortured, fearful, confused, vain. He had sought truth and meaning in gurus, drugs, eroticism, religious philosophies, radical politics, and therapies, but had not found it.

Later he wrote in his diary of being seized with "Ecclesiastian melancholy," of glimpsing "God's robe sweeping relentlessly through the infinite expanse of space." At a birthday bash for the Marquis de Sade at a midtown disco to promote a string of SM boutiques, he spotted Judith, whom he had not seen in months. Dressed cabaret style, she was leading two slaves on a chain. She had become an artist, living out her erotic roles in public theaters and in writing. She did not recognize him. And he understood that all the time he was seeing her as a character in his play, she was shaping him as a character in hers.

THE MUSTARD-COLORED HOUSE on Wonderland Avenue in Hollywood's Laurel Canyon had once belonged to the rock group Paul Revere and the Raiders, but by June 1981 its occupants were Joy Miller, William Ray Deverell, and Ron Launius, all of whom had a long string of arrests. One of the frequent guests was John Curtis Holmes, whose droopy mustache, skinny frame, and pallid good looks were familiar to tens of thousands of Americans, though his most famous feature was his alleged fourteen-inch-long penis. (In fact, it measured a mere twelve and three-quarter inches—still sufficiently long, however, for him to boast about it as "fourteen inches of dangling death.") At thirty-six, John Holmes was at the height of his fame. In a business dominated, at least on screen, by females, he was porndom's only authentic male superstar.

On June 30, Launius invited his estranged wife, Susan, to come stay at the house in an attempt at a reconciliation. After eating pizza and watching TV, they went to sleep. A visitor, Barbara Richardson, was curled inside a sleeping bag on the couch. Upstairs Deverell and Miller watched TV. At three forty-five in the morning, other visitors returned to the house to discover that the house had been ransacked and Deverell, Miller, Ron Launius, and Richardson had all been bludgeoned to death with a length of pipe. Susan Launius was found slumped against a bedroom wall but still alive, one finger severed in a futile attempt to defend herself.

Even to a town that had survived the Manson murders, the Freeway Killer, and the Hillside Strangler, the carnage seemed sensationally savage. Immediately the press speculated that drugs were involved. But the police stonewalled. Within two days they thought they had solved the case. Richardson's boyfriend, David Lind, thirsting for revenge and believing she and not Susan Launius had survived, had gone to a Hollywood police station and told his story. The key to the mystery, he said, was porn star John Holmes.

A pathological liar, Holmes usually told interviewers he had been born in New York, was raised in Europe by a rich aunt, and lost his virginity to a nanny. In fact, he had been born John Curtis Estis in Columbus, Ohio, on August 8, 1944, and raised in nearby Pataskala. His father of record was Carl L. Estis, a railroad worker. Two years later his name was legally amended to John Curtis Holmes, and no father was given, with the surname taken from a local carpenter. Little Johnny was raised in a strict Christian household and for twelve straight years maintained a perfect attendance record at Sunday school. In his young adulthood he also dabbled in sculpting, supported the Greenpeace movement, took vitamins, jogged, and considered himself a health nut.

After being discharged from the army at the age of twenty-one, Holmes headed for Hollywood. Though he was ambitious and charming, it soon became apparent even to himself that he had no talent. But he did have one attribute nobody else in Tinsel Town could boast of. Not only was his penis twice the length of most men's, but he could ejaculate repeatedly.

In the beginning Holmes earned pocket money posing for porn stills, but in 1972 he graduated to Super 8 loops, sometimes shooting two or three a day, both straight and gay. When the porn industry expanded into feature-length films, he earned between $1,500 and $3,000 a day—top porn dollar. During the course of his career he made more than twenty-five hundred features and loops, initially under the name Johnny Wadd and many of them for Reuben Sturman's Caballero company.

Sometime in the late seventies, though, his fabled sexual powers began to fail and he turned to cocaine to get aroused. Before long he was freebasing, smoking a version of cocaine that had been "cooked" to remove hydrochlorides—the procedure that nearly cost comedian Richard Pryor his life. By 1981 Holmes was ripping off friends and fencing stolen goods. He had not made a feature film in two years and had fallen in with the Wonderland crowd. Another new friend during this time was a Palestinian named Adel "Eddie Nash" Nasrallah, proprietor of a string of topless and gay bars. An old friend of Holmes's, porn actress Gloria Leonard, recalls that on a visit to her home in Los Angeles Holmes looked painfully thin and seemed "all cock." By nine in the morning he had already freebased three grams of coke. When she returned from an errand, she found that $25,000 worth of jewelry, electronic equipment, and guns had disappeared, and Holmes along with it.

In the summer of 1981 Joy Miller was facing drug charges, while Deverell and Lind had assorted legal problems in Sacramento. In recent months everybody in the house spent all of their time shooting up. To support their heroin and cocaine habits, the Wonderlanders had turned to stealing cars and burgling houses between Los Angeles and Sacramento. Holmes served as go-between, delivering drugs purchased from Nash, who lived five minutes away. On June 26 Holmes delivered some stolen property to Nash as collateral for drugs. Three days later, with nothing left to barter with, the group decided to rob Nash—in effect, rip off their supplier. Holmes was the key because he knew the house and could help them gain entry.

The plan was for Launius, Lind, and Deverell to pose as detectives in order to deal quickly with Nash's three-hundred-pound bodyguard, Gregory DeWitt Diles, a karate expert whose favorite weapon was a short length of steel pipe. The robbery went reasonably well. Flashing fake badges, the three robbers quickly handcuffed Diles, though Lind's gun accidentally went off, leaving Diles with a powder burn on his thigh. Fearing the worst, Nash dropped to his knees, pleading to be spared. Launius started to cut Diles's throat, trying to find out where more drugs were hidden, but Lind dissuaded him. Eventually the trio fled with two Ziploc bags full of cocaine, vials of heroin, and Quaaludes, as well as jewelry, guns, and $20,000 in cash.

Soon after Lind went to the police, Holmes was picked up on an unrelated charge. Detectives shunted him from one hotel to another, grilling him around the clock. But he insisted he knew nothing about the killings. After being released on his own recognizance, he disappeared.

On July 10, 1981, the police caught up with Holmes again, and this time he admitted his part in the Nash robbery and to being at the Wonderland house on the night of the murders. But he claimed he had been forced to go to the house by a group of strange men with guns. He also said Nash—the "most evil man" he ever met—would kill him if he knew Holmes was cooperating with the police. Yet an hour after leaving the police station, a detective observed Holmes's car parked outside Nash's house. When the police raided Nash's house a few weeks later, they found a million dollars' worth of cocaine. Nash's lawyer said it was for his client's personal use.

Subsequently, Nash received eight years on drug charges, while Diles was given seven years for shooting at a policeman at the time of his arrest. Unfortunately, Susan Launius had lost her memory, while blood and hair samples taken at the scene of the murders were inconclusive. To make matters worse, Holmes suddenly disappeared once again. The police now theorized Holmes either led the murderers into the house or participated himself.

While Holmes was on the lam, his last film, *Exhausted,* was rushed into release. Suzanne Atamian, also known as Julia St. Innocent, a twenty-two-year-old former girlfriend of Holmes, produced the documentary pastiche of interviews, clips, and testimonials. Holmes once claimed that in twenty-four years he had appeared in 2,274 films and had sex with 15,000 women. Every time he did a shoot he dropped a pea in a bucket. At the screening, the police rushed in, hoping Holmes might be attending incognito. But he had grown a scraggly beard and migrated to Montana, where he visited with his sister, painted his car, and frequently changed license plates.

IN APRIL 1979 *Hustler* publisher Larry Flynt, paralyzed now from the midthigh down, appeared as a guest on the TV talk show *Donahue.* Flynt's spinal cord had not been injured, but a bullet had lodged in a bundle of nerves at the bottom of the spinal cord, severing some of them. Flynt told Donahue that he was shot "largely because we were going to win that particular verdict in Georgia. It was a neighboring county and the jury took a straw vote the next day after I'd been shot and acquitted me. . . . I was shot from—by a person right there in Lawrenceville, simply because they knew that they could not get me on the obscenity law, so they wanted to get me some other way."

Psychologically, Flynt said, he accepted his injury. But he complained not only of the intense pain, but of the fact that he could not take narcotics for relief because of the danger of addiction. "I got hooked on them when I was in the hospital and it was a very bad experience," he confessed, admitting also to loss of bladder and bowel control—though no loss of sexual function.

As if his medical condition were not tribulation enough, he had recently been convicted on eleven counts of obscenity, and his magazine had been banned from the state of Georgia. To make matters worse, Bob Guccione had also filed an $80 million suit, claiming *Hustler* had both libeled him and invaded his privacy by printing a touched-up photograph showing Guccione's superimposed head on a male body engaging in a homosexual act. In his suit Guccione declared that Flynt had attacked him in *Hustler* from the very first issue.

On March 1, 1980, after a ten-day trial and two days of deliberation, a common pleas court jury ordered Flynt to pay Guccione an astonishing $39.3 million in damages. In April a judge reduced the award to $4 million. *Penthouse* protested the reduction of damages, even though at the same time it was challenging the order of a federal jury in Wyoming that it pay $25 million in punitive damages and $1.5 million in compensatory damages to a young woman named Kimerli Jayne Pring. In her libel suit the former Miss Wyoming had claimed she was libeled in a *Penthouse* short story satirizing beauty pageants and featuring a fictional Miss Wyoming. That judgment was later overturned; though one of the most litigious men in America, and one of the most often sued, Guccione never lost a suit.

Yet *Hustler* was in robust shape, with an estimated sale of 2.5 million, mostly to working-class men who thought the magazine gave good value. Unlike *Playboy* and *Penthouse,* whose pictorials were segregated into distinct sections and adhered to a high standard of photography, *Hustler* was jammed with photographs laid out without much attention to lighting, cropping, or composition. A common pose for a *Hustler* model was to sit on a backed chair with her knees pulled back to her shoulders, arms surrounding her buttocks, and fingers spreading open her vagina. Mouth, vagina, and anus were thus all in vertical alignment.

Hustler satire continued to be equally crude. In 1983 Flynt ran a parody advertisement suggesting that fundamentalist Jerry Falwell had sex in an outhouse with his mother. The U.S. Supreme Court later ruled it was not defamatory and turned him into a champion of free speech. Flynt claimed the case was the most important defense of the First Amendment since *Ulysses.*

ON NOVEMBER 30, 1981, Miami Beach police discovered John Holmes hiding out with a girlfriend, Dawn Schiller, in a hotel where he had found work as a painter. He was arrested on a fugitive warrant from California, extradited to Los Angeles, and charged with first-degree murder in the deaths of the four Wonderland Avenue victims, based on a palm print found on the premises and on statements made to the police.

On May 20, 1982, the Holmes trial began in superior court, sensationally headlined the "Four on the Floor" murder trial. The prosecution claimed he had double-crossed his friends and had beaten at least Ron Launius to death himself. Among those testifying were Lind and Detective Frank Tomlinson, who insisted Holmes had confessed to taking the murderers to Wonderland, while strongly denying having done the killing himself. Wanting revenge, Nash allegedly had threatened him and his family. Holmes's unique defense, later incorporated into law school textbooks, was that he was "the man in the middle," acting under duress. The defense also took a gamble and called no witnesses. To keep his mind off his troubles, Holmes concentrated on writing his autobiography while not in the courthouse. On June 26, 1982, the jury brought in a verdict of not guilty. In a subsequent trial Nash and Diles were acquitted of the murders. In all, the Four on the Floor media extravaganza extended over nine years, four trials, two mistrials, and one retrial.

One day at the 1983 International Winter Consumer Electronics Show in Las Vegas, *Screw* publisher Al Goldstein encountered Holmes signing autographs for Caballero Control, one of Sturman's former video companies. "You're gaining weight, Goldstein," Holmes remarked. "You should be on the same diet I'm on, the cocaine diet."

Goldstein looked hard at the emaciated ex–porn star and remembered Gloria Leonard's remark. Then he asked about the large diamond signature ring Holmes used to wear in all of his films.

"Gone," Holmes replied, "with the rest of it. Up my nose in a couple of toots."

"So this whole thing was coke, John?"

Holmes looked away, his eyes narrowing painfully. But Goldstein knew cocaine merely helped the process along. Suddenly a quote from Bruce Jay Friedman floated into Goldstein's mind: "Don't let that little frankfurter run your life." They never saw each other again. Holmes soon vanished into lonely obscurity, dying of colon cancer complicated by HIV in 1988.

Among pornography's other famous dead were superstar Shauna Grant, who blew out her brains in 1984 in the bathroom of her boyfriend's apartment; Veri Knotty, who could tie her labia in a knot; Jill Munro, probably the first transsexual to do a hard-core film in *Consenting Adults,* whose death was rumored to be drug related; Tina Russell, the hippie of porndom, dead of cirrhosis of the liver in 1978; Kathy Harcourt, who was fished out of New York's East River; Melba Bruce, a suicide in 1977; Wade Nichols, who either died of AIDS or committed suicide; Savannah, Megan Leigh, Cal Jammer, Nancee Kellee, and Alex Jordan, all suicides; and Laurien Dominique, who choked to death.

Chapter 11

Missionary Positions

On Halloween 1976, a woman named Christina Regnery was violently assaulted at her home in an affluent suburb of Verona, just outside Madison, Wisconsin, while her husband, Alfred, campaigned for county attorney at a nearby shopping mall. Christina, who was eight months pregnant, claimed she had been standing naked in the bathroom, getting ready to take a bath. Her oldest child was with friends at an ice show, and the two youngest were taking an afternoon nap. According to the police report, Christina became "suddenly aware of someone else in the room, and turned to see two men standing there," a white "hippie" and a black man with a gold-capped tooth, both around thirty. The report continued, "She was startled, and did not say a word, but reached for a towel . . . to cover herself. One of the men told her to step out of the bathroom and into the bedroom, as they wanted her to smell something. . . . They also told her to leave the towel behind, so she dropped it. Upon entering the bedroom, the men asked her if she could smell the gas." They had turned off the stove's pilot light and turned up the burners, and they threatened to open the doors to the children's rooms if she did not cooperate.

Christina knelt down as commanded, and the white male grabbed her by the hair and jerked her to floor. When the men called her a "sweet little cock-sucker," she recognized their voices from obscene phone calls the household had received during the campaign, warning her husband to quit the race. Her assailants, she claimed, said her husband should have taken their advice.

While the white man sucked her nipples, the black man retrieved a paring knife from the kitchen. She begged them not to cut her, but they took turns slashing at her stomach. When the knife proved too dull, they got a razor blade. The white man also stuck an embroidery needle into her nipple. Then the black man found a condom in a night table drawer, and the perverse pair took turns shoving such items as a condom-clad can of hairspray, a can of feminine deodorant spray, and assorted jars into her vagina. Finally she screamed that she would make any "deal" they wanted.

They told her they would stop if she gave them a blow job. She asked what that was, then dutifully fellated both men in the bathroom. After they fled, a distraught and still naked Christina ran down the stairs and rushed outside. Seeing no sign of the men, she returned to shut off the gas and open the windows. Then she splashed water on herself to remove the sticky sperm, drank glass after glass of water and rinsed her mouth with Listerine, vomited several times, used disposable wipes to remove blood from her nipples, breasts, sides, stomach, and thighs, then flushed them away and got dressed. After waking her two children, she fled to a neighbor's house, sobbing, "Oh, what they did to me. They cut me with a razor. They raped me."

The neighbor urged Christina to call the police, but she refused, wanting to talk with Alfred first. A half hour later he returned home, found no one there, went to the neighbor's house, and called Dane County police. Christina was taken to the hospital and given emergency treatment for seventy-three slash marks, including at least seventeen lacerations around the nipples. The left nipple had been punctured fifteen times.

The son of far-right publisher Henry Regnery, the thirty-three-year-old Al was a past official of the Wisconsin Young Americans for Freedom club. Now he was running for office as a law-and-order candidate in Dane County, home of the University of Wisconsin, a hotbed of post-sixties radicalism. While his wife was being treated, he talked first to an investigating officer, then to a reporter from the *Capital Times*. Regnery told the reporter the attack was aimed at getting him to withdraw his candidacy.

But by the eve of the election, Regnery had a serious credibility problem; the police did not believe the rape story. Christina had said the two assailants left through a basement door, but that door was blocked by dust-covered boxes that showed no sign of disturbance. The police also found no sign of a struggle in the master bedroom or even a speck of blood.

What they did find in the nightstand was a stash of hard-core pornography and catalogs for sex toys. Curiously enough, some of the photographs depicted acts strikingly similar to those Christina ascribed to her alleged assailants. Though a can of feminine hygiene spray with a condom stretched over it was found on the bed, the packet of prophylactics had been carefully cut, not ripped open as might be expected under the circumstances. Also, it was almost impossible to relight the dirt-clogged stove. When the police confronted Al with their suspicions, he confessed to his own misgivings that her wounds might have been self-inflicted. Regnery went down in defeat in the polls, but Christina was not charged with filing a false police report because his opponent, the new county attorney, did not want to appear vindictive. In 1978 the Regnerys moved to Washington, and Al found his niche, appropriately enough, in the pro-family movement. After joining the staff of Nevada senator Paul Laxalt, he went to work lobbying for the Family Protection Act.

BY THE LATE SEVENTIES the Playboy Philosophy had found its most ardent converts in the world of TV evangelism, where a crop of Hugh Hefner wannabes had sprouted up, replete with beautiful women, luxurious mansions, private jets, and unlimited expense accounts. All that was missing was porn, though of sex advice there was plenty.

For example, *The Missing Dimension in Sex,* a book of sexual advice distributed by the Worldwide Church of God (WCG) and written by its founder, Herbert Armstrong, proclaimed that the "most important dimension in knowledge about sex and marriage has been MISSING—unpublished until this book." What was MISSING from all other sex manuals were proper instructions on how to deflower a virgin on her wedding night—an etiquette Armstrong thoughtfully supplied in detail. Still MISSING from his sex manual, though, was any mention of birth control. As for masturbation, he believed there was "no greater plague." Sexual intercourse between an engaged couple was condemned as being "as great a crime as MURDER," although "this is not to say that a fond embrace and a kiss—if not prolonged—are wrong. But remember, the male is sexually aroused in five to ten seconds—or less."

For Herbert Armstrong's son, Garner Ted, much less.

By 1978, Garner Ted's TV ministry was raking in $75 million tax-free dollars per year—more than the gross revenues of rival evangelists Billy Graham and Oral Roberts combined. But in May 1978 Herbert removed Ted from his ministry for incurring heavy gambling losses in Las Vegas and attempting to seduce one of his father's secretaries to boot. It was not Ted's first "leave of absence."

Ted had a used-car salesman's good looks and had once aspired to be an actor in Hollywood. As a sailor during the Korean War he had earned a reputation as a ladies' man, sporting tattoos on his arms and legs of spread-legged girls wearing only cowboy boots. In 1953 he was hurriedly married to the daughter of a wealthy WCG member, and six months later the new Mrs. Armstrong gave birth to a "miraculous" seven-pound "premature" baby.

But Ted's prodigal ways continued unchecked. At a meeting of some seventy WCG ministers in Big Sandy, Texas, on March 4, 1974, convened in response to rumors of Ted's profligate ways, several ministers accused Ted of committing adultery for decades. Since the WCG condemned divorce and refused to give its members permission to remarry, Herbert knew this scandal would hurt church income, and in September 1971 he relieved Ted of his duties as the golden-haired, golden-voiced heir apparent of his TV ministry.

A few weeks later, a repentant Ted was back in the trenches, at a church convention in Squaw Valley, California, preaching a sermon entitled "What the World Needs Now Is Love, Sweet Love." That night he felt the need for some love, sweet love, with his favorite stewardess at a Lake Tahoe cabin loaned by a church member. Again found out by Dad, and again relieved of church responsibilities, Ted was exiled to Hawaii with his wife and a chaperon.

A few months later, Ted was again back at headquarters and back to his old ways. On January 30, 1972, an angry Herbert Armstrong, accompanied by a church attorney and several WCG vice presidents, waited at Ted's home for his son to return from a Los Angeles Lakers basketball game. When Ted arrived home and discovered they had come to interrogate him about his sex life, he became furious. When Herbert asked just how many women Ted had affairs with, he grabbed his father by the lapels, looked him in the eye, and screamed, "Hundreds!"

After that, Ted was officially excommunicated from the church. The membership was informed that he had "a personal emotional problem" and was in the "bonds of Satan." Ted retreated to his Colorado home. But when WCG income plummeted once again, Ted was reinstated a third time, in July 1972.

The story of Garner Ted set a pattern for many greed-driven fundamentalist TV ministries throughout the seventies and eighties. Feeding into the fears of a gullible Middle America, televangelists like the Armstrongs grew inconceivably wealthy denouncing sexual immorality—as exemplified by pornography, adultery, a decline in family values, abortion, sex education, and homosexuality—while pursuing a sybaritic lifestyle worthy of Hefner himself.

While the congregations of most mainstream churches were dwindling, membership in conservative churches was exploding. The Gallup organization found that in 1976, when Jimmy Carter was elected president, fifty million people described themselves as born-again Christians. About half that number were fundamentalists, though not all fundamentalists were necessarily conservative on social and political issues.

The man who was to capitalize on the rightward drift of the nation more than any other religious figure was Jerry Falwell. Born a twin on August 11, 1933, in Lynchburg, Virginia, Falwell grew up in a home where religious instruction was virtually nonexistent, although his mother did make him listen to the *Old-Fashioned Revival Hour* broadcast by the Reverend Charles E. Fuller, a pioneer of radio evangelism, on Sunday mornings. His father, a drunk and a bootlegger, had killed his brother during an argument. Jerry himself became the town rowdy for a time, but his hell-raising days were short-lived.

In 1950 Falwell enrolled in Lynchburg College. During his sophomore year he experienced an unaccountable need to attend church. One winter night he drove his blue Plymouth sedan into the parking lot of the Park Avenue Baptist Church, accompanied by best friend and drinking buddy Jim Moon. Sitting in the front row, he listened to a sermon on hell and the Second Coming, and a half hour later was led to the altar by an elder, where he made a profession of faith. He was not so transported as to be unaware of the charms of the pianist, Macel Pate, however.

The next day Falwell bought a Bible. Turning down an offer to play professional baseball with the St. Louis Cardinals, he gave up drinking, dancing, dating, movies, and most of his friends. At the end of the school year he quit Lynchburg and transferred to the Baptist Bible College in Springfield, Missouri.

After marrying Pate in 1956, Falwell returned to Lynchburg and, with thirty-five supporters, founded the Thomas Road Baptist Church in the former Donald Duck Bottling Company factory. Within twenty-five years it had become the largest congregation in town, claiming eighteen thousand members, even though Lynchburg was largely run by Old Dominion Episcopalians.

Along with others on the Christian Right, Falwell was particularly alarmed by the rise in premarital sex and pregnancy among single women. Premarital sex was perhaps the most popular and closely watched index among sociologists of whether or not a sexual revolution was in progress, and to what degree, even though most surveys were confined to middle-class, white, college-going young women. In the fifties and early sixties, the number of men and women having premarital sex had remained fairly stable— roughly two in five women and two out of three men. But by 1972 the rate for both men and women had increased dramatically to 73 percent. Yet the number was deceptive because the overwhelming majority of such women who had premarital coitus had it with only one partner, either the man they would eventually marry or one to whom they had a strong emotional commitment. Nearly half, or 45 percent, of white women had sex by age twenty, while the figure for black women was 80 percent.

Falwell was determined to buck this seeming tide of promiscuity among teenagers. In 1971 he established the Liberty Baptist College, to train students in evangelism, liberal arts, and sophisticated broadcasting techniques. For years an undergraduate population of two thousand struggled along without benefit of campus, gym, or library. In his preaching he gave specific instructions for daily conduct—no alcohol, tobacco, drugs, cursing, dancing, rock 'n' roll—along with a dress code. His followers turned off their TV sets at night, while their car radios were replaced by tape decks stacked with cassettes of religious music. Falwell's purpose: to develop "Christian character" in what was, for all practical purposes, a laboratory of sexual repression. His rules for marriage were outlined in a book called *The Total Family* by Edward Hindson, the family guidance pastor of the Thomas Road church, who declared: "The Bible clearly states that the wife is to submit to her husband's leadership and help him fulfill God's will for his life."

In the mid-seventies Falwell changed the focus of his preaching from railing against the evils of drink to attacking pornography, homosexuality, abortion, and the Equal Rights Amendment. In 1977 Falwell associated himself with entertainer Anita Bryant's antihomosexual campaign. A former Miss Oklahoma and runner-up for Miss America, Bryant successfully campaigned in Dade County, Florida, to repeal a ban on housing and employment discrimination on the basis of sexual orientation. In 1978 Bryant also campaigned successfully for the passage of an Oklahoma law allowing state-run schools to fire pro-gay teachers. This time gays organized and struck back, boycotting Florida oranges, which led to the dismissal of Bryant as spokeswoman for the growers. Eventually her twenty-year marriage ended in divorce, and when she later attempted to open a women's clothing shop in Selma and to get into TV work in Atlanta, gay protesters again forced her out.

But in the meantime, in 1980, Bryant and Falwell teamed up to launch their Clean Up America drive against pornography, abortion, and homosexuality. On a typical Sunday Falwell could be heard warning his followers against falling prey to liberals, Socialists, humanists, pornographers, abortionists, feminists, drugs, television, movies, rock lyrics, Communists, Jane Fonda, Gloria Steinem, and Hugh Hefner. Yet he never attacked the printing plant in his hometown of Lynchburg, where *Penthouse* was printed.

Though he possessed none of the smooth preaching style of the 700 Club's Pat Robertson or Oral Roberts, Falwell was the most energetic of the lot. Preaching in an avuncular bass against a backdrop of American flags and a college choir, he used every available medium to spread his message.

By 1979 Falwell had succeeded in raising $35 million from mailing lists of a mere 2.5 million. His grosses placed him just under Garner Ted, Oral Roberts, Pat Robertson, Jim Bakker, and Billy Graham and substantially ahead of Rex Humbard and Jimmy Swaggart. His *Old-Time Gospel Hour,* with an annual budget of $56 million, was now seen on 324 TV stations in the United States, Canada, and the Caribbean—a larger distribution than late night TV's top-rated *Tonight Show.* Yet even though other nonprofit organizations might look askance at some of Falwell's practices, they did not appear to be technically illegal.

That same year, the press also began reporting on a movement called the Moral Majority, whose grand ambition was to mold conservative Christians into political voting blocs. A combination of right-to-life groups and conservative political action committees, the Moral Majority united behind an antiabortion, pro-family stance, claiming a constituency of fifty million Protestant evangelicals and thirty million "morally conservative" Roman Catholics, as well as a few million Mormons and Orthodox Jews. Though presidential candidate Ronald Reagan was sympathetic to their causes, he rejected their candidate for the vice presidency, North Carolina Republican senator Jesse Helms.

During the presidential campaign, Falwell used the Moral Majority to create a series of state organizations headed by local pastors and handed out moral report cards on candidates and incumbents. To the media outside his constituency, he posed as a moderate conservative, telling *The Washington Post,* for example: "I have no objection to a homosexual teaching in the public classroom as long as that homosexual is not flaunting his lifestyle or soliciting students." Yet his fund-raising letters continued to declare: "Is our grand old flag going down the drain? . . . Just look at what's happening here in America: Known, practicing homosexual teachers have invaded the classrooms."

Who exactly created the Moral Majority is a matter of conjecture. Though Falwell—its most conspicuous spokesman—and his followers later tried to take credit, right-wing journalist Paul Weyrich also played a significant and perhaps key role. Regardless, the Moral Majority was within two years the most powerful of all fundamentalist lobbying groups, promoting candidates to local, state, and national office who shared its antiwelfare, antiabortion, anti-ERA, antigay, and pro-family sentiments. And although the forty-seven-year-old Falwell remained a teetotaler and a devoted husband and father, he was now also the ruler of a media empire and the owner of a mountaintop mansion complete with pool and private jet.

A small but potentially dangerous backlash was building against him. After the election, President Reagan maintained a hands-off attitude toward the Moral Majority leader. Billy Graham told *People* magazine, "The Moral Majority is not my cup of tea. . . . I do not intend to use what little influence I may have on secular, non-moral issues like the Panama Canal." (Graham later wrote Falwell a Dear Jerry letter, admonishing him for failing to take up such issues as social injustice and the arms race.) But by now *The Old-Time Gospel Hour* was televised on 380 stations, and 1981 revenues for Falwell's ministry were projected at $80 million.

ONE SUMMER NIGHT in 1979, in a tiny storefront on New York's Ninth Avenue, a former soul-food restaurant and hangout for transvestites, a dozen women watched a slide show not too different from the other varieties of adult entertainment in sex emporiums up and down nearby Times Square. One image that flashed past was a photo from the satirical magazine *Slam,* showing a man in a hard hat holding a drill between a woman's legs under the caption "At Last, a Simple Cure for Frigidity."

More provocative images flashed past in quick succession: a Rolling Stones publicity poster portraying a bound woman in torn clothing over the caption "I'm Black and Blue from the Rolling Stones—and I Love It!" Fashion shots from women's magazines, including several by Helmut Newton, typified what the narrator described for the audience as "brutal chic." A cologne advertisement showed a woman being dragged across the floor by a man, a look of pleasure on her face. "Part of what contributes to a rape culture is the making of women into objects," the narrator continued. "It is easier to abuse an object than a human being." The last image to appear was the infamous *Hustler* cover depicting a woman's body being fed, headfirst, into a meat grinder. Grimly overlooking the photo's diabolically satirical intent, the narrator reiterated its literal meaning, that "a woman is a piece of meat."

The narrator was Dolores Alexander, a former reporter with *Newsday* and one of two full-time organizers for a new but already battle-scarred group whose name said it all—Women Against Pornography (WAP). Charter members included *Ms.* magazine founder Gloria Steinem, former New York congresswoman Bella Abzug, and writer Susan Brownmiller. Alexander and Lynn Campbell, who formerly worked for the United Farm Workers in California and was WAP's other full-time organizer, were already gearing up for a New York City–wide antipornography conference in September, and in October a massive march against smut peddlers in Times Square.

Only a couple of years earlier, the Commission on International Women's Year, convened in Houston in November 1977, had declined to include pornography among issues it touched on in the twenty-five resolutions it passed. Pornography was not considered to be a "woman's issue." But that attitude was rapidly beginning to change among feminists.

After the slide show at WAP headquarters, maps of Times Square were passed out, along with the evening's itinerary: visits to sex supermarkets, peep shows, live sex shows at Show World and Harmony Burlesque, a brief look at a bookstore specializing in Nazi materials, and a full tour of an old-fashioned dirty bookstore. Final stop was a topless bar called Mardi Gras. Scheduled by appointment only, the two-hour tour was held twice weekly— on Thursday evenings and Sunday afternoons. On this particular evening, the leaders of the tour were novelist Lois Gould, Andrea Dworkin, Steinem, and Brownmiller.

The tour began with members of the quartet gesturing up and down Forty-second Street, noting which underworld figures owned what buildings, their tawdry histories, the working conditions and wages of the women

employed in each, and other depressing details. So professional was their delivery that some tourists stopped to listen in along with the women in the
group, who ranged in age from their mid-twenties to their late forties.

First stop was the peep show. Approaching a brightly lit booth, a tour
guide dropped coins and waited as metal curtains ascended to reveal two
young women dancing naked. One of the dancers blinked. "Ladies!" she
cried, pointing to the faces in the booths. "One . . . two . . . three ladies!"

Everybody giggled. "You with a religious group?" the dancer asked.

"No, no," came the reply. "We're feminists."

The dancer laughed and shook her hips. "I bet you feminists think we're
awful for selling our bodies like this."

But the feminists made it clear they did not blame the dancers. "Look," said
one of the onlookers, "we can't condemn you if that's how you make a living."

"Right on, honey," the dancer said. "It's better than doing it for free."

As the group departed, though, their comments reflected their common
revulsion: "Sick and brutal. Nothing to do with sex. Sad."

Next came the strobe-lit supermarkets featuring live sex shows, nude juice
bars, and cubicles for patrons. In the brightly lit bookstores, the women
gaped at paperbacks and magazines on such themes as rape, incest, and pedophilia. One typical cover showed a girl of about ten years old, her hair in
pigtails and nude body posed suggestively.

Beginning in 1976, many U.S. cities had begun to crack down on XXX-
rated movies and massage parlors by enacting tougher local laws resulting
from the Supreme Court's 1973 ruling that gave states and cities the responsibility for defining community standards on obscenity. Some cities resisted
what they perceived as an invasion of individual freedoms—Houston, for example, where porn film theaters were flourishing. But in San Antonio eighteen porn theaters were closed down after a jury found *Deep Throat* obscene.

According to a 1978 report by the California Department of Justice, the
nation's pornographers did $4 billion a year in business, or as much as the
conventional motion picture and record industries combined. *Forbes* magazine suggested that this estimate was "grossly conservative." The ten leading
men's magazines, with a total circulation of sixteen million, accounted for
$475 million in gross revenues, $400 million in circulation alone. The adult-
film business had an average of two million admissions per week at an average $3.50 per ticket at 780 adult film theaters for an annual gross of more
than $365 million. Another $100 million was spent on sex toys, lubricants, vibrators, and other so-called marital aids, much of it by direct mail. Though
the postal service declined to estimate the size of the sex industry mail-order
business, back in 1970 a survey indicated it pumped something like fifty million advertisements into the mail every year, and by now the figure had probably at least doubled.

The biggest component by far was the thousands of adult bookstores and peep shows around country. A large adult bookstore in Times Square easily grossed $10,000 a day, and the Los Angeles Police Department estimated that the city's sex merchants did $125 million a year. But even such impressive figures did not add up to more than about $1 billion total, and some of them were probably inflated. Most bookstores and peep shows were substantially smaller and less lucrative than those in Times Square. A more realistic assessment of soft-core's and hard-core's combined annual gross revenues was probably in the neighborhood of $1.5 to $2 billion.

In any case, whatever the government was doing to control the porn industry was not enough to satisfy the extremist wing of WAP, which was headed by Marcia Womongold, a Boston feminist who advocated the use of noxious chemicals like butyl mercaptan to close down a store and herself shot out the window of a Harvard Square bookstore selling men's magazines. Not all WAP members endorsed her methods, but all endorsed her goals.

All this discontent culminated in October 1979 with a major antiporn march in Times Square, site of the nation's heaviest concentration of commercial sex. Five thousand marchers, mostly women, showed up. The march underscored the very real aggravation many women felt about their role in society. Abortion rights and equal pay were still problems, solutions were slow in coming, and this new issue helped focus their disaffection. Opinion surveys also showed the country was becoming more conservative, with only 8 percent of high school students favoring couples living together before marriage. Back in 1971, 47 percent had approved.

By this time WAP had succeeded in removing *Hustler* from two stores in Oakland, California, closed showings of erotic movies like *The Story of O* in several cities, and forced Atlantic Records to take down a billboard advertising the Rolling Stones' *Black and Blue* album.

But the simplism of the antipornography movement also alarmed many feminists, such as Nancy Borman, editor of *Majority Report,* one of the most respected feminist weeklies, who wrote: "An antipornography campaign avoids the real feminist issues of economic oppression and abortion. . . . If feminists go on this self-righteous campaign against pornography the way Carrie Nation did against alcohol, the real causes of violence will be avoided, just like the real causes of alcoholism were avoided by the Prohibitionists."

Nonetheless, the WAP minority proved so successful that for nearly a decade the pornography issue overshadowed more important feminist concerns. Some, like Steinem, clumsily explained the problem away by trying to draw a distinction between erotica and pornography: "Pornography is the product of woman hatred, marked by cruelty and violence, and shouldn't be confused with erotica, which is rooted in the idea of free will and love." That distinction was popular within the ranks of WAP because it allowed them to acknowledge the sexual liberation movement among women. Ironically, Anaïs Nin became a popular "eroticist" of antipornography feminists, even though she had been the lover of the despised male chauvinist Henry Miller and, like the madam in a literary brothel, had presided over one of the major pornography-producing cartels of the American 1930s and 1940s. Being literary, though, Nin porn was so much nicer than the products sold in the sleazy precincts of Times Square, and it also had the merit—even though much of it was about incest and SM—of being written by a woman.

WAPers denied that pornography could be a harmless entertainment or a healthy avenue for the release of sexual tension. Rather, it was a "theory" of which rape was the "practice" (Robin Morgan), "antifemale propaganda" (Brownmiller), "the ideological basis for the systematic persecution of females by males" (Womongold). Brownmiller supported Chief Justice Warren Burger's majority opinion in the pivotal 1973 *Miller* v. *California* case that called the inclusion of "obscene material" "a misuse of the great guarantees of free speech and free press." She claimed, "We live quite comfortably with a host of free speech abridgments," citing restrictions on false advertising and on shouting "Fire!" in a crowded theater. "Restriction on the display of pornography belongs in this category," she maintained.

But if pornography was theory, ideology, or propaganda, then censoring it meant censoring a political idea, freedom of speech. In response to such fuzzy thinking, Harvard law professor (and *Penthouse* columnist) Alan Dershowitz shrewdly pointed out: "The more they say pornography is a form of racist, sexist propaganda, the more they support the argument against censoring it. Protection for propaganda is the core of the First Amendment."

In Middle America, school boards and libraries were under constant attack for stocking books like Studs Terkel's *Working,* the sex education film *Achieving Sexual Maturity,* Alex Comfort's *The Joy of Sex,* works by Harlan Ellison, Kurt Vonnegut, and J. D. Salinger, video games, and countless other scabrous and scatological amusements. In a tradition going back to Anthony Comstock, not to mention the Roman Catholic Church's *Index Librorum Prohibitorum,* moral vigilantes were everywhere.

ACCORDING TO CATHARINE MACKINNON and Andrea Dworkin, "radical feminism" was the only true form of feminism because it alone spoke for all women; liberal feminism, they claimed, promoted the interests of only a relatively few privileged women while helping to conceal the oppression and abuse of the vast and silenced majority. "If this is feminism, it deserves to die," Dworkin contemptuously declared.

Yet MacKinnon avoided biological determinism, refraining from universal generalizations about the victimization of women and the villainy of men.

Rather, she grounded her position by asserting the primacy of social forces over biological ones. Gender, in her view, was a system of dominance rather than difference. Her point was not to emphasize the familiar feminist distinction between sex and gender, according to which sex referred to nature, biology, maleness or femaleness and gender to culture, social norms, and masculinity or femininity. MacKinnon regarded that distinction as a liberal construct.

"On the first day that matters, dominance was achieved," she wrote, "probably by force." Men, the dominant gender, had assumed the power to define both differences and "the differences gender makes." Current understandings of sexual differences, in her view, were masculine constructions, leading her to conclude that the biological and social were inseparable in this area. Thus she used the words "sex" and "gender" interchangeably. In her usage the word "male" functioned as "a social and political concept, not a biological attribute; it is a status socially conferred upon a person because of a condition of birth." At the same time, men were also capable of becoming feminists.

Consequently, MacKinnon argued, radical feminism had a "dominance perspective," while liberal feminism adopted a "difference perspective." The former revealed aspects of public policy "invisible to liberal feminists"—for example, that allegedly gender-neutral reforms sometimes even contributed to the subordination of women. A case in point: sex discrimination laws, which benefited only those women whose biographies approximated the male norm. Most women's injuries from male dominance were so deep, they appeared merely as natural sex differences. The inability of sex discrimination laws to address those injuries meant, in effect, that such laws ended up rationalizing inequity.

MacKinnon was also critical of attempts to ground the right to abortion on an alleged gender-neutral right to privacy. From the dominance perspective, the so-called private realm had never guaranteed women a sphere in which they could act as autonomous individuals. Rather, the distinction between public and private provided an ideological rationale for allowing men an arena in which to exercise their power over women free from the restraints imposed, at least theoretically, in the public realm. In the private realm that often meant forced sex, which in turn created the need for abortions that the feminization of poverty often made unavailable.

Yet the biggest contrast between a "dominance" and a "difference" perspective was over pornography. MacKinnon claimed pornography was a central mechanism of women's subordination because it eroticized the relation of domination between men and women and simultaneously reinforced the prevailing definitions of gender and sex. "Violation of the powerless is part of what is sexy about sex, as well as central in the meaning of male and female," she declared.

If dominance was experienced as erotic, through pornography-induced orgasm, that made gender inequality appear natural and rendered it pleasurable not only to men, but also (though not equally) to women. Allegedly gender-neutral rights to freedom of speech affected men and women very differently because the sexes were not "similarly situated" in relation to pornography. As a result, "the free speech of men silences the free speech of women." In the antipornography ordinances that she was later to coauthor, MacKinnon defined pornography as sex discrimination, made actionable through civil rights law. This difference in ideology was to become the driving wedge that split feminism and transformed pornography into the battle-ground of a feminist civil war throughout the eighties. Spoiling for a fight, MacKinnon taunted feminists who opposed censorship by comparing them to "house niggers who sided with the masters," and organizations like the Feminist Anti-Censorship Task Force (FACT) to labor scabs and Uncle Toms.

PART FOUR

ORGASM

1979 - 1984

Chapter 12

Après Nous the Spermathon

THROUGHOUT THE UNINHIBITED 1970s, the most notorious, self-celebrating adulterer in the land was a New York journalist named Gay Talese. For a time he even displaced Hugh Hefner—a main character in the product of his investigations, a book titled *Thy Neighbor's Wife*—as America's best-known (and most envied) sybarite. Talese's pretext was investigative journalism. In *The Kingdom and the Power,* his best-selling history of *The New York Times,* he described fellow journalist David Halberstam as having "rats in the stomach," meaning that he was one of those reporters who were "driven, totally involved, . . . [and] unencumbered by conventionalism or the official version of events." That was the way Talese also wanted to cover the Sexual Revolution.

Born in 1932 in Ocean City, New Jersey, Gaetano Talese was the elder of two children of a father born in Italy and a mother of Italian descent. His upbringing was traditional Catholic, Italian style. A poor student and bad athlete, Talese was a late bloomer to boot; he claimed he did not even masturbate until age twenty. He majored in journalism at the University of Alabama, graduating in 1953, then signed on for a two-year hitch in the army.

While serving as a public information officer at Fort Knox, Talese made a visit to New York, where he was introduced to Nan Ahearn, the convent-educated daughter of a prosperous banker who was working as a copy editor at Random House. They had lunch at P. J. Clarke's, the legendary East Side watering hole, and on their second date helped close it down at four A.M. He and Nan stayed in touch, and when Talese headed back north in 1955 to take a job as a copy boy for *The New York Times,* they began to date steadily.

Over the next decade, Talese earned a reputation as one of the paper's—and country's—foremost journalists. In the summer of 1959 the *Times* sent

Talese to Rome to cover the making of Fellini's *La Dolce Vita*. A few days after his arrival in Italy, he cabled Nan and asked her to join him. They married in Rome in a civil ceremony that marked Nan's formal break with the church, which Talese had left many years earlier. Their first child was born in 1964, the same year Nan became an acquiring editor, and a second child arrived three years later.

Talese left the *Times* in 1965 with a hefty advance to write a book about the paper, the best-selling and critically acclaimed *The Kingdom and the Power,* which appeared in 1969. Two years later he issued the less successful *Honor Thy Father,* about the Bonanno Mafia family. As his career prospered, Talese was able to buy the East Side brownstone in which he had once rented a small bachelor flat. William Styron wrote some of *The Confessions of Nat Turner* on the second floor. Many of Talese's other friends were writers as well—Halberstam, A. E. Hotchner, Michael Arlen. In the evenings, Nan often remained at home with their two daughters while he went out to Elaine's or to a ball game.

In March 1971, Talese, nearing the end of his Bonanno family saga, was searching for the subject of his next book. One afternoon, as he and Nan were leaving P. J. Clarke's, his eye caught a garish red neon sign that read "Live Nude Models."

"Let's go up and see what it is," he suggested.

Nan declined, but suggested he go up alone. Though he went home, he returned the next noon hour. Perhaps it was a sign from the muses that Talese's pretty, topless masseuse had been from Alabama. But the sexual upheaval of the sixties had long fascinated Talese. Apart from his own occasional infidelities, he had been intrigued by the sexual exploits of Bill Bonanno, a principal character of *Honor Thy Father.*

During his massage session, the masseuse had masturbated Talese. When he returned home, he told Nan that he had found the subject for his next book—America's changing sexual mores. Following several more visits to the masseuse, he decided to embark on the book by taking a job as manager of two massage parlors, which became his laboratory for studying the buying and selling of sex under semiclinical conditions. The job also came with several agreeable perks.

So began Talese's excellent adventure, a sexual odyssey that many men would gladly, thoughtlessly have exchanged for wife, children, and whatever kingdom and power they possessed. Talese, though, wanted it all—not just the fringe benefits that came with this newest innovation in New Journalism, but Nan, their beloved daughters, his reputation. It is a tribute to his ingenuity as both a journalist and a husband that he found a way to do for adultery what Linda Lovelace did for fellatio while somehow managing to keep his marriage intact.

Talese hoped to do three things that had never been accomplished by a serious journalist: to report on sexuality as it really happened, without trivializing it; to write about the people who had helped to redefine morality in America; and to tell through their stories the sexual and social history of America, with an emphasis primarily on the previous thirty years. It was time, he thought, that sexuality got some journalistic respect.

For starters, Talese's publisher, Doubleday, gave him a $600,000 advance. But although the manuscript delivery date was June 1974, as of June 1975 Talese had not written a word. He did not begin writing for another two years, and it was 1979 before he was able to work on it with any seriousness and industry. Meanwhile, the research dragged on and expenses mounted to a staggering $800,000. Talese received the advance in installments of $200,000 per year in 1972, 1973, and 1974. So great were publishers' and booksellers' expectations that Dell paid another $750,000 for paperback rights, also before a word was written.

Talese explained that the book took so long to write because it was difficult to get people to open up about their sex lives. He also claimed that researching extramarital sex was not half so glamorous as some people might imagine. That was partly true, but it was more the case that Talese, mired in midlife crisis, had grown so bored with his subject that he could barely manage to produce a single magazine article during this long dry period. But despite (or perhaps because of) Talese's epic case of writer's block, *Thy Neighbor's Wife* became one of the most talked-about works in progress of the seventies, and his name continued to appear regularly in the gossip columns.

One of Talese's first extended adventures involved Sandstone Ranch, John Williamson's upscale swingers' community in the Malibu hills. Talese first learned about Sandstone in the underground *L.A. Free Press,* where Williamson had placed an advertisement describing the community as a "growth center" dedicated to eliminating "jealousy and possessiveness between couples." Intrigued, Talese paid a visit, and during the summer of 1972 he went back for six weeks.

When he returned to Ocean City, where he and Nan had a summer home, he tried to get her to accompany him to a nudist camp. Talese's grand plan was for Nan to take a leave of absence from Random House, pack up the kids, and come with him to Sandstone as his co-researcher, his Virginia Johnson—maybe even his coauthor. Nan did accompany him to a nudist camp—Sunshine Park in Mays Landing—one summer afternoon, but she found the experience to be no big deal and refused to join him at Sandstone.

So Talese went back to the ranch alone and virtually took up residence there for a time. Along with Hugh Hefner's Los Angeles mansion, it was a major focus of his book, a place that he viewed as a "Reichian experiment" where women could be the sexual aggressors, having sex with whomever they desired. At one point Talese wrote a brief piece on the commune for *Esquire*—a hosanna of ecstatic drivel that so dismayed the editors that they called in Dr. Robert T. Francoeur, a scholarly ex-priest researching Sandstone for his book, *Hot and Cool Sex,* to rewrite it. The article eventually ran without a byline. Francoeur, a frequent Sandstone visitor, had observed that Talese seemed in a state of near panic and near constant impotence as he wrestled with the demons of Catholic guilt.

Talese's relationship with the Williamsons was also strained. They perceived him as aspiring to the status of sex guru, but to Sandstone regulars he was just another person with his share of shortcomings and hangups, an attitude that infuriated and frustrated him. Gradually, though, his genuine admiration for the Williamsons led to his acceptance by the community.

Talese's first experience with group sex was an awkward one. A married couple who lived nearby invited him and his female companion into one of Sandstone's private bedrooms. Talese tried to stall by attempting conversation, but before long all four were fondling and groping. Though excited by seeing the man making love to his companion, he also felt frustrated at the lack of more than an immediate sexual connection to his own new partner. After lying impotent for some time on the bouncing bed, Talese finally invited the other woman to go somewhere else, where they had sex. Then they returned to the room, all embraced, and later they had foursomes frequently. And although Talese never explored bisexual or homosexual sex with that man or any other during his adventures, he enjoyed for the first of many times the freedom to be gentle with other males.

On several subsequent occasions at Sandstone, Talese took part in group sex in the company of Alex Comfort, who had not yet published *The Joy of Sex.* (The sequel, *More Joy,* would devote an entire chapter to the commune.) Two of the major characters in Talese's own book were Sandstone regulars John and Judith Bullaro. In one long scene, which Talese believed to be the most sexual scene he would ever write, he recalled how Bullaro watched Judith make love to John Williamson. Although just moments before Bullaro himself had made love to Barbara Williamson, he collapsed at the scene, finding the sight of his wife making love to another man unbearable. (Ultimately, Bullaro left both Sandstone and Judith and became an expert in wilderness survival.)

As Talese slowly progressed on his work, he twice became a hot story himself. The first occasion was a profile by Aaron Latham that appeared in *New York* magazine, Talese's old stomping grounds, in July 1973, under the title "An Evening in the Nude with Gay Talese." Talese had made the mistake of allowing Latham to trail him to the Fifth Season, Manhattan's most exclusive brothel, and to watch as he frolicked naked with a nude masseuse, who playfully tugged on his penis. "I love it. I love it," he told her. "I have dreams about it." Later, journalist confided to journalist, "Getting head from an NYU student is not going to threaten a marriage of fourteen years."

After the article appeared, friends and foes alike were shocked that someone of Talese's stature had been so brazen about his sex life and so inconsiderate of his wife's feelings. Her friends told her she was crazy to put up with him. A. E. Hotchner, whose best-selling *Papa Hemingway* she had edited, was scandalized. Even Talese's mother and father were offended by remarks such as his wisecracking regret that he did not have incest with his parents. In many people's view, Nan was either the country's biggest sap or its greatest stoic, or both. In a story without a hero, she ultimately emerged, as have other wives of straying husbands, as a heroine.

Though the article dealt his marriage a wicked blow, Talese refrained from attacking Latham for the seeming betrayal of confidence, telling friends that his personal code of ethics forbade him from criticizing a fellow journalist's assessment of himself. *New York* later printed a number of letters both attacking and defending Talese, though it refused to print David Halberstam's spirited condemnation of the magazine for what he characterized as its cheap treatment of his friend.

A far more devastating piece appeared in *Esquire* in December of that year. This time the author of the profile was Philip Nobile, a fellow Italian Catholic and the only other journalist in the country who knew the contours of America's sexual landscape half so well as Talese. Worse, Nobile had a reputation for being both a meticulous researcher and an unsparing critic. When Nobile approached Talese for an interview, Talese told him, "My marriage can't stand another tough piece, and you're a tough guy." Nan counseled him not to give an interview, saying, "The first time you may seem foolish, but the second time you seem to be looking for it."

Only after several angry exchanges among all three did Gay and Nan finally decide to talk. The *New York* article had been so damaging that Talese could not resist an opportunity to improve his public image. Nan reluctantly agreed to be interviewed because she was fearful that holding back, as she did with *New York* magazine, would only confirm that Talese slept in a cold bed at home. But she refused to reveal any sexual intimacies that might help explain how their marriage survived.

In his background research for the piece, Nobile interviewed Al Goldstein, whom Talese had interviewed extensively. "You ought to talk to my former wife, Mary Phillips, about Gay Talese," Goldstein advised Nobile. "She knows him pretty well." Nobile did.

Talese had interviewed Phillips about a year before the *Esquire* piece appeared. Though they talked mainly about Al, Talese was amazed that this refined southern woman could have married Goldstein, by his own description a fat pornographer. He mentioned to Phillips during their first couple of sessions that in his experience subjects opened up after sexual intimacy. Phillips welcomed the overture, as she found him attractive and was herself trying to escape the confines of sexual exclusivity. Though she had been monogamous with Goldstein, she and her current lover were experimenting.

After lunch one day, Talese and Phillips spent the afternoon in bed at his town house. Phillips recalled not being able to make any noise, and she told Nobile that "the whole scene suggested that sex was dirty. Then somebody knocked on the door as we were getting dressed. I had to hide in the kitchen. It was like an episode from a soap opera. It was the maid knocking." Before she left, though, Mary remarked that she wanted to tell her lover, an unproduced playwright, of her afternoon in bed with the famous Gay Talese.

Over another lunch Talese tried to get Phillips to swear to secrecy, even though neither felt any guilt. She replied that she wanted to meet Nan. Talese refused, questioning her motives and her discretion. "You'll embarrass me," he said. "I don't want my wife to know about it. I don't want your boyfriend to know about this."

"Why?" said Phillips.

"I don't want any more enemies," said Talese. "What's your purpose?"

"Well," she said, "I believe in honesty."

Talese begged her again not to say anything, and he again refused to tell Nan. Phillips replied that she would never have sex with him again, nor did she. Talese remained silent about the affair, but for weeks he dreaded the possibility of an angry man calling him on the phone and threatening him or, worse, calling Nan at her office.

Phillips read the *New York* profile and was pleased to find him fairly candid in it. But she still thought that for him sex was more of an ego trip than a pleasure cruise—that he was more interested in conquest than research, and that he reveled in his image as not only a literary but a sexual lion. When the *Esquire* piece appeared, his afternoon with Mary Phillips was included in full, much to Talese's surprise and chagrin.

Nan read it there, and she was dismayed and humiliated. Moreover, their daughters were now old enough to be vulnerable to the taunts of schoolmates. On two occasions she left their home briefly, though quietly, once alone and once with the children.

In the piece Talese was asked whether he could countenance Nan taking a lover. He replied that his relationship with Nan would probably survive intact if the affair did not change her or affect their marriage, friendship, or love. Nobile persisted, asking point-blank whether their relationship would survive if she shared his attitudes.

"Would I feel about Nan as I do?" Talese asked.

"Would you have the confidence that I have?" asked Nan, who had been sitting in on the interview.

"I think it's fair to say no," Talese admitted uneasily. "I just have to be honest about that. Nan would be a different person. She'd be like most people, and I wouldn't marry most people. . . . The marriage would survive. I'd live with her, but it wouldn't be special."

The contradiction was obvious: though Talese did not want Nan to have an affair, he was apparently willing to share her at Sandstone or, in Nobile's words, to offer "his wife up for sexual sacrifice." Would that not ruin their romantic idyll?

Talese's rejoinder: "You have to take risks. Let me give you a line from Sinatra, which is really a line from Talese." He then read from his own profile of Sinatra in a collection of his journalism entitled *Fame and Obscurity:* "He is the champ who made the big comeback, the man who had everything, lost it, then got it back, letting nothing stand in his way, doing what few men can do: he uprooted his life, left his family, broke with everything that was familiar, learning in the process that the one way to hold a woman is not to hold her."

Nobile theorized that Nan was a Catholic sex widow, a fairly common phenomenon. But he gave Talese credit for his compassion for lonely people and reported how Talese had once upbraided consumer activist Ralph Nader and a group of fellow liberal types associated with incumbent mayor John Lindsay for ignoring the mayor's antipornography drive. "Loneliness is a problem in this city," Talese had passionately proclaimed to the group. "The lonely middle-aged man—the priest, the policeman. Massage parlors deal with loneliness better than any city agency." Talese mentioned that he was writing a book on the subject, "but it's so unfashionable that none of you would be interested."

Loneliness was indeed an important theme of Talese's book when it was eventually published. In one memorable passage, he observed: "On any given night, in any given city in America, there are going to be many more men who are interested in, craving, casual sex than there are women. . . . And that's why you will find large numbers of men all over America going to prostitutes and massage parlors and peep shows and X-rated movies. And relying on the visual stimulation they get from men's magazines, masturbating to those pictures in hotels and motels at night, in lieu of the company of a woman." He added: "The millions made by porn kings come from lonely men. When they left the massage parlors where I worked, they were happier. There is tremendous sexual frustration in this country."

ON A RAINY NOVEMBER EVENING in 1979 the Sexual Revolution reached its high-water mark—appropriately, within the clammy precincts of New York's Plato's Retreat—when an occasional porn actress named Tara

Alexander took on eighty-six men, four at a time, in a nonstop six-hour spectacle dubbed the Spermathon.

Wanting to make a "splash," the lanky, long-haired Alexander had approached Al Goldstein and his high school buddy Larry Levenson, Plato's proprietor, asking them to dream up a sexual stunt that might bring her fame and fortune. Putting their libidos together, the decadent duo concocted a friendly little gang rape, with Levenson to host and Goldstein to film the event for his X-rated cable TV show, *Midnight Blue.*

Cable sex had begun in the mid-seventies when New York and San Francisco, among other cities, were wired for cable. *Midnight Blue* debuted in 1975, followed by *Ugly George,* featuring a roving cameraman who convinced women to strip for him in building vestibules and back alleys. Around the same time, the newly launched HBO started beaming R-rated movies into America's living rooms, while *Playboy at Night* offered viewers a highly censored peek inside the Hefner mansion, with the *Playboy* publisher himself acting as party host to hangers-on, introducing second-tier celebrities, and on occasion crooning a song.

Arriving with her husband on the well-publicized appointed evening, Alexander appeared nervous, especially after glimpsing a line of nearly one hundred naked men, each holding a number. A nurse stood by to rub down each man with alcohol and hand out condoms. In a modest concession to Alexander's dignity, the Spermathon took place in a partial enclosure, where only the next four men in line could freely observe the preceding quartet. Voyeurs, though, had no trouble finding peepholes.

Alexander's modus operandi was simultaneously to masturbate two men and fellate one, while having sexual intercourse with a fourth. Overcoming her initial anxiety, she eventually reached twenty-four orgasms during the course of the evening. Only one man asked to leave. Most did their duty with aplomb; only one offered to perform cunnilingus, and she accepted. Wanting anonymity, the owner of a restaurant participated with a paper bag over his head.

In a fairy-tale ending of sorts, Alexander and her broad-minded husband made love after the last foursome. Later she starred in two porn films, *October Silk* and *Nightmare,* and with her husband managed Show World, a live sex show near Times Square. Then, when her fifteen minutes were up, she was forgotten.

DURING THE DECADE that Gay Talese chose to plumb American morals, Bob Guccione resolved to do the same for human decadence. In the process, he hoped to liberate mainstream moviemaking from its R-rated bonds. A man who thrived on pushing the limits, the erstwhile painter and ex-actor seemed to have found in celluloid the ideal mass medium to tinker with.

Traditionally, the film and television industries, along with their close cousin, advertising, lagged well behind publishing and the arts in testing the limits of sexual expression and provocation. Primarily, perhaps, the reasons were economic. Millions of dollars in potential profit and loss rode on the average feature film or prime-time series, which was incentive to market them as family entertainment to appeal to as large a segment of the market as possible. A less obvious reason was the creative culture of those media, which had not yet nurtured an individual determined, powerful, and talented enough to break with sexual convention and steer a bold new path—no Ginzburg, Hefner, Guccione, John Updike, William Burroughs, Philip Roth, Kenneth Tynan, Diane Arbus, Robert Mapplethorpe, or Jim Morrison.

Guccione now decided to make film history by creating the first sexually explicit first-run movie in history, sparing no expense and hiring only the finest talent. He had the imagination, the contempt for convention, and the wealth to work outside the Hollywood studio system, and he very nearly succeeded. If all had gone according to plan, *Caligula,* based on the cruel, brief life of the most decadent of Roman rulers, might have been a masterpiece. Unfortunately, absolutely nothing went according to plan, and the result was the most expensive sexually explicit film ever made. If it was not the worst, that was only because the genre excelled at being mediocre.

The idea of making a movie about the tyrant Caius Caligula Caesar, who ruled from A.D. 37 to 41—four years marked by sadistic violence and a voracious sexual abandon virtually without parallel in ancient history—originated with the Italian director Roberto Rossellini, who wrote a treatment for it but never progressed beyond that point. But Rossellini's nephew Franco showed the treatment to American novelist Gore Vidal, who was intrigued and recognized that Guccione was probably the only individual in the world who could bring it off. Vidal agreed to write the screenplay and to introduce Rossellini to Guccione.

Guccione had invested in a few feature films—*The Day of the Locust* and the profitable *Chinatown* and *The Longest Yard* among them. But he wanted to do more than sit on the sidelines. *Caligula* gave him the opportunity to co-produce with the more experienced Rossellini. As soon as he got Vidal's treatment, Guccione contacted a number of top directors. But John Huston's agent was difficult, and Lina Wertmüller wanted to jettison Vidal, call the film *Lina Wertmüller's Caligula,* and cast Jack Nicholson as the lead.

So Guccione proceeded with casting, signing up an impressive cast for what was already being touted as the world's first major X-rated film. Malcolm McDowell, best known for his portrayal of a punk hoodlum in Stanley Kubrick's *A Clockwork Orange,* agreed to play Caligula. The rest of the cast included Peter O'Toole as the aged and syphilitic emperor Tiberius, Caligula's grandfather; Helen Mirren as Caesonia, Caligula's mistress; John

Gielgud as the noble senator Nerva; and Maria Schneider, who had starred opposite Brando in *Last Tango in Paris,* as Drusilla. Thirteen *Penthouse* Pets, including Pet of the Year Anneka di Lorenzo and Lori Wagner, helped round out the cast.

Meanwhile, Guccione ordered the reconstruction of half of ancient Rome at Dear Film Studios outside the city. Sets included a mile-long facsimile of a first-century street, a 100-yard-long stadium, and a 175-foot floating bordello encrusted with gold leaf, where the wives of Roman senators were forced into prostitution to fill Caligula's treasury. Guccione spared no expense in his determination to make a movie—he frequently invoked *Citizen Kane* as an apt comparison—that would make history.

Exasperated at his inability to find a suitable director while his first-rate cast languished and his bills mounted, Guccione agreed to have lunch with a distinctly second-rate Italian director named Tinto Brass. In preparation for the meeting, Guccione viewed a couple of reels of Brass's *Salon Kitty,* a spy thriller set in a Nazi brothel. But that did not dissuade him from signing Brass, a Falstaffian figure with a temper to match. Naively, Guccione assumed that the sheer magnitude of the project would keep Brass in line.

Vidal had already revised the script five times, partly in response to Guccione's concern that only one of the sex scenes was heterosexual—the one between Caligula and his sister. But almost immediately Brass declared Vidal's script too bourgeois, "the work of an aging arteriosclerotic." He threw Vidal out of the studio and rewrote the screenplay yet again with the help of McDowell. Where Vidal had envisioned Caligula as a good boy gone bad, Brass made him a born monster. Where Vidal had been liberal with sex scenes, Brass was profligate, tossing in orgies, decorative phalluses, and naked girls at will.

On the first day of shooting, early in 1976, Brass announced that the one thing banished from the set was sexual inhibition. Then—with his wife, an astonished Guccione, and cast and crew members looking on—he proceeded, with the help of a female extra, to demonstrate the proper way to perform cunnilingus. Schneider so objected to her nude scenes that she walked off the set and was replaced by Teresa Ann Savoy.

The movie covered Caligula's rise to power, his brutal four-year rule, and his bloody assassination. Among his vile deeds, as concocted by Vidal and Brass, were crashing a wedding and sexually abusing both the bride and the groom, playing out erotic fantasies with his sister, and turning the imperial palace into a brothel. Increasingly, though, Guccione came to perceive that Brass was mishandling the film's sexuality.

Production soon divided into two camps, Guccione and his Pets versus Brass's mob of extras, which consisted of ex-convicts, thieves, political anarchists, and wrinkled old women, while the stars kept mostly to themselves.

As the film progressed, with Gielgud and O'Toole primly mingling with naked Pets, Brass shot 120 miles of film, or fifty times the length of the original *Ben-Hur.*

Finally, on Christmas Eve, shooting was completed, and everyone went home for the holidays. But although Guccione had not seen a single frame of film, he had seen enough from the sidelines to know that, for all Brass's crudity, the movie that had been touted as mainstream's first venture into X-rated moviemaking contained no explicit sex whatsoever.

Shortly after Christmas, Guccione sneaked back into the studio with his new co-director, Giancarlo Lui, a dozen Pets, and a skeleton crew. Raiding the prop room, they created out of the remaining odds and ends a few little sets. The imperial boat was still intact, and they reoutfitted that as well. The next day they cast thirty extras. Then, with Guccione—who had never before even touched a thirty-five-millimeter camera—operating one camera and Lui the other, they worked for five nights to stage, direct, and film enough sexually explicit scenes to make a difference, including a lesbian scene between Anneka di Lorenzo and Lori Wagner of which Guccione was especially proud.

The secrecy was necessary because of European laws that protected a director's creative rights. Guccione then had to sneak the sole 120-mile negative out of the country. Once he reached England he fired Brass, setting off a series of lawsuits. Brass sued Guccione, Guccione sued Brass, Brass sued Vidal, and Vidal threatened to sue everybody. Ultimately, Vidal surrendered his right to a percentage of the profits, in exchange for getting his name removed from the movie's title, though he continued to be listed in the credits as author of the screenplay.

Meanwhile, the negative was hidden in the musty vaults of Twickenham Studios, in cans marked *The Pecos Kid, My Son, My Son,* and similar prosaic titles, while Guccione proceeded to edit the film. Then Technicolor, which had been doing the printing, grew alarmed at the explicit nature of some of the scenes and threatened to stop work. Guccione also feared that Technicolor might tip off the police that under British law he was making an obscene film. By now, British unions had sent out word that no one was to work on *Caligula.* Worried that the unions had begun to search for the negative and might know how to find it, Guccione conducted another midnight raid, this time on Twickenham Studios. Once again he smuggled his negative out of the country under cover of darkness, this time to Paris, where he made several prints before returning to New York to continue the endless editing process.

Finally, on February 1, 1980, the movie opened as *Caligula* at Guccione's own movie theater, the Penthouse East, not far from his town house. The ticket price was a steep $7.50, which some thought was a tactical error. Convinced that the film would get a bad review because his name was attached to it, no matter how good it was, Guccione also declared a press blackout. Nor did he seek any rating for the film, even an X rating, which he regarded as "demeaning."

As predicted, critics were contemptuous, while the public seemed either baffled or indifferent. Fans of hard-core were less than shocked by the artsy, and occasionally laughable, scenes of decadent Rome, while mainstream viewers who had gone slumming at their local porn houses to see *Deep Throat* stayed away in droves. Despite exquisite sets and costumes and exceptional cinematography, the result seemed to be, by consensus, a poor man's *Satyricon*. Vidal himself dismissed the film as a "Copenhagen sex show" and sneered that several of the sets resembled "the lobby of the Fontainebleau Hotel in Miami Beach." To a TV interviewer he cattily explained, "Caligula—that's a Latin word meaning 'turkey.' "

The total cost of the film was $17.5 million—$22 million including lost interest, or enough to make two hundred top-of-the-line porn films. Guccione paid for it all in cash, another first. Rossellini claimed the movie killed his love of the industry. In later years, though, he insisted that it had made a great deal of money. Guccione confirmed that this was the case, much of the profit having derived from video. Rossellini himself saw only a few million of the earnings, and with the subsidy of his good friend Doris Duke, he sued Guccione. But despite a long and ugly court battle, Rossellini did not prevail. He died of AIDS in 1992, consumed by his suit and his hatred of the *Penthouse* publisher.

Anneka di Lorenzo, however, succeeded where so many others had failed. During a promotional tour for the movie, Guccione fired her, though the two were having an affair, when she balked at the last moment at going to Japan. In 1989 she sued him in Manhattan Supreme Court, charging that he had failed to deliver on his promise to make her a star and had used her as his sex slave within the *Penthouse* organization; her explicit nude scenes in *Caligula*, she claimed, had been particularly detrimental to her career. Guccione bitterly fought the case, which was followed widely and luridly in the tabloids. Eventually the case wound up in the court at a time when the issue of sexual harassment had become national news. On the advice of his attorneys, Guccione finally settled out of court—for him, another first.

In May 1980, five years behind schedule, Gay Talese's *Thy Neighbor's Wife* was published to the kind of hoopla usually reserved for royal weddings, papal elections, and the passing of presidents. The book that nearly broke his marriage made him rich. Even before publication it had earned $4 million, including $2.5 million from Hollywood, the most ever paid for movie rights to a book.

One person not very pleased with the book was Hugh Hefner, who after reading an advance proof promptly sent Talese a twenty-two-page single-spaced memo. Among the facts Talese allegedly got wrong was the assertion that the *Playboy* publisher had a perspiration problem during seduction. Hefner also felt the string of sexual anecdotes involving him created a two-dimensional character, and he regretted that his serious romances with Barbi Benton and Playmates Janet Pilgrim and Karen Christy were treated only as passing liaisons. In the *Playboy* interview with Talese slated to coincide with the book's publication, the author described Hefner as one of the few millionaires he knew who was really happy. Yet Hefner did not think that was the portrait of him that emerged from the book, which in his view served up too much titillation.

Talese flew out to the publisher's Los Angeles mansion to discuss some of Hefner's reservations, and a few facts were straightened out. But for the most part Talese stuck to his story, portraying Hefner as a terminal adolescent "unable to deal with women older than twenty-four." And Hefner acknowledged that Talese had captured him better than anyone else had.

Talese declared that despite its title, the book was not about marriage at all, but about "love and lust, about experimentation and male fantasy"—a distinction whose subtlety was perhaps lost on most married male readers. His tales of Hefner, Sandstone's John Williamson, and *Screw* publisher Al Goldstein were told mainly as case studies of grown men living out their boyhood sex fantasies. In the process they escaped from oppressive marriages and, by extension, from an oppressive, moralizing society. Alex Comfort was roundly praised as "a major figure in the sexual revolution" and his *Joy of Sex* a "pioneering" work, famous because the middle class bought it. Talese further claimed that some figures—the Williamsons, for example—represented "future sex" because they were the forerunners of a new sexual candor and openness.

The Playboy Philosophy, on the other hand, was barely mentioned. Also bypassed, virtually or altogether, were Guccione, the subterranean world of sexual adventurers like Marco Vassi and Annie Sprinkle, gay liberation, and the antipornography efforts of Andrea Dworkin and others. Masters and Johnson and Reuben Sturman, each a pillar of the Sexual Revolution, received only passing mention. Hard-core, like homosexuality, was simply ignored.

Playboy struck back, though perhaps unintentionally, by hiring acid-penned *New York Times* cultural commentator John Leonard to review the book. Leonard dismissed the book as "a pile of anecdotes, stapled together at random, of recipes instead of people, of ingredients and tics of personality and vehement longings: new uses for old organs! The enigmatic anus! . . . In *Thy Neighbor's Wife,* nobody seems ever to have graduated from junior high—and certainly not Talese." For its $2.5 million, Leonard whooped, United Artists had bought such platitudinous conclusions as, "While I can't prove it, I think that middle-class American husbands now, more than ever before in American history, can live with the knowledge that their wives were not virgins when they married—and that their wives have had, or are having, an extramarital affair. . . . The contemporary husband, unlike his father and grandfather before him, is not so shocked by such news, is more likely to accept women as sexual beings, and only in extreme cases will he retaliate with violence against his unfaithful wife or male rival."

Leonard also had his pontificating moments. He suggested that people like Goldstein and Flynt stood for nothing more complicated "than the right to cash in on loneliness; what they have achieved is to make America safe for pubic hair." Leonard further took Talese to task for almost totally ignoring feminism, trivializing Freud, and not even mentioning Marx. "For Talese the sexual revolution seems to mean that more people are getting more of it and not feeling quite so bad afterward. Off, then, to California, where we remove our disposable clothes and discuss 'primary' versus 'secondary' relationships."

Though Hefner and Talese outwardly remained friends, Talese came to suspect that Hefner and his editorial director, Art Kretchmer, had been out to get him, with John Leonard the weapon of choice. Actually, novelist Erica Jong was Kretchmer's first choice, and Hefner had learned of the Leonard review only when he read it in page proofs. He wrote Talese a note that read in part: "I'm almost as unhappy with the John Leonard review as you presumably are—not just because of our friendship, and the manner in which this review attempts to trivialize an important work, but because I think *Playboy* should applaud any serious effort of this sort that attempts to humanize our sexuality." Hefner later disavowed the review completely, saying, "I'm sorry that it ever appeared in *Playboy.*"

The *Playboy* interview was some consolation, especially since it touted *Thy Neighbor's Wife* as *the* big book of the year—and even "a bench mark for the decade." Never shy about praising his own work, Talese concurred, allowing that he regarded his accomplishment as "a great book," and beautifully written to boot. Yet he feared the critics would find it otherwise because of the subject matter, sex being something "everyone thinks he knows something about."

Pressed by *Playboy* on whether he had focused too much on Hefner's sex life, at the expense of examining at greater depth his role in the Sexual Revolution, Talese replied: "Hefner is one of the most influential men in the United States in the mid–twentieth century, no question about it, and the book does credit to his contribution. . . . But the fact is that he does have an extraordinary amount of energy for those sorts of new experiences."

Talese also revealed that writing the book had transformed him into a First Amendment absolutist utterly opposed to government restrictions on pornography. He was also critical of Susan Brownmiller and other "female liberationists," whom he deemed both "antimen" and "antisex—asexual." Radical feminists who "want to close down sex shops and adult bookshops and porno movies and massage parlors are really against heterosexual male pleasure." As for Brownmiller and women like her, they were "people with sex-negative experiences. Men have failed them; men have been irresponsible. Sex, to them, is dirty."

Talese further disclosed that he had become more comfortable with his own sexuality, had learned to enjoy nudism, and had found a new ease in showing affection toward his male friends—as with movie actor Ben Gazzara, whom he was now able to kiss on the mouth ("a Latin thing with us") and not worry about being called a homosexual.

As Talese suspected, most critics were either hostile or lukewarm in their reception of his complex saga of middle-class wrestling with morality. Many seemed more interested in what Nan thought about the book and her philandering researcher-husband.

In *Playboy* and in other interviews, Talese admitted that on several occasions he had come close to falling in love while doing research, and he acknowledged that there were times when he was not eager to go back to New York, his wife, and his married life. Yet he chose to remain married because Nan was "an extraordinary woman." "Nan and I love each other," he explained in an interview. "During the past 21 years, I have never felt any less in love with my wife. In fact, the reverse seems to be true. I'm more in love now; the love I feel for her has grown with time and she has remained throughout the marriage physically desirable to me. Now, if you say I'm not faithful to my wife sexually, I might say I'm faithful to her in a spiritual sense."

At the time of publication, Nan was forty-six and a vice president at Simon & Schuster, editing such high-profile authors as Oriana Fallaci and Judith Rossner. She had also gone over every page of *Thy Neighbor's Wife* before Talese showed it to his own editor at Doubleday. Nan did not applaud her husband's conduct, and in interviews she admitted that she preferred matters were otherwise. But her remarkable dignity and transparent love of her husband always shone through. "The fascination that this isn't threatening to me is only an indicator of the naïveté of other people," she said. "Unfaithfulness is no longer loving and no longer being involved. Sexual infidelity is simply sexual infidelity."

To the dismay of feminists outraged over her husband's betrayal of their marriage vows, she replied: "The fact is I am more liberated than most women's lib members who sit around tables drinking coffee and talking about the frustrations in their own lives. I have everything." Mary Phillips, for one, was impressed, remarking that Nan was the only person she knew who distinguished between sex and love.

Thy Neighbor's Wife made it just under the wire before the Sexual Revolution, at the popular level, shut down altogether. Though no masterpiece, and undervalued by critics, the book shared with the work of Kinsey, Masters and Johnson, and Money the virtue of being the first of its kind to accord sexuality the high seriousness it deserved—to report on the sexual trends and mores of a nation with a narrative breadth and forthright attention to intimate detail never before seen in mainstream journalism. Though he refrained from drawing any grand conclusions, Talese's life and work underscored his passionate conviction that uncompromising honesty and freedom of expression lie at the basis of both authentic selfhood and an authentic erotic relationship.

On the other hand, there was something terribly naive in Talese's utopian belief, derived in part from associating with the likes of Williamson, Hefner, the Bonannos, and Sinatra, and in part from simple hubris, that sexual openness was the best policy. The stratospheric divorce rate, the epidemic of battered women, the plague of STDs, the date rape and sexual harassment debates dominating the ensuing decade, the ever-burgeoning professions of sex therapy and marriage counseling, and numerous other evidence all attested to the contrary: that sexual jealousy, aggression, and good old-fashioned cheating are human constants and cannot easily be abolished by mere sexual sophistication or wishful thinking, and that lusting after thy neighbor's wife always spells trouble.

THOUGH *Thy Neighbor's Wife* garnered all the media attention, perhaps the most important book on sexuality published in the early eighties was *Sexual Preference: Its Development in Men and Women* (1982), by Alan P. Bell, Martin S. Weinberg, and Sue Kiefer Hammersmith, all former researchers at the Institute for Sex Research. Its explanations for the causes of homosexuality refuted or cast doubt on most lay and professional assumptions and beliefs.

Freud had claimed that homosexuality was caused by unresolved difficulties with the Oedipus complex. His successors pointed to possessive mothers and remote fathers. A typical example in literature: the young hero of Marcel Proust's *Remembrance of Things Past,* who suffered from insomnia whenever his mother forgot to kiss him good night.

Bell, Weinberg, and Hammersmith interviewed 979 homosexual and 477 heterosexual men and women in the San Francisco Bay Area, taking care to avoid the built-in biases of many previous studies, which drew their samples from such unrepresentative sources as lists of psychotherapy patients or even prison populations. Working from this unprecedented sample, Bell, Weinberg, and Hammersmith analyzed every known hypothesis, idea, or suggestion about the origins of homosexuality and found most of them were wrong.

"Boys who grow up with dominant mothers and weak fathers," they discovered, "have nearly the same chances of becoming homosexual as they would if they grew up in 'ideal' family settings." Nor was a lack of friends in childhood a significant factor; the small extent to which gay men and women were less involved with peers while growing up was more a result of feeling different than a cause. Being gay did not appear to be a self-fulfilling prophecy; the researchers found no evidence that a man who was labeled as effeminate, for example, became homosexual for that reason. They ruled out traumatic experiences with the opposite sex, too, along with rape, punishment by parents for sex play, and seduction by an older person of the same sex. In fact, contrary to the suspicions of Middle America, the data showed that "recruitment" played little if any role in creating gays and lesbians.

Although the researchers demolished a number of worn-out theories, they failed to identify what did, finally, cause homosexuality. But they did make some interesting observations. By the time most women and men reached adolescence, they concluded, their sexual identities have been determined. Homosexual feelings, moreover, played a much more significant role in the process of becoming a homosexual adult than did actual homosexual experiences. "What we seem to have identified," they concluded, "is a pattern of feelings and reactions within the child that cannot be traced back to a single social or psychological root; indeed, homosexuality may arise from a biological precursor."

Such a finding would have gone against Kinsey's grain. In their quest for a universal explanation, the researchers ignored a vast bibliography of research that correlated the origins of same-sex preference with the time of puberty, the amount of early sex, masturbatory patterns, and other factors that psychologists traditionally skipped over. Rather, Bell and company argued for the "naturalness" of homosexuality and insisted that "society would do well to examine its expectations and the extent to which its rigid standards of behavior contribute to untold misery."

By now the homosexual capital of the country was San Francisco, where one-fourth of the city's 750,000 residents were gay—a demographic that led one female journalist to write a rueful lament titled "Why Women Can't Get Laid in San Francisco." (Another vast homosexual ghetto was Los Angeles' West Hollywood, two square miles of rowdy bars and garish stores whose residents called it Boys Town.) Evidence of the city's homosexual ethos was everywhere: more than thirty gay activist groups, gay parades, gay political slates, gay neighborhoods, gay businesses, gay political officials. As local novelist Herb Gold described it: "If one imagines a world of hairdressers and interior decorators, painted flowered window boxes and poodles, one imagines wrong. Nevertheless, the prevalence of the gay style affects the city in important ways. Having relatively high disposable income (usually no children, often two working in a couple), they help to support restaurants, recreation, improved housing, gardens, theaters, bookstores, music."

The annual gay rights parade was a gaudy spectacle involving two hundred thousand participants, many in drag or flaunting their love of leather, SM, and other fetishes. But gay rights were a serious issue, even in the city that had been the first in the country to pass an ordinance banning discrimination based on sexual orientation, in employment, housing, and public accommodation. Acting mayor Dianne Feinstein, though she voted for the ordinance, qualified her approval, saying the right to live a gay lifestyle could not be interpreted in an offensive way, that there was a need to set some standards.

The bisexual population of the country posed an even more difficult problem since so many lived as gays, lesbians, or heterosexuals, and bisexuality itself was difficult to define. Ultimately Weinberg and two colleagues applied the 0–6 Kinsey Scale to the sexual behaviors, sexual feelings, and romantic feelings of 435 men and 338 women. The result, which they summed up in their 1994 book, *Dual Attraction,* was a typology of five kinds of bisexual: the pure type who enjoyed men and women almost equally, those who favored their own sex, those who favored the opposite sex, those whose fantasies and behavior were at variance (for example, men who fantasized about other men but had sex mostly with women), and those whose psychosexual profile did not fit any other category.

By 1980, the country was awash in an epidemic of sexually transmitted diseases—although the rates of infection could be attributed partly to the fact that some diseases had only recently been recognized as venereal. By far the most common STD was nongonorrheal urethritis, while venereal warts and herpes genitalis vied for second place.

Known as the love virus, herpes was reaping nearly one hundred thousand victims a year and was particularly painful and embarrassing to women. Typically, a woman infected by the virus developed small red blisters on her vulva several times in the course of a year. When they surfaced, the herpes sores were highly communicable, and they often tended to reappear when a person was depressed or anxious. Uncircumcised men were particularly prone to herpes, which invaded not only the urethra but the prostate and seminal vesicles—and the anus.

Like the common cold, herpes simplex was a viral disease that baffled the medical world. Type 1 infected the lips, inside of the mouth, and the area near the eyes; Type 2 appeared on the genitals. Though the virus could not be cured, an antigen for Type 2 called Lupidon G was mildly successful in treating symptoms. Syphilis, on the other hand, was no longer considered by STD specialists as a major threat. Not only was it easily treatable, but many people inadvertently cured themselves by taking antibiotics for colds and other infections. Epidemiologists' biggest concern was gonorrhea, which raged without symptoms in half the women and up to 15 percent of the men it infected. The most widespread STD was chlamydia, whose symptoms for both sexes was painful urination and, in women, pelvic inflammation and bleeding.

The epidemic of STDs was fueled by the burgeoning rates of sexual activity. In the fifties and sixties, the number of men and women having premarital sex had remained fairly stable—about 46 percent of women and 56 percent of men as of 1968. But by 1973 those figures had leaped to 73 percent for both sexes, though without any significant change in the number of sex partners (with half of all women confining themselves to one partner and nearly all the rest to anywhere from two to five men). Among white women, 45 percent had sex by age twenty, while the corresponding figure for black women was 80 percent. (A 1975 *Redbook* survey put the rate of premarital sex even higher, at 82 percent among its respondents, half before age seventeen.)

Adultery among women, meanwhile, had risen from 26 percent in Kinsey's day to 30 percent, according to the *Redbook* survey, or 36 percent, according to *Psychology Today*. Among males there was little change—an ever-constant 40 to 50 percent.

Despite all the publicity attendant on the struggle among gays and lesbians for equal civil rights, homosexual activity had not significantly increased. A very small percentage of heterosexual women admitted to experimenting with lesbianism as a political gesture, but no men seemed to have chosen their homosexuality, except perhaps a few male prostitutes. Similarly, rates for paraphilias and SM remained largely independent of social change.

Reflecting on the state of sexual affairs in a ruminative, wide-ranging essay published in 1980, Dr. Paul Gebhard, the grand old man of sexology, noted that perhaps the greatest change affecting the world of sexuality in the past quarter century was the collapse of censorship. Abortion was also now legal. Nineteen states had changed their sex laws so that what consenting adults did in private was not subject to legal sanctions.

"Another welcome development," Gebhard wrote, "is the abolition of ancient, vague, and poorly defined sex offenses which could be interpreted so as to indict almost anyone. There were until recently some fantastic examples. One state defined sodomy as the insertion, however slight, of the penis into any 'unnatural orifice' of the body. Setting aside the problem of what bodily orifice is unnatural, a strict interpretation of that law would mean that a man who, in impetuous haste, missed the vulva and struck the navel would be guilty of sodomy."

Gebhard's thoughtful analysis, like Talese's rambling but insightful examination of American morality, was among the last rose-colored assessments of the Sexual Revolution before the onset of AIDS, the Meese Commission, and the puritanical crusade of the Christian Right and their radical feminist allies against the heretics and pagans of the new sexual morality.

Chapter 13

Dark Night of Sexology

In 1975, WHEN HE REACHED THE AGE OF SIXTY, WILLIAM MASTERS RETIRED FROM surgery. A few years later the biochemical laboratory, having become more onerous than profitable, was sold and the Masters & Johnson Institute moved to a new location with a staff of twenty-five and a long waiting list.

In the mid-seventies Masters and Johnson also published *The Pleasure Bond,* which espoused such worthy values as sexual fidelity, emotional commitment, and communication. The institute was severely strapped for cash, and the two researchers hoped to capitalize on the booming market for sex manuals. Though written in an attempt at popular English, unlike their two previous works, the book proved just as dull, and it bombed.

Then in 1979 the pair published *Homosexuality in Perspective,* based on research they had begun in 1962. With publication came a sustained attack on Masters and Johnson's heretofore unassailable reputation.

One aspect of the book that drew fire was the example of Phil, a thirty-one-year-old white man living near San Francisco's Castro district, one of the largest homosexual neighborhoods in the United States. A frequenter of gay bars, Phil also worked for a gay-related business. But then Phil met a black woman named Janet, whom he liked a lot. There was one little problem, though. She did not arouse him sexually. The only way to surmount that difficulty, they decided, was for Phil to become a heterosexual. Phil wrote to Masters and Johnson, explaining his plight. The researchers wrote back, offering Phil and Janet a reduced rate for their intensive, two-week therapy course in St. Louis, because Juliet and her would-be Romeo did not have a lot of money.

In St. Louis, Phil and Janet underwent a series of interviews in which they learned how heterosexuality worked—positions, response cycles, and so on. When Phil told Masters and Johnson of his feelings about men, they suggested he was perhaps taking the wrong course of action by seeking treatment and that he should perhaps just be gay. But at the time Phil was unprepared to admit that to himself. Nor were Masters and Johnson—believing as they did that a homosexual could learn to be a heterosexual—prepared to admit it, either. The researchers then forbade Phil and Janet from having sex initially, in order to relieve them of any pressure to perform. At night they engaged in "sensate focus," or foreplay. The next day they reported on their experiences.

Finally they reached a point where they told Masters and Johnson they could complete the sex act if they wanted to. Even so, Masters and Johnson gave them specific instructions not to concentrate on intercourse, but instead to focus just on their own pleasure—in a sense, to concentrate more on themselves than on their partner. Counselors also urged them not to adopt the missionary position, but for Janet to be on top, where she could insert Phil's penis into her vagina herself.

At the end of the first week, Phil and Janet reported back: mission accomplished. But Phil felt disappointed. The therapy did nothing to change his fantasy life. The counselors told him that if fantasizing about men would work for him, then he should fantasize about men while making love to Janet. She was also given permission to fantasize about other people. At the end of two weeks, Phil and Janet met with the counselors for a wrap-up session. They reported that they thought they could continue to progress back home. Masters and Johnson considered the treatment a success.

Back home, though, Janet found it difficult to get on top all the time because she found that position psychologically uncomfortable. Soon all that expensive, if discounted, therapy began to unravel. No follow-up plans had been made. The St. Louis clinic relied on patients to call them if a problem developed. Janet did call once, and the clinic did call back once, but that was it. A couple of months later, Phil decided it was not fair to either of them to continue and broke off the relationship.

Even so, Phil was one of Masters and Johnson's success stories in *Homosexuality in Perspective*. They did not regard homosexuality as a disease, a mental disorder, or a sign of retarded psychosexual development. But they did claim a 35 percent nonfailure rate (giving no criteria for what constituted nonfailure) in their efforts to treat an admittedly small number of homosexuals who wanted to convert their sexual orientation to heterosexuality.

Masters and Johnson claimed that *Homosexuality in Perspective* was as much about heterosexuals as homosexuals. Among its other claims: that male heterosexual and homosexual erections and orgasms were physiologically identical, with both groups having the same 3 percent failure rate to reach orgasm. After one year, homosexual couples had a better understanding of their partner's sexual needs than heterosexual couples after a similar period. Lesbian couples, in particular, devoted an "extraordinary" amount of time to sexual play in lovemaking. Yet Masters and Johnson found that at least half of U.S. couples had some kind of sexual problem (which they claimed a steady overall success rate of 80 percent in treating). And the problem of premature ejaculation—which they had intimated in *Human Sexual Inadequacy* would be eradicated in ten years—was still around.

The researchers disputed the latest notions of various sex clinicians that there were, in fact, distinct vaginal, clitoral, and even uterine orgasms and reaffirmed not merely the primacy, but the singularity of the clitoral orgasm. Johnson in particular was violently opposed to the recent practice of surgically realigning the clitoris in an anorgasmic woman, condemning it as a form of mutilation. They also responded in the book to John Money's charge that they relied too heavily on instruments to measure human sexual response and overlooked the erotic imagination. From 1957 to 1970 they had collected volumes of sexual fantasies, which they now reported on. One of their most striking findings was that the most common fantasy of both straight and gay men and women was forced sex. The only other fantasy common to all four groups: cross-preference, that is, gay men having sex with women, or straight women with other women. Such data suggested innumerable possible interpretations—for example, a gay male fantasizing about sex with a woman did not necessarily make him a latent heterosexual; rather, the diagnosis of homosexuality in his case may not have been so reliable as previously thought.

In *Homosexuality in Perspective,* Masters and Johnson also came up with a new sexual classification: the ambisexual, whom they defined as uniquely devoid of sexual prejudice and consistently comfortable and successful in sexual performance, regardless of a partner's sex, orientation, or activity preference. Ambisexuals were distinguished from bisexuals by their unwillingness or inability to become involved in sustained relationships. It was a definition Marco Vassi might have approved.

But it was their theories on the origins and "treatment" of homosexuality that aroused the greatest controversy. Taking a stand in the great debate, Masters and Johnson speculated that sexual orientation was a result of environment. In their view, people were born sexual beings, genetically male and female, whereas both homosexuality and heterosexuality were learned behaviors.

But the homosexuals Masters and Johnson studied were far from a representative cross section of the gay population at large, a fact the authors underscored but that most media accounts missed. With homosexuals as with heterosexuals, the authors chose to work mostly with well-educated men and women in their thirties and forties who were in committed relationships. Masters and Johnson also tended to ignore sexual practices they did not choose to deal with—anal or dildo sex, for example—merely asserting that only a minority of their sample showed much interest in either. (Kinsey, however, had suggested a far higher rate of anal sex among gay men.)

And the fact remained that as of 1980, a year after *Homosexuality in Perspective* was published, Phil—cited as a successful heterosexual convert in the book—still had a gay lover. As several critics of the book pointed out, the desire to please the therapists—and all the time and money he had invested—probably prevented Phil from ending his relationship with Janet even sooner.

The severest critic of Masters and Johnson's attempts to convert homosexuals was Dr. Damien Martin. Though a professor of communications at New York University and not a sex researcher, Martin had founded the Institute for the Protection of Lesbian and Gay Youth with his companion, psychiatrist Emory Hetrick. Martin claimed that conversion therapy verged on malpractice and raised serious ethical issues, even though some therapists who undertook it were obviously sincere. (Oddly, the American Psychiatric Association had created a loophole that encouraged such practices when it removed homosexuality from its list of mental disorders in 1973. The exception was ego dystonic homosexuality, which referred to an individual uncomfortable with her or his behavioral tendencies, though the APA made no recommendations on how to treat such unhappiness.)

Appearing on the TV talk show *Donahue,* Martin confronted Masters, who appeared to wither under Martin's pointed and repeated insistence that sexual orientation was impervious to reversal. Martin claimed that not a single case history in the literature of psychology documented such a change and asked Masters to explain his criteria for success. Masters replied that he never claimed success. When Martin asked him to explain his confusing statistics, again Masters did not answer. Nor did he respond when Martin asked why the book contained no report on the dangers of conversions.

Martin and other critics were especially alarmed at the prospect of conversion therapy for children who were still confused by sexuality, and especially for adolescent males, to whom they thought such therapy could cause inestimable harm. They were also leery of the Ex-Gay Movement, a mostly Protestant fundamentalist group with 12-Step overtones. Unlike the Episcopal and Catholic gay groups, Dignity and Integrity, which affirmed the self-worth of homosexuals while encouraging them to live celibately, the Ex-Gay Movement was dedicated to getting men to renounce their sinful homosexuality altogether. Much like AA groups, Ex-Gay members met informally under church sponsorship. Yet a 1980 article in the *American Journal of Psychiatry* reporting on one church's Ex-Gay group found that of three hundred individuals who sought treatment over a five-year period, only thirty claimed to have "converted" to heterosexuality; and of those, only eleven agreed to take part in the study; and of those, five continued to evidence "persistence of homosexual impulses."

Masters and Johnson were not alone in practicing "conversion therapy." Helen Singer Kaplan had created a new diagnosis for gay men called "situationally inhibited sexual desire," a variation of a recognized difficulty in becoming sexually aroused. In Kaplan's view, gay men suffered from this new mental disease simply because they were inhibited in desiring women. Yet homosexuality was, by definition, a desire for a member of the same sex with a corresponding lack of desire for the opposite sex. Kaplan considered homosexuality a deviation because it involved "desire for an object or situation which does not interest the majority of persons." In short, gays were damned if they did and damned if they didn't.

Masters and Johnson had started from a more traditional premise, that homosexuality originated in some prior negative experience like incestuous seduction, rape, or ridicule of a prior heterosexual performance. But their reasoning, too, was sloppy, claiming causality where they had established only chronology. And they neglected to provide any explanation of how heterosexuality was learned. Moreover, their views appeared to be colored by what they saw as the inherent long-term disadvantages of homosexuality—a limited number of techniques and the putative "my turn, your turn" character of gay lovemaking as opposed to the "our turn" of heterosexual coupling.

Dr. Kevin Gordon, a San Francisco psychotherapist, criticized *Homosexuality in Perspective* for homogenizing homosexuals and diminishing the "otherness" of gays and lesbians. Masters and Johnson were in "over their clinical heads," he charged, and the "perspective" in the title was "not so much a service in scientifically exploring gay sexuality, but rather a self-serving apologia for Masters and Johnson's previously published magisterial pronouncements of orthodoxy and orthopraxies in human sexuality."

THINGS ONLY GOT WORSE for Masters and Johnson.

Dr. Bernie Zilbergeld was a young sex therapist from Berkeley, laid-back but with a distinctly un-Californian streak of skepticism. He suspected that Masters's reputation was built on deception—maybe unintentional, maybe not. A respected author in his own right, Zilbergeld had first launched his attack in an August 1980 cover story in *Psychology Today,* when he and fellow therapist Michael Evans ripped into the phenomenal success rate Masters and Johnson claimed in treating sexual dysfunctions. What did the famed St. Louis therapists mean by success? "Masters and Johnson's sex-therapy research is so flawed by methodological errors and slipshod reporting that it fails to meet customary standards—and their own—for evaluation of research. . . . It is impossible to tell what the results were. Because of this, the effectiveness of sex therapy is thrown into question."

The article hinted at a cover-up. Carried away by their own enthusiasm and the pressure to publish, the authors claimed, Masters and Johnson had rushed to clinical judgment, then withheld their data from the scrutiny of peers. Though they had faced vociferous professional criticism in the past, the embrace of the media had conferred on them near mythological status, so that by 1980—despite whispers in the hallways of sex conventions—no one wanted to challenge them head-on.

In *Human Sexual Inadequacy,* Masters and Johnson had claimed that approximately 80 percent of men suffering from impotence and premature ejaculation, and a similar percentage of women afflicted by an inability to achieve orgasm, experienced a so-called symptom reversal during their intensive two-week course in the late fifties and early sixties. With that kind of success, though, their reputations soared, and an 80 percent success rate became the gold standard of the profession. Dr. Helen Singer Kaplan, who had also published therapy outcome statistics without giving criteria, asserted that 63 percent of her patients were "cured" of their sexual problems.

Even more startling were Masters and Johnson's five-year follow-up statistics, which indicated that less than 2 percent of these clients constituted "treatment reversals." "The abiding guide to treatment value," they wrote, "must not be how well patients do under authoritative control but how well they do when returned to their own cognizance without therapeutic control. This result finally must place the mark of clinical failure or success upon the total therapeutic venture."

In working with Masters and Johnson on his 1969 *The Sex Researchers,* the first book to deconstruct Masters and Johnson for the educated public, journalist Edward Brecher, who specialized in human sexuality, had come to suspect that many of their contentions were not supported by data. But only to his colleagues at the Institute for the Advanced Study of Human Sexuality in San Francisco did he confide his doubts. For thirteen years Masters and Johnson withheld their criteria from outside scrutiny, although they themselves said that the acid test of a study was replicability: others must be able to do it over and over again, using the same methods to achieve the same results.

Two psychiatrists trained by Masters and Johnson reported a relapse rate of 54 percent; in another study by another researcher, the rate was 37 percent. Hoping to replicate Masters and Johnson's study with a college population, Evans had even visited the researchers in St. Louis to determine what he needed to know to repeat their study, but they gave him little information. Even the number of hours of actual treatment during the two-week course was not known. Evans and Zilbergeld began to wonder if the research could be repeated.

Ultimately, they concluded that, for whatever reasons, Masters and Johnson had not provided the information necessary for either an intelligent interpretation or replication of their work. *HSI* was full of gaps—essential information about the duration of therapy had been withheld, and the criteria and measures used to assess treatment effects initially and on follow-ups were absent. Masters and Johnson had given only one general definition of failure: "Initial failure is defined as indication that the two-week rapid-treatment phase has failed to initiate reversal of the basic symptomology of sexual dysfunction."

Initiating reversal could mean several things. Did it mean, for example, that an anorgasmic woman might feel less guilty about sex, or become less performance oriented during sex, or enjoy sex more, or have an orgasm with masturbation, or have an orgasm during intercourse? What exactly led Masters and Johnson to classify an anorgasmic woman as a nonfailure? They defined a premature ejaculator as a man who could not control his ejaculatory process long enough during intercourse "to satisfy his partner" at least 50 percent of the time. But in a 1976 seminar Masters said that "satisfaction" referred not to orgasm but to subjective satisfaction and that "only the female can judge whether the male is prematurely ejaculating."

In short, Masters and Johnson not only did not define success, they did not define failure. Yet they denied that "nonfailure" meant success, contrary to a widespread assumption in the sex profession. "It must be emphasized," they said, "that a 20 percent failure rate should not automatically be converted into the suggestion that the therapy program was blessed with an 80 percent success rate. A 20 percent treatment failure rate means just that—and nothing more." So was a premature ejaculator who learned to control himself for hours and still failed to bring his partner to orgasm a failure or a success?

And how to account for Masters and Johnson's extraordinarily low relapse rate of 7 percent when other researchers using similar methods had failed to come anywhere near it? Perhaps many couples viewed a trip to St. Louis as a romantic interlude rather than a desperately needed treatment, or perhaps they were more highly motivated than couples who sought treatment nearer to home. But perhaps, suggested Zilbergeld and Evans, Masters and Johnson simply had more flexible criteria for relapse.

One problem was that no consumer regulatory agency had ever been established to overlook sex therapy. It had no counterpart to the Food and Drug Administration, no Ralph Nader. Yet Zilbergeld and Evans were not alone in their skepticism. Psychiatrist Natalie Shainess of the Columbia College of Physicians and Surgeons called their work an "unprecedented snow job" on the entire psychiatric profession, claiming they merely treated symptoms, not causes, to achieve their phenomenal success rates. As far back as 1970 she had written, "Strangely, nobody to date has verified the Masters and

Johnson research, nor has anybody duplicated his experiments. This is unusual in a normally skeptical scientific community."

Moreover, as Shainess and many others in the sexological community pointed out from time to time, a close comparison of the Kinsey report and *Human Sexual Response* showed virtually no significant findings in the latter that had not been documented in Kinsey's 1948 book, which contained four long chapters on the physiology of sexual response. For that matter, as early as 1912 pioneer sexologist Albert Moll had identified four stages of "voluptuary pleasure": onset, equable voluptuous sensation, acme, rapid decline. Sixty-four years later, Masters and Johnson renamed those phases excitement, plateau, orgasm, and resolution and tacked on a preliminary stage, desire. "As far as I'm concerned," Shainess wrote, "they've done little more than produce a second-rate rehash of work that Kinsey got a good start on twenty years ago and used it as an entrée to an immensely profitable profession."

Other early critics included Dr. Rollo May and Yale psychologist Kenneth Kenniston, and several sharp critiques appeared in British medical and psychiatric journals. Dr. Thomas Szasz, a maverick libertarian psychiatrist at the State University of New York at Syracuse, stoked the fires of criticism with a series of inflammatory books and articles. In his view sex therapy was a pseudoscience and sex therapists no more effective than prostitutes and pornography in the treatment of sexual problems. "When you go to [Masters and Johnson's] clinic," he noted, "you can deduct payment as a medical expense on your tax form. Why can't you likewise deduct the cost of a subscription to *Playboy* or *Penthouse* magazines?" He called the researchers frauds, pointing out that while they "constantly agitate for the licensing of sex therapists . . . Virginia Johnson doesn't even have a college degree."

In light of all this criticism, Masters and Johnson's consistent rejection for funding by the National Institute of Mental Health (except for the brief period from 1956 to 1959) could look less like discrimination against sex therapy per se and more like a considered response to sloppy methodology and ill-defined criteria. In fact, a flat refusal by the NIH for research of any merit was reputed to be rare. But by the time their first book was published, Masters and Johnson had stopped applying for government grants, and most of their donors were not only private but anonymous. (Masters claimed he was blackballed by the organization under pressure from "politicians opposed to sex research.") One of the few public donors—and one of the largest—was Hefner's Playboy Foundation. Christie Hefner sat on the board of directors of the Masters & Johnson Institute, and Masters served as a consultant for the magazine's *Playboy* Adviser, though the magazine never attempted to influence the nature of his research.

* * *

To OTHER RESEARCHERS, the *Psychology Today* article might have dealt a fatal blow. But so secure was Masters and Johnson's public reputation that the article went virtually unnoticed, and many sex therapists continued to cite the institute's statistics as evidence of the effectiveness of sex therapy. In the months after the article was published, Masters and Johnson themselves maintained a stoic silence. Dr. Robert Kolodny, associate director of the Masters & Johnson Institute, attempted a rebuttal in a dry 1981 monograph in the *Journal for Sex Research,* declaring that Masters and Johnson's research statistics had been misinterpreted, but he still did not reveal the mysterious data.

In the face of Masters and Johnson's silence, Zilbergeld kept up the attack in a series of public lectures, including a talk at the annual meeting of the Society for the Scientific Study of Sex (SSSS) in San Francisco in the fall of 1982. But this time Masters's protégé Mark Schwartz sat in the audience, and Masters himself was attending the conference.

Schwartz listened as Zilbergeld repeated his objections. Specifically Zilbergeld zeroed in on Masters and Johnson's treatment reversal of symptoms of female orgasmic dysfunction. Did success mean a woman with such a problem now had an orgasm every time she had sex, or half the time, or once in ten times, or what?

After the lecture, Schwartz approached Zilbergeld and asked: "Why are you acting like we won't tell you our criteria? We'd be happy to tell you." He offered to arrange a meeting with Masters the next day in the hotel lounge. Schwartz showed up with Masters and another colleague, Dr. Ruth Clifford. Zilbergeld brought along Evans and Dr. Bernie Apfelbaum, director of the Berkeley Group for Sexual Development. Zilbergeld asked permission to take notes on a legal pad. Masters nodded his assent. Masters and Schwartz then went on to describe the criteria for primary and situational orgasmic dysfunction. Zilbergeld subsequently read his notes back to Masters to make sure he had them correctly, and Masters agreed the notes were accurate.

Armed with this new ammunition, in the summer of 1983 Zilbergeld resumed the attack in the pages of *Forum,* in collaboration with editor Philip Nobile. At the meeting in San Francisco, Zilbergeld wrote, Masters had said "that the criteria for non-failure in both primary and situational orgasmic functions in women were one orgasm in St. Louis and just one more orgasm in the five-year follow-up period." No wonder other sex therapists had difficulty matching Masters and Johnson's success rates—no one had assumed so low a standard!

Although Evans and Apfelbaum confirmed Zilbergeld's account of the meeting with Masters, Masters released a statement claiming that it was "not an accurate representation of my meaning." Nor, said Masters, did it accurately reflect methodological policy at the institute. But he declined any further discussion of the matter until it was fully explored in a scientific setting.

Meanwhile, Dr. Sallie Schumacher, one of three collaborators cited on the acknowledgments page of *Human Sexual Inadequacy,* admitted to Nobile that while she was in training with Masters and Johnson in St. Louis, so far as she understood there were no clear outcome criteria.

In his book *The Shrinking of America* Zilbergeld accused sex therapists of enticing as many customers as possible into their offices by creating new sex myths and new expectations. Masters and Johnson, Zilbergeld claimed, had even invented a dysfunction for women who were orgasmic in intercourse but not in masturbation. Such women allegedly suffered from "masturbatory orgasmic inadequacy." Not that Zilbergeld believed their work to be entirely without merit. In the end, he suggested, the two researchers would be remembered mainly for having popularized brief, symptom-oriented treatment of sexual dysfunctions and for some of their physiological work.

THE MASTERS-ZILBERGELD CONFRONTATION was not the only high drama at the November 1982 SSSS meeting. A controversial luncheon feting Shere Hite was also on the agenda, even though many of the sexologists in attendance were opposed to honoring a researcher whose work they considered scientifically flawed. Virginia Johnson herself had criticized *The Hite Report* and similar sex studies that she claimed "suffered from a lack of funds and investigative expertise and therefore provide insufficient or questionably adequate interpretation of data." For example, *The Hite Report* finding that up to 70 percent of American woman were unable to reach orgasm in intercourse, Masters and Johnson argued, was merely a commentary on a culture that taught generations of women to deny their sexual needs; it did not reveal anything new about the female capacity for sexual response.

The editor of the society's own journal boycotted the luncheon, but most invitees ended up attending. Hite herself had selected the two panelists who talked about her work. Making light of the fuss, the organizer of the symposium joked that while a 50 percent rate of anorgasmia in females was considered natural, a 50 percent rate of impotence in males would be considered an epidemic.

In an editorial in *Forum,* Nobile—who had disrupted the luncheon with a string of embarrassing questions directed at Hite—dubbed the meeting a Tower of Erotic Babble, fuming that "the study of sex will never be scientific until the day when the scientists drive the charlatans out of the erogenous zones." Hite—who was a friend of Kathy Keeton and *Forum* publisher Bob Guccione—promptly sued Nobile for $18 million for implying she was a charlatan. Nobile was called on the carpet by a company executive and told to shut up or be fired. With three children to support, he chose prudence over valor and temporarily abandoned a chase he had begun years earlier with a devastating review of the first *Hite Report* in the pages of *New York* magazine.

A very angry Bill Masters also contemplated suing Nobile for what he considered to be an attack not only on his methodology, but on his person. Instead, he decided to go on the offensive. At a May 1983 meeting of the Sixth World Congress of Sexology in Washington, D.C., an agitated Masters finally gave the outcome data demanded of him and received a standing ovation. "As many of you know," he stated, "our work has recently been attacked by author Bernie Zilbergeld and by Philip Nobile, an editor of *Forum*, in two articles and an accompanying editorial in the June 1983 issue of *Forum*. Since it is distressing to us to see such distortions and inaccuracies about our work, we want to take this opportunity to set the record straight."

Zilbergeld's central accusation, according to Masters's fifteen-page response, hinged on the claim that *Human Sexual Inadequacy* described the criteria for successful treatment of primary anorgasmia, situational orgasmic dysfunction, and impotence in terms bordering on the ludicrous. Masters further noted that he had already issued a denial of the accuracy of Zilbergeld's alleged "quotations." Yet Masters had declined to discuss the matter in the popular press until he had addressed it in a scientific setting. That moment had now arrived.

In his clarification, Masters stated that the Masters & Johnson Institute had never considered a single orgasm during therapy and one orgasm during the next five years to be an indication of therapeutic success in the treatment of female anorgasmia. The criterion used in the work on which *Human Sexual Inadequacy* was based was that a woman became orgasmic in at least 50 percent of her sexual opportunities. Nor, he claimed, was a 50 percent rate of failure to maintain erections accepted as evidence of successful therapy of impotence. In his original *Psychology Today* critique, a confused Zilbergeld had written: "A premature ejaculator is defined by Masters and Johnson as a man who cannot control his ejaculatory process long enough during intercourse 'to satisfy his partner' at least 50 percent of the time. The crucial phrase is 'to satisfy his partner.' Satisfaction has been almost universally taken to mean orgasm. But is this what Masters and Johnson had in mind?" Now Masters claimed that the criterion for success in treating a premature ejaculator was the ability to get and keep erections on more than 75 percent of "coital occasions."

Finally, said Masters, the *Forum* articles had seriously distorted and misstated statistics listed in *HSI*. Zilbergeld had said that "only 5 of the 276 women who were successfully treated for [primary and situational anorgasmia] in Masters and Johnson's St. Louis clinic were listed as failures in a five-year follow-up study." Masters pointed to Table IIA in *HSI*, which clearly showed that only 137 women were available for a potential five-year follow-up. Another table showed that the overall failure rate for female orgasmic dysfunction was 20.8 percent. Masters claimed that Nobile had similarly distorted and misread statistics on treatment reversals.

He also insisted that Zilbergeld's "own track record of hyperbole and inaccuracy in critiquing others should also be acknowledged." He noted that recently, under threat of legal proceedings, Zilbergeld had been forced to issue a public retraction of "derogatory statements he had previously made about the methodology and motives of another sex researcher." He concluded that Zilbergeld harbored "notions that are being perpetrated on the public through media hype in the name of science and methodological purity," even though his own work was full of "distortions, hyperbole and inaccuracies."

Nobile responded angrily in yet another *Forum* diatribe. Zilbergeld was not Masters's only critic, the journalist pointed out, reminding him of Evans and Apfelbaum. More to the point, Masters had given "vastly different criteria" in San Francisco and in Washington. Even in the pages of *Human Sexual Inadequacy,* their responses revealed, they had mixed apples and oranges in order to cast their findings in a more positive light than was justified. Finally, asked Nobile, why attempt to smear Zilbergeld by alluding to legal difficulties with another sex researcher when Masters and Johnson themselves had been the object of a suit in a celebrated sex-surrogate case?

There, in limbo, the matter was left. And again, despite enormous attention paid to the brouhaha within the sexological ranks, the world at large remained indifferent. As late as 1985 Masters told *Newsweek* that in more than 2,300 cases he and Johnson treated from 1959 to 1985, a phenomenal 84.4 percent of the men and 77.8 percent of the women reported long-term cures.

During his fiery six-year reign at *Forum,* however, Nobile nevertheless managed to transform the magazine into a healthily abrasive watchdog of the sex industry—the only one of its kind in any language, before or since. In the process he had outraged and alienated not only Bill Masters, Virginia Johnson, and Shere Hite, but Wardell Pomeroy and Ted McIlvenna, as well as a score of pop-sex charlatans. Nobile later resumed his assault on Hite, appearing as a guest on radio and TV talk shows, denouncing her as a charlatan, and daring her to sue him again.

In 1987 Hite published *Women and Love,* which claimed that 98 percent of American women were dissatisfied with their relationships with men—a thesis roundly discredited by reviewers, though some feminists like Susan Faludi, who chronicled the counterattack against feminism in *Backlash,* were sympathetic. Bitter that her work had been "trivialized and trashed" by the American media, and professing to fear for her physical safety, Hite moved to Europe, regarding herself as a political exile. With her concert pianist husband, twenty years her junior, she divided her time between Paris, London, and Germany and continued to write on such themes as male anger against women, and women as agents of revolutionary change.

In 1983, desperate for money, Masters and Johnson attempted to exploit the aborning human potential movement by sponsoring "Sexual Health and Wholeness Weekends" for $485 per couple at various spas around Middle America, complete with mineral baths, pool, massage service, and steam rooms. No children were allowed, and the weekends consisted mostly of associates of the famed sex researchers cheerleading couples into regenerating their relationships. Courses were devoted to explorations of myths about sex, the use of anatomically correct dolls to illustrate sex positions, slide shows of fondling couples, and preaching the gospel that sex was play for its own sake, without goals. The weekends had a success rate of zero and were soon abandoned, though the fee for couples treatment in St. Louis was upped to $5,000 for the two-week course, and eventually to $7,500.

In 1984 Masters and Johnson embarked on a $5 million fund-raising campaign, with a series of gala parties in New York, Chicago, and Los Angeles. They had changed the name of their Reproductive Biology Research Foundation to the Masters & Johnson Institute mainly in order to facilitate the raising of funds, which were always in desperately short supply.

In February 1985 the two researchers contracted with ABC to dramatize their life stories. Producer Joan Marks had also presented *A Bunny's Tale,* the story of Gloria Steinem's experience as a *Playboy* Bunny. But the two writers hired to write the story found Johnson condescending and contemptuous and eventually resigned. Johnson and Marks then wrote a version together, but at the last moment Johnson vetoed it.

Chapter 14

Tristis Post Coitum

MARCO VASSI HAD BEEN LIVING MONOGAMOUSLY FOR A TIME WITH A WOMAN named Sara, first on her houseboat in Sausalito, then in Woodstock, then again in Sausalito. But after a number of months their relationship had deteriorated to the extent that Marco, during a particularly heated argument, got carried away and slapped her. Immediately he regretted his action, apologized, and suggested she strike him back. But she only glared and walked off the boat. Marco packed his suitcase, phoned for a cab, and flew back to his beloved Woodstock.

Four months of letters and phone calls followed, then in 1981 she came to visit him in his Woodstock cabin. They made passionate love, but the next morning Marco remembered with a sinking heart that he wanted to be a bachelor. His four months in the woods had only reinforced his need for solitude. Yet here was Sara, wanting monogamy again. "Hello, Vassi," she said brightly when he looked up from his pillow.

After dressing, Marco went off to a coffee shop to eat breakfast and read the *Times*. On his return he found Sara sitting up in bed sipping tea, looking sexy and sympathetic.

"You still wake up in a bad mood?" she asked.

"Not when I wake up alone, or with someone I know will be leaving sometime," he replied.

Sara shook her head, her blue eyes wide in disbelief. "After last night you still won't admit that what you really want is me?"

"I want you, and I want my freedom," he explained. "And if I can't have both, I have to make a choice."

"Well, you can relax," she continued, a slow, sensuous smile inviting him back into bed. "I'm only going to be here for a month. I've decided to play it your way, if that's the only way I can have you. I'd rather have some of you than none at all."

"You can have all of me. But only for limited periods of time."

Sara opened her legs wide. "So since I'm leaving, and you don't have to be afraid I'm trying to trap you, why don't we relax and have a good time?"

Three weeks later, though, Sara admitted she had spoken of leaving only as a ploy. She revealed that she had an offer on the boat—enough to buy a house in Woodstock and still have enough to live on for two or three years. She could get back to her painting, she proposed, and Marco could write his novel at last. Marco was tempted: a home of his own, a woman crazy about him, maybe even children, a chance at enjoying a "normal" life. Yet he knew he had to refuse, even though there would be nights when he would kick himself for saying no.

Sara's last week was difficult, as they swung between sorrow and ecstasy and their lovemaking grew more desperate. On the night before she was to leave they fell asleep in each other's arms, their faces wet with tears.

"This is the last time," Marco vowed to himself, not for the first time. "This is the last time I fall in love or let somebody fall in love with me."

The next day Sara left. "I'll always love you," she said as she boarded the bus back to New York. "But I'll probably never forgive you for rejecting me."

"I'm not rejecting you," he replied forlornly. "I'm rejecting monogamy."

In the weeks after Sara's departure, Marco fell into a severe depression. He was approaching forty, an event he had prepared for by reading Gail Sheehy's best-selling *Passages*. But acquiring a serene philosophical acceptance of middle age was one thing. Actually experiencing it was another.

Judith, his old lover and still an important member of the Family, fist-fucked him for his birthday, a gift he had requested as a symbol of his resignation from a life of excess. A seminomadic sexual tribe, the Family was the informal name of a loosely knit New York erotic arts community who made the same scenes and helped each other when in need.

"Moving her fingers in a wild dance deep in my bowels," he wrote in his diary, Judith fellated him at the same time, pulling her fist out suddenly as he came. "The earth seemed to shake and the room dissolved and I came close to knowing what a woman goes through in childbirth. It was the first and the last time that I will do this. I consider it a high-water mark in my psycho-erotic explorations."

But the experience did not stem his fall into depression for long. During this dark night of the libido, Marco reflected that over time, despite his full and varied erotic life, he had begun to accept quantity over quality, to settle for superficial excitement instead of deeper involvement, almost reeling from embrace to embrace, scene to scene, without counting the cost. Finding himself in bed one evening with a young woman almost half his age, Marco could not help but notice that she was still plump with baby fat. He had seduced her with his standard routine—marijuana, wine, and music, followed by a few choice passages from some of his books.

By now Marco's repertoire ranged from spanking and bondage to water sports and fantasy games. He was trying to decide which trick to use next with the girl, as they lay on the bed half undressed, when she pulled back, fear in her eyes, and said, "Wait, I just realized I don't know who you are. I've read your work, but actually you're a stranger to me."

From long experience, Marco knew how to deal with that kind of temporary rebuff, usually by launching into a long, soul-baring monologue guaranteed to win over the most reluctant virgin. But now he was attacked by a sharp sense of insecurity: he did not know who he was, either. Desire drained from him. He took her home and spent the rest of the night in troubled, solitary sleep. He awoke frightened. Sex had always been central to his life. Now he was no longer sure he could handle it.

Two nights later he called on Judith, who laughed and told him, "Oh, you're just going through male menopause." To comfort him, she unzipped his pants and began to fellate him. But he felt like a robot performing a mechanical function.

In the ensuing months, Marco's depression only deepened, despite occasional sex highs that occurred mainly thanks to drugs or an orgiastic atmosphere. He all but abandoned masturbation, and even his sex fantasies seemed dull. As depression edged into despair, he stopped reading his mail, answering his phone, cleaning his apartment, or doing the laundry. After a time, he realized he was bottoming out. Though his sex life was still stagnant, he began to look upon this passage in his life as a necessary evil, like a cleansing fever. For the first time in his adult life he went nearly three months without having an orgasm.

He wrote in his diary: "I have ransacked all the gurus, teachers, therapists, philosophers, revolutionaries, artists, sages, scientists to try to find the material for a synthesis. And I can honestly say that in the area of conceptual comprehension, I have reached the farthest stretches of the mind." Comparing himself with other self-styled sex gurus, he asked: "What, for example, do Masters and Johnson do in bed, are they as inventive as their experiments might indicate? Is the supposed tantric master Bhagwan Shree Rajneesh a good fuck, or does he just talk a good game? Is Harold Robbins as horny as his characters?"

He concluded that no one since Henry Miller had been so capable of talking about his or her own metasexual life "with simplicity, passion, richness of physical description and fullness of emotion and feeling without getting either pornographic or literary about it." Though he greatly admired Miller and was pleased that he had been compared with the great bohemian adventurer, Marco hoped to eclipse him in at least one respect by "being more personal than anyone has ever attempted to be in this area, including the Old Master himself who, after all, had no precedent and who restricted himself to conventional relations with women."

During this period he decided to reverse Casanova's secret of success— "Lower your standards and double your efforts." Marco would double his standards and lower his efforts. Though he continued to live periodically in serially monogamous relationships with different women, for periods lasting up to eight months, there always came a moment when Marco grew bored and restless. Besides, as he told his diary, "I want to be remembered for what *I* am like in bed, not what *we* are like in bed."

By 1980, when she turned twenty-seven, Annie Sprinkle had transformed herself into a one-woman sex industry, making scores of films, writing for sex magazines, turning tricks. Then at a party she met Gary. If ever there was a case of opposites attracting, this was it. Gary was a gemologist and a devout Christian. He had never seen a porn film or heard of Annie Sprinkle. They fell in love.

Annie credited Gary with saving her sex life. Having strayed so far off the beaten track, she, like Marco, had begun to think that she no longer knew what sex was really about. Gary and Annie had straight, mostly missionary-style sex—her favorite position—every day, and she regarded it as the best sex she ever had. Except for the tricks she turned to make a living, they lived monogamously, and she stopped going to the Hellfire Club.

The relationship lasted a year, but ultimately Gary was too much of a straight arrow to get along with Annie's friends. The truth was, he had fallen in love with Ellen Steinberg, not Annie Sprinkle. But even after they broke up, the sex business remained just a job to Annie; it paid the rent, but it no longer offered her any excitement.

Deciding to turn her New York apartment into a tattoo parlor, Annie rented out half of it to Spider Webb, who had tattooed her right buttock when she was nineteen. Tattooing, body piercing, and other forms of decorative physical mutilation were just coming into fashion in the radical undergrounds of New York, San Francisco, and a few other big cities. But New York City had a law banning tattoo parlors. To show his defiance, Webb announced to the world—via press releases sent to all the major media—that he was going to tattoo porn star Annie Sprinkle's wrist on the steps of the Metropolitan Museum of Art. He hoped to get arrested so the issue could be brought before the courts.

Dutifully, a respectable representation of the media showed up to record the event. Unfortunately, the police failed to make an appearance, even after a desperate Annie and her co-conspirators called them from the pay phone inside the museum, pretending to be enraged citizens witnessing a crime. Soon after this unheeded challenge to authority, tattoo parlors began springing up all over town, even though tattooing remained illegal.

Webb taught Annie to tattoo, and after she became an expert, she tattooed Webb and his entire family, as well as numerous friends. After he had drunk a couple of six-packs, Webb would let her tattoo any part of his anatomy she wanted to. Once, after he passed out, she tattooed a can of Budweiser on his calf. She also began an affair with Fakir Musafar, a San Francisco advertising executive and the editor of a publication called *Piercing Fans International Quarterly,* whom she met after she wrote him a fan letter.

Musafar had been inspired to explore the world of piercing after witnessing an American sundance ceremony (as seen in the movie *A Man Called Horse*). After making two large permanent piercings through his chest, Musafar performed his own sundance ceremony once a year "to seek the Great White Spirit." A colorful, widely beloved figure within the piercing community, Musafar saw his discipline as primarily a spiritual experience, and he became the country's foremost practitioner of an art form he virtually invented called "body play."

In body play, as piercing and related activities were called, the sexual act itself either played a subordinate role or was sublimated altogether. Musafar and his disciples went far beyond conventional SM—bondage, masks, latex sheathing—to turn the body into not only a sexual object but a living erotic work of art. Body players painted themselves to resemble fantastic birds of paradise, pierced their genitals, walked barefoot on broken glass, slept on a bed of nails, or—a favorite Musafar pastime—hung for hours from chains attached to pins piercing their breast muscles.

Previously a practice reserved for Gypsies, prostitutes, primitive people, and SM radicals, piercing by the early eighties was quickly becoming the ultimate symbol of neoradical chic—and also, in the dawning age of AIDS, a form of safe sex. As punks, bikers, gays, masochists, porn stars, and other sex radicals made piercing and other forms of bodily mutilation commonplace, piercing increased exponentially in popularity in urban populations, especially among the young and disaffected. The ubiquitous ponytailed, Gucci-loafered, multiearringed hipster male executive was emblematic of just how pervasive the culture of piercing had become.

Perhaps the country's foremost innovator in the art of body piercing was Jim Ward, who owned and operated a "piercing shop" called the Gauntlet on Santa Monica Boulevard in Los Angeles, where patrons could choose from a variety of jewelry designed especially for places besides earlobes. In the back of the shop was a private room like a doctor's office where the shopper could have his or her jewelry inserted into his or her body for free by Ward or an experienced employee. Ward also sold piercing equipment and jewelry by mail.

Piercing enthusiasts spared nothing—nipples, belly button, labia, clitoris, penis, scrotum, perineum, tongue, lip, nose, eyebrows, cheek. Some claimed it increased their sex drive; others regarded the act of piercing as a romantic, deeply intimate, and sexually intense act that bound lovers more closely than ever—as when a chain linked the tongue of one partner with the penis of another. Still others, perhaps the majority, flaunted their pierced body parts as a show of radical individuality or a come-on.

In Manhattan, the Body Arts Society—the majority of its members pierced—met once a month at the Sixth Sense Gallery, occasionally having a piercing night. The Janus Society, the SM group in San Francisco, also had evening meetings devoted to piercings, sometimes with live demonstrations. People in the Scene also occasionally threw piercing parties where guests were able to get new piercings if they so desired. But most piercing was done at home by the gritted-teeth method, though usually in some kind of sexual context, so that the ordeal was often more exciting than excruciating. Anesthetic sprays were generally spurned and most infections cleared up with soap and water.

Serious devotees of the art subscribed to Musafar's *Piercing Fans International Quarterly,* the first of its kind. Along with sometimes mind-boggling stories and photos, it provided step-by-step instructions for do-it-yourself types, as well as personal advertisements called Pin Pals.

Also in the early eighties, Annie and Marco Vassi finally met while appearing as guests on a cable-TV talk show in New York. At the time, Marco was apartment-sitting for a gay acquaintance whose bed was covered with black leather sheets. The two uninhibited adventurists celebrated their meeting with a night of kinky experimentation that commenced with Annie peeing into Marco's ear.

BY 1982 the classic age of SM was over. Serious SMers continued to congregate—from ten at night until nine in the morning—at the Hellfire Club, where the practice of fetishism was not only tolerated but encouraged. Tourists were now discouraged because they inhibited the regulars, and the club also eschewed telephones and advertising. But for the most part, SM, no longer the most forbidden fruit in the garden, had become a sideshow for the curious, the kinky minded, and the lonely. The sex was gone, and all that remained, in most latter-day New York clubs, was theater.

Billing itself as "the friendly SM club," Paddles catered to a mostly gay clientele, along with the usual quota of doms and wimps. The Loft was Manhattan's most elegant SM retreat, a clean, well-lighted place with beautiful women galore (an SM club rarity) that looked more like an after-hours club than a part of the Scene. Here, on any given night, a woman in mink might take on three muscle boys at one time, with one man wearing an executioner's hood, the second (likely her husband) watching and masturbating, and a third grinding his heels into the expensive fur as he penetrated her.

Even Plato's Retreat got in on the act, renting out its premises once a month to the SM crowd, offering "Hellfire parties" under heavy security. In contrast with club policy on other nights, single males were allowed admittance. Black leather drag was de rigueur. The highlight of the evening was a choreographed show performed against a thumping disco beat. A leggy mistress danced to Donna Summer's "Love to Love You, Baby" as she playfully whipped a "slave girl" bound in chains. Then, as Master Ron with many an elaborate flourish trussed, nipple-clipped, spanked, and dildo-fucked Slave Girl Marie, who remained immobile as a corpse, the emcee—taking his cue from network game shows—pumped the crowd at every moan and groan with, "Let's hear it for Master Ron and Slave Girl Marie!"

Out in the audience, meanwhile, men jostled one another or scaled the walls of adjoining rooms for a view of the action, while club security stood on the sidelines, shaking their heads in disgust at all the weirdness. But the only real problem on SM night was too many womanless men and too many curiosity seekers—dilettantes of desire.

True, the Scene was not entirely dead. Fist fucking—now known as brachioproctic eroticism (BPE)—was growing in popularity among women, who performed it mostly in private but increasingly at clubs, with multiple participants stimulating a single woman. Women who were into BPE tended to defy easy categorization as homosexuals, heterosexuals, or bisexuals. In BPE vernacular, the inserter was the top, the insertee the bottom. Both tops and bottoms described good BPE as verging on religious ecstasy. A popular variation was for the top to insert her hands simultaneously or sequentially into the vagina and rectum of the bottom. Some bottoms described a psychic state of trust and abandon that included a very long-lasting orgasm that approached transcendence; tops confessed to a feeling of beneficent power.

For the most part, however, the SM Scene of the eighties was pure vanilla, in which actually hurting somebody—an integral part of lovemaking in serious SM—was the biggest taboo of all. This soft and mushy version of SM was symptomatic of the confused, sexless, and often moronic outlook of the sex industry at large at the dawn of the Reagan administration and the birth of the Moral Majority.

IN THE LATE SEVENTIES and early eighties an antisex mood began to settle on the country, as symbolized by such hit movies as *Looking for Mr. Goodbar* and *Cruising,* which stressed the dangers of casual sex. The Christian Right was in ascendancy, and the antipornography movement was cranking out propaganda around the clock.

One of the principal antisex gurus to capitalize on this poisonous mood was George Leonard, the former West Coast editor of *Look*. A high priest of the human potential movement, whose temple was Esalen, Leonard had once suggested in *Look* that "sexual intercourse and birth could be shown on network television and in family magazines." Now he argued that the Sexual Revolution had failed to live up to its promises, at least the outlandish ones he had envisioned. Renouncing the whole mess, he now claimed to sense a mood of boredom and despair among friends and others he interviewed for his 1982 book, *The End of Sex,* which concluded, "But I believe . . . that love will prevail, that love will eventually join us in a family as wide as all humankind that can laugh together, weep together and share the common ecstasy." Except for the politically correct substitution of "humankind" for "mankind," the passage just happened to be identical to the conclusion of his sexual manifesto "Why We Need a New Sexuality," published in *Look* a scant five years earlier.

In August 1982, *Time* magazine mercifully put the Sexual Revolution (at least at its popular and more egregious level) out of its misery, with a moralizing cover story on herpes that called the disease the "new scarlet letter" and linked sexual promiscuity to sin. The timing was perfect. The baby boom generation—the first to enjoy the benefits of the pill, safe abortion, and virtually unrestricted access not only to pornography but to a wide variety of other sexual information and entertainments—was getting ready to settle down and have families. Its collective interest in sex, along with its ability to perform, was (allegedly) on the decline.

In fact, the country at large was suffering from collective libidinal burnout. There was too much pornography, too many erotic boutiques, too much nudity, too many sex surveys. Meanwhile, sex therapy had become infested with legions of charlatans, mediocrities, and prostitutes of both sexes posing as trained surrogates. Masters and Johnson were under fire from both the gay and sexological communities. Transsexual surgery was under intense attack from psychiatry's right wing. The circulations of *Penthouse* and *Playboy* were in inexorable decline.

In response to the changing social climate, *Playboy* had jettisoned its book publishing division and closed all but three of its twenty-two clubs. Hoping to boost the Playboy Channel's subscriber base, it also began programming nonsex fare, an effort that ultimately failed. *Penthouse,* though, stuck with sex. Guccione now no longer saw *Playboy,* but X-rated videocassettes, as his main competitor.

Herpes was an answered prayer to the antisex forces, which had long labored to establish an inevitable connection between sexual freedom and disease. *Newsweek* had bannered its coverage "The Misery of Herpes II," but it was the *Time* story that put herpes virtually on a par with the bubonic plague.

John Leo, a former editor of the Catholic weekly *Commonweal* who wrote the story, had assembled various sexual horror stories not unlike a priest sprinkling a sermon with cautionary tales—for example, that of three women who were consciously spreading herpes in a crusade of revenge on male partners. "They were just one-night stands, so they deserved it anyway," one of them was quoted as saying. Leo also quoted a Philadelphia man who boasted that he had transmitted herpes to twenty women.

Incurable and easily transmitted, herpes affected an estimated five to twenty million Americans, according to the article; the numbers were difficult to estimate because doctors were not required to report new cases as with other STDs. Even so, by conservative estimates up to a half million people were contracting the disease each year. In addition to the inconvenience of enforced abstinence for herpetics with open sores, the disease also bestowed the stigma of shame and guilt. Moreover, women were more vulnerable to the disease and to long-term harm from it. Women with herpes were five to seven times more likely to develop cervical cancer, and researchers wondered if there was a causal link. Some even wondered if cervical cancer itself was a sexually transmitted disease.

Only in the final paragraph of his story did Leo find anything good to say about herpes, noting that the threat of infection might "be a prime mover in helping to bring to a close an era of mindless promiscuity. The monogamous now have one more reason to remain so. For all the distress it has brought, the troublesome little bug may inadvertently be ushering in a period in which sex is linked more firmly to commitment and trust."

Yet an ABC/*Washington Post* poll published around the same time revealed that only 9 percent of Americans reported altering their sex lives to avoid contacting herpes. And a survey of an unprecedented 106,000 women commissioned by *Cosmopolitan* magazine and carried out by the New York–based Simmons Market Research Bureau found that an extraordinary 90 percent of women now reported having sex for the first time before the age of twenty.

But *Time* magazine seemed determined to declare the party over. In April 1984 it published a cover story entitled "Sex in the '80s: The Revolution Is Over." The story began: "From cities, suburbs and small towns alike, there is growing evidence that the national obsession with sex is subsiding. . . . Veterans of the revolution, some wounded, some merely bored, are reinventing courtship and romance. . . . Many individuals are rediscovering the traditional values of fidelity, obligation and marriage." The sermon concluded, " 'Cool sex,' cut off from emotions and the rest of life, seems empty, unacceptable or immoral."

Again Leo was the author of the piece, and again no evidence was presented. As survey after survey affirmed, people were having the same amount of sex. The human sex drive appeared to be a constant factor in history and, allowing for individual variation, little had changed over time except that it was easier in recent years to have sex and prostitution was flourishing. In fact, by 1984 the age of first intercourse had dropped to a record 16.2.

Though the kinds and amounts of sex that most people were having continued to increase at a steady rate, some forms of high-risk behavior—one-night stands, swinging, SM—were becoming decidedly unfashionable. As events soon proved, the herpes scare brought on not so much the end of a promiscuous era as the dawn of a much longer and darker season of sexual despair and tragedy that no one could have foreseen, though already there had been a few published reports of male homosexuals dying of a mysterious disease. Pornography was also under attack by the federal judiciary, the Christian Right, and radical feminism. Sex, having escaped from the clutches of puritanism for one giddy decade, was being viewed as a sin again, except within the context of monogamous marriage.

Only members of the Family, and others on the far fringes of the erogenous zone, seemed not to notice that the Sexual Revolution was going into a nosedive.

THE PRO-SEX MOVEMENT was certainly not helped by the surfeit of second-rate sex manuals and how-to books that publishers inflicted on the public in the last days of casual promiscuity. The truth was, sex authorities generally had a shortage of problems to cure. The solution was to invent a few "epidemics" that universalized the inadequacies of a few. Journalist Alexandra Penney capitalized on the alleged lack of sexual desire in marriage in her best-seller *Great Sex*. So did Carol Botwin in *Is There Sex After Marriage?* Penney's book hit the bookstores with a red band announcing it was "So Hot We Had to Seal It" and guaranteeing to give the reader at least one night of unsurpassed sex. Penney talked of "ultimate sensations" and "ultimate sex," suggesting that women should emulate Japanese geishas if they wanted "nights of endless pleasure." Similarly inane advice had been offered in 1970 by Christian fundamentalist Marabel Morgan, who in *The Total Woman* had urged women to dress up in Saran Wrap or cowgirl outfits to inject excitement into marriage.

But as most married people knew, marriage was not designed as an aid to sexual excitement; neither were children. The sex rates of married couples almost universally declined from the birth of their first child until the last grown child left home. Though over the years many women's (and later men's) magazines and some popular books published articulate, intelligent, and empowering information and advice on a variety of sexual issues, helping to demystify behavior too often burdened with guilt, taboos, and ignorance, the shoal on which sex advice routinely foundered was the attempt to reverse monogamous sex rates with silly and often demeaning bedroom games.

Among the most popular of the so-called sexperts was Dr. Ruth Westheimer, a woman with a thick, high-pitched, almost comical German accent who burst onto the scene with her radio program, *Sexually Speaking,* in early 1980. A typical exchange went like this:

Male caller: "Dr. Ruth, I think you're the greatest, and I hope you can help me with my problem."

"Well, I'll try."

"Okay. I started about a year ago, when I was having some problems with my sexual encounters. Ho-hum, you know, in the sack. So I went out and bought some pornographic magazines, and looked at them just before and during intercourse. And then my wife started buying these magazines. Well, we have an eight-millimeter film projector and she bought some eight-millimeter porno films, and now she shows those while we're in bed having sex. She turns on the projectors and watches movies while we're going through our routine."

"Do you have good orgasms?"

"Oh, yeah."

"And she has good orgasms?"

"Yeah."

"Nothing to worry about, then. You have found a way that is right for the two of you, and enjoy it, okay? Bye-bye."

Female caller: "Yes, how ya doing, Doctor?"

"Fine, how are you?"

"I'm great, but this very close friend of mine confided in me about a problem that she has. She's been seeing this gentleman for a while, and it seems as though he's been making her engage in fantasies every week. And recently it seems like these fantasies have been getting a little bit out of hand. At what point should she draw the line?"

"Does she get paid for it?"

"No, she doesn't get paid for it. She does it because she cares for this gentleman."

"Ah-ha. Then you'll have to explain a little bit more. Can you give me an example?"

"Golden showers is what he suggested to her the last time."

"I would say that she certainly should find the courage to say she doesn't like that. Okay? That's very simple, to just say, 'I do not like that,' and tell her that Dr. Westheimer said to take a stand and be counted and say this is something she doesn't like. Okay?"

Within the year *Sexually Speaking* became the hottest program on the American airwaves. Neither host nor callers had any concern for the Federal Communications Commission (FCC), which only forbade the broadcast of seven words, most of them four lettered and none of them in Dr. Ruth's vocabulary. A fiftyish mother of two with a doctorate in family studies from Columbia— the accent helped to reinforce the scientific gloss—Dr. Ruth was not only warm and witty, but permission-giving. Masturbation was recommended this way: "Use it or lose it." By 1984 she was on cable TV with a show called *Good Sex,* accompanied by a seemingly endless stream of ghostwritten books and magazine articles bearing her name that covered every sexual subject under the sun.

Possibly the worst (and best-selling) sex advice book of all time was Naura Hayden's 1983 *How to Satisfy a Woman Every Time . . . and Have Her Beg for More!* A volume of fewer than twenty thousand words, it advanced the all-she-needs-is-a-good-fuck philosophy as a universal remedy for anorgasmic women, while insisting that the missionary position was the best way to achieve results. Hayden's secret formula: The man should tease the woman's clitoris with his penis. When she begged him to penetrate her, he should continue to tease until she was nearly wild with excitement, then push in only an inch, then another half inch, and so on by half-inch stages to full penetration. Never mind that when such tactics failed to work the unfulfilled woman was burdened with an increased sense of failure and guilt.

As if ordinary anorgasmia, impotence, ebbing marital passion, and the fruitless search for "ultimate sex" were not enough to occupy it, the professional sex community outdid itself in 1983 with the alleged discovery of a new erogenous flashpoint that promised orgasmic bliss to women beyond anything the mere clitoris could accomplish. The sighting was announced in a slender volume entitled *The G-Spot and Other Recent Discoveries about Human Sexuality* by sex therapist John Perry, and his coauthors, sex researchers Beverly Whipple and Alice Ladas, and sent thousands of women probing their vaginal walls, tapping for orgasmic tremors.

The G-spot was a tangle of glands the size of a coin, located just under the bladder near the urethra, about halfway between the backside of the pubic bone and the front edge of the cervix and about one inch beneath the vaginal surface. Named for German gynecologist Ernst Grafenberg, who reported the discovery in 1944, it was also called the female prostate to emphasize its similarity to the male prostate. The phenomenon of female ejaculation was first mentioned in 1672 by a Dutch physician, Regnier de Graaf, though scientists continued to disregard his claim for more than three hundred years. Victorian pornographers referred to female ejaculation frequently, but most physicians dismissed female patients who consulted them about their ejaculations as "hypersecreters."

Kinsey had known of the glands but thought they were "only vestigial structures." Similarly, Masters and Johnson had dubbed female ejaculation an "erroneous but widespread concept." A common view among skeptics was that women suffering from urinary stress incontinence usually had weak vaginal muscles and accidentally wet the bed during sex; moreover, some women do urinate during sex.

In 1978 a young law student, Josephine Sevely, published a documented history of references to female ejaculation in Western medical books. Sevely suggested that the fluid received scant attention from scientists because of a simple language problem. In most ancient languages, "semen" was used to describe the ejaculate of either sex. But with the invention of the microscope, only male ejaculate was seen to contain sperm. Since female ejaculate did not contain "seed," those fluids were left with no word to describe them. As a result, the phenomenon vanished from scientific texts.

Intrigued by Sevely's texts, various researchers began looking anew at the evidence of female ejaculation. In 1981 Dr. Edwin Belzer and others at Dalhousie University in Halifax, Nova Scotia, published the first case study of a female ejaculator. They found that the substance she expelled during orgasm was probably not urine, nor did the substance stain the sheets. A chemical analysis showed the ejaculate contained prostatic acid phosphatase (PAP), an enzyme characteristically found in secretions of the male prostate. Since Dr. Belzer had proved that at least one woman could ejaculate, it could no longer be considered an impossibility.

However, in a 1982 study at the Jefferson Medical College in Philadelphia, researchers analyzed "ejaculate" from six women and found no evidence of prostatic secretions, concluding that "the ejaculate and urine seem to be one and the same." Yet they acknowledged that women who said they ejaculated described the fluid they emitted as being quite different from urine in smell, taste, and appearance. And Dr. Daniel Goldberg, who headed the study, emphasized that the findings did not necessarily contradict Belzer's, because the studies had used different methodologies.

Later reports stated that at least some of the fluid contained in female ejaculate came from the so-called female prostate. Researchers in Bratislava, Czechoslovakia, analyzed ejaculate obtained from ten women by several methods, including scanning electron micrographs. Their results were published in the British *Histochemical Journal*. Many of the cells in the female ejaculate came from the women's urethras and paraurethral ducts and glands. Other studies found that prostatic markers such as PAP were found in secretory cells around the female urethra.

Yet the alleged link between the G-spot and female ejaculation remained ambiguous. A 1984 study published in Colombia showed that women did not always ejaculate when they had vaginal orgasms resulting from G-spot stimulation, while other women reported ejaculating without direct stimulation of the G-spot.

Perry insisted that all women had G-spots and that the G-spot was always the source of the ejaculate, although it did not have to be directly stimulated for ejaculation to occur. But direct stimulation did cause more and quicker ejaculation, possibly because muscular contractions occurring around the gland during orgasm forced the ejaculate from the so-called female prostate. Perry explained that, as with the clitoris, psychological and physiological factors could inhibit normal functioning; unresponsive women simply needed to relearn what was essentially a natural response. He also hypothesized that lesbians were able to find their G-spots more easily than heterosexual women did because they used their fingers extensively during lovemaking, with greater dexterity than the penis and greater motivation than male hands to find pleasure spots.

The G-spot was also touted as a way to bring many anorgasmic women to their first orgasm, either with a vibrator or via a lover. Direct stimulation, in fact, often caused multiple orgasms. G-spot stimulation also resulted in distinctly different pleasure from clitoral stimulation. Some experts assumed the difference between clitoral and uterine orgasm was psychological, while others pointed to evidence of a physiological distinction. Like the stimulation of the glans of the penis, clitoral stimulation provoked a muscle reaction closer to the surface of the pelvis—the pubococcygeal muscles, or what Masters and Johnson called the orgasmic platform. Stimulation of the G-spot led to contractions of deeper pelvic muscles and of the uterus itself. Women familiar with both kinds of orgasm reported that ejaculation occurred during the "deeper" orgasms produced by either intercourse or digital penetration. Women who favored the deeper orgasm caused by uterine spasm said they preferred men with shorter penises, since a short penis was more readily in contact with the G-spot than a larger one that, as it were, overshot the mark.

Among those who contested the pervasiveness of female ejaculation was Shere Hite, who reported that only fifteen out of her three thousand respondents in *The Hite Report* claimed to ejaculate. Like Masters and Johnson, she also continued to dispute the idea that women could have orgasms without direct clitoral stimulation. "To try to insist women have orgasms because of simple penetration puts women back in the kitchen," she protested. Dr. Howard Ruppel Jr. of the Iowa School of Social Work also suggested to the Sixth World Congress of Sexology in 1983 that 43 percent of the 189 heterosexual women he interviewed for a study said they had ejaculated during orgasm. But after viewing a film of a woman who emitted copious amounts of fluid during sex, only 22 percent claimed they did.

PHONE SEX had been around since 1973, when Prism Productions in New York instituted the first phone-sex service, though customers had to order calls by mail. A woman (or, in the case of gay phone sex, a man) would then phone the customer at the appointed time, and the two would talk until the amount of time paid for ran out. However, the phenomenon did not take off until 1983, when the FCC ruled that the Bell network could no longer monopolize "enhanced services" that outside companies were able to supply. For example, the telephone company could no longer provide prerecorded announcements of the time or weather but had to lease its forty-four "dial-it" lines to outside suppliers.

Within a month pornographers were running New York Telephone's dial-it lines, providing an assortment of messages being read by breathy women. Customers could choose length and type of message—lesbian, threesome, a woman masturbating, sex-hungry or voracious women, SM (sadistic or masochistic), and numerous other fantasies. Leading the way was *High Society,* cornerstone of a major porn empire run by the publicity-shy Carl Ruderman. These prerecorded, noninteractive messages quickly became a national novelty, not only among sexual lonely-hearts, but among children, adolescents, and office pranksters. After parents complained that their children were calling the lines, Congress passed a law ordering the FCC to restrict access of minors. Hard-core messages were allowed only from nine P.M. to eight A.M., on the assumption that minors would be under adult supervision—or asleep—during those hours.

The dial-it trade was big business, ultimately earning about $25 million a year for telephone companies and twice that for pornographers. Even more lucrative was the introduction of credit card pornography offering men the opportunity to talk dirty with live girls. Live phone sex was not only the first big breakthrough in porn technology since the introduction of video—it was truly the first interactive form of the genre—but a lucrative lifeline for soft-core magazines like *Penthouse, Hustler,* and their scores of imitators. As mainstream advertisers continued to drop out of soft-core publications under pressure from the Christian Right and radical feminists, their place was taken by ever steamier advertisements offering readers the opportunity to indulge in virtually any scenario fantasy could contrive. Like old-fashioned print pornography, however, phone sex depended entirely on the user's imagination without providing any visual clues. That little problem was resolved in late 1996 with the introduction of the first "cyberbrothel," live two-way video technology that permitted members to engage in sex fantasies from their home PCs.

IN THE MID-EIGHTIES Bob Guccione reached a career apex in controversy. At the same time, he was making magazine history, with the single most profitable issue of a magazine ever published. The cause of all the frenzy was a woman seldom seen in the pages of *Penthouse*—a black woman who, moreover, seemed to personify the girl-next-door comeliness and comparatively wholesome values associated with the magazine's only serious competitor. Best of all, she was officially the most beautiful woman in the country—Miss America herself.

Vanessa Williams had been an undergraduate at Syracuse University before becoming the first black woman to win the crown. But one summer when she was trying to prove her independence and begin her career in entertainment, Williams had posed in the nude on two separate occasions for photographers Tom Chiapel and Greg Whitman. As Williams's reign was ending, Chiapel had approached Hefner with his set of photographs, which depicted Williams in a series of erotic poses with a young white woman. *Playboy* turned the set down because it considered Chiapel's price too high and because without a model's release it considered the risk of a lawsuit too great. Chiapel took the photographs to Guccione, who also found the documentation insufficient. But eventually Chiapel produced a model's release, and Guccione bought the pictures for a reputed $100,000—the highest sum the magazine had ever paid for a contribution.

Even before the issue hit the newsstands in September 1984, copies were being pilfered and hawked on the black market. The issue sold a total of 5.5 million copies (at the time the average sale was 3.4 million), even though for this issue the newsstand price was upped from $3 to $4, bringing Guccione a single-issue gross of about $11 million. The ensuing uproar pushed the Olympics and the nomination of Geraldine Ferraro as vice president off the front pages. For a time it even looked as if it could propel soft-core into a second birth, reversing its steady decline in readership in the wake of the video revolution.

Albert A. Marks Jr., executive director of the Miss America Pageant, was so distressed that he could barely choke out a statement: "As a man, a father, a grandfather, as a human being, I have never seen anything like these photographs. . . . I can't even show them to my wife." Venus Raymey, Miss America of 1944, denounced Williams as a "slut." Even *The New York Times* chimed in with an editorial that accused Guccione, like the beauty pageant itself, of exploiting the market for beautiful young women.

Williams herself was on a promotional tour at the time. When she first heard that *Penthouse* was publishing photos of her, she assumed they were the ones by Whitman, for which she remembered signing a model's release. She decided to resign as Miss America because she was afraid the second set of photos would surface eventually and the public would not forgive a second mistake. The controversy was not directly responsible for the breakup of her relationship with a man she had been dating for the past four years, but it did cost her a number of endorsements, including a six-figure, nine-year contract with Gillette that was being negotiated at the time.

Guccione had made no attempt to contact Williams or ask her permission beforehand, explaining: "My first obligation is to my readers. Anyone who seeks the limelight must realize that they are newsworthy." But when he saw how matters were playing out, he was remorseful, claiming he did not know the story would be so big and never suspected Williams might lose her crown. He contacted Williams's lawyers and offered to help, saying that if she were fired, he would hire her at twice her current salary, namely, $250,000 per year. For that fee she would not be obliged to pose for any more photographs and would appear on TV and radio only to promote the magazine. But Williams declined the offer.

That was about the extent of Guccione's remorse. He proclaimed the photos to be "the most controversial publication of our time" and—correctly—the biggest media stir about sex since *Deep Throat*. He also pointed out to his critics and to an outraged Middle America that Williams did, after all, pose voluntarily and that it had been the pageant, not he, that forced her to resign.

When an undoubtedly envious Hugh Hefner publicly painted him as the heavy, Guccione responded by characterizing Hefner as "an unmitigated hypocrite." "For the nineteen years I've been publishing *Penthouse*," Guccione pointed out, "I have scrupulously avoided a public mention of his name. To me, it's unethical to personalize the competition between us. Business is business and personal is something else." He noted that *Playboy* had purchased photographs of actress Suzanne Somers taken years earlier, which it had published to great furor when she became famous. Then there were all those policewomen, cheerleaders, and female marines who lost their jobs after their pictorials appeared in *Playboy*. "I didn't see Hefner offering to help them out," Guccione commented.

After Williams chose to bring suit against Chiapel, Guccione paid for his defense while intimating that further details of Williams's past would be brought out. In the wake of the uproar he received 2,000 death threats and 250 bomb threats. His response was characteristic: he published a second set of Chiapel's photos of Williams, while hinting that the magazine was negotiating to buy even more shocking photos from another photographer, Greg Whitman.

Williams acknowledged that she had signed a model's release for Whitman's photographs. Yet she continued to deny signing the release for Chiapel, even though Guccione insisted a handwriting expert had verified her signature. In January 1985 *Penthouse* published the third set of photographs starring Vanessa Williams, this time wearing chains, handcuffs, and leather restraints. Humiliated and disgraced, she retired from public view—only to rise from the ashes years later as a major recording star and Broadway actress, the only Miss America in history to achieve a level of stardom that guaranteed she would be remembered for more than a perfect figure and expertise with a baton.

PART FIVE

R E S O L U T I O N

1984 - the Present

Chapter 15

The Bonfire of the Fantasies

EARLY IN THE EVENING OF JULY 10, 1984, A DISTURBED, HEAVYSET YOUNG WOMAN named Ruth Christenson approached Shinder's bookstore in downtown Minneapolis, doused herself with gasoline, and sparked a lighter. As Christenson ran screaming through the store, a frantic clerk and several bystanders wrapped her in rubberized carpets and smothered the flames. After the ambulance left, the bystanders noticed a carton of bullets spilling out of the backpack she had left behind, along with leaflets attacking pornography. At nearby Hennepin County Medical Center, Christenson reportedly mumbled something to a nurse about mounting a protest against pornography. But why choose Shinder's, which offered a wide range of books and magazines and by no stretch of the imagination could be considered an adult bookstore?

Raised in a local suburb, the daughter of a Methodist minister, Christenson was a loner who changed religions frequently and opposed smoking, drugs, and drinking. As a teenager she had been abducted and raped, and four years prior to her immolation attempt she had committed herself to a mental health center in south Minneapolis for several years. Christenson subsequently told a female friend she had been raped a second time during a walk around a nearby lake while on a day pass from the institution. Some time after her discharge, Christenson became active in the peace movement and volunteered at a shelter for battered women. In the spring of 1984 she began showing up at antipornography demonstrations, where she came under the thrall of Andrea Dworkin.

The previous fall, Dworkin and Catharine MacKinnon had begun teaching a class at the University of Minnesota on pornography that examined how it lay at the root of every form of exploitation and discrimination of women by men. But when Dworkin and MacKinnon were invited to appear before a public hearing on a new Minneapolis zoning law intended to contain the city's adult business, they testified against the zoning strategy and offered a surprising new tactic instead. Railing at the city council for tolerating pornography in the first place, Dworkin and MacKinnon suggested a civil rights approach to eliminate, rather than merely regulate, the problem.

In response, the city council hired MacKinnon and Dworkin to draft an ordinance defining pornography as a violation of women's civil liberties and allowing any woman acting "as a woman" to sue to prevent the distribution of words or pictures presenting women "as sexual objects" through "postures or positions of submission or servility or display." The ordinance was based on the claim that pornography reinforced male attitudes that encouraged rape. Although MacKinnon and Dworkin acknowledged that no amount of research could predict whether a given man would commit rape after being exposed to pornography, that was not the issue, because when a man did rape a woman, he was targeting not her as an individual, but the entire female sex.

Opponents of the ordinance testified before the city council that its broad definition of pornography—"graphic, sexually explicit subordination of women, whether in words or pictures"—could encompass everything from romance novels geared primarily toward women to works of literary merit like *Ulysses* and Anaïs Nin's diaries. During a debate between MacKinnon and Nan Hunter of the Feminist Anti-Censorship Task Force (FACT) on a Sunday morning TV program, a young woman in the audience asked what the proposed Minneapolis legislation meant to lesbian publications like *On Our Backs* that dealt explicitly with sexuality. MacKinnon's reply was that a woman who needed pornography as part of her sexuality had no right to that sexuality.

Dworkin and Christenson were among those who addressed the city council. In an earnest but rambling presentation, Christenson read from a thirty-page agenda she had prepared, which included a warning to male doctors to keep their "hands off assault victims" and calling for the death sentence for "all pimps, rapists, wife-beaters of women." Linda Lovelace Marchiano—now a Long Island housewife and mother of two—also testified: "Every time someone sees *Deep Throat,* they're seeing me being raped."

Dr. Edward Donnerstein, a University of Wisconsin psychologist, testified that it was the violent context of pornography, and not its sexual explicitness, that stimulated aggressive behavior in men. In his controlled experiments, college men were first aroused to anger by a woman, then shown different films, some violent, some pornographic but without violence, some featuring violence toward women but with no sexual content, and the fourth lacking both sex and violence. Then they were asked to administer an electrical shock to the woman who had angered them.

The main factor contributing to their willingness to administer higher shocks was "the aggressive nature of the film," Donnerstein said, concluding that aggressive pornography was linked to lessened inhibitions about rape and "a general pattern of behavior and attitudes" that encouraged a negative reaction toward women. He defined aggressive pornography as including "objectification and female submissiveness"—in other words, as including R-rated movies and magazines like *Playboy* and *Penthouse*.

After hearing such testimony, the city council approved the ordinance, but Mayor Donald Fraser vetoed it. The council then ratified a slightly amended version of the ordinance, but the mayor again vetoed it. Council member Charlee Hoyt, a Republican feminist who sponsored the antipornography bill, kept a candle burning in her office since the first defeat of the measure that she refused to extinguish until the bill passed.

In the meantime, the mayor of Indianapolis, having learned of MacKinnon and Dworkin's legislative strategy, invited them to introduce similar legislation in his city. The Indianapolis ordinance passed, but not before legislators had narrowed the definition of pornography to concentrate on violent pornography—"a compromise we're not too happy about," said Dworkin. Her supporters called it "the *Playboy* exemption."

Nevertheless, the law—framed as an amendment to Indianapolis's civil rights ordinance—made the city the first to define pornography as a form of sex discrimination. The legislation allowed individuals to sue in civil court to ban sexually explicit materials and to collect damages. It also marked the first time that radical feminists had joined forces with conservative Republican politicians and fundamentalists.

Less than ninety minutes after the legislation was signed into law, a collection of publishers, booksellers, broadcasters, and librarians joined with the ACLU to seek an injunction against it. The injunction was upheld in federal court, prompting the city of Indianapolis to file an appeal. The Minneapolis City Council decided to await the ruling before taking up the matter for a third time themselves.

It was at this juncture that Christenson attempted to immolate herself. Before heading off to Shinder's, she mailed copies of a four-page letter to Mayor Fraser and Charlee Hoyt. In the letter, which was an attack on pornography, Christenson said that "society has never and will never recognize me but as a piece of meat." Later, employees of the downtown YWCA where she had checked in a few days before found a rifle in her fifth-floor room.

At the end of September 1984, Christenson was discharged from the hospital to recuperate in seclusion. In 1985, a U.S. Federal Appeals Court ruled the proposed Indianapolis law unconstitutional.

* * *

AFTER RONALD REAGAN was elected president in 1980, Al Regnery, the former Wisconsin also-ran for county attorney and husband of alleged rape victim Christina, published a paper under the auspices of the conservative Heritage Foundation urging that the new administration put an end to the Legal Services Corporation, which provided free legal counseling for the poor. Soon afterward, his mentor, Paul Laxalt, a conservative senator from Nevada, urged Regnery to apply for the office of president of Legal Services. The American Bar Association, which strongly supported the continuation of Legal Services, immediately opposed the appointment.

Before long, rumors about what had happened in Madison on Halloween eve 1976 were circulating around the Beltway. Legal Services rejected Regnery's application, and he moved to another Justice Department office. But in 1982 he was appointed acting director of the Office of Juvenile Justice and Delinquency Prevention (OJJDP), and his name was put forward for Senate confirmation. The OJJDP's $67 million budget soon became an issue, however, since up to 30 percent of that amount was given over to discretionary grants. The purpose of the office was to encourage states to adopt policies that would help deter juveniles from committing criminal offenses. But the discretionary aspect of the budget, combined with Regnery's dubious reputation, led the *Capital Times* and other local newspapers to demand copies of Madison police reports, and soon they were pointing out contradictions in Regnery's statements about the attack. Even Regnery's former law partners in Madison expressed skepticism. The doctor who treated the baby Christina had been carrying at the time of the attack revealed that it was born with a drug dependency. In view of the mounting questions, the Senate moved to delay consideration of the appointment until an FBI field investigation was completed.

But by April 1983 the Senate Judiciary Committee was immersed in the nomination of Sandra Day O'Connor to the Supreme Court and presumably did not give the FBI report (which contained details of Christina's alleged rape, her drug problems, and the couple's hard-core porn collection) on Regnery its full attention. Though opposed by both Wisconsin senators, the nomination was approved in early May.

The very next month, Regnery's office released a memo written by deputy Robert Heck, the former canine supervisor for the Massachusetts State Police bloodhound unit. Heck's memo called for $8 million in grants to study the impact of pornography on the divorce rate, homosexuality, and the abuse of women. As Reagan's de facto porn czar, Regnery was eager above all to subsidize the research of Dr. Judith Reisman, a former songwriter for the children's television show *Captain Kangaroo* and a self-proclaimed expert on pornography.

In 1981 Reisman had collaborated with Edward Eichel, a Manhattan psychotherapist, on a then unpublished book titled *Kinsey, Sex and Fraud: The*

Indoctrination of a People, which claimed that Kinsey was a statistic-inflating charlatan intent on transforming America into a bisexual nation that considered homosexuality and sex with children normal. They maintained that Kinsey made and collected films of children's sexual behavior. The institute did possess some films of children's sexual behavior, but they had been donated to the institute for research purposes by individuals or by police and law enforcement agencies. One such film, for example, was made by a professional filmmaker who inadvertently filmed his son masturbating while documenting a day in his son's life.

On a 1983 radio program, right-wing columnist Patrick Buchanan interviewed Reisman about a particularly inflammatory claim, that Kinsey had routinely kidnapped and drugged ghetto boys to conduct secret experiments on orgasm and to indulge his pedophilic penchant. A zealous opponent of pornography who also took a jaundiced view of sex research, homosexuality, abortion rights, and sex education, Buchanan endorsed the unpublished book as "social dynamite."

But although Reisman held a doctorate in speech from Case Western Reserve University, she had never published a scientific article or book and had held a full-time appointment at the American University for only three semesters. In her résumé she listed membership in eight "professional organizations," but six of them required no professional credentials.

Nevertheless, Regnery tried to get Congress to approve a staggering $800,000 grant for Reisman to measure neurological changes in men and boys as they looked at sexually explicit photos. When that proposal floundered in the wake of congressional and media criticism, Regnery repackaged the study into the biggest antipornography boondoggle of the century— $734,000 for the ex-songwriter to evaluate the images of children in *Penthouse, Playboy,* and *Hustler* cartoons. Furthermore Regnery proposed to funnel Reisman's grant through the American University, which stood to collect a substantial fee in exchange for hiring her as a professor. When some university officials balked, White House counselor Ed Meese's office called to urge the appointment. Meese's wife, Ursula, was a member of the university's board of directors.

In her study, Reisman clipped cartoons from every issue of *Playboy, Penthouse,* and *Hustler* published since their foundings. She then went on to identify 2,016 cartoons and 3,988 other visuals involving children, such as photographs or drawings. Of these latter, 681 were pseudochildren—that is, adults posing as children. The total count came to 6,004 child-linked images—an average of 6.4 per issue for *Penthouse,* 8.2 for *Playboy,* and 14.1 for *Hustler.* Reisman also condemned the cartoons of Gahan Wilson and the photographs of Helmut Newton for featuring shaved genitals, "a troublesome new phenomenon."

Reisman's study proved so embarrassingly unscientific it was never released by the Justice Department. Regnery, meanwhile, resigned his post just days before the *New Republic* published his admission that he kept erotic magazines in his house. Reisman later charged that her "research effort was wrongfully gutted and subverted" by American University.

In 1984, when President Reagan signed the Child Protection Act, he also directed Attorney General William French Smith to establish a commission "to determine the nature, extent, and impact on society of pornography in the United States" and to recommend ways it could be contained, consistent with constitutional guarantees.

On February 22, 1985, Smith's successor, Edwin Meese III, established the commission, with a budget of $500,000. Henry E. Hudson, who as a commonwealth attorney in Virginia had closed down every adult bookstore and theater in Arlington County, was appointed chairman, prompting ACLU legislative counsel Barry Lynn to remark, "I'm afraid there is a train marked 'censorship' which has just left the station." Executive director Alan Sears, another antiporn zealot, had been chief of the Criminal Division of the U.S. Attorney's Office for western Kentucky. Other commission members included radio evangelist James C. Dobson, author of *Dare to Discipline*, the bible of tough-love parenting, and Father Bruce Ritter, founder of Covenant House, which operated shelters for homeless children in New York, Houston, and Toronto. Revered on the antipornography circuit, Ritter had once charged in a fund-raising advertisement that a Fortune 500 company operated a sex ring, providing young boys to pedophiliac clients. A few years later, Ritter himself would be exposed as a practicing pedophile.

In November, the Department of Justice also created the National Obscenity Endowment Unit (NOEU) in Washington, D.C. Consisting of a law center and task force, and headed up by Meese's special assistant Robert Showers, NOEU planned to go after a "$6–$8 billion industry" that Showers claimed was "responsible for abusing thousands of American women and children every year." Clearly the Reagan administration, in tandem with the Christian Right, had elevated pornography to a major issue.

The hearings of the Meese Commission were scheduled to be held in six cities across the country, focusing respectively on First Amendment issues, research into the effects of pornography on sexual and aggressive behavior, the production and distribution of pornography, child pornography, and the involvement of organized crime within the industry.

At the first hearing, in Washington, D.C., Andrea Dworkin asserted that pornography was an $8-billion-a-year industry, or more than the conventional film and record industries combined. Yet FBI special agent Kenneth

Lanning, who also testified at the hearing, had once declared that kiddie porn was essentially a cottage industry in which private practitioners traded photographs of young children on the black market "like baseball cards." Later he admitted privately that no one knew the scope of the pornography industry at large.

At the Houston hearings, University of Wisconsin psychologist Edward Donnerstein was billed as a star witness. Yet the darling of the antipornography movement refused to make a direct causal link between pornography and violence and generally repeated his testimony before the Minneapolis City Council. "The most calloused [sic] attitudes and the highest percentage [among the college males in his study] indicating some likelihood to rape were found in the aggression-only condition. The X-rated, sex-only film was the lowest. The research thus suggests that violence against women need not occur in a pornographic or sexually explicit context for the depictions to have an impact on both attitudes and behavior."

Violent films without sex such as *Rambo,* according to Donnerstein, caused the same changes in attitude as sexually violent ones. But the commissioners did not want to hear that kind of testimony because *Rambo* star Sylvester Stallone was a frequent visitor to the Reagan White House (as were Ritter and Dobson).

John Money also testified in Houston, lecturing the panel on the biology of arousal and dismissing the notion that perversion was contagious. A man's taste in pornography, he argued, was determined by his early sexual development, or "lovemap." "The sequence is that the lovemap comes first, the homemade pornography second, and the commercial pornography third," he testified. "Commercial pornography, if it matches the lovemap, is a ready-made, mass-produced substitute for the homemade variety." But since lovemaps developed in each generation independently of commercial pornography, the prohibition of commercial pornography would only succeed in creating a black market for professional racketeers.

Not surprisingly, pornography found a friendlier audience at the hearings in Los Angeles, the hard-core headquarters of the world, where 80 percent of XXX-rated videos were produced and distributed, grossing $550 million annually. Los Angeles also consumed more pornography than any other city in the world, with forty-nine adult motels showing hard-core films, thirty-eight adult bookstores, twenty-five adult theaters, and twenty-seven known prostitution-related parlors. Bill Margold, a veteran porn actor, critic, and publicist, beseeched the panel not to bomb the trade back into the stone age of grainy blue movies, warning: "Forcing it underground would only result in encouraging unconscientious factions to spuriously create and unpalpably supply lesser materials of a far more objectionable nature."

On the other hand, former *Playboy* centerfold Miki Garcia, who had risen quickly in the *Playboy* organization to become coordinator of Playmate Promotions before leaving the organization, emotionally testified to the presence of indiscriminate drug use in Hefner's Los Angeles mansion, as well as forced sex (including her own rape at the hands of an unidentified celebrity), a prostitution ring involving Playmates, and the bought silence of the police.

Dr. Ted McIlvenna, head of the Exodus Trust archives in San Francisco, also testified. The Exodus Trust owned perhaps the largest collection of historic and contemporary pornography ever assembled. The contemporary collection, which began around 1960, contained an estimated 525,000 items, including 193,000 books, magazines, and periodicals; 260,000 photographs; 61,000 films; 5,000 sexual enhancers; and 8,000 videotapes. In subsequent years McIlvenna's collection of videotapes was to soar into the hundreds of thousands as pornographers dumped their merchandise into his warehouses as a tax write-off. McIlvenna explained to the commissioners that 95 percent of the pornography industry was "commercial"; the rest was divided between "educational" products (so-called better sex videos) and a private network of home producers who traded videos and still photography.

In Miami, where child pornography was the official topic, detective Mike Berish, head of the city's antiporn squad, noted that kiddie porn was "very, very tough to get"—even under the counter. This assessment was echoed at the New York hearing, when FBI agent William Kelly, the agency's foremost expert on pornography, confessed, "People don't like me to say this, but it's true. Kiddie porn has never been more than 1 percent of the total problem. But it gets 99 percent of the grease."

But in New York questions about child pornography were eclipsed by feminist intramural politics. Defenders of pornography, including a number of porn actresses and some members of FACT, pointed to inconsistencies in feminist ideology. For example, they asked, if a pro-choice position on abortion meant defending women's rights to control their own bodies, why could not women choose to exhibit their bodies in pornography? Author Nancy Friday poured fuel on the fire by suggesting in her testimony that the real reason many women objected to pornography was their deeply ingrained feeling that their genitals were unclean. Feminists' opposition to pornography, she went on, had come to see the biological attractiveness of women to men as a wrong in itself.

The high point of the New York hearing was the appearance of Linda Lovelace Marchiano, pornography's most famous victim, who once again revealed that she was forced by threat of death to make *Deep Throat*. In her testimony, Marchiano made a strong appeal for early sex education. "The biggest mistake my parents made was that they protected me too much," she told the panel. "Growing up, I didn't know what a prostitute or a hooker was. If I had known . . ." But the radical feminist contingent emphasized porn films' victimization of women, whom they claimed were routinely beaten, humiliated, forced to have sex with animals, tortured, hung from trees, and sometimes even murdered. The hearings reached an emotional peak when Andrea Dworkin pleaded with the commissioners "to go and cut that woman down and untie her hands and take the gag out of her mouth, and do something, for her freedom." Several commissioners were visibly moved, Commissioner Dietz to tears.

Dworkin also testified that, although she herself had never seen a snuff film, they were allegedly available in the Las Vegas area for $2,500–$3,000 per print. "We have information from prostitutes from all parts of the country that they are being forced to watch snuff films before then being forced to engage in heavily sadomasochistic acts," she said. None of the commissioners asked for proof.

Perhaps sensing a stacked jury, such pro-sex celebrities as Dr. Ruth Westheimer, Alex Comfort, Betty Friedan, and Dr. June Reinisch, director of the Kinsey Institute, were no-shows. Writers Gay Talese and Kurt Vonnegut, however, were among those who issued denunciations of the hearings.

IN THE EARLY 1980s a boyhood friend of Reuben Sturman's paid him a visit in Los Angeles, where he kept a condo.

"There's a girl I want you to meet," the friend told him.

"How old is she?" Sturman asked.

"Twenty-one."

"Are you out of your fucking mind?" Sturman said. "Do you know how old we are?"

But the friend persisted. "She wants to meet you. I told her all about you. She wants an older man."

Sturman insisted that he wasn't interested, but six months later the friend tried again, and Sturman agreed to meet the woman. Her name was Naomi Delgado. He took her to dinner in the Valley and found her mature beyond her years, very bright, and more beautiful than any woman he had ever seen.

After dinner Sturman said, "I'll take you home now."

But Naomi asked, "Don't you live around here somewhere?"

Twenty minutes later they were in bed, and it did not take much longer for Sturman to be smitten. He began to see Naomi frequently and even got a face lift. After Naomi got pregnant, they were married. The King was convinced theirs was one of history's great love affairs.

Sturman also maintained his defiance toward the feds, who were regrouping in the courts for another attack on his empire. At a 1984 Christmas party for his employees at Swingo's restaurant in Cleveland's Statler Hotel, Sturman gave an uncharacteristic pep talk on the limitless future of the video market and vowed to fight any government agency barring his way. Then he signaled for a screen to drop from the ceiling of the grand ballroom, and the revelers were treated to a fifteen-minute mock porn flick featuring Sturman in a variety of skits—as Pinocchio, as a cowboy looking at a Wanted poster of himself, as a dreamer awakened by Naomi. Everybody laughed at the boss's antics until the final scenario, in which Sturman portrayed a "dirty old man" approaching a group of schoolgirls playing ring around the rosey. In the fade-out Naomi pulled him away to the accompaniment of Maurice Chevalier singing "Thank Heaven for Little Girls." As all of Sovereign's nervous employees knew, even joking about child porn was not funny. And pornography in general was so heavily under fire that during the Meese Commission hearings Sturman parked eighteen-wheelers outside his Shaker Heights home to deter picketers.

Meanwhile, IRS agent Richard Rosfelder and up to seventy-five other agents slaved away, trying to figure out who owned what and where in the smoke-and-mirrors kingdom of kink that Sturman had created. Eventually Rosfelder wrote to the Swiss government, informing it that a certain Reuben Sturman belonged to a hierarchy of U.S. crime families and had been involved in twenty-eight murders. Unknown to Sturman, a treaty existed between the United States and Switzerland that allowed IRS investigators to examine secret bank accounts if the holder of the account was a "leader" of organized crime. When a highly placed Swiss friend quietly informed Sturman of the letter, he replied: "What? Twenty-eight murders! I was involved in only one death, and that was when some guy in Buffalo masturbating at a booth had a heart attack. And he died with a smile on his face."

In 1985 the U.S. Justice Department brought a sixteen-count indictment in Cleveland against Sturman, his thirty-three-year-old son, David, and four other associates, charging that they had funneled more than $7 million through Swiss bank accounts held under a variety of fictitious corporate names and accounts. Meese himself announced the indictment to underscore its importance. Sturman was arrested in Los Angeles and held on a $3 million cash bond. Among those who put up bail money was his fellow Ohioan and confidant, Larry Flynt.

Cocky as ever, Sturman arrived for his grand jury appearances in an assortment of disguises, most notoriously as Groucho Marx, partly to hide his face from the press, but also as a signal to the opposition that his lawyers would squash this latest nuisance like a fly. Meanwhile an item in *The Wall Street Journal* describing the Porn King's tax troubles had him besieged by investment bankers wanting to take him public.

Soon after the grand jury handed down its indictment, Sturman secretly began to sell off his enterprises to his many partners. By 1988 Sturman claimed he no longer owned anything and was out of the pornography business. But because many of his sales contracts were verbal, it was impossible to determine whether he had genuinely divested himself or was only trying to elude the IRS with another layer of obfuscation. Meanwhile, he and his associates spent weeks shredding documents.

When they were subpoenaed, members of his inner circle either invoked the Fifth or perjured themselves. But Rosfelder, in tandem with Assistant U.S. Attorney Craig Morford, kept up the pressure, subpoenaing employees and threatening them with jail time and fines if they perjured themselves or colluded in Sovereign's various schemes to launder money or evade taxes. The warehouse employees worked in constant fear of infiltration by undercover agents and informers. Sturman's management team routinely administered lie detector tests, while video cameras peered into every corner.

Finally, two Sturman loyalists cracked. A bookkeeper tipped Rosfelder off to hundreds of corporate documents that had not yet been shredded, and the IRS found them in the basement of the home of Sturman's housekeeper. And Sturman's longtime private secretary testified that she had plucked the names of corporate officers from telephone books and novels like *Lost Horizon.*

In the fall of 1989, fifteen years after Rosfelder began his manhunt, Morford finally succeeded in bringing Sturman to trial in Cleveland. Simultaneously, Sturman was facing trial in Las Vegas, where federal prosecutors claimed he and Ralph Levine were selling obscene materials. Unknown to Sturman, Levine began cooperating with the prosecutors, revealing corporate secrets.

In Cleveland, Sturman was convicted of evading $3.5 million in taxes, and in February 1990 he was sentenced to ten years in prison and fined $2.5 million. The IRS wasted no time in placing liens on his homes in Van Nuys and Shaker Heights and even confiscated his beloved 1964 Rolls-Royce and several valuable Dutch and Belgian paintings when he tried to move them out of the house. The Rolls was later returned, but little else.

Things really began to unravel for Sturman following the death of the owner of Pleasure World, an adult bookstore in Phoenix. After his widow took over, she noticed that $1,000 monthly payments were being made to a certain Reuben Sturman, but she failed to find a bill or contract to justify the outlay. When she stopped making the payments, Sturman called to explain the arrangement—her husband had "bought" the store—but she ignored his threats and harangues. Around Thanksgiving of 1991 Sturman decided to send her a serious message. He arranged through intermediaries for thugs to smash up the store's video machines. The message was very effective, and the payments immediately resumed.

In March 1992, Sturman again arranged through the same intermediaries to smash up eight porn shops in Chicago and four in Milwaukee that were also not paying what federal prosecutors characterized as extortion money but Sturman later insisted were mortgage installments. To further complicate matters, the twelve stores were now making their "monthly payments" directly to the IRS, which wanted to collect back taxes from Sturman.

This time, though, the thugs decided to use bombs instead of hammers. Driving east on Chicago's Division Street, one of the men reached into the backseat, took a bomb out of a bag, and put it on his lap. Moments later it exploded, killing him almost instantly. A few days later, the dead man's three accomplices turned themselves in, knowing they were as good as convicted. The ringleader had unwisely used a Visa card to rent the blown-up car.

And so, with a small but deadly bang, did the biggest XXX-rated empire in the history of the world come to an uncertain end. The whimpering came later, when all the co-conspirators turned state's evidence, including even David, the prodigal son in pornography's biggest kingdom.

In October 1984 *The New York Times* ran a feature on the front page of the science section on Dr. Patrick Carnes and his organization, Sex Addicts Anonymous (SAA). A tall, reddish-haired man in his forties, Carnes claimed that one in twelve Americans were sex junkies who needed help. At the registration desks at workshops he gave around the country, applicants were asked to fill out a twenty-five-item "Sexual Addiction Screening Test." A sex addict was anyone who answered "yes" to such questions as "Have you subscribed [to] or regularly purchased sexually explicit magazines like *Playboy* or *Penthouse?*" and "Do you often find yourself preoccupied with sexual thoughts?" Respondents then computed their score, in this singularly unscientific test, to determine how much of a sex addict they were or might become.

Carnes, who described himself as a "recovering academic," preached his gospel with evangelical fervor at the workshops, which cost $175 apiece. He also directed the Family Renewal Center at Fairview Southdale Hospital in Minneapolis, a hospital program treating sex addiction in more than six hundred families per year. According to Carnes, sexual activity became an addiction when it led to financial burden, lost work time, or a disrupted family life. Carnes, who had once been obese, thought overeating was a more useful analogy for sex addiction because while alcoholics had to give up drink altogether, food and sex were basic needs that addicts had to learn to consume in moderation. Carnes did, however, ask sex addicts to enter into a twelve-week celibacy contract that excluded even masturbation, because it "keeps the fantasy alive at an addictive level."

The guidelines for treating sex addicts in the SAA were identical to the ones used by AA—confession of addiction and constant peer support and encouragement in order to keep from regressing to former patterns of behavior. Most sex addicts, according to Carnes, were overly involved in masturbation, pornography, prostitution, and habitual heterosexual or homosexual promiscuity. Those activities became addictions when they began to interfere with daily living. At the pathological level were such sex addicts as rapists and child molesters.

But most sexologists scorned the notion of sex addiction. "No one can really define sexual excess," William Masters observed. "Like premature ejaculation, such concepts are defined within the couple unit." Dr. Paul Gebhard thought it was "almost impossible for males to overdo sex. Erectile capacity has a built-in safety catch." Helen Singer Kaplan also denied the existence of sexual addiction, except in cases of pathological hypersexuality. Yet hypersexuality, referring to people with unusually high libidos, was an imprecise term that varied according to culture and psychiatric standard. Sex anthropologist Helen Fisher noted that most Kuikuru Indians of Brazil copulated daily, as did many Polynesians, who believed that sex was good for the circulation, muscles, menstrual cramps, and the maintenance of a loving relationship. But the last word belonged to Mary Calderone, the doyenne of sex educators, who once declared: "There is no such thing as too much sex."

One issue that divided therapists, however, was how to treat promiscuity among gay men, a question that divided gay men themselves. Even more than herpes, which heightened concerns about promiscuity among heterosexuals, AIDS precipitated the issue among gay men; but many were also motivated by dissatisfaction with a promiscuous lifestyle. Sexual Compulsives Anonymous, a gay group that met weekly at New York's Gay and Lesbian Community Services Center in Greenwich Village, consisted mostly of white, well-dressed men from twenty to their late forties, although the only requirement for membership was a desire to stop having compulsive sex. The SCA Preamble declared that the group's purpose was not "to repress our God-given sexuality, but to learn how to express it in ways that will not endanger our mental, physical, and spiritual health." Most members were less interested in learning safe sex than in achieving chastity, however. Members called one another on the phone if they felt an urge to cruise the bars or baths. If SCA kept gay men from engaging in high-risk sex, members asked, what was so wrong?

What was so wrong was the SCA's self-flagellating approach to sex, said critics. Michael Quadland, a Manhattan sex therapist and regular contributor to the gay magazine *New York Native,* thought the issue was not sexual frequency, but impulse control. Truly compulsive people did not choose when to have sex or with whom; rather, anxiety dictated their behavior. The proper recourse for treating such behavior was not attendance at a sex addicts group, but a visit to a therapist.

* * *

THANKS TO EXAGGERATED CLAIMS about their prevalence and profitability, the emotionally charged subjects of child pornography and snuff movies remained easy and perennial targets for fundamentalists and radical feminists. Snuff films, in fact, got their name in the 1970s from a group led by Charles Keating that called itself Citizens for Decency in Literature (later the Campaign for Decency through Law, or CDL), which alleged that the hard-core porn industry was torturing and killing female performers on camera and claimed to have proof. But when Adult Film Association of America (AFAA) president David Friedman called on the CDL to hand over its evidence to the authorities so that action could be taken, nothing happened.

Major pornographers had everything to lose and little to gain by producing pornography that focused on pathological depravity rather than on the usual mindless pleasures. Less than 2 percent of all pornography even depicted fantasy rape or other forms of violent sex. Moreover, in countries where SM and rape-fantasy porn was readily available, it nevertheless failed to attract more than a negligible male audience. But the issue of snuff films was kept alive not only by fanaticism but by film footage allegedly circulating among antipornography organizations that depicted real sexual atrocities inflicted on both male and female civilian populations by members of the Argentine and Chilean armies; and by assorted other footage showing Honduran, Guatemalan, and Colombian torture teams raping and then murdering women, often simultaneously. Some of this gruesome material was purportedly spliced into a few routine porn flicks—and, in at least one instance, into one of the *Emmanuelle* movies. However, though antiporn activists repeatedly claimed to have either knowledge or actual possession of such films, no evidence to back up such assertions was presented to the Meese Commission, and as recently as September 1996 a spokesman for Amnesty International in New York admitted that no one on staff had ever seen such a film. When U.S. porn producer Alan Shackleton made a sexploitation film shot in Argentina called *Snuff,* about a Charles Manson–like gang, complete with faked mutilations, liberal feminists were justifiably outraged. The AFAA even picketed the Los Angeles cinema showing it, on the theory that with such friends, who needed enemies?

As the prosecution of pornography proceeded inexorably, the inventory of forbidden practices increased exponentially. Bestiality had always been proscribed, but now the censors began to ban scenes depicting golden showers, defecation, pain, and SM. At the same time, it became acceptable to show formerly taboo acts like anal sex, double insertion, orgies, and group sex—a reflection of society's increasing sanction of such acts in private, but also a reflection of the arbitrary and subjective criteria of obscenity on the part of federal prosecutors.

Another antipornography stratagem made life particularly difficult for hard-core pornographers. Under Section 266i of the California penal code, any person procuring another person for the purpose of prostitution was guilty of a felony and subject to three years' imprisonment, with prison mandatory. Since performers were paid to engage in sexual acts for money, some prosecutors attempted to apply the code to hard-core pornographers operating out of North Hollywood. As a result, the production of porn movies was forced underground, with shooting being done in secret locations and, if possible, on Sundays, when more law officers were on holiday.

Another recurring charge leveled against the pornography industry was that the Mafia controlled it, just as it controlled drugs and prostitution. Here, too, the smoke exceeded the fire. It was true that in the late 1960s Robert "Debe" DiBernardo, a leading member of New Jersey's DeCavalcante crime family, had purchased the New York firm Star Distributors Ltd., which specialized in pinup magazines until DiBernardo switched its focus to hardcore. Crime experts had also frequently linked pornographer Mike Thevis both to Star and to New York Mob boss Carlo Gambino. In the fall of 1969 Thevis had attended a Las Vegas convention of porn manufacturers and distributors, where he claimed, according to Mob informant Jimmy Fratianno, to own 90 percent of all peep-show machines in the United States. That brought a sharp retort from DiBernardo. "Don't forget, Mike," the mobster said in a soft voice, "you *manage* those machines. The family is in charge."

Asked why he had sold his percentage of *Deep Throat* for a pittance, director Gerard Damiano said he could not talk about it, explaining, "Do you want me to get both my legs broken?"

Yet the consensus among most people in the pornography industry was that Mob involvement was no more extensive there than in unions, sports, gambling, construction, real estate, politics, and garbage disposal. Though the Mob had a long-term interest in pornography—primarily in distribution, not its manufacture—it did not dominate. Moreover, despite FBI allegations, the American pornography industry was not a cartel but, in the words of porn film critic and insider Bill Margold, more like "the last vestige of independent, rugged individualism." If pornography were a Mafia cartel, why did bootlegging continue to be a major problem?

Charges of child pornography were harder for the industry to evade. By the mid-seventies, magazines and other pornographic media depicting children engaged in explicit sex acts had begun to appear on the shelves of adult bookstores in New York, Los Angeles, Chicago, Minneapolis, and other major cities. Much child pornography was manufactured in Denmark and Holland and, to a lesser extent, in Sweden and West Germany. About 20 percent of what was sold as child pornography was in fact lifted from nudist magazines and depicted children engaged in innocent play. But hard-core child pornography was also readily available in many adult bookstores, inside magazines bearing such titles as *Chicken Little, 200 Boys, Kids, Playtime Pals,* and *Rascals.* A national magazine called *Boy Gazette* even featured classified advertisements for boy lovers from around the world.

Outraged citizens took up the cause and soon gained the support of newspaper editorialists across the country. Within a year or two, in the face of mounting public pressure, adult bookstores removed most child pornography from their stocks, though many continued to sell it under the counter. The 1977 Protection of Children Against Sexual Exploitation Act officially proscribed the sale and commercial exchange of child pornography, which was defined as any obscene visual depiction of a person under age sixteen engaged in any sexual activity, in a state of sexual arousal, or posed in such a way that the genital or anal area was lewdly exhibited. Lewd exhibition of the genital or anal area was defined as extending even to simple nude photographs of a minor under sixteen, since they were subject to the prurient delectation of pedophiles, so that the manufacture, distribution, or possession of any photograph of any nude person under sixteen became a federal crime punishable by up to ten years in prison.

Even after the strict new laws were passed, however, the issue continued to be exploited by law enforcement officials, moral crusaders, politicians, and the media. Legitimate concern passed into moral panic, and news articles, workshops, exposés, and TV programs warning parents and children about kidnappings and sexual advances from strangers, neighbors, and relatives proliferated at an astonishing rate. Laws were passed requiring psychologists, teachers, and other professionals to report any suspicion of sexual abuse or illegality involving a minor. Such requirements made it extremely difficult for counselors like John Money to reach potential sex offenders and to establish a trusting relationship with them. And as claims of sexual abuse reached epidemic proportions, many innocent individuals, parents and nonparents, teachers and day care workers, were falsely accused of crimes involving children that ranged from child brothels, child auctions, and toll-free numbers for ordering child prostitutes to snuff films, Satanic molestation rituals, and motorcycle gang rapes involving children.

Seldom were such charges accompanied by any persuasive evidence. According to Douglas Besharov, director of the conservative American Enterprise Institute, up to 65 percent of all child abuse reports in the United States was probably unfounded, if not malicious. But the impression of a genuine crisis was reinforced by the formation of special units and interagency task forces within the U.S. Customs Office, the U.S. Postal Inspection Service, and the FBI, as well as within various state and local law enforcement and social service agencies, to combat child pornography and pedophilia. Dozens of "sting" operations were launched to entice individuals into trading, selling, purchasing, or receiving child pornography through the mails, resulting in the arrest of hundreds of individuals. Nudists and photographers were particularly fearful of arrest. As a result, the number of depictions of nude children in the pages of art photo books and nudist publications declined significantly, and most sex education books depicting children were permanently withdrawn from the market or heavily censored.

But the crusade continued. Among the most outspoken of the self-appointed experts on child pornography was Judianne Densen-Gerber, founder of the multinational drug rehabilitation organization Odyssey House. In a 1979 mailing to every member of Congress, followed by a highly publicized national tour, Densen-Gerber told stories of forced prostitution, drug addiction, kidnapping, and even murder. She claimed that 264 kiddie porn magazines were being produced monthly and shipped to adult bookstores across the country. She also claimed that 1.2 million children were victims of child pornography and child prostitution. This figure was an extrapolation from a claim made by journalist Robin Lloyd, who in his book *For Money or Love: Prostitution in America* declared that there were three hundred thousand male prostitutes in the United States under the age of eighteen. Densen-Gerber surmised there must be at least as many female prostitutes under eighteen, then doubled the overall figure on the assumption that the problem had been grossly underestimated.

In 1982 the *Albany Times-Union* reported that child pornography was a "$46 billion national industry—a loose network involving 2.4 million youngsters, according to federal statistics." That same year, in *New York* v. *Ferber,* the U.S. Supreme Court ruled that child pornography was not the kind of expression that warranted First Amendment protections and that New York State had the constitutional right to bring criminal charges against someone who "produces, directs, or promotes any performance which includes sexual conduct by a child less than sixteen years of age."

Still, public outcry and pressure from children's advocacy groups continued to tighten the loopholes in the federal antichild porn laws. New legislation increased the penalties for producing, selling, buying, trading, or owning child pornography to as much as fifteen years' imprisonment. The Child Protection Act of 1984 further amended the existing laws against child pornography by removing the stipulation that the depiction be obscene or be commercially exchanged; by extending the age range of the children protected from sixteen to eighteen; and by making it a crime to receive or import child pornography. That year President Reagan also approved the formation of a National Bureau for Missing and Exploited Children to deal with all forms of child abuse.

By the mid-eighties, the subjects of child pornography and child sex abuse had become white-hot subjects for sensational treatments. *Reader's Digest* and HBO (in its movie version of Joseph Wambaugh's *The Glitter Dome*) offered exposés of kiddie porn rings, and the NBC documentary *The Silent Shame,* which aired in August 1984, purported to delve into the world of child pornographers. Masquerading as a pornographer, a reporter interviewed mail marketers in Denmark and a pedophile in Chicago. On the basis of such skimpy evidence, the show claimed that kiddie porn was a "$2 to $3 billion business in America" alone and alleged that child pornography was still pervasive in Denmark.

Shortly after the airing of the documentary, Danish officials conducted a thorough investigation. Berl Kutchinsky, professor of criminology at the University of Copenhagen and Denmark's foremost expert on pornography, reported in 1985: "When the two NBC reporters came back to Denmark to give evidence about their undercover sessions with Danish porn dealers, they also handed over specimens of what they claimed to be Danish-produced child pornography. Examination of these specimens as well as the stocks of the alleged porno exporters showed, however, that no children were involved. Although some of the material may have been considered 'child pornography' according to American laws (the federal age limit appears to be eighteen years), not one single magazine or film contained pictures which qualified as child pornography according to the Danish law."

In April 1986 the issue of child pornography once again made national headlines when a young woman named Nora Kuzma appeared as a centerfold in *Penthouse* magazine, then shortly afterward made national headlines as Traci Lords, West Coast porn superstar. As it turned out, Lords had appeared in dozens of movies and magazines produced between 1984 and 1986 while under the age of eighteen. Soon after, her mother complained to a reporter that her daughter was a minor who had no business being involved in X-rated films. With the issue of child pornography still very much in the news, Lords instantly became a media sensation—even as *Penthouse* executives and porn producers in Hollywood scrambled to destroy every print and negative of Lords in their possession.

On the face of it, both the magazine and the makers of the movie *Such Young Girls* had violated the U.S. Child Protection Act—a serious federal offense, even though it did not appear that Lords had ever complained to anyone about her work in the adult film industry. Moreover, she was deceptively mature in appearance, and she was not portrayed in the magazine as a child. (The title of the film obviously left the viewer to infer Lords's age for himself.) Later it transpired that Lords had used a fake driver's license and fake passport to establish herself as an adult. Subsequently Lords's agent and the producer of *Such Young Girls* were indicted, though *Penthouse,* which destroyed every copy of Lords's photographs in its files, was not. Though the film was withdrawn from circulation in the United States, it continued to be popular in Europe, where the age of legal consent was sixteen.

In 1988 Congress passed the Child Protection and Obscenity Enforcement Act, which required publishers and distributors to document the ages of nude models and performers and to ascertain that they were at least eighteen at the time a photograph or film was made. Because the legislation was retroactive, the photography libraries of soft-core magazines were rendered virtually worthless overnight. Most models and performers who had appeared in existing work could no longer be tracked down, and record keeping for future work promised to become a bureaucratic nightmare.

For even the staunchest champions of freedom of speech, the logic behind most of the legislation and court decisions governing child pornography was unassailable. As the Supreme Court put it in its ruling in *New York* v. *Ferber:* "The prevention of sexual exploitation and abuse of children constitutes a government objective of surpassing importance." But some First Amendment scholars did express concern over a separate concurring opinion in the case by Justice Sandra Day O'Connor that stressed that material with serious literary, scientific, or educational value was not necessarily exempt.

Among those who vigorously opposed such laws and rulings was St. Martin's Press, which in 1975 had published a book titled *Show Me!* by Helga Fleischhauer-Hardt and photographer Will McBride that the new laws made illegal to sell, distribute, or receive. An adaptation of a German sex education book, *Show Me!* contained numerous photographs of young children with their genitals exposed, for the purpose of teaching children their proper names. Yet FBI special agent Kenneth Lanning once called the book "the single item most commonly found in the possession of pedophiles in the United States," illustrating a fundamental truth about child pornography: not only was much of it produced without the informed consent of its subjects, but once produced, it became a tool that child molesters also used in the seduction of other children.

And pedophilia did in fact exist, although with nowhere near the frequency that antipornography crusaders often claimed. Many researchers found that sexual desire toward minors was quite common among "normal" heterosexual men and women. Most pedophiles were male and made no distinction in their affection for boys or girls; the child's innocence was the fetish, which also explained why facial expression was so important in child pornography. And while the pornographic depictions of children ranged from mere nudity to explicitly sexual acts, pedophiles mostly wanted to believe that the child was having a good time.

However, the only active pedophile group in the country, the North American Man-Boy Love Association (NAMBLA), operated entirely within the law, as a lobbying and support organization. Investigations between 1982 and 1986 by the Postal Inspection Service in New York and the U.S. Permanent Subcommittee on Investigations failed to uncover any evidence of ille-

328   ■   WHAT WILD ECSTASY

gal activities by the group. Anyone seeking entrée to an underground of pedophiles was more likely to encounter a vast network of postal inspectors and
police agents. Most practicing pedophiles were loners whose network, if it
existed at all, seldom extended beyond a few other individuals like themselves.

All in all, claims about the extent and nature of child pornography made
during the antipornography fever of the seventies and eighties were greatly
exaggerated. Knowledgeable experts put the number of minors who participated in child pornography from its beginnings to its alleged demise at between five thousand and seven thousand worldwide, most of them between
the ages of seven and fourteen. Relatively few were runaways, drug addicts,
prostitutes, or victims of kidnappings. Most were from middle-class homes
and were well acquainted with the adults for whom they posed. Fewer than
550 commercial child pornography magazines were produced in the United
States and Europe from the late sixties onward that actually showed children
engaged in sexual activity with other children or adults or in lascivious poses;
while another 460 depicted boys in naturist or erotic nude settings. Never a
lucrative business in the United States, kiddie porn was most often cheaply
produced for a very limited audience.

Today there is no commercial production of magazines or videotapes depicting child sexual activity in either the United States or Europe; where it
does exist, it is mostly on an amateur basis and created primarily for private
viewing.

WHILE THE MEESE COMMISSION met in Chicago, Sheena Easton danced at a
celebration of her "Sugar Walls" ("The blood races to your private spots /
Lets me know there's a fire . . ."). From the oppressive censorship of the late
fifties, music had now come around 180 degrees to the point where no sexual
subject was forbidden. Rock plumbed perversion: boot fetishism (Iggy Pop's
"Sixteen"), coprophilia (Lou Reed in "Dirt"), statutory rape ("Lost
Paraguayos" by Rod Stewart), male hustling (the Rolling Stones' "When the
Whip Comes Down"), and father-daughter incest ("Janie's Got a Gun" by
Aerosmith). Two of the most notorious rock songs of the eighties were
Prince's "Darling Nikki," about a young woman in a hotel lobby "mastur-
bating with a magazine"; and Madonna's celebration of a young woman's loss
of virginity in "Like a Virgin."

Alarmed by such antics, in 1985 a group called the Parents' Music Re-
source Center (PMRC) formed. Its members were mothers who lived in the
Washington, D.C., area, many of them the wives of powerful men: Tipper
Gore, wife of Al Gore, then a senator from Tennessee; Susan Baker, wife of
Secretary of the Treasury James Baker; Georgie Packwood, wife of Senator

Robert Packwood of Oregon; and Nancy Thurmond, wife of Senator Strom Thurmond of South Carolina. Before long the PMRC had attracted favorable attention from *Newsweek, The Washington Post, U.S. News & World Report,* and various TV shows and had persuaded the Senate Commerce Committee (of which Al Gore was a member) to hold full-scale hearings on the rising plague of rock lyrics, noting that some lyrics "promote defiled sexuality, satanic worship, violence, and even rebellion."

Back in 1971 Vice President Spiro Agnew had launched a similar effort to clean up the lyrics of rock songs, grimly intimating that otherwise radio stations would lose their licenses. His warning was itself an echo of an effort by Asa Carter, executive director of the North Carolina White Citizens Council, who in 1956 proclaimed the start of a national purge of jukeboxes because the NAACP had "infiltrated" southern white teenagers with "rock and roll music." (Never mind that country music and blues had featured bawdy lyrics for decades, such as this Arkansas square dance call:

> Goose that gal and watch her prance.
> Ladies do the shimmy, down goes her britches,
> In goes a little thing about six inches.)

At the time, the record industry was trying to get Congress to approve a bill allowing it to collect a royalty on blank tapes in compensation for the home copying of commercial record releases. The PMRC wanted a quid pro quo. It proposed that LPs and CDs be labeled according to a rating system: X for sexually explicit or profane lyrics or lyrics containing heavy references to violence or suicide; D/A for lyrics glorifying the use of drugs or alcohol; O for occult; V for violence. Through its well-publicized hearings and letter-writing campaigns, the Parents' Music Resource Center succeeded in persuading record companies voluntarily to identify recordings with explicit lyrics, though the ratings system was rejected.

In February 1986, just months before the Meese Commission was set to issue its final report, the commission dealt soft-core a blow from which it has never recovered. Perhaps sensing that, though all the battles had been won, the media war against pornography was lost, that the commission itself was no more than a sop to the Christian Right and radical feminists whose findings would change nothing, executive director Alan Sears wrote a letter on behalf of the commission, on Justice Department stationery.

The letter was addressed to twenty-three companies identified during the hearings as "major players in the game of pornography." Attached to the letter was a copy of testimony, with the name of the witness removed. The testimony stated that 7-Eleven was the single most important outlet for

Penthouse and that the chain also sold 20 percent of all copies of *Playboy.* Other major venues of soft-core included the Rite-Aid drugstore chain and Kmart, owner of Waldenbooks. Though the letter did not charge that any laws were being violated, he gave the companies three weeks to respond to the charges, threatening to publish the testimony in its final report if they did not. He concluded ominously, "Failure to respond will necessarily be accepted as an indication of no objection."

That testimony had been presented, in fact, by pornography's most outspoken male foe, the fundamentalist Reverend Donald Wildmon. Wildmon, the son of a VD investigator for the Mississippi Health Department, was the founder of both the National Federation for Decency, headquartered in Tupelo and claiming 350 chapters nationwide, and the American Family Association, the most effective pro-censorship group in the history of the United States, with more than 500 chapters around the country. For years Wildmon had been putting pressure on the CVS drugstore chain to drop *Playboy* and *Penthouse* from its 600 shops.

The letter had the intended effect—7-Eleven, Rite-Aid, and some others dropped *Playboy, Penthouse,* and other sexually explicit magazines from their inventory. If they could not inspire widespread grass-roots antipornography campaigns, Sears and Wildmon would settle for corporate capitulation for the time being. But in May *Penthouse,* the American Booksellers Association, and others filed suit against Meese, Sears, and the Meese Commission, seeking a retroactive injunction against Sears's letter. *Playboy* put out a call for a December pictorial entitled "Women of 7-Eleven." Meanwhile, Ron Reagan Jr. remained a regular contributor to the magazine, and Reagan's daughter Patti would eventually pose nude in its pages.

Judge John Garrett Penn of the Federal District Court in Washington, D.C., ruled that Sears's threat amounted to "a prior restraint of speech" and granted the injunction, directing the commission to send out a second letter to the twenty-three companies informing them that their names would not be listed in the final report. But the damage had been done. The removal of *Playboy* and *Penthouse* from ten thousand stores across the country, including the mammoth 7-Eleven and Rite-Aid chains, sent the circulations of both magazines plummeting. Even after the injunction had been issued, and long after the Meese Commission became only a memory, the cowed retail giants refused to reinstate the two magazines, even though they had been an extremely lucrative source of revenue.

Sears's maneuver was a sign of the times. The baby boom generation that had turned sexual morality on its head during the giddy sixties and seventies was sliding into comfortable middle age. Pornography, singles bars, and promiscuity were on the wane and were fast being replaced by marriage, monogamy, and children—not to mention herpes, AIDS, and a relentless

litany of bad news about sex: sexual harassment, sex addiction, satanic pedophilia, date rape. A 1986 *Time* magazine poll reported that 63 percent of
women now thought sexually explicit movies, magazines, and books led men
to commit rape; 47 percent of men thought so, too. Some 49 percent of men
also wanted homosexual acts between men to be outlawed by federal or state
governments, and 40 percent of women concurred. The entire country was
taking a long guilt trip, with no end in sight.

IN 1985, Donald Wildmon had determined that 74.3 percent of all sexual intercourse depicted on TV was between unmarried people. As a result, his
American Family Association began targeting such TV shows as *The Wonder
Years, Head of the Class,* and *A Different World.* In 1989 it made headlines by
successfully pressuring General Mills, Ralston Purina, and Domino's Pizza
to withdraw advertising from the highly rated *Saturday Night Live,* many of
whose skits it also deemed offensive.

Wildmon's biggest weapon was the boycott, whether threatened or actual.
By threatening a boycott, he was able, for example, to persuade Pepsi-Cola,
in a much publicized brouhaha, to discontinue a TV commercial featuring
Madonna because she used religious symbols in her videos. Other targets that
Wildmon successfully opposed, insofar as he succeeded in persuading advertisers to drop sponsorship, were such TV shows as *L.A. Law, Cheers, In the
Heat of the Night, The Magical World of Disney,* and *60 Minutes.* He was also
in the forefront of censors attacking Martin Scorsese's allegedly blasphemous
The Last Temptation of Christ. In 1989, learning of an Andres Serrano photograph entitled *Piss Christ* and its indirect funding by the National Endowment for the Arts (NEA), Wildmon instigated—through full-page
newspaper advertisements and a barrage of letters to Congress—a furious
and still ongoing debate in and out of Congress about the organization's future.

Another enemy of the NEA was Wildmon's fellow southerner, North
Carolina senator Jesse Helms, who considered himself a spiritual leader in
the battle "for the preservation of Western civilization as we have known it
for thousands of years." A strong opponent of federally funded abortions,
Helms was a former TV and radio editorialist who had parlayed his stock-
in-trade invective, innuendo, and guilt by association into a statewide political base. Like his forerunner Joe McCarthy, he was not just another
politician, but an avatar of America's deepest sexual and racial fears and anx-
ieties. He was also a shrewd judge of the political dynamics of cultural issues.

In October 1990 Helms introduced a legislative amendment to prevent the
use of federal funds to "promote, disseminate, or produce obscene or indecent materials, including but not limited to depictions of sadomasochism, ho-

moeroticism, the exploitation of children, or individuals engaged in sex acts, or material which denigrates the objects or beliefs of the adherents of a particular religion or nonreligion." To attract the attention of the media, Helms obtained photographs taken by Robert Mapplethorpe, including one of a black man performing cunnilingus on a white woman. After requesting all women and young pages present to leave—a throwback to another century—he then exhibited the photographs on the floor of the Senate.

Though the amendment was defeated, its sponsorship was a victory for Helms, who did force Congress to approve an amendment that, for the first time in the country's history, restricted federal funding of the arts on the basis of content. A censorial precedent had been established. Though the term "indecent" was omitted from the new law, "obscene" remained, as did the language about sadomasochism, homoeroticism, and other taboo sexual acts.

Another major censor was the city of Cincinnati, which in the seventies and eighties became what Boston had been in the late nineteenth century. Not only did Cincinnati banish all adult bookstores, but it was difficult to find even a *Playboy* or a *Penthouse* within its limits. In April 1990 the city made national headlines when police went to the Contemporary Arts Center, removed visitors viewing a traveling exhibition of Mapplethorpe photographs, and photographed the photographs for evidence. Indictments were later handed down against museum director Dennis Barrie and the museum itself on charges of pandering, obscenity, and the illegal use of a minor (nude but nonobscene pictures of two young children that had been commissioned by their mothers). Barrie was later acquitted.

THOUGH THE PUGNACIOUS MEESE was Reagan's moral point man and was widely regarded as the driving force behind the commission, he had not actually established the commission, nor had he sat in on any of its hearings. He had also refrained from calling for sweeping bans on pornography, urging instead that state and local governments rule on such issues without federal intervention. A week before accepting the commission's report formally, he admitted to not having read it. Nevertheless, on July 9, 1986, the Meese Commission issued its final report, which Meese accepted from commission chairman Henry E. Hudson in the lobby of the Capitol building, with a statue depicting a bare-breasted Spirit of Justice behind him.

Published in two volumes totaling 1,960 pages, the report defined anyone below the age of twenty-one as a child; women and men could marry, vote, join the army, and still not be responsible for their own sexuality. The report also infantilized women by placing them on a par with children, who required similar protection and surveillance by the law. It also contained so many explicit sexual descriptions of such practices as asphyxiation and anilingus, or fetishes like collecting toenail clippings and sniffing sweat, that many Christian bookstores refused to carry it. Its nucleus was a paper entitled "The Question of Harm," written by First Amendment scholar Frederick Schauer, a professor of law at the University of Michigan, which focused on a distinction between primary and secondary harm.

Primary harm referred to "intrinsically harmful" practices such as rape, murder, and sexual discrimination, though the commissioners could not agree on whether to include masturbation, homosexuality, and premarital sex. As that dispute demonstrated, the commissioners had no consensus about objective standards. Anything that offended an individual commissioner's sensibilities—in the case of Chairman Hudson even fellatio and cunnilingus—was potentially a primary harm.

Secondary harms were defined as not harmful in and of themselves but harmful because they incited or caused illegal or "offensive" behavior. To the extent that the commission could determine that pornography caused rape, it constituted a secondary harm. (The commission conceded that the causal link between rape and pornography was admittedly "tentative.") As a result, secondary harm became the central focus of the final report.

The commission eliminated pornographic books from its discussion of harm (such materials had gone virtually unexamined during the various hearings anyway) on the basis of First Amendment protection. In a close vote (Commissioner Hudson and four others still wanted to censor erotic literature), the panel recommended that books be given special immunity from prosecution except in cases of child pornography. The implication was that men who read pornographic books rather than watching hard-core videos were less apt to sexually assault women, although there was no evidence for such an assumption.

That left still images and film. Schauer next discussed the criteria used to determine that a particular pornographic image was harmful, rejecting a standard of harm based on "conclusive proof" as a polemical device that could be manipulated by those who wished to reject a particular causal inference. He also rejected a standard based on "some evidence" as too weak to sustain a causal inference. Instead he took the middle ground, settling on a standard somewhere between "conclusive proof" and "some evidence," which in practical terms permitted him to use the term "cause" to describe the relationship between pornography and a variety of primary harms.

Only two commissioners dissented from the majority report. Significantly, both were women. Troubled by the tendency of their colleagues to go beyond the available data in concluding that laboratory aggression was equivalent to rape, both Judith Becker, a clinical psychologist at Columbia University, and

Ellen Levine, editor of *Woman's Day,* wrote that "efforts to tease the current data into proof of a causal link between these acts cannot be accepted."

A *New York Times* editorial on the report judiciously observed that, though pornography offended some people, consumers also had rights and that the commission's purported connection between pornography and crime "outruns its own evidence and its cure of censorship is worse than the disease."

Chapter 16

Ecce Homo

IN THE SIXTIES AND SEVENTIES, WHILE THE GREAT WHITE HETEROSEXUAL PENIS was under siege left and right, the gay penis was experiencing its greatest period of liberation since ancient Greece. A significant percentage of gay men probably enjoyed more sex more often with more sex partners than had happened in two thousand years—astronomically high sex rates, moreover, that very few heterosexuals, male or female, had ever equaled.

Like women, gay men were an oppressed sexual minority. But gays transformed their most intimate symbol of powerlessness and rejection into one of pride and strength. They decorated, pierced, and groomed their penises, wore cock rings, even underwent painful surgery to restore their foreskins— circumcision being a barbarity invented by the high priests of the Great White Penis. The more extreme participants in Gay Pride demonstrations insisted on marching with as little covering their genitals as was legally permissible.

Just as gay men were taking hold of their political destiny and making incredible strides, however, they were brought up short by a tragedy that transcended issues of sexual orientation. In July 1981 *The New York Times* ran a brief item under the headline "Rare Cancer Seen in 41 Homosexuals," and the public read about a new immune-deficiency virus for the first time. Homophobes rejoiced, declaring that God and nature were exacting retribution for the penis being put to a perverse use. Repellent and ignorant as this attitude was, indisputably the penis had become an agent of death as well as life, and in the wake of AIDS the gay subculture lay devastated.

AIDS made herpes, the STD of the seventies, seem like a mere rash. With the Sexual Revolution already in a tailspin, media hysteria about the new sexual scourge was instant and high volume. The May 31, 1982, issue of *New York* trumpeted a cover story entitled "The Gay Plague." In October the ailing *Saturday Evening Post* did an AIDS story titled "Being Gay Is a Health Hazard." *Rolling Stone* followed suit the following February with a story headlined "Is There Death after Sex?"

The decade of death had begun in earnest in early 1981 when Dr. Linda J. Laubenstein, a Manhattan hematologist, discovered some of the earliest mysterious cases of what was soon to become a worldwide epidemic. With Dr. Alvin Friedman-Kien she wrote the first article in a medical journal on the alarming prevalence of Kaposi's sarcoma, a previously rare disease of lesions of skin and other tissues, among young men, most of them gay, who appeared to be suffering a puzzling collapse of their immune system.

One of Dr. Laubenstein's first cases involved a thirty-three-year-old man with two purple spots behind his ears. Initially he had responded to cancer drugs, but eighteen months later he was dead, his body covered with seventy-five lesions. Many more cases soon followed. By May 1982 Dr. Laubenstein had sixty-two patients with AIDS—a fourth of the known national total at the time. She had a premonition that a terrible epidemic was about to sweep across the land.

In July 1982 the disease was also found in hemophiliacs and IV drug users and acquired the name AIDS from U.S. health officials. By January 1983 two women whose partners had AIDS contracted the disease. An editorial in the *Journal of the AMA* dated May 6, 1983, raised the possibility that AIDS could be acquired through ordinary nonsexual contact with a victim. Wire services and *The New York Times* moved that story along. On *20/20* Geraldo Rivera added to the panic by suggesting that since AIDS could be spread by transfusion, the nation's blood supply might be contaminated and the best precaution was to begin storing your own blood. Rivera was correct, though, in pinpointing blood banks as a potential source of AIDS infection. The shortsightedness and incompetence of those responsible for ensuring the integrity of the blood supply eventually led to tragic results—thousands of infected hemophiliacs and other victims.

Yet gay men remained the group at highest risk. A study of 250 gay men infected with the AIDS virus published in the April 1987 *American Journal of Public Health* showed that all but four had been the receptive partner in anal intercourse. There were other factors that put some groups at higher risk than others. Hepatitis B, which affected far more gay men (up to 80 percent of whom carried the virus, according to some studies), and IV drug use were thought to render the immune system more susceptible to the AIDS virus. The presence of other STDs was another serious cofactor. Not only did they help weaken the immune system, but they caused ulcerations that allowed the virus direct access to the bloodstream, particularly during anal intercourse. People infected with genital herpes, according to a 1987 study, were found to have a three or four times greater risk of contracting AIDS because of such lesions. Yet another cofactor was the use of non-IV drugs such as amyl nitrite, which also undermined the immune system even as it greatly enhanced sexual pleasure.

A survey of New York City victims found that, during an average month in the year they came down with the disease, each gay victim had an average of ten or more partners. Even considerably less promiscuous behavior could produce the same tragic result.

As Dr. Laubenstein's private practice grew to consist primarily of AIDS cases, she and her associate Dr. Friedman-Kien convened the first full-scale medical conference on AIDS, at New York University in 1983. The pair also helped to found the Kaposi's Sarcoma Research Fund that same year. Laubenstein herself suffered from severe asthma and in the view of colleagues was often sicker than some of her patients. Getting about on a motorized wheelchair, she often made house calls and visited emergency rooms in the middle of the night. Though an outspoken critic of the government, which she accused of foot-dragging in the fight against the disease, Dr. Laubenstein was nevertheless unpopular with some gay groups for advocating that bathhouses be shut down to discourage unsafe sex.

In 1989 Dr. Laubenstein and Dr. Jeffrey B. Greene, another colleague, founded Multitasking, a nonprofit organization that sold office services to other businesses and employed people with AIDS. The doctors' concern was for patients who had lost their jobs—work being vital to their emotional and physical health as well as their financial well-being.

Meanwhile, scientists in France and the United States were racing to discover the mysterious cause of AIDS, with millions of dollars in annual patent royalties and incalculable honor and prestige among the prizes. The French seemed to be winning when, in May 1983, Dr. Luc Montagnier of the Institut Pasteur reported that he and his team had discovered the virus—which they named LAV—linked to AIDS. Nearly a year later, Dr. Robert Gallo of the National Cancer Institute in the United States announced in a report published in the April 1984 issue of *Science* that he and his team had isolated the AIDS virus, which they called HTLV-3B, later known as HIV. In March 1985 the United States approved the first test to detect HIV antibodies.

Still, researchers could not understand the method to the virus's madness. Like all viruses, HIV was simply a strand of genetic material, in this case the nucleic acid RNA, surrounded by a protein coat. Like any virus, it lacked the tools to reproduce unless it invaded a living cell and took over the host's molecular machinery. A favorite HIV target was the CD4 T-cell, an important player in the human immune system. But why did HIV lie dormant in human cells, often for years, before producing a full-blown case of AIDS? What triggered the deadly phase of infection? Why did cells not harboring the virus die off almost as fast as those that did? Some researchers thought HIV somehow provoked cells into destroying themselves.

One prominent theory was that the virus needed an assistant assailant, or cofactor, but the search for cofactors proved inconclusive. While the presence of genital sores made transmission easier, for example, neither the sores nor the microbes that caused them were necessary for HIV to spread. Cytomegalovirus, a common form of herpes, was also ruled out.

In April 1985 AIDS hysteria spread to the heterosexual community when Dr. James Curran of the Centers for Disease Control (CDC) announced that AIDS, like other STDs, "can be readily transmitted to heterosexuals as well as homosexuals." At the time, only about 1 percent of one hundred thousand AIDS cases in the United States had been attributed to heterosexual transmission alone. Some experts predicted a sexual apocalypse.

Before 1960, according to one theory about the cause of AIDS, rural Africans had contracted a benign form of HIV, which spread so slowly that it never became virulent. That changed beginning in 1960, when war, drought, commercialization, and urbanization caused HIV to spread rapidly throughout the continent. By 1975 global travel placed it in even broader circulation, abetted by shifting sexual mores and modern medical techniques such as blood transfusions. Though drug use in Africa was relatively minimal, another quicksilver catalyst was needle therapy. In city and countryside alike, at ersatz dispensaries called Croix Rouges, a single unwashed hypodermic needle was often used to administer repeated doses of calcium carbonate, adrenaline, and vitamin B_6, all quick energy boosters. The African-origin theory gained support when researchers isolated STLV-3 (later called SIV), a simian version of the human agent HTLV-3, in infected macaques, African green monkeys, and some chimps.

However, what most people did not understand was that heterosexual practices in Africa were quite different from practices in much of the rest of the world. In many African countries female genital mutilation was nearly universal. In a gruesome rite of passage, a prepubescent girl was "circumcised"—that is, her clitoris was removed, seldom with a clean knife in a sterile environment. In some cases an extreme form of circumcision called infibulation was performed, which entailed removing all the vulval tissue, including the clitoris and labia. (In the Sudan, an unimaginable barbarity involving "enlarging" the vagina into the bladder and rectum of women thought to be suffering from various disorders was also practiced.) After the tissue was removed, the sides of the wound were sewn together, leaving an opening the size of a wooden matchstick. Intercourse was then accomplished through forcible entry by the husband, which often led to hemorrhaging. It was not surprising that Dr. Uli Linke, an anthropologist at the University of

Toronto who studied female genital mutilations in Africa, found a direct correlation between prevalence of female mutilation and AIDS outbreaks.

In October 1985 AIDS claimed its first national celebrity with the death of Rock Hudson, who throughout his leading-man career passed as heterosexual; but not until 1986, with the untimely passing of Charles Ludlam, a gifted playwright and founder of New York's beloved Ridiculous Theatrical Company, was the first AIDS-related death reported on the front page of *The New York Times.*

AMONG THOSE WHO READ the small item in *The New York Times* in July 1981 about the rare cancer affecting gays was another playwright, Larry Kramer, who immediately went to see Dr. Friedman-Kien because all of the men discussed had a history of STDs—syphilis, gonorrhea, hepatitis B. Kramer had contracted every one of them. The doctor told Kramer that he was fine. But while he was in the office, two friends accompanying him were diagnosed with AIDS literally under his nose. The experience transformed Kramer into an activist.

At the time, the gay community had no national organization with more than five or six thousand members, no nationally known leaders, no lobbyists in Washington. With a few concerned homosexuals like himself, Kramer founded the Gay Men's Health Crisis (GMHC) in New York City in 1982, with the purpose of inaugurating AIDS activism. But instead of rallying around, many gay men thought he was overreacting or even demented. Meanwhile, as the number of reported AIDS cases steadily rose from forty-one to one thousand in eighteen months, *The New York Times* grudgingly published seven more short articles on its inside pages about the epidemic (versus fifty-four articles in three months on a Tylenol scare that caused seven deaths).

After a two-year wait, Kramer got a meeting with New York mayor Ed Koch, in which Kramer recommended that gay bathhouses be closed. In 1985 GMHC began sending counselors into some of the city's ten gay bathhouses to distribute literature on safe sex. That fall the New York State Sanitary Code was amended to permit the closing of commercial places for so-called high-risk sex. Many gays were furious, blaming Kramer, Dr. Laubenstein, and others who saw a conclusive link between the AIDS plague and the promiscuous sex practices prevalent among gays since the late sixties. Even the majority of Kramer's associates at GMHC disagreed. For many gay men, as for a number of heterosexuals, the right to have unlimited amounts of uninhibited sex was virtually a civil rights issue.

Concluding that by and large the gay community seemed to be intent on refusing to look at both the problem and its solution squarely, Kramer went to Europe, after being thrown out of the GMHC, where he started writing his play *The Normal Heart,* which told the story of his entry into gay activism. He visited Dachau, where he was mesmerized by a plaque that read "Opened in 1933." "Where was everybody for eight years before the war started?" he asked himself. Kramer knew that American Jews had tried to work from the inside to oppose the Nazi regime but had accomplished nothing. The analogy with the gay community seemed striking. Gay leaders, in Kramer's view, did nothing but stab each other in the back, and as a rule, gays refused to join activist organizations at all. Kramer thought it was time for gays to stop being accomplices in their own deaths. Certainly the government was not going to rescue them. As of August 1985 President Reagan still had not mentioned the word "AIDS" in any context.

In 1987 Kramer—by now diagnosed as HIV-positive—founded ACT UP, a high-profile AIDS activist organization that used extremist tactics to heighten public awareness of the plight of AIDS victims and to pressure the government and research laboratories into stepping up efforts to find a vaccine and to formulate interim treatments that would provide HIV-infected individuals with a better quality of life. Along with Queer Nation, ACT UP changed forever the relationship between medical researchers and patients by forcing the former to consider alternative treatments and to abandon control-group studies that gave some subjects placebos instead of the experimental treatments they desperately needed. Kramer—himself a long-term HIV survivor—exhorted HIV and AIDS patients to take an active role in the search for a vaccine.

Ultimately, Joseph Papp, head of New York's Public Theater, agreed to produce *The Normal Heart.* Ironically, the play was in the vanguard of an extraordinary renaissance of gays in the arts even as AIDS was decimating their ranks. By 1993 gay theater was dominating Broadway, with Tony Kushner's *Angels in America: Millennium Approaches,* the first of a two-part, seven-hour epic, as well as with *Kiss of the Spider Woman* and *The Sisters Rosensweig,* the latter about a man who romances one of the title siblings, then leaves her because he prefers men.

Angels became the first gay-centered play to win the Pulitzer Prize in drama. The runner-up was also gay centered, as was the best show of the Off Broadway season—Kramer's *The Destiny of Me,* in which the playwright confronted having contracted the AIDS virus himself. Sadly, Dr. Laubenstein could share neither Kramer's agony nor his ecstasy, having died in August 1992 at her summer home in Cape Cod at the age of forty-five.

IN 1985 the strain of HIV that Dr. Robert Gallo had presented to the world the year before turned out to be virtually identical to the strain isolated by Dr. Luc Montagnier in 1983. As part of an ongoing exchange between the NIH and the Institut Pasteur, Montagnier had provided Gallo with a sample of the virus being studied by the French researchers, and Gallo had worked extensively with it to extend his own discoveries. Cross-contamination of cultures was a frequent occurrence in academic laboratories. The big question: Did Gallo and his senior research assistant Dr. Mikulas Popovic take deliberate advantage of the cross-contamination, or did they—as Gallo claimed—have no knowledge of it?

At the heart of the issue was the millions of dollars in royalties from manufacturers of HIV blood tests that the respective governments stood to reap. Lawyers for the Institut Pasteur wanted the United States to turn over half of the $50 million in profits that had accrued since 1985. Gallo himself had received about $100,000 a year from royalties, as had Montagnier. In 1987 the United States and France reached a deal: 80 percent of the royalties would go to neither government nor to individual scientists, but to AIDS research in their respective countries, with the remainder to be split equally.

Yet the controversy continued to simmer. Two years later, following an investigation by the *Chicago Tribune,* the Department of Health and Human Services began to look into charges that Gallo was guilty of deception in failing to give enough credit to the French for their role in finding HIV. In 1991 Gallo and Montagnier had their staffs analyze the original HIV samples again, and this time the mystery was solved. The strain that Gallo presented as an AIDS virus and used to develop a blood test for the disease had been accidentally contaminated by a virus from a French sample. Gallo insisted that the mistake did not diminish the achievement of his researchers because they also isolated several other strains of HIV. But lawyers for the Institut Pasteur and other critics claimed that the U.S. government's investigation into the Gallo affair—ultimately six different agencies conducted inquiries—had been weakened by its desire to keep its share of patent royalties.

Meanwhile, a further scandal erupted. In June 1992, four former French health officials went on trial in Paris for authorizing (in 1985) distribution of blood products known to be contaminated with the AIDS virus. As a result, 1,506 hemophiliacs were fatally infected with the virus, and 256 of them had already died. Lawyers for the victims were incensed that the matter was being treated in a lower court that usually dealt with trade-related misdemeanors, arguing that the four officials should be tried for poisoning. But French jurists said that charge would apply only if there was intent to kill. Dr. Michel Garretta, director of the National Blood Transfusion Center at the time, was ultimately sentenced to four years imprisonment "for falsifying the nature of a product." After serving only two and a half years, he was released with time off for good behavior, prompting widespread protests among the victims and their supporters.

On December 30, 1992, after three years of investigation, the Federal Of-

fice of Research Integrity found that Gallo had committed scientific misconduct, saying he had "falsely reported" a critical fact in his 1984 paper in order
to gain credit for himself and diminish credit due his French competitors.
His false statement also "impeded potential AIDS research progress" by di-
verting scientists from potentially fruitful work with the French researchers.
Gallo and Popovic appealed the verdict, and in early 1993 the panel exoner-
ated Popovic, concluding that his lack of familiarity with English had led the
Czech-born researcher to make several sloppy but innocent mistakes. By the
end of the year the government also withdrew all misconduct charges against
Gallo. Still, Popovic's reputation was so tarnished that he eventually relocated in Sweden to find work.

In 1993 Gallo published a memoir, *Virus Hunting: AIDS, Cancer, and the
Human Retrovirus,* which gave his account of all that happened. Two years
later he opened the Institute of Human Virology in Baltimore. Backed by
powerful local bankers and affiliated with the University of Maryland, the
institute was devoted to advancing the fight against AIDS and other diseases.

AFTER PUBLISHING THEIR MASTERPIECE, *Human Sexual Response,* in 1966, and
their flawed but history-making *Human Sexual Inadequacy* four years later,
Bill Masters and Virginia Johnson went on to issue eight other books for both
the sex professional and the general public. Most were unmemorable, and at
least one—*Homosexuality in Perspective*—was a disaster. But in March 1988
they published their worst book of all—*Crisis: Heterosexual Behavior in the
Age of AIDS,* whose apocalyptic message was that the disease was "running
rampant in the heterosexual community."

As always, their timing—if nothing else—was perfect. The AIDS scare
was at its height, and the pair had scheduled coast-to-coast press conferences,
a cover story in *Newsweek,* and syndication through the *Los Angeles Times* to
coincide with publication. The rush to publication may have been spurred by
the shaky finances of the Masters & Johnson Institute. Frustrated by his inability to obtain funding for a small research project to determine if HIV was
carried by male preejaculatory discharge as well as by semen, Masters hoped
royalties would allow him to increase staff and to expand the institute into a
major sexological research center, perhaps even including a psychosexual
think tank.

Masters and Johnson based their work on a survey they conducted among
heterosexuals in New York, St. Louis, Atlanta, and Los Angeles, claiming to
have found surprisingly high levels of HIV infection among fifty non-
monogamous men and women in each city while a control group of four
hundred monogamous heterosexuals had turned up only one infected per-

son. Extrapolating from those findings, Masters and Johnson estimated that as many as three million people in the United States were carrying the AIDS virus, triple the figure used by the federal government.

Gay critics called such claims "breeder hysteria." The medical community turned on the pair, too. Surgeon General Dr. Everett Koop, who advocated sex education, condoms, and abstinence as a way to avoid AIDS, branded them as irresponsible. Both the Public Health Service and the American Federation for AIDS Research questioned the authors' research, noting that some people in the survey who had identified themselves as heterosexual were in fact bisexual or were IV drug users who had contracted the virus from sharing needles. The researchers were also criticized for releasing the book before submitting it to scientific review, a charge to which Johnson petulantly responded, "Do we have to wait and wait to speak out?"

But when asked at a New York press conference about how he could justify his assertion that the AIDS virus was "running rampant" among heterosexuals, Masters could only reply, "I simply believe this." When Johnson was asked the same question, she appeared to cast the blame on collaborator Robert C. Kolodny, noting, "I'm not sure we chose the word 'rampant' ourselves." At a news conference in St. Louis, Kolodny himself compounded their troubles by stating that it was likely people would become infected with the AIDS virus in the exchange of blood in athletic events such as football. Immediately a variety of health officials and AIDS experts disputed this reckless generalization as well, leading Masters and Johnson to cancel speaking engagements in San Francisco, Miami, Atlanta, and New York to promote the book.

Though *Crisis* wildly exaggerated the risk of heterosexual AIDS and was virtually devoid of research citations, some of its findings—such as that some 5 percent of the most sexually active heterosexual population with no other risk factors carried the virus, or that many gay men slipped back into high-risk behavior after learning of their infection—were later confirmed by other studies. But the damage was done. At the Masters & Johnson Institute, patient inquiries fell off drastically. Quietly the board disbanded and the staff dwindled. Johnson moved into semiretirement, separating herself professionally from Masters. Insiders waited for the other shoe to drop—the announcement of a divorce.

Masters and Johnson were not alone in fanning the flames of heterosexual AIDS hysteria. *Time* magazine reported in December 1986 that one hundred million people would be stricken by 1990. In 1988 New York City health officials urged the state to add vaginal intercourse to a list of risky sex practices. But AIDS simply was not spreading at the anticipated rate among non-IV-drug-using straights. Gay men remained at the highest sexual risk for one reason above all: their predilection for anal intercourse, which often caused bleeding and torn tissue in the receptive partner, dramatically increasing the likelihood of infection.

The myth fostered by a profoundly misinformed media was that the Sexual Revolution was killed by AIDS. The public, weary, confused, and threatened by too many choices, bought it readily. The thesis also made for simple reading. People did not want to read about the mutilation of female genitals in Africa. Most newspapers even avoided describing how transmission occurred through anal sex. In a misguided effort to be politically correct, most media simply failed to differentiate between homosexual and heterosexual risk. The media further confused readers by employing the term "exchange of bodily fluids" instead of saying "commingling of blood and semen." As a result, many people also believed AIDS was transmitted by kissing.

Prostitutes were immediately made a scapegoat for heterosexual AIDS, even though the evidence of any kind of heterosexual transmission remained scant. The average street prostitute saw an estimated 1,500 customers a year. If only 5 percent of New York's estimated 20,000 prostitutes were infected in 1978, in the years just before AIDS was identified by Dr. Laubenstein, then 4,000 hookers times 1,500 customers times 3 years to allow for incubation times 20 percent (one estimate of the rate of female-to-male transmission) equaled 360,000 diagnosed cases of AIDS among the client population. But as of December 1986, among those for whom the only known risk factor was heterosexual contact with a person who had AIDS or was at risk of AIDS, only 557 men and 533 women had been diagnosed with the disease. And by 1987 only 70 men diagnosed with AIDS claimed contact with prostitutes as their only risk.

The CDC in Atlanta maintained no records on prostitutes diagnosed with AIDS. COYOTE knew of only five women thought to have AIDS who had been identified specifically as prostitutes. Yet the CDC continued to identify prostitutes as a high-risk group, along with "women who have used drugs intravenously for nonmedical purposes; women who were born in countries where heterosexual transmission was thought to play a major role . . . and women who are or have been sex partners of men who . . . are bisexual, have hemophilia," or are members of high-risk groups and/or have evidence of HIV infection.

A persistent AIDS myth was that women could readily transmit the HIV virus to men. Yet by the mid-nineties most HIV-infected males between the ages of twenty and twenty-four (who represented 77 percent of all AIDS cases) had contracted the virus through sex with men (63 percent), IV drug use (13 percent), or both (11 percent). By the mid-nineties, the proportion of AIDS cases among women had more than doubled, with 58,448 cases accounting for 13 percent of all infected adults and adolescents. But women were most likely to become infected via IV drug use (41 percent) or sex with infected men (38 percent). A prostitute was more likely to contract HIV from a john than to give it to him.

Ironically, AIDS was a boon to the legitimate prostitution business. Brothels such as the Cherry Patch Ranch in Lathrop Wells near Las Vegas averaged forty customers a day who made the long hot trip because they knew the prostitutes were given a blood test every month. AIDS hysteria also turned "safe sex" into a growth industry. From 1984 on, AIDS boosted the sale of products ranging from condoms to cocktail napkins illustrating safe-sex techniques, not all of them directed at gays. The Crown Zellerbach Corporation in San Francisco, which made Sanitary Safe T Gard covers for toilet seats, reported that sales increased noticeably with media attention to AIDS.

History of sorts was made with the first gay safe-sex porn movie, Henry Mach's *Inevitable Love,* about two high school wrestling pals. In the opening sequence, a series of extreme close-ups focused on sweat dripping down foreheads, panting chests, a hand gripping at a jockstrap during the struggle for supremacy. Gary finally pins Hal as the referee declares him the winner. Both collapse like exhausted lovers after a furious orgasm. Later Gary takes the low road and becomes a street hustler, while Hal goes on to college and meets a famous gay activist writer who teaches him about condoms. When the two friends are finally reunited, flashbacks of the wrestling match are juxtaposed with images of Hal, his penis sheathed, anally penetrating Gary.

But the biggest winners in the AIDS bonanza were condom manufacturers. In 1982 Reuben Sturman's Doc Johnson began making the first condoms geared toward gay men, called Man-to-Man. Sales soon doubled with the AIDS crisis. Some industry estimates suggested that the condom market was expanding at a rate of about 25 percent per year.

Researchers at the Mariposa Foundation, a charitable organization specializing in the prevention of STDs, discovered that an ingredient called Nonoxynol-9 that was present in a number of spermicides marketed as contraceptives for women seemed to kill the HTLV-3 virus associated with AIDS. Some experts recommended using a spermicide containing 5 percent Nonoxynol-9 in cream, foam, gel, lubricant, or suppository form. Contraceptol and Ramses condoms containing Nonoxynol-9 became so popular that independent dealers made a tidy profit selling them through mail order at twice the drugstore cost. The AIDS virus was also killed on any surface by a 10 percent solution of standard hydrogen peroxide, a 30 percent solution of rubbing alcohol, or even 160-degree hot water (the hottest temperature a normal person can tolerate without getting burned), which could be used to detoxify dildos, vibrators, nipple clamps, and other standard sex gear.

Yet the CDC refused to endorse the use of Nonoxynol-9, to say that condoms prevented AIDS, or to pass on other such information about safe-sex practices; nor would the government allocate even the few thousand dollars necessary to find out whether condoms blocked the AIDS virus. Biologist and gay activist Dr. Bruce Voeller, who developed a cream containing Nonoxynol-9 for the Mariposa Foundation, tried in vain to persuade the CDC to run clinical tests on humans. Voeller charged that Dr. James Curran, the director of the AIDS division of the CDC, had put a gag order on his staff, informing Voeller that endorsing such practices would make him and his division look bad in a sex-phobic administration. Voeller theorized that many in the CDC were not only homophobic but opposed to any practice that might appear to promote sex.

Despite the intransigence of the CDC, the NIH, and the FDA, they and other government agencies were full of many anonymous heroes, both gay and straight, who quietly shared information. In the private sector, moreover, despite gay activists' claims to the contrary, never in the history of science was so much research mobilized so quickly against a disease. By 1992 nearly a dozen anti-HIV vaccines were in clinical trials, the result of a race among dozens of pharmaceutical companies to claim what analysts said could be a $2-billion-a-year market for a preventive medicine by the end of the decade.

A few preparations had proved mildly effective in delaying onset, but actually preventing the disease was another story. HIV could hide in cells and even vary its chemical makeup, like an actor changing costumes. Comparing HIV with protein molecules that made up human cells, Gerald Myers, a biophysicist at Los Alamos National Laboratory and director of a data bank that tracked genetic changes in the virus around the world, found that since its discovery HIV had already evolved as much as "all human proteins in the history of mankind." At least five distinct subtypes of HIV-1, the principal form, had now been identified. As if in evolutionary fast-forward, the virus—a newcomer to the human body—was like an animal species entering a new continent, where it adapted quickly, spinning off new species. Some researchers hoped that meant it would become less virulent, as viruses often evolved into forms that allowed them to coexist with their hosts rather than kill them. HIV-2 in Africa was not so lethal as HIV-1; SIV, its older cousin, did not kill monkeys.

HIV had a particular affinity for T4 lymphocytes, a type of white blood cell that orchestrated the activity of the immune system. By invading such cells, HIV gradually subverted the body's defenses. As the number of healthy T4 cells in the bloodstream declined, the HIV victim might display symptoms that made up so-called AIDS-related complex (ARC): chronically swollen glands, recurrent fevers, weight loss. As the immune system collapsed, the patient fell prey to cancers and viruses, bacterial infections, and parasites the body normally fended off.

For most diseases, vaccines consisted of a dead or weakened virus; injected into the body, they caused a mild infection, which was quickly suppressed by the immune system. But vaccine makers avoided introducing any form of HIV into healthy patients for fear that even a single virus particle slipping into a cell could lead to AIDS. Some companies, such as Bristol-Myers Squibb and Abbott Laboratories, eventually abandoned vaccine research altogether, fearful of lawsuits that might result if a clinical trial went awry. Instead, researchers concentrated on turning HIV's changeability against it, attempting to zero in on the molecular structures and genetic sequences that were indispensable to its survival and to stimulate the immune system with harmless, genetically engineered vaccine cocktails.

The most dramatic gain in the fight against AIDS was in the war against Pneumocystis pneumonia, a major killer of AIDS patients. In 1986 the antiviral drug AZT became available, later to be joined by DDI and DDC. Though some patients found them too toxic to tolerate, some evidence suggested that these drugs could delay the onset of serious illness. All three attacked the virus at the same point, interfering with an enzyme called reverse transcriptase, which was critical to HIV reproduction.

Other researchers continued to search for the origins of the disease. In 1992 some researchers speculated about a link between the polio vaccine and AIDS, insofar as the population in Zaire, which had the first significant outbreak of the disease, had been the first large group to receive an experimental polio vaccine in the 1950s, when that country was also being devastated by outbreaks of paralytic polio. The oral vaccine had been developed by Dr. Hilary Koprowski of Philadelphia's Wistar Institute and was derived from weakened polio viruses in a culture of green monkey kidneys. The conclusion: The kidneys of those monkeys might have been contaminated with the deadly HIV. Yet it was not known if HIV could survive oral ingestion. Moreover, how could the spread of HIV infection have gone unnoticed for so many years?

Meanwhile, epidemiologists were discovering a wide variation in infection rates that suggested a significant range of susceptibility in the population. Instances of heterosexual transmission were documented both from men to women and from women to men, mainly through vaginal intercourse. But while in one case transmission was reported after only one sexual contact with a sexual partner, other individuals remained uninfected despite hundreds of sexual contacts with an infected partner. Some researchers suggested that transmissibility was influenced by variations in strains of the virus, but there was no data to support that theory. There was some evidence that HIV was transmitted more easily from men to women than vice versa. Some studies suggested that heterosexual anal sex posed a higher risk, while other studies concluded it posed no higher risk than vaginal intercourse. Though oral sex presented a theoretical risk, its magnitude could not be quantified with current data.

348 ■ WHAT WILD ECSTASY

It was harder to get a clear picture of transmission among IV drug users. Many crack users provided sexual services to finance their habits, but there was virtually no data quantifying or qualifying those services.

By the end of March 1992, the number of AIDS cases reported in the United States had reached 218,000, with 139,000 deaths. Allowing for under-reporting, the CDC believed that, with between forty thousand and eighty thousand new cases per year, the number of Americans infected with HIV was approaching one million. Both new cases and deaths from the disease were expected to level off at approximately fifty thousand per year. By the time of the Eighth International AIDS Conference in Amsterdam that year, AIDS was eleven years old and billions had been spent on scattershot research and halfhearted prevention efforts, with no vaccine, no cure, and not even an effective treatment in sight. The World Health Organization, meanwhile, predicted that 40 million people would be afflicted with the disease by the year 2000. Some experts put the number at 110 million.

The biggest buzz at the conference was about a new kind of AIDS. Dr. Jeffrey Laurence of New York Hospital–Cornell Medical Center described five instances of people suffering from an AIDS-like illness, though none showed any trace of HIV. Was a deadly new microbe on the loose, or some other illness whose symptoms simply mimicked those of AIDS? Among the skeptics—and the more optimistic—at the Amsterdam conference was the short, stocky, bespectacled figure of Luc Montagnier. Unlike many of his American counterparts, he was not persuaded by arguments that there was a new virus; instead, he thought, HIV was simply changing its disguise again. He remained hopeful that a vaccine would be found before the year 2000.

THE MOST FANATIC HOMOPHOBE of the eighties was Dr. Paul Cameron. A former member of the ACLU turned reactionary, Cameron was a frequent guest on the talk-show circuit in the eighties. Pudgy and sandy haired, he liked to taunt the liberal establishment with inflammatory sound bites, suggesting that homosexuals be castrated or exterminated. Since homosexuality was no longer a shocking taboo, he coupled it with child molestation—suggesting, for example, that gay teachers preyed on students. He liked to tell audiences that homosexuals were instrumental in the founding of the Nazi Party, which later turned on them, that 15 to 20 percent of all STDs were linked to homosexuality, and that a disproportionate number of mass murderers were gay. In 1982 the American Psychological Association expelled him for violating its code of ethics with his hate-filled rhetoric, although Cameron later claimed to have resigned, charging that the organization was stacked with homosexuals.

In 1985 Cameron created the Institute for the Scientific Investigation of

Sexuality, primarily a one-man show. For $1,000 a day he eagerly testified as an expert witness in sex-crime cases, asserting that homosexuals were far more likely to molest children, commit violent crimes, and spread diseases than were heterosexuals. He also wrote a book, *Sexual Gradualism.* Yet despite his gospel of hatred, Cameron seemed strangely preoccupied with anal sex in his book. "The anus is potentially 'sexy,' " he wrote. "Animals do not use the anus to sexual advantage, but many humans do." His fascination with anal sex did not prevent him from campaigning for antisodomy laws in twenty-six states that did not yet have them, however, or from helping to defeat gay rights amendments in Baltimore, Columbus, and Houston.

In 1986 such efforts got a boost from the Supreme Court when Chief Justice Warren Burger declared: "To hold that the act of homosexual sodomy is somehow protected as a fundamental right would be to cast aside millennia of moral teaching." In a decision written by Justice Byron White, the Court upheld the right of individual states to outlaw homosexual sodomy. It seemed that the evolution of the constitutional right to privacy, which had been enshrined during the past two decades in decisions such as those allowing the use of contraceptives and asserting a woman's right to have an abortion, would not be allowed to continue unchecked.

Though Cameron was the most abominable homophobe of the decade, perhaps the most influential in a more collective sense was the Catholic Church, which condemned homosexual unions in the strongest possible terms and actively worked to deny homosexuals legal, social, moral, and sexual parity with heterosexuals. Bishops cautioned seminaries to turn away effeminate candidates, even though the National Catholic Bishops Conference had no official policy against ordaining homosexuals and homosexuality was not an official impediment to ordination. Only if a candidate was "active in the lifestyle" was he considered unfit. Yet Father John McNeill, a Jesuit and author of the controversial best-seller *The Church and the Homosexual,* was forbidden by the Vatican for seven years to speak publicly about homosexual issues relating to the church. The church also revoked the imprimatur, or formal permission to publish, that had previously been granted to the book. Yet the book remained in print; and after temporarily observing the enforced silence, McNeill left the Jesuit order to become a gay activist.

Ironically, a 1982 study conducted by the Archdiocese of San Francisco found that almost one in three Catholic priests in the United States was gay. The author of the report was Kevin Gordon, a professor of human sexuality at Brooklyn College who canvassed Roman Catholic clergy in workshops across the country. Though the study was not based on a scientific sample, Gordon's statistic probably erred on the side of conservatism. Ex-priest Robert T. Francoeur, author or editor of a score of books on sexuality, guessed that as many as half of all American priests were homosexual.

Another powerful homophobic force in U.S. society was the military. Official discrimination against homosexuals had begun during World War II, been consolidated into policy during the fifties, and reached its apogee, in terms of witch-hunts and administrative repression, during the eighties. Though the General Accounting Office said chasing suspected homosexuals out of the service cost the Pentagon about $27 million annually, that estimate did not reflect the actual human cost of ruined careers and disrupted lives.

The first real blow to homophobia in the military occurred in the mid-1970s, when Sgt. Leonard Matlovich was discharged from the air force on the grounds of his sexual orientation. He later collected $160,000 in back pay when the service—unwilling to clarify what would constitute an exception to its policy of banning all homosexuals and hoping to avoid defending its exclusion policy before the Supreme Court—declined to rebut his claim to an exemption from the no-gays policy.

In the 1992 presidential race, candidate Bill Clinton, governor of Arkansas, staked out a position on homosexuals in the military during an appearance at Harvard's Kennedy School of Government in October 1991. Clinton boldly announced that he would do for gays what Harry S. Truman did for blacks in 1948—eliminate the military's discriminatory policies by executive order. But after his election he encountered widespread opposition in the ranks and stonewalling from the Joint Chiefs of Staff and eventually backed down. The resulting compromise—a "don't ask, don't tell" policy—relegated the matter of gay rights and self-respect to a legal and moral limbo. But in late 1992 the Supreme Court's upholding of a lower court ruling that demanded the military services provide "a rational basis" for banning gays at least signaled an end to the Pentagon's active persecution of homosexuals.

The fourth estate—at least its mainstream—was of astonishingly little help in combating homophobia. Possibly the most virulent instance of homophobia in modern journalism was an article by columnist Patrick Buchanan that appeared in the August 1984 issue of the *American Spectator.* Coauthored with J. Gordon Muir, M.D., the piece, entitled "Gay Times and Diseases," identified homosexuals as "sodomites" whose lifestyle consisted almost exclusively of random, promiscuous sex. Describing gays as proselytizers and child molesters who presented a special danger to the young and impressionable, Buchanan and Muir concluded that homosexuals deserved the most atrocious punishment God or fate could inflict: in other words, AIDS. The tirade concluded with a plea that the general populace reconsider the privileges given to homosexuals and proposed that they be denied work as food handlers, bartenders, teachers, attendants in medical care facilities, and aides in day care centers for young children.

Even so distinguished and even-handed a publication as *The New York Times* had a legacy of homophobia. For many years its policy was to refuse to list a deceased gay's significant other as a survivor. But by the fall of 1985 the vast increase in AIDS deaths and the paper's own increasing coverage of the disease had forced a reexamination of that policy, at least on a case-by-case basis. Yet the *Times* maintained its odd rule against using the word "gay" as a synonym for homosexual.

The ban dated to 1975, when a freelance writer had contributed a piece to the travel section titled "The All-Gay Cruise: Prejudice and Pride." The story was about three hundred homosexuals and fifteen heterosexuals who had cruised from the Everglades to the Yucatán, the highlights being assorted high jinx in the staterooms and a cast of characters that included "leathermen in black cowhide outfits trimmed with chains, zipper and metal studs." It caused a sensation. Publisher Punch Sulzberger's mother, then in her eighties, hit the roof; allegedly, Sunday editor Max Frankel was called on the carpet and fired, then rehired six hours later. Frankel later denied that he had ever been fired, but the word "gay" was henceforth banned from the paper.

Despite resistance from many quarters, homosexuals were making progress. In April 1993, hundreds of thousands of gays and lesbians and their supporters rallied in the capital to celebrate the right to free sexual expression and to demand an end to discrimination. That same year, Hawaii's supreme court ruled that its ban on same-sex marriages probably violated the state's constitution. Still, homophobia was ever-present. One index: In its 1993 survey of five metropolitan areas, the National Gay and Lesbian Task Force reported that antigay crimes were up 172 percent over the past five years.

Most of the causes of homophobia were deeply ingrained in the culture, but civil war within the ranks of sexual minorities contributed indirectly to it. To the distress of hard-line gay activists, a burgeoning bisexual movement was attempting to capitalize on and even to join the gay rights movement, transforming places like the New York Lesbian and Gay Community Center into a Balkan state.

The crux of the conflict was over what actually constituted a bisexual. Many homosexuals freely conceded they had fantasies about the opposite sex, while remaining gay or lesbian in their sexual lifestyles. A few even acted on them from time to time without revising the label they gave themselves. Bisexuals, on the other hand, had sex with both men and women but these days seemed to be coming from the ranks of avowed homosexuals. These "queer" bisexuals considered their bisexuality a second coming out and held up icons like David Bowie and Madonna as role models. Before long the media had picked up on a new fad. Hollywood threw a bisexual ice-pick murderer into *Basic Instinct,* while TV's highly rated *L.A. Law* added a bisexual regular, C. J. Lamb. In a 1991 segment, C. J. (Amanda Donohoe) and Abby (Michele Green) also shared prime-time TV's first lesbian kiss—followed in a few years by Roseanne and Mariel Hemingway on the nation's top-rated show..In the meantime, bisexuals accused the gay establishment of biphobia, and gays in turn charged bisexuals with bichauvinism and of availing themselves of "heterosexual privilege" when convenient.

How DID A PERSON arrive at her or his sexual preference? Some scientists and activists sought the answer in genetics, or in prenatal hormones, or even in the kind of food their mother ate when pregnant. Some homosexuals viewed their sexual orientation as a moral choice. But in the opinion of John Money, the original cause of homosexuality was irrelevant. What mattered was that science had been unable to change straights into gays and vice versa. A gay man might be able to have sex with a woman, but he could not fall in love with her, which was key.

Even so, in 1980 Dr. Gunter Dorner, an East German endocrinologist, tried to prove that homosexuality was caused by hormonal differences. According to Dorner, gay males had a bigger response to estrogen injections than did straight males. The effect of the injections on levels of luteinizing hormones (a pituitary regulator that triggers the gonads to secrete sex steroids) in homosexuals resembled that of heterosexual women and differed from that of heterosexual and bisexual men. Four years later Brian Gladue of Stony Brook University on Long Island obtained similar findings. But in 1986 researchers in Amsterdam not only failed to replicate those findings, but showed that variations in receptivity were due to a previously overlooked variable—poor functioning of hormone-producing cells in the testicles, a phenomenon that occurred in both gay and straight men.

A much larger issue—not what caused homosexuality, but who was a homosexual—emerged in 1990 when John de Cecco, editor of the *Journal of Homosexuality,* identified a fundamental problem in Kinsey's definition of sex. For the great Indiana sex researcher, sex had equaled physical expressions or "outlets." In each sex history he tried to calculate the "total outlets." How often did a person experience "the sudden release of local spasms and all-consuming convulsions"? Did orgasm result from masturbation, nocturnal emission, petting, intercourse, or animal contact? What was the gender of the actual or fantasized partners in those orgasms? He had ignored the psychological character of attraction and fantasy that made orgasms so varied but also made sexual histories almost unmanageably complicated. To Kinsey, an orgasm was an orgasm.

Another problem with Kinsey's methods, according to de Cecco and others, was his tendency to view sexual response in mechanistic terms. To Kinsey, healthy sex meant a lot of sex. This strictly zoological view of sex ignored the fact that in every human culture, past and present, sexual behavior occurred in a social context. Even permissive cultures assigned values to when people had sex, with whom, and why. By ignoring the emotional side of sex, according to de Cecco, Kinsey advanced a view of sex as fast food; this burgeoned in the late sixties and early seventies, leading in turn to a need for a more holistic, playful view of sex that was less obsessed with performance and orgasm.

On a pragmatic level, scientists were also reevaluating Kinsey's conclusions about the prevalence of homosexuality, heterosexuality, and bisexuality. It was now common for scientists to distinguish among gender identity, gender role, and gender orientation. Money and others now thought that gender identity (awareness of self as male or female) was irreversibly set by age three. On the other hand, gender role (the balance of masculine or feminine behaviors adopted to signal that one was male or female) changed throughout life. Gender orientation, which most scientists thought was set by age five, was reflected in sexual fantasies and attraction, in the gender of sex partners, and in the gender of persons one fell in love with.

Kinsey died before any of these ideas had been conceived, let alone assimilated into the mainstream. As a result, he concentrated solely on the gender of the partners with whom his subjects reached orgasm or about whom they fantasized, using the average to place each subject on a scale of 0 to 6. Someone whose real and fantasized sexual partners were always of the opposite gender was a Kinsey 0, exclusively heterosexual. A Kinsey 6 had sex and fantasized about it only with same-sex partners. Nor had Kinsey asked whether a married person who had sex with his or her spouse was fantasizing about sex with a same-sex partner, or what the imagined sexual orientation of the fantasy partner was, for that matter. In the gender landscape of the 1990s, however, crowded as it was with transsexuals, transgenderists, cross-dressers, and others with conflicts among gender identity, gender role, and sexual orientation, categorizing people as gay, straight, or bisexual seemed as foolhardy as trying to pigeonhole someone by racial ancestry.

Meanwhile, the search for the cause of homosexuality continued. A 1991 study of twins provided strong evidence that homosexuality had a genetic basis. The study examined fifty-six identical twins, fifty-four fraternal twins, and fifty-seven adopted brothers. (Identical twins are genetic clones, developed in the womb from a single egg split after being fertilized by a single sperm; fraternal twins develop from two separate eggs fertilized by two separate sperm cells.) The researchers found that 52 percent of identical twin brothers of gay men were also gay, compared with 22 percent of fraternal and 11 percent of genetically unrelated brothers.

In 1991 researcher Simon LeVay reported that a portion of the hypothalamus was smaller in homosexual men than in heterosexual men and was equal in size to that portion in heterosexual women. Though widely discussed in the media, this claim was seriously flawed, owing to the size and composition of the study

354 ■ WHAT WILD ECSTASY

group, and was ultimately judged meaningless. But in 1992 researchers found another anatomical idiosyncrasy in the brains of gay men. A cord of nerve fibers that allowed the two halves of the brain to communicate with each other was larger in homosexual men than in either heterosexual men or in women. Though brain structure did not influence sexual behavior directly, researchers concluded that the subtle differences in the brain structures of homosexuals and heterosexuals were signs of a deeper biological difference.

Further confusing the matter was an article in the March 1993 issue of the *Archives of General Psychiatry* that suggested lesbianism was perhaps genetically induced. Following up their similar study of gay men, Northwestern University psychologist J. Michael Bailey and Boston University psychiatrist Richard C. Pillard looked at 108 lesbians with identical or nonidentical twin sisters, and 32 additional lesbians with adoptive sisters. Each pair grew up in the same home, which neutralized parental influence on sexual orientation. In almost half of the identical pairs, both twins were homosexual, compared with only 16 percent of nonidentical pairs and 6 percent of genetically unrelated sisters.

While the balkanization of gender identity increased, and the debate among feminists, social theorists, and sexologists intensified over what constituted gender, and whether it was biogenetically inherited or socially constructed, sex surveys—the last bastion of traditional sexology—continued to codify the sexual universe in reactionary, almost colonial, terms.

The most notable was a 1993 survey of the sexual practices of 3,321 American men in their twenties and thirties conducted by the Battelle Human Affairs Research Centers in Seattle, which claimed that its survey was the first scientifically valid one of its kind and boasted that for once the results were not astonishing. The median number of sex partners over a lifetime was 7.3. The median age at which white men in the survey lost their virginity was 17.2; for blacks, 15. The median frequency of sexual intercourse was slightly less than once a week, slightly more for married men. Only 2.3 percent of the men surveyed reported any homosexual contact in the past ten years, and only half of those, or just over 1 percent, said they were exclusively gay in that period. This was, in fact, astounding—a much lower incidence of homosexuality and bisexuality than Kinsey had asserted decades before.

Gay activists worried that the finding would lend weight to antihomosexual crusaders like Phyllis Schlafly, whose son had recently admitted he was gay. And indeed Schlafly asserted that the survey showed politicians "they don't need to be worried about 1 percent of the population." But critics pointed out that the survey was limited to men between twenty and thirty-nine, an age at which many men had yet to come to terms with their sexual orientation. In addition, the survey merely compiled statistics on the frequency of vaginal, oral, and anal sex and the gender of the partners, without dwelling on the matter of sexual identity.

Some doctors, researchers, and gay activists were also developing reservations about the burst of interest in the biological aspects of homosexuality. If homosexuality was found to be a largely biological phenomenon, they feared, it might come to be seen as a physical illness in need of a cure, just as it had once been seen by psychiatrists as a mental illness in need of treatment.

DESPITE THE GAINS in gay rights in general, lesbians were still a largely invisible minority throughout most of the eighties. Various surveys put their number at between two million and three million in the United States, with activists guessing that most were still in the closet. But things began to change in 1992 with the much publicized coming out of Patricia Ireland, president of the National Organization for Women (NOW).

During the 1970s NOW's leadership had purged open lesbians; notably, lesbian novelist Rita Mae Brown's departure from the New York chapter after antagonizing fellow members over the primacy of lesbianism as a feminist issue. Also adding to the lesbian-straight split throughout feminist organizations was Kate Millett's acknowledgment in late 1970 that she was bisexual. By 1993, however, NOW's membership had grown to 280,000 and the organization now regarded gay rights as a principal objective. During an interview with the *Advocate,* a biweekly gay magazine, Ireland, a married woman, disclosed that she had a female companion in Washington, D.C. The cover story was headlined "America's Most Powerful Woman Comes Out."

Though Ireland refused to label herself, the controversy shook both her personal and professional lives, especially since the *Advocate* publicized her disclosure before she had an opportunity to alert the NOW board and its various chapters—though the issue soon died down. About the same time, country singer k. d. lang also came out to the *Advocate,* giving new meaning to her hit "Constant Craving." Even more successful was Melissa Etheridge, an openly lesbian singer whose top-forty hits included "Come to My Window" and "If I Wanted To."

That same year *Out* magazine was launched as the first glossy general-interest magazine for gays and lesbians, with fashion designer Calvin Klein among its advertisers. Gay-themed films that succeeded in the mainstream included *My Own Private Idaho; Paris Is Burning;* and, soon after, *The Adventures of Priscilla, Queen of the Desert; Boys on the Side;* and *Fried Green Tomatoes.* Homosexual politics also went mainstream, as prominent gays and lesbians like Massachusetts representative Barney Frank, one of two openly gay members of the House, became players for the first time in a presidential election.

Within a year a hot new sexual trend—lesbian chic—was being celebrated

by such nationally known lesbians or bisexuals as comedian Sandra Bern-
hard, Madonna, Dee Mosbacher (a San Francisco psychiatrist and daughter
of Bush cabinet member Robert Mosbacher, who came out in a college commencement speech), and tennis star Martina Navratilova. Dorothy Allison's
riveting autobiographical novel, *Bastard Out of Carolina,* hit the best-seller
lists. Designer Calvin Klein used lesbian themes to advertise his perfume.
President Clinton nominated the openly lesbian Roberta Achtenberg as assistant secretary in the Department of Housing and Urban Development.
Lea DeLaria, a lesbian comic, broke the late night talk-show barrier on *Arse-
nio.* Even *Cosmopolitan* put a lesbian story on its cover. Along with "Check
Out These Super Hunks" and "How to Make Your Man Better in Bed" was
"A Matter of Pride: Being a Gay Woman in the '90s."

Lesbians were also at the forefront in defining nontraditional family concepts, from arranging to have children through artificial insemination or
adoption to nurturing long-standing friendship circles that constituted a chosen extended family. While lesbians had the lowest rates of STDs of any sexual orientation group, they also faced some unique health issues, particularly
with hospitals that did not recognize the consultation or visitation rights of a
nonmarital partner.

By the mid-nineties, despite the numerous challenges lesbians still faced,
they had indisputably established themselves as a fully visible, highly articulate, and well-organized cultural and political force. Towns like Northamp-
ton, Massachusetts, and Provincetown on Cape Cod were becoming lesbian
meccas. In contrast with the fragmentation of the gay community in the
wake of AIDS, lesbians were growing visibly stronger and more united.

WHILE MANY LESBIANS were instrumental in AIDS activism and in caregiving
for victims, many gay men who became infected with HIV had to contend
not only with the prospect of dying at an early age, but with enduring treatments that often seemed worse than the disease. Adding to the gloom was an
ominous trend—more AIDS patients were developing tuberculosis, in a
deadly form that was resistant to traditional treatments. Not surprisingly,
men with AIDS had a high suicide rate, although it declined between 1987
and 1989 when the prospects for a vaccine looked more hopeful.

The pressure on the medical establishment from AIDS activists to use virtually any new drug that showed promise in a clinical trial, without a control
group taking a placebo, had also led to therapeutic anarchy. For a long time
no one was quite sure if a drug like AZT really worked. So many people with
AIDS were experimenting with so many drugs that it was impossible to evaluate the effectiveness of a single drug. In the early 1990s the FDA approved
a second anti-AIDS drug, DDI; and then a third, DDC.

Meanwhile gay men who managed to escape HIV infection had to contend with guilt, cumulative grief, and identity crises created by the connection between gay identity and HIV infection. Some gay men were simply unable to alter their sexual behavior to reduce the risk of HIV infection. In 1992 a new national study by the Medical College of Wisconsin found that 31 percent of gay men surveyed outside of big cities still engaged in high-risk sex. Particularly disturbing was a new trend toward high-risk sex among gay men in their thirties and early forties who had managed to remain HIV-negative for twenty years. After burying so many friends, some men no longer wanted to live into old age.

The scourge continued to reap famous and unknown alike: the entertainer Liberace; eighteen-year-old hemophiliac Ryan White; tennis great Arthur Ashe, who contracted the virus through a blood transfusion; artist Keith Haring; ballet star Rudolf Nureyev; choreographer Michael Bennett; photographer Robert Mapplethorpe; fashion designers Halston and Perry Ellis; actors Tony Perkins and Denholm Elliott; and another victim of an infected blood transfusion, Elizabeth Glaser, whose husband, Paul Michael Glaser, was a star of TV's hit series *Starsky and Hutch.*

One who escaped the AIDS plague was Boyd McDonald, the angry old man of gay sexology, who in September 1993 succumbed to lung cancer in his room in an Upper West Side transient hotel. His legacy was his *Straight to Hell* anthologies, which chronicled what their creator called the "classical period of homosexuality—1940 to 1980." Some questioned whether, in the age of AIDS, it was morally responsible of the *New York Native* to publish McDonald's pornography. His response was that such critics were not happy about being gay.

But he also acknowledged that "AIDS is very sad for the young homosexuals of today. I didn't face anything like it when I was young. I had sex with some two thousand men, which was not really extreme. Everybody back then [in the fifties] had sex with two thousand men. The only thing I ever got was syphilis, which was no problem—you just got a couple of needles for it." And in recognition that the classical period was over, he had begun to include a fact sheet with safe-sex guidelines on the back of each book. McDonald himself had retired from sex as of 1985, after which his books were his sex life.

Hopes for finding an imminent cure for AIDS reached a low point in the early nineties, though by 1993 researchers had a clearer idea of how it began—most thought through direct contact with the blood of infected primates, through an accidental needle jab or a skin lesion, for example, or having sex with a chimp. The virus was now considered to be not new and inherently deadly, as commonly assumed, but an old one that had only recently acquired deadly tendencies. Paul Ewald, an evolutionary biologist at

Amherst College, thought HIV might have infected people benignly for decades, maybe centuries, before it started to cause AIDS. Ewald traced the virulence of AIDS to the social upheavals of the sixties and seventies, which sped its movement through the population.

Such theories reflected a growing awareness that parasites evolved by natural selection, just like everything else in nature, changing character to adapt to the environment—except, in the case of HIV, tens of thousands of times faster than plants or animals, too fast for a drug or immune reaction to stop it in its tracks. Few researchers, though, had tried to exploit that quality in the virus until a Boston medical student, Yung-Kang Chow, made headlines when he showed that the technique of speeding up the evolution of HIV worked perfectly in a test tube. If the rapid spread of HIV turned it into a killer, then condoms and clean needles might actually do more than prevent new infections. If used widely enough, they might even drive the AIDS virus into a benign form like the one researchers claimed to have sighted in an eighty-one-year-old man in Australia who lacked any symptoms of the disease.

The scientific community was further encouraged in its quest for a vaccine when in 1995 scientists in Australia discovered a rare strain of the AIDS virus in a group of people who had carried it for up to fourteen years without developing the disease. Perhaps a weakened or attenuated virus could be the basis for an AIDS vaccine after all.

Despite the horrifying statistics, the AIDS plague in some ways remained almost invisible. Although it was talked about incessantly in the media, outside of scientific circles and coastal urban centers the disease was barely evident to most people.

After years of enduring bad news, however, all those whose lives had been touched by the disease were filled with a sense of anticipation and hope at the Eleventh International AIDS Conference, held in Vancouver, British Columbia, in July 1996. Experiments using a combination of three drugs—a protease inhibitor called saquinavir with AZT and DDC—had removed all measurable evidence of HIV in some patients' bloodstreams, and some were even experiencing a dramatic return to health. At the same time, researchers stressed that the drug combination was not a cure, and no one knew if the reduction in HIV was permanent.

Chapter 17

Twilight of the Gods

ON MAY 10, 1985, THE SEXUAL REVOLUTION TRIED TO GET IT UP ONE LAST TIME. On that date, Larry Levenson's sons, daughter, and niece, who had managed Plato's Retreat while he spent forty months in Allenwood Prison in Pennsylvania on tax evasion charges, threw the self-styled "King of Swing" a homecoming party.

During Levenson's incarceration, the club had limped along with floor shows, SM nights, and mud wrestling. On an average weekend night only thirty couples showed up, and most did not even bother to take off their clothes anymore. It was not unusual to see the once brimming mat room occupied by only two couples. The backroom maze of private rooms was almost deserted. The stripper nights intended to lure in the crowds on weekends were a flop. Plato's had gone from a swingers' paradise to just another hangout for voyeurs in towels.

Levenson's loyal family attributed the decline to his absence, and for one brief, shining moment it looked as if they were right. For the homecoming, five hundred loyal patrons, friends, and fans showed up, ranging in age from eighteen to seventy and running the sexual gamut from gorgeous to gross. Levenson himself appeared wearing a fake leopard robe with a matching hat and a long red train trimmed with white fur—looking like, in the words of one observer, a cross between Santa Claus and Tarzan. His date for the night was a heavyset dom accoutred in black teddy, white fur stole, and riding crop. The guest of honor was Al Goldstein, who had once bet Levenson $6,000 that he could not have fifteen orgasms in twenty-four hours. Levenson—who claimed that he had sex with four thousand to six thousand women a year (on weekdays five to seven women a night, ten to fifteen on weekends)—had accomplished the feat with ten hours to spare.

The last hurrah was short-lived. On November 22, 1985, the New York City Department of Public Health closed Plato's down. Earlier it had posted an ominous warning on the front door: "Absolutely No Anal Sex or Fellatio Permitted on Plato's Premises/Violators Will Lose Their Membership." With the Sexual Revolution dying of its own accord, along came the sex police to apply euthanasia. The club was padlocked not for high-risk sex, but for prostitution and failure to obtain an occupancy permit.

Though Levenson denied the prostitution charge, Plato's had earned a well-deserved reputation as a place where some women sold their services, even advertising in *Screw* their willingness to accompany men to the club. The ACLU leaped in to defend Plato's, arguing that many of the city's famous hotels and bars would also have to be closed if equal justice were applied. The real reason the club was busted, the ACLU accurately pointed out, was that gay activists were protesting the closing of gay clubs, so the city moved to close a heterosexual club.

In November 1985 New York also closed down the Mine Shaft, a multilevel SM-oriented social club for gays. The Anvil, another gay club, shut voluntarily. After the Hellfire Club closed, the city padlocked the gay New St. Mark's and the Everard Spa. In 1988 and 1989 three movie theaters that boasted dark lounges and glory holes were also shuttered. Sexual alternatives to clubs and baths became instantly available, however, with commercial masturbation parlors like the Locker Room, J's/The Hangout, and Shooting Stars soon attracting gays who synchronized their masturbation rituals while watching hard-core videos.

A quarter of a century earlier, in 1964, exotic dancer Carol Doda had been the first stripper to shed her bra, a historic performance that took place at San Francisco's Condor Club. Now the naked woman atop the club's giant neon sign wore a corset. In North Beach, where once tourists could obtain both topless and bottomless shoe shines, the number of topless clubs had shrunk to exactly four.

Sleaze was in a big squeeze. In the Combat Zone in Boston, the Block in Baltimore, Times Square in New York, strike forces of federal and local law enforcement officials were making life miserable for porn shops and peep shows, employing an array of legal weaponry ranging from statutes and ordinances involving everything from obscenity, narcotics, prostitution, gambling, and alcohol to public health, building maintenance, child labor, income taxes, zoning, and immigration.

In addition, a confluence of technological and economic forces was further eroding pornography's power base. An estimated twenty million Americans now rented X-rated movies from their local video store. The number of porn theaters nationwide had declined from more than eight hundred to less than four hundred. Seventeen of the Combat Zone's twenty-two sex clubs had vanished largely because of the real estate boom of the eighties. Not even the sleaze merchants could afford the high rentals brought on by the tide of gentrification that was an urban hallmark of the eighties. Similar uprootings had also taken place in Pittsburgh, Baltimore, and Washington, D.C.

ONE DAY IN 1986 Bob Guccione received through the mail an article that had originally appeared in *Soldier of Fortune* magazine. The article was about a mercenary who had advertised his services in that magazine but had suddenly dropped dead. Police investigating his death found on his body an uncashed check for $1 million made out to the dead man. It was signed by Larry Flynt. According to *Soldier of Fortune,* over dinner in Los Angeles the *Hustler* publisher had offered the mercenary a seven-figure payoff if he killed Guccione, Hugh Hefner, and Frank Sinatra. (Flynt later claimed the offer was a joke.)

Guccione had heard the story before, from three of Flynt's ex-bodyguards, two of whom claimed to have fled Flynt's employment after he torched their houses, possibly during a bout of drug-induced paranoia. During his recovery Flynt and his wife, Althea, had become addicted to painkillers and, later, other drugs. Numerous detox attempts failed. Now confined to a gold-plated wheelchair, he spent much of his time in his eight-bedroom Mediterranean mansion in the Hollywood Hills above Los Angeles, where with the help of trusted associates he continued to look after his dwindling empire from afar.

Meanwhile, Flynt's would-be assassin had not been found, though white supremacist Joseph Paul Franklin, who by now was serving four life sentences for racially motivated killings in Utah and Wisconsin, was linked to the shooting. Prosecutors had not brought him to trial, however, because of inconsistencies in the evidence.

In 1987 Althea, the only woman Flynt had ever claimed to love, drowned at the age of thirty-three in a bathtub. Previously, she had been diagnosed with HIV, which she may have contracted through IV drug use, though she and Flynt were also members of an SM group based in Long Beach, California. Other members of this group—the same one once "audited" by Ruth Carter Stapleton—included a prominent businessman. Flynt possessed a videotape of an orgy involving the businessman, a *Hustler* executive, and several government agents, and threatened to go public with it as a means of ensuring a continuing flow of drugs for his addiction. Flynt was also deeply in hock to Mob-controlled moneylenders based in south Florida. Unknown to him, they considered Althea Leasure a "loose cannon" who "knew too much," and it was they who arranged her murder in the guise of an accidental drowning induced by a drug overdose.

(Several years later, Nicole Brown Simpson, ex-wife of football player O. J. Simpson, accompanied a black professional football player to one of the SM parties in Long Beach, and it was there that she first met Ron Goldman. According to members of the group, Nicole—a battered wife—had little interest in pursuing SM and did not return a second time. In one of the most celebrated trials of the century, Simpson was later acquitted of the grisly murder of both Goldman and his former wife.)

Haunted by the loss of Althea, Flynt began to call others by her name. Yet in 1992 he began a romance with a former nurse, Liz Berrios. She oversaw his care, though after Althea marriage seemed out of the question.

In August 1993 Larry Flynt launched a new magazine for mothers called *Maternity Fashion & Beauty.* The first cover featured all-American TV host Kathie Lee Gifford, pregnant with her second child. Only after the magazine appeared did she learn that its publisher was the same man who put out *Busty Beauties, Barely Legal,* and *Hustler,* but she had signed a photo release and there was nothing she could do. She had also posed for the May cover for *Longevity,* a Guccione publication that had been launched in 1989 with a $5 million kickoff campaign.

Pornographers had gone mainstream with a vengeance. Flynt's $100 million empire now contained thirty magazines, among them *PC Laptop Computers* and *Camera & Darkroom Photography.* Guccione had purchased the revered *Saturday Review* in October 1987 from Manhattan Media Corporation for an estimated $3.5 million and also published such mainstream monthlies as *Omni* and *Four Wheeler.*

In the aftermath of *Penthouse*'s Vanessa Williams coup, the feud between Guccione and Hefner had moved onto new turf—celebrity bodies. In 1985 the most famous woman in the United States, and probably the world, was pop singer Madonna, whose earthy past emerged when both men's magazines published sets of unremarkable black-and-white nude photographs taken of the singer years earlier. Guccione claimed he had first crack at the set *Playboy* published and had turned them down in favor of other and better photos. Hefner printed 5.9 million copies, or fifty thousand more than the magazine's normal run, and *Penthouse* shipped 5.2 million instead of 4.9. But Madonna's response to the exposure—refreshingly, it seemed to bore rather than to haunt her—ensured a lackluster response on the part of her millions of fans as well.

In 1987 the feud rekindled over the biggest sex story of the eighties. It all began one summer day when a twenty-eight-year-old prostitute and part-time church secretary named Jessica Hahn appeared on TV screens and in newspapers and magazines, saying she had been forcibly deflowered by charismatic TV evangelist Jim Bakker, who with his wife, Tammy Faye, operated the highly profitable and influential PTL (People That Love) televangelism empire out of North Carolina.

Born a Catholic, Hahn first set foot inside the Full Gospel Tabernacle Church in Massapequa, Long Island, as a chubby fourteen-year-old. She quickly became a devoted member of the congregation, volunteering for duties like cleaning the church toilets. After graduating from high school in 1977, she signed on as a church secretary. Friends soon noticed that Hahn seemed to be very close to the congregation's flamboyant pastor, the Reverend Gene Profeta, who carried a pistol, drove a Lincoln, wore a mink coat and tinted eyeglasses, and flew his own airplane. She also appeared to be living in a style far beyond what her $80-a-week salary could support. A gospel groupie, Hahn was also friendly with a number of visiting preachers. Profeta's wife, Glenda, urged her to tone down her plunging necklines and tight sweaters, but to no avail.

Among the preachers Hahn was close to was John Wesley Fletcher, a televangelist and friend of Bakker who had duplicated the success of his mentor, Pat Robertson, with his own talk show and religious network. Hahn frequently baby-sat for his children when the Fletcher family came to Long Island for revivals. In February 1980, when Hahn was seventeen, she later told friends, she had lost her virginity to Fletcher at a New York hotel. But when Fletcher flew home to Oklahoma, treating her as a one-night stand, Hahn grew furious.

To placate her, Fletcher invited her to Florida to meet Bakker in December 1980. A friend remembers her calling from her room at the Sheraton Sand Key Hotel, where she was waiting for Bakker and Fletcher to return from the telethon they were conducting. "I'm so excited," said Hahn. "I met Jim Bakker! We sat and talked for two hours. He's so sweet and wonderful! You couldn't speak to a nicer man. I'm sitting here drinking wine and watching TV."

When Hahn returned to her church after that weekend, she confided to a friend that she had slept with both Fletcher and Bakker. She claimed that Bakker had told her that Tammy Faye's vagina was too big for him and that he could not be satisfied with her. But later Fletcher came back to the room and told her that Bakker was in a fetal position, "sobbing and crying his heart out because he is sick about what he did. He's calling you a New York bimbo." Jessica was outraged.

A few days later Bakker called to apologize, but Jessica was still furious. She mused to her friend that perhaps she could make some money off the affair.

"You mean blackmail?" the friend asked.

"You never know," Jessica replied.

Hahn then apparently consulted with Profeta, who introduced her to Paul Roper, a California businessman and lay preacher. After taking her sworn affidavit, Roper negotiated a hush-money payment, collecting $265,000 in fees and expenses from PTL. However, Hahn had no intention of keeping silent, knowing that Bakker was powerless to enforce her agreement not to talk.

Hahn then attempted to sell a version of the story to Guccione, whose earnest manner on television had impressed her. Her portrayal of herself quickly evolved into a media con not seen since Clifford Irving's hoax biography of Howard Hughes in the early seventies. She told Guccione that she had been a virgin until Bakker drugged and brutally raped her in a Florida hotel room. Guccione said he was "hungry" for her story in order to "get" TV evangelists like Bakker, whom he suspected of being an éminence grise of the Meese Commission, and maybe even Jerry Falwell, if she could network her way into his circle. He offered Hahn $350,000, but she broke off negotiations with him when he asked her to wear a tape recorder in an attempt to entrap Bakker and Falwell into making incriminating remarks.

Next Hahn went to Hefner, who shared Guccione's low opinion of Bakker and was still eager to settle the Vanessa Williams score. *Playboy* offered Hahn a contract (reputedly for $1 million, but more likely in the $350,000 range) in exchange for her agreement to bare not only her soul but her upper torso. *Penthouse* tried to scoop its competitor by publishing a detailed description of her encounter with Bakker based on a transcript it had "obtained" of a tape recording Hahn had made while trying to squeeze hush money out of Bakker's organization. *Playboy* countered with a two-part interview of Hahn by Robert Scheer, a reporter for the *Los Angeles Times,* that had Bakker murmuring, "When you help the shepherd, you're helping the sheep," and other unconvincing pillow talk.

Scheer later told *The Washington Post* he had found Hahn's account "credible," though he stressed that his interview was not an investigative piece. *Washington Post* reporter Art Harris, a protégé of Bob Woodward whom *Penthouse* hired to look into the matter, at first believed Hahn, too. Harris and his *Post* colleague Michael Isikoff had begun investigating the seamier side of the PTL in the spring of 1987, while scouring topless bars in North Carolina looking for other Bakker mistresses.

But Harris began to have doubts about Hahn after receiving several anonymous phone calls saying that the citizens of Massapequa, Long Island, were irate that she was passing herself off as the virginal prey of a manipulative preacher. Harris tracked down a woman named Evelyn Riccobono, a former secretary at the Full Gospel Tabernacle Church. Riccobono in turn led Harris to her ex-husband, Rocco Riccobono, who confirmed that he had had a sporadic affair with Hahn beginning in 1978, two years before her alleged deflowering by Bakker. Harris also located Joanne Posner, a former friend of Hahn, who claimed to have witnessed at least one sexual encounter between Hahn and Rocco. Further research turned up other witnesses who remembered Hahn boasting of losing her virginity at age seventeen to

Fletcher. And in a lurid sidebar that ran with the *Penthouse* article, a woman identified as Roxanne Dacus claimed to have been Hahn's "madam" in 1977 and 1978. Dacus had operated an escort service out of her house in Nassau County, New York, and she claimed that Hahn had oral sex and intercourse with up to forty men at a single party.

By now the scandal was playing out on the front pages of newspapers across the land. The energetic *New York Post* dug up two more alleged ex-lovers, while *The Washington Post* introduced a pre-Bakker lover of Hahn's who disputed her claim of sexual inexperience. Even shock-radio host Howard Stern, a friend of Hahn's, seemed aghast; he had also believed.

Bakker was now under federal investigation for alleged frauds at PTL stemming from the hush-money cover-up and assorted tax-, mail-, and wire-fraud charges. He called Hahn a professional "who knew every trick in the trade" and said his private detective had located eighteen ex-lovers of hers. But eventually he confessed to a fifteen-minute sexual encounter with the shapely ex-church secretary back in December 1980 and resigned his multi-million-dollar TV ministry. He was eventually sentenced to eighteen years in jail for defrauding his TV flock. Tammy Faye found another man.

Hahn continued to deny all allegations about her sexual past, along with those made by two alleged ex-lovers when a New York grand jury began looking into the extravagant lifestyle of Gene Profeta, tax fraud at his church, and his possible role in the Wedtech defense-contracting scandal. Hahn testified in that grand jury session and another probing PTL irregularities in North Carolina only under a grant of immunity.

Meanwhile, *Playboy* maintained an awkward silence, although it abruptly canceled Hahn's East Coast promotional tour in October 1987 as witnesses to her secret sex life were stepping forward. Nevertheless Hahn went on to get substantial plastic surgery on her lips, nose, cheeks, and breasts, and ultimately took up residence in the Playboy mansion in Los Angeles. In 1988 Hahn became a sultry radio voice in Phoenix for $350 a week plus car and hotel room. Ratings climbed at first, then fell, and she was dismissed, although she remained a frequent radio and TV guest. Eventually a new preacher came into her life—ex-minister turned comedian Sam Kinison, with whom she had a stormy affair. As late as 1992 *Playboy* ran a third pictorial of Hahn under the headline "My Fifteen Minutes of Fame Are Up. Not." But they were.

In July 1988 *Penthouse* unmasked the hypocrisy of another prominent televangelist. In a sixteen-page layout sealed by a perforated strip to prevent casual drugstore browsers from peeking, it featured a series of grainy black-and-white photographs re-creating the various "pornographic" poses that the Reverend Jimmy Swaggart had asked a streetwalker named Debbie Murphree to assume. The pictures showed what Swaggart had paid for, first cheaply ($20), then dearly (loss of his TV empire): a crude "Debbie" tattoo on her arm, coarse linen, an unshaded bulb hanging from the pasteboard ceiling of the actual motel room where Swaggart, according to Murphree, had instructed her: "Pull your panties up your crack like a magazine I've seen. . . ." After the exposé, Swaggart vanished into obscurity, reemerging briefly in the headlines a few years later after he picked up another streetwalker.

Though the falls from grace of Jim Bakker and Jimmy Swaggart captured the biggest headlines, they only culminated a decade of fundamentalist scandals, financial and otherwise. Perhaps the most notable was the 1976 downfall of Dr. Billy James Hargis, king of the McCarthy-era anti-Communist preachers and a prime denouncer of sex and satanism, when *Time* revealed he had sodomized male and female students at his tiny fundamentalist college. There was also a continuing public scandal involving sexual abuse of minors by the Catholic clergy, a problem that had traditionally been treated as an internal problem within church jurisdiction and not reported to police.

The silence ended with national media coverage of a case involving James Porter, a Massachusetts priest who between 1960 and 1972 victimized, often sadistically, more than two hundred minors in several states. Between 1984 and 1994 an estimated five thousand survivors reported their abuse to church authorities, and by early 1995 more than six hundred cases were pending in court, with more than half a billion dollars already paid out to plaintiffs and several dioceses approaching bankruptcy. By some estimates one in six priests was involved in sex with a minor, with a three-to-one preference for boys.

THE SAME MONTH that *Penthouse* published its black-and-white photos of Swaggart's hooker, *Playboy* ran a rare black-and-white spread of supermodel Cindy Crawford in a bathing suit. The contrast between the sordid and the fashionable exemplified the difference between the two magazines and epitomized the latter's ongoing attempt to become mainstream and to distance itself from its pornographic essence. Hefner now lived in semiretirement in California, his diminished empire run out of Chicago by his daughter, Christie. The magazine had long since dropped its Playboy Philosophy, its ratings of porn videos, the photos of Hef with pipe and robe surrounded by Bunnies. The text accompanying the layouts was full of girl-next-door banalities ("She hates rainy days, loves animals").

The long-running battle between *Playboy* and *Penthouse* moved to video in the late eighties. Here again, *Penthouse*'s offerings were racier and initially sold extremely well, outselling such popular favorites as *Thelma and Louise* and *Fantasia*. Though some chains such as Blockbuster refused to touch *Penthouse*'s unrated products, soft-core was one of the fastest-growing segments in the home video market.

In August 1987, while the Jessica Hahn–Jim Bakker scandal was still un-folding, Guccione made other headlines when he threw his eldest son, Bobby, and the entire staff of Bobby's pop-music monthly, *Spin,* out of the corpora-tion's offices. For months the two had quarreled over the ownership of the magazine, which Guccione had helped to launch with a loan of $6 million. Guccione wanted General Media to acquire 100 percent ownership of the trademark, which was licensed to Bobby. Bobby Jr. refused. The day after his father ejected him, Bobby Jr. announced his plans to keep the publication alive without Guccione's support.

Skeptical about the future of print, in 1993—a year ahead of *Playboy*—Guccione launched an on-line service featuring erotic electronic mail and the opportunity to download high-resolution images from the magazine, as well as *Penthouse Interactive,* a CD-ROM that permitted viewers to pose one of three Pets for a centerfold shoot "critiqued" by Guccione himself. Despite the popularity of the *Penthouse* home site on the Internet, reputedly garnering more hits than any other (three million daily), electronic profits proved to be elusive.

In fact, Guccione's empire was now in serious trouble. Circulation of *Pent-house* was dropping precipitously. Though Guccione's holding company, General Media Ltd., avoided junk bond financing in the eighties, his con-suming obsession with opening a casino in Atlantic City had drained the company of more than $200 million, mostly in lawyers' fees and interest on loans. Unable to get bank financing, Guccione ultimately sold the property to real estate developer Donald Trump for $44 million. In need of cash, Guc-cione finally succumbed to temptation and put the company in hock with $95 million in junk bonds.

Meanwhile, *Longevity* and *Omni,* the company's two high-profile main-stream publications, had never showed a significant profit and in 1996 were finally closed down. Another $25 million was lost when the company arranged with a Moscow publisher to issue a Russian edition of *Penthouse.* The "publisher" turned out to be the Moscow Mob, who simply kept all the profits—the first few issues sold out—until Guccione ended the disastrous arrangement.

Matters only got worse. While Guccione's wife, Kathy Keeton, battled lymphoma, his second son, Anthony, a Harvard MBA and the heir apparent, was also booted out of the company in a dispute over General Media's bid to launch an X-rated cable network. As *Penthouse* circulation hovered at the million mark, with newsstand sales at around 600,000, Guccione saw his net worth—which had once reached a high of $310 million—plummet to minus $70 million. Media and company insiders measured the company's future in terms of days and months, as a desperate Guccione resorted to such pathetic "scoops" as publishing a picture of a Hollywood prop that he had been persuaded by an enterprising photographer was the first snapshot ever of a space alien.

Yet Guccione remained as self-confident as ever, vowing not only that *Penthouse* would survive, but that he would one day live to see the opening of his dream casino in Atlantic City. Even as his company dwindled into inconsequence, if not obscurity, Guccione was making plans to direct the world's *second* mainstream XXX-rated film, this one based on the life of Catherine the Great. This time, unlike the *Caligula* debacle, *he* would direct.

Hefner's family situation was also in flux. In 1985 he had suffered a minor stroke, which he later referred to as a stroke of luck. During his recovery he asked himself, "What is the future?" and the answer came to him in a single word: "Death." He decided that he had reached the end of the second act of his life, with its business commitments and its obsessive series of romantic relationships, and he wanted to enjoy the third. He literally stopped going to business meetings, and in July 1989 the sixty-three-year-old publisher married twenty-six-year-old Kimberley Faye Conrad, the Playmate of the Year, who later bore him two children. Before long, houseguests found themselves tripping over toys on the stairway. Playboy Mansion West had become a home at last.

Playboy was also faring considerably better than its longtime rival, with newsstand sales at about half a million and a total circulation of slightly more than three million. Though the subscriptions were mostly bargain-rate giveaways, they ensured a healthy revenue flow from advertisers. The battle between the hare and the tortoise, as Guccione once described his competition with Hefner, had for once been won by the hare.

Larry Flynt, meanwhile, had not been idle. In early 1993 the Wyoming State Supreme Court ruled that he had a constitutional right to call Andrea Dworkin a "repulsive presence," a "foul-mouthed, abrasive man hater," and a "shit-squeezing sphincter," not to mention "a crybaby who can dish out criticism but can't take it." Dworkin, for some reason, had claimed the statements were defamatory. Flynt was not faring as well on the newsstands, however, where *Hustler* now claimed a circulation of four hundred thousand.

In late 1996 Flynt finally got some mainstream respect when Oliver Stone produced and Milos Forman directed a movie version of his life titled *The People vs. Larry Flynt*. As played by Woody Harrelson, Flynt emerges as a drug-abusing, foulmouthed lowlife but also as a genuine American folk hero and staunch defender of the First Amendment. Flynt's contribution to enlarging the legal definition of the First Amendment was certainly as enormous as it was colorful and obnoxious (he once called Justice Sandra Day O'Connor a "token cunt" to her face before getting thrown out of court). But the movie glossed over Flynt's ties to the Mob and perpetuated his preposterous claim that he was shot by right-wing enemies of pornography.

Al Goldstein's porn empire was in a state of near collapse. The circulation of *Screw* had dwindled to about ten thousand, with most sales in New York. The publication survived precariously on phone-sex and prostitution ads catering to out-of-town businessmen. With the heady days of the First Amendment wars long behind him, the restless Goldstein spent his weekends at the Playboy mansion in Los Angeles with other forgotten celebrities and the rest of the time commuting between homes in Florida and New York.

LIKE LEAR, his kingdom in ruins, his sons and knights plotting against him, Reuben Sturman waited for nightfall on the evening of December 7, 1992. Earlier in the year he had exhausted all appeals on his tax conviction. Meanwhile jurors in the Las Vegas trial had cleared him of one obscenity charge but could not reach agreement on nine others, and prosecutors were threatening to try him again. And he still faced trial in Chicago on extortion and murder charges. Feeling betrayed by Ralph Levine and his other closest friends, and bereft of allies in the porn industry, Sturman had struck a deal with the Department of Justice in April. He had agreed to plead guilty to one count of racketeering and seven counts of shipping obscene materials, including child porn and bestiality films, across state lines. In exchange, the sentence was to run concurrently with his ten-year sentence in the tax case.

Two months later, at age sixty-eight, he had entered the minimum-security federal prison in Boron, California. In an attempt to keep Naomi out of jail, he had divorced her, though she remained his only friend and confidante. Then he learned that federal prosecutors were going to bring charges against her anyway, for attempting to bribe a juror in the Cleveland tax case with sex and/or money.

Recently Sturman had heard a rumor that two hundred prisoners at Boron, including probably himself, were being transferred to a new camp in Colorado. That meant he would be separated by a thousand miles from Naomi and their six-year-old daughter, Erica, who now lived a convenient hour's drive away in Los Angeles. Desperate to be reunited with them during the upcoming holidays, and dreading his approaching murder trial, Sturman took the longest walk of his life, out to the prison softball field, which bordered the highway. He was dressed in blue fatigues and tennis shoes, and he sported the beard he had recently begun to grow. As the sun slowly set over the sand dunes, mesquite, and Joshua trees, he waited.

Sturman had plotted his escape with the aid of Michael Colella, a small-time California pornographer who lived in the Los Angeles suburb of Encino. It was a secret even from Naomi. At seven o'clock, on schedule, a jeep appeared on the horizon. As it pulled up, Sturman glanced around one last time to make sure he was unobserved, then got in and drove off. "Good-bye and good luck," he murmured defiantly. "I'm leaving." Characteristically, his prison escape was as low-key and undramatic as the antlike perseverance and marketing genius that had helped him create his XXX-rated empire.

Back in Cleveland, where the escape was front-page news, IRS investigator Richard Rosfelder, who had spent most of his career tracking Sturman's paper empire from Switzerland to the Cayman Islands, was devastated. His longtime colleague Tom Ciehanski, who had retired in 1987 partly because he thought Sturman would never be brought to trial, was despondent, too. So was Cleveland's hard-driving assistant U.S. attorney, Craig S. Morford, whose crusading tenacity had finally led to Sturman's conviction of evading $3.5 million in taxes—a token but nevertheless crushing victory. (Government prosecutors claimed to have evidence that Sturman actually evaded $42 million in taxes and penalties, but thought presenting that case to a jury would take years.) Homer Young, the FBI's longtime porn expert and another career Sturman watcher, noted with irony that the escape fell on the fifty-first anniversary of another day of infamy in American history, the predawn bombing of Pearl Harbor.

If the law enforcement community found it difficult to savor this or any other aspect of Sturman's escape, North Hollywood was soon ablaze with gossip. Rumors quickly spread that the King had been cooperating with the government or that he had arranged to be picked up by an all-terrain 4WD vehicle, hustled to a waiting plane in the middle of the desert, and flown to the south of Spain or maybe the Algarve. Ensconced in a sumptuous seaside villa on some almond-scented coast, the myth had it, he would live out his last years drawing on his secret banks accounts and enjoying the company of Naomi and his daughter.

But the reality, like Sturman himself, was both simpler and much more complicated. Colella had arranged with Sturman's secretaries, Stephanie Friedman and Sylvia Richards, for Friedman's brother to bring Sturman to Colella's home, where he would stay temporarily. Convinced that prosecutors and insiders alike would think he had fled to Spain or Tangier, Sturman decided the best place to hide was in his own backyard. From Colella's home he contacted Naomi, who visited him on several occasions and talked to him frequently by cellular phone. After she had installed a false light fixture to conceal a stairway to the attic if he needed to hide, he moved to their Sherman Oaks home. Naomi asked her brother to open a bank account under the name Escape, Inc., to receive overseas transfers. In January, fearful he might be discovered, Sturman moved into a furnished one-bedroom apartment, rented under the name of Abe Levine, in Anaheim, only 110 miles from Boron.

Meanwhile, federal marshals—under the direction, ironically, of Henry E.

Hudson, who had headed the Meese Commission when it had investigated Sturman seven years earlier—put a tail on Naomi and other Sturman associates. Eventually the two secretaries and the brother confessed. At seven-thirty in the morning on February 10, 1993, Sturman was sleeping in his Anaheim apartment when three U.S. marshals, using a passkey, entered.

"Hey, Rube!" one of them called out good-naturedly.

Sturman's eyes widened, and slowly he raised his hands. He had no intention of reaching for the loaded .38 revolver lying on a nearby dresser.

Later Naomi was arrested in Los Angeles and charged with conspiracy to bribe a juror in the Cleveland tax case. After pleading guilty, she was sentenced to twenty-one months in prison. Sturman also pleaded guilty and received a similar sentence. Around the same time, their luxurious Sherman Oaks home was lost in a mudslide. But the worst was yet to come. In the Chicago trial relating to the bombing incident, Sturman was found guilty of conspiring to commit murder and received a sentence of twenty years—making it unlikely that he would ever again be a free man.

Sturman also had the shock of learning, from evidence presented by the prosecution during the Chicago trial, that his son, David, had been cooperating with the U.S. government ever since their conviction in the Cleveland tax case. David had wanted his father to plead guilty in the case, ostensibly to get everybody else off, but Sturman had been certain they would win. What Sturman did not know was that David, who drew a four-year sentence, had instructed his lawyers not to cross-examine his father in any way that would force Sturman to incriminate himself. Now, of all the children from his first marriage, only Peggy, his adopted daughter, remained close, and Sturman harbored especially bitter feelings toward David.

Some porn insiders continued to suspect that Sturman himself was cooperating with federal prosecutors to get his sentence commuted. They knew, for example, that after being captured in Anaheim, Sturman had told authorities that Doc Johnson, the crown jewel of his empire, which he had sold to partner Ron Braverman in the great 1985–1988 divestiture, was his. The company was immediately closed down and its bank account seized. Only when the authorities were shown proof that Braverman was the owner of record was the company allowed to resume business. Sturman angrily insisted that Braverman had never paid him for the purchase, but he could not prove it. Indeed, in the end nothing Sturman had to say about Doc Johnson or any of his other former holdings interested prosecutors sufficiently to get his sentence reduced.

In September 1995 a mysterious fire nearly leveled the Doc Johnson plant in North Hollywood. Soon after, a bank in the Cayman Islands was blown up. The two events amounted to a last battle for control of what remained of Reuben Sturman's once vast empire, though the circumstances and players in the power struggle remain known only to a very few. According to insiders, three major factions were vying for control of the porn industry, and the retaliatory bombing targeted a place where a significant amount of one of the faction's assets resided. That bombing decisively concluded the struggle, and the three groups—one of them headquartered in Paris—agreed to divide the international porn market into three equal shares.

THROUGH THE YEARS, numerous porn stars had tried—and failed—to succeed in the Hollywood mainstream. Aspiring technicians routinely learned their craft in the porn industry. Directors Peter Bogdanovich and Francis Ford Coppola also worked on the fringes of the business, although neither actually made a porn flick. It was also possible for porn actors who had managed to remain unburdened by reputation to cross over, most notably Sylvester Stallone, who had starred in a forgettable 1970 porn flick, *Party at Kitty and Stud's*. (After he achieved superstardom, the movie resurfaced as *The Italian Stallion*. When rights were offered to Stallone for $100,000 to "save him embarrassment," he replied, "I wouldn't buy it for two bucks.") But the experience of veteran porn actress Georgina Spelvin—whose mainstream high point was a role as a prostitute who gives a blow job to the commander in *Police Academy*—was typical. Crossover attempts by male actors like Harry Reems usually failed even more dismally.

Nor were the salaries of porn actors much consolation. Top female stars like Seka were rumored to make $25,000 a film, but many insiders remained skeptical that anyone was this well paid. In general, in 1988 the top rate for an actress was about $1,000 a day, with shooting seldom lasting for much longer.

Some porn actresses supplemented their incomes with tie-ins with porn magazines, which offered the stars long-term contracts in exchange for the exclusive use of their names and bodies. Gloria Leonard of *High Society* and Marilyn Chambers of *Club* were two notable examples of porn stars who were featured each month in a pictorial in their respective magazines; each also had a column that offered sex advice and worldly wisdom. Two or three times a year the more successful porn stars also toured the United States and Canada, performing in well-paying strip shows. But only the most industrious of even this select group earned more than $100,000 a year. The situation was even worse for most male porn stars, who had virtually no opportunity to pick up a few extracurricular dollars.

Not everyone got into porn for money, however. There was the occasional amateur like Susie Bright, an aspiring San Francisco writer and lesbian activist. Bright was only fourteen years old when *Behind the Green Door* premiered in 1972. On the six o'clock news she learned that the film's star was

Marilyn Chambers, who was also the woman pictured on the Ivory Snow box. Searching the cupboard, she found a box of the detergent and scrutinized Chambers's well-scrubbed, maternal glow. Chambers looked pretty and nice, and Bright thought it was very unfair of the soap manufacturer to cancel her contract.

Exactly fourteen years later Bright found herself cast as an orgy extra in *Behind the Green Door: The Sequel.* In recent years she had shed her orthopedic shoes and braces, but she insisted on wearing her glasses so as not to miss any detail of this, the first ever safe-sex heterosexual porn movie. The film, which was produced by the Mitchell brothers, Arnie and Jim, also boasted another, more dubious first: all eighty of its performers were amateurs.

"Raise your hand if at any time you believe you are not having safe sex," director Sharon McNight ordered the cast when filming began. "The staff will now be handing out a bag of condoms, surgical gloves, dental dams, and Nonoxynol-9 lubricant. No penis will be touched without a rubber on it. No fingers will get sticky without a rubber glove. All pussies must be covered with a dental dam before they are licked. I want to be able to smell your lubricant a yard away. Is that clear?" Bright and her fellow cast members agreed that they were prepared to teach the home audience how to have safe sex even if they had to cover *Green Door* with rubber from wall to wall.

Later Jim Mitchell announced: "Okay, everyone, loosen up. We'll be coming over to your tables, one at a time, for some close-ups, so start your action." Panic set in as people realized they could no longer just sit there, flexing their empty condoms. Bright and her lover Fanny Fatale, a dancer at the Mitchell brothers' O'Farrell Theater, were sitting in a booth with two other women. Fatale turned to one of them and said—casting Susie an apologetic glance—"Vanessa, you have the nicest breasts."

"Yes, can't we use the champagne on them somehow?" Bright suggested.

"But we have to use the rubber goods," Fatale reminded them. Suddenly the movie began to seem like a last-minute audition for *The Gong Show.*

Arching her back, Fatale began to serve up great Method moans. Realizing she had better look busy, Bright stretched a dental dam over Fatale's labia and took a long plastic lick. But by then the camera had moved on to the next table.

None of the cast knew that the Mitchell brothers were feuding over the future direction of their partnership. With the rise of video their chain of porn theaters was fast collapsing, numerous lawsuits were pending, and their jointly owned O'Farrell Theater in the Tenderloin district was in financial difficulty.

In February 1991 a drugged-out Jim shot Artie to death in what most porn insiders, despite the feud, viewed as an accidental shooting. Artie's wife, Karen, later accepted an $800,000 wrongful death settlement from Jim

Mitchell and Associated Indemnity Co., which had written Artie's home-owners insurance policy and would have been responsible in a negligence suit. In February 1992 a Marin County judge sentenced Jim Mitchell to six years and a $10,000 fine for voluntary manslaughter in the death of his brother.

In 1991 Berl Kutchinsky published a follow-up to his study of Danish pornography for the Johnson Commission, which had shown a correlation between decriminalizing pornography and a decline in sex crimes.

According to Kutchinsky, the theory that pornography was a direct cause of rape originated in 1960 with Tennessee senator Estes Kefauver, who at the time was chairing a Senate subcommittee investigating the possible link between juvenile delinquency and pornography as typified by such airbrushed magazines as *Good Times;* with J. Edgar Hoover in 1965 in a diatribe against pornography; and with the minority report (coauthored by longtime porn foe Charles Keating) of the U.S. Presidential Commission in 1970. More recently the theory had been embraced by coalitions of feminists and Christians not only in the United States but in Canada, Great Britain, Norway, Sweden, and other countries. It had even penetrated the ranks of behavioral and social scientists.

The most severe criticism leveled against the 1970 presidential report, Kutchinsky noted, was that it had not sufficiently investigated the long-term effects of violent pornography. Instead of taking up the challenge, most new research was limited to the immediate effects of exposure. Kutchinsky further pointed out that violent pornography was not very common in the late sixties, when the research sponsored by the commission was carried out.

Referring to Edward Donnerstein's 1984 experiment, which suggested that males became more sexually aggressive after watching such violent full-length movies as *The Texas Chainsaw Massacre,* Kutchinsky observed that the subjects did not choose to see those movies, let alone five in one week. Second, they knew they were part of an experiment and could hardly be unaware of what was expected of them. Third, repeated viewing might well lead to reduced sensitivity in some subjects, as a result of reduced anxiety. Kutchinsky's conclusion: "These experiments, when they are best, pose an intelligent question—they do not answer it."

Kutchinsky also took note of studies that examined the reactions of rapists to pornography, such as the comparative studies of sex offenders and non–sex offenders undertaken by the U.S. Commission on Obscenity and Pornography. Sex offenders generally reported sexually repressive family backgrounds, immature and inadequate sexual histories, and rigidly conservative attitudes toward sex. Sex offenders generally had less experience as teenagers with erotica and as adults did not use pornography more frequently than others. But a major drawback of such studies was their reliance on their subjects' own reports about their reactions.

According to Kutchinsky, the only reliable way to prove or disprove a causal connection between pornography and rape was to examine rape statistics in countries where hard-core was widely available, making allowances for the incidence of other social problems. Kutchinsky looked at Denmark, Sweden, and West Germany, which had legalized pornography in 1969, 1970, and 1973, respectively, and the United States, where pornography, though not legalized, was readily available in major cities. "A twenty-year period would therefore be sufficient to trace any influence of the 'porno wave' on the rape statistics," Kutchinsky declared.

Only in the United States was there a marked increase in officially recorded incidence of rape, and that might have been partly a result of increased reporting as rape victims no longer felt so stigmatized. Moreover, since rape was by definition both a violent crime and a sex crime, it seemed reasonable to compare rape with nonsexual violent crimes and with nonviolent sex crimes. Kutchinsky found that in the European countries rape was clearly not part of either the general crime pattern or a pattern of violent crimes in particular; in all three, nonviolent sex crimes decreased, while the incidence of rape remained constant. (As for the United States, Kutchinsky cited a lack of statistical evidence that made it impossible to compare assault and rape with nonviolent sex crimes.)

Kutchinsky also refuted Andrea Dworkin's undocumented claim that in most pornographic films "real women are tied up, stretched, hanged, fucked, gang-banged, whipped, beaten, and begging for more." An analysis of 430 sexually explicit magazines on sale at an adult bookstore in Times Square revealed that only 1.2 percent contained SM material. SM was defined as activity "in which one person hurts another for the purpose of mutual sexual gratification." Bondage and discipline ("in which at least one person is relatively immobile and subject to discipline, usually as a result of being tied, and another person engages in sexual interaction with the person in bondage") accounted for another 4.9 percent. The woman was the submissive partner in 60 percent of the films and in only 3 percent of magazine pornography. Moreover, in all cases the brutality was obviously staged or faked.

Kutchinsky quoted a historical survey of porn movies undertaken in 1984 by J. W. Slade showing that, unlike mainstream film culture, "the hard-core film . . . rejected violence almost entirely." Slade himself disputed the myth of the "secret circulation of 'snuff films,' i.e., reels that depict actual intercourse climaxed by the literal murder of the female. To date, despite a thorough investigation by the FBI, despite a large reward posted by the publisher of the sex tabloid *Screw,* and despite frenzied searches by collectors of the bizarre, no authentic snuff film has come to light."

IN THE DARK AND GLOOMY NIGHT of political correctness that enveloped much of the early nineties, one bright sunbeam of good news was the discovery that the most famous pinup girl of all time was alive and well and living in Southern California—a born-again fundamentalist no less, completely oblivious of her vast underground fame but still proud of the modeling work that had earned her such sobriquets as "Dark Angel" and "Queen of Bondage."

Born in 1923 in the mountains of Tennessee, Bettie Page traveled to Hollywood in 1944, where she failed a screen test with Twentieth Century–Fox. She then got married and moved to Pennsylvania, and when the marriage broke up in 1948 she headed for New York. She got a job as a typist on Wall Street. She did not smoke or drink, but she did carry a brick to ward off attackers drawn by her voluptuous figure.

One day in 1950 while wandering a beach on Coney Island she met Jerry Tibbs, a Brooklyn policeman and amateur photographer, who suggested she minimize her high forehead with bangs. The rest was history. Over the next eight years Bettie posed for more photographers and camera clubs and appeared on more magazine covers than any other model until the current era of "supermodels." Nearly a half million photographs of her were taken in all, the majority by her friend Irving Klaw, perhaps the most prolific supplier ever of girlie photographs to both underground and legitimate magazines. She was sought after by the rich and famous, including Howard Hughes, whom she dated. (Yet when Weegee tried to cop a feel after climbing into a bathtub with her to get a shot, she gave him a smack.)

Many of the photographs of Bettie were classic forties-style cheesecake, some showing her completely nude or half-nude, others with her wearing a swimsuit. Yet partial or full nudity was never the real attraction. Bettie's mystique lay in her perfectly proportioned body and innocent looks. Even the mild SM photos showing her trussed up in rope seemed more hokey than suggestive of some dark fantasy. While on a Florida vacation with fellow model Bunny Yeager, a photographer in her own right, Bettie posed for Yeager in a leopard-skin outfit. That photograph became among the most prized by her fans. Later she also appeared in eight-millimeter films showing her dancing a hula, wandering about in stiletto heels, modeling her homemade lingerie, brushing her hair, or getting bound and gagged, kidnapped, or spanked, ever so mildly, as if it were all part of some corny game.

Around the same time that Bettie was discovered, a young California girl named Norma Jean Baker made her first movie for Twentieth Century–Fox under the name Marilyn Monroe. The following year, to the consternation of studio executives, Marilyn posed for a calendar photo that brought her a much-needed $50. That photo later became the most famous nude in history, the body that launched a thousand soft-core magazines, when in December 1953 aspiring publisher Hugh Hefner used it as the centerfold of the first issue of his new magazine, *Playboy.*

In January 1955 Hefner used Bettie as a centerfold as well. But around the same time, Senator Estes Kefauver, from her home state of Tennessee, was chairing a committee investigating Irving Klaw. A claim had been made that the body of a murdered Florida man found in full bondage gear looked like something out of a Klaw catalog. Expert witnesses claimed there were links between pornography and organized crime, juvenile delinquency, and madness—the first time such a charge had ever been made.

The process broke Klaw, who made a deal to destroy thousands of photographs in return for his freedom. Withdrawing from the business, he died years later, a bitter man. Fearful that she might also face prosecution, and tired of posing for girlie magazines, Bettie moved to Florida in 1957, where she modeled fashion for a few years, then dropped out of sight, finding work as a fifth-grade teacher. On New Year's Eve in 1959 she walked into a little church in Key West and accepted Jesus as her savior. Two years later she enrolled in the Moody Bible Institute in Chicago. After another failed marriage and a nervous breakdown that required hospitalization, Bettie—her dark period over—moved to California.

Meanwhile, thousands of fans kept her memory alive with a pocket-size (and misspelled) magazine called *The Betty Pages,* a series of Betty Page collector cards, *The Betty Page 3-D Picture Book,* and Betty Page postcards. The Atlanta Comics Expo even sponsored a Betty Page look-alike contest; some entrants were men. In Chicago a full-length play was staged, *The Betty Page Story.* Paintings and lithographs of Bettie in bondage outfits adorned the walls of apartments, houses, and art galleries around the world and also made a few sly appearances in feature films. Her likeness was one of the most popular tattoo selections in the United States. But all through the sixties, seventies, and eighties, nobody knew what had become of this most famous of sex goddesses, although rumors abounded: she was the wife of a sheik, a nun, on the run from gangsters in Europe, had undergone plastic surgery and secretly married a film star.

In early 1989, *Hot Talk,* a Penthouse publication, published a pictorial retrospective of Bettie's career and tried unsuccessfully to locate her. *Rolling Stone* and *Playboy* joined in the pursuit, with the latter also publishing a pictorial retrospective in December 1992. One week after the issue hit the stands, the TV show *Lifestyles of the Rich and Famous* aired a segment on Bettie that included a big surprise—they had found and interviewed her.

The Dark Angel was amused by the *Playboy* article but pointed out that her name had been misspelled. At nearly seventy, she lived in a retirement village and spent her time taking day trips or going window-shopping. She seemed happy. Though she admitted to being the naughty girl next door, Bettie maintained she never did pornography. "Pornography is open poses—legs open," she explained, still sounding as charmingly naive as she had once looked in her photographs. "I worked for Irving Klaw, and he never allowed that. But if you worked for Irving Klaw, you had to do bondage. We just laughed at the bondage scenes when we were doing them. I mean, certainly no one actually wants to be whipped or spanked, right?"

Chapter 18

Linda Montano's Pubic Hair

ANNIE SPRINKLE'S NEW YORK APARTMENT FEATURED A FISH TANK, TWO CATS, A red-and-white plastic Infant of Prague statue serving as a lamp, and a show-biz-style, bulb-bedizened mirror smothered with photographs of friends, family, gurus, and lovers, both male and female. Also her diploma. In 1982, having just passed her thirtieth birthday, Annie had enrolled in New York's School of Visual Arts. She chose photography as her major and was a straight-A student. The following year she stopped making traditional porn movies.

In her new career Annie succeeded in publishing some of her work—photos of the Times Square sex scene—in *Newsweek* and other national publications. But money was always a problem. To supplement her income, she wrote a monthly column about porn stars for XXX-rated *Adam* magazine, occasionally performed in burlesque shows, and worked as a prostitute. Increasingly, though, she was finding sex boring. Her fantasy was to be an artist, to live like Brassaï in Paris in the thirties. Yet she had no regrets about her past.

For nearly twenty years her favorite (and in recent years only) trick was a man named Lester, whom she had met while shopping in his general merchandise store on New York's West Thirty-fourth Street. At the time, she was nineteen and he around fifty. They made a barter: one smoky topaz ring for one blow job, though later she learned the ring was worth only half the usual price for such a service. Yet she continued to shop at his store, trading oral sex for a camera, a toaster oven, a gold bracelet, and many other goods.

Lester had introduced her to other shop owners, some of them his relatives, who allowed her to barter her services for more consumer goods. As his own business expanded, however, Lester had less privacy in his back office. He began to visit Annie in her apartment, paying cash. He was one of the few tricks she ever allowed into her home. Over the years Lester and Annie became good friends, and he helped her out in several financial emergencies, including lending her the services of his accountant during a tax audit. Yet their sexual relationship never went beyond a long, languorous blow job. Always he arrived stressed out and tense, and afterward, invariably, a grateful Lester confessed that Annie gave him the most ecstatic, blissful, peaceful moments he ever had on earth. Theirs was the longest-running relationship she ever had with any man.

In 1983 Annie met a fiery young Greek porn star and aspiring writer named Veronica Vera, who was having an affair with Marco Vassi. The two women immediately became best friends. Like Annie, Vera was at the end of her porn career. Together they started the Sprinkle Salon Mail Order, producing their own magazines, audiotapes, and eight-millimeter loops of some of Annie's films. They sold small bottles of their urine for $35, including instructions to consumers on how they could give themselves a golden shower. Pubic hair in a velvet box went for $25, soiled panties for $15. They received so many orders for the latter that they were unable to wear enough to meet demand, especially since their standards were high—two or three days' wearing apiece—and neither liked wearing panties in the first place. To solve the problem, they upped the price to $100. Dubbing themselves the only two members of the School of High-Heel Journalism, they also published *Annie Sprinkle's ABC Study of Sexual Lust and Deviation, Love Magazine #83,* and *Post Art Art in America,* all designed by Willem de Ridder and published by Prince Mickey Leblovic.

During her burlesque shows, Annie began inviting men up on stage to suck her breasts, then simulating orgasm. Every performance was different, except that each lasted twenty minutes and was followed by a session in the lobby when male patrons were invited to take Polaroid shots of Sprinkle's vagina for $5 apiece. Annie enjoyed the audiences and the shows but in general despised the owners as tightwads.

In December 1984 Richard Schechner, head of performance studies at New York University and creative director of the sixties avant-garde theater sensation *Dionysus in 69,* caught her Nurse Sprinkle Sex Education act at Show World on Times Square. He invited her to be in an upcoming performance, *The Prometheus Project,* at the Performance Garage in SoHo. Soon Annie found herself performing for an entirely different kind of audience—not the raincoat crowd, but highbrows. Her appearance consisted of presenting a series of graphs charting her sexual career: 5.1 quarts of semen swallowed, 1,475 feet of penis sucked, 17 hours of work a week, $4,000 average weekly income (a gross exaggeration; most of the time she was desperately poor). Best of all, the show was reviewed in *The New York Times*. Performance art, Annie decided, was a great way for an ex–porn actress to stay in sex and yet remain respectable. In 1985 she made her solo debut as a performance artist at the Franklin Furnace.

Around that time Annie also joined PONY (Prostitutes of New York), an offshoot of COYOTE whose members were a handful of prostitutes who wanted to decriminalize their profession. PONY had been reorganized by Veronica Vera after she and Annie attended the Second International Whores' Conference at the European Parliament building in Brussels, where proceedings were translated simultaneously into eight languages. A PONY project, Club 90 (named after its East Village address), served as a support group for porn stars, call girls, and other women in the sex industry and included such members as porn stars Veronica Hart, Gloria Leonard, and Candida Royalle. One brainstorm: free sex entertainment for the homeless.

But after fifteen years of intense sexual experience, Annie continued to struggle with a severe case of erotic burnout. At the same time, she increasingly saw sex in terms of healing—of exploring the cosmos through her vagina—as she tried to come to grips with certain incidents in her past. The time she had had sex with five hitchhikers in the Arizona desert—was it rape? Had she joined in only as an unconscious way of protecting herself? Was peeing on somebody really a joyous celebration of self and sex or an act that degraded both of them? Though she had never been coerced into making a porn film, had she in fact been exploited by the men who directed those films and paid her a pittance for her performance? How much was she herself to blame? Was there even call for blame, guilt, regret?

These and other questions led her to embrace a purifying form of vegetarianism and to consult a succession of New Age gurus. An early mentor was Jwala, an itinerant preacher of New Age sex who traveled the world giving tantric workshops. In January 1987 Annie attended one of Jwala's workshops in a private home in a quiet Philadelphia suburb, where she learned about the seven psychic and physical centers in the body called chakras. The goal of the workshop was to cleanse and purify the chakras so that participants could draw energy from them. Annie left with a sense of enthusiasm she had not known since her early days in porn, only now it was directed not toward sexual exhibitionism but toward sexual introspection and healing.

Another of Annie's gurus was an American Indian named Harley Swift-Deer, a Native American shaman, healer, and teacher. At a three-day workshop in a suburb of Milwaukee, Annie and a dozen other participants learned a technique for inducing the firebreath orgasm, a prolonged orgiastic state achieved through breathing exercises, without genital stimulation of any kind.

But the person who was to change Annie's life most profoundly was the longtime performance artist Linda Montano. Raised a strict Catholic (a religion she once described as "pretelevision theater") in upstate New York, Montano had joined the Maryknoll Sisters after a period of adolescent sexual confusion. But she became anorexic in the order and left after two years, weighing only eighty-two pounds. After enrolling in college as an art major, she traveled to Italy to study sculpture but found herself compulsively making statue after statue of Jesus on the cross. When performance art, an offspring of the happenings of the sixties, began to flower in the early seventies, Montano knew she had found her calling.

In her performances Montano strove to erase the distinction between art and life, claiming that attitudes, intent, and awareness could transform life into art, which she believed should be viewed not as a commodity, but as a state of mind. She had dressed as a dead chicken (lying inside the Berkeley Museum in Berkeley, California, from noon to three on a platform while wearing a blue prom dress with a twelve-foot wingspan, tap shoes, and a feathered headband); remained handcuffed for three days to conceptual artist Tom Maroni; and spent another three days in 1975 blindfolded inside a gallery without speaking.

In 1983 and 1984 Montano had made national news by living for an entire year attached to, but never touching, fellow performance artist Tehching Hsieh, a former lover, via a six-foot length of rope tied around their waists. At the end of 1984 Montano launched her "7 Years of Living Art," in which, for each of the following seven years, she wore clothes of only one color; listened to one pitch on an oscillator for seven hours a day; stayed inside a similarly colored space for three hours a day; and spoke in a different accent. During that time she also wrote five books, produced twenty videotapes, and lectured as an art instructor at the University of Texas in Austin.

It was also during that time—in 1987—that Montano and Annie Sprinkle met. Annie was still doubting that she could truly call herself an artist, despite the encouragement and assurances of such friends as Willem de Ridder. When she expressed her doubts to Montano, Montano set up a performance ritual at her lesbian-holistic retreat in Kingston, New York, in which she blindfolded Annie for six hours, then baptized her as an official artist. As a graduation gift and talisman, she gave Annie an envelope containing clippings of Montano's pubic hair. After the ceremony Annie burst into tears, crying, "I always wanted to be an artist." For a time she called herself an "arthole," de Ridder's term. She also changed her name briefly to Anya.

In the summer of 1993 a hard-core porn film titled *Revelations* received a thumbs-down review in the "Gonzo" section of *Adult Video News,* which was where the trade journal reviewed weird, sleazy, and exploitative tapes, most of them produced by amateurs. *Screw*'s reviewer, David Clark, called it "pretentious," noting that the camera even looked away as the stars climaxed and expressing irritation not only at the absence of cum shots, but at the short shrift given to fellatio, "while cunnilingus is dwelt upon with endless (softcore) fascination." Contradicting the verdict of his own publication, though, Al Goldstein gave *Revelations* a favorable review in his video column in *Penthouse.*

Set in a totalitarian future, *Revelations* tells the story of the sexual awakening of Ariel, a young woman married to a militaristic drone who will copulate only procreatively. When a neighbor is arrested, she steals into his apartment and discovers his cache of pornography tapes, watches them, and learns how to masturbate. The film had an unusually high budget—$115,000, or ten times the average for a porn movie. But what most distinguished it was that its creative team was composed entirely of women, working under the auspices of ex–porn star Candida Royalle and her company, Femme Distributors, Inc.

Born on Long Island in 1950, Royalle had studied fashion illustration at the Parsons School of Design. By 1968 her involvement in the antiwar movement, the women's movement, and a relationship took precedence over school, and she dropped out and took a job as a secretary. But after her boss sexually assaulted her, Royalle joined the Bronx Women's Coalition and went back to college. During this time she continued to remain sexually active. By 1971, though, feeling her sense of humor and creative energy ebbing amid the grayness and politics of New York, and aware that the women's movement was fragmenting, she decided to go to Europe.

As an ex-Catholic, Royalle felt guilty about having had so much sex, and in Europe she became celibate for two years. But she also discovered in this period an identity as a woman that was neither traditional nor feminist in the sense she had known in the United States. Soon she began modeling herself on the stars of the silver screen in the forties and fifties, wearing glitzy clothing and purple nail polish—a glorious release after her radical-feminist phase, when she had not allowed herself to wear makeup or shave her legs. When she returned to the United States she moved to San Francisco, where she appeared in nude skits with avant-garde theater groups and sang jazz, gospel, and pop in nightclubs. She also began sleeping with men again.

Then her world fell apart. The play she was currently appearing in closed after its star, transvestite cult figure Divine, died. Her boyfriend was becoming a drug addict, and her friends, who despised him, were not supportive. She had no money. An acquaintance offered her a job in a porn film. She thought, "Why not?" The job paid well. It also seemed safe. The only person who touched her was the other paid actor, while the thousands of men who were going to pay to see her could never touch her. Despite what her former colleagues in the radical-feminist movement thought, Royalle sensed a kind of control in that. She liked being able to manipulate men sexually.

She took her *nom de porn* from Voltaire's rebellious hero. Among the films she starred in were *Hot Rockers, Fascination,* and *Sizzle.* During a casting call she met producer Per Sjostedt and married him. But once she was married, she had a difficult time doing sex scenes. She also began to long for work that was more secure financially. To resolve her ambivalence about her work and to explore her feelings about family, guilt, sex, and self-worth, Royalle went into therapy. Ultimately she concluded that there was nothing wrong with having made erotic movies except that they were unfair to women.

Then as now, hard-core porn had scarcely evolved from the days of stag films showing men in black socks and women in too much mascara. The primitivism was not even tempered by a veneer of technical sophistication. Though XXX-rated films were at least shot in color, the dialogue was juvenile at best. The problem with hard-core was not so much that it was created by and for males, but that it was just plain outdated in its worldview and aesthetic. In reaction against this monopoly, more dreary than offensive, a group of porn actresses on the radical fringes of the feminist movement had begun to meet to discuss the seemingly inherent contradiction of being both porn stars and feminists. Ultimately, they decided, the problem lay with their inability to express themselves fully in the formulaic, stifling roles male directors cast them in. Pornography, they believed, was an artistic medium whose potential had not yet been realized.

The group decided to create an alternative pornography that appealed as much to the sensibilities of women as to men. One of the first efforts was a film called *Femme,* independently produced by Royalle and, as the credits noted, "conceived, written, directed, produced, and shot by women." The only male contribution was that of half a dozen porn actors doing what they did best.

An intelligent, sensual film, *Femme* consisted of six unrelated vignettes done in MTV style, with music and a little dialogue, each segment shot with different actors and different sets. In one shot a punk couple skirmish on a staircase. They kiss madly, she licks his fingers, he pushes her face into his crotch, then he bends her over and takes her from behind, with sharp, hard thrusts, as her face flushes with excitement. He comes inside her, with no cum shot. A publicity flyer claimed the film offered eroticism not only for women but also for "couples, the educated man, and maybe even the raincoat crowd."

Royalle's philosophy was to find people who were "artists at fucking," encourage them to get comfortable and wear what they liked, then do whatever kind of scene turned them on. Direction was minimal, and interrupting the actors to get a close-up was unthinkable. Conventional porn wisdom dictated that the viewer wanted to get "inside" the action and not just be an observer. But Royalle held that her approach allowed for both: some women liked to spread their legs for the camera, while others were more modest. At the same time, she did not resort to romantic fade-outs and dissolves. Though women liked romance, Royalle knew that many of them also liked sex low-down and nasty.

Royalle began to produce her own porn, with the financial backing of her husband and her father-in-law and her old friend Lauren Niemi, a photographer, as her cinematographer and business partner. Other women had assumed executive positions in pornography by this time. Anne Perry Rhine, Joyce Schneider (director of *Raw Heat*), Sharon Mitchell, and Veronica Rockett were producing their own films or tapes. Porn actress Kay Parker oversaw promotion for Caballero, Reuben Sturman's former company and one of the world's largest distributors of porn videos. Stephanie Martin started a company that promoted and sold to retailers materials that would appeal to women and couples.

But Royalle was unique in the degree to which she challenged conventional wisdom and techniques. Her films were far more polished than the usual XXX-rated fare, paying particular attention to the visual setting and camera technique. Usually, in hard-core filming, two cameras were set on tripods. To obtain a different angle, the film crew had to shift everything around and relight while the porn actress was getting a sore jaw trying to keep the penis of her leading man erect. Royalle used only one camera and gave Lauren free range of the set. The result: no static shots of the male actor endlessly pumping away.

Royalle also devoted much more footage to cunnilingus than did the average fellatio-obsessed porn film. And unlike male-produced and male-oriented porn, which got down to action virtually instantaneously, Royalle's erotica also depicted a progression of intimate events, as in most actual lovemaking. Yet she was cautious about gay and lesbian sequences, mindful that some women were turned off by lesbian sex, some men by gay sex. Also she made an effort to find men who were as attractive as the women, which was palpably not the case in most porn films.

The biggest challenge Royalle faced was distribution. Mainstream distributors would not handle her tapes, and although smaller distributors agreed to, no women's magazine would accept her advertisements. It was a classic catch-22: there seemed to be no way to tell women about porn for women.

The breakthrough came in November 1985 when *Glamour* did a piece entitled "How Women Are Changing Porn Films" and called *Femme* one of the "best of a new breed." Impressed, her distributor, Video Company of America, put time and money into advertising Royalle's next film, *Urban Heat,* released the following year. Other publicity soon followed, and within ten months of *Femme*'s release Royalle had made back all of her expenses plus a substantial profit. Porn by, for, and about women—an idea whose time had literally come—was now a mainstay of American sex entertainment.

IN THE FALL OF 1975, around the time Gay Talese was enjoying the unparalleled amenities at Hugh Hefner's Los Angeles mansion in the name of giving sex journalism a good name, a twenty-four-year-old gay hippie named Randy Shilts arrived in San Francisco's Castro district. He might have been just another of the five thousand gays who migrated to the Bay Area each year during the mid-seventies. But he was also destined, like Talese, to write an important chapter in the history of American journalism and to emerge as the most prominent and successful of a remarkable generation of gay and lesbian essayists, reporters, and novelists who were fashioning a seemingly golden age of homosexual arts and letters. Notable books by homosexuals in the late eighties and early nineties included Dale Peck's *Martin and John* (literary pornography), Gary Indiana's *Gone Tomorrow* (sodomy at Dachau), Rita Mae Brown's pansexual *Venus Envy,* and Dorothy Allison's autobiographical novel *Bastard Out of Carolina.*

In 1981 Shilts became the first openly gay reporter to be hired by the *San Francisco Chronicle.* His first book, *The Mayor of Castro Street,* recounted the events leading up to the assassination of San Francisco supervisor Harvey Milk, and rights were later sold to Hollywood. On March 16, 1987, he tested positive for the HIV virus. That same day he finished his second book, *And the Band Played On,* which chronicled the spread of the AIDS virus and made him famous.

In the book, Shilts portrayed Gaetan Dugas, a Canadian airline steward and the earliest known carrier of the HIV virus, as the Typhoid Mary of AIDS. Known in AIDS research circles as Patient Zero, Dugas traveled widely and had an estimated 250 sex partners per year. His promiscuous behavior continued until his death in March 1984, even though he had been diagnosed with Kaposi's sarcoma in June 1980 and warned he was endangering his sex partners.

A brusque, easily misunderstood man, Shilts found he was regarded with suspicion, if not outright hostility, by many gay and lesbian colleagues. His critics charged that he associated promiscuity exclusively with illness and death. Some pointed out that Shilts's reporting of the role of Dugas was based on conjecture, not fact. Andrew Kopkind, *The Nation*'s openly gay editor, complained that Shilts never made it clear that "you can't have a healthy sex life in an unhealthy society" and that his work lacked "a sociological framework" for its conclusions about gay sexuality. Gay novelist John Preston thought that Shilts, a recovering alcoholic, viewed bathhouse owners in the same light as bar owners—merchants who exploited the compulsions of the gay community. Shilts was also accused of being "puritanical." Shilts in turn claimed that many gay and lesbian journalists were jealous of his stature in the straight community.

And the Band Played On went on to sell more than 130,000 copies, positioning Shilts to receive an advance of nearly $1 million for his next book, *Conduct Unbecoming,* about the struggle of gays and lesbians in the military. His books thus addressed three of the most significant developments in the gay rights movement in the past fifteen years.

But Shilts remained bitterly disappointed that *Band,* despite its best-selling status, did not persuade substantial numbers of gays to avoid high-risk sex. (In Preston's view the book was virtually a 12-Step program for gay sex addicts.) In December 1992 Shilts came down with *Pneumocystis carinii* and he died in February 1994.

AIDS had also divided the porn industry, mostly pitting men against women. A case in point was the Adult Video Association (AVA), which had been founded by director Henri Pachard (real name Ron Sullivan) when it occurred to him that pornography had made no obvious First Amendment gains in twenty-five years. Former porn star and *High Society* spokeswoman Gloria Leonard served as the AVA's administrative director, helping to defend the industry's First Amendment rights on college campuses, on radio and TV talk shows, and in debates with pro-censorship feminists, fundamentalists, and repentant ex-porn actresses. But Leonard, sister activist Royalle, and others in the industry—particularly women—favored safe sex on the set, while most male producers were opposed to it. They supported a boycott of male actors who refused to work without a condom. In 1992, when AVA merged with the Free Speech Legal Defense Fund to form the Free Speech Coalition, a new organization that preempted much of its constituency and clout, Leonard was sacked—another example of the industry's myopia, greed, and squandering of a valuable resource. Commercial pornography simply had zero tolerance for women who proposed to meddle with its basic formula, regardless of any risk to the actors of AIDS or other STD.

Two other prominent pro-porn feminist activists were Debi Sundahl and her friend Nan Kinney, founders of Blush Entertainment Corporation, the parent company of Fatale Video, the only ongoing lesbian porn production company in the country, and *On Our Backs,* the preeminent magazine of lesbian erotica. Among Fatale Video's groundbreaking lesbian porn offerings were *Clips, Shadows, Private Pleasures, BurLEZk Live!, Hungry Hearts,* and *Suburban Dykes.*

Sundahl and Kinney had been inspired to make lesbian porn back in the early eighties, when, as students at the University of Minnesota in Minneapolis, one of the hot zones of antiporn activism, they were active in

Women Against Violence Against Women. But when the organization changed its focus and name to Women Against Violence and Pornography, the atmosphere got too oppressive for them. Now even lesbian sexuality—especially including the SM and penetration Sundahl and Kinney liked—was frowned on. After moving to San Francisco, they found immediate acceptance with Samois, the most visible SM group, and Sundahl began writing for its newsletter. When Samois dissolved a year later, she and Kinney started On Our Backs, and in the mid-eighties they began making videos.

Like Royalle, they encountered resistance when they tried to recoup their substantial investment by wholesaling their videos to distributors for about $15, as opposed to the usual $6 to $12. An even bigger problem for Sundahl and Kinney was the homophobia and/or ignorance of distributors, who thought heterosexual tapes with girl-girl scenes (frequently with a man coming along at the end to finish things off) would satisfy the lesbian market. Though Sundahl and Kinney's partnership eventually collapsed, they succeeded in being the first to establish a genuinely viable market for lesbian erotica, both print and video, though national distribution has continued to be elusive for such materials. Most lesbian erotica and other sex products for women continue to be sold primarily through mail order. Among the oldest and best mail-order operations is that run by Good Vibrations, an offshoot of a sex aid store founded in San Francisco in 1977 by Joani Blank. Unlike such larger mail-order businesses as Adam and Eve and Xandria, Good Vibrations refuses to sell sex novelties or lingerie, and concentrates on what women (whether lesbian, bisexual, or heterosexual) and not men want—vibrators, informative books, and high-quality erotica on video.

Another powerful female presence in erotica, one verging on a mass cult, was novelist Anne Rice. Like her literary forebears, the pseudonymous Pauline Réage, author of Story of O, and Elizabeth McNeill, author of the modern classic 9 ½ Weeks, Rice specialized in SM, particularly vampirism and spanking. (In a celebrated 1995 essay in The New Yorker, journalist John de Saint-Jorre unmasked Réage as Dominique Aury, an aging Parisian woman of letters. In fact, Aury was itself a pseudonym. The author's real name is Anne Desclos.) At the same time, Rice enjoyed the respectability and acceptance accorded to only one other major pornographer in this century—Henry Miller.

Rice entered the literary scene in 1976 with Interview with the Vampire, her deadly serious portrait of Lestat de Lioncourt, an eighteenth-century vampire talking about his centuries of ruin, of the eternal struggle between good and evil, of the meaning of death and immortality. The book became an instant cult classic and the basis for a series of novels, The Vampire Chronicles. Rice also experimented with pornography. Her first effort, The Claiming of Sleeping Beauty, which appeared under the pseudonym of A. N. Roquelaure, related how the Prince awakened Beauty both literally and sexually in a sadomasochistic version of the fairy tale. Much of the book was devoted to detailed descriptions of spanking and paddling, two perennial SM fantasies. Under the name Anne Rampling, Rice also wrote *Exit to Eden,* set in an unusual sex club on a Caribbean island.

Rice's foremost rival in SM fiction was gay writer John Preston, a former Green Beret and a founding editor of *The Advocate,* who lived in Portland, Maine. In 1992, while dying of AIDS, Preston got enormous satisfaction from seeing three of his books on a gay best-seller list at the same time—*Mr. Benson* (BadBoy Books), an anthology of his fiction entitled *Flesh and the Word* (Plume), and *Hometowns: Gay Men Write About Where They Belong* (Dutton). When Preston died in April 1994, Rice took out a full-page memorial advertisement in *Publishers Weekly,* the journal of the book trade, to express her admiration and her grief.

By 1983, long before the public at large became aware of the devastating potential of the AIDS plague, Marco Vassi had ceased all sexual activity that was considered to be high risk. Already too many of his friends were dying. That same year he moved in with Annie Sprinkle. It was largely a relationship of expedience. Marco had broken up with another woman and had wearied of supporting himself as a dishwasher in a local restaurant. Annie had a spare room, and Marco slept in it. But then their sex life, which had always been casual, suddenly became very intense. They began to talk about having safe sex. At a party thrown by PONY to celebrate the Second International Conference of Whores in Brussels in late 1986, Annie and Marco were dancing when she plunged her tongue into his mouth and kissed him. Marco drew back, suggesting that they start now, and Annie realized he was afraid of contracting the HIV virus from her.

Like many other sex radicals, Annie and Veronica Vera had also become more cautious about whom they slept with and how they did it. Finally they worked up the courage to get blood tests. Then Marco decided to get tested also. When Annie's and Veronica's results came back negative, they were so overjoyed that Annie even printed up new stationery with her results on the back (a celebration quickly abandoned when she realized how thoughtless it was). A few days after Annie got her clean bill of health, however, Marco received word that he had tested positive.

From that moment on his sex life changed radically. For five months he was despondent and felt no sexual desire at all. But then the "ancient itch" returned, and he wondered how it might be scratched. After two decades of unbridled bisexual promiscuity, it seemed inconceivable he could confine himself in the straitjacket of safe sex. Risk had always been an aphrodisiac to him. But now he had to take into account the risk to his partners.

Marco and Annie decided not to have intercourse or oral sex, but to explore new ways of having sex, experimenting with tantric, Native American, and Taoist techniques, forgoing Western orgasm-oriented practices in favor of rhythmic breathing, hour-long bouts of eye gazing, and conversations about how sex was really more about tapping into and circulating energy than it was about fucking and sucking. Toward the end of his career and approaching fifty, Marco claimed he had gone from being polymorphous to promiscuous to monogamous, and he predicted that he would one day be celibate again, just as he had been, briefly, as a Franciscan novice.

Later, in a vague and somewhat halfhearted search for a holistic cure, Marco flew to San Francisco. While there he received a phone call from Marsha, a woman with whom he had had a brief affair ten years earlier. At first they confined their get-togethers to movies and poetry readings, trying to ignore their mutual lust. But one night they agreed to try safe sex, after first listing all forbidden behaviors: no soul kissing, no fondling of one another's genitals without surgical gloves, no intercourse without a condom. Marco further consented not to perform cunnilingus under any circumstances, while she was permitted to fellate him only if he wore a condom.

Despite the many constraints, their affair began to take on emotional overtones. Soon they were talking about living together. Fate intervened when Marco received an urgent phone call from his father, who had landed in a hospital in New York with a collapsed lung. His mother, who used a walker, was now home alone. Having no other family members to rely on, Marco decided to fly back to New York. Marsha wept at the news. During the flight home, Marco felt as if he was being swept into darkness, away from the embrace of a woman willing to risk her life to be with him. Many phone calls ensued, and there was talk of her going to New York or vice versa when the family crisis passed. But nothing happened. Marco returned to living with Annie and later came up with a name for his experience with Marsha—he called it sexual outercourse.

MEANWHILE, Annie took her formidable talents to Europe. Her performance art show *Post Porn Modernist* featured her "greatest performance hits"—including such old favorites as the "Bosom Ballet Folklorico," "A Public Cervix Announcement," "How to Be a Sex Object," "Pornstistics," "A Bible Reading," "Introduction to New Age Sex," and "Tits on Your Head Polaroids." Joining her as art director at Hamburg's Reeperbahn, where the performance was sold out for its thirty-day run, was her ex-lover and longtime friend Willem de Ridder. Every night he sat in the balcony, operating the sound system and slide projector.

Like Annie, de Ridder was exploring various Eastern sexual techniques, including deep genital massage. After one session in which his partner had spent an hour massaging his scrotum while he practiced his shallow-breathing techniques, de Ridder finally signaled her that he wanted to stop. Suddenly his entire body began to shake, as if he were having an epileptic fit. Heavy shocks seemed to pass through every limb. At the same time he was aware of a very deep quiet at the core of his being, of having no thoughts. His partner was alarmed at first, thinking he was having convulsions. Finally, though, he sat up. For a long time they embraced. He wanted to talk but could not utter a word.

At their next session the following week, the electrical storm commenced almost as soon as the woman touched him and he began his shallow breathing. After three more such experiences, de Ridder called an end to the massage sessions because he found them unbearable.

Annie always ended her show with a firebreath orgasm that she had learned from her workshop with Harley SwiftDeer. Sometimes the energy orgasm was faked, but most of the time it was authentic. One night, while watching Annie, de Ridder decided to see if he could induce the electrical storm in his body just by breathing. As soon as he started, he began to shake all over and cry uncontrollably.

After all the patrons departed, he went downstairs to visit Annie in her dressing room. While she took off her makeup, he sat beside her and said, "Listen, something very weird just happened to me. I just had an incredible orgasm. Maybe it was the power of your ritual. I want to find out more."

The next day de Ridder made an appointment with a masseuse who had attended Annie's show and offered both of them a free massage. Annie went first. When it was his turn, de Ridder tried to reexperience what had happened to him the day before by breathing shallowly. Instantly his body again began to shake, leaving him hardly time to catch his breath. That night, after the show, he demonstrated for Annie what was now happening to him almost instantaneously with thought. It seemed that whenever he wanted to enter that deeper realm of the senses, there it was.

From that time on, that powerful state was de Ridder's constant accompaniment to sex. Orgasm began to seem like little more than the tip of a vast sensual iceberg.

IN THE SPRING OF 1987 an impoverished and depressed Marco Vassi took an apartment on New York's Upper West Side. To support himself, he cranked out formulaic erotica whose recurring themes were all familiar territory: old lovers, partings, sorrow, not daring to think about the future, enjoying only blissful moments.

Around the same time, the Permanent Press, a small literary house on

Long Island, published his last novel, *The Other Hand Clapping*, a nonerotic work written at the insistence of his publisher, Martin Shepard. A reviewer in *The New York Times Book Review* praised it as a novel of "intricate intelligence, tremendously witty and well constructed, with a plot whose tiny, focused center is like the eye of a hurricane."

All his life Marco had bounced from glee to depression and back again, and he continued to seesaw between them. He even joked about his several failed suicide attempts—most of them halfhearted, though one night he had climbed onto a ladder, with a rope around his neck, and leapt off, only to have the rope break. The attempt left a deep rope burn on his neck that literally provided gallows humor to friends desperate to cheer him up.

One day Marco complained to Annie, who still looked in on him often, that he had never received an award for anything. He was the new Henry Miller, yet all of his works had gone virtually ignored.

"Well, what do you really want?" she asked him.

"The respect of my peers," he replied.

So Annie threw a party for Marco. Forty people were invited, and all forty attended. Each person was instructed to give the guest of honor an award. Gloria Leonard arranged for a star in the firmament to be named in his honor. Everybody gave a speech. It was like a memorial service, except that Marco was still alive, and he felt very loved and appreciated. Not long after, though, he got very sick for the first time.

During this period he joined Alcoholics Anonymous, though he had always drunk moderately. He had also become a vegetarian, as part of an overall attempt to rid himself of all unnecessary desires and appetites. He became active in a privately owned facility for AIDS victims in Tribeca called the Renwick Project, which was underwritten by Gerald Duval, a wealthy real estate developer. But as he grew sicker, he found himself in desperate circumstances. The electricity in his apartment was turned off, garbage was strewn everywhere, and he could not even look after his bodily wastes, let alone cook for himself. Finally he moved into the AIDS facility.

At one point he became so ill that volunteers transferred him to Metropolitan Hospital. During this time he was visited by a priest, who told him, "Whatever you have done in your life, you are still welcome back." Later the priest heard his confession and gave him communion. Friends visiting Marco at the hospital found him in good shape mentally and unusually serene for a man given to an operatic style. At seven o'clock in the morning, on January 14, 1989, Marco Vassi died at Metropolitan Hospital. Annie had been with him the day before, as had other former lovers, and knew the end was near.

At a second memorial service held some weeks after Marco's death, Norman Mailer, a fan, described Vassi as "the foremost erotic writer in America . . . a sexual explorer . . . his own experiment, and, ipso facto, a rare mortal," though also deeming him "by any average standard, a minor writer." Though sales of Marco's works continued to be very large in Europe and Japan, he remained virtually ignored in the United States. The Permanent Press later reissued his complete works.

Annie Sprinkle, meanwhile, continued to preach the gospel of mirthful sex in her performance art, announcing at the opening of each engagement: "Let there be pleasure and ecstasy on earth, and let it begin with me." Jesse Helms, hearing of her act and having just emerged from a battle to remove state funding for artists Robert Mapplethorpe and Andres Serrano, called for a congressional investigation into whether Annie and her ilk received federal funding for their "pornographic" performances.

Refusing to be a victim of sex, life, or men, Annie chose this moment to launch yet another career, giving her own adult education sex workshops, titled "A Guide to Sex for Healing, Meditation and Enlightenment." By 1993 she had reinvented herself as the ultimate sex-radical performance artist. Willem de Ridder described her as being "as open as a human being can be. She embraces people that our culture judges as gruesome, she faces situations that most of us desperately try to avoid."

In 1995 Annie gave up her Manhattan apartment, eventually settling year-round in Provincetown on the tip of Cape Cod, where she spends her days jogging, meditating, reading, and cooking, just as she had two decades earlier when she and de Ridder retreated to his kingdom by the sea. Several times a year she emerges to go on tour, particularly in Europe, where she remains a major attraction. Most of her lovers, as well as her fans, are lesbian. Her best friend, Veronica Vera, flourishes as founder of Miss Vera's School for Boys Who Want to Be Girls, the world's only academy for aspiring transvestites. Willem de Ridder also prospers as a well-known Dutch radio personality.

Chapter 19

Sex Among the Ruins

ON FEBRUARY 20, 1992, WILLIAM YOUNG, DIRECTOR OF WHAT WAS LEFT OF THE Masters & Johnson Institute and son-in-law of Virginia Johnson, issued a press release announcing that "the First Couple of Sexology" were getting divorced after twenty-one years of marriage. Officially the blame was put on incompatible priorities regarding work and play. She wanted to spend more time with family and friends, while he remained deeply absorbed in his research and therapy, helping to treat the institute's current caseload of some two hundred patients. Unofficially they strongly disagreed on the future course of the institute and who should succeed them. In her semiretired state Johnson, though no longer active in patient therapy, continued to be involved in all executive decisions. Her most potent prerogative—the power of veto.

Johnson was sixty-seven. Masters was seventy-six and in the first stages of Parkinson's disease, but as some insiders knew, he already intended to marry for a third time. Still, he and Johnson remained on cordial if somewhat formal terms—a handshake, not a buss on the cheek, when they met. Johnson had taken with her most of the institute's archives when she moved out of Masters's home, however, not trusting their safekeeping to whoever might succeed them.

Johnson favored Robert C. Kolodny, M.D., who had been with them since the late sixties and had coauthored several of their books, as the institute's successor. In 1983 Kolodny had left to set up his own Behavioral Medicine Institute in Connecticut. Masters preferred Mark Schwartz, who had done his postgraduate training at the Masters & Johnson Institute after earning his doctorate in behavioral medicine at Johns Hopkins, where he had studied under John Money. Since 1982 Schwartz had directed the institute's treat-

394

ment of victims and families involved in child abuse. After leaving the institute, he set up a private practice and his own inpatient sex trauma unit in
New Orleans, where he specialized in treating the victims and perpetrators
of child sexual abuse. In his work with families where incest had occurred, he
discovered that not only all male abusers but 80 percent of female abusers
whose sexual environment was permissive to begin with had deviant arousal
patterns. (For example, a woman who was sexually aroused by dogs was
more likely to abuse a child sexually than a woman who was either sexually
inhibited or whose sexual behavior was more or less average.) He became an
expert in the long-term negative effects of child abuse, which allowed him to
develop a profitable sideline as an expert witness specializing in cases involving sexual abuse by priests.

The Masters & Johnson Institute had never concentrated on child abuse
for the very reason Schwartz did—treatment was expensive. But Schwartz
managed to persuade the sexologists not only to appoint him director of research, but for the first time to lend their names to a project outside the Masters & Johnson Institute—a "sexual compulsivity program" focusing on
everything from sexual trauma and vandalized lovemaps to eating disorders.

Schwartz had hired a social worker named Lori Galperin, who had
trained with him at Tulane University while pursuing her master's degree.
Before long they got involved and decided to marry. Together they set up the
Masters and Johnson Sexual Trauma Unit at a psychiatric hospital in New
Orleans, and later a second one in Kansas City. Patients suffering from sex
trauma—whether recent, recurrent, or repressed—were treated on an outpatient basis at a cost of $300 a day. A month of inpatient care cost $10,000.

On weekends Schwartz and Galperin toured the lecture circuit with an
enfeebled Masters, preaching the gospel that previously untreatable and un-
diagnosable—or, in the case of multiple personality disorder, often just plain
unbelievable—cases were based on childhood sexual trauma. Among the
controversial techniques Schwartz and Galperin employed was clinical hyp-
nosis to "scan" for past abuse and treat multiple personality disorder.

It was a provocative road show, leading *Vanity Fair* to dub the two younger
members the "Sonny and Cher of sex trauma." Though they had not published any books, they did have an air of youthful, gregarious sophistication—
she tall, blond, quick-witted, he boyishly suave, with blond shoulder-length
hair and Italian designer suits. They also had a brand name that allowed them
to surf the wave of child abuse hysteria just then threatening to wash over the
country. (In a distinction whose subtlety was perhaps lost on all but Masters,
Johnson, and the IRS, Schwartz was allowed to advertise his association with
"Masters and Johnson," while "Masters & Johnson"—using an ampersand—
denoted the carefully guarded nonprofit status of the institute.)

In the wake of Schwartz and Galperin's success in treating victims of child abuse, Masters and Johnson decided to open a new center in a sparklingly renovated former St. Louis mental hospital. They charged only about $5,000 for two weeks—half what Schwartz and Galperin charged—to patients referred by doctors and therapists around the country. Though few insurance companies paid for such programs, most did pay for the St. Louis program because it was less expensive than hospital care. At the Masters & Johnson Institute, a staff of ten counselors could treat up to fifty patients at a time.

The truth was, Masters was having a difficult time treating his nonabuse patients. They were younger than those of an earlier period, many had previously tried psychotherapy, and their problems were different. Far less common in the post–Sexual Revolution era were such relatively "easy" problems as premature ejaculation or vaginal spasms, since physicians, pastoral counselors, and the couples themselves could figure out how to treat them from the available literature. A full half of all patients now suffered from loss of sexual desire or simple aversion to sex.

In the waning days of 1994 an aversion to sex—at least at the professional level—finally overtook Masters himself. On December 15, a few days before his seventy-ninth birthday, he closed down the Masters & Johnson Institute after fifty years of seven-day weeks. His reason: "I'm tired." There was also the chronic lack of funding, Masters's declining health, and an ever-decreasing number of patients. No successor acceptable to both Johnson and Masters had been found. As a result, only two full-scale sex research organizations remained: the Kinsey Institute in Bloomington, Indiana, though riven by deep divisions within its ranks; and the Institute for the Advanced Study of Human Sexuality in San Francisco.

Earlier that year Masters had married his third wife, Dody, the sister of his former roommate at Hamilton College. In retirement Masters and his wife spent their winters in Tucson and their summers in upper New York state. Johnson, when not spending time with friends and grandchildren, devoted herself to writing a "tell-all" memoir, a long-term project.

BY SOME ESTIMATES, more than three million children were abused in the United States every year, and more than two thousand died of their injuries. Another shocking and widely cited figure came from a 1985 survey showing that one in four women suffered childhood sexual abuse. It was clear that abuse occurred at all socioeconomic levels and in all kinds of families. Yet statistics in this area were notoriously unreliable and prone to manipulation. A 1965 national survey suggested that the incidence of abuse was 4 percent, while in Morton Hunt's *Playboy*-sponsored sex survey a decade later, 20 percent of respondents reported having engaged in noncoital incest and another 7 percent reported having engaged in incestuous vaginal intercourse. In a

1979 survey of students at six New England colleges, 32 percent reported having been the victim of some form of incest, while a 1982 study suggested that perhaps as many as 70 percent of children with alcoholic parents encountered some form of sexual abuse.

The National Center on Child Abuse and Neglect defined child sexual abuse as "contact and interactions between a child and an adult when the child is being used for the sexual stimulation of the perpetrator or another person." That definition left open the question of who was a child, with professionals setting the cutoff age at anywhere from twelve to seventeen. It was also not clear who was an adult, with some criteria requiring perpetrators to be at least sixteen years old, and others specifying an age difference between victim and perpetrator of five years or ten years. Finally, what was abuse? Legally speaking, it might include anything from a single glimpse of a flashed penis to forced intercourse. And the assessment of injury could be complicated by a victim's report that an incestuous experience, for example, had been positive—although such an assertion did not preclude the possibility of severe psychological injury.

In short, epidemiological estimates of child sexual abuse were among the most worthless in sexological literature, ranging from 6 to 62 percent for women and from 3 to 31 percent for men. Yet studies limited to girls under fourteen that defined abuse as sexual contact with a man at least five years older showed a fairly consistent rate of 10 to 12 percent since the 1940s.

Freud was notorious for having attributed reports of incest made by two of his female patients not to experience, but to childhood fantasy. Kinsey was hardly more sympathetic. Although approximately 24 percent of his subjects reported frightening childhood sexual experiences, he concluded gruffly that "children should not be upset by these experiences. If they were, this was not the fault of the aggressor, but of prudish parents and teachers who caused the child to become 'hysterical.' "

Wardell Pomeroy, Kinsey's successor, also maintained that incest was not necessarily a catastrophic experience. In instances of father-daughter incest, the daughter's age, in Pomeroy's view, was the most important factor. The older she was, the likelier it was that the experience would be positive. A negative reaction might be attributable not to the incest per se, but to restrictions imposed by the father—for example, that the daughter could not date. "The best sort of incest," Pomeroy flippantly suggested, was between a son and a mother who educated him sexually, then encouraged him to go sow his oats.

Such attitudes curtailed research into incest for a long time. But more recent and responsible inquiries suggested that the incestuous father or stepfather was usually a domineering, introverted figure who, although often hardworking and a good provider, was insecure and unable to relate to people his own age. He considered females inferior and viewed his children as possessions. Often churchgoing and imbued with a deep if perverted moral sense, he might rationalize his incestuous behavior as preferable to seeking sex from prostitutes or in an affair and as a way of protecting his daughter from the dangers of sex with males her own age.

The role of the mother in father-daughter incest was often that of facilitator, though some stood by silently for fear of being abused themselves. In some families daughters were groomed to take their mother's place sexually. Most incestuous relations developed gradually, beginning on average when the child was between the age of nine and eleven, before puberty and its accompanying psychological autonomy. Only very rarely did a precocious Lolita type actually "seduce" her father. But most daughters (and sons) did not protest their abuse, either because they did not fully understand what was being done to them, because they believed they were protecting a younger sibling, or because the father bribed or threatened them.

As they grew older, many adults also suppressed their memories of being sexually abused as children. Some developed post-traumatic stress disorders, particularly severe depression. (In one study, one in five college women reporting a history of childhood sexual abuse was hospitalized for depression, compared with one in twenty-five who had not been abused.) Yet not all abuse survivors suffered such severe effects; in most studies up to a third were symptom free.

As increasing numbers of adult women and men came forth to disclose childhood incidents of sexual abuse, a further complication arose—so-called false memory syndrome. In some cases abuse survivors always knew what had happened but had never before spoken out or sought help. In other instances, however, some adults reported "remembering" or retrieving lost memories of childhood sexual abuse. Genuinely remembering and confronting unresolved issues connected to childhood sexual abuse might explain why a victim suffered from such lifelong afflictions as obesity, sleep disturbances, problems with intimacy, sexual disorders, or compulsive behavior. Yet false reports by both children and adults, often at the prompting of poorly trained therapists, teachers, and others, led to a witch-hunt atmosphere in numerous communities around the country.

While some investigations led to convictions, many other accusations of child abuse were found to lack substance. One of the worst instances of child abuse hysteria was the McMartin Preschool case, tried between April 1987 and July 1990, the longest criminal trial in U.S. history. Defendants Raymond Buckey and his mother, Peggy McMartin-Buckey, along with five teachers employed by them, were charged with one hundred child molestations at their preschool in suburban Manhattan Beach, California. Eventually the charges against the teachers were dismissed for lack of evidence, and only the two Buckeys remained, to stand trial on sixty-five charges.

Though the pair was ultimately acquitted on fifty-two of the charges, the jury remained deadlocked on the rest. Raymond, who had already spent five of the last seven years in jail, stood trial alone on the remaining charges, which were subsequently trimmed to eight. On July 27, 1990, a mistrial rang down, setting him free. Since then, more than a dozen other verdicts of mass molestation of children were overturned, though fifty-six adults remain incarcerated as they await appeal in similar cases.

One of the most controversial self-help books for women who suffered child abuse was *The Courage to Heal* by Ellen Bass and Laura Davis, which contained this infamous passage: "If you don't remember your abuse, you are not alone. Many women don't have memories, and some never get memories. This doesn't mean they weren't abused." Mark Schwartz could not have said it better himself. In their child abuse workshops for therapists around the country, he and Galperin stressed the higher end of the epidemiological scale without offering, much less examining, an iota of evidence. Schwartz also intimated that satanic cults and the ritual torture of children were rampant.

Like many sexologists, John Money was skeptical of the faddish interest in sexual abuse and its exploitation by professionals like his former protégé. In a society permeated by sexual taboos, he noted, some children subjectively experienced, for example, a physical examination by a doctor both as an invasion of privacy and the equivalent of sexual assault. Moreover, in many states the law required that a doctor consulted by a pedophile in effect assume the role of undercover cop and, instead of treating him, report him to the criminal justice system.

Money favored a nonadversarial model for dealing with sexual abuse that freed the medical and therapeutic communities to treat offenders without interference from the law. Like many sex professionals, Money believed that pedophilia, like alcoholism, was incurable, but that with innovative treatments (rather than radical solutions like castration) sex offenders could learn to manage their sexual impulses.

Yet by one estimate 75 percent of pedophiles and other sex offenders in prison received no help at all. In 1990 state and federal prisons had a population of 85,647 sex offenders, or 1 in 6 of all prisoners, with that number growing as victims became increasingly willing to report crimes. As the regular prison population grew 20 percent from 1988 to 1990, the incarceration of sex offenders increased by 48 percent—second only to those convicted of drug-related crimes.

Perhaps the most significant exploration into the causes of child abuse occurred in the mid-seventies, when Dr. James W. Prescott of the National Institute of Child Health and Human Development of the National Institutes of Health studied a group of infant monkeys separated from their mothers at birth. Building on the work of Harry Harlow and others in the late fifties and early sixties, Prescott similarly studied monkeys reared in cages by themselves in a colony room with other animals, where they could establish social relationships with other animals based only on seeing, hearing, and smelling, but deprived of all body contact with other animals.

Those infant monkeys deprived of physical affection through lack of maternal touch developed many abnormal emotional-social behaviors: self-mutilation, impaired pain perception, aversion to touch, aberrant sexual behavior, poor grooming, and a pathological violence toward other animals. Curiously, they also rocked themselves incessantly. What Prescott succeeded in demonstrating for the first time was that the failure of "mother love" in the primate resulted in developmental brain dysfunction and damage. Only artificially induced maternal-like rocking was able to soothe those orphaned, emotionally deprived monkeys.

After further investigation into four hundred so-called primitive or preindustrial cultures, Prescott found that child sexual abuse was most likely to occur in a culture where women's status was inferior, mothers and fathers showed little physical affection toward their children, and nurturing skills were almost nonexistent. By contrast, the incidence of child abuse was very low or nonexistent in cultures where parents showed strong affection for children.

Prescott concluded that child abuse was above all a failure of parenting. But he emphasized that the solution was not to criminalize abusive mothers and fathers who had themselves been abused. Rather, an entire society had to learn or relearn nurture—the most important sex education class of all.

In February 1992 the Canadian Supreme Court unanimously endorsed Catharine MacKinnon's theory of pornography, upholding a law suppressing "obscene" material that "subordinates" women and has "a negative impact on the individual's sense of self-worth and acceptance." Though the Court admitted its decision limited freedom of expression, it cited a superseding need to halt "the proliferation of materials which seriously offend the values fundamental to our society." The decision was the latest incursion of Canadian censorship, which over the preceding decade had become increasingly intolerant not only of pornography, but also of seditious material, hate propaganda, and even Saturday morning children's TV programs that were perceived as excessively violent. It was a major victory for MacKinnon. But the following fall she ended up on the losing side of a major battle on her home turf.

MacKinnon had been the moving force behind a three-day conference called "Prostitution: From Academia to Activism" sponsored by the University of Michigan Law School in Ann Arbor, where MacKinnon had tenure. A newly organized, MacKinnon-influenced student publication, *The Michi-*

gan Journal of Gender & Law, had set up the art exhibit to accompany the conference, which featured works about prostitution by five artists, including two former prostitutes.

MacKinnon had long favored legislation allowing women to show they had been harmed by pornography and to sue producers and distributors. But Carol Jacobsen, a Detroit artist who put together the art exhibit at the request of the *Gender & Law* staff, supported abolishing laws against prostitution. Her exhibit, which opened a week before the conference, included her own video interviews with Detroit prostitutes, who were referred to as "sex workers" by conference organizers. Entitled "Pornimagery: Picturing Prostitutes," the show also contained a videotape by Veronica Vera that featured explicit footage from sex films, including a segment depicting her performing cunnilingus on a menstruating Annie Sprinkle, as well as a brief clip showing her testifying against an antipornography measure before a U.S. Senate committee.

Some law students found Vera's segment so offensive that they removed both it and Jacobsen's tape, saying they were acting in response to complaints by two of the speakers, Evelina Globbe, director of an antiprostitution group in St. Paul, and John Stoltenberg, Andrea Dworkin's significant other. In response, the artists involved closed the exhibit altogether and threatened a suit against the university for violating their First Amendment rights. Though not involved in the decision, MacKinnon supported the students' action.

MacKinnon had settled in Ann Arbor after an itinerant decade as a visiting professor at assorted law schools. During this period she was also widely credited as a legal theorist with defining sexual harassment. She had been frequently cited during the 1991 confirmation hearing of Supreme Court nominee Clarence Thomas, whose accuser, Oklahoma University law professor Anita Hill, made the issue of sexual harassment front-page news.

Though only 29 percent of Americans believed Hill, in the ensuing decade the number of women filing sexual harassment claims doubled, and in 1993 the U.S. Supreme Court that Thomas now sat on ruled that sexual harassment could be determined if a worker demonstrated that the workplace environment was "hostile" or "abusive" to a "reasonable person."

Another itinerant lecturer and controversial national figure who wound up at Ann Arbor around the same time was Jeffrey Masson, a psychoanalyst who had been hired as director of the Freud Archives in 1980. While sorting through Freud's letters to his friend Wilhelm Fliess, Masson had begun to suspect that Freud had once believed his patients' stories of sex abuse by their parents but had repressed that knowledge because it was too shocking and might interfere with the acceptance of his new science of psychoanalysis among the Viennese bourgeoisie, who were possibly abusing their children. Instead Freud had developed one of his major theories, that children devel-

402 ■ WHAT WILD ECSTASY

oped an "Oedipus complex" that caused them to fantasize about sexual abuse by parents. To become healthy, adults had to "resolve" the complex by understanding the fantasies as expressions of their own unconscious sexual desires.

Masson eventually elaborated on his theories about Freud's alleged suppression of the seduction theory in *The Assault on Truth,* published in 1985. Two years prior, though, in a profile of Masson for *The New Yorker,* journalist Janet Malcolm previewed Masson's theories at great length but also portrayed him as wanting to have sex and wild parties in Anna Freud's house in London, the sanctum sanctorum of psychoanalysis. Malcolm said that Masson told her he had slept with nearly one thousand women.

After *The New Yorker* articles appeared, the Freud Archives fired Masson. Though he sued for wrongful dismissal and eventually received a settlement of $150,000, he had grown so disenchanted with psychoanalysis that he soon stopped practicing. In 1984 he filed suit for libel against Malcolm, *The New Yorker,* and Knopf—publisher of the book version of Malcolm's articles—though Knopf was later removed as a defendant by the court. Meanwhile, Masson opened a sandwich shop in Berkeley with a friend and began publishing books debunking psychiatry. *A Dark Science* chronicled psychiatry's abuse of women and children in the nineteenth century. In 1989, in *Against Therapy,* he took on the entire profession, detailing the sexual exploitation of women by therapists. By now Masson was a vocal opponent of all forms of psychotherapy.

Masson spent nine years trying to recover from the *New Yorker* profile and attendant publicity and trying to find another job. Though he had authored twelve books, the best he could muster was a part-time position paying $8,000 a year to teach a course at the University of Michigan on "media harms." In 1985 Masson was introduced to MacKinnon by a mutual friend. They met at a bookstore for lunch, partly because of her concerns about reprisals by organized crime for her attacks on pornography.

In her work MacKinnon had come to know many people—prostitutes, for example, or men with disreputable pasts—who had reformed their lives. Masson's womanizing, therefore, did not preclude him from her friendship. Moreover, they discovered a number of mutual passions—a commitment to social justice, outrage over the sexual abuse of women, the Holocaust. They became close friends.

In June 1991, after breaking up with another girlfriend, Masson went to see MacKinnon, seeking consolation. She came out wearing jeans with her hair down. Masson thought, "She's really lovely, and I hadn't noticed." She said, "Tell me all about it." She agreed to go out to dinner with him, and a year later they were living together in Ann Arbor. Many feminists were surprised at the news of their cohabitation since, in her courses, MacKinnon taught that the institution of marriage had served throughout history to oppress women.

Masson kept a photograph of MacKinnon on the dashboard of his car, after the manner of a taxi driver with a holy card of the Virgin Mary. It showed MacKinnon in a blue tunic, her long hair flowing to the waist, gazing demurely at the ground while Masson looked at her adoringly. "She is the greatest mind at work in the world today," he once exclaimed. "Hearing her lecture often makes me cry. I am immensely privileged to be living with her. It is like living with God!"

Masson read MacKinnon's work and for the first time correlated his promiscuous behavior with the way men were socialized to take pleasure from their dominant position in the sexual hierarchy. A convert to the cause, he came to believe that the root of sexual abuse lay in pornography, or in the attitudes that created it. To atone, Masson attended antipornography conferences and read the professional literature on pornography. The fact that he had not looked at pornography when he was younger did not matter, since pornography determined how men saw women whether they actually looked at it or not.

In May 1993 Masson's suit against *The New Yorker* and Janet Malcolm went to trial in San Francisco. Masson was asking for $13 million in damages. That October, in a settlement reached with legal help from the ACLU, the University of Michigan Law School reinstated its exhibition. MacKinnon and her radical feminist disciples had lost. So did Masson: in November 1994, after a first trial found Malcolm guilty but could not decide on damages, a federal jury in a retrial found Malcolm innocent of libel. Later Masson and MacKinnon broke up, and he found another girlfriend, a thirtysomething pediatrician with whom he had a child.

In 1993 MacKinnon published *Only Words,* which like much of her and Dworkin's writing continued to do a great imitation of pornography: "You grow up with your father holding you down and covering your mouth so another man can make horrible searing pain between your legs. When you are older, your husband ties you to the bed and drips hot wax on your nipples and brings in other men to watch and makes you smile through it."

Yet again MacKinnon reiterated that pornography was a significant cause of sexual crime, though yet again she could cite no reputable study that had ever proved such a contention. She insisted pornography was not "only words" because it was a "reality." Sometimes referring to her readers as "you," she invited women to see themselves as victims of appalling sexual crimes and reinforced the idea that all women were passive, innocent, and oppressed.

MacKinnon's fiercest critic was also her academic and feminist opposite, Camille Paglia, lesbian author of the best-selling *Sexual Personae,* a sexual tour of Western literature. In Paglia's view, MacKinnon was the classic WASP, a modern-day Puritan raised in a body-denying Protestant culture.

She was also a totalitarian who believed that "rules and regulations will solve every human ill and straighten out all those irksome problems between the sexes that have been going on for five thousand years."

As for the heavyset Dworkin, said Paglia, like Kate Millett she had "turned a garish history of mental instability into feminist grand opera. Dworkin publicly boasts of her bizarre multiple rapes, assaults, beatings, breakdowns, and tacky traumas, as if her inability to cope with life were the patriarchy's fault rather than her own. She pretends to be a daring truth teller but never mentions her most obvious problem: food. Hence she is a hypocrite." Paglia recognized Dworkin as a type: the Girl with the Eternal Cold, a pudgy, clumsy, whiny kid who was always spilling her milk or getting a cramp on the hike.

"MacKinnon and Dworkin detest pornography because it symbolizes everything they don't understand and can't control about their own bodies," Paglia proclaimed. Their basic error was to identify pornography with society, which they then simplistically defined as patriarchal and oppressive. In fact, pornography, which historically erupted into the open only during periods of personal freedom, "shows the dark truth about nature, concealed by the articles of civilization."

Despite the steep decline in the circulations of soft-core men's magazines, and the suffocating glut of hard-core in North Hollywood, the genre of pornography itself was alive and well. By the mid-nineties, most of its problems no longer stemmed from its foes in the Department of Justice or on the religious or radical-feminist Right so much as from a rapidly changing technological marketplace.

In the six years since the Justice Department had set up its special Child Exploitation and Obscenity (CEO) unit to fight pornographers, the number of adult video makers and their videotapes had actually risen, cheap amateur videos proliferated, and the industry had expanded far beyond magazines and videos to telephones and computer networks. The CEO was created to enable federal and local prosecutors to pursue pornography operations aggressively and, if possible, to apply the Racketeer Influenced and Corrupt Organizations (RICO) statute—a law used primarily against organized crime figures, drug traffickers, and Wall Street criminals and providing for harsher fines and prison sentences.

Since the unit's inception it had obtained 135 convictions, 50 involving mail-order companies. The RICO statute had applied to only 4 of those convictions. Paul Fishbein, publisher of *Adult Video News,* the industry trade journal, estimated that the industry's rental and retail sales had grown from $992 million in 1989 to $1.6 billion in 1992.

The Internet had played an increasing role in pornography and the exchange of sex information in recent years, though the Internet itself was not responsible for a rise in fetishism and other unorthodox sexual practices, as some conservative critics believed. Rather, according to Robin Roberts, an Internet guru in California and founder of Backdrop, one of America's oldest fantasy and bondage clubs, the Internet served as a magnet for lurkers (voyeurs), flamers (those who insult), and those who enjoyed posing as someone else (for example, a man posing as a lesbian). What attracted all such individuals to sexual cyberspace was its anonymity.

Several of pornography's most outspoken enemies, in the meantime, had come to an unhappy end, most notably Charles Keating, financier and director of the Citizens for Decency through Law. In 1993 Keating was found guilty on all seventy-three counts for defrauding depositors and creditors in two savings institutions, Lincoln Savings and Loan and American Continental Corporation. The two S&Ls had funneled more than $800,000 to the antipornography group, and their bailout ultimately cost the U.S. government $2.6 billion. After a protracted series of appeals, Keating began serving a ten-year prison sentence. Meese commissioner and Franciscan friar Bruce Ritter was exposed on the front pages of the nation's newspapers as a pedophile, resigned his position as head of Covenant House, and disappeared from public view. Keating's S&Ls had also contributed more than $400,000 to Covenant House and provided it with another $33 million in questionable loans.

In November 1995, Texas evangelist Garner Ted Armstrong resigned as head of the Church of God International after a licensed masseuse filed suit, alleging that he had tried to force her to perform oral sex, explaining that his work was so important to God that any sin would be overlooked. Jerry Falwell's Liberty University, as it had been rechristened, was $73 million in debt and facing bankruptcy.

In July 1992, transsexual pioneer Roberta White showed up at a big family reunion in Indiana. Two of her brothers had not spoken to her since her surgery more than a quarter of a century before. One of them told her she was a disgrace to the family even for appearing; several other brothers shunned her. But at one point she stole off with a nephew to tell him some of the family history. The following April, Roberta learned to her considerable pleasure that, when her uncle Gill died, she would become the family matriarch.

The nineties saw the emergence of a new trend in changing gender roles and behaviors, as seen in the appearance in 1995 of a newsletter entitled *Hermaphrodites with Attitudes,* published by cross-gendered persons who wanted the medical community to recognize gender diversity and cease using surgery and gender reassignment to force true hermaphrodites (herms), female pseudohermaphrodites (ferms), and male pseudohermaphrodites (merms) into the dichotomous mold of male and female. Fueling this trend in changing gender roles and behaviors was an explosion of knowledge in molecular biology—genetics and endocrinology especially, as scientists sought to discover the role of hormones in gender coding on the brain—the emergence of a "queer" (gay, lesbian, bisexual, cross-gender) community; and the influence of computer technology, which enabled hundreds of sexual minorities to communicate with each other and keep abreast of medical developments on virtually a daily basis.

With the collapse of so-called gender rigidity, which had been derived from the male-female anatomy of *Homo sapiens,* a new sociocentric gender model arose, based on three basic parameters: perception, social role, and presentation. A cross-dresser was a male or female who wore apparel usually worn by the other gender, and this denomination now included people previously known as transvestites or female impersonators or drag queens. The number of cross-dressers was unknown, but *Tapestry,* a quarterly, distributed ten thousand copies per issue in 1995, compared with only two thousand in 1990. *Transformation,* a newer cross-dressing publication, had an international circulation of fifty thousand in 1995.

A cross-gender male or female was someone who desired to explore a gender role different from that usually associated with his or her biological sex. A transsexual, male or female, wanted anatomical congruity with that gender role preference, usually through hormone therapy and sex reassignment surgery. Finally, the transgenderist was a person who crossed gender boundaries to adopt traits usually associated with the opposite sex but did not necessarily want to change his or her anatomy (as in the case of a woman who impersonated a male and related sexually only to another woman).

By the mid-eighties, swinging had fallen on hard times, a victim of antisex forces, the AIDS epidemic, and collective erotic burnout. None of Bob and Geri McGinley's eight children or stepchildren had become a swinger, and Bob's oldest, Gary, was a born-again Christian and ordained evangelist in the Earth Church of the Pacific. Another son, David, looked after the family's travel agency, sending golden-yeared remnants of golden age swinging around the globe, though declining to participate. Bob and Geri wound up divorced but remained business partners in both the swinging and travel agency ends of their ventures, the latter of which prospered. And despite the decline of swinging, the McGinleys' North American Swing Club Association still listed more than one hundred active, organized swing clubs, while the swing community published more than a dozen publications for members.

In 1990 Bhagwan Shree Rajneesh died of a heart attack. But three years after "leaving his body," and seven years after his Oregon commune collapsed, the guru was again drawing spiritual seekers from Bombay to San Francisco.

Now renamed Osho, he had been resurrected by a group of longtime devotees, who had also expanded his ashram in Poona, just outside Bombay, into
a Club Med–like meditation spa that drew thousands of Japanese, German,
American, and Indian followers. Swimming, tennis, facials, and pedicures—
and an AIDS test—had now been added to the traditional menu of meditation and avant-garde psychotherapy techniques. Many of Bhagwan's new
generation of followers were only vaguely familiar with his life and teachings
but had been attracted through books and videos articulating principles that
attracted aging hippies, altered-state junkies, and disaffected yuppies.

Bhagwan's new commune—Osho Ranchana Commune—was situated on
a fifteen-acre farm in Redmond, Washington, two hundred miles northwest
of what was once Rajneeshpuram. The commune was no flash in the pan. An
astounding 348 other Osho centers also flourished around the world. Like
Scientology, the Hare Krishnas, and the Way International—or, for that
matter, Christianity—the teachings of Bhagwan had survived the death of a
charismatic leader.

AROUND THANKSGIVING 1994, the media with much hoopla announced the
publication of the most ambitious American sex survey since Kinsey. It could
not have been worse news—a revisionist reversal of fifty years of sex research. After three decades of radical feminism, antipornography activism,
and the sex abuse and sex harassment consciousness-raising of the early
nineties, the survey was the logical culmination of the new and improved puritanism of the United States, dressed out in the guise of objective science.

Some of its more dubious findings, based on a random stratified sampling
of 3,432 people aged eighteen to fifty-nine:

- A resounding 94 percent of Americans claimed they were faithful
  to their spouses. (Kinsey's infidelity figure of 26 percent for
  women had risen to 30 percent and 36 percent, respectively, in the
  Redbook and *Psychology Today* surveys. The figure for males had
  long remained at a constant 40–50 percent.)
- The median number of sex partners for a woman over her lifetime was two. For men, the figure was six.
- Only one-third of Americans, whether heterosexual or homosexual, had sex twice a week or more.
- Married couples had more sex and more orgasms than singles
  did. Divorced people ranked third.
- Only 2.7 percent of men and 1.3 percent of women engaged in homosexual sex per year. Since puberty, the percentage figures for
  each sex were, respectively, 7.1 and 3.8.

- Only 63 percent of men and 42 percent of women masturbated in the course of a year. (Kinsey, Morton Hunt, et al., put the figures respectively at about 100 percent and about two-thirds.)
- Only 23 percent of men and 19 percent of women engaged in oral sex in the course of a year.
- Only 54 percent of men even thought about sex daily, while a scant 19 percent of women did.

Jesse Helms, Jerry Falwell, and Donald Wildmon could not have asked for better numbers if they had written the survey themselves—which, in a sense, they had.

The survey was conceived back in 1987 by the National Institutes of Health as a response to the AIDS crisis. In order to mount a defense against the plague, the NIH needed to find out how many Americans were engaged in such high-risk behavior as anal sex. The officials decided that the available data—in Kinsey and such subsequent sex surveys as those by Masters and Johnson, *Redbook,* and Morton Hunt—were unreliable and insufficient. One of the biggest areas of controversy was Kinsey's finding that 10 percent of the population engaged in homosexual behavior, a statistic that stood at the very epicenter of AIDS research.

Aware that in the Reagan-Bush era government funding for sex research was virtually impossible to obtain, NIH officials tried to sneak the project past Congress by asking for money to conduct a survey with the insipid and redundant title "Social and Behavioral Aspects of Fertility Related Behavior." Researchers were invited to apply for a grant to design such a study.

Working with the National Opinion Research Center associated with the University of Chicago, sociology professor John Gagnon and his colleagues at the State University of New York at Stony Brook, Long Island, won the contract. Tragicomedy soon struck, however, when North Carolina's Jesse Helms realized "fertility related" and "behavior" must have something to do with his favorite subject. That meant he could indulge in his favorite pastime—funding interruptus.

Over the next four years Gagnon fiddled with the design of the survey, even agreeing to drop out all questions about masturbation—which would have made it one of the oddest sex surveys in history. Another concession: If an interviewer somehow determined that an interviewee was not at risk of AIDS, the interview was to be cut short. All to no avail. In September 1987, Helms introduced an amendment to a bill on funding the NIH that specifically prohibited the government from subsidizing any prying into the sex lives of citizens. The measure passed by a margin of two to one.

By that time, though, Gagnon and company had their ducks in a row and were quickly able to secure $1.6 million in private funding from the Robert

Wood Johnson, Ford, and Rockefeller Foundations. Theoretically, they were now free from political constraints and able to embark on the biggest and most ambitious sex survey since Kinsey.

Many sexologists, though, like Ted McIlvenna, director of San Francisco's Institute for the Advanced Study of Human Sexuality, were alarmed. Sometime in 1991, Gagnon visited McIlvenna and told him what the survey was going to find out. Expressing doubts about Kinsey's statistics on homosexuality, Gagnon claimed he was also going to demonstrate that people were not as sexually active as the Kinsey report said. As the two men talked about methodology, McIlvenna sensed that Gagnon's survey had been created to reflect his own politically conservative point of view.

McIlvenna's guess was that Gagnon and his associates designed their survey with the disastrous aftermath of the Kinsey surveys in mind. After the Rockefeller Institute withdrew its financial support, Kinsey never quite recovered and died a disappointed man only a few years later. Having failed to get funded the first time, Gagnon was determined not to make the same mistake—or Kinsey's—the second time around.

The political climate in which Gagnon and company operated was virtually a cofactor in their survey. For all its flaws, the Kinsey survey was conducted in relative scientific freedom. So were those by Masters and Johnson, *Redbook*, Morton Hunt, Shere Hite, *Cosmopolitan,* and a half dozen others, all of which tended to support Kinsey's basic general observation: more people were having more and different kinds of sex than anybody ever imagined. The Morton Hunt survey of 1974, for example, had reported that more than 80 percent of unmarried persons were having oral-genital contact—reflecting a continuing steady rise from 20 percent in Kinsey's time.

Even as recently as late 1993, befuddled American newspapers around the country were bannering "the Second Sex Revolution" in the wake of yet another sex survey by the wife-and-husband team of Dr. Cynthia L. and Dr. Samuel S. Janus, this one purporting to surpass all previous sex surveys in scope and breadth.

Though virtual unknowns in the small world of sexology, the Januses— she an obstetrician-gynecologist, he an associate professor of psychiatry at the University of Virginia—embarked on their study using 210 graduate student volunteers. Basing their findings on 2,765 satisfactorily completed questionnaires divided almost equally between women and men in twenty-seven states, the Janus team found, for example, that 61 percent of men and 55 percent of women reported more than ten sex partners over a lifetime. The Janus survey also asked respondents: "Are you functioning at your biological maximum sexually?"—that is, are you having as much sex as you can comfortably handle? Lining up in the "Yes" column were 53 percent of all singles, 43 percent of all divorced persons, and 49 percent of married couples.

The Janus team further determined that 5 percent of males identified themselves as homosexual, with another 4 percent admitting to same-sex behavior at one time or another.

Those and other findings strongly validated Kinsey's original data, and *The Janus Report* itself received the warm endorsement of none other than Dr. William H. Masters, who claimed it brought the art of the sex survey into the twenty-first century.

Then along came John Gagnon to cast doubt on all the surveys that had preceded his. He argued, for example, that the sampling methods used by Kinsey and the Januses produced only "junk statistics" that usually overestimated the incidence of certain sexual behaviors. Such surveys, though perhaps understandable in Kinsey's time, were today—in Gagnon's words—"inexcusable—a willful blindness."

The conflict boiled down to methodology vs. methodology, sexologists vs. social scientists, veteran sex researchers who had spent a lifetime peering into the labyrinths of the libido vs. number crunchers with their mystical belief in the art of a well-designed questionnaire. It seemed to be an unbridgeable gulf. Sexologists insisted that getting just about any woman or man on the planet to talk about his or her sex life with something approaching honesty was next to impossible. Some sexologists who specialized in medical anthropology—setting up camp, for instance, in a gay bathhouse or a brothel to track the spread of sexually transmitted diseases—went so far as to insist that even after six months of getting to know and trust a researcher, a person still lied about certain facets of his or her sex life.

Social scientists, on the other hand, set great store in probability sampling—conceding a certain margin of error, but insisting that women and men who filled out a questionnaire about the most secret, intimate, and maybe scariest or guiltiest aspects of their existence were going to let it all hang out. They considered sex just another kind of demographic data that a skilled interviewer, working with a carefully crafted instrument or questionnaire, could elicit from the general population along with its preferred brand of cigarette or favorite long-distance telephone company.

What particularly riled sexologists was the method behind the statistical madness. Kinsey thought it was impossible to create an exact socioeconomic and demographic picture of America in miniature through random sampling, preferring instead a "sample of convenience." That meant he and his colleagues interviewed anybody and everybody willing to talk to them and tell the truth, which they considered more important than going for a balanced demographic sample. If eighteen thousand people (one hundred thousand was his ambition) from all walks of life told something very much like the truth, the result was likely to be a near accurate overall demographic picture anyway.

By contrast, Gagnon and his team asked the computer to randomly select 9,004 addresses across the country. Immediately 1,121 were eliminated because official occupants and actual residents did not match up. Another 3,514 did not qualify for the age limits imposed on the study—eighteen to fifty-nine. Of the remaining 4,369 households, the interviewers visited 3,432—or 80 percent of the target audience, which by social science standards was quite an achievement. By sexological standards, however, 20 percent of a supposed representative sample were completely ignored. The 200 Gagnon interviewers were mostly white middle-aged women—just like the mothers of two-thirds of the respondents, who were also white.

What really differentiated the Gagnon study from other surveys, however, was not so much its demographic sophistication as the appalling lengths to which the researchers went to wring answers from interviewees. Many respondents, for example, were reluctant to be interviewed. Yet in some cases the researchers visited—or harassed—them with up to fifteen home visits to get their answers, and the more recalcitrant were bribed with $100 fees. The Chicago team even set up a "hot line" to coax the hesitant to respond. In one case a local professor wrote a letter that tried to persuade a reluctant interviewee to answer the questions.

Did such methods, reminiscent of a bill collector's dunning tactics, really lend a veneer of scientific credibility to the survey? Or did they spur delinquent respondents to give whatever answer would get the researchers off their back?

Kinsey, one of the most charismatic interviewers who ever lived, conceded that any interview was beset by two potential dangers: the respondent might be lying (either by exaggerating or by covering up) or might have a faulty memory. Confident in his own trustworthiness as an interviewer, he considered the latter more of a problem and developed various statistical procedures to test reliability. Still, despite the public furor that greeted his work, Kinsey considered his data somewhat on the conservative side and explained that even his nonjudgmental, artful probing failed to pierce the armor of a person determined to cover up a past sexual incident in her or his life.

In fact, another survey taken around the time Gagnon was extracting his responses found that among 422 California college students aged eighteen to twenty-three, 68 percent of men and 59 percent of women had lied about sex in the past, and 43 percent of men and 34 percent of women claimed they would never disclose even a single incident of infidelity.

But for the Gagnon team, an answer was an answer was an answer—despite the fact that in 6 percent of its interviews a spouse or sex partner was present, and in 15 percent children were present. Even Gagnon and his coauthors noted that "when interviewed alone, 17 percent of respondents reported having two or more sex partners in the past year, while only 5 percent said so when their parents were present during the interview." Respondents were also permitted to answer potentially "embarrassing" questions about masturbation by mailing in a confidential form. Quarantining masturbation in such a manner further eroded the questionnaire's neutrality and indirectly suggested that such a practice was something the respondent might be ashamed of.

Yet when the Gagnon survey was published, headlines proclaimed: "Sex in America: Faithfulness in Marriage Thrives After All" (*New York Times*), "Survey Finds Most Adults Sexually Staid: Americans' Average Is Once Per Week" (*Washington Post*). *Time* trumpeted the survey on its cover, while its parent company, Time Warner, published a pop version through its publishing arm Little, Brown with the help of *New York Times* science writer Gina Kolata.

The weightier, more scientific tome containing all of the tabulated data was published by the University of Chicago Press under the title *The Social Organization of Sexuality: Sexual Practices in the United States*. Gagnon's coauthors were Edward O. Laumann, a professor of sociology at the University of Chicago; Robert T. Michael, dean of the Harris Graduate School of Public Policy Studies at the University of Chicago and former director of the National Opinion Research Center; and Stuart Michaels, a researcher at the University of Chicago.

The message, of the Gagnon survey, in short, was that the conformist, pre–Sexual Revolution (and completely mythical in the first place) fifties were back. Homosexuality was practically back in a tiny 3-percent-of-the-population closet. Far from engaging in orgies, group sex, and other subversive bedroom activities, most men much preferred to get a good night's sleep. In short, the Gagnon survey told people like Jesse Helms exactly what they wanted to hear. The fact that Helms had once opposed the study was irrelevant. What he now had in John Gagnon was an ally, a man of science.

In the new American sexual landscape devised by John Gagnon and company, the homosexual and the bisexual were invisible. So were the transvestite, the transsexual, the sadomasochist, the pornographer, the consumer of pornography, the paraphiliac, the horny guy, the sexually adventurous woman, and just about anyone else who was not monogamous and heterosexual, and completely content to be so.

THOUGH SOCIAL REVOLUTIONS are of, by, and for the people, the average woman and man invariably remain the invisible players in the upheavals that so dramatically affect their daily lives. Yet at the end of a revolution, long after the heroes and visionaries, the fanatics, the charlatans, the counterrevolutionaries, and all the rest have left the barricades, the people remain to sort out the legacy that everyone has wrought, in one way or another, by their silence or indifference, grass-roots involvement, or informed consent to or repudiation of the great issues.

In the half century that sex has been out of the closet, it has gone from being a forbidden topic to serving as the vehicle of mindless sensationalism in the media. Yet the very ubiquity of sexuality sometimes obscures the ongoing agenda of the permanent Sexual Revolution.

This revolutionary continuum can be roughly divided into four stages. The first occurred in Germany and Austria at the beginning of the century, when sexual scholarship and clinical research first flowered in the work of Freud, Magnus Hirschfeld, and numerous others. That nascent period ended in the early thirties when a Nazi goon squad plundered Hirschfeld's Institute for Sexology.

The second, overlapping stage emerged in the giddy postwar years of the twenties, when urban American middle-class women and men first began to challenge two hundred years of puritan morality. Serious work on sexual reform also began around this time—above all by Margaret Sanger, a New York nurse, who had been appalled by the misery of women among whom she worked in some of the city's poorest sections. In 1921 she founded the American Birth Control League, later to become the Planned Parenthood Federation, and the long, difficult march toward artificial contraception began. In 1938 Kinsey embarked on his zoological study of human sexuality, which culminated in 1948 with the publication of *Sexual Behavior in the Human Male* and, five years later, its companion volume on female sexual behavior—two landmark works that endure as the twin Everests of sexual research.

This book has been a chronicle of the third and most important Sexual Revolution so far. Out of its ruins will come the fourth, which will gather force some time after the millennium. This momentous next phase will be worldwide, affecting all nations large and small, rich and poor, and will strike at the very heart of deeply ingrained antisexual traditions, whether cultural, tribal, or religious. One great engine of this next stage will be technology—satellite television and the Internet, which are exporting liberal Western views of sexual equality—if occasionally at a very distorted level—into the remotest villages of Africa and the Middle East, and giving inspiration and strength to the women who will be the primary revolutionaries overthrowing centuries of patriarchal tyranny and ignorance.

All stages of the permanent sexual revolution share one principal goal: to eradicate the fear and loathing of sex itself, the sheer inability to enjoy sexuality. In that sense, the third Sexual Revolution, like its predecessors, was an unequivocal failure. Despite great strides in clinical research, greater freedom of expression for some sexual minorities and nonconformists, the liberalization of laws regulating erotic literature, film, and art, the universal availability of birth control, and other successes, the United States and most other Western countries remain more deeply polarized over sexual issues than at any time in their history.

"Unfortunately, as a society we still value innocence and lack of information," Ted McIlvenna, still a card-carrying Methodist traveling elder, has remarked. "Maybe not enough people benefited personally from the Sexual Revolution. Maybe that's why a lot of people, and not just those in religion, want to regulate everybody else's sex life. Loretta Haroian, my late colleague, used to say what we need is lust. What's wrong with celebrating it? Everybody hides behind Jesus and children when it comes to sex, she used to say. We're just wrong all the time."

McIlvenna's pessimism is almost universally shared by sex professionals who as teachers, counselors, or therapists work with sexually troubled or uninformed people every day. His prescription—the celebration of lust, or, more prosaically, the enjoyment of sex for its own sake—is more a vision of paradise regained than a practical goal. We are such slaves to sexual fear, guilt, and ignorance that we scarcely even understand what sexual freedom means.

Yet the road to sexual emancipation, though long and difficult, is not endless. Someday we will find the courage to declare that freedom of sexual expression does not mean merely a license to cast off sexual inhibitions. Rather it means the freedom to love another person on a consensual adult basis without fear of penalty or recrimination. Such freedom implies that sex is morally neutral—a position increasingly being adopted by enlightened elements within the Christian and Judaic traditions. Such freedom reinterprets natural law to affirm that interpersonal bonding, not heterosexual procreation, is the primary purpose of any sex act. Such freedom allows homosexuals, transsexuals and transvestites, bisexuals, heterosexuals, drag queens, SM leathermen, masochists, tops, paraphiliacs, and celibates alike to live out their sexual lifestyles with honor and integrity. Finally, universal freedom of sexual expression means that no one sexual group has any claim to the moral high ground, nor has it any business regulating the consensual adult sexual behavior of any other group.

When all of us become sexual revolutionaries, we will also find a way to put an end to sexual violence, the greatest scourge of our time.

To the barricades, then—the grass-roots organizations, the voting booth, libraries and bookstores, the Internet, the public demonstrations and boycotts, the classrooms and pews, the letters to the editor and legislator. A fourth great battle to reform our sexual doctrines, mores, and laws awaits us.

Sources and Acknowledgments

The archives of sexuality both in the United States and in Europe are virtually nonexistent and where they do exist often suffer the intolerable indignity of either censorship or neglect. At the Mary Calderone Library of the Sex Information and Education Council of the United States (SIECUS) in New York, a politically correct sensibility has banished or even discarded certain publications, potentially a source of invaluable information, because they were deemed pornographic. The archives of the now defunct Masters & Johnson Institute reside, at last word, in the home of Virginia Johnson and have never been made available to scholars or journalists.

One of the most valuable collections of sex-related materials is housed in the Institute for the Advanced Study of Human Sexuality in San Francisco— a vast and mostly uncataloged potpourri of books, magazines, newspapers, and pamphlets, many of them exceedingly rare and obscure, as well as many thousands of videos, sixteen-millimeter and eight-millimeter films, photographs, posters, and countless miscellaneous items, all of which constitute a sex-archaeological treasure trove of unparalleled proportions.

Similarly, the library of the Kinsey Institute in Bloomington, Indiana, contains priceless literature and journalism, art, and other materials that can be found nowhere else on earth. At both of these institutions it was my pleasure to spend many days and weeks, poring through the shelves, and to the very capable staffs of both I am deeply indebted.

I especially wish to thank Ted McIlvenna, director of the Institute for the Advanced Study of Human Sexuality, whose sexual erudition and familiarity with the byways of sexual culture are second to none. To Dr. John Money, whose achievements will not receive the public recognition they so richly deserve for decades to come, and who continues his solitary struggle in a scandalously hostile academic environment, I am also obliged for his insights, advice, and ironic perspective.

My thanks also to the staffs of the Library of Congress, the National Archives, the St. Louis Mercantile Library Association, the St. Louis Public Library, the New York Public Library, the Cleveland Public Library, the

415

Chicago Public Library, and countless other librarians across the country who have invariably provided me with courteous and often shrewd assistance when I was, as usual, at a loss.

Less friendly, though understandably so, were the staffs of the Metropolitan Correctional Center in Chicago and the Lake County Jail in Painesville, Ohio. I thank them, as well as the U.S. Marshal's Offices in Chicago and Youngstown, for allowing me to do my job without interference.

One of the great pleasures in researching a book is the opportunity it affords to interview people who know much more about a subject than you do. For taking time out from their busy schedules to instruct and enlighten me, I thank Joe Brooks, Hall Call, John de Cecco, Tom Ciehanski, "Daniel," Jackie Davison, Albert Z. Freedman, Ralph Ginzburg, Bob Guccione, Muriel Guccione, Samuel S. Janus, Virginia Johnson, Kathy Keeton, Luis Kremnitzer, L. (an anonymous disciple of Bhagwan), Ed Lange, Louis Lieberman, Phyllis Lyon, Ron McAlister, Ted Marche, Del Martin, Merv Mason, William H. Masters, V. K. McCarty, Bob McGinley, Ray McIlvenna, Ted McIlvenna, John Money, Chris Moran, Anne Ogborn, Michael Perkins, Wardell Pomeroy, Ira Reiss, Willem de Ridder, Maggi Rubenstein, June Reinisch, Howard Ruppell, Pepper Schwartz, Annie Sprinkle, Reuben Sturman, Laird Sutton, Clark Taylor, Veronica Vera, Roberta White, James D. Weinrich, and David L. Weis.

Since 1982, when I first took a professional interest in the world of sexuality, many individuals have provided me with their unique perspectives on assorted sexual issues as well as on their own lives and careers. In particular I wish to thank Mistress Antoinette, Susie Bright, Dr. Robert T. Francoeur, Al Goldstein, Dr. Erwin Haeberle, Jwala, Ray Lawrence, Linda Montano, Dr. James W. Prescott, Tracy Quan, Candida Royalle, Marcy Sheiner, and the late Marco Vassi for sharing their insights, knowledge, and experiences with me.

For background assistance and advice I also wish to thank Angela Bell, Peter Bloch, Adam Bourgeois, Clarence Cranford, Barbara Corellas, Mara Drew, Kate Fleming, Steve Friedman, Dolores Friesen, Maggie Harter, Jane Homlish, Debra Hughes, Marty Lubin, Jackie Markham, Craig Morford, Diane O'Connell, Terry Sare, Jim Shortridge, Roger Wharton, and William Yarber.

Citing sensitive ongoing investigations into the affairs of Reuben Sturman and other pornographers, both the Federal Bureau of Investigation and the Internal Revenue Service declined to make agents available for interview, even for background or to explore unrelated cases. I encountered a similar reluctance at the U.S. Attorney's Offices in both Cleveland and Chicago.

As usual, my agent, Thomas C. Wallace, has proven to be a rock of support and editorial sagacity. I could not have written the book without him. To

Ann Patty, who first gave this project life, I am also most grateful. I also wish to thank Dr. C. J. Scheiner for volunteering to read the manuscript, point out errors of commission and omission, and serve as a devil's advocate on a variety of issues.

Above all, though, I owe a very heartfelt thank-you to my editor, Becky Saletan, whose unerring criticism, judicious counsel, painstaking editing, and unwavering encouragement permeate every page of this book. Under her guidance, the labor of revision was both a learning experience and a pleasure. I am equally indebted to her assistant, Denise Roy, on whose competence and good cheer I relied at every stage of the editorial process.

Finally, my wife, Pat, and our four children, Mary, John, James, and Margaret, warrant a gratitude that is too deep for words. I thank them for their boundless love and support, for patiently reading the manuscript at various stages, and for their own often spirited—and inspired—insights and recommendations.

In the notes that follow I have provided only the most essential or obscure references, while forgoing countless citations from the daily press or from the vast number of magazine and newspaper articles in my overstuffed files. Similarly, I have provided only a few basic book titles. On virtually any sex-related topic, the Kinsey Institute is able to provide researchers with a reasonably comprehensive bibliography covering books, scholarly journals, and assorted periodicals, and there is no need for me to duplicate that process here.

Abbreviations used below include *TNY* (*The New Yorker*), *NYRB* (*New York Review of Books*), *NYT* (*New York Times*), and *VV* (*Village Voice*).

CHAPTER 1: THE ORGASM THAT CHANGED THE WORLD

BOOKS: William H. Masters and Virginia Johnson: *Human Sexual Response*, Little, Brown, Boston, 1966; *Human Sexual Inadequacy*, Little, Brown, Boston, 1970. Fred Belliveau and Lin Richter, *Understanding Human Sexual Inadequacy*, Bantam Books, New York, 1970. Ruth and Edward M. Brecher, *An Analysis of Human Sexual Response*, New American Library, New York, 1966. Edward M. Brecher, *The Sex Researchers*, Little, Brown, Boston and Toronto, 1969. Vern L. Bullough, *Science in the Bedroom*, Basic Books, New York, 1994. Seymour Fisher, *The Female Orgasm: Psychology, Physiology, Fantasy*, New York, Basic Books, 1973. Erwin J. Haeberle, *The Sex Atlas*, Seabury Press, New York, 1978. Helen Singer Kaplan, *The New Sex Therapy*, Brunner/Mazel, New York, 1974. Nat Lehrman, *Masters & Johnson Explained*, Playboy Paperbacks, Chicago, 1970. Wilhelm Reich, *The Sexual Revolution*, fourth edition, Farrar, Straus and Giroux, New York, 1974. Jhan and June Robbins, *An Analysis of Human Sexual Inadequacy*, New American Library, New York, 1970. John D'Emilio and Estelle B. Freedman, *Intimate Matters:*

A History of Sexuality in America, Harper & Row, New York, 1988. ARTICLES: "New Contraceptive Pill Declared Safe by U.S.," *NYT,* February 6, 1962. Susan Crain Bakos, "Help Yourself to a Richer Sex Life," *St. Louis* magazine, March 1980. Tom Buckley, "All They Talk About Is Sex, Sex, Sex," *New York Times Magazine,* April 30, 1969. Leslie Farber, "I'm Sorry, Dear," *Commentary,* November 1964. Steve Friedman, "Everything You Always Wanted to Know about Masters & Johnson," *St. Louis* magazine, June 1988. Margaret Mead, "Margaret Mead Answers Questions About . . . ," *Redbook,* October 1966. Bette-Jane Raphael, "Why Women Can't Climax," *Forum,* March 1973. OTHER: Virginia E. Johnson and William H. Masters, "Contemporary Influences on Sexual Response: The Work Ethic," a paper presented at the Second Annual SIECUS Citation Dinner, October 18, 1972, New York.

CHAPTER 2: THE MERCHANTS OF VENUS

BOOKS: Stephen Byer, *Hefner's Gonna Kill Me When He Reads This* . . . , Allen-Bennett, Chicago, 1972. Al Di Lauro and Gerald Rabkin, *Dirty Movies,* Chelsea House, New York and London, 1976. David Hebditch and Nick Anning, *Porn Gold,* Faber & Faber, London, ·1988. Bob Hoddens, *The Porn People,* American Publishing Corp., Watertown, Mass., 1973. Walter Kendrick, *The Secret Museum,* Viking, New York, 1987. Russell Miller, *Bunny: The Real Story of Playboy,* Holt, Rinehart & Winston, New York, 1984. Michael Milner, *Sex on Celluloid,* MacFadden-Bartell, New York, 1964. Gary W. Potter, *The Porn Merchants,* Kendell/Hunt, Dubuque, Iowa, 1986. Kenneth Turan and Stephen F. Zito, *Sinema,* Praeger, New York, 1974. ARTICLES: "Bertrand Russell Wins Suit Against a British Publisher," *NYT,* March 6, 1965. "Hollywood's Morality Code Undergoing First Major Revisions in 35 Years," *NYT,* April 7, 1965. Frank Brady, "The Private Life of Hugh Hefner," *Swank,* August 1975. Stanley Kauffmann, "Sex Symbols," *New Republic,* November 2, 1968. Carrie Rickey, "Great Movie Orgasms," *Forum,* December 1982. "A Curator Who Doesn't Blush Easily," *NYT,* January 31, 1996. OTHER: *Report of the Longford Committee Investigating Pornography,* Coronet Books, London, 1972. *The Report of the Commission on Obscenity and Pornography,* Bantam Books, New York, 1970. *The Millionaire Pornographers,* a special issue of *Adam* magazine, February 1977. I also wish to acknowledge my debt to the Cleveland *Plain Dealer,* which reported on Reuben Sturman's career in pornography from beginning to end.

CHAPTER 3: THE PUBIC WARS

BOOKS: George Paul Csicsery, ed., *The Sex Industry,* New American Library, New York, 1973. Ralph Ginzburg, *An Unhurried View of Erotica,* Helmsman Press, New York, 1958. Henry Anatole Grunwald, ed., *Sex in America,* Bantam Books, New York, 1964. Morton Hunt, *Sexual Behavior in the 1970s,*

Playboy Press, Chicago, 1974. Phyllis and Eberhard Kronhausen, *The Sex People,* Playboy Press, Chicago, 1975. Nat Lehrman and Frank Robinson, eds., *Sex American Style,* Playboy Press, Chicago, 1971. Geoffrey Neil, *An Illustrated History of the Stag Film,* Graduate Enterprises, Canoga Park, Calif., 1972. Vance Packard, *The Sexual Wilderness,* David McKay Company, New York, 1968. Jeremy Pascall and Clyde Jeavons, *A Pictorial History of Sex in the Movies,* Hamlyn, London and New York, 1975. Carolyn See, *Blue Money,* David McKay Company, New York, 1974. Carol Tavris and Susan Sadd, *The Redbook Report on Female Sexuality,* Delacorte Press, New York, 1977. ARTICLES: Benjamin De Mott, "The Anatomy of *Playboy,*" *Commentary,* August 1962. "The Second Sexual Revolution," *Time* cover story, January 24, 1964. "Not on Marquee, but in Spotlight: The Audience," *NYT,* February 7, 1965. Ralph Ginzburg, "Eros on Trial," *Fact,* vol. 2, issue 3, n.d. "Hugh Hefner: 'I Am in the Center of the World,' " *Look,* January 10, 1967. "Think Cheap," *Time* cover story on Hugh Hefner, March 3, 1967. "Anything Goes: Taboos in Twilight," *Newsweek,* November 13, 1967. Alan Rich, "Miss Moorman's Thing, or: Nudity Is No Cover," *New York,* July 8, 1968. Richard Goldstein, "The Theatre of Cruelty Comes to Second Avenue," *VV,* October 31, 1968. Natalie Gittelson, "The Erotic Life of the American Wife," *Vogue,* July 1969. Wardell B. Pomeroy, Ph.D., "A Comment on the Report of the Commission on Obscenity and Pornography," *SIECUS Newsletter,* April 1970. "*Penthouse* Plays Peek-a-Book Pussy," *Screw,* September 13, 1971. Al Goldstein and Bob Weiner, "Simon on the Mount," interview with John Simon, *Screw,* November 29, 1971. Gregory Battcock, "Art On: New Frontiers in Erotic Art," *Screw,* December 6, 1971. Eric Norden, "The Ralph Ginzburg Story," *Hustler,* February 1976. D. Keith Mano, "Tom Swift Is Alive and Well and Making Dildos," *Playboy,* March 1978. Calvin Tomkins, "Mr. Playboy of the Western World," *Saturday Evening Post,* April 23, 1966. Sidney E. Zion, "The Ginzburg Decision," *NYT,* March 24, 1966. OTHER: *Eros,* vol. 1, nos. 1–4. REMARKS: I have not been able to ascertain where two photocopied articles I unearthed originally appeared: Tom Prideaux, "The Man Who Dared to Enter Paradise," and Chloe Aaron, "Group Grope Theatre."

CHAPTER 4: A LOVE THAT DARED TO SPEAK ITS NAME

BOOKS: John Money: *Man & Woman, Boy & Girl* (with Anke A. Ehrhardt), Johns Hopkins University Press, Baltimore and London, 1972; *Gay, Straight, and In-Between,* Oxford University Press, New York and Oxford, 1988; *Biographies of Gender and Hermaphroditism in Paired Comparisons,* Elsevier, Amsterdam, New York, Oxford, 1991. Eli Coleman, Ph.D., ed., *John Money: A Tribute,* Haworth Press, New York, London, Sydney, 1991. John J. McNeill, S. J., *The Church and the Homosexual,* Sheed, Andrews and McMeel, New York, 1976. ARTICLES: "Women Deviates Held Increasing," *NYT,* December 11, 1961. Paul Welch, "The 'Gay' World Takes to the City Streets," *Life,* June 26, 1964. "Lords Vote to Ease Homosexuality Ban," *NYT,* May 25, 1965. "A Changing of Sex by Surgery Begun at Johns Hopkins," *NYT,* November 21, 1966, p. 1. "Surgery to Change Gender," *NYT,* November 27, 1966. Lucian Truscott IV, "Gay Power Comes to Sheridan Square," *VV,* July 3, 1969. Jonathan Black, "Gay Power Hits Back," *VV,* July 3, 1969. Will Roscoe, "Politics and Visions: The Story of Gay Liberation," *Vortex,* July 1987. David Franks, "Dangerous Sex with John Money," interview, *Harry,* October 1991. OTHER: "Roberta's Autobiography," private manuscript of twenty-one pages, n.d. "Statement on the Establishment of a Clinic for Transsexuals at the Johns Hopkins Medical Institutions," Office of Institutional Public Relations, November 21, 1966. John Money, "Explorations in Human Behavior," *The History of Clinical Psychology in Autobiography,* vol. II, Brooks/Cole Publishing Company, Pacific Grove, Calif., 1993. *Last Call at Maud's,* a documentary film directed by Paris Poirier, 1993.

CHAPTER 5: INTIMATIONS OF IMMORALITY
BOOKS: Andrea Dworkin: *Letters from a War Zone,* E. P. Dutton, New York, 1988; *Our Blood: Prophecies and Discourses on Sexual Politics,* Harper & Row, New York, 1976. Kate Millett, *Sexual Politics,* Doubleday, New York, 1970. ARTICLES: Shana Alexander, "Singular Girl's Success," *Life,* March 1, 1963. Joan Didion, "Bosses Make Lousy Lovers," *Saturday Evening Post,* January 30, 1965. James Kaplan, "The Mouseburger," *Vanity Fair,* June 1990.

CHAPTER 6: VIRGINS AND GYPSIES
BOOKS: Marco Vassi: *The Saline Solution,* Olympia Press, New York, 1971; *Metasex, Mirth & Madness,* Penthouse Press, New York, 1975; *The Stoned Apocalypse,* Second Chance Press, Sag Harbor, N.Y., 1991; *A Driving Passion,* Permanent Press, Sag Harbor, N.Y., 1992. Linda Lovelace, with Mike McGrady: *Ordeal,* Citadel Press, Secaucus, N.J., 1980; *Out of Bondage,* Lyle Stuart, Secaucus, N.J., 1986. *The Deep Throat Papers,* introduction by Pete Hamill, Manor Books, N.Y., 1973. Germaine Greer, *The Female Eunuch,* McGraw-Hill, New York, 1971. Andrea Juno and V. Vale, eds., *Angry Women,* Re/Search Publications, San Francisco, 1991. Peter Michelson, *The Aesthetics of Pornography,* Herder & Herder, New York, 1971. Annie Sprinkle, *Post Porn Modernist,* Torch Books, Amsterdam, 1991. ARTICLES: "Publisher Turns New (Clean) Leaf," *NYT,* May 5, 1956. "The Famous and Infamous Wares of Monsieur Girodias," *NYT Book Review,* April 17, 1960. Marilyn Meeske, "Memoirs of a Female Pornographer," *Esquire,* April 1965. Israel Shenker, "Girodias Sees Rich Vein of Erotic Interest in U.S.," *NYT,* October 16, 1968. "Dirty Writers of America Unite to Fight for 'Our Dirty Money,' " *NYT,* June 25, 1971. Germaine Greer, "Lady Love Your Cunt,"

Screw, June 28, 1971. "Revolting Pornographers," *Screw,* July 13, 1971. Germaine Greer, "Riding High on the Hog," *Screw,* August 9, 1971; "Do You Like Boobs a Lot?" *Screw,* October 4, 1971. Al Goldstein, "City of Wet Dreams: The 2nd Dutch Fuckfilm Festival," *Screw,* November 22, 1971. Marco Vassi, "My Scene: Bisexuality, Therapy and Revolution," parts I and II, *Screw,* November 1 and November 8, 1971; "Contours of Darkness," *Screw,* December 20, 1971; "Beyond Bisexuality," *Screw,* February 21, 1972. "Gerard Damiano Speaks his Mind," interview, *Stud,* March 1975. James Martin, "Gerard Damiano," interview, *Hustler,* March 1975. OTHER: *The Virgin Sperm Dancer* (*Suck* special issue), Amsterdam, 1972. *Suck: The Last Number,* Amsterdam, 1974. Newsletter of the Lifestyles Organization (Web page: http://www.PlayCouples.com). REMARKS: No one is quite sure how many times Marco Vassi was married, though most estimates range from eight to nine. Several were heavily SM in orientation. Since his liaisons, both legally recognized and casual, are far too numerous to chronicle, and were both heterosexual and homosexual in nature, this book provides only a representative sampling of his career as one of the century's foremost sexual adventurists. Marco also unknowingly fathered out of wedlock a son whom he later legally adopted.

CHAPTER 7: THE SCENE

ARTICLES: R. Allen Lieder, "Harry Reems: From Stag Film Stud to Sex Superstar," *Sir!,* March 1976. Martin S. Weinberg, Colin J. Williams, Charles Moser, "The Social Constituents of Sadomasochism," *Social Problems,* April 1984. OTHER: Pat Bond, "Living in Leather VII," keynote speech at a meeting of the Eulenspiegel Society, October 9, 1992.

CHAPTER 8: SEX FOR ADVANCED STUDENTS

BOOKS: John Money: *Lovemaps: Clinical Concepts of Sexual/Erotic Health and Pathology, Paraphilia, and Gender Transposition in Childhood, Adolescence, and Maturity,* Prometheus Books, Buffalo, N.Y., 1986; *Vandalized Lovemaps* (with Dr. Margaret Lamacz), Prometheus Books, Buffalo, N.Y., 1989. Anna K. and Robert T. Francoeur, *Hot & Cool Sex,* Harcourt, Brace, Jovanovich, New York and London, 1974. Tom Hatfield, *Sandstone Experience,* Crown, New York, 1975. Shere Hite, *The Hite Report,* Macmillan, New York, 1976. Nena O'Neill and George O'Neill, *Open Marriage,* M. Evans and Company, New York, 1972. Bhagwan Shree Rajneesh, *The Orange Book,* Rajneesh Foundation, Poona, India, 1980. Gabriel R. Vogliotti, *The Girls of Nevada,* Citadel Press, Secaucus, N.J., 1975. ARTICLES: Eleanore A. Luckey and Gilbert D. Nass, "A Comparison of Sexual Attitudes and Behavior in an International Sample," *Journal of Marriage and the Family,* May 1969. "W.U. Sex Researchers Sued by Irate Husband," *St. Louis Post-Dispatch,* August 25, 1970.

"Sex Suit Secrecy Studied," *St. Louis Post-Dispatch*, December 5, 1970. Leonard Baker, "California Weekend," *Forum*, March 1972. " 'Who Keeps Score?': Masters' Wife Ducks Question," *St. Louis Globe Democrat*, May 3, 1973. ". . . At Home They're 'Stuffy as Hell,' " *St. Louis Globe-Democrat*, August 9, 1973. Robert Westbrook, "The Twenty-Minute Orgasm," *Penthouse*, June 1975. Marco Vassi, "A Fistful of Fucking," *Hustler*, September 1976. Wardell B. Pomeroy and Leah C. Schaefer, "*The Hite Report:* Two Professional Views," *SIECUS Report*, November 1976. Wardell B. Pomeroy, "The New Sexual Myths of the 1970s," *SIECUS Report*, July 1977. Marco Vassi, "Diary," *Forum*, January–December 1978. Zbigniew Kindela and Michael Stott, "The Reverend Ted McIlvenna: Apostle for Sexual Rights," interview, *Hustler*, April 1979. Verna Betts and Peter Betts Good, "Morehouse—A Sensual and Educational Commune," *Forum*, August 1979. Wardell Pomeroy, "Kinsey Co-author Speaks Out," *Chic*, February 1981. Robert Blair Kaiser, "Sandstone—a Love Community," *Penthouse*, September 1982. Mark Christensen, "Rancho Rajneesh," *Penthouse*, July 1985. Bernie Zilbergeld, "How Good Is Nancy Friday?" *Forum*, March 1986. George de Stefano, "The Most Outrageous Homosexual in America," *Forum*, October 1986. REMARKS: Files of the George E. Calvert case remain sealed at St. Louis County Court House.

CHAPTER 9: THE SLEAZING OF AMERICA

ARTICLES: "High Court's Obscenity Rulings Provoke Confusion and Debate," *NYT*, June 23, 1973, p. 1. "Chuck Traynor," interview, *Hustler*, January 1975. Patrick William Salvo, "Larry Rosenstein," interview, *Hustler*, December 1975. Donald R. Myrus, "Going Down in Bunnyland: The Decline and Fall of the *Playboy* Empire," *Hustler*, March 1976. "The Porno Plague," *Time* cover story, April 5, 1976. Lowell Bergman and Jeff Gerth, "La Costa: Syndicate in the Sun," *Penthouse*, April 1975. "Althea Leasure: The Feminine Side of *Hustler*," interview, *Hustler*, July 1976. Alan Dershowitz, "Screwing Around with the First Amendment," *Penthouse*, January 1977. Tim Conaway, "*The Hite Report* Exposed," *Hustler*, April 1977. Bruce David, "*Hustler* on Trial," parts I and II, June and July 1977. Dr. Wardell B. Pomeroy, "Sexual Contact with Animals," *Forum*, October 1977. Dan Dorfman, "Upstairs, Downstairs at the Ansonia," *New York*, November 28, 1977. Al Goldstein, "Doing Slime," interview with Larry Levenson, *Screw*, October 25, 1982. OTHER: Bob Guccione: *Drawings & Paintings*, privately printed catalog, n.d.

CHAPTER 10: SEE DICK RUN

BOOKS: Alex Comfort, *Sexual Behaviour in Society*, Gerald Duckworth and Co. Ltd., London, 1950. Dr. William Hartman and Marilyn Fithian, *Any*

Man Can, St. Martin's Press, New York, 1984. Germaine Greer, *Sex and Destiny,* Harper & Row, New York, 1984. Rodney A. Smolla, *Jerry Falwell v. Larry Flynt,* St. Martin's Press, New York, 1988. ARTICLES: Ethel Reed Strainchamps, "Why We Can't Say B——shit," *[More], a Journalism Review,* July 1972. "The New Merchant of Venus," *Newsweek,* June 24, 1974. G. Denison, "Sultan of Smut," *Reader's Digest,* November 1975. Marco Vassi, "Tattoo Tripping," *Hustler,* June 1977. "Bell Denies Young Is Target of Inquiry," *NYT,* October 19, 1977. "A Pornographer's Saga: Wealth, Disrepute, Jail and Now Escape," *NYT,* May 18, 1978. "Pornographer Indicted on a Murder Charge," *NYT,* June 13, 1978. "Jersey Is Investigating *Penthouse* Casino Bid," *NYT,* July 10, 1978, p. 1. "Supplementary Material from *New York Times* News Service," August 17, 1978, on hunt for Michael G. Thevis. "Supplementary Material from *New York Times* News Service," October 26, 1978, on assassination of Roger Dean Underhill. Ron Ridenour, "Conspiracy Against Truth: The Shooting of Larry Flynt," *Hustler,* September 1978. "Fugitive Pornographer Captured," *NYT,* November 10, 1978. "Murder Indictment Awaits Millionaire Pornographer Seized at Bank," *NYT,* November 11, 1978. "Pornographer Gets Life in Plot to Kill Key Witness," *NYT,* October 27, 1979. "55 Indicted by U.S. as Pornographers and in Film Piracy," *NYT,* February 15, 1980, p. 1. Dennis R. Hall, "A Note on Erotic Imagination: *Hustler* as a Secondary Carrier of Working-Class Consciousness," *Journal of Popular Culture,* Spring 1982. Al Goldstein, "The Harder They Fall," *Playboy,* April 1983. "John C. Holmes," interview, *Adult Video News,* June 1985. Eric Nadler, "Sex and the *New York Times,*" *Forum,* October 1985. Earl Arno, "The Good, the Dead and the Ugly," *Screw,* May 26, 1986. Mike Bygrave, "Darkness on the Edge of Tinsel Town," *Weekend Guardian,* February 9–10, 1991. OTHER: Anne Koedt, "The Myth of the Vaginal Orgasm," *Notes from the Second Year: Women's Liberation; Major Writings of Feminists,* New York, Radical Feminism, 1970. *Donahue,* with guests Larry Flynt, Herald Fahringer, and Hinson McAulisse, broadcast April 3, 1979 (show #04039).

CHAPTER 11: MISSIONARY POSITIONS
ARTICLES: Helen Dudar, "America Discovers Child Pornography," *Ms.,* August 1977. John Trechak, "In Bed with Garner Ted," *Penthouse,* September 1978. Mary Murphy, "The Next Billy Graham," *Esquire,* October 10, 1978. Georgia Dullea, "In Feminists' Antipornography Drive, 42nd Street Is the Target," *NYT,* July 6, 1979. Mark I. Pinsky, "Helmsman of the Right," *Progressive,* April 1980. Elizabeth Drew, "Jesse Helms," *TNY,* July 20, 1980. Sasthi Brata and Andrew Duncan, "Reverend Jerry Falwell," interview, *Penthouse,* March 1981. Frances Fitzgerald, "A Disciplined, Changing Army," *TNY,* May 18, 1981. Larry M. Lance and Christina Y. Berry, "Has There Been a Sexual Revolution? An Analysis of Human Sexuality Messages

in Popular Music, 1968–1977," *Journal of Popular Culture,* Winter 1981. L. J. Davis and Ernest Volkman, "Jerry Falwell," *Penthouse,* December 1981. Arthur Weidel, with L. J. Davis, "Praise the Lord and Pass the Contributions," *Penthouse,* January 1982. Judy Klemsrud, "Joining Hands in the Fight Against Pornography," *NYT,* August 26, 1985. Larry Bush, "The Truth and Alfred Regnery," *Penthouse,* November 1985.

CHAPTER 12: *APRÈS NOUS THE SPERMATHON*
Books: Gay Talese, *Thy Neighbor's Wife,* Doubleday, New York, 1980. Articles: "Nobody Serves Onion Dip at Sandstone," *Esquire,* October 1972. Aaron Latham, "An Evening in the Nude with Gay Talese," *New York,* July 9, 1973. Philip Nobile, "Gay Talese Has a Dilemma," *Esquire,* December 1973. William Mead and Michael Feinsliber, "The American Way of Sex," *Penthouse,* April 1980. "On the Avenue," profile of Gay Talese, *Avenue,* April 1980. John Leonard, "Thy Neighbor's Wife," book review, *Playboy,* May 1980. Larry DuBois, "Gay Talese," interview, *Playboy,* May 1980. Frank Fortunato, "Gay Talese Talks about Sex—California Style," interview, *Forum,* June 1980. Uta West, "Can Sandstone Survive Talese?" interview with John and Barbara Williamson, *Forum,* October 1980. Rebecca Nahas, "Whatever Happened to Tara Alexander?" *Forum,* December 1985. Other: Paul H. Gebhard, "Sexuality in the Post-Kinsey Era," *Changing Patterns of Sexual Behaviour,* Academic Press, London, New York, and Sydney, 1980.

CHAPTER 13: DARK NIGHT OF SEXOLOGY
Books: Dr. William H. Masters and Virginia Johnson: *The Pleasure Bond* (in association with Robert J. Levin), Little, Brown, Boston, 1974; *Homosexuality in Perspective* (with Robert C. Kolodny), Little, Brown, Boston, 1979; *On Sex and Human Loving* (with Robert C. Kolodny), Little, Brown, & Co., Boston and Toronto, 1982. Articles: "Hefner Helps Pay for Research of Masters, Johnson," *St. Louis Globe-Democrat,* March 6, 1975. "Masters and Johnson Interview," *Advocate,* May 21, 1979. Kevin Gordon, "Latest Study 'Homogenizes' Homosexuals," *National Catholic Reporter,* October 12, 1979. Bernie Zilbergeld and Michael Evans, "The Inadequacy of Masters and Johnson," *Psychology Today,* August 1980. Lenny Giteck, "Kevin Gordon Takes a Critical Look at Masters and Johnson," *Advocate,* December 11, 1980. Robert C. Kolodny, "Evaluating Sex Therapy: Process and Outcome at the Masters & Johnson Institute," *Journal of Sex Research,* November 1981. Philip Nobile, "The Sex Establishment," editorial, *Forum,* March 1983; "Dr. Bernie Zilbergeld," interview, *Forum,* June 1983; "Masters and Mead," editorial, *Forum,* June 1983; "Masters & Johnson Finally Reveal Missing Criteria at Sex Congress," *Forum,* September 1983. Dr. Bernie Zilbergeld, "Masters, Johnson and Me," *Forum,* November 1983. Eric Nadler, "Inside Masters and

Johnson's New Sex Spa," *Forum,* February 1984. Philip Nobile, "Dr. Damien Martin," interview, *Forum,* August 1984. "Masters and Johnson TV Film Is Set," *NYT,* February 6, 1985. Jane Brody, "Personal Health" column, *NYT,* October 31, 1989. Victoria McKee, "Exile's Riposte," *NYT,* February 27, 1994. OTHER: William H. Masters, M.D., Virginia E. Johnson, D.Sc., Robert C. Kolodny, M.D., and J. Robert Meyners, Ph.D., "Outcome Studies at the Masters & Johnson Institute," a paper presented at the Sixth World Congress of Sexology, Washington, D.C., May 26, 1983.

CHAPTER 14: *TRISTIS POST COITUM*
ARTICLES: Marshall McLuhan and George B. Leonard, "The Future of Sex," *Look,* July 25, 1967. "Porno Pets," *Time,* March 10, 1980. John Perry and Beverly Whipple, "The Varieties of Female Orgasm and Female Ejaculation," *SIECUS Report,* May 1981. "Marco Vassi's Journal," *Forum,* February, April, June 1982. "Herpes: The New Scarlet Letter," *Time* cover story, August 2, 1982. Frank Fortunato, "Those Wild and Wacky S&M Clubs," *Forum,* October 1982. Philip Nobile, "George Leonard," interview, *Forum,* April 1983. "Sex in the '80s," *Time* cover story, April 9, 1984. Dr. Bernie Zilbergeld, "The End of Excitement," *Forum,* September 1985.

CHAPTER 15: BONFIRE OF THE FANTASIES
BOOKS: F. M. Christenson, *Pornography: The Other Side,* Praeger, New York, 1990. Joan Delfattore, *What Johnny Shouldn't Read,* Yale University Press, New Haven, Conn., and London, 1992. Edward Donnerstein et al., *Question of Pornography,* Free Press, New York, 1987. Eric Nadler and Philip Nobile, *The United States of America vs. Sex,* Minotaur Press, New York, 1986. Dr. Judith A. Reisman and Edward W. Eichel, *Kinsey, Sex and Fraud,* Lochinvar-Huntington House Publications, Lafayette, La., 1990. Lynne Segal and Mary McIntosh, eds., *Sex Exposed: Sexuality and the Pornography Debate,* Rutgers University Press, New Brunswick, N.J., 1993. Nadine Strossen, *Defending Pornography,* Scribners, New York, 1995. ARTICLES: Mary Kay Blakely, "Is One Woman's Sexuality Another Woman's Pornography?" *Ms.,* April 1985. Karen DeCrow, "Strange Bedfellows," *Penthouse,* May 1985. George De Stefano, "The Gay Sex Addict Controversy," *Forum,* January 1986. Lisa Duggan, "Censorship in the Name of Feminism," *VV,* October 16, 1984. Andrea Dworkin, letter to the editor, *VV,* November 6, 1984. Walter Kendrick, "Prudes and Prejudice," *VV Literary Supplement,* September 1986. Berl Kutchinsky, "Pornography and Its Effects in Denmark and the United States: A Rejoinder and Beyond," *Comparative Social Research,* vol. 8 (1985). Robert Love, "Furor Over Rock Lyrics Intensifies," *Rolling Stone,* September 12, 1985. Eric Nadler, "Inside Sexaholics Anonymous," *Forum,* September 1984. Anna Quindlen, "Life in the 30's," *NYT,* July 23, 1986. Dawn Stover,

"The Sexaholism Hustle," *Forum*, October 1985. Lindsay Van Gelder, "Pornography Goes to Washington," *Ms.*, June 1986. Philip Weiss, "Porn Martyr," *Forum*, January 1985. "The War Against Pornography," *Newsweek*, March 18, 1985. "Sex Busters," *Time* cover story, July 21, 1986. "Defeated by Pornography," editorial, *NYT*, June 2, 1986. "Pornography: A Poll," *Time*, July 21, 1986. "Domino's Pulls 'Saturday Night' Ads," *NYT*, April 11, 1989. "Pornography: An Exchange," correspondence between Catharine A. MacKinnon and Ronald Dworkin, *NYRB*, March 3, 1994. OTHER: Meese Commission testimony of Andrea Dworkin, Dr. Loretta Haroian, Linda Lovelace Marchiano, Dr. Ted McIlvenna, Catharine MacKinnon, Dr. John Money, Terese Stanton, Donald Wildmon.

CHAPTER 16: *ECCE HOMO*

BOOKS: Dr. William H. Masters and Virginia Johnson, *Crisis: Heterosexual Behavior in the Age of AIDS* (with Robert C. Kolodny, M.D.), Grove Press, New York, 1988. ARTICLES: Paul Cameron, "A Case Against Homosexuality," *The Human Life Review*, Summer 1978. "Linda Laubenstein," obituary, *NYT*, August 17, 1982. Andrew Kopkind, "Once upon a Time in the West," *Nation*, June 1, 1985. Paul R. McHugh, "Psychiatric Misadventures," *The American Scholar*, Autumn 1992. "Gay Americans Throng Capital in Appeal for Rights," *NYT*, April 26, 1993, p. 1. Jeanie Russell Kasindorf, "Lesbian Chic," *New York*, May 10, 1993. Vince Aletti, "Boyd McDonald, 1925–1993," *VV*, October 12, 1993.

CHAPTER 17: TWILIGHT OF THE GODS

BOOKS: Roy Grutman and Bill Thomas, *Lawyers and Thieves*, Simon & Schuster, New York, 1990. ARTICLES: *"Playboy* vs. *Penthouse,"* *Business Week*, December 6, 1982. "The Rocky Porno Show," *Hustler*, March 1979. "Beauty Sale," editorial, *NYT*, July 25, 1984. *"Penthouse* Sales Soar for Miss America Issue," *NYT*, August 1, 1984. John Skow, "Bob Guccione," *People*, December 17, 1984. "Bob Guccione," interview, *Penthouse*, January 1985. Hariette Surovell, "Larry Levenson Comes Home," *Forum*, September 1985. Frank Fortunato, "Orgy of Recrimination," *Forum*, April 1986. "Deshabille to Doomsday," *Forbes*, July 28, 1986. Susie Bright, "Safe Sex: Behind the Green Door," *Forum*, December 1986; "Two Days on a Porn Set," *Forum*, January 1989. Allen Sonnenschein, "I Was Jessica Hahn's Madam," interview, *Penthouse*, January 1988. Mark Hosenball, "Like a Virgin," *New Republic*, January 4–11, 1988. J. W. Slade, "Violence in the Hard-Core Pornographic Film: A Historical Survey," *Journal of Communication*, vol. 34, pp. 148–163. Patrick M. Reilly, *"Penthouse* Profits Fuel Guccione Buying," *Wall Street Journal*, August 7, 1990. Berl Kutchinsky, "Pornography and Rape: Theory and Practice," *International Journal of Law and Psychiatry*, vol. 14, 1991. "10 Hottest

Magazines 1991," *Adweek*, February 17, 1992. "Top Retailer Profit Performers," *Magazine & Bookseller*, May 1992. "Mitchell Widow Settles Lawsuit from Slaying," *San Francisco Examiner*, November 16, 1992. "Family Man. No Mansion. This Guy Really Runs *Playboy?*" *NYT*, November 22, 1992. "The Playboy Philosopher," *Buzz*, November/December 1992. Buck Henry, "The Betty Boom," *Playboy*, December 1992. Jessica Hahn, "My Fifteen Minutes of Fame Are Up. Not!" pictorial, *Playboy*, December 1992. "Strictly Maternal," *People*, August 2, 1993. Christopher Byron, "While *Penthouse* Slowly Goes Bust, Guccione Lives High on Its Hog," *New York Observer*, January 3, 1996. OTHER: *Hugh M. Hefner*, a documentary film directed by Robert Heath, 1992.

CHAPTER 18: LINDA MONTANO'S PUBIC HAIR
ARTICLES: Lisa Katzman, "The Women of Porn," *VV*, August 24, 1993. Annie Sprinkle, "Not Just Your Average Orgy," *Forum*, May 1987. John Weir, "Reading Randy," *Out*, August/September 1993. "Double Reissue of Literary Erotica," *Publishers Weekly*, May 31, 1993.

CHAPTER 19: SEX AMONG THE RUINS
BOOKS: Samuel S. Janus, Ph.D., and Cynthia L. Janus, M.D., *The Janus Report*, John Wiley & Sons, New York, Chichester, Brisbane, 1993. Albert D. Klassen, Colin J. Williams, and Eugene E. Levitt, *Sex and Morality in the U.S.: An Empirical Enquiry Under the Auspices of the Kinsey Institute*, Wesleyan University Press, Middletown, Conn., 1989. Catharine A. MacKinnon, *Only Words*, Harvard University Press, Cambridge, 1993. Edward O. Laumann, John H. Gagnon, Robert T. Michael, and Stuart Michaels, *The Social Organization of Sexuality*, University of Chicago Press, Chicago and London, 1994. Robert T. Michael, John H. Gagnon, Edward O. Laumann, Gina Kolata, *Sex in America*, Little, Brown, New York, 1994. John Money, *Reinterpreting the Unspeakable*, Continuum, New York, 1994. A. W. Richard Sipe, *A Secret World*, Brunner/Mazel, New York, 1990. ARTICLES: Dawn Stover, "The Red Hot Center of Swinging," *Forum*, December 1985. "Canada Court Says Pornography Harms Women," *NYT*, February 28, 1992. Stephen Fried, "The New Sexperts," *Vanity Fair*, December 1992. "Religious Cult Flourishes Despite Bhagwan's Death," *San Francisco Examiner*, December 7, 1992. Lisa Katzman, "The Women of Porn," *VV*, August 24, 1993. "Falwell's Gospel Hour Fined for Political Activity," *NYT*, April 7, 1993. "Proof Lacking for Ritual Abuse by Satanists," *NYT*, October 31, 1994. Catharine A. MacKinnon, "Turning Rape into Pornography: Postmodern Genocide," *Ms.*, July/August 1993. Richard Bernstein, "Guilty If Charged," *NYRB*, January 13, 1994. Lawrence A. Stanley, "The Child Porn Myth," *Cardozo Arts & Entertainment Law Journal*, vol. 7, no. 2, 1989. "Sex in America," *Time* cover

story, October 17, 1994. OTHER: James W. Prescott, Ph.D., "NIH Violence Research Initiatives: Is Past Prologue?" presentation before the Panel on NIH Research on Anti-social, Aggressive and Violence-Related Behaviors and Their Consequences of the Center for Science Policy Studies, National Institutes of Health, Bethesda, Md., September 22–23, 1993. Mark F. Schwartz, D.Sc., and William H. Masters, M.D., "Treatment of Paraphiliacs, Pedophiles, and Incest Families," *Research Handbook of Rape,* 1984. *Masters and Johnson Report,* vol. 1, no. 1, Winter 1992, and no. 2, n.d. The author also attended a three-day workshop on child abuse conducted by Dr. Mark F. Schwartz, Lori Galperin, and Dr. William H. Masters in Newport, R.I., in March 1993.

Index

448 ■ *Index*

Printed in the United States
36813LVS00004B/1-51